The Art of Musical Ciphers,
Riddles and Sundry Curiosities

The Art of Musical Ciphers, Riddles and Sundry Curiosities

R. Larry Todd and Katharina Uhde

THE BOYDELL PRESS

© R. Larry Todd and Katharina Uhde 2026

All Rights Reserved. Except as permitted under current legislation no part of this work may be photocopied, stored in a retrieval system, published, performed in public, adapted, broadcast, transmitted, recorded or reproduced in any form or by any means, without the prior permission of the copyright owner

The right of R. Larry Todd and Katharina Uhde to be identified as the authors of this work has been asserted in accordance with sections 77 and 78 of the Copyright, Designs and Patents Act 1988

First published 2026
The Boydell Press, Woodbridge

ISBN 978 1 83765 303 4 (hardback)
ISBN 978 1 83765 304 1 (paperback)

The Boydell Press is an imprint of Boydell & Brewer Ltd
and of Boydell & Brewer Inc.
website: www.boydellandbrewer.com

Our Authorised Representative for product safety in the EU is Easy Access System Europe
– Mustamäe tee 50, 10621 Tallinn, Estonia, *gpsr.requests@easproject.com*

A CIP catalogue record for this book is available
from the British Library

The publisher has no responsibility for the continued existence or accuracy of URLs for external or third-party internet websites referred to in this book, and does not guarantee that any content on such websites is, or will remain, accurate or appropriate

Typeset in Minion Pro by
Sparks Publishing Services Ltd—www.sparkspublishing.com

Toutes les choses de ce monde ne sont qu'un vray chiffre
Everything in this world is only a true cipher

Vigenère, Blaise de, *Traicté des chiffres, ou secrètes manières d'escrire* (Paris: 1586)

Contents

List of Illustrations		viii
List of Music Examples		ix
List of Tables		xviii
Preface		xix
Acknowledgements		xxiii
1	A Musical Riddle	1
2	The Riddles of Music	17
3	The Rise of Cryptography	49
4	Sounding Numbers, Fickle Anagrams, Chameleonic Alphabets and Carved Vowels	69
5	Sonic Monuments, Alchemy, Hexachords and Lunar Discourses	101
6	BACH: His Way and Ours	129
7	Enlightened Ciphers, *Ars combinatoria* and Masonic Secrets	147
8	Censors, *Unsinn*, Nominal Ciphers and *Solrésol*	175
9	Riddles of the Sphinx	203
10	Stenographic Mysteries, Dark Sayings, Magic Squares and Foul Balls	229
11	Queer Liaisons, Mystic Chords, *DSCH* and Tombstone Monograms	261
12	*Hommages, Tombeaux*, Triskaidekaphilia and *Langage communicable*	291
13(12a)	Mystics, Numerologists and Modernists	321
14	Round Trips, Gothic Skyscrapers, Thunderwords and Fallen Angels	347
Bibliography		377
Index		417

List of Illustrations

2.1	Da Vinci, Musical Rebus (Windsor Castle 12697) © Royal Collection Enterprises Limited 2025	Royal Collection Trust. An example of da Vinci's mirror writing, by which he recorded material backwards. By holding the rebus against a mirror one can discern the intended message.	29
2.2	Mendelssohn, Rebus (1831), (Staatsbibliothek zu Berlin Preußischer Kulturbesitz, Mendelssohn Archiv Nachl. 22/B, 1 Spiegel)	30
3.1	Hildegard von Bingen, *Lingua ignota*, Alphabet (Wiesbaden, Hessische Landesbibliothek Hs. 2, fol. 464a)	59
4.1	Machaut, 'Ma fin est mon commencement' (Paris, Bibliothèque Nationale, fr. 22546, fol. 153r)	75
6.1	J. S. Bach, *Musicalisches Opfer*, Acrostic on 'Ricercar' (first ed., Leipzig, 1747)	140
7.1	William Hooper, *Rational Recreations* (1774), vol. 1, pl. III (p. 152)	150
7.2	Joseph Haydn, First Commandment (1791), autograph, Mary Flagler Cary Music Collection (The Morgan Library & Museum, New York)	167
8.1	Auguste Bertini, *Mélographie, nouvelle Manière de noter la musique* (1812), p. 11 (Paris, Bibliothèque Nationale)	179
10.1	Elgar, Dorabella Cipher (1897), Powell (1937), 98	233
12.1	Lili Boulanger, Monogram, title page, *Pie Jesu* (first edition, 1922)	307

List of Music Examples

1.1	BACH	1
1.2	Malcolm Arnold, *Fantasy on a Theme by John Field*, Op. 116	4
1.3	C. G. Hering, CAFFEE Cipher	5
1.4	Webern, Sketch for TENET	11
1.5	Webern, Row for SATOR Square	11
1.6	Webern, Row for 'Das Sonnenlicht'	12
1.7	Charles Koechlin, Marlene Dietrich Cipher	15
1.8	Charles Koechlin, Cipher Key for Marlene Dietrich	15
1.9	Charles Koechlin, Emil Jannings Cipher	15
1.10	Charles Koechlin, Charlie Chaplin Cipher	15
1.11	Charles Koechlin, Chaplin Cipher and Its Inversion	16
2.1	Joseph Haydn, Symphony No. 47 in G major, Minuet	19
2.2a–b	Beethoven, Piano Sonata in B-flat major, Op. 106, 'Hammerklavier', Finale	20
2.3	Friedrich Kuhlau, *Musikalisches Anagramm*	25
2.4	Beethoven, Canon, WoO 191	25
2.5	Beethoven, String Quartet in C-sharp minor, Op. 131	25
2.6a–b	J. S. Bach, Fugue in F minor (*Well-Tempered Clavier II*); Joseph Haydn, String Quartet in F minor, Op. 20 No. 5, Finale	26
2.7a–b	Stravinsky, Symphony in C, First Movement; Beethoven, Symphony No. 1 in C major, First Movement	26
2.8	Bartók, *Music for Strings, Percussion and Celesta*, First Movement (1936)	27
2.9	G. J. Werner, *Musical Calendar*, January (1748)	27
2.10	Robert Schumann, *Rebus* (1848)	31
2.11	Bartók, *Music for Strings, Percussion and Celesta*, Third Movement	45

3.1a	Phrygian Mode	62
3.1b	Hildegard von Bingen, 'O orzchis Ecclesia'	62
3.2	*Ut queant laxis*	65
3.3	Guido's arrangement of *Ut queant laxis* with text of Horace's 'Ode to Phyllis'	66
4.1	Trithemius, *Steganographica* (1606)	81
4.2	Trithemius, Key to Ex. 4.1	81
4.3	Schott, *Schola Steganographica* (1665)	82
4.4	Schott, *Schola Steganographica* (1665)	82
4.5	Schott, *Schola Steganographica* (1665)	82
4.6	Schott, *Schola Steganographica* (1665)	82
4.7	Gustavus Selenus, *Cryptomenitices et Cryptographiae* (1624)	86
4.8	Josquin, *Missa Hercules, Dux Ferrariae*	87
4.9	Busnois, *In hydraulis*	94
4.10a	Obrecht, *Missa Graecorum* (Agnus Dei)	97
4.10b	Obrecht, *Missa Graecorum* (Agnus Dei)	97
4.10c	Obrecht, *Missa Graecorum* (Agnus Dei)	97
4.10d	Obrecht, *Missa Graecorum* (Agnus Dei)	97
4.11a	Obrecht, *Missa De tous biens plaine* (Kyrie)	98
4.11b	Obrecht, *Missa De tous biens plaine* (Credo)	99
4.11c	Obrecht, *Missa De tous biens plaine* (Et incarnatus est)	99
5.1	Romano Micheli, 'Maria est fons signatus' (1650)	107
5.2	Biagio Pesciolini, 'Surrexit pastor bonus'	107
5.3	P. F. Valentini, Polymorphous canon	109
5.4	P. F. Valentini, Polymorphous canon	109
5.5	Michael Maier, *Atalanta fugiens* (1617)	112
5.6	Athanasius Kircher, 'Fama latere nequit' (1650)	120
5.7	Frescobaldi, *Capriccio* No. 11 (1624)	122
5.8	Frescobaldi, *Fiori musicali*, Ricercar (1635)	123
5.9	Francis Godwin, *The Man in the Moone* (1638)	124

5.10	Francis Godwin, *The Man in the Moone* (1638)	124
5.11	John Wilkins, *Mercury, or the Secret and Swift Messenger* (1641)	125
5.12	Philip Thicknesse, *A Treatise on the Art of Decyphering* (1772)	126
5.13	Philip Thicknesse, *A Treatise on the Art of Decyphering* (1772)	127
5.14	Philip Thicknesse, *A Treatise on the Art of Decyphering* (1772), bars 1–12 ('All that of love can be')	127
6.1	BACH Fugue in B-flat major (BWV 898), perhaps by Johann Christian Kittel	131
6.2	J. S. Bach, Brandenburg Concerto No. 2 in F major (First Movement, bars 109–12)	131
6.3	J. S. Bach, English Suite No. 6 in D minor (BWV 811), Gigue (bars 22–4)	132
6.4	J. S. Bach, English Suite No. 6 in D minor (BWV 811), Gigue (bars 40–5)	132
6.5	J. S. Bach, Sinfonia No. 9 in F minor (BWV 795), bars 16–18	133
6.6	J. S. Bach, *Canonische Veränderungen über ein Weihnachtslied* (BWV 769), *Variatio* 4, bars 37–42 (BACH)	133
6.7	J. S. Bach, *Art of Fugue*, Contrapunctus 4	135
6.8	J. S. Bach, *Art of Fugue*, Contrapunctus 14	135
6.9	C. P. E. Bach, Canonic Cipher Draft	144
6.10	J. C. F. Bach, 'Fughette'	144
6.11	C. P. E. Bach, Symphony in C major, Adagio (1773), bars 1–4	145
6.12	C. P. E. Bach, Rondo in C major (1780), bars 137–9	145
7.1	Joseph Haydn, String Quartet in E-flat major, Op. 76 No. 6, 'Alternativo' (1799)	155
7.2	Mozart, *Musical Game*, K 561f	157
7.3a–j	Mozart, Comparisons between K 551 and 561f	157
7.4	Mozart, *Jupiter* Symphony, K 551, Finale, Stretto (1788)	158
7.5	Mozart, *Die Zauberflöte*, Overture (1791)	164
7.6	Michael Haydn, Cipher Key	165
7.7	Michael Haydn, Cipher	166

7.8	Joseph Haydn, String Quartet in C major, Op. 76 No. 3, Cipher (1799)	169
7.9	Joseph Haydn, String Quartet in C major, Op. 76 No. 3, 'Emperor's Hymn' (1799)	169
7.10	'Haydn' Cipher	170
7.11	John McCabe, 'Franz Joseph Haydn' Cipher (1982)	172
7.12	John McCabe, *Lamentation Rag* (1982)	172
8.1	J. J. H. Buecking, *Anweisung zur geheimen Correspondenz* (1804)	176
8.2	J. J. H. Buecking, *Anweisung zur geheimen Correspondenz* (1804)	177
8.3	Beethoven, Sketch for *Missa solemnis*, 'Dona nobis pacem'	183
8.4	Beethoven, *Grosse Fuge*, Op. 133 (1827)	183
8.5	Beethoven, String Quartet in E-flat major, Op. 127, Finale (1827)	184
8.6	'Salvum me fac, Deus'	184
8.7	Schubert, Fugal Sketch (1828)	185
8.8	Abbé Stadler, Fugue in C minor (1828)	186
8.9a–c	Abbé Stadler, Fugue in C minor (1828); Simon Sechter, Fugue in C minor, Op. 43 (1828); Schubert, Fantasy in F minor, 1828 (D 940)	187
8.10	F. E. Fesca, Theme	190
8.11	Louis Spohr, String Quartet, Op. 29 No. 1	190
8.12	F. E. Fesca, String Quartet in B-flat major, Op. 1 No. 3 (1815)	191
8.13	Fanny Mendelssohn, Klavierstück on the Name of Begas, H-U 41 (1821)	192
8.14	Mendelssohn, Fugue for String Quartet in C minor (1821)	193
8.15	Mendelssohn, Fugue for String Quartet in C minor (1821)	193
8.16	Mendelssohn, Chorale Harmonization of 'O Haupt voll Blut und Wunden'	195
8.17	Mendelssohn, Organ Sonata in F minor, Op. 65 No. 1 (1845)	197
8.18	Fanny Hensel, *Hiob* (1831)	197

LIST OF MUSIC EXAMPLES   xiii

8.19	B. E. A. Weyrich, *Die Instrumentalton-Sprechkunst* (1830)	199
8.20	François Sudre, *La langue musicale* (1823)	199
8.21	François Sudre, *La langue musicale* (1823)	199
9.1	Robert Schumann, *Abegg* Variations, Op. 1 (1830)	205
9.2	Robert Schumann, Fantasy, Op. 17, First Movement (1837)	206
9.3	Robert Schumann, *Carnaval*, Op. 9, Sphinxes (1837)	207
9.4	Robert Schumann, *FAE* Sonata, Intermezzo (1853)	210
9.5	Brahms, Double Concerto in A minor, Op. 102, First Movement (1887)	213
9.6	Brahms, Sextet No. 1 in G major, Op. 36, First Movement (1865)	214
9.7	Agathe Cipher in Joachim's Letter to Brahms of 27 September 1894	214
9.8	Brahms, *Fünf Gedichte*, Op. 19 No. 3, 'In der Ferne' (1858)	215
9.9	Brahms, Fugue in A-flat minor, WoO 8 (1856)	215
9.10	Brahms, String Quartet in C minor, Op. 51 No. 1, First Movement (1873)	216
9.11	Brahms, Intermezzo in A minor, Op. 116 No. 2 (1892)	217
9.12	Robert Schumann, 'Nordisches Lied', Op. 68 No. 41 (1848)	219
9.13	Niels Gade, Violin Sonata No. 1 in A major, Op. 6, Second Movement (1843)	219
9.14	Grieg, *Lyric Pieces*, Op. 57 No. 2 (1893)	220
9.15	Proposed Ferenc Liszt Cipher (after David Brown)	221
9.16	Proposed Ferenc Liszt Cipher (after David Brown)	221
9.17	Liszt, Piano Sonata in B minor, First Movement (1854)	221
9.18	Cipher for Carolyne zu Sayn-Wittgenstein (after David Brown)	222
9.19	Liszt, *Präludium und Fuge über das Thema B-A-C-H* (1856)	223
9.20	Liszt, *Präludium* (1856)	223
9.21	Joachim, 'Abendglocken', Op. 5 No. 2 (1853)	223
9.22	Reger, *Phantasie und Fuge über BACH*, Op. 46 (1900)	227

9.23	Robert Schumann, Organ Fugues on *BACH*, Op. 60 Nos. 1 and 6 (1845)	227
9.24	Reger, Violin Sonata No. 4 in C major, Op. 72 (1903)	227
10.1	Elgar's Cryptograms and Key	234
10.2	Possible Key to Elgar's Liszt Cipher	235
10.3	J. H. Schooling, Musical Cipher from the Time of George II (1796)	236
10.4	Elgar, *Allegretto* for Violin and Piano (1885)	239
10.5	Elgar's Musical Signature	239
10.6a	Elgar, *Enigma* Variations, Op. 36 (1899), Bass Line	241
10.6b–c	*Scala enigmatica*; Verdi, *Ave Maria* (1898)	241
10.7	Elgar, *Enigma* Variations, Op. 36 (1899)	242
10.8	Elgar, *Caractacus*, Op. 35 (1898)	243
10.9	Brahms, Fourth Symphony, Op. 98 (1885)	243
10.10	Elgar, *Enigma* Variations, Op. 36 (1899)	244
10.11	Granville Bantock, *Helena* Variations (1900)	244
10.12	Holst, *The Planets*, 'Uranus' (1920)	245
10.13	Holst, *The Planets*, 'Saturn' (1920)	246
10.14	Walton, *Variations on a Theme by Hindemith* (1963)	247
10.15	Humphrey Searle, Symphony No. 1, Op. 23 (1953)	247
10.16	Humphrey Searle, *Passacaglietta*, Op. 16 (1949)	248
10.17	Humphrey Searle, *Passacaglietta*, Op. 16 (1949)	248
10.18	Thea Musgrave, *Homage to B.A.C.H.* (2013)	249
10.19	Thea Musgrave, Chamber Concerto No. 3 (1967)	251
10.20	Thea Musgrave, Chamber Concerto No. 3 (1967)	251
10.21a–b	*Ave maris stella*; Peter Maxwell Davies, *Ave maris stella* (1975)	253
10.22	9 × 9 Magic Square	253
10.23	Peter Maxwell Davies, Magic Square for *Ave maris stella* (1975)	254
10.24	Amy Beach, Prelude and Fugue, Op. 81 (1918)	258

11.1	Désirée Artôt Cipher	264
11.2	Tchaikovsky, Piano Concerto No. 1, Op. 23, First Movement (1875)	264
11.3	Tchaikovsky, *Fatum*, Op. 77 (1869)	265
11.4	Tchaikovsky, *Fatum*, Op. 77 (1869)	265
11.5	Tchaikovsky, Piano Concerto No. 1, Op. 23, First Movement (1875)	265
11.6	Tchaikovsky, Suite No. 1 in D minor, Op. 43 (1878)	266
11.7	Cui, Scherzo, Op. 1 (1857)	267
11.8	Rimsky-Korsakov, *Paraphrases*, 'Chopsticks' (1879)	269
11.9a–b	Lyadov, String Quartet, Scherzo (1886); Debussy, String Quartet in G minor, Scherzo (1893)	270
11.10	Myaskovsky, String Quartet in D minor, Op. 33 No. 3 (1930)	271
11.11	Scriabin, Mystic Chord	271
11.12	Prokofiev, Third Piano Sonata, Op. 28 (1917)	273
11.13	**BACH** and **DSCH** Ciphers	273
11.14	Stravinsky, *Symphony of Psalms*, Second Movement (1930)	274
11.15	Shostakovich, Tenth Symphony, First Movement (1953)	277
11.16	Shostakovich, Tenth Symphony, Third Movement (1953)	277
11.17	Shostakovich, Elmira Cipher (1953)	277
11.18	Ronald Stevenson, *Passacaglia on DSCH* (1963)	281
11.19	Edison Denisov, *1969 DSCH* (1969)	283
11.20	Schnittke, Third String Quartet (1983)	289
12.1	Honegger, *Prélude, Arioso et Fughetta sur le nom de Bach* (1932)	292
12.2	Poulenc, *Valse-Improvisation sur le nom de Bach* (1932)	293
12.3	Koechlin, *Offrande musicale sur le nom de Bach*, Op. 187 (1942)	294
12.4	Roger-Ducasse, String Quartet No. 1, Finale (1902)	296
12.5	Ravel, String Quartet, First Movement (1903)	297
12.6	Ravel, Berceuse (1922)	299

12.7	Aubert, *Esquisse sur le nom de Fauré* (1922)	299
12.8	Roger-Ducasse, *Poème symphonique* (1922)	301
12.9	Roger-Ducasse, *Poème symphonique* (1922)	301
12.10	Honegger, *Hommage à Albert Roussel* (1929), Key	302
12.11	Honegger, *Hommage à Albert Roussel* (1929)	303
12.12	Pierné, *Prélude sur le nom de Paul Dukas* (1936)	303
12.13a–d	Ropartz, *A la Mémoire de Paul Dukas* (1936); Dukas, *L'Apprenti sorcier* (1897); Dukas, *La Péri* (1912); Dukas, Symphony in C (1896)	304–305
12.14	Lili Boulanger, *Clairières dans le ciel*, 'Elle était descendue' (1919)	308
12.15	Lili Boulanger, *Clairières dans le ciel*, 'Elle était descendue' (1919)	309
12.16	Lili Boulanger, *Clairières dans le ciel*, 'Par ce que j'ai souffert' (1919)	310
12.17	Langlais, Symphonie n°2, ©1977 Editions Combre, Paris. All right reserved. Used by permission	311
12.18	Messiaen, *Méditations*, Musical Alphabet (1969)	315
12.19	Messiaen, *Méditations*, 'Être' and 'Avoir' Motives (1969)	315
12.20	Messiaen, *Méditations*, 'Relation en Dieu est identique à essence de Dieu' (1969)	317
12.21	Rivier, *Nocturne* (1956)	318
13.1	Bruckner, Fifth Symphony, Adagio (1877)	325
13.2a–b	Bruckner, Ninth Symphony, First and Third Movements (1894)	326
13.3	Mahler, *Ewigkeit* Motive	328
13.4	Schoenberg, String Quartet No. 2, Scherzo (1908)	335
13.5	Schoenberg, Suite, Op. 29 (1925)	335
13.6	Schoenberg, Suite, Op. 29 (1925)	335
13.7	Schoenberg, Variations, Op. 31 (1928)	336
13.8	Schoenberg, Variations, Op. 31, BACH (1928)	337

13.9	J. S. Bach, *Art of Fugue, The Musical Offering*; Schoenberg, Variations, Op. 31, Tone Row (1928)	337
13.10	Berg, 'Über den Bergen' (1905)	341
13.11	Wagner, *Tristan und Isolde*, Vorspiel (1859)	343
13.12	Berg, *Lyric Suite*, Tone Row (1926)	345
13.13a–b	Berg, *Lyric Suite*, Tone Rows, Second and Third Movements (1926)	345
14.1	Hindemith, Sonata for Althorn and Piano (1942)	350
14.2	Bartók, Scherzo in B-flat minor (1900)	351
14.3	Webern, String Quartet, Op. 28, Tone Row (1938)	353
14.4	Stravinsky, *Symphony of Psalms*, Second Movement (1930)	353
14.5	Stravinsky, *In memoriam Dylan Thomas* (1954)	353
14.6	Sacher Cipher	355
14.7	Dutilleux, *Trois strophes sur le nom de Sacher* (1976)	357
14.8	M. E. Bossi, Fugue (1888)	357
14.9	Malipiero, *Prélude à une fugue imaginaire sur le nom de Bach* (1932)	357
14.10	Castelnuovo-Tedesco, Greeting Card No. 4 (Walter Gieseking) **Mirages on the Name of Gieseking** Music by Mario Castelnuovo-Tedesco from *Greeting Cards – 18 Pieces for Piano from Opus 70* Edition by Luca Ciammarughi © 2021 Casa Ricordi Srl, part of Universal Music Publishing Classics & Screen International Copyright Secured. All Rights Reserved Reprinted by Permission of Hal Leonard Europe BV	359
14.11	James Joyce, *Finnegans Wake* (1939)	363
14.12	Tōru Takemitsu, SEA Cipher	367
14.13	Górecki, Fourth Symphony, *Tansman Episodes* (2014)	373

List of Tables

6.1	Bach's Signatures, after Tatlow (2016), 67	137
6.2	Ruth Tatlow's Analysis of Title Words in the *Musical Offering*, First Edition	142

Preface

∾

*L*IKE a riddle reluctant to surrender its solution, this book has been long in gestation. Its origins extend back to 2015, when the authors performed at the conference The European Salon: Nineteenth-Century Salonmusik the cipher-laden *FAE* Sonata for violin and piano (1853), a collaborative effort by Albert Dietrich, Robert Schumann and Johannes Brahms to honour Joseph Joachim. It is a singular work, with shifting moods shaped by the contributors' personalities – the brooding introspection of Dietrich, adamantine assertions of the young Brahms, and baffling Eusebius-Florestan pairings of late Schumann. When Joachim first read the sonata with Clara Schumann, he identified the authorships of all four movements and recognized their two quintessential ciphers – *FAE*, for 'frei aber einsam' ('free but lonely'), his personal motto, and its transposed inversion, G-sharp-E-A, for Gis-e-la von Arnim, daughter of Bettina von Arnim and source of his romantic infatuation.

The Schumann circle was just one group of musicians who manipulated ciphers to practise musical cryptography, the art of concealing messages in compositions through correspondences between pitches and letters of the alphabet. These encrypting enterprises reflected enduring traditions: the experiments of Franco-Flemish composers with solmization syllables during the Renaissance; the adoption by the Bachs and legions of later Bachians of B-flat, A, C and B-natural to 'sign' the Thomaskantor's surname; the French practice of honouring Haydn, Fauré and others through specialized keys that transformed their letters into musical motives; and the cryptic art of the Russian polystylist Alfred Schnittke, who elevated cipher composition by overlaying onto his Third Symphony (1981) a veritable catalogue of composers' names, like pieces of a composite puzzle about the history of Western music.

Our volume sketches a cultural history of these phenomena as they developed in Western art music. Of course, riddle culture has also engaged rock, film music, jazz, hip hop and video games. Our discussion of cryptography could be enhanced, for instance, by considering the appearance of ambigrams on album covers of rock bands, or the technique of backmasking, recording material in reverse to be added to a track, as in The Beatles' sound collage *Revolution 9* (1969). As for film, Josef von Sternberg's *Entehrt* (*Dishonored*, 1931), in which

Marlene Dietrich plays a secret agent for the Austrian military during World War I, is a pertinent example. In one scene she deciphers at a piano intelligence gathered behind Russian lines and concealed in musical notation. Owing to limitations of space, these and other examples must await another occasion for full discussion.

The fourteen chapters build upon work of scholars such as Siglind Bruhn, John Daverio, Minos Dounias, Willem Elders, Constantin Floros, Douglas Jarman, George Perle, Eric Sams, Katelijne Schiltz, Gerhard Strasser and Ruth Tatlow. The book also extends the purview of musical cryptography to treat other riddle-like techniques, some peculiar to music, such as puzzle canons and *Augenmusik* ('music for the eye'). Still other relevant techniques are indebted to mathematics – for example, musical realizations of the Golden Section and Fibonacci Series – and to the literary and visual arts – for example, palindromes, numerology, chronograms, rebuses, calligrams, anagrams and acrostics (one, readers be advised, unfurls itself across the chapters of the book).

To offer an outline of the book: Chapter 1 poses a five-part riddle after which Chapter 2 reviews cryptographic and related procedures. Chapter 3 considers how cryptography might have entered Western music through innovations in notation of the tenth-century Italian monk Guido d'Arezzo and the 'unknown language' of the twelfth-century abbess Hildegard of Bingen. In Chapter 4 the focus shifts to Guillaume de Machaut, whose fourteenth-century music and poetry drew on numerology, palindromes, puns and anagrams, sometimes revealed, but more often not. A highpoint of musical riddle culture then emerged in the richly layered Renaissance polyphony of Franco-Flemish composers such as Dufay, Busnois, Ockeghem, Obrecht and Josquin, whose musical forays often required solving labyrinthine Latin puzzles to unlock concealed meanings. Josquin developed what Gioseffo Zarlino described as *soggetto cavato dalle vocali di queste parole*, a musical subject 'carved from the vowels of … words', represented by the solmization syllables *ut, re, mi, fa, sol* and *la*. Honorific names or short messages were embedded in Masses, motets and instrumental works, as in seventeenth-century keyboard fantasies on the hexachord (Chapter 5). Around this time, cryptography affected too the music of English recusants such as Thomas Tallis, the proliferation of the Rosicrucian (Rosy Cross) movement, and the interdisciplinary visions of polymaths such as Francis Bacon, Gottfried Leibniz and Athanasius Kircher.

In the annals of musical cryptography BACH remains the most celebrated cipher, followed perhaps by DSCH (D-E-flat-C-B-natural), which permeated the scores of Dmitri Shostakovich and his followers, sparking debates about whether his music, if promoting the Soviet state, also concealed critiques of the regime. In the case of BACH (Chapter 6), that cipher formed part of the chromatic scale (A, B-flat, B-natural, C …), in effect a synecdoche, or (musical) figure of speech that limned the severe chromaticism of Bach's music and its latent meanings.

What J. J. Winckelmann described as the 'noble simplicity and quiet grandeur' of the classical art of antiquity might apply to the high classicism of Haydn and Mozart (Chapter 7), though that view might easily minimize ways in which cryptography informed the composers' lives and music. Haydn's brother, Michael, employed a musical code in his correspondence, and Mozart routinely encrypted sensitive topics in letters to his father. The entertaining quality of cryptography manifested itself in musical dice games and the practice of *ars combinatoria*, evidenced in Haydn's String Quartet in E-flat major, Op. 76 No. 6 and Mozart's *Jupiter* Symphony. Finally, both composers joined Masonic lodges, where they participated in the secret rituals of Freemasonry. Mozart's final opera, *Die Zauberflöte*, often impressed as a Masonic work, as recognized early on by Goethe.

During the Napoleonic wars and Restoration musical cryptography figured in manuals about secret writing (Chapter 8). The potential of ciphers attracted Beethoven, who drafted ideas for an overture on BACH, and Schubert, who at the end of his meteoric life crafted fugal expositions on a subject derived from his own name. The inveterate Bachian Mendelssohn improvised on BACH at the Thomaskirche in Leipzig, while his colleague Robert Schumann constructed six learned organ fugues from the cryptogram. The members of Schumann's circle (Chapter 9), which included Brahms, Gade, Joachim, Liszt and others, forged their own Romantic cipher paths, guided by Beethovenian veneration and, in the case of Joachim, also Weimarian temptations. Quite a different direction was pursued by the visionary French violinist François Sudre, who developed a *langue musicale* ('musical language'), one of several attempts to realize a universal language that might bind all nations.

In England (Chapter 10), Sir Edward Elgar, inclined to solving *and* creating puzzles, beguiled audiences with the iconic *Enigma* Variations. In the last quarter of the twentieth century, Maxwell Davies resorted to magic squares to determine the pitch content and structure of his esoteric scores. Several Russian and Soviet composers (Chapter 11) pursued the play of ciphers and other procedures in their music, whether Tchaikovsky, members of the Russian Five, the mystic Scriabin, or Shostakovich and his followers. In France (Chapter 12), when Maurice Ravel, Raoul Bardac, Paul Ladmirault and Jean Roger-Ducasse collaborated on a string quartet in honour of Gabriel Fauré (1902), they made sure to derive thematic material from a cipher associated with his name, FAGD. Lili Boulanger, the first woman to win the Prix de Rome (1913), appears to have been drawn to the number thirteen (her name contains thirteen letters), which she worked into her scores in various ways. And Olivier Messiaen tested the limits of music to convey spiritual truths by developing in his *Méditations sur le mystère de la Sainte Trinité* for organ the *langage communicable*, which relied upon a musical alphabet and coded leitmotifs.

All these examples manifest composers' intentions to veil in their music extrinsic messages, ideas and meanings. Few, if any, embraced more fervently the role of what James Joyce termed the 'cypherjugglers … on the great quest' than the second Viennese school (Chapter 13), whose triumvirate of Schoenberg, Berg and Webern brought to culmination several musical strategies explored in this volume, whether ciphers, palindromes, numerology or concern for absolute musical symmetry. If Hindemith, Bartók and Stravinsky explored related directions, later composers, including Torū Takemitsu and John Cage, pondered Joyce's obverse art – hiding musical allusions within literary contexts. Chapter 14 summarizes these trends and concludes with two relatively recent examples from Henryk Górecki and John Luther Adams. There our narrative rests, for wherever the future of riddles in sound leads remains anyone's guess.

Durham/Munich
September 2024

Acknowledgements

༄

WHILE envisioning and writing this book the authors accrued debts that should be recorded here. The critical reactions of many scholars and musicians, disposed or not toward the meanderings of cryptography, have informed much that follows. Among them are Styra Avins, Emanuel Ax, Claire Catenaccio (Georgetown University), David Cooper (*emeritus*, University of Leeds), Nancy Green, Paul Hawkshaw (Yale School of Music), Mikołaj Górecki, Stephen Hefling (*emeritus*, Case Western University), Kerry McCarthy, Jennifer Oates (Carroll College), Kirsten Santos Rutschman, Katelijne Schiltz (Universität Regensburg), David Schulenberg (Wagner College), Conrad Tao, László Vikárius (Bartók Archives, Budapest) and Giovanni Zanovello (Indiana University, Bloomington). At Duke University several colleagues, including Thomas Brothers, Roseen Giles, Bryan Gilliam, Anthony Kelley, Ieva Jokubaviciute, Scott Lindroth, Phil Rupprecht, Caroline Stinson, Nick Stoia, John Supko, Jacqueline Waeber and Andrew Waggoner, brought fresh perspectives to the subject, and patiently tolerated the perplexing vagaries of two cipher addicts.

Research funds from the Office of the Dean of Trinity Arts & Sciences at Duke University supported completing the manuscript and travelling to conferences where we presented early versions of material from several chapters, for which we remain grateful.

It is a pleasure to thank as well libraries and institutions that facilitated our work and granted permission to reproduce primary sources: Deutsche Staatsbibliothek, Mendelssohn Archiv, Berlin; the Morgan Library & Museum, New York; Bibliothèque Nationale, Paris; Hessische Landesbibliothek, Wiesbaden; Windsor Castle, Windsor; and Elgar Birthplace Museum, Worcestershire. The director of the Duke Music Library, Laura Williams, and her able staff, Sarah Griffin and Jamie Keesecker, went well beyond the call of duty to maintain a steady flow of library materials, especially during the difficult, claustral period of the Covid epidemic.

To Michael Middeke, Crispin Peet, Nick Bingham and the staff at Boydell Press our heartfelt thanks for expert advice and smoothing the production process, and to Dr. Emily Shyr our thanks for dispatching the index and unravelling its thorny complexities. To Kirsten Santos Rutschman our sincere thanks for her assistance in proofreading the book. To Dr. Karin Yoch our special thanks for diligent proofreading and assistance of many kinds during the final stages of production. Our thanks also go to Katharina's and Larry's whole families for their continuous support. We are pleased as well to acknowledge Kerry Jesberger (Aero Gallerie, https://aerogallerie.com/) for designing the cover and reminding us that silence is golden.

If, as Sir Edward Elgar famously observed, 'there is music in the air, music all around us', so too are we never far removed from cryptography, musical or not, hidden though it may be. And so, we would like to acknowledge one special friend, J. P., who habitually spins palindromic mysteries and captures their inaudible music with unflagging aplomb and precision – never odd or even.

R. L. T. / K. U.
March 2025

The authors and publisher are grateful for the generous funding provided by the Claire and Barry Brook Fund of the American Musicological Society (AMS).

CHAPTER 1

A Musical Riddle

'What can promote innocent mirth, and I may say virtue, more than a good riddle?'
– George Eliot, *Middlemarch*, Ch. 60

Question: What do J. S. Bach, beef cabbage, coffee, the SATOR Square and Marlene Dietrich have in common?
Answer: Composers have enciphered these and many other words into music.

SINCE time immemorial riddles have intrigued us, partly for their mirthful manner of connecting incongruous ideas, partly for their arresting way of opening fresh perspectives on our shared human condition. When we think of riddles, we normally recall verbal conundrums from cultures around the globe. But riddles can penetrate non-verbal aspects of our existence as well. Masking messages in music so that they lurk beneath the sonorous surface is an august Western tradition spanning the Middle Ages to the present. Known as musical cryptography, this puzzling pursuit is the subject of this book, construed broadly enough to capture not just musical ciphers and codes but also a curiosity shop of related techniques, which arguably *can* advance the greater virtue. They entertain and edify, but also bedevil and bewilder, and, when unsolved, perplex and perturb.

To illuminate our question, let us begin with **Johann Sebastian Bach**. For many the epitome of the Baroque, he applied two methods of enciphering 'Bach' into his scores, in effect 'signing' them, 'as in paintings where the partially concealed name of the artist appears'.[1] The first involved translating the four letters into pitches (ex. 1.1), so that B, A, C and H mapped onto B-flat, A, C and B-natural (in German musical nomenclature, B=B-flat, while H=B-natural).

Ex. 1.1: BACH

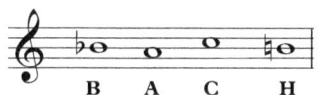

---
[1] *Neue Zeitschrift für Musik* 15 (1841), 44.

Already in 1732, the musical lexicographer J. G. Walther, second cousin of the composer, acknowledged the cipher for its 'melodic' quality.[2] As Bach himself recognized, these telltale pitches form a reordered segment of a chromatic scale (A, B-flat, B-natural, C) that divides the octave into twelve semitones, the equidistant steps of Western music. A salient feature of Bach's style was indeed its intense chromaticism, evidenced by liberal applications of flats and sharps that invested his music with a melodic/harmonic opulence that placed him among the most cerebral musicians. In essence, Bach's name spawned a metaphor for the chromaticism that saturated his music. Extending the cipher's mystique, several of his children deployed the eponym. Then, as the Bach Revival erupted in the nineteenth century, the cipher became a homage to the Baroque titan, revisited by scores of composers, from Beethoven to Schoenberg, Liszt to Poulenc, Busoni to Dallapiccola, Borodin to Gubaidulina. During the Bach tercentenary (1985), German scholars compiled four hundred instances of BACH in music history;[3] recent decades betray few signs these tributes have slackened.

More contentious, though, was Bach's second method of 'signing' his name – through numbers instead of pitch letters. There is evidence that he used number alphabets, according to which he counted letters, so that BACH equated to 14, the sum of their values:

B	A	C	H	
2	+1	+3	+8	= 14

Further, 'J. S. Bach' could be reckoned as 41, the reverse of 14:

J.	S.	B	A	C	H	
9	+18	+2	+1	+3	+8	= 41

There were different alphanumeric codes, some dating back to Hebrew gematria (aleph = 1, tav = 400) and Greek isopsephy (alpha = 1, omega = 24). Bach would have employed a version of the Latin alphabet from 1 to 24. How did he insinuate these numbers into his scores? In 1947 Friedrich Smend noticed that Bach's four-part canon for J. G. Walther (BWV 1073) was *fourteen* bars long (BACH), and comprised *forty-one* sounding notes ('J. S. Bach'), half the numerical sum for his cousin ('Walther'):[4]

---

[2] Walther (1732), 64.
[3] Prinz, Dorfmüller and Küster (1985).
[4] Smend (1947), III, 9–10.

W	A	L	T	H	E	R	
21	+1	+11	+19	+8	+5	+17	= 82

We cannot hear these correspondences, but that has not discouraged numerologists from divining a wealth of information in Bach's music. According to Smend, 'When Bach uses the number alphabet in his compositions, it is by no means always a matter of his own name alone … [W]ords of a religious and theological nature, are regularly… found also'.[5] And so, in the monumental Mass in B minor, Smend detected that the numerical equivalent of 'Christus' was 112, that Bach invoked 'Christus' in the *Credo* seven times, and that the *Credo* had 784 bars (112×7). But were these relationships deliberate? Not everyone concurred; number symbolism, whether regarding Bach or others, remains in dispute to this day.[6]

※ ※ ※

Beef Cabbage: We usually remember the Irish pianist/composer John Field (1782–1837) for creating the piano nocturne. Though he did not routinely explore musical ciphers, according to Eric Sams he did seize one occasion to generate two melodies from the words BEEF CABBAGE, to acknowledge a culinary hostess who prepared an especially savoury dish for him.[7] Surveying the Field thematic catalogue[8] yields no gustatory incipits, so presumably the composition never advanced far, or was lost. Nevertheless, in 1975 Field's name attracted the attention of the English composer Malcolm Arnold, who featured it in the *Fantasy on a Theme by John Field*, Op. 116. A one-movement piano concerto, this work contraposes reminiscences of Field's Nocturne No. 7 in C major (1821) against periodic sorties into Arnold's brash, cinematic style that typify his nine symphonies (1949–86) and film scores, *The Bridge over the River Kwai* (1957) among them.

What concerns us are Arnold's ciphers that run like leitmotifs throughout the Fantasy, including one for John Field, and three more for cities significant to his career – Dublin, Naples and St. Petersburg. To convert the ciphers into pitches, Arnold first wrote out the alphabet from A to Z, numbered from 1 to 26. Next, he notated a chromatic scale, assigning 1 through 13 above the pitches, and 14 through 26 below. From the plaintext, JOHN FIELD, Arnold

---

[5] Ibid., III, 20; trans. in Tatlow (1991), 9.
[6] For a critique of Smend's theories, see Tatlow (1991).
[7] Sams (2001), 755.
[8] Hopkinson (1961).

Ex. 1.2: Malcolm Arnold, *Fantasy on a Theme by John Field*, Op. 116

re-employed the musical namesakes of four letters, H, F, E and D, or B-natural, F, E and D. What remained was to quantify J, O, N, I and L as 10, 15, 14, 9 and 12, which became A, C-sharp, C-natural, G-sharp and B (ex. 1.2).[9] The first two bars enciphered JOHN FIELD; the last two bars extended the melody in retrograde order, re-concealing the Irishman's name in the pitches' compact musical palindrome.

Arnold then generated cryptograms for the three cities. And, in the case of Naples, he provided a clue – a melody suggestive of a madcap saltarello, the infectious Neapolitan folk dance. Together with Field's nocturne, the four ciphers gave Arnold sufficient material to flesh out his composition, which now transported the listener to Field's perfumed character piece from 1821, and now concealed his name and sites of influence in a game of ciphers.

※ ※ ※

Coffee: By most accounts, this indispensable beverage first captured the Western imagination in late seventeenth-century European coffeehouses, transforming 'civilized conversation into a popular sport'.[10] What facilitated the embrace of coffee was the Turkish siege of Vienna (1683), ultimately raised by Polish forces who ended Sultan Mehmed IV's expansionist designs. The hastily retreating Turks abandoned prized sacks of coffee beans; soon, Viennese merchants were peddling the black elixir. From the early 1730s dates J. S. Bach's *Coffee Cantata*, BWV 211, in which the addicted Lieschen exclaims, 'If I can't be allowed three times a day to drink my little cup of coffee, then my torment will turn me into a withered, roasted goat'. Fittingly, Bach performed this musical satire in the Café Zimmermann, where a growing clientele of middle-class Leipzigers could enjoy his music while sipping their preferred brew. But a few decades later in Berlin Frederick the Great mandated that his subjects imbibe beer instead. And so, platoons of *Kaffee-Schnüffler* ('coffee sniffers') rounded up vendors illegally selling coffee without royal permits. The effort proved futile, and Berlin commoners avidly joined the committed legions of caféphiles.

---

[9] See further, Jackson (2003), 164ff.
[10] Allen (1999), 129.

Ex. 1.3: C. G. Hering, CAFFEE Cipher

Bach seems not to have noticed the musical potential of the word 'Caffee', but in the nineteenth century, other Germans did. In 1831, the pianist Eduard Marxsen, remembered for instructing the young Brahms, composed a *Fantasie 'alla moda' über den Kaffee*, a virtuoso piano work on a theme drawn from the pitches C, A, F, F, E, E, and subjected to five variations.[11] Then, in 1844, the Austrian Hieronymous Payer offered his Op. 139, *Variationen über das Buchstaben-Thema C, A, F, F, E, E*, also filtered through five variations, the last a fashionable waltz. Why did Payer choose to celebrate coffee in 1844? His title page explained: 'Introduced from Africa to France in 1644, and to Germany in 1744, coffee now celebrates its jubilee in 1844'.[12]

Sometime before 1846, the music pedagogue Carl Gottlieb Hering exploited the CAFFEE cipher in a round composed for elementary-school children learning the musical alphabet. This time the six pitches served as a mnemonic device, periodically reinforced as each vocal part imitated them in turn, spelling out 'coffee' letter by letter, even though the text admonished children from consuming the 'Turkish drink', which, it was thought, weakened the nerves (ex. 1.3).

---

[11] The Fantasy survives in manuscript at the Gesellschaft der Musikfreunde in Vienna. See also Jaffe (2009).

[12] *Wiener Allgemeine Musik-Zeitung* 4 (1844), 290.

The SATOR Square: Among the oldest surviving verbal riddles in the West is the SATOR Square, which for two millennia has cast its spell over five continents, often as a 5 × 5 array in squared form:

S	A	T	O	R
A	R	E	P	O
T	E	N	E	T
O	P	E	R	A
R	O	T	A	S

Since the latter nineteenth century enigmatologists have probed the meaning of these words, which translate roughly as: 'The sower Arepo keeps the works rotating'.

Setting aside for the moment the cryptic 'Arepo', absent in Latin lexicons, we can parse the remainder without difficulty. 'Sator', in the nominative and hence the subject, is 'sower'. 'Tenet', third person singular, present tense, is from 'tenere', the verb 'to hold', 'to keep'. 'Opera', or 'works', is in the accusative, and thus the object. Finally, 'rotas', again accusative plural, means 'wheels', and syntactically is an accusative of direction. So, 'the sower keeps the works rotating'. As for Arepo, it could be the sower's fabricated name. But why 'Arepo'? Viewing this 'nonsense' word in the context of the entire square provides the answer. When spoken backwards, 'Arepo' becomes 'opera', and thus completes a perfect word square that can be read row by row (left to right or right to left), and column by column (top to bottom or bottom up).[13] Indeed, pursuing the paradigm in any direction reproduces the same five words, one of which ('tenet') is a strict palindrome, while the other four turn back on themselves in a special type of double meaning known as an *emordnilap* (literally, 'palindrome' backwards) – that is, a word which, when read in retrograde, produces another meaningful word (e.g., 'stressed' and 'desserts').

All these relationships piqued the curiosity of scholars intent upon extricating a hidden message from the square. By most accounts, the 'Sator-Arepo-Formel', as the German ethnologist Reinhold Köhler described it in 1881,[14] dates to Roman antiquity. As early as 1868, a graffito-like specimen surfaced on a plaster wall in Cirencester (Corinium), Gloucestershire, site of a Roman fortification from *ca.* 49 CE. By the early 1930s, more squares were emerging

---

[13] Another option is to read in a zigzag manner, left to right, then right to left, etc. (or down up, down up), a pattern known as *boustrophedon*, Greek for 'as the ox ploughs'.

[14] Köhler (1881).

from Roman ruins, perhaps from the third century CE, in Dura-Europus on the Syrian Euphrates River, along with 'inscriptions … of cabbalistic character: alphabets, magic signs and symbols, pentagrams, evil eyes, a magic animal, and several hermetic texts in mystic alphabets'.[15] Further afield, Sator paradigms materialized on Scandinavian runes and in Ethiopian Coptic churches; they penetrated medieval European monasteries, and found accommodations in sumptuous parchment manuscripts.

Strengthening the square's association with magic were its palindromic loops. Many cultures, including those of Graeco-Roman antiquity, shared the belief that one could countermand baneful spells by reciting them in retrograde. Occasionally the practice of retrogression spilled over into Latin poetry. Thus, in Ovid's *Metamorphoses*, when confronted by Ulysses for having transformed his men into swine, the sorceress Circe reversed her magical charm: 'words were spoken contrary to the spoken words' (*verbaque dicuntur dictis contraria verbis*).[16] And Horace implored the witch Canidia, the 'dark antimuse'[17] of his poetry, who had cast a spell on him by spinning a *turbo*, or magical wheel, to negate its effects by rewinding its rotations.[18]

If the SATOR Square bore magical associations, it also penetrated spiritual/religious realms. According to one interpretation, 'sator' referred to Christ. The seventeenth-century polymath Athanasius Kircher discovered that Abyssinian Christians had adopted corruptions of the square's words – Sador, Alador, Danet, Adera and Rodas – to symbolize the five nails of the Cross.[19] What was more, the two strategic placements of 'tenet' highlighted the Cross within the square, as if a cruciform had been positioned at the centre:

S	A	T	O	R
A	R	E	P	O
T	**E**	**N**	**E**	**T**
O	P	E	R	A
R	O	T	A	S

Yet another reading upended interpretations of the square in the 1920s, when researchers uncovered in the charm an anagram for 'Pater noster', the opening of the Lord's Prayer. Furthermore, they discovered that once realigned, these words could assume the shape of a cruciform, with the letters 'a' and 'o' (alpha

---

[15] Sheldon (2003), 238.
[16] Ovid, *Metamorphoses*, XIV, 301.
[17] Paule (2017), 1.
[18] Horace, *Epodes*, XVII: 7. See also Schwartz (1883).
[19] Sheldon (2003), 242.

and omega), the beginning and apocalyptic ending announced in the Book of Revelation, serving as the four endpoints[20]:

```
                        A
                        P
                        A
                        T
                        E
                        R
        A P A T E R N O S T E R O
                        O
                        S
                        T
                        E
                        R
                        O
```

Reshuffling the twenty-five letters of the secular SATOR array thus reshaped the square into the iconic symbol of Christianity. For many this discovery solved the mystery of the Latin talisman, now presumed to have been a device early Christians had encrypted to profess their faith secretly during the waning years of the Roman Empire.

There the matter rested until another stunning turn, in 1929. This time, an Italian archaeologist, Matteo Della Corte, announced the recovery of two more SATOR Squares, one a fragment in the ruins of Pompeii. Presumably they antedated 79 CE, when the roiling eruptions of Mount Vesuvius eviscerated the Roman city. Della Corte's discovery was doubly significant: first, the Pompeiian artefacts were the earliest surviving specimens of the square, but second, their dating now raised doubts about the validity of Christological interpretations altogether. In brief, 1) no hard evidence suggested that early Christians had populated Pompeii; 2) had they been active there, they would likely have communicated in Greek, not Latin; 3) the symbolism of alpha and omega would have been borrowed from the Book of Revelation, usually dated from *ca.* 95 CE, probably during the reign of the Roman emperor Domitian, and thus *after* the destruction of Pompeii; and 4) not until the second century CE did the cross emerge 'as an esoteric sign of Christianity'.[21]

New interpretations now challenged the 'Pater noster' solution. There were efforts to relate the square to Gnosticism, to Judaism by way of the Kabbalah,

---

[20] Grosser (1926); Sheldon (2003).
[21] Sheldon (2003), 253; also Jerphanion (1938).

and to the esoteric Orphic and Mithraic cults. Or, coming full circle, the square remained simply a reversible, if ingenious, word game, a clever palindromic construction not unlike another found in Pompeii: 'Roma tibi subito motibus ibit amor' ('In Rome, love will come to you suddenly, by [my] exertions').

We do not know when the Austrian composer Anton von Webern (1883–1945), member of the Second Viennese School, encountered the SATOR Square, though he was aware of it by 1931, just two years after the discoveries at Pompeii, for he referred to the 'berühmte alte Spruch' ('famous old proverb') and charted its palindromes in a letter to the poet Hildegard Jone.[22] The composer Ernst Krenek relates that Webern became preoccupied with the square.[23] A committed miniaturist, he promoted the greatest unity and symmetry in his music. Anything deemed redundant Webern meticulously removed, sculpting instead into the void terse, arabesque-like gestures. Hence his attraction to palindromes, whether verbal or musical. Webern's music invited the listener to enter, as it were, a hall of mirrors and to contemplate its perpetual symmetries.

Like Schoenberg and Berg, Webern was among the first to emancipate himself from tonality, with its centuries-old teleological triadic hierarchies. What Schoenberg began describing around 1908 as pantonality, which avoided tonal anchors in favour of 'egalitarian' distributions of the 'total chromatic',[24] rendered traditional distinctions between consonance and dissonance obsolete. Hostile critics, however, rejected pantonality, and soon found an alternative, decidedly pejorative tag – 'atonality' – to label Schoenberg's radical experiments. Nonetheless, by the early 1920s, the composer was promoting another new musical system, this one more rigorously regulated than the aimlessly drifting pantonality of his earlier scores. The result was dodecaphony – twelve-tone music – a type of pantonality based on tone rows (*Reihen*), orderings of all twelve chromatic pitches that could also appear in retrograde, flipped upside down in mirror inversion, or delivered simultaneously in retrograde *and* inversion. Through transposition, the four basic rows – prime, retrograde, inversion and retrograde-inversion – could start on any of the twelve chromatic pitches, yielding a total of forty-eight rows (4 × 12). Drawing from his preplanned row chart, Schoenberg would then invent the thematic and harmonic material for a new composition and winnow out unneeded rows. He confidently believed that dodecaphony would ensure the supremacy of German music for the next century. That prediction was too sanguine, though Webern and Berg did not hesitate to adopt dodecaphony, as did generations of committed twelve-tone

---

[22] Webern (1959), 17–18.
[23] Krenek (1965), 395.
[24] All twelve pitches of the chromatic scale.

10   THE ART OF MUSICAL CIPHERS, RIDDLES AND SUNDRY CURIOSITIES

composers who followed them. For Webern in particular, 'the row ensure[d] unity',[25] which explains why in 1931 he found validation in the SATOR Square.

What he saw in the Latin paradigm was a visual instantiation of the ideal he aspired to achieve in his own music. And so, he attempted to recreate the symmetries of the five words in purely musical terms, converting their rotating, self-perpetuating acrostics into abstract cells of pitches. His surviving sketches from 1931 reveal how he wrestled with the daunting task of transforming the verbal five-by-five pattern from classical antiquity into modernist music predicated upon twelve-tone rows. Webern's initial, laconic attempt, probably from mid-January, required just six rising and falling pitches, describing a simple musical palindrome above which he notated the verbal counterpart, TENET (ex. 1.4).[26]

By early February he had devised a complete twelve-tone row with its own, special symmetrical properties, and recorded it along with its retrograde version to produce a palindrome of twenty-four pitches that read identically, forwards and backwards. In turn, each row subdivided into four three-note segments, which Webern demarcated with vertical lines (ex. 1.5).

The eight segments, known as trichords, reflected each other in various ways, and thus added another layer of symmetry that could play off the square. For example, the first trichord (*a*) related to the second trichord (*b*) through retrograde-inversion (RI); to the third (*c*) through retrograde (R); to the fourth (*d*) through inversion (I), etc. Similarly, the second row, the retrograde of the first row, also partitioned itself neatly into four trichords linked to each other, and to those of the first row.

How, though, to underscore the derivation of the tone rows from the words of the 'famous old saying' proved formidable. Webern made a start by writing 'Sator Arepo tenet opera rotas' beneath his tone rows, either syllable by syllable, or letter by letter (see ex. 1.5). For example, he divided the disyllabic 'Sator' as 'S-a-tor', deliberately setting it beneath the first *three* pitches of the row. He seems not to have pursued the project further, and yet the idea of achieving unity through 'as many connections as possible'[27] did take hold and left a clear imprint on one of his major compositions, the Concerto, Op. 24, begun in July 1931 and finished in 1934. Now regarded as a *locus classicus* of twelve-tone composition, Op. 24 reused Webern's tone row created in February 1931 for the SATOR Square, with all its triplicating symmetries.

The result was a chamber work of remarkable concision, replete with miniature pitch squares that some scholars have interpreted as masterful transformations of the old Latin saying.[28] Sadly, when an American soldier mistakenly shot

---

[25] Webern (1959), 55.
[26] For facsimiles of Webern's autograph (Paul Sacher Stiftung, Basel), see Oesch (1991), 119 and Webern (1968), Plate 34.
[27] Webern (1959), 56.
[28] See, in particular, Gauldin (1977).

Ex. 1.4: Webern, Sketch for TENET

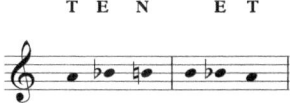

Ex. 1.5: Webern, Row for SATOR Square

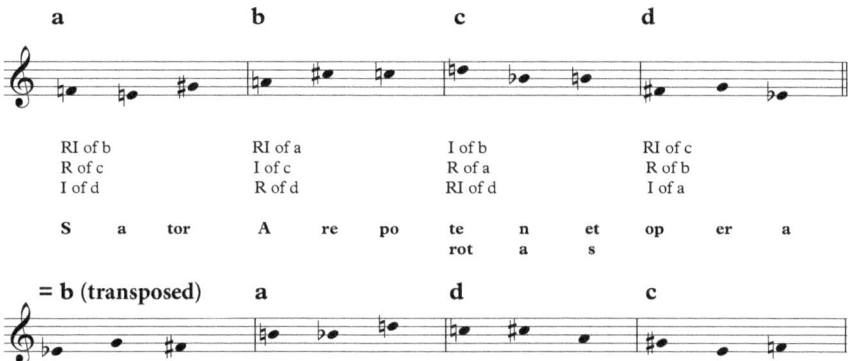

Webern to death in September 1945, the composer left preliminary sketches for what promised to advance his quest to entirely new orders of symmetry and uniformity. Contemplating early in 1944 another, 'purely instrumental' chamber concerto akin to Op. 24, Webern had begun recasting his new work as a cantata on a poem by Hildegard Jone, 'Das Sonnenlicht' ('Sunlight'), his *opus ultimum*, Op. 32,[29] but was unable to progress further after his son, Peter, died during an air raid in March 1945. Of interest here is the row Webern crafted for Op. 32, for it constricted the trichords to purely chromatic gestures moving by half-steps – four taut musical aphorisms in which the retrograde and inverted forms were identical (through transposition), as were the prime and retrograde-inversion (ex. 1.6).

At the time of his death, Webern was still pursuing the ultimate concinnity of the SATOR Square and approaching what the French composer Pierre Boulez described a few years later after a painting by Paul Klee as 'At the limit of the fertile land'.[30]

And what about the allure of the square? In 2019 the Italian composer Fabio Mengozzi found fresh inspiration in its verbal riddles and released a nine-minute work for soprano and string quartet titled *SATOR*. Not limiting himself

---

[29] Todd (1980b), and Oesch (1991), 132ff.
[30] Boulez (1976), 55.

Ex. 1.6: Webern, Row for 'Das Sonnenlicht'

to the five words of the square, Mengozzi considered smaller three-letter segments, triangulations formed from adjacent words, for example, 'TEP' (*templum*, temple) from Sator and Arepo, and 'RET' (*recte*, in a straight line) from Opera and Rotas:

S A **T** O R O P **E** R A
A R **E** P O R O **T** A S

Then, in 2020, director Christopher Nolan released the epic film *Tenet*, a two-and-a-half-hour science-fiction thriller. It explores temporal reversibility through palindromic, labyrinthine scenes shifting from the present to the past or future – sometimes simultaneously – as the protagonist (John David Washington) endeavours to prevent the destruction of the world through inverted entropy. Of course, palindromes being palindromes, there is already talk of a sequel – or perhaps a prequel?

❧ ❧ ❧

Marlene Dietrich: By 1931, as the SATOR Square was captivating Webern, a new musical medium was entertaining mass audiences and transforming the landscape of popular culture. Film music, limited during the preceding 'silent' era to live music performed in cinema theatres, now emerged as a potent new genre, a consequence of the new technology that synchronized moving images with sounds. As the eerie spectres of silent films gave way to speaking, emoting actors of the 'talkies', composers developed techniques to advance the dramatic narratives on the silver screen, and to fill the space between the (mostly silent) audiences and their emancipated, sounding counterparts.

Not all silent film stars flourished in the new medium. The swashbuckler of *The Thief of Bagdad* (1924), Douglas Fairbanks, had limited success in sound pictures. Charlie Chaplin, the empathic, down-and-out 'tramp' who found his forte in 'silent' pantomime, remained sceptical of the new art form, though he tested its potential in another creative way – retrofitting his silent films of the previous decade with newly composed film scores, giving a musical voice, at least, to the muted vagabond. Other actors happily crossed the divide. They included the flapper Clara Bow; singer/dancer Lilian Harvey; and seductive Swede Greta Garbo (*née* Gustafsson), whose stage name may have originated in an inadvertent acrostic in a critique of her acting, '**G**ör alla **r**oller **b**erömvärt opersonligt' ('performs all roles in a manner admirably impersonal'). Still others, including Marlene Dietrich in *Der blaue Engel* (*The Blue Angel*, 1930), effectively launched their international careers in sound (her co-star, Emil Jannings, did not fare as well, owing to his thick German accent and involvement in Nazi propaganda films).

Mentioning these seven film stars of the 1920s and 30s may seem to digress from our topic, so we might pull the main thread into prominence. In 1933 the Frenchman Charles Koechlin (1867–1950) completed a major orchestral score titled *The Seven Stars' Symphony*, Op. 132, a suite-like composition comprising musical portraits of the actors just mentioned. A former pupil of Gabriel Fauré (he will make a cameo appearance in Chapter 12) Koechlin was a prolific, multi-talented composer. His catalogue includes a wealth of songs, chamber and orchestral works (among them, three symphonic poems based on Rudyard Kipling's *The Jungle Books*). But Koechlin's preoccupation with the cinema and obsession with the 'insolent beauty of certain female stars'[31] interest us here.

Initially, Koechlin was not particularly attracted to the talkies. He made an exception for the silent films of Chaplin, who 'represented eternal hope in misfortune'.[32] But when Koechlin saw *Der blaue Engel* (*The Blue Angel*) in 1933, he imagined that a score for a sound film could add 'profound comment, as well as being faithful to the details and mood of the subject and forming a self-contained, balanced musical work in its own right'.[33] *The Seven Stars' Symphony* was his first response to the new medium. Infatuated with Lilian Harvey, he wrote over one hundred album pieces for her, as well as dances for Ginger Rogers; and after the tragic death of Jean Harlow at twenty-six in 1937, he memorialized the 'platinum blond' in a moving *Épitaphe* for flute, alto saxophone and piano, Op. 164. As for the symphony, its lush score is notable on several counts – for instance, Koechlin's introduction of the newly invented *ondes martinot* in the third movement, intended to intone a 'pagan chorale' for Greta Garbo; and the sensual colours of the saxophone and oboe d'amore in the fifth, devoted to Marlene Dietrich, temptress of *Der blaue Engel*.

By using ciphers Koechlin optimized another way to celebrate three members of his cinematic pantheon – Dietrich, Jannings and Chaplin – in effect adding their musical signatures to the last three movements of his score. Conveniently for us, in the case of Dietrich, Koechlin identified the *femme fatale* by superimposing the fifteen letters of her name above her theme (ex. 1.7).

But how did he assign, for instance, 'm' to the pitch E, or 'r' to B-flat? Ex. 1.8 reveals the answer, exposing one way that French composers, from Debussy

---

[31] Orledge (1971), 2.
[32] Ibid., 1.
[33] Ibid., 4.

and d'Indy to Ravel, Dukas and Poulenc, transformed letters into note names. First, Koechlin wrote out the eight letters from 'a' to 'h', then a second row from 'i' to 'p', and a third from 'q' to 'x', leaving 'y' and 'z' for the fourth. Observing German practice, he interpreted 'b' as B-flat, and 'h' as B-natural. The remaining letters of the alphabet aligned beneath the first eight, facilitating the conversion of plaintext letters beyond 'h' to pitches in the first row of letters. And so, 'm' became E; 'r', B-flat; 'l', D; 'n', F; 'i', A; and 't', D. The residual letters – 'a', 'e', 'd', 'c' and 'h' – required no conversion, which explains why, for instance, the pitch D could serve triple duty as 'd', 'l' or 't'. The advantage of the system was that every letter of the plaintext, not just its 'musical' letters, could be encoded. Though efficient, the process was not uncontroversial. When Camille Saint-Saëns was invited in 1909 to write a piece on Haydn's name for that composer's centenary, based on the musical cipher B-A-D-D-G, the Frenchman wondered to Fauré whether 'the two letters Y and N can signify D and G', and then admonished, 'It would be annoying to get mixed up in a farcical business that would make us the laughingstock in the German musical world'.[34] Though an ardent admirer of Haydn's music, Saint-Saëns (and Fauré) declined.

Koechlin had no scruples about encrypting all letters of the alphabet, and so fashioned his enchanting melody for Dietrich, presented first by the bass clarinet alone, to become the common adhesive binding seven fetching variations. Each one exudes the fragrant theme, dispersed through shifting instrumental timbres in the flute, clarinet, saxophone, English horn, oboe d'amore, cello and double bass, and French horn and saxophone. This sultry music – slowly changing in timbre yet replicating the theme – contrasts strikingly with the tensely dissonant movement that follows for Jannings. It charts the demise of Immanuel Rath, the repressed, pedantic Gymnasium instructor smitten by the siren-like cabaret singer Lola-Lola (Dietrich), and pilloried mercilessly by his students as Professor '(Un)rath' ('garbage'). In contrast to her rising theme, marked *pp dolcissimo*, his *fortissimo* theme (ex. 1.9) descends brusquely; together, the two signify the fated misalliance of utterly dissimilar souls.

Koechlin also applied his encrypting skills to the final movement of the symphony, devoted to the slapstick mishaps of Charlot (Charlie Chaplin) in silent films such as *The Gold Rush* (1925) and *The Circus* (1928). Curiously, the composer did not generate the theme from the same method applied in the previous two movements. Instead, Koechlin wrote out the letters from 'a' to 'g' for the first row, and then continued the process but with the letters in retrograde for the subsequent rows (see ex. 1.10), as if to capture cryptographically the madcap reversals of Chaplin's screen character.

---

[34] Saint-Saëns to Gabriel Fauré, 16 July 1909, in Nectoux (2004), 88.

Ex. 1.7: Charles Koechlin, Marlene Dietrich Cipher

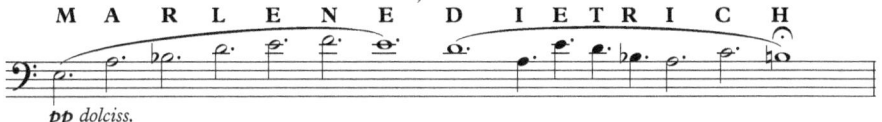

pp dolciss.

Ex. 1.8: Charles Koechlin, Cipher Key for Marlene Dietrich

```
A B C D E F G H
I J K L M N O P
Q R S T U V W X
Y Z
```

Ex. 1.9: Charles Koechlin, Emil Jannings Cipher

Ex. 1.10: Charles Koechlin, Charlie Chaplin Cipher

```
A B C D E F G
G F E D C B A
N M L K J I H
U T S R Q P O
  Z Y X W V
```

Having assigned the theme to a muted solo viola, Koechlin added an inverted form commencing a third below (ex. 1.11).

Why these manipulations – a code with letters reordered in retrograde, a theme that undergoes inversion – that serve to dissemble the 'little fellow's' name, and throw listeners off the track? Perhaps Koechlin's cryptic tinkering has to do with the disorientations of the tramp that drive Chaplin's narratives – scenes that move backwards and forwards in a cycle reeling from misfortune to renewed hope.

We have already encountered the culturally charged meaning of retrograde in the SATOR Square, and the use of reversed motion in classical antiquity to undo spells. Projecting a film backwards, thereby seemingly upending the concept of causality, was recognized perhaps as early as 1896, in Louis Lumière's short film *Démolition d'un mur*, which shows a wall being demolished and then

Ex. 1.11: Charles Koechlin, Chaplin Cipher and Its Inversion

magically restored *à l'envers*. Chaplin understood the technique and exploited it in his films, if for no other reason than to facilitate the production of his more dangerous escapades. Among the memorable scenes of *Modern Times* (1936), for example, was one in which the blindfolded Chaplin skated forwards and backwards, nearly losing his balance and plummeting from a height. In another scene, set in a factory, he was swallowed whole by the grinding cogwheels of a soulless machine, then regurgitated in reverse and restored. Koechlin could not have enjoyed *Modern Times* in 1933, when he composed the finale of his symphony. But he most likely would have known the maze of mirrors scene in *The Circus* (1928). Here a policeman chased the vagabond into a hall of mirrors, where their infinitely multiplying likenesses moved forward and backward in a dizzying whirlwind. Perhaps Koechlin's inversion of his Chaplin theme was a musical response to the anxieties of an alienated figure trying to find meaning in a modern world.

CHAPTER 2

The Riddles of Music

'Leverkühn was not the first composer, nor will he have been the last, who loved to insert secret messages as formulas or logograms in his work, revealing music's innate predilection for superstitious rites and observances charged with mystic numbers and alphabetical symbols.'

– Thomas Mann, *Doctor Faustus*, Ch. 19[1]

AFTER elucidating our riddle, we may consider other ways composers conceal messages in their scores. By and large, these techniques parallel well-established devices in other arts, suggesting that even if, as Walter Pater observed in 1877, 'all art constantly aspires towards the condition of music',[2] not infrequently music has responded in kind to sibling disciplines. Thus, Webern's attempt to realize the Sator Square as music led him to consider not only palindromes, but also acrostics and anagrams, all supported by literary traditions stretching back to classical antiquity.

Originating possibly with the poet Sotades, active in Alexandria during the fourth century BCE, the **palindrome** (Greek for 'running back again') is one example. The Roman epigrammatist Martial turned his mordant wit on sotadic verses: '… I don't pride myself on palindromes or read pathic Sotades backwards'.[3] Nevertheless, Roman poets exploited the emordnilap *Roma-amor*, which infiltrated Pompeian word squares. In the third book of *Ars armatoria* (*The Art of Love*) Ovid contrived at the ends of lines 507–10 a telestich spelling 'amor' when read vertically, while the last word of line 510 was 'amor', or 'Roma' spelled backwards, completing the word pair:

> *Vos quoque si media speculum spectetis in ir**a***
> *Cognoscat faciem vix satis ulla sua**m***
> *Nec minus in vultu damosa superbia vest**ro***
> *Cornibus est oculis alliciendus **amor***

---

[1] Mann (1999), 166.
[2] Pater (2018), 78.
[3] *Epigrams*, 2:86; Martial (1993), 195.

And you, should you in mid-passion behold a mirror, scarce one of you would know her own features. Not less harmful in your looks is pride; by gentle eyes must love be enticed.[4]

Why this literary conceit? Book III advises lovers to communicate through hidden messages. Mathias Hanses, who uncovered Ovid's hinged *amor-Roma* in 2016, argues that 'this interest in clandestine communication makes [Ovid's] poem an obvious hunting ground for … ancient word play'.[5] Sometimes, these verbal manipulations affected poetry in more profound ways. Thus, for Jay Reed the broad themes of Virgil's *Aeneid* derive from three words forming anagrams of each other: the reversible *amor-Roma* pair – love (Aeneas is the son of Venus, goddess of love); *Roma* (Aeneas is destined to found the Roman empire) – supplemented by *mora*, 'delay' (having fled the Trojan War, Aeneas lands in Carthage, where, postponing his departure for Italy, he falls in love with Dido).[6]

When musicians began reorienting pitches backwards remains unknown. An early example appears in the mid-thirteenth-century manuscript Florence Pluteo 29,1, a primary source for the *Magnus liber* of Léonin (*ca.* 1150–1201), a repository of early two-part polyphony (*organa*) associated with the Cathedral of Notre Dame in Paris. Here we find gatherings of substitute *clausulae* – short passages with freely composed upper parts set against plainchant in the tenor voice – designed to replace parallel passages in preexisting *organa*. One particular *clausula* reorders the chant text, *Dominus* ('Lord'), as *Nusmido*, specifying that it be sung in syllabic retrograde.[7] By the fourteenth century retrograde procedures had developed into elaborate palindromes, the most famous being Guillaume de Machaut's *rondeau*, 'Ma fin est mon commencement' ('My end is my beginning').[8] Franco-Flemish composers of the fifteenth and early sixteenth centuries applied retrograde techniques in their cyclic polyphonic Masses, sometimes in the *Agnus Dei*, to underscore symbolically the Lamb of God, who 'taketh away the sins of the world' (*qui tollis peccata mundi*).[9]

In time, retrogression became associated with arcane musical pursuits; indeed, the device was often activated by a Latin riddle such as *Ut prius, sed dicitur retrograde* ('As before, but said in retrograde').[10] These types of enigma canons were a means of testing a composer's contrapuntal mettle. Thus, J. S.

---

[4] Ovid (1962), 154–5.

[5] Hanses (2016), 199.

[6] Reed (2016).

[7] Fol. 150v; facsimile in Dittmer (1960), vol. 1.

[8] See also Ch. 4, pp. 74–77.

[9] Schiltz (2015), 106–7; Todd (1978), 71–8.

[10] For other examples see Bonnie J. Blackburn, 'Catalogue of Enigmatic Canonic Inscriptions', in Schiltz (2015), 367–477.

Ex. 2.1: Joseph Haydn, Symphony No. 47 in G major, Minuet

Bach practised the art of retrograde or 'crab' canons, most conspicuously in the *Musical Offering* (1747), where two palindromic parts commence simultaneously but from opposite ends, meeting midway before reversing course. But sometimes composers wore their learning lightly and applied retrograde motion for comic relief. Thus, Joseph Haydn included a *Minuet al rovescio* in his Symphony No. 47 in G major (1772), likely inspired by the *Menuetto cancrizante* for June in the *Neuer und sehr curios- Musicalischer Instrumental-Calender* (*New and Very Curious Musical Instrumental Calendar*, 1748) by G. J. Werner, Haydn's predecessor at the Esterházy court.[11] In Haydn's symphony, the second half of the minuet proper (and trio) reverses the first half, made droller by the placement of dynamics, so that a strong *forte* downbeat in the first half returns as an intrusive *forte* on a normally weak upbeat (ex. 2.1).

Haydn was pleased enough with this humorous effect to redeploy it in a piano sonata.[12] Then, in the twentieth century, the palindrome enticed the English composer Robert Simpson, who based a set of piano variations on it in 1948,[13] and crafted two palindromic slow movements for his First String Quartet (1952) and Second Symphony (1956), before returning to Haydn's theme to amass no fewer than thirty-two variations (all palindromic) and a fugue for his Ninth String Quartet, produced just in time for the semiquincentennial of Haydn's birth (1982).

---

[11] Todd (1980), 175–7.
[12] Hob. XVI: 26 (1773).
[13] Pike (1993).

Ex. 2.2a–b: Beethoven, Piano Sonata in B-flat major,
Op. 106, 'Hammerklavier', Finale

Fuga a tre voci, con alcune licenze

a)

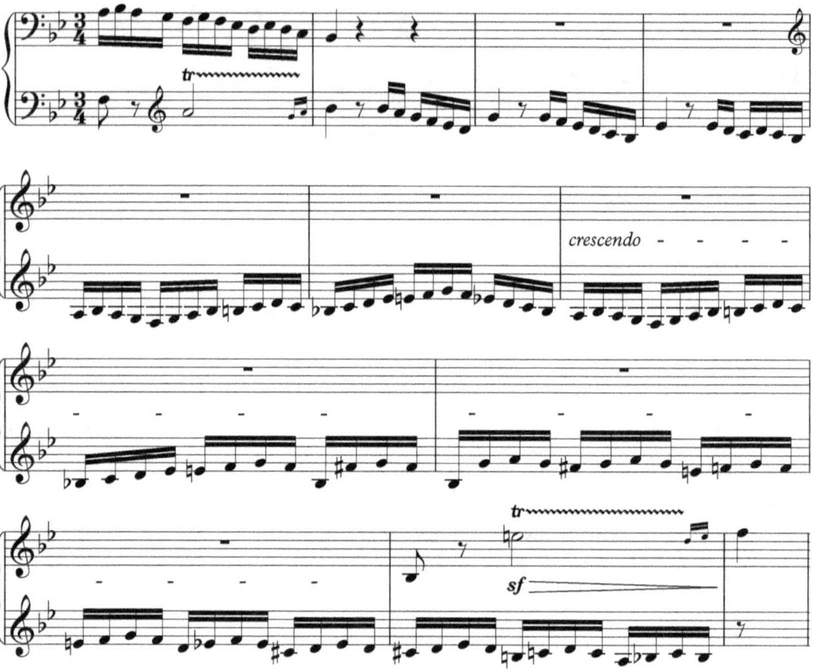

b)

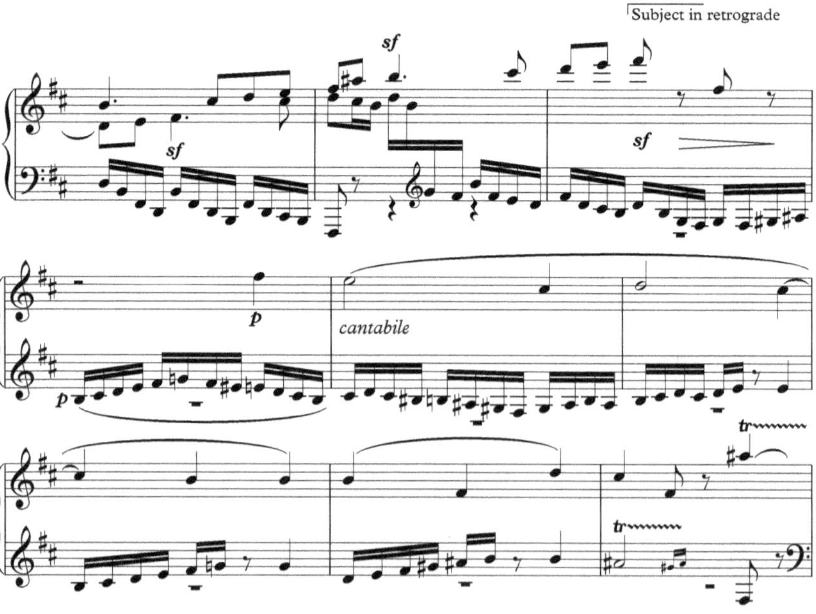

The two minuets by Werner and Haydn, supplemented by a third from C. P. E. Bach (H 216), are among the few documented usages of retrogression in the eighteenth century. Not many more accrued during the nineteenth. One was Beethoven's reversed presentation of the fugal subject of the monumental finale of his *Hammerklavier* Sonata, Op. 106. Usually missed by listeners, this *cancrizans* passage lasts but a few seconds before disappearing into a contrapuntal thicket (ex. 2.2a–b).

Two other examples include a *Lento al rovescio* by Friedrich Kuhlau,[14] and a palindrome in the third number of Schubert's melodrama *Die Zauberharfe* (*The Magic Harp*, 1820). Though the music for this play survives, the complete libretto does not, apart from a few cues for the spoken dialogue, leaving us pressed to understand the dramatic significance of the palindrome. Most likely it has to do with an unwinding of events engendered by a demonic agent. Schubert went to considerable trouble to conceal his artifice: the nineteen-bar orchestral passage does return in exact retrograde, but only after an interim gap of some three hundred bars. This 'split-palindrome' escaped attention until 1992, when Brian Newbould discovered it, conceding that Schubert was probably 'one of the least likely [to perpetrate] the cerebral deed'.[15]

Not so the members of the Second Viennese School, all of whom used palindromes for symbolic, extra-musical reasons. We have already seen how the SATOR Square promoted Webern's quest to achieve a penetrating musical unity. Palindromes were often utilized by Schoenberg and Berg as well.[16] Advancing a musical narrative only to negate it by moving in the opposite direction was an essential feature of Berg's music, as in his unfinished opera *Lulu* (1935). For the midpoint of the central second act Berg planned to show an interlude-like silent film 'whose images would depict aspects of Lulu's arrest, detention, trial, and imprisonment; these images then reversed by parallel events leading to her escape from prison: a revival of her will to live, illness, and medical consultation, subsequent isolation, and freedom'.[17]

∽ i

Acrostics and **anagrams** are two more literary devices that inspired musical treatments. Well represented in the Hebrew Bible (e.g., Lamentations, Proverbs and Psalm 119), acrostics figured prominently as well in classical antiquity. Thus,

---

[14] WoO 201 in Kuhlau's works without opus number.
[15] Newbould (1992), 214.
[16] See Ch. 13.
[17] Simms and Erwin (2021), 351.

the arguments prefacing the comedies of Plautus exhibited acrostics spelling the titles of his plays. From the fourteenth century, Chaucer's *An ABC* (1369?) was an early example of an alphabet poem, in which the initial letter of all twenty-three stanzas progressed from *a* to *z*,[18] constructing, as it were, a 'half-way house to the acrostic'.[19] Of Dante, Petrarch and Boccaccio – all created acrostics – the last was unmatched in zeal, especially in *Amorosa visione* (*The Amorous Vision*, 1343): 'Boccaccio first wrote three sonnets, … which together contain 1502 letters; and he then composed his long poem in *terza rima*, in such fashion that the initial letters of the 1502 successive tercets and single final lines of his fifty *capitoli* correspond exactly to the 1502 letters of the sonnets'.[20]

In medieval and Renaissance music Machaut, Busnois, Dufay and Josquin set texts containing acrostics, sometimes of their own fashioning. Often these revealed a dignitary's or composer's name, as in Josquin's motet *Illibata dei virgo nutrix*, published in Venice in 1508.[21] Absorbed into J. S. Bach's Cantata No. 150, *Nach Dir, Herr, verlanget mich*, is an acrostic dispersed over three of seven movements and uncovered only in 2010. Its text, 'DOKTOR CONRAD MECKBACH', refers to a town councillor in Mühlhausen,[22] where Bach arrived in 1707.

A few other cases display acrostics as defining features. The Russian Anton Rubinstein, for instance, wrote two sets of piano pieces titled *Akrostichon*, Op. 37 (1856) and 114 (1890). Before each movement he placed a capital letter that, when combined with the others, spelled a word. The letters for Op. 37, for instance, 'LAURA', revealed these five to be character sketches of Laura Sveykovskaya, an invalid whom Rubinstein met in Warsaw; those for Op. 114, 'SOFIA', referred to Sofia Poznańska, one of his pupils. Still other composers turned to texts by authors with a propensity for acrostics, including Lewis Carroll, whose many interests included photography, cryptography and writing in retrograde. In 1976 the late David Del Tredici inserted into his opera 'in concert form', *Final Alice*, the 'Acrostic Song', an aria based on a poem of Carroll displaying the acrostic 'ALICE PLEASANCE LIDDELL', the original inspiration for the eponymous protagonist of *Alice's Adventures in Wonderland* and *Through the Looking Glass*. More recently, in 1993, the Korean composer Unsuk Chin returned to children's fantasy literature in her *Akrostichon-Wortspiel* (*Acrostic Word Play*), for soprano and chamber ensemble. It comprises seven scenes from Carroll's *Through the Looking Glass* (1871) and Michael Ende's *Die unendliche Geschichte* (*The Neverending Story*, 1979), of which the third bears the intriguing title *Die*

---

[18] See Haresnape (2015). Chaucer omitted j, u and w.
[19] Knox (1924), 4.
[20] Wilkins (1951), 101.
[21] Elders (2013), 179–80.
[22] Schulze (2010).

THE RIDDLES OF MUSIC 23

Spielregel-sträwkcüR tieZ (*The Rules of the Game-sdrawkcab emiT*). Throughout the composition Chin manipulates her texts beyond recognition through various word plays – conjoining vowels and consonances from dismembered words, for example, and presenting syllables backwards, allowing verbal fantasy to blur into asemic musical fantasy, so that 'only the symbolic meaning remains'.[23]

Another challenging category, musical **anagrams** (Greek for 'art of rewriting'), can be difficult to discern; though, like their literary cousins, they, too, may hide in thinly veiled, if not plain, sight. When Shakespeare, for instance, begins *Twelfth Night* with these familiar lines,

> If music be the food of love, play on;
> Give me excess of it, that, surfeiting,
> The appetite may sicken, and so die

we focus on the lovelorn Duke of Orsino's infatuation with Lady Olivia, who, mourning the death of her brother, has declined to marry for seven years. Few suspect, though, that through a network of anagrams, Shakespeare's text might also divulge the play's date, authorship and even some of its sources. In an ambitious analysis, William Bellamy has argued that '"sub-textual" anagrammatism is not only pervasive in Shakespeare's verse, but fundamental to his verbal art'.[24] And so, if we highlight strategically spaced letters in the poem of *Twelfth Night*, additional meanings seem to germinate:

If **m**usic be the foo**d** of love, play on;	M D
Give me ex**c**ess of **i**t, that, surfeiting,	C I
The appetite may sicken, and so die.	
That strain again! it had a dying fall:	
O, it came o'er my ear like the sweet sound,	
That **b**reathes upon **a** bank of violets,	B A
Stealing and giving odou**r**! E**n**ough; no more:	R N
'Tis not so sweet now **a**s it was **be**fore.	A B E
O **s**pirit of love! **h**ow quick and fresh **a**rt thou,	S H A
That, notwithstanding thy **c**apaciti**e**	C E
Receiveth a**s** the sea, nought enters there,	S
Of what validity and **p**itch so **ere**,	P E R E W
But falls **i**nto abatement and low price,	I
Even in a minute: so fu**ll** of shapes is fancy	L L
That it alone is high fantastical.	

---

[23] See further, Lee (2017), 276–93.
[24] Bellamy (2015), 1.

Thus, lines 1 and 2 may yield the date of composition, **MDCI** (1601), an example of a **chronogram**; lines 9–14, the authorship (Shacespere Will); and lines 6–12, Barnabe Riche, author of 'Apolonius and Silla', on which Shakespeare drew for his comedy.[25]

While one might debate whether such filtered evidence is coincidental, there is no denying the long history of anagrams. After Shakespeare, they were in vogue at the seventeenth-century court of Louis XIII, who appointed a royal anagrammatist, tasked with discovering examples propitious for the monarch's reign. But by the early eighteenth century, such literary conceits were out of favour, so that Joseph Addison, co-founder of *The Spectator*, dismissed them as 'false wit'.[26] The question remains, though: in the case of music, did composers appropriate parallel anagrammatic techniques?

Friedrich Kuhlau (1786–1832), for one, did so. A German pianist and composer who fled to Copenhagen in 1810 to escape the Napoleonic Wars, Kuhlau had a propensity toward puzzle canons and other learned musical endeavours. And so, in 1819 he published a 'Musikalisches Anagramm' in the Leipzig *Allgemeine musikalische Zeitung*.[27] It is a curious piece of work, with six pitches gingerly fitted on and between two lines of a treble stave, with a third line below for a figured-bass part (ex. 2.3).

Though Kuhlau did not provide the solution, the four central pitches of the treble part would seem to spell BACH, so that Kuhlau likely had in mind a contrapuntal riddle on the Thomaskantor's name. When Kuhlau visited Vienna in 1825, he may have shared his 'anagram' with Beethoven, who responded with a punning canon (WoO 191) on '**Kühl**, nicht **lau**' ('cool, not tepid'); suitably, the first four notes of Beethoven's canon were B-A-C-H[28] (ex. 2.4).

Apart from these minor *pièces d'occasion*, the concept of *musical* anagrams does not seem to have gained currency. To search for them, we might consider the poet/composer Guillaume de Machaut (*ca.* 1300–77), whose narrative poems teem with *literary* anagrams, deciphered by solving clues strategically placed in the poet's verses.[29] We have already mentioned Machaut's palindromic 'Ma fin est mon commencement', in which the music and text mirror each other directly. But whether Machaut might have translated his poetic anagrams into musical counterparts remains an open question. That said, we might adduce a

---

[25] See Bellamy (2015), 494ff, from which this example is drawn.
[26] *The Spectator* (11 May 1711).
[27] *AmZ* 21 (1819), col. 832.
[28] On Kuhlau's visit to Beethoven, see Platen (1987).
[29] See in particular De Looze (1988).

Ex. 2.3: Friedrich Kuhlau, *Musikalisches Anagramm*

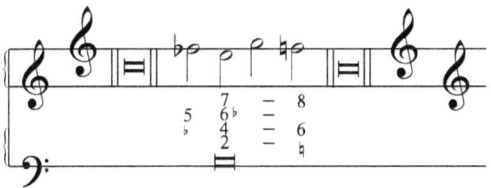

Ex. 2.4: Beethoven, Canon, WoO 191

Ex. 2.5: Beethoven, String Quartet in C-sharp minor, Op. 131

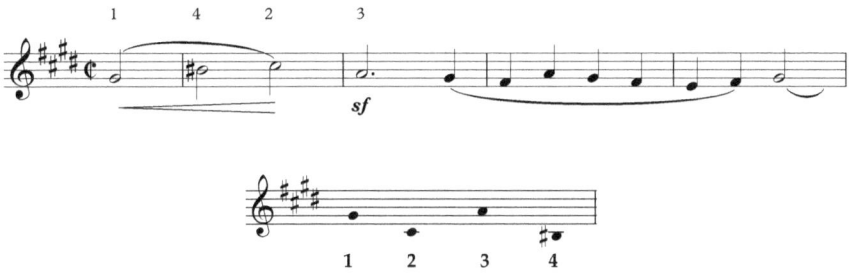

few examples from later composers that do seem to manipulate musical gestures in an anagrammatic way. Consider, for instance, the first four pitches of Beethoven's String Quartet in C-sharp minor, Op. 131 (1826), the beginning of an austere fugue from his penultimate year (ex. 2.5).

If we 'unscramble' the order of these pitches, we can trace their historical antecedent to a stock Baroque fugal subject visited by Bach (*Well-Tempered Clavier*, Book II, Fugue in F minor), Joseph Haydn (String Quartet in F minor, Op. 20 No. 5) and many others (ex. 2.6).

In short, Beethoven's opening impresses as a musical anagram of an older model. Similarly, we might read the motive propelling the first movement of Stravinsky's Symphony in C (1940), B-C-G, as an anagrammatic respelling of the persistent three-note motive, C-G-B, that drives forward the first movement of Beethoven's Symphony No. 1, Op. 21, also in C major (ex. 2.7).

Ex. 2.6a–b: J. S. Bach, Fugue in F minor (*Well-Tempered Clavier II*);
Joseph Haydn, String Quartet in F minor, Op. 20 No. 5, Finale

Ex. 2.7a–b: Stravinsky, Symphony in C, First Movement;
Beethoven, Symphony No. 1 in C major, Op. 10, First Movement

Or, the opening fugal subject of Bartók's *Music for Strings, Percussion and Celesta* (1936), based on a chromatic cluster spanning the third from A to C-sharp, appears to subsume B-A-C-H in an anagrammatic reordering (ex. 2.8).

Before leaving anagrams, we might mention one specialized subtype, the **chronogram** ('time writing'). Historically this device has appeared on buildings, monuments and coins, figured in coronations, and decorated poetry and prose, as a means of commemorating dates, often by inscribing Roman letters with numerical values (M, D, C, L, X, V and I) that, in the aggregate, produce the relevant year.[30] Like acrostics and anagrams, chronograms fell out of favour in the eighteenth century; Joseph Addison dismissed them as 'the results of monkish ignorance'.[31] But that did not dissuade the English eccentric James Hilton from compiling thousands of examples in three hefty volumes published during the 1880s. The title page of the first conceals this chronogram: 'The QVaInt bVt not aLtogether VnsChoLarLy ConCeIts whICh thIs LIttLe

---

[30] See Hilton (1882) and Marschall (1997).

[31] *The Spectator*, 9 May 1711.

Ex. 2.8: Bartók, *Music for Strings, Percussion and Celesta*, First Movement (1936)

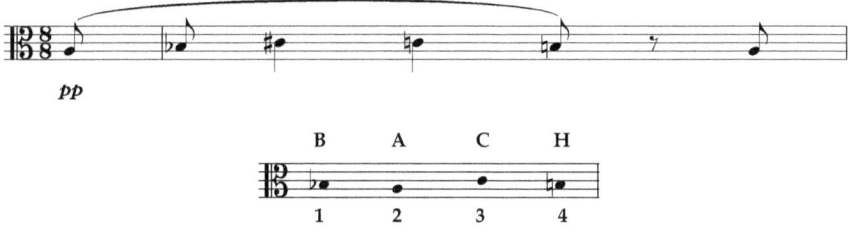

Ex. 2.9: G. J. Werner, *Musical Calendar*, January (1748)

book ContaIneth DespIse not O CoVrteoVs reaDer', rather arduously confirming 1882 as the year of publication.

How have composers recorded specific years in their music? The preface to Johannes Pachelbel's keyboard variations, *Hexachordum Apollinis* (1699), incorporates a chronogram by converting 'Johannes Pachelbelius Organista Noriberghensium' into four numbers, the sums of which (243 + 423 + 378 + 655 = 1699) yield the year of issue.[32] Katelijne Schiltz has uncovered two early musical chronograms, one of which, by Martin Agricola, appears in a collection of vocal canons, *Suavissimae et iucundissimae harmoniae* (*Sweetest and Most Delightful Harmonies*), published in 1567.[33] The other example occurs in a chanson by Tilman Susato printed in 1543. Agricola merely requires the reader to count the number of notes and rests in the music to discover the pertinent year; Susato provides a verbal rubric with instructions about how to determine the year, month and day.

A few other composers pursued more active, interventionist approaches in their time riddles. When G. J. Werner, for example, wrote music for the month of January in his *Musical Calendar* suite, he composed a fugue on a subject generated from intervals forming the year 1748, *viz.*, an ascending seventh, descending fourth and ascending octave (ex. 2.9).

---

[32] See Tatlow (2016), 47–8.

[33] Schiltz (2012 and 2015, 350–8).

Similarly, Bedřich Smetana's album leaf for piano in C major displays thematic material that privileges scale degrees 8, 6 and 2, so that, once again, a chronogram divulges the year of composition, 1862.³⁴

～ ii

The techniques discussed so far relate letters or words to music – for example, enciphering a text to conceal it; presenting it backwards, as in a palindrome; or reordering the letters of a word to generate an anagram. But some word plays exploit not only verbal but visual elements. One of these brain teasers is the **rebus**, from the ablative plural of *res*, Latin for 'thing' – so, 'with things'. These visually oriented 'things' play on homophones – words sounding the same but conveying different meanings. Typically, a rebus transforms a verbal text into a succession of letters, visual objects and perhaps numbers. When one reads aloud the entire rebus the process activates the homophonic equivalents. Thus, the word 'I' might trigger a drawing of an 'eye'; in a German rebus, the word 'ein' might appear as a drawing of an egg ('Ei') followed by 'n'.

The origins of the rebus may reach back to the logograms of Sumerian cuneiform and Egyptian hieroglyphics.³⁵ During the Renaissance, the *grands rhétoriqueurs* of the late fifteenth and early sixteenth centuries experimented with the device in their poetry. In 1572 the jurist Étienne Tabourot released *Les Bigarrures* (*Medleys*), which, playing on the ambiguities (équivoques) of words, reminded readers that in sixteenth-century France 'language was just as much a matter for the ears as for the eyes'.³⁶ Among the volume's conceits were *précis* of different types, including rebuses that used musical pitches, identified by their solmization syllables to substitute for syllables of words. Thus, in the case of 'Hola Monsieur, vous estes / L'ami fat resolu' ('Greetings, Monsieur, you are / our conceited, determined friend'), one could visualize the second line in musical notation as the pitches *la, mi, fa, re, sol* and *ut*.³⁷ Not to be outdone, Leonardo da Vinci concocted over one hundred Italian picture-puzzles, mostly preserved at Windsor Castle, including eighteen with musical notations. One clever invention, recorded on a hand-drawn musical stave, begins with a fishhook (*amo*) followed by the notes *re, sol, la, mi, fa, re, mi*, then *rare* (written out). The second portion continues with *la, sol, mi, fa,*

---

[34] Large (1970), 33.
[35] See further, Schenk (1968); and Céard and Margolin (1986).
[36] Glidden (1982), 245.
[37] Tabourot (1584), 128.

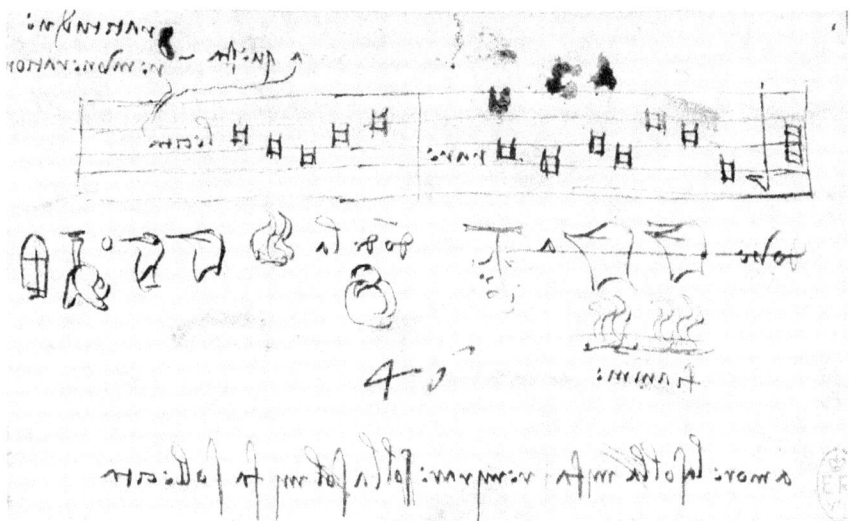

Illustration 2.1: Da Vinci, Musical Rebus (Windsor Castle 12697) © Royal Collection Enterprises Limited 2025 | Royal Collection Trust. An example of da Vinci's mirror writing, by which he recorded material backwards. By holding the rebus against a mirror one can discern the intended message.

sol and *lecita* (again written out). The result is: 'Amore sol la mi fa remirare, la sol mi fa sollecita' ('Love only makes me remember, it alone makes me alert').[38]

Several Renaissance composers devised rebuses for their signatures, primarily by appropriating relevant solmization syllables.[39] Guillaume Du Fay, for example, designed a rebus-like escutcheon that appeared on the four corners of his tombstone. Within a large Gothic G 'Du' rested above the notated pitch 'fa', while below, the letter 'y' completed his name.[40] The signature of Pierre de la Rue separated 'de' and 'Rue' with a notated 'la',[41] while that of Matthaeus Pipelare showed an image of a pipe followed by the pitches 'la' and 're'.[42] The surname of the music copyist, merchant and sometime spy of Henry VIII, Petrus Alamire, easily accommodated the pitches 'la', 'mi' and 're' for his rebus-like signature. Alamire was the pseudonym of Petrus Imhoff, prompting some scholars to surmise that he chose it on account of its potential for word play.[43]

---

[38] See further, Winternitz (1974), 114; and Marinoni (1954).
[39] Schiltz (2015), 343ff.
[40] See Turrentine (1986).
[41] Meconi (2003), 3–4.
[42] Kellman (1999), 21.
[43] Schiltz (2015), 345.

Illustration 2.2: Mendelssohn, Rebus (1831), (Staatsbibliothek zu Berlin Preußischer Kulturbesitz, Mendelssohn Archiv Nachl. 22/B, 1 Spiegel)

Ex. 2.10: Robert Schumann, *Rebus* (1848)

Later musicians, too, honed their skills at rebuses, among them the sedulous Felix Mendelssohn Bartholdy, who, when not contriving Bachian puzzle canons might invent *Bilderrätsel* (picture puzzles) for the amusement of family and friends. One rebus from 1831 presents in succession the number 8, drawings of a piano and spool of wool, the letter 'n', an egg, the syllable 'len!', the word 'wenn', syllable 'Ad', an elephant and continent labelled 'Asien' and, finally, the word 'spielt'. The solution converts the gibberish of 'acht Klavier Wolle n Eilen! Wenn Ad Elefant Asien spielt' into the intelligible 'Ach Thekla, wir wollen eilen, wenn Adele Fantasien spielt' ('Oh, Thecla, we want to hurry, when Adele plays fantasies').[44]

Two of Mendelssohn's circle, Robert Schumann and Niels Gade, labelled their compositions after similar types of word play. When in 1848 Schumann sketched his *Rebus*, intended for the *Jugendalbum* (*Album for the Youth*), Op. 68, he began with a chiasmic literary maxim, 'Laß das Fade, faß das Echte' ('Leave the tasteless, grasp the genuine'), and then exchanged each letter save 'L' (appearing alone at the beginning of the rebus) and 't' into musical pitches, generating this melody (ex. 2.10).

A few decades later, Schumann's younger Danish colleague, Niels Gade, published three *Claveerstykker* titled *Rebus* (1875), into which he folded his own name (G-A-D-E) and the BACH cipher, both of which appeared in multiple iterations subjected to rhythmic and harmonic modifications, and presented in different registers.[45]

In the twentieth century, at least two composers attempted musical applications of the rebus. In 1931 the Ukrainian Igor Markevitch, who worked in Paris and was hailed as the second Stravinsky, completed his orchestral score *Rébus*, originally intended as a ballet. Its internal scenes were planned to act out the words 'pauvreté' ('poverty'), 'nez' ('nose'), 'pas' ('steps') and 'vices' ('vices'), or,

---

[44] Wehner (2017), 114. Adele is Adele Schopenhauer, author and sister of the philosopher.
[45] On Gade, see further, Chapter 9 below, and Todd (2023).

when slightly adjusted, 'pauvreté, n'est pas vice' ('poverty is no vice').[46] Then, during the waning months of the Battle of Britain in 1940, Frank Bridge completed his final work, *Rebus*. Scored for orchestra, it 'depict[ed] a simple rumour which, when spread from person to person, gradually becomes distorted until it bears little resemblance to the original'.[47] Indeed, the music germinates from a basic cell (E-F-sharp-A-B) that undergoes multiple transformations.

One other category that blends sonorous and visual elements is **eye music** (*Augenmusik*) – the use of distinctive designs within notated music to create visual layers of meaning in the score. As the musical pedagogue Wendell Kretzschmar in Thomas Mann's novel *Doktor Faustus* observes, 'composers in every age had tucked away some things in their notation that were meant more for the reading eye than for the ear'.[48] Some significant twentieth-century examples include George Crumb's *Makrokosmos I* and *II* for piano solo (1972 and 1973), in which the composer notated six of the twenty-four pieces in various shapes – in Vol. 1, a cross for No. 4 (*Crucifixus*), circle for No. 6 (*Magic Circle of Infinity*) and spiral for No. 12 (*Spiral Galaxy*); in Vol. 2, two circles for No. 4 (the *Doppelgänger*-like *Twin Suns*), a mollusc shape for No. 8 (*Prophecy of Nostradamus*) and the peace sign for No. 12 (*Agnus Dei*). For Crumb's contemporary Donald Martino, *Augenmusik* could serve a satiric purpose, as in his reaction to mixed-media creations of the 1960s: *Augenmusik: A Mixed Mediocritique*, for 'actress, danseuse, or uninhibited female percussionist and pre-recorded tape' (1972).

A literary analogue to eye music is the **calligram** (Greek for 'beautiful writing'), coined by the French poet Guillaume Apollinaire in 1918, with the appearance of *Calligrammes: Poèmes de la paix et de la guerre, 1913–1916*. Here Apollinaire offered syntheses of poetry (devoid of punctuation) and art by subjecting his abstract verses to graphic designs related to his subjects. Partly inspired by cubism, Apollinaire sought to replace the conventional layout of a poem with a fusion of verses and images that might encourage readers to consider the work simultaneously from a variety of perspectives. But the idea of dissolving disciplinary borders separating the poetic and the visual was not the Frenchman's innovation. Antoine Coron has traced a long tradition of 'poèmes figurés' to Greek antiquity.[49] Be that as it may, Francis Poulenc did not hesitate to add a musical dimension to Apollinaire's poetic/artistic syntheses, in which 'poetic

---

[46] See further, Hillebrand (2000), 103–13.
[47] Programme note by John Bishop (London, Boosey & Hawkes, 1978).
[48] Mann (1999), 67.
[49] Coron (2005), 7; see also, Schiltz (2015), 275ff.

metaphor spars with raillery'[50]; in 1948, the composer set seven of Apollinaire's calligrams as songs with piano accompaniment. The cycle's midpoint, 'Il pleut' ('It rains'), shaped by the poet into five slanting columns of verbal precipitation, inspired from Poulenc a busy, étude-like piano accompaniment of 'sixteenths attached to vertical lines that resemble a Hokusai rain painting – the first of Poulenc's several attempts to mirror Apollinaire's designs with the sound of the music *and* its appearance on paper'.[51] Pierre Bernac, the French baritone who premiered the cycle, revealed that Poulenc's intention was indeed 'to achieve a kind of musical calligram'.[52]

After Apollinaire's death one of his creations, 'Mon coeur pareil à une flame renversée' ('My heart resembles an inverted flame'), was inscribed on his grave in Paris. The poet had fabricated this calligram in the shape of a heart. He was perhaps unaware, though, that some four centuries before, near the turn of the fifteenth, the composer Baude Cordier had created a heart-shaped love song, 'Belle, bonne, sage' ('Beautiful, good, wise [lady]'), in an early efflorescence of novel *musical* notations that encouraged multivalent, aural/visual readings.[53] Preserved, like 'Belle, bonne, sage' in the lavish Chantilly Codex,[54] Cordier's rondeau 'Tout par compas suy composés' ('Entirely from a compass am I made') featured as well a graphic design, this one laid out on concentric circular staves, and conceived in three voices, with the upper two unfolding a strict canon supported by a tenor. Here the choice of circles reflected the textual references to the compass, playing visually on the metaphor in Christian iconography of God as creator and architect of the universe, typically depicted with compass in hand.[55] Yet another 'picture song', 'La harpe de melodie' by Jacob Senleches, also dates *ca.* 1400; in this case, a drawing of a harp provides the frame for the chanson, conveniently notated in two voices on the strings of the harp which do double duty as staves (in addition, a verbal canon advises how to derive a third, canonic voice from the upper part). The text declares that the author has played his melody on his harp and had an intimate dialogue with the instrument, 'his second I, that follows him like a shadow'.[56] Senleches's music is rep-

---

[50] Shattuck (1958), 234.

[51] Johnson (2020), 326.

[52] Bernac (1977), 86.

[53] See Anheim (2005), 7, for whom 'the figure of the heart appears like a signature of the musician'. Thus, Baude Cordier is almost surely a pseudonym, a play on the Latin 'cor' ('heart'). In addition, the composer places a drawing of a small heart within the piece to substitute, rebus-like, for the word 'coeur'.

[54] Chantilly, Musée Condé 564.

[55] For other Renaissance examples, see Schiltz (2015), 279–301.

[56] Strohm (1988), 315.

resentative of an intricate, avant-garde style emanating from Avignon during the Papal Schism (he served as harpist for the cardinal who became anti-Pope Benedict XIII in 1394), and known as the *Ars subtilior* ('more subtle art').

During the Renaissance, painters and composers found new ways to relate the musical and the visual in their work, secular and sacred.[57] Thus, the Ferrarese painter Dosso Dossi (*ca.* 1490–1542) incorporated into his *Allegory of Music* (Horne Museum, Florence) two precisely notated puzzle canons, one (unidentified) in the shape of a circle, the other (by Josquin), in that of a triangle; for H. Colin Slim both symbolized perfection.[58] One worldly musical genre that attracted composers privileging visual imagery was the Italian madrigal. Alfred Einstein described it as an active gymnasium (*Turnplatz*) of *Augenmusik*,[59] and adduced numerous examples from Palestrina, Marenzio, Lassus and Giovanni Gabrieli. For example, in 'Occhi, dolci e suave' ('Sweet and suave eyes', 1587) Luca Marenzio inserted a visual pun for 'Occhi' by writing two semibreves (whole notes: o o). As a type of constrained composing, using exclusively voided white notes (semibreves, minims for example) could depict 'daylight', 'white' or 'open'. On the other hand, when Josquin created his *déploration* on the death of Ockeghem, *Nymphes des bois* (1497), he blackened the notes, a striking visual response to his selection of plainchant from the Introit of the Requiem Mass, which served as a foundational *cantus firmus* in the tenor part.[60]

Augenmusik had its proponents and detractors. The Bergamese theorist Pietro Cerone deemed the practice significant enough to include an enthusiastic endorsement in his *summa* of music theory, *El Melopeo* (1613), which, weighing in at some 1,100 pages, led satirists to lampoon the tome as 'el monstruo musical'. Considerably less charitable was Vincenzo Galilei (father of the astronomer), who reacted to musical riddles of any kind, including eye music, as 'abuses' that were more properly the purview of a carnival.[61] Nevertheless, composers persevered in manipulating sounds *and* images in their music. Thus, the crescent and waning stages of the lunar cycle found apt musical metaphors in mensuration signs (for example C for the crescent moon; O for the full moon).[62]

---

[57] For fifteenth- and sixteenth-century examples, see Abele (2008).

[58] Slim (1990).

[59] Einstein (1913), 9.

[60] See also Gioseffo Zarlino's motet *Nigra sum sed formosa* (1549) from the Song of Solomon ('I am black but comely').

[61] Galilei (1581), 88.

[62] Schiltz (2011).

Another type of eye music that engendered a venerated tradition – for instance, Ludwig Senfl left several examples[63] – was the puzzle canon notated in the shape of a cross, the Christian emblem of salvation. Often accompanied by verbal annotations, these riddles were typically realized as 'double retrograde canon[s], with the voices starting from opposite ends of the cross's arms'.[64] Visual representations of the Cross included Heinrich Biber's creative applications of scordatura for solo violin in his *Rosary* Sonatas (*ca.* 1676), especially in No. 11 ('Resurrection'). Here the re-tunings of the four open strings literally required the second and third to 'cross' each other (for example instead of the normal disposition, g-d'-a'-e", the scordatura adjustment g-g'-d'-d"), and yielded concentrated clusters of chromatic sharps (*Kreuz*, the German word for 'sharp', also means 'cross'), and compact chiasmic motives that suggested a cruciform.[65] The summit of this tradition came in the sacred music of J. S. Bach, who applied cross symbolism in several compositions, chiefly in the cantatas and Passions. Some scholars, including the Bach biographer and colleague of Brahms, Philipp Spitta,[66] viewed the BACH cipher itself as a chromatically crossed motive that affirmed not only the composer's surname but also his Lutheran faith. Later composers, too, found additional ways to imprint cruciform imagery into their scores. For instance, the Second Symphony of Alfred Schnittke ('Invisible Mass', 1979), written in memory of Anton Bruckner, combines horizontal, chant-like melodic lines and vertical, harmonic blocks of sounds to suggest cross shapes; and various works of Sofia Gubaidulina, including *In croce* for cello and bayan (1979) and *Sieben Worte* (*Seven Last Words*) for cello, bayan and strings (1982), represent the Cross through instruments that gradually exchange high and low registers, or through glissandi that traverse each other, symbolic gestures that leave visual traces in the scores.[67]

Augenmusik of a quite different kind emerged in Telemann's *Gulliver's Travels* Suite for two violins, composed two years after the release of Jonathan Swift's sensational novel in 1726, and comprising an *Intrada* and four programmatic movements depicting the fantastic voyages in the satire. For the second movement, a brisk chaconne, Telemann chose the microscopic time signature of 3/32 for the diminutive scampering of the six-inch Lilliputians. In contrast, the third movement provided a lumbering gigue in a hyperbolic 24/1 for the sixty-foot-tall Brobdingnagians. Of course, these extreme metres, offering a visual

---

[63] Schiltz (2015), 305ff.; Braun (2004).
[64] Schiltz (2015), 305.
[65] Giles (2018), 91ff.
[66] Spitta (1880), vol. 2, 379n.
[67] See also, Tsenova (2001b), 6–8.

reductio or *augmentatio ad absurdum*, were perceptible only to those perusing the score, not to casual listeners. But other musicians intrigued with the concept of *Augenmusik* endeavoured to place it on a firmer scientific footing by investigating 'the demonstrable physical relationship between colour and musical sound'.[68]

In particular, the eccentric Jesuit mathematician Louis Bertrand Castel (1688–1757) spent the greater part of his life trying to develop a 'clavessin pour les yeux' ('harpsichord for the eyes'), drawing selectively on Newton's *Opticks* (1704). Newton had argued that the bandwidths of colours in a spectrum corresponded to the harmonic ratios that generated the pitches of a scale. And so, Castel designed an instrument that, when its keys were depressed, enabled lanterns to project contrasting hues. Through this means the keyboard could transmute sounds into brilliant arrays of colours, so that 'a deaf listener could enjoy music that was originally written for the ear'.[69] After visiting the inventor in Paris, Telemann was convinced, and in 1739 released a German pamphlet heralding the new invention.[70] But no working models materialized, deferring synaesthetes' gratification until the invention in 1895 of a 'colour organ' by Alexander Wallace Rimington, who 'performed' Chopin preludes and the Overture to Wagner's *Rienzi* in London, leaving spectators to wonder whether 'beautiful music necessarily produces beautiful colours, and ugly music ugly colours'.[71]

Then, in 1911, the Russian mystic Alexander Scriabin introduced his phantasmagorical *Prometheus: The Poem of Fire*, Op. 60, for large orchestra that included a 'clavier à lumières' to project a train of shifting colours, ultimately culminating in a blaze of bright blue, associated with the pitch F-sharp (the work ends in F-sharp major, symbolizing spirit). There is some evidence that Scriabin's '*Augenmusik*' was meant not only to be seen, but to serve a larger pan-sensory project designed to introduce stimuli of touch and smell into listeners' experiences.[72] In large part Scriabin's ecstatic visions reflected his immersion into mystical theosophy, but in a strange enough way brought to fruition what Castel had been unable to achieve in the eighteenth century, so that, at least, 'the experience of colour would enhance the experience of sound, as any devotee of psychedelia will agree …'[73]

---

[68] Mason (1958), 104.

[69] Hankins (1994), 143.

[70] Wolff (1982). Telemann may have composed some pieces for the instrument, though none have survived.

[71] 'Colour Music', *The Sydney Morning Herald* (20 September 1895).

[72] Hugh Macdonald (1978), 56.

[73] Ibid.

Scriabin would perhaps not have imagined that in 1990, the Russian composer Sofia Gubaidulina would revisit the idea of 'colour-music' in her *Alleluia* for chorus, orchestra, boy soprano and colour keyboard, as a corrective to the rapidly turning tints in his score. For Gubaidulina, Scriabin had erred by interpreting light in a 'purely melodic' way, so that the 'colour/light component' became 'too mobile and dynamic'.[74] Instead, Gubaidulina opted for a relatively static treatment. She chose seven colours, ranging from a vibrant yellow to a pale violet. The first movement, for example, required only orange, gradually intensifying before fading away completely in a crescendo-decrescendo effect in the ratio of 6:2, the 'proportion of reflected and absorbed rays in the orange colour', allowing this example of *Augenmusik* to breathe, as it were.[75]

~ iii

There remains another category to introduce, the symbolic use of numerical relationships (**numerology**) in music. The idea of music as sounding numbers is familiar enough from Greek antiquity, when it was attributed to the philosopher/mathematician Pythagoras,[76] who established ratios for consonant intervals with simple integers: 2:1 for the perfect octave; 3:2, the perfect fifth; and 4:3, the perfect fourth. Pythagoreans celebrated the mathematical underpinnings of the cosmos by imagining that the heavenly bodies generated an inaudible 'music of the spheres' resonating according to these ratios. In turn, Plato's writings betrayed strong Pythagorean influences, as did those of the early Church fathers, including St. Augustine of Hippo (354–430 CE), for whom 'reason has perceived that numbers govern and make perfect all that is in rhythms … and in song itself'.[77] Not surprisingly, early Western music theory privileged Pythagorean number theory, as in the anonymous, ninth-century *Scholia enchiriadis*, where we find one of the earliest descriptions of polyphony, and read, 'sounds pass quickly away, but numbers, … obscured by the corporeal element in sounds and movements, remain'.[78]

Supporting numerological pursuits was **gematria**, the alphanumeric system of codes that assigned numbers to Hebrew letters. Various number alphabets were employed, not only in Judaism, in which numeric symbolism was associated with the esoteric practices of the Kabbalah, but also in early Christianity.

---

[74] Lukomsky (1998), 28.

[75] Tsenova (2001a), 23–8; Lukomsky (1998), 28–30.

[76] On Pythagorean numerology, see especially Butler (1970), 1–11.

[77] St. Augustine, *De ordine* II, quoted in the *Scholia enchiriadis*; Strunk (1998), 137.

[78] Ibid.

The New Testament Book of Revelation (13:18) identified the 'number of the beast' as 666, leading some to 'unmask' Nero as the Antichrist, because the emperor's numerological sum also equalled 666. Applications of gematria in Western art music occurred at least as early as Machaut, whose music sometimes literally referred to numbers.[79] An early zenith of musical gematria occurred in the sacred polyphony of the fifteenth and early sixteenth centuries by prominent Franco-Flemish composers. The Dutch scholar Willem Elders has amassed evidence that their names in Masses and motets were encrypted through numbers – 54 for Dufay; 97 for Obrecht; 64 for Ockeghem; and 88 for Josquin.[80]

Were these correspondences, though, part of a systematic use of gematria, or mere coincidence? After all, a determined enough researcher can excavate scores until 'striking' veins of numerological ore, with or without corroborating evidence. In particular, the case of J. S. Bach became a flashpoint during the twentieth century for proponents and critics of numerology. Bach was compared after his death in 1750 to Sir Isaac Newton, and, to the extent that Bach's music was known then (he saw only ten compositions of his output of over a thousand through the press), there was a sense that it was 'best appreciated by real connoisseurs'.[81] Small wonder, then, that his music's complexity, his interest in puzzles, deep immersion in theology and, finally, membership in the Society of Musical Sciences eventually raised the question: had Bach employed a number alphabet 'to incorporate significant words into his music as part of a grander scheme of compositional number symbolism'?[82]

Friedrich Smend was the first to propose this thesis in 1947. Noticing that the word 'Credo' appears 43 times in the chorus 'Credo in unum Deum' of the B-minor Mass, and that the same chorus and its successor, 'Patrem omnipotentem', add up to 129 bars (3 × 43), Smend confidently concluded: '... Bach's setting of the first article of faith, in the very number of its bars, states: CREDO, CREDO, CREDO. That means: there is no true belief in God outside belief in the Trinity. And Bach makes this affirmation at the very period when Deism was beginning to flourish'.[83]

In 1991 Ruth Tatlow published *Bach and the Riddle of the Number Alphabet*, a comprehensive review of Smend's theories that urged caution in applying number alphabets to Bach's music. Tatlow observed that some forty

---

[79] Hoppin (1978), 403; Kellner (1981).
[80] Elders (1994), 144; Elders (2013), 84–5; and Vellekoop (1966).
[81] Wolff (2000), 6.
[82] Tatlow (1991), 1.
[83] Smend (1947), III, 21, trans. in Tatlow (1991), 9.

number-alphabets were in use during his time; there was 'no certainty, however, that Bach used any eighteenth-century number-alphabet forms, even assuming that he knew about them'.[84] Still, she could not totally disprove Smend's thesis, which she viewed rather as a 'conjectural hypothesis'. Among the supporting, circumstantial evidence: Bach's close association in Leipzig with the poet C. F. Henrici (pseudonym, Picander), librettist of several cantatas and the *St. Matthew Passion*, who experimented with poetic paragrams that relied on number alphabets; and Bach's knowledge of the *Musicalische Vorstellung einiger Biblischer Historien* (*Biblical Sonatas*, 1700) by his predecessor at the Thomaskirche, Johann Kuhnau, who included in his preface an 'Algebraisches *Problema*'. It contained clues directing the reader to a number alphabet to reveal the name of a celebrated musician, Agostino Steffani.[85] In the end, Tatlow remained sceptical about Bach's knowledge of number alphabets, though she conceded: 'it is quite plausible that Bach hid messages or names in his compositions with cryptographic intent'.[86]

If Bach's numerology provoked debate, the American composer Leonard Bernstein openly acknowledged his own interests in gematria and the Kabbalah. Here the relevant work is his score for Jerome Robbins's ballet *Dybbuk* (1974). Based on a Hasidic play by S. Z. Rappoport (pseud., S. Ansky, 1914), *Dybbuk* 'explores Jewish mysticism and numerology, explicitly hovering between the worlds of the dead and the living, and dealing with the tension between the more rational Talmudic study and the rituals, spells, word play, and sorcery associated with Kabbalah'.[87] In the play, Channon falls in love with Leah, but in the end is able to win her only by turning into a dybbuk, a ghostly possessing spirit. Leah's numerological equivalent is 36, and Channon's is 54, both multiples of 9, and thus mathematically compatible. Also, Leah's number is twice that of 'chai' (18), the Hebrew word for 'life', so that in numerological terms she symbolizes 'double life'. These relationships drew from Bernstein an esoteric composition, in which he explored nine-note scales and rigorous serial procedures employing tone rows. Bernstein went so far as to assert that 'every note in the ballet was arrived at by Kabbalistic or mystical manipulation of numbers'.[88]

Not every application of musical numerology has utilized number alphabets. Composers could also underscore, for instance, the symbolic meaning of

---

[84] Tatlow (1991), 127.

[85] See Tatlow (1991), 52–3; and Kellner (1980).

[86] Tatlow (1991), 128.

[87] Shawn (2014), 231.

[88] Richard F. Shepard, 'Kaballah Numerology Inspires a Bernstein "Dybbuk"', *New York Times*, 9 May 1974.

specific numbers. Thus, in analyzing Guillaume de Machaut's Motet 15 (*Amours qui ha le povoir/Faus samblant/Vidi dominum*), Margaret Bent noted the significance of 3 and 30, as possible allusions to 'Peter's threefold denial and the thirty pieces of silver paid for Judas's betrayal', asserting that 'the choice of these numbers for a motet about deceit may be far from accidental'.[89] Machaut's polyphonic Mass (*ca.* 1360s) has prompted a similar approach highlighting certain numbers. For Owen Rees, 7 and 12 'feature prominently in the construction of *Kyrie*, *Credo*, and *Agnus Dei*', so that their symbolic meaning can be interpreted 'within the tradition of Christian exegesis'.[90] The length of the complete *Kyrie* is 210 longs, or 7 × 30, and the length of the *Kyrie*, *Agnus Dei* and *Ite missa est* is 276 longs, or 12 × 23. In turn, 7 and 12 – both are laden with Christian symbolism – are related because they are the sum and product of 4 and 3. As to why, for instance, Machaut favoured 7, Rees turns to its symbolic value, after noting that the *Kyrie* and *Agnus Dei* are essentially 'petitions for forgiveness'. Thus, 'if Machaut had wished to employ numerical symbolism to reflect their principal theme ... he would have chosen the number 7, which was regarded as the number of sin, repentance, and forgiveness'.[91]

'If', of course, does not mean that Machaut planned to use numerical symbolism in his Mass. What is more, counting longs in different movements to uncover recurring numerical meanings might seem a dubious enterprise, for 'the dangers of playing with numbers are many and legendary'.[92] But sometimes the case for numerical symbolism is plausible enough. Thus, Willem Elders has proposed that the fivefold repetition of the word 'Benedictus' alternating between the bass and tenor in Josquin's *Missa Pange lingua* may have a straightforward numerological explanation – 'the five blessings in the prayer "Unde et memores", said immediately after the consecration at the moment the singers start the Benedictus: the celebrant offers to God the sacrificed Victim (Christ), making the Sign of the Cross five times'.[93]

Yet another trend in numerological analysis of music has been to privilege the architectural blueprints of compositions, and the proportions of their internal sections. For Brian Trowell, the isorhythmic motets of John Dunstable (1390–1453) are 'built on mathematical and proportional principles that the ear can discern',[94] namely the arithmetical and harmonic progressions 9: 6: 3 and

---

[89] Bent (1991), 15.

[90] Rees (2003), 96.

[91] Ibid., 106. For the association of 7 with sin, Rees references Luke 17:4 and Matthew 18:21.

[92] Tatlow (2016), 3.

[93] Elders (2013), 91.

[94] Trowell (1978), 100.

6: 4: 3, which not infrequently demarcate the formal divisions of Dunstable's music. A mathematician himself, Dunstable achieved these ratios easily enough by compressing the time signatures from section to section.

Of course, proportional analysis too has not been immune to controversy. In 1973, Charles W. Warren published a study of Dufay's motet *Nuper rosarum flores*, performed in 1436 at Florence Cathedral for the consecration of Brunelleschi's dome. Warren argued that the proportions of the motet's four sections – 6: 4: 3: 2 – paralleled the architectural design of the dome.[95] Warren's thesis was refuted by Elders[96] and Craig Wright,[97] for whom Dufay's inspiration betrayed itself rather in 1 Kings 6, which describes the dimensions of the Temple of Solomon as 60 × 40 × 30 × 20 cubits. Several more works of Dufay, including Masses[98] and motets, have spurred others to apply proportional techniques. Margaret Vardell Sandresky, for instance, noticed that Dufay's three motets inspired by events in the Byzantine Empire, including the fall of Constantinople to the Turks in 1453,[99] have tenor parts with lengths divisible by the number 13. Supposing that the unusual recurrence of this number could carry symbolic significance, Sandresky interpreted it as a marker of the Byzantine emperor, memorialized since the reign of Constantine as the thirteenth apostle. But there is also a special mathematical property of 13, one that has challenged the validity of numerological analysis. Thirteen is a term of the Fibonacci sequence: 0, 1, 1, 2, 3, 5, 8, **13**, 21, 34, … whereby each term is generated by adding the previous two. What is more, the Fibonacci series relates directly to the Golden Section (GS) – the ratio formed by dividing a line into two unequal parts (a and b), so that the longer part (a) to the entire length ($a + b$) is the same as the shorter part (b) to the longer (a):

$$\frac{a}{a+b} = \frac{b}{a}$$

When these two ratios are equivalent, the GS is present, an irrational number rendered approximately as .618033. As for the Fibonacci connection, the further one proceeds in the sequence, the closer the ratio of any two successive terms approaches the GS – so, 1/2 = .50; 2/3 = .66; 3/5 = .60; 5/8 = .625; 8/13 = .615, 13/21 = .6190, etc.

---

[95] Warren (1973).
[96] Elders (1994), 13–15.
[97] Wright (1994), 404.
[98] See Nosow (1993).
[99] *Lamentatio Sanctae Matris Ecclesiae Constantinopolitanae*. The other two motets are *Vasilissa, ergo* and *Balsamus et mundus*.

Mathematicians have pondered the GS since the time of Euclid (*fl.* 300 BCE), who described it in his *Elements* as the 'extreme and mean ratio'. That composers employed it is not difficult to imagine, not to mention simple Pythagorean ratios, 'in a manner similar to the geometric calculations that painters used to create perspectives or architects used in the designs of buildings'.[100] Analyzing Dufay's early ballade *Resvellies vous et faits chiere lye* (1423), Allan Atlas went further, to argue that 'beneath the "sumptuous" audible surface' of this single composition 'lies a three-tiered system of number and proportion that draws on gematria, Pythagorean number symbolism, and the linear ratio known as the Golden Section, all of which work together in the service of symbolic, structural, and aesthetic ends'.[101] Written for the wedding of Vittoria di Lorenzo Colonna and Carlo Malatesta, the ballade appears to encode several key words in the music through their numerical equivalents. By using gematria, Dufay thus 'names the newlyweds, identifies the place, bears the blessings of the pope [Martin V, uncle of the bride], and carries the signature of a witness – Dufay'.[102] As for the second tier, Pythagorean number symbolism, Atlas finds that 5, 6 and 7, all associated with marriage, permeate the music. The search for the third and final tier, the GS, surely approaches a new limit in this type of analysis. First, Atlas locates the GS of the entire ballade on the 271st minim, the downbeat of bar 45, which he describes as the 'melodic and articulatory high point'[103] of the work. But he then specifies five other Golden Sections (including one 'reverse' Golden Section) active within the subdivisions of the whole, for a total of six. All told, Atlas concludes, the ballade offers a 'treat for the ultramontane scholastic intellect; a musical allegory of the wedding that it celebrates.'[104]

There remain some practical difficulties in applying the GS, and, by extension, Fibonacci numbers to this music.[105] For one, the GS is an irrational number that does not accommodate itself to precise divisions of music determined by bar numbers or rhythmic values. Second, to 'discover' the GS in a composition does not mean that the composer deliberately placed it there. And third, the Fibonacci Series, frequently invoked with the GS (though not in Atlas's study), did not become a viable term until 1878, when the French mathematician Édouard Lucas[106] invented it. That early composers such as Dufay or

---

[100] Planchart (2018), 371.

[101] Atlas (1987).

[102] Ibid., 116.

[103] Ibid., 123.

[104] Ibid., 126.

[105] See in particular Tatlow (2006).

[106] After whom the Lucas sequence was named.

even J. S. Bach[107] were aware of it is at best unlikely. What we know today as the Fibonacci Series began with the early thirteenth-century work of Leonardo da Pisa (*alias* Fibonacci), a medieval mathematician instrumental in introducing Arabic numerals to the West, and author of the *Liber abbaci* (*Book of Calculation*, 1202). Da Pisa's unusual path to the series named after him began when he started calculating how many progeny a pair of rabbits produced in one year.[108] Enumerating the burgeoning generations yielded results that corresponded to the Fibonacci Series, though da Pisa never made the connection between those numbers and the GS, which was left for the later nineteenth century. And his name – Fi [*filius*] *Bonacci*, son of Bonacci – was largely a product of the nineteenth century as well.

That does not mean, however, that composers from the late nineteenth century on neglected the GS and its relation to the Fibonacci Series. Candidates who plausibly did not include two seminal modernists, Debussy and Bartók. More recently, Sofia Gubaidulina has acknowledged her deep numerological interests, including the GS, Fibonacci and related Lucas Series, while Brian Ferneyhough has manipulated the Fibonacci Series in various works, including his Second String Quartet (1980), where the series becomes an 'interactive game with procedures, algorithms and structured data, played according to the composer's own "musical feeling."'[109] The case of Debussy first piqued the interest of Roy Howat, who argued that the Frenchman frequently resorted to the Golden Section and Fibonacci relationships to strengthen a 'feeling of proportional correctness or inevitability'.[110] Howat gleaned several examples in which 'well-defined sections in Debussy's music follow Fibonacci's numbers at strategic places'[111] – for instance, the introduction to the finale of *La mer* (fifty-five bars). In 'Reflets dans l'eau' from *Images I* (1905), Debussy placed the *ff* climax with its dramatic modulation to E-flat major in bars 58ff., marking out of the total ninety-four bars the GS. Even the wave-like contours of its opening phrase, peaking on the fifth or sixth quavers in groupings of eight, approximated the golden division on the local scale.

One reason that Howat's numerological approach is inviting is that Debussy's music resists traditional analyses. If Debussy applied the GS and Fibonacci ratios routinely, that might unlock the mystery that cloaks the sensuous appeal of his music. Its ostensible formlessness might mask underlying proportions

---

[107] See Tatlow (2016), 105.
[108] See further, Powell (1979); and Devlin (2017), 126ff.
[109] Albert (2015), 60.
[110] Howat (1983a), 25.
[111] Ibid., 3.

that yield aesthetically pleasing results. There is little hard evidence from the composer to substantiate this hypothesis, though he did leave at least two valuable clues. One appears in an essay about Jean Philippe Rameau, of whom Debussy observed: 'To the end, [Rameau] never for a moment doubted the truth of the old Pythagorean theory that music should be reduced to a combination of numbers: it is the "arithmetic of sound" just as optics are the "geometry of light".'[112] In 1903 Debussy wrote to his publisher, Jacques Durand, about a missing bar in the proofs for 'Jardins sous la pluie': 'it's necessary, as regards number, the divine number... .'[113] Indeed, as Howat discovered, the restoration of that missing bar maximized the accuracy of the placement of the GS in the composition, so that *le divin nombre* in Debussy's letter 'is more likely to signify *nombre d'or*, the usual French term for GS, than any other known possibility'.[114]

Béla Bartók was the second modernist to stimulate numerological readings, in part because of his fascination with mirror formations, palindromes and symmetrical arch schemes. His leading apologist was the Hungarian theorist Ernő Lendvai, who maintained that the GS and Fibonacci Series were as important for Bartók's compositional process as symmetrical thematic periodization had been for the Viennese classicists.[115] Lendvai found that the GS appeared at critical structural breaks in many of Bartók's works, including the recapitulations of the first movements of the Sonata for Two Pianos and Percussion, *Contrasts* and *Divertimento*. One composition especially laden with Fibonacci relationships was the *Music for Strings, Percussion and Celesta* (1936). Lendvai endeavoured to show, for instance, that the eighty-eight bars of the opening fugue reached their *fff* climax in bar 55, a Fibonacci number that approached the GS of the movement (55/88 = .625).[116] Furthermore, Lendvai argued, Fibonaccian partitions determined some internal proportions. Thus, the 55 bars subdivided conveniently into 34 and 21; and in bar 34, Bartók directed the strings, muted since the beginning of the fugue, to remove their mutes, an audible marker of that structural break.

Occasionally, as Howat has shown, Lendvai overstated his case by indulging in 'wayward arithmetic'.[117] Still, there is evidence to support the thesis that Bartók was sensitive to Fibonaccian proportions. The third movement, cast in a symmetrical arch form (*ABCBA*), begins and ends with a xylophone solo

---

[112] Debussy, 'Jean Philippe Rameau' (November 1912), in Lesure and Smith (1977), 255.

[113] Debussy (1927), 10.

[114] Howat (1983a), 7.

[115] Lendvai (1971), 18.

[116] Ibid., 28n.

[117] Howat (1983a), 187; also, Howat (1983b).

Ex. 2.11: Bartók, *Music for Strings, Percussion and Celesta*, Third Movement

that, appropriately, is not only a palindrome, but rhythmically based on the series (ex. 2.11).

Furthermore, Tibor and Peter Bachman have found 'Fibonaccian superstructures' in Bartók's music, especially after 1918.[118] The composer was particularly meticulous about temporal spans in his music, and often notated timings for his major works, such as in the four movements of the *Music for Strings, Percussion and Celesta*, which elicited from him approximate preferences: *ca.* 6'30", 6'55", 6'35" and 5'40".

After Bartók, other composers were more forthright about their Fibonaccian constructions. Among them was the *enfant terrible* of the post-war avant-garde, Karlheinz Stockhausen, in at least three works: *Klavierstück IX* (1954–5); *Mixtur* for orchestra, sine-wave generators and ring modulators (1964); and *Adieu* for wind quintet (1966). Here the relevant techniques were: deriving from the series a sequence through an additive process, 1, 3, 6, 11, etc. (*1, 1 + 2 = 3; 1 + 2 + 3 = 6; 1 + 2 + 3 + 5 = 11*)[119]; determining the proportions of twenty 'moments' by multiplying a Fibonacci segment (2, 3, 5, 8, 13) by 6 to obtain 12, 18, 30, 48 and 78; and generating sectional divisions from the series from 1 to 144, then allying them with different articulations or textures (for example trills or note repetitions). In 1964 Ernst Krenek composed *Fibonacci Mobile* for piano (four hands) and string quartet, in which chance procedures brought blocks of Fibonaccian materials together in random formations, somewhat like a mobile by Alexander Calder.[120] Then, in 1995, the late Dmitri Smirnov, who succumbed to Covid in 2020, released his Symphony No. 3 (*Voyages*) – dedicated to the memory of Fibonacci.

None of these composers, however, relied more extensively on the Fibonacci and derived sequences than the Tatar-Russian Sofia Gubaidulina, who since the 1980s and 1990s has created individually crafted 'numerical plots' for her music

---

[118] Bachmann and Bachmann (1979).
[119] Frisius (2008), 86.
[120] Stewart (1991), 310–11.

to guide 'the proportional calculation of the whole form'.[121] An early example was *Im Anfang war der Rhythmus* (*In the Beginning Was Rhythm*, 1984) for percussion ensemble, totally generated from the series, and betraying in its opening timpani solo a palindromic reminiscence of the xylophone solo in Bartók's *Music for Strings, Percussion and Celesta*. By the 1990s, Gubaidulina was experimenting with the Lucas Series as well as the *Evangelium* Series (3, 2, 5, 7, 12, etc.), after Matthew 14 and 15, in which Jesus feeds the multitudes with two fish, five loaves and, again, seven loaves of bread. The next step was to combine different series, as she did in *Gerade und Ungerade* (*Even and Odd*) for percussion and piano (1991), and *Heute früh, kurz vor dem Erwachen* (*Early in the Morning, Right Before Awakening*) for seven Japanese kotos (1993). Both compositions drew upon the Fibonacci and Lucas Series.[122] A work particularly redolent of number series but also of gematria and number symbolism was the *Meditation on the Bach Chorale 'Vor Deinen Thron tret ich hiermit'* for harpsichord and string quintet (1993). Here Gubaidulina took her inspiration from Bach's chorale prelude for organ (BWV 668), dictated on his deathbed in July 1750.[123]

As is typical of Bach's chorale preludes, BWV 668 alternates between 'free' sections and the chorale, intoned phrase by phrase:

Free   Chorale 1 Free   Chorale 2 Free   Chorale 3 Free   Chorale 4
                                        GS

In her *Meditation*, Gubaidulina preserved Bach's basic structure, with a few adjustments. For much of the composition, she drew only on the first phrase of the chorale, before allowing the strings in the ultimate section to offer the entire melody in octave doublings. Diffusing the spirit of Bach over her score, at the end she assigned the harpsichord four tonal chords, with the top voice articulating BACH. The proportions of her eight formal divisions derived from the Fibonacci Series; the GS, for instance, fell at the 115th quaver (of a total of 187, for a ratio of .6149), just after the fifth of the eight sections.

These calculations, though, were just the beginning. Returning to the number 14 and its reverse, 41 ('Bach' and 'J. S. Bach'), Gubaidulina also highlighted 9 (J[ohann]), 23 (J. Bach) and 32 (S. Bach), for example, as well as 37 (J. Chr[istus]) and 48 (for her first name, Sofia). She then deployed them throughout the composition: 48, for instance, was the metronome marking; and there were precisely 23 beats in the last section of the work. Even the total number of

---

[121] Tsenova (2001a), 24.

[122] Tsenova (2001b), 79ff.

[123] Thorough analyses in Tsenova (2001b), 108–44; and Tsenova (2002), 258–60.

beats, 518, produced a final, well-hidden allusion to Bach: 5 + 1 + 8 = 14. And, she discovered in Bach's chorale prelude a magical sequence of numbers, a veritable Bach Row (*Bach-Reihe*): 88 51 **37 14 23 9** 32 41 73 114 187. Reading from 9, forwards or backwards, Fibonacci combinations begin to emerge around the symbolic appearances of the composer's name and reference to Christ. Gubaidulina then derived another row, this one beginning with 1 and 4 – again remembering Bach's name – and proceeded by adding terms to generate this Fibonacci-type sequence: **1, 4, 5, 9, *14*, 23, 37**, 60, ... Significantly, the series also displayed symbolic numbers subsumed in the previous *Reihe*.

Over the course of this book we shall encounter numerology further, including a type of proportional parallelism applied to Bach's music *not* based on the Fibonacci Series; the possibility that Mozart's music inspired by Freemasonry contains an underlayer of number symbolism; and the obsession of Schoenberg and Berg with the numbers 13 and 23. Although contentious, numerology remains a prominent strand running through the confounding riddles of music, whether composers deliberately resort to it or somehow intuit in their music embedded numerical processes. Ultimately, if it is true, as Lord Peter Wimsey observes in *Whose Body?* (with apologies to Apuleius), that the golden mean, 'as Aristotle says, keeps you from bein' a golden ass',[124] composers have also leveraged other methods described in this chapter, all to cloak messages in their art.

---

[124] Sayers (1923), 49.

CHAPTER 3

The Rise of Cryptography

'It may well be doubted whether human ingenuity can construct an enigma ... which human ingenuity may not, by proper application, resolve'.

– Edgar Allan Poe, *The Gold Bug* (1843)

THERE are diverse opinions about when and where cryptography arose. It was an inevitable by-product of writing, originating after the florescence of early recorded languages, whether Mesopotamian cuneiform, Egyptian hieroglyphs, Minoan tablets transmitting early Greek (Linear B) or Old Germanic runic futhark. Balancing the desire to communicate ideas through written symbols was the countervailing need to restrict them to the need-to-know few.

Probably to most Egyptians, hieroglyphs remained shrouded by veils of secrecy, even though their original purpose was not necessarily to conceal. Thus, funerary inscriptions on the pharaohs' tombs were commemorative, celebrating nobility who had entered the afterlife. But in 391 CE, when the Christian Roman emperor Theodosius closed Egyptian temples, the need for hieroglyphs abruptly declined, and they ceased to be understood.[1] In 1823 Jean-François Champollion cracked the 'code' of the Rosetta Stone, a granite slab recovered by Napoleon's engineers during the Egyptian campaign of 1799 in the western delta. Chiselled into the stele were fragments of a text in three tiers: at the top, hieroglyphs; in the middle, the same rendered in a cursive form known as demotic; and, near the base, the same in Greek letters, key to unlocking the meaning. Now a prized possession of the British Museum, the Stone revived the Western fascination for Egyptology, and spurred cryptanalysts to expose secrets of antiquity.

What Champollion deciphered were parts of an official decree promulgated in 196 BCE for the pharaonic coronation of Ptolemy V Epiphanes. The text's allure thus owed little to cryptography; on the contrary, the juxtaposition of hieroglyphics, demotic and Greek was calculated to reach as broad a literate

---

[1] In 2005 Okasha El-Daly challenged this Eurocentric view with evidence that after the Moslem annexation of Egypt in the seventh century CE Arabic scholars were able to progress in deciphering hieroglyphics. El-Daly (2005), 57–73.

audience as possible. But because hieroglyphics and demotic were obsolete long before Champollion, his success was greeted as if he had unravelled an arcane code. That said, two questions remain. First, what evidence do we have for early cryptography, that is, the *deliberate* transformation of texts to conceal their meaning? And second, how and when did *musical* cryptography arise?

∾ i

The early history of cryptography yields not so much a linear narrative as a patchwork quilt, with isolated cases from different areas of antiquity. In Mesopotamia the earliest surviving example dates from *ca.* 1500 BCE.[2] On a small cuneiform tablet, a scribe recorded a process for pottery glazes, but by applying a cryptographic substitution technique disguised the formula, enhancing its value as a trade secret. In India, where espionage was part of statecraft, 'secret writing' figured in several written sources, including the *Kamasutra* (second or third century CE). There the philosopher Vātsyāyana recommended sixty-four yoga, or arts, that women should practise, of which the forty-fifth concerned the 'writing of words in a peculiar way' – secret writing – presumably for communicating discreetly with lovers. Vātsyāyana recommended the use of *mlecchita-vikalpa*, a substitution cipher that randomly associated each letter of the plaintext with another.

Secrecy was required too for military operations, though here the early history of cryptography is not uncontroversial. The Greeks and Romans relied much more upon the counsel of oracles than clandestine intelligence to predict the outcomes of military engagements. *Haruspices*, who specialized in extispicy, 'reading' the entrails of sacrificed animals, and *auspices*, augurs who interpreted the flight patterns of birds, endeavoured to prognosticate the will of the gods, like 'seers who communicated with the divine'.[3] Nonetheless, early historians did describe subterfuges for transmitting messages, including Herodotus in his *Histories*. In the fifth book we read how Histiaeus, Greek ruler of Miletus, intending to instigate through his nephew Aristagoras a revolt against the Persians (499–494 BCE), shaved the head of a slave, inscribed a message on his scalp and, once his hair had grown back, dispatched him to Aristagoras.[4] No encryption was involved in this deceit; rather, Histiaeus had resorted to steganography ('covered writing') to conceal the message.[5]

---

[2] Kahn (1996), 75.
[3] Andrew (2018), 39.
[4] Herodotus (1965), 323.
[5] For another example, see ibid., 498.

On the other hand, a device known as a scytale, a baton wrapped with an inscribed scroll, may have encrypted military intelligence. According to Thucydides,[6] the Spartans employed the cylinder in the fifth century BCE. Plutarch included a description in his life of the Spartan commander Lysander:

> When the ephors send out a general or admiral, they prepare two cylindrical pieces of wood ... each corresponding to the other in its dimensions. One of these they keep themselves, the other being given to the departing officer ... Then whenever they want to send some important message secretly, they make a long narrow strip of parchment ... and wind it round the cylinder with the edges touching. Having done this, they write their message on the parchment in the position in which it was wrapped round the cylinder, and then they unwind the parchment and send it without the cylinder to the commander. When it reaches him ... he has to take his own cylinder and wind the strip of parchment round it. The spiral is then arranged in the correct sequence, the letters all into their proper order, and he can read round the cylinder and understand the message as a continuous whole.[7]

And what if the receiver of the unwound spiral did not have a baton of the correct circumference? This challenge attracted the attention of Edgar Allan Poe, who, when not creating macabre tales, prided himself in deciphering all manner of surreptitious writing. While editing *Graham's Magazine*, a Philadelphia literary review, he solved the problem:

> The strip of skin being intercepted, let there be prepared a cone of great length ... and whose circumference at base shall at least equal the length of the strip. Let this latter be rolled upon the cone near the base, edge to edge, as above described; then, still keeping edge to edge, and maintaining the parchment close upon the cone, let it be gradually slipped towards the apex. In this process, some of those words, syllables, or letters, whose connection is intended, will be sure to come together at that point of the cone where its diameter equals that of the *scytala* upon which the cipher was written.[8]

One cryptographic procedure from antiquity with which Poe was quite familiar was the Caesar cipher. According to Suetonius, Julius Caesar used it for confidential documents: 'to understand their apparently incomprehensible meaning one must number the letters of the alphabet from 1 to 22, and then replace each of the letters that Caesar has used with the one which occurs four numbers

---

[6] Thucydides (1966), 85.
[7] Plutarch (1964), 305–6.
[8] Poe (1841), 33.

lower – for instance, D stands for A.'[9] Caesar may have been the first military leader to value secret intelligence.[10]

Other examples of early cryptography occur in the Hebrew Bible, where some words are subjected to a substitution technique known as *atbash*. Here, the first letter of the Hebrew alphabet, *aleph*, is paired with the last, *tav*; the second, *beth*, with the penultimate, *sin* (or *shin*); the third, *gimel*, with the antepenultimate, *resh*, etc. The word *atbash* itself juxtaposes *aleph* with *tav*, *beth* with *shin*. In the Book of Daniel 'Babel' ('Babylon') appears twice as 'She-shach' (25: 26 and 51: 41), where the repeated 'b' is converted to the 'sh' of *shin*. But the second occurrence betrays the procedure by pairing 'Sheshach' and 'Babel': 'How is Sheshach taken! / and how the praise of the whole earth surprised! / How is Babylon become an astonishment / among the nations!' Kahn described this example as 'proto-cryptography', since 'the element of secrecy [was] lacking'.[11]

The search for hidden biblical codes has long challenged cryptological sleuths, including Newton, who expended considerable prose on biblical prophecies and eschatology; by his calculations, the Apocalypse announcing the end time would not occur before 2060. Among the monticule of papers left at his death in 1727 was 'Concerning the Language of the Prophets'. Here Newton argued that they spoke a secret tongue that, like the Egyptian hieroglyphs, remained undeciphered: 'John did not write one language, Daniel in another, Isaiah in [a] third, & the rest in others peculiar to themselves; but they all wrote in one & the same mystical language as well-known without doubt to the sons of the Prophets as the Hieroglyphic language of the Egyptians [was] to their Priests'.[12]

In 1997 interest in a biblical code was rekindled with the publication of Michael Drosnin's *The Bible Code*, which made an extraordinary claim: the Hebrew Bible conceals messages that foretold significant events millennia before their occurrence, including the Moon Landing; assassinations of John F. Kennedy, Anwar Sadat and Yitzhak Rabin; and a 'great terror' that would grip the world, possibly in 2113. How were these predictions conveyed? For Drosnin, 'the hidden text of the Bible was encoded with a kind of time-lock' that 'could not be opened until the computer had been invented'.[13] The first step was to convert the entire Bible into 'one continuous letter strand, 304,805 characters

---

[9] Suetonius (1965), 34–5.
[10] See Andrew (2018), 46ff.
[11] Kahn (1996), 76.
[12] Keynes Ms. 5, King's College, Cambridge.
[13] Drosnin (1997), 21.

long', by omitting spaces between the words.¹⁴ The next step was to apply an Equidistant Letter Sequence (ELS) by choosing a specific letter in the strand as a starting point, and then instructing the computer to skip a fixed number of characters, isolate the next letter, and repeat the process, before pursuing additional iterations of the text beginning on other letters. The final step was to highlight relevant words that emerged from the process, like so many spectres from the past revealing the future.

To interpret the data, the analyst could arrange portions of the strand into rectangular grids in which significant words might converge in vertical, horizontal or diagonal clusters. For advocates of the Code, the likelihood that words unmasked through this sifting were mere coincidence decreased precipitously as they cohered to suggest related meanings. Thus, the deaths of John F. Kennedy and Yitzhak Rabin were announced with specific details about their assassins. Drosnin's summary was indeed provocative: 'There is a Bible beneath the Bible. The Bible is not only a book – it is also a computer program. It was first chiselled in stone and handwritten on a parchment scroll, finally printed as a book, waiting for us to catch up with it by inventing a computer. Now it can be read as it was always intended to be read'.¹⁵

But for others these startling readings did not withstand rigorous review. A quartet of sceptics led by the Australian mathematician Brendan McKay detected inconsistencies in applying protocols for the ELS.¹⁶ Variant spellings of proper names, for instance, could provide enough flexibility to 'tune' the sifted text to promote 'revelatory' results. No less problematic was the length of the Bible; its nearly 305,000 characters were statistically sufficient in length to generate through ELS 'seemingly surprising outcomes much more frequently than naïve intuition might suggest'.¹⁷ Indeed, in a separate trial using ELS McKay was able to find the names of the assassins of Martin Luther King and Indira Gandhi in a Hebrew translation of Herman Melville's *Moby Dick*!¹⁸

So far, these examples primarily concern cryptography, the technique of enciphering secret messages, but not its reverse, cryptanalysis, the technique of deciphering concealed texts without knowledge of the key. The question arises, when did cryptography and cryptanalysis converge? By most accounts, this confluence coincided with the rise of the Abbasid caliphate, which reigned from 750 CE, ushering in the Golden Age of Islam until Mongol forces besieged

---

¹⁴ Ibid., 25.

¹⁵ Ibid.

¹⁶ McKay, Bar-Natan, Bar-Hillel and Kalai (1999).

¹⁷ Kass (1999), 149.

¹⁸ 'Assassinations Foretold in *Moby Dick*!', Cs.anu.edu.au. Accessed 29 October 2021.

and conquered Baghdad in 1258 CE. Over this stretch of time Baghdad became 'the largest urban centre of the medieval world,'[19] a major metropolis of scholarship that produced significant advances in algebra, statistics and linguistics. The expanding literacy rate increased the need for secret communications, so that cryptology flowered in this greenhouse of intellectual ferment.[20]

Through a curious etymology the term 'cipher' (Latin, *cifra*; Italian, *zefiro*; French, *chiffre*; German, *Ziffer*), from the Arabic for 'zero' (*sifr*), became associated with the incomprehensible. Instead of Roman numerals, commonly used in the West until the thirteenth century but lacking a sign for zero, Arab mathematicians had adopted around the ninth century the Hindu decimal system, in which zero provided an empty space. As Muslim influence expanded into the Iberian Peninsula, Arabic numerals spread to other parts of Europe. Initially, Europeans found the concept of zero difficult to apprehend, so that *sifr* took on the additional meaning of something hidden or enciphered.

By the eighth century the Arab linguist Al-Khalīl was writing a treatise about cryptology, though it has not survived. Then, in the ninth century, the remarkable polymath Al-Kindī (*ca.* 801–73) produced *A Manuscript on Deciphering Cryptographic Messages*. A prolific author with wide-ranging interests, Al-Kindī is perhaps best remembered as the father of statistics, and the first to use letter-frequency analysis for solving encrypted messages. In this method, the cryptanalyst first examines an unrelated plaintext in the same language sufficient in length to determine an average range of letters in decreasing order of frequency (for instance, in English the most common letter is the vowel *e*; the least, *q* and *z*). Next, the targeted text undergoes the same process to reveal the most frequent and least frequent of the encrypted letters. Then, by replacing these letters with their corresponding letters from the unencrypted text, the concealed text gradually emerges. Perhaps unwittingly, Al-Kindī may have triggered the cryptological race that continues to this day, pitting nimble cryptographers pursuing foolproof methods of secret writing against equally avid cryptanalysts bent upon unmasking any system, and confirming Edgar Allan Poe's sanguine assertion from 1843.

༄ *ii*

If the Arab Renaissance marked the great cultural awakening of the early Middle Ages, in the West much of this period stagnated, 'a void … in which all commercial and intellectual activity … ceased after the decline and fall of

---

[19] El-Hibri (2021), 5.

[20] See in particular, Al-Kadi (1992).

Rome.'[21] To the extent cryptography managed to gain a foothold in Europe, flickering feebly, 'like a single candle guttering in a great medieval hall,'[22] it was the domain of a literate minority. That elite included the clergy, monks and scribes of the Catholic Church, slowly consolidating its far-flung authority from Rome over Western Christianity in the emerging urban centres and monastic outposts.

Cryptographic techniques of classical antiquity were largely forgotten, though there were exceptions.[23] When Archbishop Isidore of Seville (ca. 559–636) compiled his widely distributed *Etymologiae* (*Etymologies*), which preserved 'the accumulated learning of the classical world,'[24] he described the Caesar substitute cipher mentioned by Suetonius. In *The Reckoning of Time* (*De temporum ratione*), a treatise about how to calculate time in the Christian calendar, the Venerable Bede (672–735) recommended a clandestine system of hand signals to facilitate counting large numbers, by which 'one may either signify necessary information by secret intimation, or else fool the uninitiated as if by magic.'[25] As an added measure of security, Bede exchanged Greek letters and numbers for the familiar Roman numerals.

Yet another English proselytizer, Boniface (ca. 675–754), Archbishop of Mainz, may have introduced to German realms cryptographic techniques, such as replacing the five vowels by their adjacent consonants (*a* became *b*, *e* became *f*, etc.), or by substituting in their stead one to five dots.[26] And Boniface's successor, the learned Rabanus Maurus (780–856), had deep interests in cryptology, evidenced by his pattern poems arrayed on grids of thirty-six lines, with thirty-six letters per line, forming perfect squares. Here Rabanus encrypted his poems and wove visual figures, as in *De laudibus sanctae crucis* (*Concerning the Praises of the Sacred Cross*), in which he embedded cruciform images within swirling blocks of letters, like the artwork of an inveterate cruciverbalist. These literary/visual creations later caught the attention of the sixteenth-century cryptographer Johannes Trithemius, generally credited with inventing the polyalphabetic substitution cipher system, leading the scholar Gerhard Strasser to suggest Rabanus as a possible source for Trithemius's innovation.[27]

---

[21] Lombard (2004), 1.
[22] Kahn (1996), 89.
[23] See, for instance, Colker (1971).
[24] Barney, Lewis, Beach and Berghof (2006), 13.
[25] Bede (1999), 11.
[26] Levison (1973), 138–9, 290–4.
[27] Strasser (2010).

During the early thirteenth century, a new type of numerical notation using cipher-like figures appeared in England and spread through monastic centres on the Continent. Perhaps designed to replace the more cumbersome Roman numerals, this innovation accommodated numbers from 1 to 9,999, produced by adding 'to the side of a vertical or horizontal stem a series of nine shapes corresponding to the numbers from 1 to 9'.[28] The placement of these strokes determined whether to read the numbers in tens, hundreds or thousands.

During the same century the versatile Franciscan friar Roger Bacon (1220–92), whose curiosity contemplated flying machines and gunpowder, enumerated seven different ways to communicate secretly.[29] For some time Bacon was a candidate for the authorship of the mystery-shrouded Voynich Manuscript,[30] copied probably in the early fifteenth century in an unknown or enciphered language that has frustrated many attempts at decryption, including those of Alan Turing, the cryptanalyst generally credited with breaking the codes of the Nazis' enigma machine. Most recently, in 2019 Gerard Cheshire of the University of Bristol proposed that the text transmitted a 'calligraphic, proto-Romance language', and that a Dominican nun had prepared it for Maria of Castile, Queen of Aragon (1401–58).[31] But Cheshire's claim that he deciphered the manuscript in a fortnight provoked reactions from incredulous medievalists, so that this episode of the Voynich affair counted as another false start.

Along with Roger Bacon, no less a luminary than Chaucer played a role in the history of cryptography, though here, too, not without controversy. We have already mentioned his alphabet poem (see p. 22). Chaucer's other interests included astronomy, so that when, in 1951, Derek Price discovered a Middle English treatise at Cambridge University titled *Equatorie of the Planetis*, he initially assumed it was a missing part of Chaucer's *Treatise on the Astrolabe* (1391), also written in English instead of Latin, and concerning an instrument for calculating the positions of the stars and the sun. In contrast, the subject of the *Equatorie*, thought to date from 1393, was a larger instrument known as an *equatorium*, capable of tracking the trajectories of the moon and planets. The temptation to assign the authorship to Chaucer proved irresistible, made more intriguing by the appearance of five encrypted passages in astronomical tables that appeared to employ a substitution cipher.[32] But, as with Roger Bacon, here again Chaucer's authorship was challenged, and in 1993, after an exhaustive review of the evidence, Kari Anne Rand Schmidt could only equivocate: 'The

---

[28] King (2001), 32.
[29] David (1923), 39–41.
[30] See Clegg (2003), 176–83, and Clemens (2016).
[31] Cheshire (2019).
[32] See in particular Price (1955), 182–7.

style of the *Equatorie* is not sufficiently unlike that of the non-Chaucerian texts and like that of the *Astrolabe* to be identified as Chaucer's work'.[33]

༄ iii

We may now take leave of these early demonstrations of cryptology in medieval Europe. There remains, though, the second question: when did cryptography expand its purview into music? We can approach this problem through three more examples from the ninth, tenth and twelfth centuries. Two involve celebrated figures. One was Notker Balbulus, who composed verses for sequences (*sequentiae*), textless melismatic *jubili* of the Alleluia Proper chants for the Mass (sung to the syllable -*ia*). The second was the visionary Abbess Hildegard of Bingen, founder of a convent at Rupertsberg on the Rhine, who invented her own esoteric language (*lingua ignota*). And the third occurred in one of the earliest surviving manuscripts to transmit musical notation.

Notker 'the Stammerer' (840–910 CE) was a Benedictine monk, poet and scholar who worked at the Swiss Abbey of St. Gallen, a centre of early Western musical notation using neumes. Today he is remembered primarily for his *Liber hymnorum* (*Book of Hymns*), a collection of texts for forty-nine sequences, forming a cycle of these chants for the liturgical calendar. Describing himself as 'least of the monks of St. Gallen',[34] Notker related how, attempting to memorize the long melodies of sequences, he set to them fresh verses that accommodated the melodic flourishes of the older neumes, with generally one syllable for each pitch. Notker designed his texts as mnemonic devices, so that 'he who would be retentive may grasp the wind'.[35] To be sure, we have no evidence that Notker's *sequentiae* drew upon cryptography to conceal additional levels of meaning. Still, he was aware of ciphers that safeguarded ecclesiastical correspondence dating back to the Council of Nicaea (325), which involved substituting Greek letters (and numerical equivalents) for Latin words, creating, in effect, a xenocrypt that blended two different languages.[36]

Our next example, the Léon Antiphoner (*ca.* 902–20),[37] presents an exceptional case in which musical neumes *did* substitute for letters of the alphabet. Here, the scribe appropriated neumes as abstract signs for use in unrelated, non-musical cryptographic messages. Elsa de Luca has identified ninety-three tenth- and eleventh-century primary sources, all Visigothic in origin and

---

[33] Rand Schmidt (1993), 98.
[34] Bower (2016), vol. 1, 129.
[35] Ibid., vol. 2, 9.
[36] Harris (2018), 71, and Kaczynski (1988), 33–4.
[37] Léon, Archivo de la Catedral, 8.

centred around Léon in northern Spain.[38] The great majority concern cartularies inscribed by clerics or monks, who also served as public notaries. In the margins of these documents they enciphered short texts, identifying, for example, the scribe or where the manuscript was prepared. The neumes were no longer 'just music notes in the modern sense, but also *figurae* intended to transmit meanings having little to do with the execution of this or that trope or motet'.[39] That musical neumes became part of an 'elitist code used only by skilled notarial scribes'[40] added considerably to the mystique of this clandestine process.

Similarly, with the advent of rhythmic (mensural) notation in the thirteenth century, trained musicians found another way to underscore the idea of notation as 'opaque, esoteric writing for a literate few'.[41] John Haines has argued that the term ligature (*ligatura*), which came to designate a compound of two, three or four pitches connected together and performed according to rhythmic modes, derived from the considerably older meaning of the term to refer to an amulet tied to the body and associated with magical, chant-like incantations for promoting healing.

This projection of esotericism certainly applied to the seer-like 'Sibyl of the Rhine', Hildegard of Bingen (1098–1179), one of the few named composers from the twelfth century. She was an extraordinary polymath – a poet, natural scientist, theologian, hagiographer and composer – who with the assistance of the monk Volmar recorded startling visions from her monastic cell. Though corresponding with popes, archbishops and emperors, much of her creative work, including what may have been the first musical morality play, *Ordo Virtutum* (*Order of the Virtues*, 1151), fell into obscurity until centuries later; indeed, not until 2012 was she named a Doctor of the Church by Benedict XVI, and canonized as a saint.

Hildegard invented her own language, the *lingua ignota* (*Unknown Language*), 'the only systematically constructed imaginary language that has come down to us from the Middle Ages'.[42] It is relevant here for its possible deployment of cryptography. All that survived of this ambitious project was a glossary of words 'never before heard'[43] and a secret alphabet of twenty-three newly designed, cipher-like characters that cloaked the whole in an obnubilant aura of mystery (see Illustration 3.1).

---

[38] De Luca (2017).

[39] De Luca and Haines (2018), 30.

[40] Ibid., 34.

[41] Haines (2011), 217.

[42] Schnapp (1991), 283.

[43] Higley (2007), 3.

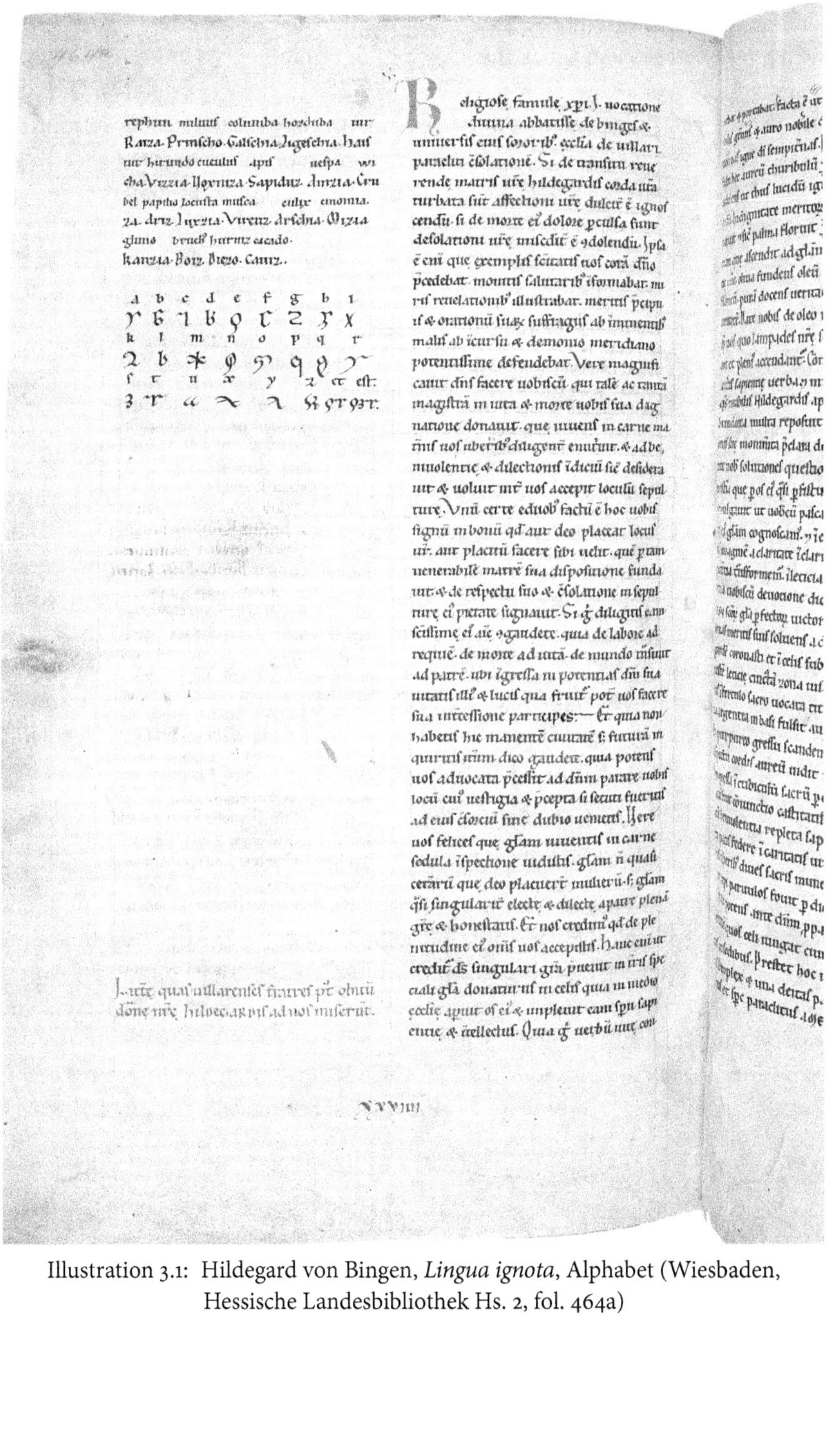

Illustration 3.1: Hildegard von Bingen, *Lingua ignota*, Alphabet (Wiesbaden, Hessische Landesbibliothek Hs. 2, fol. 464a)

Today, we can only conjecture about the purpose of the language. In a time when letters were viewed as the 'foundation of literacy',[44] Hildegard von Bingen's spontaneous way of connecting words and music resulted in a highly individualized style of composing that sometimes exceeded the conventions of plainchant. For instance, not infrequently she subordinated syllabic settings, with one pitch per syllable, to flights of free-floating melismas that Joseph Schmidt-Görg labelled *Melismenfreudigkeit* ('melismatic joyfulness').[45] Some of these rhapsodies consume for just one syllable scores of pitches that seem to escape terrestrial bounds and offer breathless intimations of the hereafter. Words *and* music were inseparable for the abbess as she endeavoured to convey her mystical experiences.

The *lingua ignota* encompasses more than a thousand nouns Hildegard invented and glossed in Latin, with some in Middle High German. Conspicuously absent are verbs, leading some scholars to conclude that the *lingua* 'could not have been spoken'.[46] According to Schnapp, the neologist arrayed her nouns in taxonomical order, beginning with the supernatural and human domains, proceeding through churchly and secular affairs to temporal measurements, and concluding with the socio-economic sphere and natural world, 'spanning everything from the highest to the lowest, from God and the angels to the humble grasshopper and hornet'.[47] To peruse the vocabulary of the *lingua* is to enter a 'regressive linguistic fantasy-world' that relies on 'simple vowel / consonant / vowel / consonant patterns', often fitted within bisyllabic words. A good measure of 'alien phonetic matter' lends them an exoticism that maintains its 'distance from the always concealed mother tongue(s)'.[48] Shadowing the artful juxtaposition of those tongues and now and then impressing as free-ranging glossolalia is a Germanic vernacular 'in which Latin, Hellenic and Semitic elements appear fully integrated within a strongly Teutonic phonetic and orthographic grid'.[49] The critical question, though, remains: how might the *lingua* have interacted with Hildegard's music? Could her 'unknown words' have created counterparts in 'unknown sounds', as if to summon forth some poetic/musical vision of Eden before the Fall?

Hildegard herself provided evidence in a letter dispatched to Pope Anastasius IV around 1153. Here we find in the earliest reference to the *lingua ignota* a

---

[44] Ellison and Kim (2018), 8.
[45] Hildegard von Bingen (1969), 10.
[46] Newman (2013), 459.
[47] Schnapp (1991), 284.
[48] Ibid., 293.
[49] Ibid., 291.

connection to her musical visions: 'But He without defect, who is great, has just now touched a lowly dwelling, so that it might see a miracle, and might form unknown letters, and might utter an unknown language, and also that by itself it might sound forth multitudinous, harmonious melodies'.[50] Elsewhere, in the *Proemium* to her *Book of Divine Works* (*Liber divinorum operum*), she compares her music to a 'harmonious symphony of celestial revelations' and links it to her unknown language and letters,[51] suggesting perhaps that the *lingua ignota* was more extensive than the surviving sources betray, that it may have been intended to work in tandem with her music.

Supporting these conjectures is Hildegard's tantalizing antiphon for the dedication of a church, 'O orzchis Ecclesia'. Of the seventy-odd monophonic melodies in her musical corpus, this antiphon is the only one to offer a macaronic text in which the primary language, Latin, is embellished with five 'unknown' words, marked in bold italics:

O **orzchis** Ecclesia	Oh, immense Ecclesia
armis divinis praecincta,	girded with divine arms,
et hyazintho ornata,	and bedecked in hyacinth,
tu es **caldemia**	you are the fragrance
stigmatum **loifolum**	of the wounds of people
et urbs scientiarum.	and the city of knowledge.
O, o, tu es etiam **crizanta**	Oh, oh, you are truly anointed
in alto sono et es **chorzta** gemma.	amidst lofty sounds and are a sparkling gem.[52]

The significance of this unicum cannot be overstated: the only applied example of the *lingua ignota*, it occurs in the context of a musical inspiration. Of the five invented words only one, according to Schnapp, appears exactly in extant manuscripts of the *lingua: loifolum*, 'of people'. Still, 'the adjectives *orzchis* and *chorzta*, as well as the participial adjective *crizanta* and noun *caldemia* are clearly cast in the same linguistic mold'. For Schnapp, these four words 'intrude' into the song 'like rough ornaments into an angelic song'.[53]

Regarding the meanings of the five secret words, Sarah Higley offers these interpretations. *Crizanta* is a version of *crizia* ('church'), turned here into a participle for 'anointed'. *Orzchis* shares its first part with *Orschibuz* (oak tree); thus, *orzchis* 'may mean "great"'. The adjective *chorzta* and noun *caldemia*, on the other hand, are not part of the surviving *lingua* and 'raise the possibility that Hildegard's invented language was larger than her list implies and could

---

[50] Cited in Higley (2007), 22.
[51] See Schnapp (1991), 292, 41n.
[52] As translated in Schnapp (1991), 293.
[53] Ibid., 293.

Ex. 3.1a: Phrygian Mode

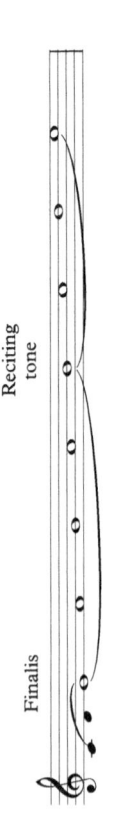

Ex. 3.1b: Hildegard von Bingen, 'O orzchis Ecclesia'

include adjectives – or that it was subject to spontaneous alterations that she drew from a wide collection of memorized words'.[54]

And, finally, what of the music for 'O orzchis Ecclesia' (ex. 3.1)?[55] It begins and ends on the pitch E, identifying the mode as Phrygian.

That pitch grounds the melody periodically throughout the composition (for example, on *Ecclesia*, *praecincta* and *loifolum*). Other pitches that carry structural weight are the reciting tone B a fifth above (*ornata*, *scientiarum*) and G, midway between the *finalis* and reciting tone (*sono*). But what lends the music its special character is Hildegard's gradual expansion of the *ambitus* from a low C two pitches below the *finalis* to the high E, so that the range of the music spans a full tenth. That climactic pitch appears three times, first on the metaphor of the Church as the 'city of knowledge' (*urbs scientiarum*), then on 'anointed' (*crizanta*), and finally at the crest of a melismatic ascent for 'amidst lofty sounds' (*in alto sono*). We might consign these manipulations of pitch and tessitura to examples of word painting, but they promote too an ecstatic, visionary quality, as Hildegard bridges the familiar with the unfamiliar, orthodox Church Latin with her uninhibited, newly constructed nouns, and the terrestrial with the celestial sublime.

℘ iv

For centuries, Hildegard was remembered primarily for her literary works; her melodies 'had much less a life of their own'[56] until their rediscovery in the nineteenth century. On the other hand, with the Benedictine monk Guido d'Arezzo (*ca.* 991–1033), we meet a musician from central Tuscany whose primary contribution, a new system of notation that specified pitches with a heightened level of precision, was soon adopted. Guido radically transformed how music was learned, and, as we shall see in Chapter 4, provided a method for encoding names and messages into music that Renaissance composers would pursue. The author of didactic writings, including the widely copied *Micrologus* (*post* 1026) 'addressed to boys learning the elements of music',[57] Guido was especially concerned about improving the musical education of singers and their efficiency in learning complex chants. In response, Guido Monaco compiled an antiphoner with its neumes placed carefully in succession above the text. He began by ruling two coloured horizontal lines, one yellow, one red, to represent

---

[54] Higley (2007), 30.
[55] Transcribed from Hildegard von Bingen (1969), 142–3.
[56] Bain (2015), 63–4.
[57] Palisca (1978), 50.

the pitches C and F. Neumes sung to these pitches appeared on these lines; neumes for other pitches appeared below, between or above the lines, thus mapping the music along vertical and horizontal axes (charting the height and temporal succession), the beginnings of what evolved into our modern, five-line musical stave.

Like Notker's earlier experiments in adding verses to textless sequences, Guido's system was intended as an *aide de mémoire*. What made the monk's grid-like notation especially efficacious, though, was his second innovation: using the solmization syllables (*ut, re, mi, fa, sol, la*) to stand for the six pitches of the hexachord we recognize today (C, D, E, F, G, A). As Guido explained in his *Letter Concerning an Unknown Chant* (*Epistola de ignotu cantu*), these syllables assisted singers in learning notated chants and in writing down unknown melodies. Guido recommended the eighth-century Hymn in Praise of St. John the Baptist, the verses of which Paul the Deacon (*ca.* 720s–799?) had fashioned as Horatian Sapphics.[58] Its first four lines read:

Ut *queant laxis* **res**onare *fi*bris	O free our sinful lips from stain
Mira gestorum *fa*muli tuorum,	That we your servants may rejoice
Solve pollute *la*bii reatum,	At your great miracles again,
Sancte Iohannes!	Holy St John, with open voice![59]

By Guido's time this text was being paired to the melody shown in ex. 3.2, which ascends with the beginning of each line of text and its midpoint progressively by step from C to D, E, F, G and A.

The syllables that Guido now joined to these sequential pitches (in bold above) became our familiar solmization syllables (eventually *do* supplanted *ut*, and *ti* was added for the pitch B to 'complete' the scale through the octave). By memorizing the melody for 'Ut queant laxis' and recognizing its embedded hexachord, singers could identify pitches in other chants, considerably sharpen their ability to sightread, and lessen their dependence on learning by mechanical rote.

Soon Guido's success in training choristers was attracting the attention of Pope John XIX (1024–33). Many assumed that Guido himself had fabricated the melody for the Hymn to St. John, incorporating into its contours the ladder-like pattern of steps that formed the ascending hexachord. But here our narrative diverges to return us to classical antiquity, and to another unsolvable mystery. For it turns out that the famous melody also survives in a medieval

---

[58] Typically arranged in verses of three hendecasyllabic lines followed by a shorter line of five syllables.

[59] Lyons (2007), 215.

Ex. 3.2: *Ut queant laxis*

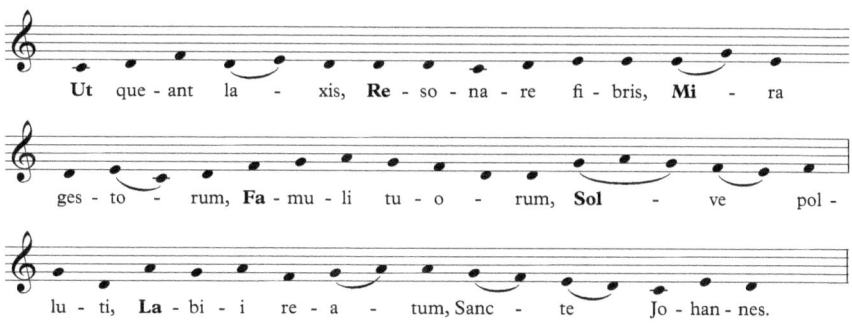

manuscript adorned with musical neumes for a different text – a secular ode of the Roman poet Horace. How that transpired requires an excursion, which brings us to the close of the French Revolution.

After the dissolution of the Directory in 1799, the newly elevated First Consul, Napoleon, ordered the confiscation of literary manuscripts from religious institutions and the estates of aristocrats who had fled the Revolution. The Oratory College of Troyes in the Champagne region southeast of Paris possessed rare items from the library of Pierre Pithou, a sixteenth-century lawyer, publisher and Huguenot who, having barely survived the St. Bartholomew's Day Massacre of 1572, renounced his Protestant faith. In 1804 Napoleon's agents transported Pithou's holdings to the School of Medicine of Montpellier University in southern France. Among them was a small codex bearing the shelfmark M425. Written in a clear, lower-case Carolingian minuscule dating most likely from the mid-eleventh century, this manuscript contained the complete works of Horace.

For the 'Ode to Phyllis' (*Odes* 4.11) the scribe took the trouble to rule horizontal lines to accommodate raised musical neumes, suggesting that this ode, at least, was not only recited but sung. What is more, Stuart Lyons, who has argued for 'Horace's odes as performance art',[60] has demonstrated that, when properly transcribed, the melody in M425 is uncannily like the melody Guido associated with the Hymn in Praise of St. John the Baptist. In short, 'there can be no doubt that Horace's 'Ode to Phyllis' and Guido's arrangement of *Ut queant laxis* are precipitations of a single musical ancestor'.[61] Guido seems to have transferred the tune to Paul the Deacon's verses which, like Horace's,

---

[60] Lyons (2010), 90.
[61] Ibid., 177.

Ex. 3.3: Guido's arrangement of *Ut queant laxis* with text of Horace's 'Ode to Phyllis'

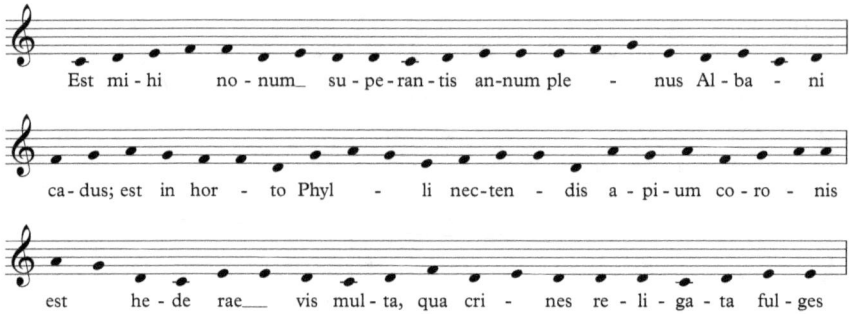

unfolded in similarly scanned, predominantly hendecasyllabic Sapphic lines. Ex. 3.3 shows the opening of the music with Horace's text.[62]

As for why Guido suppressed the Horatian text, we probably need look no further than its closing, mildly prurient lines:

Age iam, meorum Finis amorum,	Come to me now, my own last love, –
Non enim posthac alia calebo	No other girl will keep me warm, –
Femina condisce modos, amanda	Learn, learn the music! Come along,
Voce quos reddas: minuentur atrae	And with your lovely voice perform!
Carmine curae.	Dark cares will become less with song.

Lyons summarizes the matter thus: 'These were not sentiments with which Guido could associate ... Horace was short, plump, and extroverted, an Epicurean womanizer and a pagan entertainer. Guido was spare, ascetic and highly strung, a Benedictine celibate and a cathedral choirmaster'.[64]

No fewer than forty-eight medieval manuscripts transmitting Horace's odes display musical neumes,[65] suggesting that there was a tradition that connected certain odes to notated melodies. But were they medieval in origin, or did they somehow recall an older, oral musical tradition extending further back into antiquity? A careful reading of the odes does lend credence at least to the idea of Horace as a poet/musician who sang his odes, often accompanying himself on a cithara. The self-proclaimed composer of *carmina* (songs) and 'first of men to sing Aeolian song transposed to Italian measures',[66] Horace was remembered

---

[62] Adapted from ibid., 119.

[63] Lyons (2007), 195.

[64] Ibid., 39.

[65] See further, Lyons (2010) and Wälli (2002).

[66] *Odes* III. 30, as trans. in Lyons (2010), 174.

by Ovid and Juvenal as a practitioner of 'sophisticated songs' (*carmina culta*).[67] Too, the sheer number of musical references in Horace's poetry[68] suggests a musical sophistication not possessed by other poets. But with the fall of Rome in 476 CE, Horace's reception was interrupted until the mid-ninth century, a grand caesura that resembled a 'waisted hour-glass, the splendid heritage leading through a period of compression down to a brilliant reception'.[69]

That Guido evidently reused a melody associated with the 'Ode to Phyllis' – a melody that articulated the stepwise hexachord on which much medieval music theory was based – may well betray a distant memory of the Augustan age of Roman poetry. Though separated by a millennium from Horace, Guido could not ignore the heritage of the classical past. And so, in the preface to his *Regule Rithmice*, cast in versified hexameters instead of prose, we encounter this acrostic, a word game that Horace and his contemporaries would have appreciated:

> **G***liscunt corda hominum mollita meis Camenis.*
> **U***na mihi virtus numeratos contulit ictus.*
> **I***n celi summo dulcissima cantica fundo,*
> **D***ans aule Christi cum munera voce ministri.*
> **O***rdine qui dixi me primo carmina scripsi.*

> The hearts of men rejoice, made tender by my Muses.
> My single talent has brought together the counted beats.
> In heaven on high I pour out sweetest *cantica*,
> giving gifts to the palace of Christ with the voice of a servant.
> I who have stated my name in a row at the beginning am the one who wrote the *carmina*.[70]

We should not be surprised by connections, however tenuous, between Guido and Horace, any more than by the unexpected link between Guido's syllables and the American musical film *The Sound of Music* (1965). Here, in the didactic 'Do-Re-Mi' performed by Julie Andrews as she teaches the seven von Trapp children the C-major scale, Rodgers and Hammerstein awakened our own long memory of solfège and Guido's syllables, and in the process playfully re-encrypted *do-re-mi* as *doe, ray, me*.

---

[67] Ovid, *Tristia* 4.10, 49–50, and Juvenal, *Satires* 7.55, as trans. in Lyons (2010), 45–6.
[68] Lyons (2010), 91–2.
[69] Ibid., 99.
[70] Pesce (1999), 328–9.

CHAPTER 4

Sounding Numbers, Fickle Anagrams, Chameleonic Alphabets and Carved Vowels

'*Cest ce que chascuns na mie / Scens de trouver tel muserie*'
'Not every man / has enough skill to solve such a puzzle.'[1]

Machaut, *La Prise d'Alexandre*, 1391–2

O F the preeminent fourteenth-century French composers, Guillaume de Machaut (*ca.* 1300–77) also enjoyed a singular distinction as a poet during the period known as the *Ars nova* (*New Art*), in contrast to the earlier *Ars antiqua* (*Ancient Art*). He played a significant role in our narrative of early musical cryptography for finding diverse ways to project multiple authorial voices, some well enough hidden from the reader/listener to pose vexing riddles, not all of which, it seems, we possess sufficient skill to solve.

Evidently the first to use the term *Ars nova* was Jacques de Liège (*ca.* 1260–post 1330) in his *Speculum musicae* (*The Mirror of Music, ca.* 1330), a 'voluminous and spectacularly learned treatise'[2] of medieval music theory. His purpose was to expose 'errors of the composers of the *Ars nova* and to demonstrate the validity of the teachings of the *Ars antiqua*'.[3] As a result, Jacques inveighed against the innovations of the new century that Machaut embraced while acknowledging in his music the lingering influence of the *Ars antiqua*. Among them was a relaxed – for Jacques – unprincipled treatment of dissonances he likened to a 'great bestiality': 'It seemed as if an ass was dressed as a man, a nanny goat as a lion, a bird as a fish, a snake as a salmon'.[4] Above all, Jacques criticized the admission of 'imperfect' binary rhythmic values. Reaffirming Pythagorean number theory as transmitted through the scholastic philosopher Boethius, the theorist understood numbers to reflect 'the divine plan of God

---

[1] Machaut (2002), 98–9.
[2] Wegman (2016), 257.
[3] Slocum (1993), 11.
[4] Jacobus Leodiensis, vol. 7, 23, as translated in Slocum (1993), 22.

in the sensible world'.[5] Thus, if the number one encompassed the unity of the cosmos, two represented imperfection. Three, on the other hand, was the most perfect of all; in Christian exegesis, it mirrored the consummation of the Trinity, the three in one. So, Jacques privileged ternary proportions, metres, rhythmic divisions, etc. And he propounded his conservative views in the longest musical treatise surviving from the fourteenth century, the *Speculum musicae*, comprising 521 chapters in seven books, introduced with letters that form the acrostic 'Iacobus'. Machaut, too, was no stranger to games involving words, numbers and self-naming.

∾ i

Numerology offered one way to weight music with submerged meanings. But corroborating number symbolism was by no means straightforward. When Marie-Bernadette Dufourcet-Hakim pondered Machaut's twenty-three motets, she noted first the medieval view of odd numbers as more perfect than even, so that twenty-three represented the 'primordial unity' more compellingly than, say, twenty-four. Further, twenty-three was the number of letters in Machaut's alphabet, and, finally, the sum of his initials: G. d. M. = $7 + 4 + 12 = 23$.[6] But were all these correspondences unrelated, or did they convincingly demonstrate how numbers 'ruled music in its physical cause as well as artistic organization'?[7]

Sceptics might dismiss Machaut's initials as inconsequential were it not for his use of numerological anagrams, suggesting that alphanumeric transformations were more than recreation for him. One example is from *The Tale of the Alerion* (*Dit de l'alerion*), in which the poet compares the art of courtly love to falconry. As was Machaut's wont in his *dits*, in lieu of a decisive cadential 'signature' he typically concluded his octosyllabic verses with a riddle, tasking the reader to tease out his identity:

> If you would know, without a doubt,
> Who has composed all of this rhyme,
> It's easy and quite plain to see;
> You will not find it difficult,
> If you wish to amuse yourself
> With 18, 24 and 2,
> 40, 10 and 22,
> But divide them into two;

---

[5] Slocum (1993), 16.

[6] Dufourcet-Hakim (2002), 85.

[7] Ibid., 89.

> And 13, 7 and 18,
> 19, 4 and 3 and 8,
> Without adjusting them at all.[8]

Dividing the first series by two yields 9, 12, 1, 20, 5 and 11, which, when joined to the second, produces 9, 12, 1, 20, 5, 11, 13, 7, 18, 19, 4, 3 and 8. Substituting their letter equivalents, we have: *i, m, a, u, e, l, n, g, s, t, d, c* and *h*. By rearranging their order and deploying some letters twice, we may grasp a 'solution': 'Guillemins de Machaut', an alternate spelling the poet sometimes concealed in his anagrams.

He implemented a similar device in two compositions interpolated into the *Voir dit* (*True Poem*),[9] purportedly an autobiographical narrative in 9,000 verses about his relationship with a young woman, Péronne, whose name he also ensconced within an anagram. Here, Machaut again indulged in numerology, this time announced in the first two verses: 'Dix et sept, cinq, trese, quatorse et quinze / M'a doucement de bien amer espris' ('Seventeen, five, thirteen, fourteen and fifteen / has sweetly inflamed me with virtuous love'[10]). These numbers veil the letters *r, e, n, o* and *p*, which, when rearranged and supplemented by a second *e* and *n*, yield *Péronne*, the real or imagined object of the poet's affection.[11] In this case, Machaut set these lyrics as a rondeau, with the rhyme scheme *ABaAabAB*, whereby *AB* represented a framing refrain, and *ab* new text underlaid to the music of *AB*. The circling refrain recycles compact musical motives that mirror internal, pun-like rhymes within Machaut's poetry – for example, *espris, et pris* and *prise*, deft applications of *rime équivoque* ('equivocal rhyme').[12]

A second 'number rondeau' appears near the concluding verses of the *Voir dit*, with the riddle announced thus: 'Cinq, un, trese, wit nuef d'amour fine / M'ont espris sans definement' ('Five, one, thirteen, eight, nine of a fine love / have seized me without limits'). In 1906 Ernst Hoepffner decoded these numbers as *e, a, n, h* and *j*, yielding the name Jehan, possibly the noblewoman Jeanne d'Armagnac, who married Jean, Duke of Berry, in 1360.[13] That attribution is uncertain, but more difficulties confront the cryptanalyst intent upon solving the verbal anagram with which *Voir dit* concludes. Here the poet promises to reveal his name and that of his *dame jolie*, by drawing the reader to the ninth line and first eight letters of the eighth line from the end:

---

[8] Machaut (1994), 165–6 (lines 4801–11).
[9] See Leo (2005), 96–100.
[10] Machaut (1998), 441 (verses 6336–7).
[11] See Suchier (1897), 542.
[12] See further, Hahn (1993), 264–7.
[13] Hoepffner (1906), 409.

	[... I've no desire]
Pour li changier nulle autre fame	To change her for some other woman.
Ma dame le [savra de vrai]	My lady will know it for the truth.[14]

Several solutions have been proposed for reshuffling these thirty-six letters, including 'Guillaume de Machault et Agnes de Navarre', 'guillaume de machaut peronelle d'armentiere' and 'guillaume de machaut amera fille perronne'.[15] Only the third expends every letter, as opposed to the first (thirty-five) and second (thirty-seven). So, while Machaut's anagrams ostensibly pose 'as rigorous, detailed, [and] defined', they can betray 'a certain amount of ... slippage or blurring around the borders ... like playing chess with oneself'.[16]

Machaut identified himself in his *dits* with flexibility, from direct 'self-naming to not naming at all'.[17] His anagrams admitted a range of readings, from the readily explicable, confirming our presumption that Guillaume (de Machaut) *was* the real author, to the other extreme – anagrams so resistant to decryption as to cast doubt about whether the first-person narrator was Machaut, a fictive character posing as Machaut, or perhaps someone else. To make sense of these riddles, Laurence de Looze catalogued categories of Machauldian 'anagrammic logic'.[18] At one endpoint is *The Judgment of the King of Navarre* (*Le jugement dou Roy de Navarre*), in which Machaut reveals he *is* the one who has 'composed and rhymed this little book'.[19] With no need for stealth, there is no anagram. In the next stage, exemplified by *The Taking of Alexandria* (*La Prize d'Alexandre*), Machaut introduces an anagram and provides clues for its solution, yet elsewhere also names himself, releasing the answer in advance.[20] Two further stages tease the reader by removing altogether 'Guillaume [de Machaut]' as the answer. In three dits (*The Judgment of the King of Bohemia*, *Remede de Fortune* and *The Tale of the Alerion*) the author creates anagrams that yield 'an almost-Guillaume',[21] that is, 'Guillemin' or 'Gullemins'. In the final stage, activated in the *Voir Dit*, *Dit dou Lyon* and *Dit de la Harpe*,[22] Machaut contrives anagrams that, despite his clues, resist solution; the author's 'identity'

---

[14] Machaut (1998), 625 (verses 9085–7).
[15] See Suchier (1897), 544–5; Hoepffner (1906), 408–9.
[16] De Looze (1988), 545, 557.
[17] Ibid., 543.
[18] Ibid., 540.
[19] Machaut (1988), 189 (line 4202).
[20] Machaut (2002), 417 (lines 8874–85).
[21] De Looze (1988), 545.
[22] Ibid., 547–9.

remains sequestered within the anagrams, which may betray pseudonyms for the author, but not much more.

If Machaut's anagrams create 'pseudo-autobiography',[23] elsewhere he exploits different word games or numerology to conceal messages. A case in point is the isorhythmic three-part motet 'Tans doucement/Eins que ma dame/Ruina'. In 2017 Melanie Shaffer announced the discovery of a Latin acrostic buried in the French text of the middle voice, the *motetus*. By segregating the letters of the text that aligned with the beginnings of the four *taleae* – that is, the foundational rhythmic pattern repeated in the lowest sounding, tenor voice – she was able to extract the message 'Es equa' ('You are a mare'). This equine metaphor is likely an allusion to the *Roman de Fauvel* (1310–14), the political allegory of nearly 3,300 verses by Gervais de Bus, a clerk at the French Chancery of Philip IV (r. 1285–1314) and Louis X (r. 1314–16). A ribald, trenchant satire, it survives in several manuscripts, of which one[24] is lavishly appointed with illustrations and one hundred plus musical examples. A few are ascribed to Philippe de Vitry (1291–1361), a central proponent of the *Ars nova*, and significant influence on Machaut.

The title character in the *Roman* – part horse, part ass – was an acronym enumerating cardinal sins then thought rampant: **F**(lattery), **A**(varice), **U**(illainy), **V**(ariety, that is, duplicity), **E**(nvy) and **L**(aziness). Machaut's word play was, in effect, an acrostic about an acronym, placing his motet in direct dialogue with the *Roman de Fauvel*. To underscore the connection, Machaut borrowed the tenor voice (*Ruina*) from one of the interpolated motets in *Fauvel*, this one with Latin texts, 'Super cathedram/Presidentes in thronis/Ruina'.

Why did Machaut liken Fauvel to a mare (*equa*) instead of a stallion (*equus*)? In the *Roman*, the virile Fauvel seeks to wed Fortune (*Fortuna*), who dismisses him as the Antichrist. Instead, he unites with Fortune's daughter, Vainglory, with whom he begets daily offspring. As for *equa*, Shaffer argues that Machaut's second-person singular 'es' refers to 'the attributes *of the lady* – that Fortune, the female goddess, uses to deceive'.[25] Deception then plays out on several levels. For example, the upper two voices (*triplum* and *motetus*) cross several times, momentarily assuming each other's role, 'as if to display a reversal of the normal order, suggesting that Fortune is at work in this piece'.[26] Fortune's churning wheel indeed seems to encircle the unnamed Fauvel in this motet,

---

[23] De Looze (1997), 2.
[24] Paris, Bibliothèque Nationale fonds fr. 146.
[25] Shaffer (2017), 133.
[26] Ibid., 124.

encouraging Shaffer to group it with Machaut's other 'fortune' motets as a thematically related subset within a larger, cyclic whole.

In Chapter 2 we conjectured that Machaut strategically aligned significant words of his texts or portions of his music at points demarcating the Golden Section, that 'a calculating mind seems to have been at work'.[27] For instance, in the number rondeau 'Cinq, un, treze, wit, nuef d'amour fine' the Golden Section falls where the second half of the refrain (*B*) begins, as likewise obtains in the rondeau 'Vos doulz resgars'.[28] The idea of music as 'sounding number' (*numerus sonorus*) may also have inspired Machaut to use numerical relationships in symbolic ways related to the meaning of his texts. Jacques Boogaart, for example, has garnered evidence from several motets for the role of numbers.[29] In 'Quant en moy', in which 'love's perfection is central',[30] Machaut adheres strictly to ternary mensural relationships (for example, one long = three breves; one breve = three semibreves). Further, the duration of the music is 144 breves, and the *color*, or underlying melodic pattern, contains thirty notes, both divisible by three. In still other motets, Boogaart detects structural/symbolic uses of twelve and seventeen,[31] and proposes that Machaut intended the latter to represent hope.

The calculating side of Machaut is especially unhampered in the rondeau 'Ma fin est mon commencement' (see p. 24). Here, in an 'extreme example of opacity',[32] he produced not only a double musical palindrome, but supplemented it with a text that, instead of singing about love or concealing a lady's name, dispensed clues about how to perform the music. The score itself became the object of the text, music about creating music, and how the three voices of the composition – a *triplum*, *cantus* and *tenor* – were to fit together, relying on the information divulged in this cue, with its circular Delphic logic:

> My end is my beginning and my beginning my end. And the tenor in the normal way. My end is my beginning. My third voice – three times only – turns back on itself and thus ends. My end is my beginning and my beginning my end.[33]

To make the solution more challenging, Machaut notated music for only the *triplum* and *tenor* (Illustration 4.1), leaving the *cantus* to materialize as the retrograde of the *triplum*.

---

[27] Boogaart (2003), 23.
[28] Hahn (1993), 171–2, 191–2.
[29] Boogaart (2021).
[30] Ibid., 379.
[31] Regarding medieval number symbolism see Meyer and Suntrup (1987).
[32] Bain (2012), 81.
[33] Translation from Newes (1990), 226.

Illustration 4.1: Machaut, 'Ma fin est mon commencement'
(Paris, Bibliothèque Nationale, fr. 22546, fol. 153r)

Furthermore, the *triplum* appeared upside down, so the performer had to rotate the page to read both parts from left to right, once again underscoring the circularity of the music. Also, Machaut provided only half of the *tenor* part (*A*), so that the performer produced its second half (*B*) by 'turning back' the first half. Because the complete refrain emerged three times in the rondeau (***AB**a**A**ab**AB***), so did the fully realized *tenor* part appear three times. The result was a double palindrome. One existed between the *triplum* and *cantus*; each was the retrograde of the other, and, since both commenced simultaneously in the first bar, their end was literally their beginning. The other palindrome unfolded within the fully executed *tenor* part; its end, too, was its beginning.

In Machaut's time only trained musicians could assemble the rondeau from its cryptic text. But was Machaut's erudition just a clever game for the musically inquisitive, or did it conceal something else? In Chapter 1, we commented that in classical antiquity recursion could countervail a negative force. An apposite image associated with palindromes was the labyrinth, into which an intrepid wanderer might enter, circumvent false starts to reach the symbolic centre of adversity, and somehow reverse the steps to emerge from the ordeal unscathed. A famous example was the myth of the half-human, half-bull Minotaur, who inhabited the maze of Daedalus on Crete. Here the monster devoured sacrificial victims King Minos offered annually in tribute. Theseus alone was able to slay the Minotaur, retrace his steps by rewinding Ariadne's clew of yarn he had unrolled behind him upon entering the maze, and exit safely.

Viewed as 'the French counterpart to Ovid',[34] Machaut would have known this celebrated myth from the eighth book of *Metamorphoses*. Indeed, there is a reference to Theseus and the maze in Machaut's own *Judgment of the King of Navarre*.[35] But by the composer's time paved labyrinths were common within Gothic cathedrals, including at Reims, where Machaut served as a canon. By his own request, Machaut's remains were interred in the nave, not far from the cathedral's labyrinth,[36] which, for Anne Walters Robertson, mirrored 'the doubly recursive structure' of *Ma fin est mon commencement*.[37] Christians contemplating the maze would have grasped its central message: 'life is a journey and a trial, one that takes the pilgrim to some place – often a *central* place – where deadly combat occurs, and then on to a higher sphere of spiritual awareness'.[38] The pilgrim's progress imitated Christ's, including the Harrow-

---

[34] Huot (1987), 242.
[35] Wright (2001), 113.
[36] Robertson (1992), 100–1.
[37] Robertson (2002), 171.
[38] Ibid.

ing of Hell between the crucifixion and resurrection, midpoint of the Saviour's labyrinthine journey.

There is an enigmatic paradox about Machaut's aesthetics: he was Janus-faced, with one side turned to a numerological understanding of the universe and its divine perfection, the other to the newly emerging rhetorical authority of the author/composer. Music as sounding number slowly yielded to a new concept, music as poetry (*musica poetica*).[39] The changing role of authorship in Machaut's case became clear from the intrusion of his voice into his poetry and music, so that the figural 'je' remained an omnipresent protagonist.

⁌ ii

From the fourteenth through sixteenth centuries European cryptology experienced 'an explosion of cryptographic ingenuity',[40] so that ciphers became 'as much an instrument of war as the arquebus'.[41] The rise of international embassies, hubs of intelligence gathering, was one factor driving the need for enhanced cryptanalysis. There was, too, the dominance of Italian mercantile states, of which Venice remained for centuries *primus inter pares*. Enveloping that maritime affluence was a seeping fog of political deception. From spartan rooms atop the Doge's Palazzo, a small cohort of specialists led by Giovanni Soro (d. 1544) laboured over mounting jumbles of secret documents. His primary purpose was to decipher intercepted intelligence from diplomats posted abroad. No less critical, though, was to protect Venetian encryption techniques by replacing compromised cipher keys, or augmenting them with random numbers as nulls, empty symbols inserted to thwart those who would compromise the cyphers. For extra security, entire words might substitute for other commonly used words, blending ciphers and codes in highly valued keys known as nomenclators.

Security was administered not by the Doge but a patrician Council of Ten, who swore an oath of secrecy and whose clandestine deliberations could mean life or death for Venetians, even the Doge himself. Several rival states developed their own cryptological assets, whether Milan and Ferrara, governed by the Houses of Sforza and Este, or Florence, ruled by the Medici. In Florence Niccolò Machiavelli published *The Art of War* (*Dell'arte della Guerra*, 1520), in which he discussed the value of enciphered messages. Those unfortunate to be besieged, he wrote, employed various concealments in dispatching news to their friends. Some hid missives within their bodies, while others wrote 'ordinary things in a

---

[39] Niemöller (2011).
[40] Shumaker (1982), 113.
[41] Kahn (1996), 114.

letter, and then ... with water (invisible ink) between one line and another, which afterwards by wetting or scalding (caused) the letter to appear.'[42]

By Machiavelli's time cryptography had reached the New World. During Columbus's third voyage, in 1498, he resorted to ciphers to alert his brother about an official dispatched from Spain to investigate allegations of misconduct. But the letter was decrypted,[43] and provided a pretence to send the admiral back to Spain in chains. In 1521 the conquistador Hernán Cortés fared considerably better: he subdued the Aztec empire and claimed Mexico for Spain, owing in part to his superior military intelligence. Among Cortés's cryptographic tools was a non-alphabetic substitution system.[44]

Meanwhile in France ciphers played a role during the conflicts that pitted Catholics against Huguenots (1562–98). The Protestant Henry of Navarre, who, to ascend the throne as Henry IV, converted to Catholicism ('Paris is well worth a Mass', he quipped), retained the lawyer/mathematician François Viète, a pioneer of modern algebra, who boasted to foreign officials that he routinely broke their ciphers. In England, Elizabeth I developed perhaps the most extensive intelligence service of the period, directed by her Secretary of State and spymaster, Sir Francis Walsingham. The queen had reason to heed the injunction of Lord Hastings in Shakespeare's *Richard III*: 'Nothing can proceed that toucheth us whereof I shall not have intelligence',[45] among the earliest references (*ca.* 1592–4) to 'intelligence' as meaning secret information. Walsingham oversaw a covert network of agents and double agents, tracking plots to depose Elizabeth and monitoring the Spanish Armada, poised to invade England. The scheming came to a head in the Babington Conspiracy of 1586, in which Walsingham convinced Elizabeth to sign the death warrant of Mary Queen of Scots after her implication in a conspiracy to overthrow the monarch. While preparing for the axeman, Mary spent her expiring time embroidering her motto into royal garments – 'En ma fin est mon commencement'.

Another state preoccupied with cryptology was the Vatican. We can trace papal cryptography to at least the early fourteenth century,[46] though the event that accelerated the *Curia*'s need for 'secret writing' – the Great Schism – erupted in 1378, not to be resolved until the Council of Constance elected Martin V in 1417. This dramatic bifurcation summarily increased the need to strengthen cipher security. Probably the most significant innovation was the

---

[42] Machiavelli (2006), 157–8.

[43] See D'Anghiera (1912), vol. 1, 149.

[44] For one of Cortés's cipher letters, see Kahn (1996), 115.

[45] Act III, Scene 2.

[46] See Meister (1906), 1–21.

polyalphabetic substitution system developed by Leon Battista Alberti (1404–72), a prodigious polymath who, according to Jacob Burckhardt, 'in everything that wins praise ... was, from his childhood, first'.[47] Particularly revered as an architect, Alberti was a musical autodidact who preferred buildings with harmonious, numerologically derived proportions.

Alberti was also the author of the earliest surviving Western treatise about ciphers, *De componendis cifris* (*On Composing Ciphers*, 1466).[48] Here he proposed expanding the single cipher substitution method by drawing upon interchangeable alphabets so that each letter of the plaintext could assume various values, making it far more difficult to discover. To expedite encryption, Alberti employed a volvelle, two concentric circles with letters engraved upon their circumferences, of which the outer perimeter conveyed the plaintext. By aligning it above a chosen value of the inner wheel, but periodically rotating the inner circle, one could encrypt the letters of the plaintext with shifting values. In time, such polyalphabetic substitutions became the standard, replacing monoalphabetic systems far more susceptible to decryption through frequency analysis.

Of Alberti's successors the German Benedictine abbot Johannes Trithemius (1462–1516) wrote the first published volume about cryptography, *Polygraphia libri sex* (*Polygraphy in Six Books*, 1518). Trithemius was especially remembered, though, for *Steganographia* (*Secret Writing*) in three books, written around 1500 but not released in print until 1606. This curious work was ostensibly 'about using spirits – angels and demons – to send secret messages'.[49] The author invoked phantoms through gibberish-like conjurations, such as 'Padiel aporsy mesarpon omeuas peludyn malpreaxo', that effectively impugned his reputation. He was denounced as a magician of the occult arts, so that the Spanish Inquisition banned *Steganographia* and consigned it to proscribed books.

Trithemius countered that his procedures constituted 'natural' magic, not heretical necromancy. Thus, the 'oath' above concealed the beginnings of an intercalated message borne by every other letter in the second, fourth and sixth of the nonsensical words, yielding *pry[i]mus apex* ('first apex').[50] Agile cryptanalysts unearthed other plaintexts in the first two books of *Steganographia*. Only the final, third book resisted decrypting efforts until the late 1990s, when Thomas Ernst[51] and Jim Reeds demonstrated that it, too, was 'a work of cryptography oddly expressed ... disguised by the use of a figurative language of

---

[47] Burckhardt (1892), 136.

[48] Meister (1906), 125–41.

[49] Reeds (1998), 292.

[50] See further, Reeds (1998), 294. The first, third and fifth words were nulls.

[51] Ernst (1998).

demonology'.[52] Unlike the first two books, in which Trithemius buried his plaintexts within seemingly random sequences of letters, the third resorted to un-patterned rows of numbers. More vexing, the numbers also masqueraded as data about the trajectories of planets. One reference to the retrograde motion of Saturn led Reeds to ascertain that Trithemius had employed 'a reversed 22-letter alphabet'[53] to map onto the numbers. Exploiting this breakthrough, Reeds then proceeded to unlock several plaintexts, including this pangram that consumed every letter of the Latin alphabet: 'Gaza frequens duxit Libycos Karthago triumphos' ('Filled with treasure Carthage led the Libyan triumphs').[54]

One other plaintext by Trithemius deserves mention: 'miserere mei Deus secundu[m] magnum donum tuum amen', a nearly exact quotation from Psalm 51, 'miserere mei Deus secundum misericordiam tuam' ('Have mercy upon me, O God, according to Thy loving kindness').[55] This same verse also served as a cover to disguise an actual plaintext, '[Il] papa vol far la lega contro il turco' ('The pope wants to make an alliance against the Turks'), encrypted not through rows of numbers, but musical notation, (exs. 4.1–4.2).

Ex. 4.1 appears to show a musical setting of the psalm verse, and nothing more. But as anyone with a modicum of musicianship realizes, something is amiss. The jagged contours and wayward rhythmic values distort the natural declamation of the Latin, alerting us that the 'music' is in fact disguising something else. Instead of a devout rendition of the penitential psalm the notes offer only a 'musical Gallimathias' – a confused, topsy-turvy affair.[56] The solution lies in the supporting key to the music, a series of seven ascending scales, each assigned its own rhythmic value and letters of the alphabet (ex. 4.2).

Using this nomenclator, we can reveal the plaintext. To throw us off the scent, the first two pitches are meaningless nulls. The third, notated on the fourth line of the stave with an ascending stem, converts according to the key to 'p'; the next three notes, to 'a', 'p' and 'a', completing the word 'papa'. In this way, 'an apparently harmless melody' was able 'to conceal important state secrets'.[57]

Sometimes Renaissance cryptography treatises merely observed that compositions can communicate hidden messages.[58] But occasionally we gain full access to this secret musical world. Thus, Giambattista della Porta (1535–1615)

---

[52] Reeds (1998), 292.
[53] Ibid., 307.
[54] Ibid., 311.
[55] Ibid.
[56] Meister (1892), 100; and Meister (1906), 112.
[57] Meister (1892), 100.
[58] Porta (1602), V, 156–7.

Ex. 4.1: Trithemius, *Steganographia* (1606)

Ex. 4.2: Trithemius, Key to Ex. 4.1

included in his treatise *De occultis literarum notis* (*Concerning the Hidden Signs of Letters*, 1606) a chapter about how to exploit 'without suspicion' (*sine suspicione*) musical notes for cryptographical purposes.[59]

Nevertheless, Porta's interests in 'natural magic' caused him, like Trithemius, to be suspected of practising occult arts, triggering a papal audience. Paul V may have been aware of one of Porta's steganographic sleights of hand: writing messages on hard-boiled eggs with ink, absorbed through the shells to the egg whites within. Once the external ink was washed off and the shells removed, the messages rematerialized. Among Porta's cryptographic innovations was the use of digraphic ciphers – ciphers that matched each special symbol with two letters. His interest in musical cryptography found some traction: the Germans Daniel Schwenter (1585–1636) and Gaspar Schott (1608–66) drew upon Porta's

---

[59] Ibid., V, Ch. 14, 335–7.

Ex. 4.3: Schott, *Schola Steganographica* (1665)

Ex. 4.4: Schott, *Schola Steganographica* (1665)

Ex. 4.5: Schott, *Schola Steganographica* (1665)

Ex. 4.6: Schott, *Schola Steganographica* (1665)

cipher key, which assigned letters to pitch names and rhythmic durations.[60] Schwenter and Schott also shared a challenging musical riddle, converted by the latter into a bilingual teaser in *Schola Steganographica in Classes Octo Distributa* (*School of Steganography Distributed into Eight Categories*, 1665). Music figured in the closing pages of the eighth, final category, where he devoted a

---

[60] Schwenter (1620), 303–4; Schott (1665), 322–6.

chapter to exploiting notes to convey a 'secret concept' that might be read in German or Latin.⁶¹

Schott began with a musical nomenclator, twenty-four notated pitches in ascending and descending sequences beneath which he aligned the letters of the Latin alphabet in slightly rearranged order (ex. 4.3).

Next, he encrypted the German plaintext, a riddle about how to break a nail with one's hands without resorting to a hammer. Ex. 4.4 reveals the musical results, showing how the first few German words ('Nim[m] zwei Wischdichlein', or 'Take two small cloths') became pitches.

This inelegant tune motivated Schott to try a second encryption of the same text in Latin. Here, he revised the nomenclator so that the twenty-four letters appeared in regular order from *a* to *z* (ex. 4.5). Ex. 4.6 illustrates the first few pitches of the Latin version ('Duo strophiola circumvolve clavo', or 'Wind two small bands around a nail').

Once more, the ungainly melodic leaps were problematic, but for those untrained in music, the notes left no 'suspicion that the writer [had] been secretive'.⁶² Few, indeed, would have imagined that one plaintext had generated a bilingual musical brainteaser.

∽ *iii*

As cryptology advanced in sophistication, it set off an accelerating verbal arms race between cryptographers and cryptanalysts. In the age of Renaissance humanism, the pursuit of secrecy extended to many aspects of life, impelling the punning French diplomat Blaise de Vigenère (1523–96) to declare, 'Everything in this world is only a true cipher' (*Toutes les choses de ce monde ne sont qu'un vray chiffre*),⁶³ the epigram that graces our half title page. This assertion appeared in his *Traicté des chiffres, ou Secrètes manières d'escrire* (*Treatise concerning Ciphers, or Secret Manners of Writing*), a thick volume set as continuous prose, with terse callouts in the margins announcing the topics at hand. They extended well beyond cryptography to alchemy, magic, numerology, Kabbalah, Jewish phylacteries and Japanese ideographs, as well as alphabets of the world. For Vigenère the interpretation of everything rested upon the letters of the alphabet; in short, 'l'alphabet est le monde' ('the alphabet is the world').⁶⁴

---

⁶¹ Schott (1665), 322–6.
⁶² Della Porta, V, 139, translated in Shumaker (1982), 121.
⁶³ Vigenère (1586), 53v. *Chiffre* can mean 'cryptogram' or 'number'.
⁶⁴ Vigenère (1586), fol. 38r; Fanlo (2008), 30.

Today Vigenère is remembered for the eponymous, though misattributed Vigenère Square, a grid-like, polyalphabetic substitution system based on the old Caesar-shift method – raised, as it were, to an exponential level – that remained unbroken until the nineteenth century. Vigenère demonstrated that cryptographers could explore many ways to secrete messages. Late in his treatise he included this remarkable passage, which returns us to music's potential to communicate on multiple levels, some in plain view, others concealed:

> ... even music can be disguised in the form of a cipher, by making the lines and spaces between them serve as letters through the use of notes ... In truth, to be sure, [this method] is difficult since, being thus constrained and subjected to lettering, this music can be neither well ordered, nor scarcely pleasant. In all regards it exceeds its limits and range, sometimes above, sometimes below; but not everyone is an Orlando di Lasso, Adrian Willaert, or Josquin.[65]

Here Vigenère touched on a fundamental issue of musical cryptography: depending on the length and complexity of the plaintext, its transformation often produced results utterly unconvincing as music.

Not that that obstacle discouraged all. Thus, in 1564 Marco Antonio Colonna, commander of the Spanish army and later Viceroy of Sicily, produced a cipher in which letters represented geographical areas and political figures. In turn, the letters were encoded as musical notes that occupied the three internal lines and two spaces of a musical stave, leaving the bottom and top lines and spaces for nulls.[66] But the most remarkable attempt to coopt music for secret messages was a twenty-nine-bar composition commissioned by Duke August the Younger of Brunswick-Lüneburg (1579–1666), 'the highest ranking nobleman to deal extensively' with cryptology.[67]

An incorrigible bibliophile, August founded in Wolfenbüttel the Bibliotheca Augusta, a priceless collection of manuscripts, incunabula and sixteenth- and seventeenth-century prints. As author, August contrived the pseudonym Gustavus Selenus by juxtaposing an anagram of Augustus and a reference to Selene, Greek goddess of the moon, after which Lüneburg (Castle of the Moon) was named. Word play, it seems, was second nature to him. His major contribution was *Cryptomenytices et Cryptographiae Libri IX* (*Secret Intimations and Secret Writings in Nine Books*, 1624), a compendium of cryptography based on the work of 187 predecessors, all duly credited in the preface.[68]

---

[65] Vigenère (1586), fol. 278r.
[66] Devos (1950), 215–19.
[67] Strasser (1983), 194.
[68] Ibid., 196.

In the chapter 'Concerning the Indirect Transformation of Musical Notes' (*De Transformatione Obliqua Notarum Musicalium*),[69] the duke culled several encrypted musical examples, including some that used Guidonian solmization syllables to disguise a plaintext.[70] One might suppose that, like Exs. 4.4 and 4.6, these interventions would not pass muster as musically viable. But in one case, Selenus expanded considerably the cryptographic limits of the art form. He enlisted the musician Friedrich Hollandt to compose a stretch of four-part polyphony and blend an encrypted message into the tenor part without raising alarm, even among musical connoisseurs.

To produce this masterful arcanum Hollandt began with a five-by-five array of letters drawn from the alphabet in rearranged order:

Q	R	S	T	U
W	X	Y	Z	-
A	B	C	D	E
L	M	N	O	P
F	G	H	I	K

Next, he added a row and column with the first five solmization syllables reordered as *ut, fa, sol, mi, re* across the top, and *ut, sol, fa, mi, re* along the left side:

	Ut	fa	sol	mi	re
Ut	Q	R	S	T	U
sol	W	X	Y	Z	-
fa	A	B	C	D	E
mi	L	M	N	O	P
re	F	G	H	I	K

Having determined the key, he began encrypting each letter of the plaintext as a two-note musical interval. The plaintext read, 'Der Spinola ist in der Pfaltz gefallen. Vae illi' ('Spinola has invaded the Palatinate. Woe to him'). Spinola was Ambrogio Spinola, the Spanish general who laid waste to the Palatinate at the outbreak of the Thirty Years' War. The plaintext was thus a newsworthy item of contemporary relevance.

To encrypt this message Hollandt located in the key the three letters of 'Der' as the solmization syllables *fa-mi, fa-re* and *ut-fa*, charting a descending half-step, descending minor third and ascending perfect fourth. Positioning the message in the tenor, he began with the pitch c, thereby generating the motive

---

[69] Selenus (1624), Book 6, Chapter 19, 325–6.
[70] See Schiltz (2015), 348; Strasser (2000), 1009–11; Blumenberg (1992); and Weiss (1993).

Ex. 4.7: Gustavus Selenus, *Cryptomenytices et Cryptographiae* (1624)

c-b, c-a, g-c for 'Der'.[71] Next, progressing through the plaintext, he determined the appropriate intervals from the key, requiring seventy-eight pitches, or thirty-nine paired intervals. Having selected the pitches, he added rhythmic values; furthermore, he coordinated the tenor part with freely composed soprano, alto and bass parts to yield a congruent whole in four parts. Hollandt's solution was to reuse the head motive of the tenor in the other three voices. First, the bass introduced the initial four notes transposed to f (f-e-f-d), answered by the same, one octave above in the alto.[72] Then the motive appeared in the soprano on the pitch c, to which the tenor replied an octave below in bar 5, as it began its cloaked dispatch.

---

[71] In Guidonian terminology, using the hexachord on G, with g as *ut*, a as *re*, b as *mi* and c as *fa*.

[72] Using the hexachord on C (with c as *ut*, d as *re*, e as *mi* and f as *fa*).

The result was a point of imitation, with one voice introducing a subject answered by the other voices in succession (ex. 4.7).

No doubt deliberate was the placement of the tenor as the last voice to enter, drawing the least attention to itself. Noteworthy, too, was how Hollandt 'deceived' without leaving rough edges in the music. The four voices flowed convincingly, and the dissonance treatment accorded with techniques of Franco-Flemish composers such as Josquin des Prez, who, according to Martin Luther, could bend musical notes to his will. To Josquin we now turn.

↣ iv

Repurposing Guidonian syllables to convey verbal messages in music reached an early zenith in the later fifteenth and early sixteenth centuries, especially in the sacred polyphony of Josquin des Prez (*ca.* 1450–1521), possibly the first to apply the method, in the Mass *Hercules Dux Ferrariae*, written sometime between 1480 and 1505 for Ercole I d'Este, the music-loving Duke of Ferrara (1431–1505).[73] The Mass garnered an impressive reception, attested by its wide dissemination through manuscript copies and prints. By 1558, after other composers had followed Josquin's lead,[74] the Italian theorist/composer Gioseffo Zarlino (1517–90) termed the technique 'soggetto cavato dale vocali' ('subject carved from the vowels'[75]). Josquin extracted eight vowels from the duke's name (*e, u, e, u, e, a, i* and *e*) and matched them to syllables, thus, *a = fa, e = re, i = mi* and *u = ut*, and then to pitches, *fa = f, re = d, mi = e* and *ut = c*, producing the ducal subject: *d-c-d-c-d-f-e-d* (ex. 4.8).

No fewer than forty-seven ducal statements appear throughout the Mass, nearly all in the tenor, with three reserved for the soprano, and one in the alto.[76] Lest the recurring motive became stale, Josquin found ways to refresh it. First,

Ex. 4.8: Josquin, *Missa Hercules, Dux Ferrariae*

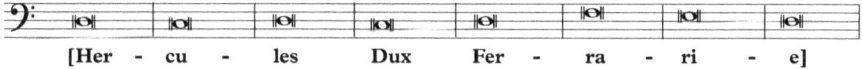

[Her - cu - les   Dux   Fer - ra - ri - e]

---

[73] See Elders (2013), 19 and 118; and Fallows (2020), 259.

[74] For example, Costanzo Festa, Johannes Ghiselin, Heinrich Isaac, Jacquet of Mantua, Orlando di Lasso, Lupus Hellinck, Cipriano da Rore and Adrian Willaert. See also Elders (1994), 79–84; Columbro (1974), vol. I, 65–102; and Agee (1996), 12–13, 18.

[75] Zarlino (1965), Book 3, Ch. 66, 267.

[76] The forty-seven statements may support a date for the Mass of 1480, the forty-seventh anniversary of the duke's knighthood. Elders (2013), 19; and Fallows (2020), 258.

while many statements entered on *d* (*re*) or *d'* an octave above, nearly a third were transposed a fifth above to begin on *a* (*a-g-a-g-a-c-b-a*), and four statements unfolded in retrograde (*d-e-f-d-c-d-c-d*). To generate the tenor part performers had to unlock a series of puzzling verbal canons. The cue for the *Gloria* mandated, 'Fingito vocales: sequentibus signis' ('Mould the vowels according to the following signs').[77] Another cue prescribed retrograde motion, 'Vertit et revertit cicius sine mora ultima longa' ('It turns and returns more quickly without the last *longa* rest').[78]

Often *soggetti cavati* transformed the names of royalty or dignitaries into pitches.[79] Among additional examples from Josquin is the *Missa Faysant Regretz*, based on a rondeau by Walter Frye, and exploring the solmization syllables *fa-re-mi-re* (*f-d-e-d*), probably derived from **Ma**r**g**u**e**rite of Austria (1480–1530), Governor of the Habsburg Netherlands. In the Marian motet *Illibata dei virgo nutrix* Josquin discovered the *soggetto la-mi-la* more directly from **Ma**r**i**a, the Virgin Mary, and echoed it dozens of times in the tenor voice. All told, the tenor part expends eighty-eight pitches, which, Elders argues, are numerologically significant[80]:

$$\begin{array}{ccccccc} D & e & s & P & r & e & z \\ 4 & +5 & +18 & +15 & +17 & +5 & +24 & = 88 \end{array}$$

Lest enumerating pitches in this way might be overlooked, Josquin manoeuvred an acrostic on his name, I O S Q V I N Des P R E Z, into the first twelve lines of the poem, further personalizing his prayer.[81]

In two other works he dissembled more elaborate messages. The instrumental fanfare *Vive le Roy*, thought to celebrate the accession of Louis XII in 1498, fashioned its subject by reading *v* and *y* as *ut* and *mi*:

$$\begin{array}{cccccc} V & i & v & e & le & r & o & y \\ Ut & mi & ut & re & re & sol & mi \\ c & e & c & d & d & g & e \end{array}$$

But the most puzzling example was Josquin's *Missa La sol fa re mi*, published in 1502. Its origins lie in a wry anecdote from the Swiss music theorist Glareanus

---

[77] Schiltz (2015), 398.

[78] Ibid., 395, 459.

[79] For other examples, including several modelled on Josquin, see Elders (1994), 79, 81–4; and Philip Jackson (1978).

[80] Elders (2013), 84.

[81] See ibid., 180; Titcomb (1963); and Sherr (1988).

in 1547: '… when Josquin sought a favour from some important personage and when that man, a procrastinator, said over and over in the mutilated French language, *Laise faire moi*, that is, "leave it to me", then without delay Josquin composed, to these very same words, a complete and very elegant *Missa La sol fa re mi*'.[82] From these syllables he fabricated the pitch sequence *a-g-f-d-e*, its transposition *e-d-c-a-b*, and retrograde *b-a-c-d-e*; the cipher permeates the composition with well over two hundred appearances, sometimes occurring in nearly every bar, and across all voices: Josquin's guileful response to the tardiness of the 'influential person'.

Related to the *soggetto cavato* was the *soggetto ostinato* – a repeated melodic pattern, whether moulded from solmization syllables or not. But at least one common pattern traversing the entire hexachord and drawn from the solmization syllables acquired a special meaning. Josquin invoked the *scala musicalis* (musical scale), the term for the Guidonian gamut of pitches, in his motet *Ut Phoebi radiis*. Here he constructed in the tenor and bass an ascending hexachord, one pitch at a time: *ut, ut-re, ut-re-mi, ut-re-mi-fa, ut-re-mi-fa-sol* and *ut-re-mi-fa-sol-la*. In the second part of the motet, he reversed the pattern in its descending (mirror inverted or retrograde) form, starting on *la*. As Elders has argued, the hexachord represented a ladder to heaven, familiar from Jacob's Ladder in Genesis; in Christian musical iconography 'the rising hexachord symbolizes the prayer to Mary and the falling hexachord the descent of God to earth through her'.[83] Supporting this reading is the division of the poem into two parts focused on the Virgin Mary and Christ. To reinforce the meaning, the syllables of the hexachord themselves are embedded through word play into the poem. In the first part, the text germinates from the word *Ut* ('as'), punning on the first syllable of the hexachord. In successive lines, a series of *Ut*-clauses then introduces successive syllables of the hexachord, thus: '**Ut** Phoebi radiis …/ **Ut re**ges Salomon …/ **Ut remi** pontum…' For the second part, the poet – Josquin? – features words beginning with *La* that progressively add the appropriate solmization syllables: '***La*** … ***Lasso*** … ***La sol fa*** …', etc.[84]

These examples project qualities in Josquin's music – now playful,[85] now sibylline – that reflect the pervasive riddle culture of the Renaissance. To some extent, this interest traced its roots to the concept of obscurity (*obscuritas*) in classical rhetoric. Opaque riddles relied upon obscurity to maximize their effect,

---

[82] Glarean (1965), II, 272.
[83] Elders (2013), 75.
[84] Ibid., 181–2.
[85] Particularly in Josquin's *Missa Di dadi*, in which images of dice establish proportional relationships between the *cantus firmus* and other voices. Long (1989).

as they required 'a certain degree of darkness'[86] that the reader confronted. Josquin was one of several Franco-Flemish composers who crossed the Alps to assume positions in Italy and elevated the cryptic into an aesthetic category.

Thus, before Josquin designed his honorific for the Duke of Ferrara, others were implanting meanings in their music, employing techniques encountered in Chapter 2. Guillaume Du Fay (1397–1474), for instance, adorned at least three works with acrostics[87]; one motet, *Inclita stella maris*, could be realized in four ways, two requiring two voices, and one each with three and four voices. No motet of Du Fay, though, attracted as much attention for its symbolic value as *Nuper rosarum flores* (see p. 41). If, as is now accepted, the work's proportions do not replicate the design of the Florence *duomo*, they can be related to 'the biblical prototype for all cathedrals and indeed, for all churches, the Temple of Solomon'.[88]

Du Fay's embrace of the enigmatic also extended to his cyclic Masses, in particular the *Missa L'homme armé* (ca. 1460–61), which spawned dozens of imitations, all based upon a secular tune still enveloped in mystery. It seems to have been associated with the Order of the Golden Fleece, founded in 1430 by Philip the Good, Duke of Burgundy, and convened in 1461 in response to Pius II's call for a crusade against the Turks. Placed as a *cantus firmus* in the tenor, the 'L'homme armé' tune charts an unusual and, for Alejandro Planchart, Christological course.[89] It appears intact in the *Kyrie*, which functions as a proemium to the remaining movements, organized into two pairs (*Gloria* and *Credo*, and *Sanctus* and *Agnus Dei*). As we proceed through the Mass, Du Fay obfuscates the melody through various stratagems. These include decorating it, verbal canons that speed it up through diminution, as well as 'incomplete statements, long-note statements, and odd segmentations that make the cantus firmus difficult to discern'.[90] The height of this obscuring arrives in *Agnus Dei* III, where Du Fay presents the melody in retrograde,[91] rendering it unidentifiable, before ultimately it emerges in clear focus in its original form, but in diminution. Plausibly enough, Planchart proposes, the 'armed man' and his progress from *obscuritas* to *claritas* is a metaphor for Christ, his death, and resurrection.

---

[86] Schiltz (2015), 40.

[87] The motets *Rite maiorem* and *Fulgens iubar*, and rondeau *Craindre vous vueil*. See Planchart (2018), II, 358, 380; and Taruskin (2010), 445–6.

[88] Planchart, II, 369.

[89] Planchart (2003), 330–2.

[90] Planchart (2018), II, 595.

[91] Here the verbal canon instructs, 'Cancer eat plenus sed repeat medius' ('Let it proceed in full, but return in half').

With Johannes Ockeghem (*ca.* 1410–97), we encounter a composer whose agendum arguably *was* 'more calculated to please the *eye* than the *ear*'.[92] The eighteenth-century German theorist Friedrich Marpurg labelled him 'the Bach of his time'.[93] Considerably less charitable, though, was Johann Nikolaus Forkel, J. S. Bach's first significant biographer, who found Ockeghem's rondeau *Prenez sur moy*, a clefless three-part canon, to be a 'stiff and unsingable' exercise (*steif und unsingbar*).[94] Surpassing it in complexity, though, were two of Ockeghem's Masses, each brandishing riddle-like designs. In the freely composed *Missa Prolationum* (*Mass of Prolations*) *a* 4, Ockeghem notated music for only two parts, but specified that each was to generate a two-part canon in different metrical prolations (2/2 and 3/2 for the first canon; 6/4 and 9/4 for the second).

All four voices began simultaneously, but at different speeds, so that the lumbering canonic strands gradually fell further behind their nimbler counterparts, until Ockeghem effected some deft rhythmic adjustments to bring them closer into alignment. Not satisfied with this feat, he accomplished another: the canonic intervals of imitation gradually expanded from the unison (*Kyrie eleison*) to the octave (*Sanctus*), rendering the Mass a cycle worthy of Bach, who would distribute a similar progressive cycle of canons in every third variation of the *Goldberg Variations* (1741). There is no evidence that Bach knew Ockeghem's work, but both composers surely shared the same motivation, summarized by the English music historian Charles Burney, who in 1776 commented on the *Missa Prolationum*, 'the performer was to solve canonical mysteries, and discover latent beauties of ingenuity and contrivance, about which the hearers were indifferent, provided the general harmony was pleasing'.[95]

Instead of providing verbal canons, Ockeghem notated just the four prolation signs, the only clue about how to germinate the double canon. On the other hand, for the *Missa cuiusvis toni* (*Mass in Any Mode*), he gave two cryptic references to Christ's encounter with the adulteress in John 8:10 above the top voice, 'Nemo me condemnat' ('No one condemns me'), and the bass, 'Nec te condemnabo' ('Neither will I condemn thee'). From these laconic cues performers somehow inferred that Ockeghem's music could be sung in any of the four principal modes then in use – Dorian on D, Phrygian on E, Lydian on F and Mixolydian on G. Because each mode had its own distinctive succession of whole-steps and half-steps, Ockeghem had to craft his score so that its sonorities were compatible with all four modes without violating the strictures of dissonance treatment. One riddle thus compounded another, as if advancing Cecil

---

[92] Burney (1775), I: 728.

[93] Marpurg (1970), 316–17.

[94] Forkel (1967), II, 533. On Ockeghem's eighteenth-century reception see Bernstein (2009) and Perkins (1990).

[95] Burney (1775), I, 731.

Gray's view that Ockeghem was 'a pure cerebralist, almost exclusively preoccupied with intellectual problems ... who ... [went] out of his way to create difficulties for the pleasure of overcoming them'.[96]

For numerologists, there is evidence that Ockeghem applied the Golden Mean to determine the internal proportions of the *cantus firmi* in his Masses through what Marianne Henze termed an 'Ockeghem Fibonacci Series', and, furthermore, that he underscored the extra-musical meaning of his music by applying gematria and embedding musically the numerical sums of critical words.[97] In the *Missa De plus en plus*, based on a rondeau by the Burgundian Gilles Binchois (*ca*. 1400–60), Ockeghem may have derived core numbers from Binchois's name.[98] Similarly, Ockeghem may have enumerated his own name as 81 (9 × 9) for Johannes, and 64 (8 × 8) for Ockeghem:

Johannes	9	+14	+8	+1	+13	+13	+5	+18	= 81
Ockeghem	14	+3	+10	+5	+7	+8	+5	+12	= 64[99]

Corroborating evidence appears in Josquin's lament on the death of Ockeghem, *Nymphes des bois*, which concludes with the text 'Requiescat in pace' ('May he rest in peace'). As Elders has observed, Josquin 'leaves no doubt concerning the intended beneficiary of the prayer',[100] for this passage requires exactly sixty-four notes. Nor does Josquin's rare use of black notation, a clear enough example of *Augenmusik*, leave any doubt as to the lament-like quality.

Latent levels of meaning also reside in the music of Antoine Busnois (1430–92), who interacted with Ockeghem in Tours, perhaps as his student,[101] and served the Burgundian court of Charles the Bold before assuming a position at St. Sauveur in Bruges. Like Machaut, Busnois was 'as much esteemed as a poet as he was as a composer'[102]; not surprisingly, he indulged in word games, not to mention musical riddles. Thus, the motet *Anthoni usque limina*, in honour of St. Anthony the Abbot, the composer's name saint, incorporated 'Busnois' in

---

[96] Gray (1931), 62.

[97] Henze (1968), 205, 224, 226.

[98] Ibid., 197. Reinhard Strohm, though, argues that Binchois constructed his chanson on 41 and 48, and that Ockeghem designed his considerably larger-scale cyclic Mass on the same mathematical relationships. Strohm (2005).

[99] Henze (1968), 200–1.

[100] Elders (2013), 84–5. Josquin's lament on the death of Obrecht, *Absolve, quesumus, domine*, concludes with the same prayer, in this case consuming ninety-seven notes, the number associated with Jacob (9 + 1 + 3 + 14 + 2) Obrecht (14 +2 + 17 + 5 + 3 +8 19), or 29 + 68 = 97.

[101] See Higgins (1986).

[102] Higgins (1991), 148.

its opening and final verses,[103] and the texts of four of his secular songs spelled out vertically various versions of 'Jacqueline d'Aqueville', whom Paula Higgins identified as a Parisian noblewoman or maid of honour to the Scottish Princess Margaret Stuart.[104]

To fathom the enigmatic, Busnois availed himself of other ruses, whether verbal, numerological or musical. Perhaps the most richly symbolic of his works was the motet *Anthoni usque limina*, possibly composed in the 1460s or 1470s for the Order of St. Anthony in Barbefosse, a lay confraternity near Havré in Belgium. Most likely, the stimulus for the motet was Busnois's acceptance into the Order,[105] which would explain his highlighted name in the poem, presumably by the composer himself,[106] and the apparently numerological emphasis on 'Saint Antoine en Barbefosse' in the score. Thus, Antoine and Barbefosse convert into 74 (1 + 13 + 19 + 14 + 9 + 13 + 5) and 88 (2 + 1 + 17 + 2 + 5 + 6 + 14 + 18 + 18 + 5) respectively, and Busnois into 108 (2 + 20 + 18 + 13 + 14 + 23 + 18). Now if we count the number of notes in the two sections of the motet, they total 666 (multiple of 74) and 792 (multiple of 88), that is, Antoine Barbefosse. And if we count in each section the basic rhythmic pulse (*tactus*), the results yield 162 (or 74 + 88, that is, Antoine Barbefosse again) and 108 (Busnois).[107] Adding yet another layer of symbolism, Busnois notated only three voices, leaving the tenor enshrouded within a verbal canon: here the musicians contrived a part for a bell that tolled intermittently.[108] A rebus-like illustration placed near the canon in the manuscript shows a bell suspended from a tau-cross, an iconographic image associated with St. Anthony.

Multiple levels are also active in two other works of Busnois that involve retrograde patterns and other recondite, numerological mysteries. The singular *In hydraulis*, on another poem by Busnois, was a tribute to Ockeghem, likened to the 'true image' of Orpheus and Cephas (Peter, the first apostle). There are references too to Pythagoras as the inventor of music, who discovered the ratios of quintessential intervals. Juxtaposing the Greek philosopher and Ockeghem afforded Busnois ample imagery to knead into the supple polyphony of his music. First, he based the motet on a palindromic *cantus firmus* in the tenor, a three-note motive (*d-c-d*) transposed a fifth above (*a-g-a*), and then a fourth above (*d'-c'-d'*), before reversing course. All told, the *cantus firmus* outlines the fifth (*d-a*), fourth (*a-d'*) and octave (*d-d'*), all mentioned in the text (ex. 4.9).

---

[103] '*Anthoni*, usque limina … Fiat in omni*bus noys*'.

[104] Higgins (1991).

[105] Wegman (1988).

[106] Appearing in red in the surviving manuscript source.

[107] Wegman (1988), 24.

[108] Blackburn and Holford-Strevens (2002), 173.

Ex. 4.9: Busnois, *In hydraulis*

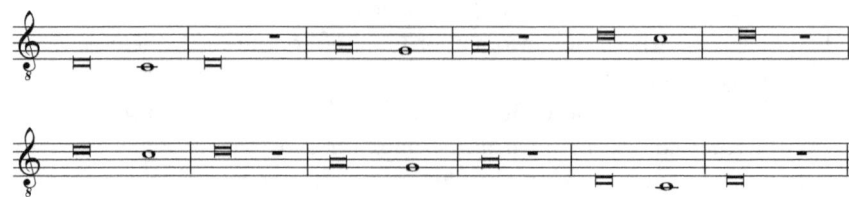

There are additional concealed layers, as Jaap van Benthem has proposed.[109] Each of the motet's two sections presents the *cantus firmus* twice, the second time in diminution, activating the Pythagorean ratio 3:2 as a metrical relationship. There is a possibility that Busnois wove Ockeghem's initials (J = 9 and O = 14) into the opening of the second section by introducing melodic figures of exactly nine and fourteen notes. Perhaps more speculative, Busnois may have activated Johannes Ockeghem's numerologically significant ratio, 81/64 (9/8 × 9/8); 9/8 is the ratio for the Pythagorean major third, and Busnois's music displays several passages with prominent sequences of thirds.

Some have understood *In hydraulis* to acknowledge Ockeghem's mentorship of Busnois,[110] and, furthermore, have heard another learned motet attributed to Ockeghem, *Ut heremita solus*, as a lament on Busnois's death in 1492. Unfortunately, the motet's full text has not survived, but its incipit could refer to St. Anthony the Abbot as the solitary hermit, and, by extension, to Busnois's *Anthoni usque limina*. Another reason links *Ut heremita solus* to Busnois, through his bergerette *Maintes femmes*. Indeed, these compositions offer some exacting verbal canons, requiring similar decryptions of elusive solmization syllables, as well as implementations of *cancrizans* motion.[111] To summarize: in the first section of *Maintes femmes*, the canon asks the cryptanalyst to extract notes of a certain rhythmic value from the upper voice, augment their value by three, and transpose them one octave lower (that is, to the tenor). For the second section, the pitches are read as solmization syllables that vary according to their placement among the Guidonian hexachords. Thus, the pitch *a* is *la* in a hexachord on *c* (*c-d-e-f-g-a*), *mi* in a hexachord on *f* (*f-g-a-b-flat-c-d*) or *re* in a hexachord on *g* (*g-a-b-c-d-e*). By adding these 'companion' (*socii*) syllables, *la* materializes in triplicate as *la*, *mi* and *re*, or *a*, *e* and *d*. Once the complete tenor is in place, it appears first in 'normal' order, then in retrograde.

---

[109] van Benthem (1999).

[110] Higgins (1986). But for another view, arguing for Alexander Agricola's authorship, see Lindmayr-Brandl (1998).

[111] Hewitt (1957); Lindmayr-Brandl (1998); Lindmayr (1988); and Schiltz (2017), 123–4, 129–31.

Recursive motion was one way Busnois rendered his music 'intentionally enigmatic'.[112] Two other techniques enabled him to organize the succession of musical pitches as he transformed the familiar into the unfamiliar. Through mirror inversion, he literally turned the music upside down; by combining retrograde with inversion, he produced an even more disorienting outcome. While retrogression was familiar enough from the palindromes of classical antiquity, mirror inversion was not. Two early examples obtain in an anonymous *Gloria* from *ca.* 1420,[113] and an isorhythmic motet by John Dunstable (*ca.* 1390–1453) on a sequence text for Pentecost, *Veni sancta spiritus et emitte*. In the latter, the Englishman placed the *cantus firmus* in the tenor in three different ways, first as written, then inverted, and finally in retrograde-inversion *and* transposed down a fifth.

Antoine Busnois may have been among the first to realize the potential of these 'proto-serial' operations, as in the *Agnus Dei* of his *Missa L'homme armé* (*ca.* 1475).[114] There the composer divided the secular tune into two portions and treated each in mirror inversion in *Agnus Dei I* and *III*. More intriguing, Busnois may have composed an imposing cycle of six Masses on *L'homme armé*, dedicated to Beatrice of Aragon, Queen of Hungary, from *ca.* 1475–90.[115] These anonymous works revel in treatments of the popular melody that require retrograde, inversion, retrograde-inversion *and* diminution, and thus were the brainchild of a musician preoccupied with specialized *cantus firmus* techniques. In the first five Masses, the composer apportioned the tune into five segments, subjected one by one to a gauntlet of verbal canons, with the first segment serving as the *cantus firmus* for the first Mass, the second for the second, and so forth. Each Mass alone was 'incomplete', as it offered only a disembodied fragment of the *cantus firmus*. The full resolution of the cycle occurred only in the sixth Mass, where the entire tune was reassembled, allowing the 'armed man' to have free rein. Here, cleverly enough, the verbal canon alluded through a pun in dactylic hexameter to the opening of Virgil's *Aeneid*: '*Arma virumque cano vincorque per arma virumque*' ('I sing of arms and the man, and I am vanquished by arms and the man').

Possibly supporting Busnois's authorship of this cycle is the version of 'L'homme armé' featured in his Mass, identical to that in the anonymous Masses, which also display stylistic traits reminiscent of Busnois and his Burgundian

---

[112] Hewitt (1957), 104.

[113] The 'Fountains Fragment'; Bukofzer (1950), 92 and 108. For an example from the circle of Du Fay, see Wright (1976).

[114] See also Perle (1950) and Seay (1971).

[115] Cohen (1968).

contemporaries.[116] All in all, this unparalleled cycle seems to celebrate more the symbolic limits of the musical art than the liturgical requirements of the Mass: 'To fuse together six whole cycles of the Ordinary into one gigantic integral cycle, which … would take six Sundays to perform, signifies a victory of the speculative aesthetic spirit over the conception of earlier centuries, which was confined within narrower liturgical limitations'.[117]

Puzzles as exacting as those of the anonymous Masses figure too in the music of the Flemish composer Jacob Obrecht (1457/8–1505), who likely overlapped with Busnois in Cambrai in the 1480s, and definitely in Bruges around 1490. Obrecht made at least two Italian sojourns to serve Ercole I d'Este before succumbing to the plague in Ferrara in 1505. Heavily influenced by Busnois, Obrecht drew the *cantus firmi* of several Masses from Busnois's chansons, and indeed modelled a *Missa L'homme armé* on Busnois's precedent, even to the detail of using a similar procedure in the *Agnus Dei I* and *III*. Here Obrecht prescribed retrograde-inversion for the first and second halves of the *cantus firmus*, recalling Busnois's analogous use of inversion in his *Agnus Dei I* and *III*.

In other Masses Obrecht experimented with 'serial' techniques to construct large-scale unifying designs. Probably the most striking example was the elusive *Missa Graecorum* (*Mass of the Greeks*), elusive because no one has explained the title or identified the *cantus firmus*. We can unravel, though, Obrecht's verbal canons, exposing the chess-like gambits of a composer intent upon maximizing the structural integrity of his music while promoting the enigmatic. Once again, a case in point is the tripartite *Agnus Dei*, with three different iterations of the *cantus firmus* produced by recalibrating the melody. As ex. 4.10 reveals, Obrecht begins by inverting the melody in augmentation, rendering it eerily familiar but remote (exs. 4.10a and 4.10b). For the central *Agnus Dei*, he transposes the original form a fifth above (ex. 4.10c), while for the third, the melody appears in retrograde (ex. 4.10d). The least apprehensible of all, this version symbolizes the restorative healing of the 'Lamb of God, who takes away the sins of the earth'.

Obrecht's mass is among the few cyclic Renaissance Masses that exploit all three 'serial' techniques of retrograde, inversion, and retrograde-inversion. But Obrecht went further in transforming *cantus firmi* into unrecognizable variants. One technique featured in the *Missae Maria zart* and *De tous biens plaine* subdivided the *cantus firmus* into several fragments (as in the anonymous *L'homme armé* Masses), and shuffled their sequence, either in different voices, as in the *Missa Maria zart*, or in one voice, as in the *Sanctus* of

---

[116] Ibid., 68–71.

[117] Ibid., 18.

SOUNDING NUMBERS 97

Ex. 4.10a: Obrecht, *Missa Graecorum* (*Agnus Dei*)

Ex. 4.10b: Obrecht, *Missa Graecorum* (*Agnus Dei*)

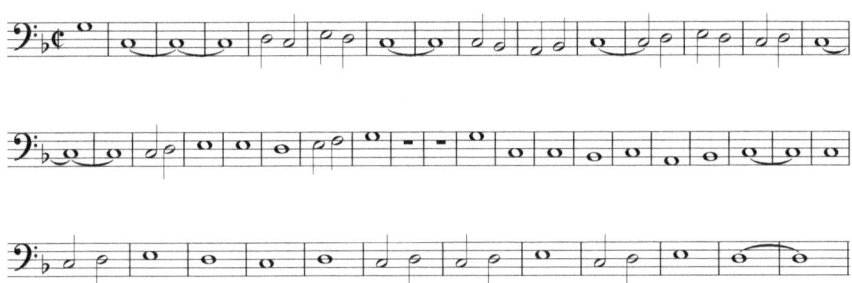

Ex. 4.10c: Obrecht, *Missa Graecorum* (*Agnus Dei*)

Ex. 4.10d: Obrecht, *Missa Graecorum* (*Agnus Dei*)

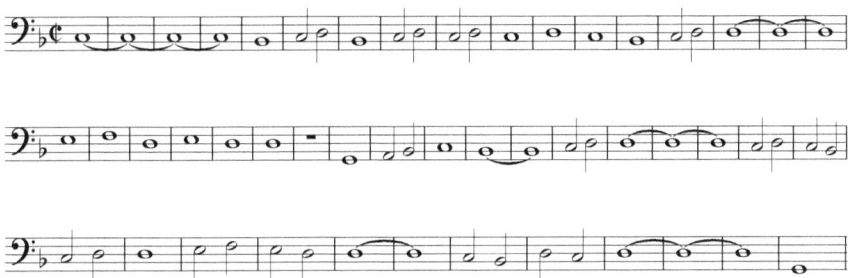

the *Missa De tous biens plaine*, where the eight portions of Hayne van Ghizeghem's chanson appear in the tenor in the (nearly retrograde) order of 1, 8, 7, 6, 5, 4, 3 and 2. Obrecht pursued this approach further in the *Credo* of the *Missa De tous biens plaine* through the canon *a maiori debet fiori denominatio* ('the name should be taken from the greater part'), a directive derived from Aristotle's *Nichomachean Ethics*.[118] In this radical alteration of the melody, he derived the new order by extracting the longest rhythmic values (*longae*, ⹀), then the shorter (*breves*, ⹁), and shortest (*semibreves*, o). Here is the *cantus firmus* as it appears in the *Kyrie* (ex. 4.11a), *Credo* (ex. 4.11b) and *Et incarnatus est* (ex. 4.11c). (In ex. 4.11a, the unaltered pitches are numbered consecutively in their original order; exs. 4.11b and 4.11c then reveal how these numbers and pitches are dispersed during the *Credo*.[119])

In the first section of the *Credo*, one discerns three series of rhythmic values, progressively increasing in speed. Then, at the *Et incarnatus est*, Obrecht inserts the superseding directive, *ut prius sed dicitur retrograde* ('as before, but stated in retrograde'), so that each rhythmic section reverses course, from the longest to shortest values, resulting in another dislocation of pitches.

Ex. 4.11a: Obrecht, *Missa De tous biens plaine* (Kyrie)

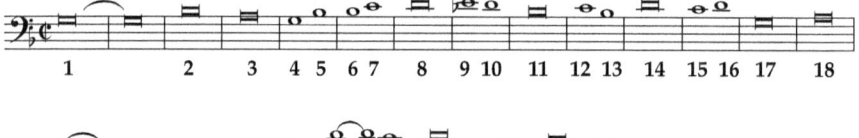

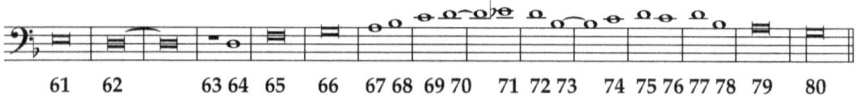

---

[118] Blackburn (2012), 195.

[119] See Todd (1978), 58–61.

SOUNDING NUMBERS 99

Ex. 4.11b: Obrecht, *Missa De tous biens plaine* (*Credo*)

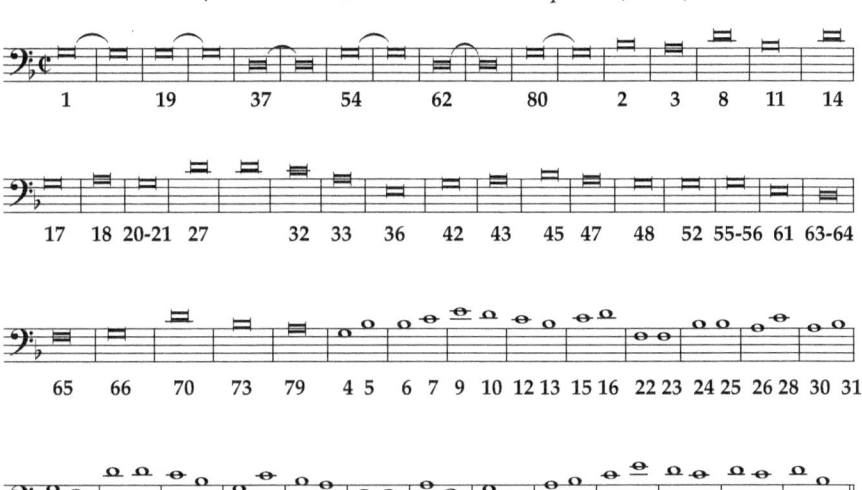

Ex. 4.11c: Obrecht, *Missa De tous biens plaine* (*Et incarnatus est*)

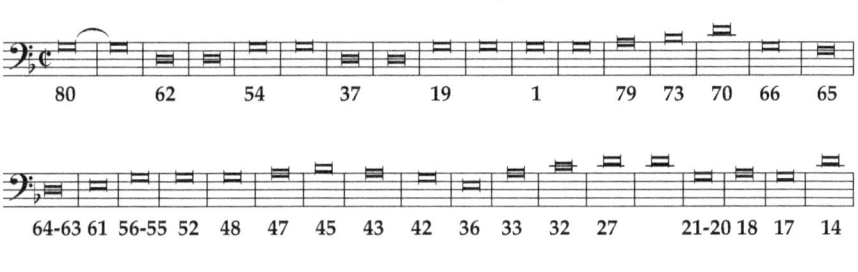
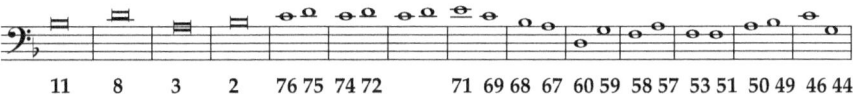
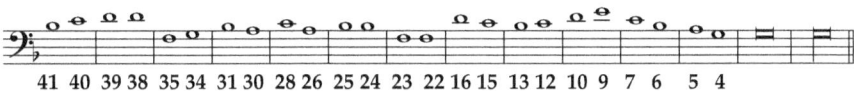

If these cerebral procedures have any overarching logic, they betray, perhaps, the wayward logic of anagrams. What appears unidimensional is duplicitous, susceptible to transformation. The wonder is the versatility of Franco-Flemish composers, who conjured so many ways to leaven their music with layers of meaning, some in plain view, others requiring solving the riddle at hand. In the case of enigmatic canons, for instance, Blackburn has proposed fourteen categories, including augmentation, diminution, retrograde, inversion, extraction, addition, rearrangement and other forms of substitution.[120] When we add techniques of numerology, of music as 'sounding number', of word plays such as acrostics, anagrams and puns, and of encrypting words through the *soggetto cavato*, the opulence of Renaissance musical cryptography emerges in full clarity.

---

[120] Blackburn (2012), 203.

CHAPTER 5

Sonic Monuments, Alchemy, Hexachords and Lunar Discourses

'A Bell no noise but *Rhetorick* affords;
Our Musick Notes are Speeches, Sounds are Words.'

John Wilkins, *Mercury or the Secret and Swift Messenger*

Reaching a brilliant culmination in the sixteenth century, Renaissance composers created sonic monuments that probed liminal spaces seemingly approaching the ends of musical architecture. Painting music on enlarged canvases was evident in the *Missa Puer natus est nobis* ('Unto us a child is born'), based upon a familiar Christmas Introit and designed for an expanded ensemble of seven instead of four choral parts. The composer was Thomas Tallis (1505–85), a Tudor musician who, together with his student William Byrd (1543–1623), dominated the turbulent English musical landscape of the Anglican Reformation and early Stuart period. Tallis's biographer Kerry McCarthy has described this Mass as possibly the 'most enigmatic piece Tallis ever composed'.[1] In addition to its lavish part writing, the music concealed an unusual rhythmic encipherment in its *cantus firmus*-bearing tenor voice, fifth from the top:

> The duration of each note is determined by the vowel to which it is sung in the original chant, with **A** (as in **na**tus) equal to one unit of length, **E** (as in pu**er**) equal to two units, **I** equal to three, **O** equal to four, and **U** equal to five … Things become even more complicated for the tenor in the second half of the mass: the chant is sung backwards in the Sanctus, the numerical code is inverted in the Benedictus (with the vowel U now producing the shortest notes), and the melody is radically redistributed in the last Agnus, with a complex interlocking scheme of notes that leaves the tune unrecognizable.[2]

By shrouding the chant, Tallis dispersed over his music the riddle-like *obscuritas* that had so captivated Franco-Flemish composers of the fifteenth century.

---

[1] McCarthy (2020), 183.
[2] Ibid., 184.

Riddles apart, *Puer natus est nobis* yielded in scale to Tallis's breathtaking polychoral motet *Spem in alium*, for forty vocal parts, conceived perhaps during the 1560s. Here Tallis appropriated a Latin Respond and Verse from the old Catholic Sarum rite,[3] with its subject drawn from the deuterocanonical Book of Judith, in which the widowed Simeonite saves the Israelites by decapitating the Assyrian general Holofernes:

[Respond:] *Spem in alium numquam habui praeter in te Deus Israel*
            Qui irasceris et propitius eris
            Et omnia peccata hominum in tribulatione dimittis.

[Verse:]   *Domine Deus, Creator caeli et terrae, respice humilitatem nostram.*

   Hope in another I have never had except in you, God of Israel,
   Who rages and yet mercifully
   Dismisses all the sins of mankind in its tribulation.

   Lord God, creator of heaven and earth, regard our humility.

Tallis apportioned his magnified ensemble into eight five-part choirs that could function separately as block-like units, answer each other in antiphonal exchanges, or muster together at strategic moments into one monolithic whole. Rather than double parts to amplify the cavernous sound, Tallis challenged the normative four- or five-part choral writing of the time, lending individual voices some independence by adding ornamental figurations to some parts while differentiating rhythmic profiles in others. The result was a euphonious complex that could foreground separate lines, creating a sublime polyphony of perceived 'boundless' parts. To dramatize the new extremes of compositional means, Tallis exploited too the use of silence, interrupting the swirling edifices of sound three times to demarcate key structural sections.

Composing in forty parts raised logistical issues, including how to shape the work into a convincing, well-proportioned edifice of sound. The motet begins unassumingly enough, with voices entering one by one, from the first through the eighth choir. Then we experience the full ensemble's gravitas before the music reverses course from the eighth to the first choir. Again, all forty parts join forces, broken only by the first intrusion of silence. In the next section, Tallis exchanges magnified double choirs of ten parts, so that the combined first and second yield to the third and fourth, the fifth and sixth to the seventh and eighth. Another pause leads to the conclusion, in which all parts attain a glowing G-major cadence.

---

[3] Doe (1970), 5–6.

Given the radically expanded dimensions of *Spem in alium*, one might wonder whether Tallis employed numerology in his score. There has been discussion of this point by the Finnish conductor Jaako Mäntyjärvi,[4] who noticed that all forty parts first align in bar 40 (out of 138, counting in breves), and that the length of the whole (counting in longs, or double breves per bar) is 69. Conveniently enough, Tallis's name sums to 69,[5] so we may have another example of a composer 'signing' his score through a number alphabet:

T	A	L	L	I	S	
19	+1	+11	+11	+9	+18	= 69

Counting again in breves, the midpoint of the composition is bar 69, as it happens the second entrance of the full ensemble, where Tallis indulges in word painting for *omnia peccata* ('all the sins'). As Mäntyjärvi observes, adding bars 40 and 69 yields bar 109, where the second silence occurs, an extraordinary moment when the rupture of sound separates two utterly unrelated sonorities on C major and A major, stretching the modal underpinnings of the music.

Whether or not one subscribes to these readings, there is another enigmatic aspect of Tallis's monument, one relating to its origins and choice of text. In 1567, Alessandro Striggio the elder,[6] composer to the Medici court in Florence, visited London, where he obtained an audience with Queen Elizabeth. Striggio was quite the virtuoso, renowned for performances on the oversized lira da gamba, which generated with its nearly twenty strings four-part harmonies. This predilection for extravagant means also marked Striggio's choral music, culminating in a large-scale motet in forty parts as well as the *Missa sopra Ecco sì beato giorno*, conceived *a* 40,[7] but including a colossal Agnus Dei *a* 60. These grandiose creations were designed to support the lavish statecraft of the Medicis. Striggio may have brought his Mass to England, where Tallis could have examined it and found inspiration for his own polychoral extravaganza.[8]

Presumably Tallis did not create his motet in isolation. But how do we explain his choice of text? Though a recusant who, like Byrd, secretly professed Catholicism in Anglican England, likely Tallis did not intend his musical monument for public performance. In 1549 the Book of Common Prayer had standardized English services for the Anglican Church. Though reversed during

---

[4] https://www.youtube.com/watch?v=Gv1zZwppTuc, accessed 15 May 2022.
[5] See Keyte (1981), 345.
[6] His son was the librettist of Monteverdi's opera *Orfeo* (1607).
[7] Arrayed in five groups of eight voices, the reverse of Tallis's scoring.
[8] See Butchart (1982) and Moroney (2007).

a five-year interim (1553–58) by 'Bloody' Mary Tudor, who restored Catholic worship, the Book of Common Prayer was re-validated with the accession of Elizabeth and passage of the Act of Uniformity, which mandated church attendance and imposed fines for recusancy.

We have discussed in Chapter 4 how Elizabeth relied upon her spymaster, Sir Francis Walsingham, to thwart several plots. Before the Babington Conspiracy came to light, an earlier attempt against the queen had been foiled in 1571. The instigator was the Florentine Roberto Ridolfi, who intended to raise an army commanded by the Spanish Duke of Alba that would overthrow Elizabeth. Mary would wed Thomas Howard, fourth Duke of Norfolk and second cousin of Elizabeth, and the two would then restore Catholicism throughout England and Scotland. But the plot was compromised, the duke arrested, tried and executed for treason in 1572.

In 1611 a law student, Thomas Wateridge, recorded an intriguing account linking the Duke of Norfolk to Tallis's *Spem in alium*:

> In Queen Elizabeth's time yere was a songe sen[t] into England of 30 parts … wch beeinge songe mad[e] a heavenly Harmony. The Duke of _____ bearinge a great love to Musicke asked whether none of our Englishmen could sett as good a songe, and Tallice beinge very skilfull was felt to try whether he could undertake ye Matter, wch was songe in the longe gallery at Arundel house wch so farre surpassed ye other that the Duke hearing of yt songe, took his chayne of Gold from of[f] his necke and putt yt about Tallice his necke and gave yt him.[9]

Perhaps '30' was a slip for '40', and the 'heavenly Harmony' referred to Striggio's Mass. The Reverend H. Fleetwood Sheppard, who published this account in 1878, identified the duke as Thomas Howard, fourth Duke of Norfolk and son-in-law of Henry FitzAlan, twelfth Earl of Arundel. Howard and FitzAlan were fervent Roman Catholics; indeed, FitzAlan 'was considered the leader of the English Catholics at the time',[10] and Howard, as we have seen, was directly implicated in the Ridolfi plot.

The earl possessed two stately residences, the nonpareil Nonsuch Palace in Surrey, begun by Henry VIII in 1538, and Arundel House in London, located between the Strand and Thames. Wateridge's account claims that Tallis's 'songe' was performed in the 'longe gallery' at Arundel House. Quite likely it was also heard at Nonsuch, where the first known copy of *Spem in alium* was preserved as 'a songe of fortie partes, made by Mr. Tallys'.[11] Also pertinent, the separate banquet hall at Nonsuch rested upon an octagonal foundation, and the two

---

[9] Sheppard (1878), 97.
[10] Moroney (2007), 30.
[11] Milsom (1993), 168–9; McCarthy (2020), 193.

imposing towers on either side of the main palace had octagonal rooms on the ground floor.[12] Indeed, Tallis may have crafted his work for an octagonal venue; if so, the motet 'falls little short of musical theatre, for it possesses at the same time a spatial and purely musical argument'.[13]

We might now attempt to fit together the puzzle pieces. Tallis perhaps composed *Spem in alium* in response to his encounter with Striggio's Mass, and the Duke of Norfolk's challenge to create a monument equally as compelling. The composer could have chosen the Latin text from the Sarum Rite to acknowledge his own Catholic faith, and that of the duke and earl, and the motet was performed at Arundel House and possibly at Nonsuch Palace, where the octagonal dimensions of the score would have resonated with the architecture. If so, these semi-private hearings perhaps obviated the need to conceal the compromising text. But 'if the text … offended some official sensibilities, in a sensitive situation the musicians could have hidden the embarrassing papist text by adding the necessary musical fig leaf'[14] – that is, substituting for the words solmization syllables, merely to dissemble the significance of Tallis's culminating masterwork, its revival of a Catholic Respond, and its possible allusion to a modern-day Judith saving the 'sceptred isle'.

ତ *i*

By the seventeenth century, the fascination with musical monuments was spurring the 'colossal baroque'. Its roots are traceable to the Venetian *cori spezzati* ('split choirs') positioned in the echoing recesses of San Marco by Andrea and Giovanni Gabrieli, though, as we have seen, the Florentine Alessandro Striggio played a role, as did Roman composers such as Orazio Benevoli, who composed several Masses *a* 16 in four choirs and *basso continuo*. Until 1975[15] Benevoli was assumed to have created the elephantine *Missa Salisburgensis* in fifty-three parts, for several choirs and a generous assortment of instruments, though that attribution has now been reassigned to Heinrich Biber, who likely produced the Mass for the Archbishopric of Salzburg in 1683. In contrast to the semi-private context in which Tallis's *Spem in alium* had appeared a century and more before, these resplendent polychoral works *were* intended for ceremonial events in public spaces. Thus, in 1633 the Roman Romano Micheli, who specialized in puzzle canons, generated one *a* 36 constructed 'upon the vowels of several

---

[12] See McCarthy (2020), 195–6.
[13] Milsom (1983), vol. 1, 192.
[14] Moroney (2007), 32, 96n.
[15] Hintermaier (1975), 965–6.

106 THE ART OF MUSICAL CIPHERS, RIDDLES AND SUNDRY CURIOSITIES

words', in honour of Louis XIII ('Louis, king and defender of all Christians'). Here is its Latin text and musical transformation:

Lu	-do	-vi	-cus	Rex	de	-fen	-sor	om	-ni	-um	Chris	-ti	-a	-no	-rum
Ut	sol	mi	ut	re	re	re	sol	sol	mi	ut	mi	mi	fa	sol	ut
G	D	B	G	A	A	A	D	D	B	G	B	B	C	D	G

Micheli claimed the enciphering device as his invention, though it clearly harkened back to the *soggetto cavato* practised by Josquin and identified by Zarlino in 1558.

Not many heeded these manipulations until Athanasius Kircher incorporated the canon for the French king into the frontispiece of *Musurgia universalis* (*Universal Musicmaking*), the polymath's musical *summa* published in Rome in 1650. Here, atop the illustration, the all-seeing eye of God surveys the universe from a perfect triangle. Just below are nine orders of angelic choirs singing Micheli's canon *a* 36 (for nine four-part choirs), unfurled on a scroll held aloft by two winged, seraphic figures. The text now reads 'Sanctus, sanctus, sanctus', a reference to the vision of Isaiah (6:3): 'Holy, holy, holy is the Lord of hosts; the whole earth is full of his glory'.[16] So, what Micheli had offered to praise a French monarch Kircher now appropriated to adorn his encyclopaedic tome, and to celebrate the penultimate part of the Ordinary of the Mass.[17]

The same year saw the release of another canon by Micheli, 'Maria est fons signatus divinae gratiae; Maria est fons misericordiae' ('Mary is the sealed spring of divine grace; Mary is the spring of mercy'). Once again, he fashioned the musical subject by enciphering vowels in the text. Thus, 'fons signatus' yielded the pitches G-E-F-C; as it happened, its transposed mirror inversion, D-F-E-A, corresponded to 'est Maria' (ex. 5.1).

For Micheli, 'Fons signatus' 'represented a mysterious and cryptic simulacrum, the custodian, through its protean virtues, of a veiled truth'.[18] In purely musical terms his canons had a considerably more limited appeal, for they possessed only a 'curious but sterile eccentricity'.[19]

Micheli was one of several seventeenth-century musicians who, according to Charles Burney, 'devoted as great a portion of their lives' in 'the construction of perpetual fugue or canon' as 'holy men ever did to severe acts of piety

---

[16] See further, Godwin (2015), 28–9.

[17] Kircher's tome enjoyed wide distribution. A copy of the canon in the hand of C. P. E. Bach survives, perhaps from the 1740s, raising the possibility that his father was aware of it. See Melamed (1995).

[18] Gerbino (1995), 98.

[19] Durante (1987), 199.

Ex. 5.1: Romano Micheli, 'Maria est fons signatus' (1650)

```
Fons    sig -  - na -  tus
Sol     mi        fa    ut

Est     Ma -  - ri -   a
re      fa        mi    la
```

and devotion, in order to be canonised'.[20] Another was Padre Lodovico Zacconi (1555–1627) of Pesaro, author of *Prattica di Musica* (*The Practice of Music*), published in two parts in Venice in 1592 and 1622. A third part, left in manuscript, was titled *Canoni Musicali*, within which was an even more specialized, esoteric digression labelled *Geroglifici Musicali* (*Musical Hieroglyphs*). The revival of this term reflected the Egyptological stirrings of the *seicento*,[21] not least of which was Kircher's *Obelisci Aegyptiaci* (*Egyptian Obelisks*, 1666), an inflated attempt in two thousand inaccurate pages to interpret the ancient logograms.[22] For Zacconi and his contemporaries, just as hieroglyphs 'spoke, in a cryptic manner, the language of access to the divine',[23] so too could music disseminate enigmatic messages. One was a visual allegory with musical pitches concealed within a vine of grapes suspended on a pergola. Another, about Christ as the good pastor, arrayed the notes of a canon as white and black sheep. Zacconi also offered examples of musical enigmas in which melodies fabricated by transforming the vowels of texts produced mysteriously encoded forms of musical poetry. He culled four from the works of a minor musician from Tuscany, Biagio Pesciolini (1535–1611), including one derived from the text 'SUR[R]EXIT PASTOR BONUS ALLELUIA' ('The good pastor has risen. Alleluia'; ex. 5.2). Here, Pesciolini used minuscule capitals and normal upper-case letters to distinguish between minims and semibreves:

Ex. 5.2: Biagio Pesciolini, 'Surrexit pastor bonus'

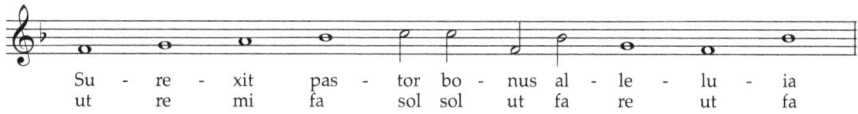

```
Su - re - xit  pas - tor bo - nus al - le - lu - ia
ut   re   mi   fa    sol sol  ut   fa   re   ut   fa
```

[20] Burney (1957), ii, 412.
[21] See Wuidar (2007), 64–5.
[22] See Godwin (2015), 59–76.
[23] Ibid., 67–77.

Pursuing a different approach, the Roman nobleman Pier Francesco Valentini (*ca.* 1570–1654) created 'polymorphous' canons that admitted multiple solutions. One, produced from the vowels of the text 'Amor, quis maior patet' ('Love, which is clearly greater', ex. 5.3), yielded forty-seven resolutions, including several that required retrograde, inversion and retrograde-inversion (ex. 5.4).

In 1629 Valentini published a canon on a text from the Marian hymn *Salve regina*, for which he engineered no fewer than two thousand solutions. But even this remarkable feat did not temper his imagination. Thus, he designed a *Canone nel nodo Salomonis* (*Canon on Solomon's Knot*) for ninety-six voices that, incredibly enough, could be exponentially raised to 144,000, moving in different metres and at different rates of speed, like a 'musical Hydra always sprouting new heads'.[24]

For Charles Burney, who found 'nothing but toil and pedantry' in these contrivances, the 'imagination [was] so manacled' that 'elegant melody [was] always precluded, and, in general, harmony... rendered so meagre and imperfect'.[25] Burney would have niggled indeed about one of the most peculiar, esoteric creations of the entire century, a part occultist, part 'learned' contrapuntal work of interest owing to its author's assertion that 'God has concealed infinite arcana in nature, which like the fire that is struck from flint can be extracted and put to use by innumerable arts and sciences'.[26] The work in question was the multimedia extravaganza *Atalanta fugiens* (*The Fleeing Atalanta*, 1617). Its author was the physician, alchemist and amateur musician Michael Maier (1568–1622), who possessed 'an appetite for the marvellous, the arcane, the weird and wonderful'.[27] Maier served as personal physician to the Holy Roman Emperor Rudolf II, who in 1583 had moved his court to Prague. There, during the years leading up to the Thirty Years' War, he collected items for his *Kunstkammer* (cabinet of curiosities) and promoted the practice of alchemy.

Maier's *Atalanta fugiens* is an emblem book comprising fifty copperplate illustrations (with epigrammatic poems in Latin and German) facing fifty short, three-part musical compositions, supplemented by explanatory interpretations. The subject is the fleet-footed Atalanta, who in the tenth book of Ovid's *Metamorphoses* compelled her suitors to race, agreeing to marry whoever prevailed, but killing the rest. Only Hippomenes, to whom Venus gave three golden apples from the Garden of the Hesperides with which to distract his love object, was

---

[24] Ambros (1968), iv, 157.
[25] Burney (1957), ii, 414.
[26] Maier (1617; repr. 1989), 101.
[27] Godwin (1987), 2.

Ex. 5.3: P. F. Valentini, Polymorphous canon

Ex. 5.4: P. F. Valentini, Polymorphous canon

able to win the hand of Atalanta, who 'loved without realizing that she was in love'.[28] But when the pair consummated their relationship near a sacred temple, they were transformed into lions that terrorized whomever they encountered.

Supporting this narrative are not only Maier's visual emblems, some of which allude to the ancient myth, but also musical supplements, a cycle of canons in which Hippomenes's part figuratively chases and ultimately overtakes Atalanta. What distinguishes Maier's singular creation further are layers

---

[28] Ovid (1955), 242.

of interpretive meaning either discernible through exegesis or hidden in plain view. Scholars have understood *Atalanta fugiens* as an allegory about alchemy, taking their cue from the subtitle, *New Chemical Emblems Concerning the Secrets of Nature* (*Emblemata Nova De Secretis Naturae Chymica*). Thus, for Hildemarie Streich, Atalanta, Hippomenes and the three apples symbolize mercury, sulphur and salt, basic materials in the alchemist's quest to find the philosopher's stone and unlock its ability to produce gold.[29] More recently, Peter J. Forshaw has explored Maier's interest in mythoalchemy, the 'premise that the Egyptian, Greek, and Latin myths were repositories of alchemical secrets, coded narratives of natural philosophy'.[30] Several emblems indeed gravitate toward the world of alchemy. Thus, the first shows the North Wind, Boreas, carrying a foetus in his stomach which Maier explains is sulphur. The twelfth illustrates Saturn consuming his own children; the fourteenth, a dragon devouring his tail – images also associated with alchemy.

In 1969 the art historian Helena Maria Elisabeth de Jong devoted a monograph to illuminating Maier's emblems. She related them to the 'rise' of the Rosicrucians, a mystical/religious/alchemical fraternity founded supposedly early in the fifteenth century by Father Christian Rosenkreuz ('Cross of the Roses'). Having lapsed into dormancy, the order suddenly reemerged in 1614 and 1615 – not long before the appearance of *Atalanta fugiens* – with the publication of two anonymous manifestos, announcing the dawn of a new age, 'a great reformation [that was] to be a millennium, a return to the state of Adam in Paradise'.[31] Maier became an outspoken apologist for this fraternity, though he never clarified whether he himself belonged; indeed, the whole affair may have been a hoax, or an attempt to propose an 'alternative to the Jesuit Order, a brotherhood more truly based on the teaching of Jesus'.[32] But the esoteric and pansophical qualities of Rosicrucianism appealed greatly to Maier, who 'endeavoured to unite science and theology'.[33]

Pursuing a different interpretation, Donna Bilak proposes that *Atalanta fugiens* affords a prime example of 'seventeenth-century ludic culture'. Maier 'engineered his musical alchemical emblem book to … conceal and reveal two books in one, creating a virtuoso work of steganography whereby a magic square is hidden in plain sight'.[34] Earlier alchemists such as the sixteenth-cen-

---

[29] Streich (1987), 21. See, in addition, Meinel (1986), 212ff.
[30] Forshaw (2020).
[31] Yates (1972); translations of the manifestos, 297–322.
[32] Ibid., 59.
[33] de Jong (1969), 337–8.
[34] Bilak (2020).

tury Swiss physician Paracelsus and German occultist Agrippa von Nettesheim had related magic squares to alchemic elements; indeed, Maier himself referred to a three-by-three perfect square associated with lead.[35] Advancing this line of inquiry, Bilak argues that Maier's fifty emblems offer strategically placed clues that reveal a far more complex seven-by-seven perfect square associated with Venus, goddess of love, who, of course, narrates the myth of Atalanta and Hippomenes in Ovid's *Metamorphoses*. Venus is also 'the consort of Vulcan, God of the forge and of the alchemist's tool of transformation: fire'.[36] Here is her magic square:

22	47	16	41	10	35	4
5	23	48	17	42	11	29
30	6	24	49	18	36	12
13	31	7	**25**	43	19	37
38	14	32	1	26	44	20
21	39	8	33	2	27	45
46	15	40	9	34	3	28

At the centre is the number 25, a factor of 175 ($25 \times 7 = 175$), obtained by summing any row, column or either of the two long diagonals.

There remains the musical component of *Atalanta fugiens*, the fifty 'fugues' (*fugae*), a word play on *fugiens*, or 'fleeing'. In Maier's time *fuga* designated the genre of the canon, which he chose for its symbolic value to depict the race. Here, strict imitation occurs between the two parts labelled Atalanta and Hippomenes, with Atalanta playing the role of *dux*, or leader, and Hippomenes, the *comes*, or companion. Not until No. 41 does Hippomenes first overtake Atalanta, so that the two briefly exchange roles. In the remaining *fugae* Maier applies several techniques to shape the outcome of the race – in No. 44, for instance, diminution in Hippomenes's part, so that, by moving in rhythms twice as fast as Atalanta's, he surpasses her again (ex. 5.5); in Nos. 45 and 46, mirror inversion, which turns the racing voices upside down.

Standing apart from the two-part canons is the third voice, *Pomum morans*, a reference to the apples that periodically distract Atalanta. Though not participating in the canonic strands, this third part offers a constant melodic line throughout the fugues. It cites the *Christe* from the troped *Kyrie* of *Cunctipotens genitor Deus* (Mass IV), lending a Christological layer of meaning to the emblem book and serving as a mediating *cantus firmus* between the two contestants. But in No. 41, the sacred chant unexpectedly appears in retrograde, as

---

[35] Tilton (2003), 98.
[36] Bilak (2020).

Ex. 5.5: Michael Maier, *Atalanta fugiens* (1617)

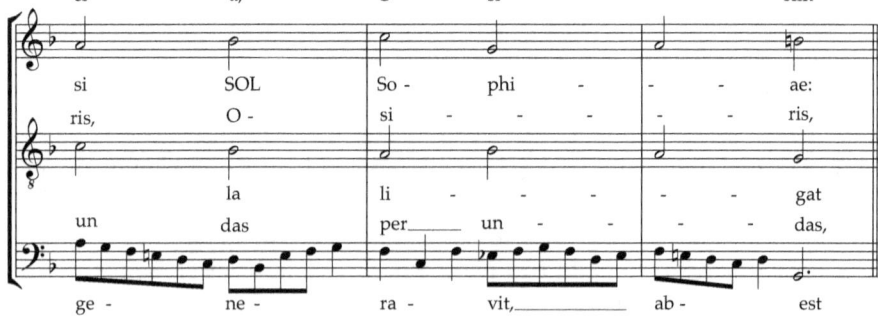

if to mark the casting of an apple, while also reviving associations of *cancrizans* motion with reversing an action.

Throughout the cycle Maier adheres to a basic template for the *fugae* – two racing canonic voices counterbalanced by an unwavering chant – though he does attempt to provide a measure of variety in three different ways. First, each *fuga* introduces a new melodic subject for the two canonic voices to exchange. Second, each part is interchangeable in register so that each may appear as the top, middle or bottom voice. And third, while the melodic contours of the chant do not change, its rhythmic values do vary from piece to piece. All these shifting musical elements impress as a kind of musical alchemy, like so many experimental retorts in the alchemist's laboratory.

That said, though, these *fugae* mask their own mysterious transmutations, revealed only recently. Prior to 2020 scholars assumed that Maier composed all fifty fugues, taking perhaps some inspiration from the *Synopsis Musicae Novae* (*Synopsis of New Music*, 1612) of the Lutheran theologian Johannes Lippius. But because Maier was an amateur musician, his *fugae* betray a vexing issue: 'In estimating the worth of this music, one must concede ... that Maier's ingenuity of idea and persistence of effort unfortunately outran his technical musical skill. Just as with the experiments of the alchemists, the attempted canons frequently meet with disaster'.[37]

Indeed, many fugues display glaring parallel fifths and octaves, unresolved dissonances and other ineptitudes that stamp the music with an unmistakable asperity, especially in the final ten pieces. Maier himself endeavoured to make amends by compiling a list of errata and encouraging the reader to continue the process,[38] but there is no avoiding the conclusion that his vision exceeded his compositional abilities, and that the music does not match the quality of the engraved emblems or epigrams.

In 2020 Loren Ludwig shed some light on this matter by establishing that Maier repurposed many of the fugues from a collection published in London in 1591 by the madrigalist John Farmer.[39] Titled *Divers & Sundry Waies of Two Parts in One, to the Number of Fortie upon one Playnsong*, Farmer's volume comprised forty two-part canons, all grounded on a plainchant as a *cantus firmus* – a phrase from the *Kyrie Cunctipotens genitor Deus*, appropriated by Maier for *Atalanta fugiens*. How he may have accessed Farmer's three-part canons we do not know, nor is it clear why Farmer in 1591 would choose a bit of plainchant from the old Sarum Rite, associated, as it had been for Tallis, with the Catholic faith, and thus still in 1591 part of a 'forbidden ritual practice'.[40] That Maier plagiarized forty canons from Farmer might explain the pronounced maladroitness of the last ten canons, which presumably Maier composed himself. But despite his limitations, *Atalanta fugiens* probably remains 'the strangest, the most beautiful and the most innovative work of esoteric alchemy in the seventeenth century'.[41]

---

[37] Sleeper (1938), 413.
[38] Godwin (1987), 179ff.
[39] Ludwig (2020).
[40] Ibid.
[41] Tilton (2003), 237.

ii

While Maier was uncovering 'infinite arcana in nature', Sir Francis Bacon (1561–1626) was engaged with 'the great instauration' – the restoration of the Edenic paradise that might finally lead mankind to full enlightenment. There is considerable evidence that, like Maier, Bacon was aware of the Rosicrucian movement,[42] though he was 'arguably no great friend of alchemists',[43] relying instead on his new, empirical method of observation propounded in the *Novum Organum* (1620). Still, Bacon was not immune to the occult or esoteric, for he viewed all natural phenomena as encryptions of hidden, universal laws.[44] Furthermore, he was no stranger to cryptography, having developed as a young man the Bilateral Cipher, which he described in *Of the Advancement and Proficience of Learning* (1605) as 'the *highest degree of Cypher*, which is to signify *omnia per omnia* [all things through all things]'.[45]

This strategy involved concealing a secret message within totally unrelated prose that, by all appearances, read as a 'normal' text. Thus, a desperate plea for military assistance might be safely tucked within one of Cicero's orations, with none the wiser. There were several stages in Bacon's process.[46] First, he devised an encryption method that linked letters of the alphabet to a sequence of five drawn from a or b: for example, a = *aaaaa*, b = *aaaab*, c = *aaaba*, etc. If the plaintext message was *Fuge* ('Flee'), its encryption using Bacon's 'Bi-literarie alphabet' would be:

F	U	G	E
aabab	*baabb*	*aabba*	*aabaa*

Next, he produced a second ciphertext to conceal the plaintext. In this case, Bacon contrived the sentence: *Manere te volo donec volero* ('I wish to stay with you until I fly'). To accomplish his task, Bacon fashioned a second alphabet, with four slightly different font styles for each letter of the alphabet, of which two were reserved for the upper case, and two for the lower. Then, above this 'bi-formed alphabet' (A*A*a*a*, B*B*b*b*, etc.) he wrote out a simple pattern alternating between the first two letters of the alphabet. In the final step, Bacon chose the appropriate font style for the letters of *Manere te volo donec volero* so that they matched the patterns of a's and b's associated with the encrypted form of

---

[42] See Frances Yates's reading of Bacon's posthumous allegory *New Atlantis*: Yates (1972), 164–9; and Dawkins (2004), 316–36.

[43] Cintas (2003), 67.

[44] Pesic (2000), 193.

[45] Bacon (1640), 265.

[46] Ibid., 266ff.

the plaintext *Fuge*. Thus, since the letter F of FUGE was transformed by the 'bi-literarie alphabet' as *aabab*, he chose the font styles for the 'M', 'a', 'n', 'e' and 'r' of *Manere* from the 'Bi-formed Alphabet' with the same values, *aabab*. If the ciphertext were intercepted, probably no one reading it deduced it was only a few stages removed from a secret message. On the other hand, anyone possessing the two alphabets as the critical keys could easily decrypt the message by working backwards, first aligning the *a*'s and *b*'s above the ciphertext, and then segmenting them into groups of five and matching those to the individual clusters of quintuple letters from the 'Bi-literarie alphabet', so that the secret imperative of the plaintext, *Fuge*, emerged. Exploiting the bilateral cipher could conceal any message within any text – *omnia per omnia*, as Bacon confidently asserted.

Ciphers preoccupied Bacon. Like his brother, Anthony, Francis was an intimate of Sir Francis Walsingham's network of spies and cryptologists during Elizabeth's reign.[47] Among Bacon's circle was Duke Augustus of Brunswick-Lüneburg (Gustavus Selenus), the author of *Cryptomenytices et Cryptographiae* (1624), which treated several different ciphers, among them some employed by Bacon. Still more intriguing is the possibility that Bacon himself may have participated in crafting the duke's *magnum opus*. The title page contains a rebus-like illustration that depicts Augustus behind the Abbot Trithemius, author of *Steganographia* (1606), one of the important sources for the duke's work. In this image the duke holds a mitre above the abbot's head. 'Mitre' (anagrammatically rearranged as 'ritem') is present within T**rithem**ius; if its five letters are removed, the remnant spells 'Thius'. By applying a substitution cipher – transposing the letters five places further in the alphabet – 'Thius' becomes 'Bnoca', a rearrangement of 'Bacon'.[48] In short, one anagram complements another: Gustavus stands for Augustus and Thius (Bnoca) for Bacon, encouraging Peter Dawkins to surmise that the philosopher was 'a second, but secular, Trithemius, and the author of at least some of the book and its ciphers'.[49]

This leap of the imagination might strain our credulity, but there is yet another provocative dimension to Bacon's cryptographic pursuits. To explore that, we may now introduce the acronym SAQ (Shakespeare Authorship Question), in which Bacon has figured over the centuries in significant, if controversial ways. What K. K. Ruthven described as the 'nightmare of paternity [in] the very heart of English literature'[50] began in the nineteenth century, when questions arose about whether the Stratford actor William Shakspere authored the plays and poems attributed to the bard in the First Folio of 1623. A growing chorus of sceptics

---

[47] Dawkins (2004), 320.
[48] Ibid., 326.
[49] Ibid., 327.
[50] Ruthven (2001), 114.

proposed Francis Bacon instead as the real author, arguing that 'plays as good as Shakespeare's must have been written not by some plebeian actor from Stratford but by a well-educated aristocrat, whose need to avoid the social stigma of association with vulgar playhouses would have obliged him to remain anonymous'.[51]

One of the first Baconians was the (unrelated) American playwright Delia Bacon, whose *Philosophy of the Plays of Shakespeare* appeared in 1857. In time several literary celebrities weighed in, including Ralph Waldo Emerson, Walt Whitman, Mark Twain and Henry James, who averred that 'the divine William is the biggest and most successful fraud ever practiced on a patient world'. To advance Bacon's candidacy, cryptologists trawled through the works of Shakespeare for ciphers that might validate their case. Among the pieces of evidence, none was more beguiling than the Latin construct 'honorificabilitudinitatibus', which appears in *Love's Labour's Lost* (V.1), where, reacting to pedantic exchanges and word plays between Holofernes and Sir Nathaniel, the rustic Costard places the word in the ablative (or dative) plural:

> O, they have lived long on the alms-basket of words.
> I marvel thy master hath not eaten thee for a word;
> for thou art not so long by the head as
> *honorificabilitudinitatibus*: thou art easier
> swallowed than a flap-dragon.

As the longest word in Shakespeare's oeuvre, this singular term was bound to attract attention; if not a fabricated nonsense word, it would translate roughly as 'worthy of being honoured'.

It did not disappoint. And so, in 1897 Isaac Hull Platt claimed to have solved this exacting tongue twister as a perfect anagram by rearranging all twenty-seven letters as *hi ludi, tuiti sibi, Fr Bacano nati* ('These plays, born of Fr. Bacon, are all his own'), slightly reworked in 1910 by Sir Edwin Durning-Lawrence as *hi ludi F. Baconis nati tuiti orbi* ('Born of F. Bacon, these plays belong to the entire world'). Platt buttressed his argument for Bacon's authorship by citing a manuscript discovered in 1867 in Northumberland House on London's Strand. Damaged by fire, the manuscript raises further mysteries even as it affords the only document from Bacon's time directly linking his name to Shakespeare.[52] Whether or not the source transmits a holograph in Bacon's hand or that of some unknown scrivener, it includes references to *Richard II* and *III*, and to our hyperbolic word, though now in the singular dative (*Honorificabilitudino*) or, possibly ablative (*Honorificabilitudine*).[53]

---

[51] Ibid., 115.

[52] See further, Pares (1960).

[53] For a more cautious interpretation, see Stewart (2013), 22ff.

This coincidence was sufficient for Platt to continue his quest for anagrams, and to inquire whether 'bacon' appears in the plays. It does, for instance, in *The Merry Wives of Windsor*, IV.1, where Mistress Quickly opines: 'Hang hog is Latten for bacon, I warrant you.'[54] As for further anagrams and word plays, Platt was able to garner several candidates, such as these two ('beacon' was evidently pronounced as 'bacon' during the seventeenth century)[55]:

> Let not our ships and number of our men,
> Be like a **bea**con **fi**red to amaze your eyes.
>
> *Pericles*, I.4

> The law of **fri**endship **b**ids me to **con**ceale.
>
> *Two Gentlemen of Verona*, III.1

Of course, several other candidates have been vetted to solve the SAQ dilemma, among them Christopher Marlowe, Edward de Vere and William Stanley. Another trend has been to view the Shakespearean corpus as a collaborative effort of several authors. Peter Dawkins, for one, concluded that 'the Shakespeare Folio [was] the careful production of a secret, cabbalistic fraternity, associated with (or comprising) the Rosicrucians and Freemasons of the sixteenth and seventeenth centuries, whose "Apollo" or "Shakespeare" was Francis Bacon'.[56] Among the most recent salvos is a monograph by Barry R. Clarke, who employs Rare Collocation Profiling (RCP), purported to identify authors more accurately than previously applied stylometric techniques relying primarily on statistical analyses of word counts. To this end, Clarke has taken full advantage of Early English Books Online (EEBO), a digitized database of over 130,000 titles comprising 'almost every book, pamphlet, or broadside published from 1473 to 1700'.[57] His research has amassed more evidence to support Bacon's involvement. For instance, in the case of *Love's Labour's Lost*, by applying RCP to the play and the *Gesta Grayorum* (1688), a pamphlet recording speeches at Gray's Inn in 1594 and 1595, Clarke has concluded that the play was likely intended for Christmas revels at the inn, and that Bacon contributed to it.[58] Baconians and Stratfordians will surely continue the vigorous debate, meaning we may never resolve SAQ, though the solution might be but a hidden cipher or anagram away.

---

[54] Platt (1897), 8–9. Other instances occur in *Henry IV*.
[55] Ibid., 12.
[56] Dawkins (2004), 350.
[57] Clarke (2019), 227.
[58] Ibid., 254–60.

iii

The seventeenth century produced other illustrious polymaths whose interests touched cryptography. Like Bacon, Gottfried Wilhelm Leibniz (1646–1716), the German philosopher and, with Isaac Newton, co-discoverer of calculus, was intrigued by ciphers, not so much as a method of espionage as one that might develop a universal language to benefit science and mathematics. Leibniz believed that ultimately his *characteristica universalis* could be realized through music; his early treatise *De arte combinatoria* (*Concerning Combinatorial Art*, 1666) sought to find 'all the possible melodies' in a given text, and offered one example that explored different combinations of the six solmization syllables as a way of generating numbers.[59] Leibniz later proposed appropriating the first nine consonants (*b, c, d, f, g, h, l, m* and *n*) to represent the first nine whole numbers, and the five vowels to establish their decimal values from 1 to 10, 100, 1,000 and 10,000 (diphthongs could denote larger numbers). Accordingly, 81,374 could be encrypted as *Mubodilefa* (*Mu* = 80,000; *bo* = 1,000; *di* = 300; *le* = 70; and *fa* = 4), creating additional options for composing poems and songs in the new language.[60]

For Leibniz, music was 'a hidden exercise in arithmetic of a soul ignorant that it is calculating'.[61] As early as 1679 Leibniz was at work on a cryptological machine that he pitched to the Habsburg emperor Leopold I, in the process contriving this musical analogy: 'Then too there is my *machina deciphratoria* with which a ruler can concurrently correspond with different ministers, and without much effort both writes in a cipher that he wishes to use and comprehend[s] a letter sent to him in cipher. This is done much as with using a musical instrument or clavichord, so that the text appears by touching the ... keys and only needs to be copied'.[62] It is unclear if Leibniz advanced far in realizing a prototype of his invention, ultimately unveiled in 2013 by Nicholas Rescher of the University of Pittsburgh. But in 1688, Leopold I was unimpressed by the device, and it languished in oblivion.

We have already mentioned another 'omniscient' seventeenth-century figure, the Jesuit Athanasius Kircher, whose interests, piqued by an encyclopaedic inquisitiveness, extended to cryptography, including its musical varieties. Remembered as an eccentric who 'never ruined a good story with facts', between 1631 and 1679 Kircher authored thirty-plus weighty tomes treating nearly as many topics – magnetism, palaeontology, Egyptology, optics,

---

[59] Leibniz (1666), 65–6.
[60] Couturat (1901), 62–3.
[61] Letter of 17 April 1712; Leibniz (1768), VI, 437.
[62] Cited in Rescher (2013), 353–4.

polygraphy, geology, ocean currents, vulcanology, alchemy, magic, Sinology, the Coptic language, comparative religions, Kabbalah, medicine, biology, acoustics and – not least – music. The two-volume *Musurgia universalis, sive Ars Magna Consoni et Dissoni* (*Universal Musicmaking, or the Great Art of Consonance and Dissonance*), published at mid-century, is often cited for its early description of the doctrine of the affections, the idea that music imitated different emotional states. Though heavily indebted to the *Harmonie universelle* of Marin Mersenne (1636), Kircher represented as his own creation at least one example that reveals a short, workmanlike composition in three-part counterpoint, arranged in several sections with shifting metres and displays of imitative counterpoint. But it is Kircher's treatment of 'cryptological musicmaking' (*cryptologia musurgica*)[63] that concerns us here.

Running throughout the Jesuit's writings is a fascination with hidden knowledge that 'could arouse wonder and awe at the marvels of God's creation'.[64] Musical mysteries were no exception, and so Kircher assiduously explored birdsongs, echo chambers and eavesdropping devices, a variety of musical automatons and even a 'musurgical ark'. This last used a proto algorithm to assist the unmusical to compose four-part polyphony. Turning to cryptography, Kircher privileged steganography and explained how one could empower musical instruments to convey hidden messages. And so, he divided the alphabet into six orders of four letters each, and paired each order with a different class of instruments:

	1	2	3	4
Fistula (winds)	A	B	C	D
Cymbalum (cymbals)	E	F	G	H
Tintinnabulum (bells)	I	K	L	M
Chorda (strings)	N	O	P	Q
Crepitaculum (rattles)	R	S	T	V
Vox (voice)	W	X	Y	Z

Thus, one could broadcast *veni cito* ('come quickly') through four shakes of a rattle, one clash of a cymbal, one stroke of a stringed instrument and one peal of a bell, followed by three blasts from a wind instrument, one peal of a bell, three shakes of a rattle and, finally, two strokes of a stringed instrument. Performed in the open for all to hear, this farrago would be meaningful to those who possessed the code.

---

[63] Kircher (1650), Part V, 360–3; Part IV, 402–14.
[64] Gouk (2005), 147.

Ex. 5.6: Athanasius Kircher, 'Fama latere nequit' (1650)

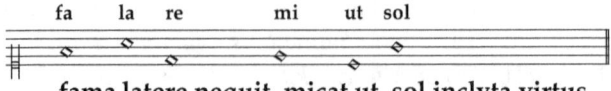

fama latere nequit, micat ut sol inclyta virtus

Elsewhere Kircher provided polymorphous canons by Pier Francesco Valentini, acknowledging him as an *insignis musicus* ('distinguished musician').[65] And Kircher presented musical nomenclators similar to those that his student Gaspar Schott discussed a few years later in his own 'school of steganography'.[66] One of Kircher's other distinctive examples mobilized the Guidonian syllables in order to distribute its message, **Fa**ma **la**tere nequit, **mi**cat **ut** **Sol** inclyta virtus ('Fame cannot hide; illustrious virtue sparkles like the sun', ex. 5.6).

In this case Kircher reissued, without identifying the source, an example previously published in 1636 by Daniel Schwenter,[67] a German orientalist and inventor credited with an early design of the fountain pen.

The solmization syllables in ex. 5.6 might seem like an atavistic nod to the old Guidonian system, though in Lionel Pike's opinion, during the late Renaissance 'the practice of mirroring solmization sounds in the text with music suggested by them was widespread'.[68] By the seventeenth century, the solmization syllables of the hexachord were enjoying a second life in instrumental fantasies, *capricci* and other works constructed on *ut-re-mi-fa-sol-la*. But well before these new genres flourished, as early as 1503 Petrucci had published a *Missa Ut re mi fa sol la* by Antoine Brumel, Obrecht's successor at Ferrara and perhaps the first to elevate the step-like hexachord to the 'authoritative' status of a *cantus firmus*; several similar Masses followed, including contributions from Palestrina and the Spaniard Cristóbal de Morales.[69] In Jane D. Hatter's view, this body of sacred music symbolizes 'music about music-making'[70]; for Wolfgang Fuhrmann, it 'thematizes musical knowledge in an over-arching master plan'.[71] The continually recurring hexachords in these settings of the Mass Ordinary could allegorize the Guidonian hand, a standard mnemonic aid in pedagogical treatises used to teach the full gamut of available pitches. In this regard, Brumel would

---

[65] Kircher (1650), II, 402ff.

[66] Schott (1665), 322ff.

[67] Schwenter (1636), 238–9; Kircher (1650), II, 363.

[68] Pike (1998), 19.

[69] For thirteen others, see Hatter (2019), 234–5; see also Brothers (1973), who traces the tradition to the early eighteenth century.

[70] Hatter (2019), 125.

[71] Fuhrmann (2015), 40.

seem to have planted a significant clue in his Mass, for it consumes in order all seven of the Guidonian hexachords (on G, c, f, g, c', f' and g'[72]), beginning with the lowest pitch of the gamut, G, and rising over the course of the composition to reach the highest, e".

That might be the end of the matter, were it not for alternate readings of Brumel's music. Fuhrmann, for example, views it as a journey from 'humble beginnings to transcendent heights … Observing that the hexachord not only ascends but sometimes descends as well … may point, for instance, to Jacob's ladder on which the angels descend and ascend between heaven and earth'.[73] Whatever special meaning these hexachordal Masses conveyed, the familiar stepwise figure soon enough became a foundational fixture for instrumental variation sets of the seventeenth century. Of the English virginalists, for example, William Byrd produced examples, including one for *My Ladye Nevells Booke* (1591), the dedicatee of which was Elizabeth Bacon, half-sister of Sir Francis Bacon. These compositions, generally comprising increasingly florid variations, could attain considerable complexity. Perhaps the most sophisticated and, indeed, puzzling example was *Ut, re, mi, fa, sol, la*, contributed by Byrd's student John Bull to the *Fitzwilliam Virginal Book*, and, like Byrd's syllable piece for *My Ladye Nevells Booke*, extending to seventeen variations. Bull boldly pushed the exploration of chromaticism to a new extreme, with twelve hexachordal entries rising by whole-steps from G to A, B, D-flat, E-flat and F,[74] and then, after skipping a minor third, again by whole-steps from A-flat to B-flat, C, D, E and F-sharp, before concluding the cycle with five reaffirming statements of the original hexachord on G (all seventeen entries presented hexachords in ascending *and* descending forms). Bull's outlier composition was thus panchromatic: most extraordinary for its time, it unfolded hexachords on *all* twelve pitches of the chromatic scale.[75]

Meanwhile, on the Continent, other virtuoso instrumentalists pursued hexachords, including J. P. Sweelinck in Holland; Juan Cabanilles in Spain; Giralomo Frescobaldi, Gregorio Strozzi, G. B. Fasolo and G. M. Trabaci in Italy; and Frescobaldi's pupil J. J. Froberger in Germany. The case of Frescobaldi (1583–1643), whose music J. S. Bach knew,[76] compels us to pause. Centred in Ferrara until a few years after the devolution of the d'Este dukedom in 1597 to the papacy, Frescobaldi spent much of his career in Rome, where he released

---

[72] For example, G, A, B, c, d, e; c, d, e, f, g, a, etc.

[73] Fuhrmann (2015), 31.

[74] For example, G, A, B, c, d, e—e, d, c, B, A, G; A, B, c-sharp, d, e, f-sharp—f-sharp, e, d, c-sharp, B, A, etc.

[75] See further, Pike (1998), 196–7.

[76] Ladewig (1991).

Ex. 5.7: Frescobaldi, *Capriccio* No. 11 (1624)

several collections of keyboard music. One, the *Capricci* of 1624, reinforced the composer's reputation as a consummate contrapuntist who ascended 'to the peak of the long tradition of works based on given subjects'.[77] Indeed, of these twelve now whimsical, now abstruse pieces, four revisited the Guidonian syllables. Further, several *capricci* betrayed allusive ties to the rich traditions of music associated with Ferrara, including works that had been 'carved from vowels'. Thus, Frescobaldi's *Capriccio sopra ut, re, mi, fa, sol, la* (No. 1) was in a direct line of succession from Brumel's hexachordal Mass, while the *Capriccio sopra la, sol, fa, re, mi, ut* (No. 4) recalled Josquin's *soggetto cavato* Mass on *La sol fa re mi*.[78] Far and away the most unusual of Frescobaldi's creations was No. 11, written in four parts in open score but performed with an obligatory fifth part that was sung. Instead of revealing the 'text', though, Frescobaldi specified only a *soggetto* on the syllables *re, fa, fa, mi, sol, fa, mi, re* (ex. 5.7), leaving open the possibility that lurking within them was an encrypted verbal message:
But what might it have been?

Through some imaginative sleuthing Patrick Macey realized that the first three syllables, *re, fa, fa*, were well 'suited to the vowels of Ferrara'.[79] By substituting *f* for *r* and *r* for *f*, 'Ferrara' indeed came into focus. Applying the same logic, he then exchanged the consonants of the other syllables (thus, *m* for *s*, *s* for *m*), so that this epigram-like phrase coalesced: 'Ferrara, [co]sì morrà, [co]sì fè [morrà] ('Ferrara, thus you will die, thus faith [will die]').[80] Conjecturing that the message was a 'covert expression of disenchantment with [Frescobaldi's] professional life in Rome',[81] Macey then set about examining another work, a ricercar for the third organ Mass from Frescobaldi's *Fiori musicali* (1635), for which he had also specified an obligatory vocal part, to be sung intermittently during the performance of the ricercar. Its *soggetto* – *re, fa, fa, mi, la, re* – appears to have been a compression and reworking of that designated for the *capriccio* (ex. 5.8).

---

[77] Macey (1994), 205.

[78] As Macey points out, Frescobaldi's student Froberger composed a ricercar on *Sol la re—la sol fa re mi*, a second allusion to Josquin's Mass.

[79] Macey (1994), 219.

[80] Ibid., 220.

[81] Ibid., 224.

Ex. 5.8: Frescobaldi, *Fiori musicali*, Ricercar (1635)

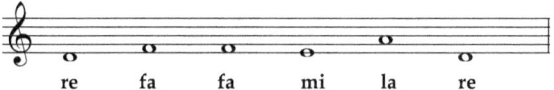

By applying the same method of 'decryption', Macey arrived at a possible solution: 'Ferrara, lì m[i]a fè' ('Ferrara, there is my faith'). Mere conjecture, of course, but plausibly one that could relate two extraordinary keyboard compositions through their shared use of symbolic vowels. That said, Frescobaldi once again left performers to their own devices to discover a suitable solution for his riddle. His only comment on the score was this open-ended quotation from Petrarch's *Canzone* No. 105: 'Understand me who can, for I understand myself'.[82]

iv

Francis Godwin (1562–1633), great uncle of Jonathan Swift, who catalogued English bishops 'since the first planting of the Christian Religion in this Island', was a cleric elevated to the sees of Llandaff and Hereford. Today we remember his 'essay of fancy',[83] *The Man in the Moone, or a Discourse of a Voyage Thither* (1638). 'The beginning of English science fiction',[84] Godwin's tale also has elements of satire and the picaresque and belongs to seventeenth-century literature concerned with a new universal language that might eventually reverse the linguistic confusion wrought by the Tower of Babel. In Godwin's imagination, music was to play a significant role in the search for a 'universal character', 'legible to all People and Countries, so that men of several Nations might with the same ease both write and read it'.[85]

In *The Man in the Moone* the Spanish adventurer Domingo Gonsales trains a flock of swans to power a twelve-day lunar flight. There, he discovers a utopian society of giant lunarians, some over thirty feet in height. They are incorruptible, do not fear death, practise a form of Christianity and live under a hereditary monarchy – perhaps Godwin's own projection of an idealized England. Their language 'consisteth not so much of words and letters as of tunes and uncouth sounds that no letters can express'.[86] Within two months, Gonsales is

---

[82] Durling (1976), 208–9. 'Intendami chi po, ch'i m'intend'io'.
[83] Godwin (1995), 71.
[84] Davies (1967b), 296.
[85] Wilkins (1641), 106.
[86] Godwin (1995), 103.

Exs. 5.9 and 5.10: Francis Godwin, *The Man in the Moone* (1638)

able to acquire some fluency, and to identify the melodic series associated with 'glory be to God alone' (ex. 5.9) and his own name (ex. 5.10).

Godwin did not provide the key to these musical encryptions, but that did not dissuade John Wilkins (*ca.* 1614–72), Bishop of Chester and another polymath interested in cryptology, from presenting the solution in *Mercury, or the Secret and Swift Messenger, Shewing How a Man May with Privacy and Speed Communicate his Thoughts to a Friend at Any Distance* (1641).[87] The key was a descending scale, with each pitch stated twice and alternating between a minim and a semibreve. 'Whence it will follow', Wilkins wrote, 'that a man may frame a Language, consisting only of Tunes and such inarticulate sounds, as no Letters can express. Which kind of Speech is fancied to be usual amongst the Lunary inhabitants, who … hath contrived the Letters of the Alphabet upon the Notes after some such order as this'[88] (ex. 5.11).

When Gonsales returns to earth, he arrives in a mountainous region of China. There he struggles with another language he 'could no way understand', further complicated when he has an audience with a mandarin, who speaks yet a different dialect 'that like that of the Lunars did consist much of tunes'.[89] The essay ends with Gonsales encountering Jesuit missionaries, and awaiting transport to Spain via Macau, so that 'by enriching my country with the knowledge of hidden mysteries I may once more reap the glory of my fortunate misfortunes'.[90]

The tonal nature of Chinese – one syllable pronounced five different ways could yield as many meanings – encouraged Godwin to pursue an artificial, universal language, located somewhere between his imagined lunar discourses and the quasi-musical inflections of Chinese. As we know, he was well acquainted with Nichola Trigault's account of the Jesuits' early proselytizing

---

[87] On Wilkins, a founding member of the Royal Society, see Shapiro (1969).
[88] Wilkins (1641), 143–4.
[89] Godwin (1995), 113.
[90] Ibid., 114.

Ex. 5.11: John Wilkins, *Mercury, or the Secret and Swift Messenger* (1641)

attempts in China.[91] Another Jesuit preoccupied with sinological pursuits was Athanasius Kircher, always eager to 'fill in the gaps in a knowledge that aspired to universality, and especially to complete the tale of how languages and religions had evolved after the Universal Deluge'.[92] Kircher's discursive *China Monumentis qua Sacris qua Profanis ... Illustrata* (*China Illustrated in Sacred and Secular Monuments*, 1667) allowed him to opine about a wide range of topics. Here, he also disclosed another repurposing of the solmization syllables, evidently appropriated as a special didactic tool: 'Hence, to make the Chinese language easier, our [Jesuit] fathers arranged its ascending and descending accents according to the musical notes *ut, re, mi, fa, sol, la*, in order to observe the accents in pronunciation'.[93]

At mid-century Godwin's lunar language became the butt of satire in Cyrano de Bergerac's *histoire comique*, *Voyage dans la Lune*, in which common lunarians communicate by jiggling the limbs of their bodies, while their superiors converse in a musical language, 'no more but various inarticulate Tones, much like to our Musick ... so that sometimes fifteen or Twenty in a Company, will handle a point of Divinity, or discuss the difficulties of a Law-Suit, in the most harmonious Consort that ever tickled the Ear'.[94] Bergerac went so far as to append a few musical motives for 'le Roi' ('the king') and 'ce méchant' ('this evildoer'); these bore no similarities to Godwin's examples, but rather represented 'just random marks on a five-line stave forming visual patterns'.[95]

There was, though, one further reaction to Godwin's lunar adventures via the music cipher Bishop Wilkins had identified in *Mercury*. In 1772, the eccentric

---

[91] *De Christiana Expeditione apud Sinas* (*Concerning a Christian Expedition among the Chinese*, Augsburg, 1615). See Davies (1967b), 301–3.

[92] Godwin (2015), 237.

[93] Kircher (1667), 12. See also Davies (1967b), 303.

[94] Cyrano de Bergerac, *The Comical History of the States and Empires of the Moon and Sun*, trans. A. Lovell (London, 1687), 42–3, cited in Cornelius (1965), 60–1.

[95] Davies (1967b), 315.

Ex. 5.12: Philip Thicknesse, *A Treatise on the Art of Decyphering* (1772)

t a e i o u s l n r y x q k w b f c d m p h g z

Philip Thicknesse, an early biographer of Thomas Gainsborough, published *A Treatise on the Art of Decyphering, and of Writing in Cypher*. Noting that Wilkins's encrypted example for *Gloria Deo soli* (see ex. 5.9) would 'instantly appear to any one the least conversant with music',[96] Thicknesse pledged to develop an improved 'alphabet by musical notes in such a manner that even a master of music shall not suspect it is to convey any meaning.'[97] His solution (ex. 5.12) employed crotchets and minims, and clustered 'the vowels in the middle of the range', while the 'least frequently used consonants [were] allotted to the two extremities of the range'.[98]

Thicknesse tried two musical realizations of his alphabet, the first of which, a setting of a couplet from Oliver Goldsmith's pastoral poem *The Deserted Village* (ex. 5.13), was marred by ungainly, awkward leaps. More convincing was the second example, a short minuet that cleverly disguised the message 'All that of love can be expressed/In these soft numbers see' by exploiting both the treble and bass lines to convey words simultaneously. In addition to this stratagem, Thicknesse inserted several non-encrypted 'empty' notes, or nulls, with tails pointing up; in contrast, the 'meaningful' notes displayed their tails pointing down (ex. 5.14).

Satisfied with his efforts, Thicknesse solicited the interest of Thomas Arne, composer of English operas, theatrical entertainments and 'Rule Britannia'. The new experiments, Thicknesse imagined, would facilitate the clandestine transmission of messages, perhaps between lovers arranging assignations at the then fashionable Grosvenor Square. At the least, they 'would disconcert even a good Decypherer'.[99] A composer, Thicknesse concluded, would 'be able to write any common epistle, with the assistance of the treble and bass clefs, so as to have very few *null-notes*'; the secret meaning would be 'instantly obtained by those who are in possession of the harmonic alphabet'.[100] Nonetheless, Thicknesse's entreaties fell on deaf ears, and nothing further came of the 'harmonic alphabet'.

---

[96] Thicknesse (1772), 43–4.

[97] Ibid., 44.

[98] Davies (1967b), 328.

[99] Thicknesse (1772), 83–4, 70–1.

[100] Ibid., 71.

Ex. 5.13: Philip Thicknesse, *A Treatise on the Art of Decyphering* (1772)

Ex. 5.14: Philip Thicknesse, *A Treatise on the Art of Decyphering* (1772), bars 1–12 ('All that of love can be')

Likely Thicknesse was unaware that notwithstanding his amateurish cryptological pursuits, Germany had already produced a musical polymath whose art would severely challenge musical enigmatologists of every stripe down through the centuries to the present. During the high Baroque, his music synthesized and brought to culmination seventeenth-century trends surveyed in this chapter. Outside German realms his vast oeuvre was little known during his lifetime, so that its full significance had to await a prolonged process of rediscovery. His name was Johann Sebastian Bach.

CHAPTER 6

BACH: His Way and Ours

'Ah, me – there are so many clever ways of hiding things in music.'
— Tortoise, *Contracrostipunctus*, in *Gödel, Escher, Bach*[1]

A CELEBRATED harpsichordist and Bach interpreter, Wanda Landowska (1879–1959) once quipped, 'You play Bach your way, I'll play him his way', as if to have the last word in a controversy involving the cellist Pablo Casals, who visited her in 1941, not long before she fled the Nazis' advance in France and embarked for New York, arriving on 7 December, Pearl Harbor Day. Then as now, apprehending Bach's 'way' was tantamount to chasing a chimera, but surely it would have recognized special features of his music relevant to us, whether ciphers, signatures and palindromes, or fascination with numbers and proportional parallelisms.

Among the most cerebral of musicians, Bach is often viewed as a composer able to turn the mysteries of contrapuntal causality to his advantage. But for the less erudite, Bach's music soon fell out of favour; by the 1730s, the critic J. A. Scheibe rejected it as turgid (*schwülstig*); not quite a century later, Eduard Devrient was contending with the abiding conviction that old Bach was an 'unintelligible musical arithmetician'.[2] The longer view embraced by Devrient and his friend Mendelssohn held otherwise – the very complexity of the Thomaskantor's music obscured its overpowering spiritual truths, apparent to those who grasped multiple levels of meaning operating in the music. There was, for instance, the chromatic aura associated with the 'Kreuzsymbol', the cross-shaped motif depicted on a musical stave by connecting the pitches B and H, A and C. Or the fugal ciphers on the plaintext 'BACH', of which the composer's own family produced several examples. Or the numerological symbolism of perfection hiding behind proportionally related sections, movements and compositions.

While the earliest mention of the BACH cipher apparently occurred in a music lexicon of 1732 by the composer's second cousin, Johann Gottfried Walther (1684–1748), the first musical applications may have been by J. S. Bach himself. The family's name originated in Hungary and was recognized as

---

[1] Hofstadter (2000), 81.
[2] Devrient (1869), 13.

particularly musical: 'all those who have borne this name, so far as is known, are said to have devoted themselves to music; which perhaps springs from the fact that even the letters "B" "A" "C" "H" are melodic in their arrangement'.[3] Difficult to overestimate is the cipher's burgeoning frequency as it passed from Johann Sebastian to his sons Carl Phillip Emanuel, Johann Christian and Wilhelm Friedemann, then to proponents of classicism before spreading throughout the nineteenth century. The Mendelssohns and Schumanns, Brahms, Liszt and many others were captivated by BACH. Toward the end of the nineteenth century the cipher attracted composers as diverse as Marco Enrico Bossi (1861–1925), Wilhelm Conradi (1816–1904), Max Reger, Rimsky-Korsakov and Vincent d'Indy. These and a plethora of others contributed to the remarkable afterlife of the cipher, which touches all the chapters that follow.

With the rise of neo-Baroque and neo-Classical directions in the twentieth century, an influx of the cipher left marks on both sides of the Atlantic, including works by Charles Ives, Amy Beach, Alberto Ginastera and the Canadian composer and educator Jean Coulthard, as well as European composers Béla Bartók, Leopold Godowsky, Hanns Eisler, Arthur Honegger and a group of Italians including Feruccio Busoni, Sylvano Bussotti, Alfredo Casella and Luigi Dallapiccola.[4] In the last seventy years or so composers working with BACH have pursued a wide range of stylistic approaches, including polystylism, spiritual symbolism and serialism, as in the music of Alfred Schnittke, Sofia Gubaidulina, Alexander Goehr, as well as Rudolf Brucci, Aldo Clementi and Luca Lombardi.

Within Bach's own oeuvre the most famous statement – and the only one he acknowledged – is the subject in the fourteenth *Contrapunctus* of the *Art of Fugue*, to which we turn below. But the motive also appears in several of Bach's other authentic compositions[5] and even in some spurious examples, for example, the 'Fugue on the Name BACH', BWV 898, a piece popular among organists by 1847 (ex. 6.1), though now thought to be by one of Bach's last students, J. C. Kittel (1732–1809).[6]

One 'genuine' example occurs in the first movement of the Second Brandenburg Concerto (ex. 6.2). As ex. 6.2 illustrates, Bach's signature appears in the bass line, propelled along in quavers. Did Bach intend this statement of the cipher? Possibly, but perhaps he merely *noticed* it later as an afterthought?

---

[3] Tatlow (2016), 61.

[4] By 1985 some three hundred instances of BACH had accrued; by 1999 the tally had grown to four hundred. Prinz, Dorfmüller and Küster (1985, 389–419); and Boyd (1999).

[5] Apart from the examples discussed in this chapter, see also Williams (1985), *passim*.

[6] Stinson (2020), 41.

BACH: HIS WAY AND OURS   131

Ex. 6.1: BACH Fugue in B-flat major (BWV 898), perhaps by Johann Christian Kittel

Ex. 6.2: J. S. Bach, Brandenburg Concerto No. 2 in F major
(First Movement, bars 109–12)

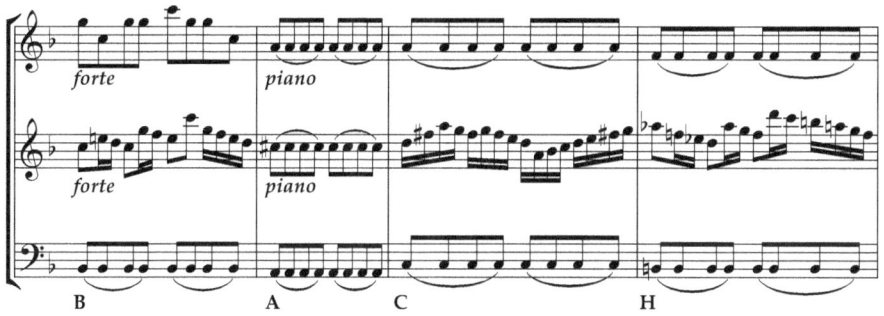

In the Gigue from the last English Suite (BWV 811) BACH, coincidentally or not, is concealed within the upper two voices, with the four letters split between the soprano in semiquaver triplets (B, A) and alto in quavers (C, H; ex. 6.3). Another appearance of BACH in this movement is more explicit, however. In bars 42–3 B, A, C and H are active in the soprano (ex. 6.4), followed in bars 44–5 by three offbeat bass iterations in sequence (B-A-C-H, C-B-natural-D-C-sharp, and D-C-sharp-E-D-sharp).

What shall we make of Bach's purported signature in the Sinfonia in F minor, where the two halves – B-A and C-H – are separated by a rest, and further camouflaged by their placement on weak beats (ex. 6.5, bar 17)? Can we still hear this cipher?

Ex. 6.3: J. S. Bach, English Suite No. 6 in D minor (BWV 811), Gigue (bars 22–4)

Ex. 6.4: J. S. Bach, English Suite No. 6 in D minor (BWV 811), Gigue (bars 40–5)

Next, let us consider one of the most intellectually demanding creations among Bach's late contrapuntal works, the Canonic Variations on 'Vom Himmel hoch da komm' ich her' for organ (BWV 769, 1746–7, published 1748). The piece contains five movements, designated in the first edition accordingly:

> Variatio 1. in Canone all' Ottava, à. 2. Clav: et Pedal. (12/8); Variatio 2. Alio Modo in Canone alla Quinta à 2 Clav: et Pedal. (C=4/4); Variatio 3. Canone alla Settima / *Cantabile*. (C); Variatio 4. à 2 Clav. et Pedal. per augmentationem Canone all'ottava. (C); Variatio 5. L'altra Sorte del' Canone all' rovercio, 1) alla Sesta, 2) alla Terza, 3) alla Seconda, è 4) alla Nona. (C).

In 1738 the polymath Lorenz Christoph Mizler founded the *Correspondierende Societät der musikalischen Wissenschaften* (*Corresponding Society of Musical Sciences*), with a membership limited to twenty. Nine years later, Bach became the fourteenth admitted (other notable musicians in the society were G. F. Handel, G. P. Telemann and C. H. Graun). Fortuitously or not, the numerological spelling of 'Bach' is fourteen, and on this occasion, he may have submitted the organ variations as a demonstration of his 'scientific learning'. Tatlow suggests that

Ex. 6.5: J. S. Bach, Sinfonia No. 9 in F minor, BWV 795 (bars 16–18)

Ex. 6.6: J. S. Bach, *Canonische Veränderungen über ein Weihnachtslied* (BWV 769), Variatio 4, bars 37–42 (BACH)

Bach did not necessarily accept membership just to 'occupy himself with deep theoretical speculations on music,'[7] though that might easily have ensued, given that Mizler was a learned mathematician and musician.

In BWV 769 Bach's signature reveals itself in Variation 4, four bars before the end and then, in retrograde order, in the antepenultimate and penultimate bars (ex. 6.6). Bach revised this work twice; the last version displays a different order of movements: here, he placed the climactic last movement between

---

[7] Tatlow (2016), 18.

the second and third variations, that is, the middle of the composition (1, 2, 5, 3, 4), so the fourth now formed the conclusion. The new plan shaped the piece into an arch emphasizing the midpoint, fittingly allowing the BACH cipher to emerge at the very end.

BWV 769 demonstrates a salient feature of Bach's approach to composition – his striving to impart a compendious 'knowledge' of the musical craft. Thus, he designed the *Well-Tempered Clavier* I to include preludes and fugues in *all* twenty-four major and minor keys, a feat repeated in the *Well-Tempered Clavier* II. Similarly, BWV 769 impresses as a cycle of canons, with intervals of imitation including the second, third, fifth, sixth, seventh, octave (two examples) and ninth; only specimens at the unison and fourth are missing, a 'defect' Bach remedied in the comprehensive *Goldberg Variations*, BWV 988, in which every third variation is canonic, starting at the unison and proceeding in order from the second to the ninth. But surely the *ne plus ultra* of Bach's display of musical learning was *Die Kunst der Fuge* (*Art of Fugue*), a nearly encyclopaedic treatment of what was creatively possible within this severe musical genre – *nearly*, because after years of work, Bach left it unfinished.

This crowning creation divides into several sections of increasing complexity: 1) simple fugues (*Contrapuncti* 1–4); 2) counter-fugues (*Contrapuncti* 5–7), where the fugal answer appears as the inversion of the subject; 3) double and triple fugues (*Contrapuncti* 8–11), where the main subject combines with countersubjects; 4) mirror fugues (*Contrapuncti* 12 and 13), in which the movement is repeated with all the intervals in inversion; and 5) canons at the octave and tenth, and in augmentation and contrary motion. The epitome (*Contrapunctus* 14) was to have been a quadruple fugue, the third subject of which exploited the BACH cipher.

The first occurrence of the signature is near the end of *Contrapunctus* 4 in the tenor part (ex. 6.7).

As mentioned, the second occurrence follows in *Contrapunctus* 14, in which BACH prominently introduces the third subject in the tenor (ex. 6.8).

Is it pure coincidence that BACH appeared in the fourteenth *Contrapunctus*, the number associated with the composer's name? According to a comment on the autograph by C. P. E. Bach, after reaching these bars, his father died. But some have challenged this assertion, arguing instead that the composer deliberately broke off work on his fugal compendium, leaving its completion to our imagination, and perhaps even providing clues about its continuation. The tantalizing final bar served in effect as enigmatic ellipses, drifting off into the unknown silence, and, for Douglas Hofstadter, turning the fragment into a metaphor for Kurt Gödel's incompleteness theorem (1931), according to which 'all consistent axiomatic formulations of number theory' – *read* Bach's cycle

Ex. 6.7: J. S. Bach, *Art of Fugue*, *Contrapunctus* 4

Ex. 6.8: J. S. Bach, *Art of Fugue*, *Contrapunctus* 14

of fugal mathematics – 'include undecidable propositions'.[8] But there is more intriguing evidence about Bach's design of the whole. For instance, in 2010 Loïc Sylvestre and Marco Costa described 'a mathematical architecture [behind] *The Art of Fugue*, based on bar counts, that the whole work was conceived on the basis of the Fibonacci series and the golden ratio'.[9] And in 2006 Indra Hughes pointed out that for whatever reason Bach broke off work on *Contrapunctus*

---

[8] Hofstadter (2000), 17.
[9] Sylvestre and Costa (2010), 179.

14 in exactly bar 239, raising again the possibility that the composer practised musical numerology: in sum (literally), 2 + 3 + 9 = 14.[10]

Given that Bach never clarified to what extent he used numerology, should we seriously consider interpretations of his music devoted to number symbolism? The nineteenth-century Bach biographer Philipp Spitta, followed by twentieth-century scholars Arnold Schering and Friedrich Smend, mentioned debates about Bach's number symbolism, but without addressing evidence *pro* and *contra*. More recently, Walter Schenkman proceeded with the hypothesis, 'if Bach had a conscious intent to insert his signature in his work by means of numbers (either 14 or 41), one logical place to do so would be at the very beginning of his work'.[11] Why fourteen or forty-one? According to Tatlow, Bach wrote his name in several ways, ranging from 'Bach' to 'Joh: Seb: Bach' and 'J. S. Bach'. Using three different number alphabets, she calculated the numerical equivalents, and demonstrated how the natural order alphabet generated fourteen and forty-one (Table 6.1).

Schenkman's findings include a reference to the first of the *Goldberg Variations*, where the right hand intones the opening motivic idea in four bars, expending forty-one notes to yield 'J. S. Bach', while the bass has groups of seven notes, with fourteen in the first two bars. Schenkman then offered one more hypothesis: 'If Bach had consciously intended to insert his name by means of number, a second logical place to do so would be at the very end of his work'.[12] The findings would seem confirming: in the quodlibet (Variation 30), Schenkman again counted exactly forty-one notes – 'a clear case of another "J. S. Bach" signature', balancing the forty-one-note signature at the beginning of the first variation in the soprano line. The last four bars offer two fourteen-note groups, 'two separate and distinct counterpoints of fourteen notes, each in the alto voice'.[13] Schenkman discovered additional examples in Variations 4, 9, 21 and 27.

One reason why scholars and music aficionados to this day are drawn to such interpretations is because word and number games, numerical interpretations and proportional parallelisms are found in 'everyday life, in every academic discipline and creative pursuit, and ... described by music theorists in

---

[10] Hughes (2006), 20. In a similar way, Anatoly Milka has interpreted the spelling of the title page on Bach's autograph (P 200), in which he altered one letter to change *Die Kunst der Fuge* to *Die Kunst der Fuga*, as a paragrammatic word play with numerological significance: *Die Kunst der Fuga* = 158 = Johann Sebastian Bach. Coincidentally or not, the digits of 158 add up to 14. Milka (2016), 179.

[11] Schenkman (2003), 88.

[12] Ibid., 89.

[13] Ibid.

Table 6.1: Bach's Signatures, after Tatlow (2016), 67

Natural Order Alphabet	Milesian Alphabet	Trigonal Alphabet	Bach's Signature Form	Resulting Number
A=1, B=2, C=3, D=4, E=5, F=6, G=7, H=8, IJ=9, K=10 [...] Z=24.	A=1, B=2, C=3, D=4, E=5, F=6, G=7, H=8, IJ=9, K=10, L=20, M=30, N=40, O=50, P=60, Q=70, R=80, S=90, T=100, UV=200, W=300, X=400, Y=500, Z=600.	A=1, B=3, C=6, D=10, E=15, F=21, G=28, H=36, IJ=45, K=55, L=66, M=78, N=91, O=105, P=120, Q=136, R=153, S=171, T=190, UV=210, W=231, X=253, Y=276, Z=300.	**BACH** J. S. Bach	14 (natural order) 46 (Trigonal Alphabet) 14 (Milesian Alphabet) 41 (natural order) 262 (Trigonal Alphabet) 113 (Milesian Alphabet)

books about how to compose'.[14] How, then, were such numerical interpretations an essential part 'of Bach's heritage'? Tatlow speaks of proportional parallelisms that created basic relationships (1:1, 1:2, etc.) between groups of bars, sections and movements of compositions. These relationships created 'a musical structure that would render his compositions the most perfect, the most beautiful, the most eurythmic, and the most lasting.'[15] Although proportions of sections within compositions are not audible, the goal was to emulate the 'created order in the universe' symbolic of 'predestined harmony'.[16]

When Bach's obituary appeared in 1754, his son C. P. E. and Johann Friedrich Agricola asserted not only that the *Art of Fugue* brandished 'all sorts of counterpoints and canons, on a single principal subject', but that it was to have culminated in a fourth fugue 'which was to contain [all] four themes and to have been afterward inverted note for note in all four voices'.[17] The autograph source known as P 200 (Berlin, Deutsche Staatsbibliotek Mus. Ms. P 200) reveals that Bach stopped composing the third fugue at bar 239, causing C. P. E. to add the comment, 'N.B., while working on this fugue, in which the name BACH appears in the counter subject, the author died'.[18] However, in the first

---

[14] Tatlow (2016), 6.
[15] Ibid., 20.
[16] Ibid., 100.
[17] David and Mendel (1998), 305.
[18] Ibid., 260.

edition overseen by C. P. E. Bach and Altnickol the unfinished fugue ended six bars earlier, at bar 233. Somehow, owing to 'a magnanimous gesture by the publishers',[19] the chorale 'Wenn wir in höchsten Nöten sein' (BWV 668) was printed on the final two pages, which the publishers were 'proud to think … will make up for his lack [of completing the unfinished fugue] and compensate the friends of his Muse'.[20]

For Tatlow, so many interpretations and reinterpretations have accumulated that what Bach may have 'originally intended for the printed version has been impossible to ascertain'.[21] Nevertheless, scholars persist in attempting to solve 'the missing final fugue'. Tatlow proposed a solution based on P 200, with twelve fugues and two canons, completed *ca.* 1742. According to Wolff, the third fugue of *Contrapunctus* 14 was deliberately broken off by Bach at bar 239. The paper he used had 'faulty ruling on the lower staff lines', so that most likely Bach 'never planned to fill the sheet from top to bottom' because the page could not accommodate a 'dense fugal setting'.[22]

Tatlow also claimed that Johann Christoph Friedrich Bach ('Bückeburg Bach'), fifth son of Johann Sebastian, 'had a larger hand in the production and printing'[23] than assumed. Much of the engraved first version of *Art of Fugue* 'was undertaken during Bach's lifetime and probably under his direction'.[24] We cannot conclusively determine whether or not Bach completed the third fugue,[25] though Tatlow's finding that Bach relied upon proportional parallelisms in the designs of his cyclical works may well be relevant: 'As parallelism has been found in all of Bach's collections and fair copies, it gives a new objective measure against which to test the status of Bach's manuscript, P 200, and the posthumously published print. Numerical results show that the design of the publication was more polished than has hitherto been appreciated and suggest that Bach had completed the quadruple fugue as far as he intended'.[26]

Another puzzling issue about the *Art of Fugue* concerns its instrumentation. According to the 'keyboard thesis', Bach arranged the work 'for use on the Clavier or organ'.[27] And yet, anomalies surrounding the composition have

---

[19] Ibid.
[20] Wolff (1991), 282; David and Mendel (1998), 258–60.
[21] Tatlow (2016), 239.
[22] Wolff (1991), 260.
[23] Tatlow (2016), 241.
[24] Ibid.
[25] Milka (2014).
[26] Tatlow (2016), 243.
[27] Dentler (2004), 88.

emboldened critics of this approach. Thus, Hans-Eberhard Dentler observes: 'Even if the "keyboard thesis" had evoked no opposition in written scholarship, it still begs an answer to the question why the work in 250 years of Bach reception history has not been able to secure an honorary place in the concert hall'.[28] Indeed, after the performance of an orchestral arrangement of the work in the Leipzig Thomaskirche on 26 June 1927, critics did not hesitate to pounce – one review lamented that the arranger, Wolfgang Graeser, had 'misunderstood the score notation of J. S. Bach by interpreting it as ensemble score without ascribed specific instruments'.[29] Furthermore, according to Dentler, the arrangement did little to shed light on an even greater question, concerning the very 'being' (*Wesenheit*) or 'meaning' of the work, which 'cannot be answered as long as the essential character of the *Art of the Fugue*, which rests on Pythagorean philosophy and music theory, remains hidden behind the mask of a particularly difficult philosophical riddle'.[30]

There is yet another possibility to consider, that the *Art of Fugue* was meant to be understood as a *quasi*-musical treatise. For Christoph Wolff this 'reading book thesis' validates the *Art of Fugue* as 'the essay for Lorenz Christoph Mizler's *Societät der musikalischen Wissenschaften*. Bach had joined the society in 1747, and in the guise of essay the work would have served the function of obligatory contribution for the year 1749, a most weighty tribute to the society's goals, which the composer was unable to complete'.[31] As Anatoly reminds us, the society's constitution required 'that each member submit at least one manual or essay of practical usefulness, endorsing the renaissance of "die Majestät der alten Musik"'.[32] Some scholars, including Hans Gunter Hoke, believe that the *Art of Fugue* was in fact Bach's contribution.[33] What are its features that made it a good fit for the Societät? The many visual elements, not least the titles and BACH signatures. However, because the *Art of Fugue* originated, at least in part, from the earlier 1740s – well before Bach entered Mizler's society – debate continues about whether the composition had anything to do with Bach's membership.

In a similar way, questions still abound about the ultimate meaning of Bach's other late contrapuntal cycle, the *Musical Offering* (*Musikalisches Opfer*, BWV 1079), a collection of canons, fugues and other pieces based on a chromatic

---

[28] Ibid., 88–9.
[29] Schlötterer-Traimer (1966), 11ff.
[30] Dentler (2004), 91.
[31] Wolff (1991), 266.
[32] Milka (2016), 18.
[33] Hoke (1979), 14–15.

Illustration 6.1: J. S. Bach, Musicalisches Opfer, Acrostic on 'Ricercar' (first ed., Leipzig, 1747)

'royal theme' composed by Frederick the Great, who during Bach's Potsdam sojourn of 1747 handed said theme to him, with the royal instruction that he improvise on the subject. To do full justice to the task, the composer returned to Leipzig and wrote out the composition in a fully elaborate version and sent it to the king with a dedication, adorned by an acrostic on the word 'Ricercar', an erudite ancestor of the fugue.

The inscription, '**Regis Iussu Cantio Et Reliqua Canonica Arte Resoluta**' translates as: 'by order of the king the theme, and the remainder resolved according to the canonic art'.

Published in 1747, the *Musical Offering* contained more puzzles than just this clever word game. 'Ricercar' derives from the Italian verb *ricercare*, 'to seek'.

As Hofstadter observes, Bach employed cryptic titles here and there, including in the fourth canon 'Quaerendo invenietis', 'by seeking you will discover' (Matthew 7:7).[34] One of Bach's pupils, J. P. Kirnberger, provided solutions for these riddles, but Hofstadter wonders if more remain to be found. Among the especially esoteric pieces in the *Musical Offering* is a *Canon per Tonos* in three voices, likened by Hofstadter to the 'strange loops' phenomenon, a concept that occurs 'whenever, by moving upwards (or downwards) through the levels of some hierarchical system, we unexpectedly find ourselves right back where we started'.[35] At work in Bach's canon is an upper voice executing the royal theme while below two voices provide a 'canonic harmonization based on a second theme'.[36] Of the two harmonizing voices, the lower is centred in C minor while the upper lies a fifth above, in G minor. By the time the canon concludes, though, somehow the music has modulated 'right under the listener's nose' to D minor, without a final cadence, and the game begins anew; after six further modulatory loops we return to C minor, despite having journeyed far from the tonic in the interim. Hofstadter believes that this 'ad infinitum' procedure reflected the king's glory, as confirmed by the composer's annotation, 'As the modulation rises, so may the King's Glory'.[37] Furthermore, Hofstadter compares the 'strange loops' phenomenon to the work of Dutch graphic artist, M. C. Escher (1902–72), celebrated for his tessellated designs. Some of them feature the paradox of endlessly descending stairs, which Hofstadter likens to the tonal steps ascending *ad infinitum* in Bach's *Canon per Tonos*.

Earlier we introduced Tatlow's thesis about proportional parallelisms in Bach's music; now, we may briefly consider if and how it undergirds the overarching architectural scheme of the *Musical Offering*. Her analysis proceeds in two steps: first, she calculates the numerical values of title words (for example, 'ricercar' = 72; 'sonata' = 66); second, she compares these values to divisions within the music at the level of bar numbers, thereby bringing into focus structural parallelisms, synchronized proportions and symbolic meanings. Also, to facilitate the numerical analysis, Tatlow treats the composition in five parts, labelled A through E, corresponding to the layout of the first edition, which was printed in five portions by different engravers: A (title page and dedication), B (Ricercar a 3 and perpetual canon on the 'Royal Theme'), C (trio sonata and *canon perpetuus*), D (five *canones diversi* and canonical fugue) and E (ricercar a 6 and two canons).

---

[34] Hofstadter (2000), 9.
[35] Ibid., 10.
[36] Ibid.
[37] Ibid.

Table 6.2: Ruth Tatlow's Analysis of Title Words in the *Musical Offering*, First Edition

Section	Title Word(s) and Value
B	Ricercar (72)
B	Canon perpetuus super Thema Regium (44 + 134 + 75 + 45 + 70 = 368)
E	Ricercar a 6 (72 + 7 = 79)
E	Canon a 2 *Quaerendo invenietis* (44 + 3 + 95 + 120 = 262)
E	Canon a 4 (44 + 5 = 49)
C	Sonata (66)
C	*sopr'il Soggetto Reale* (84 + 103 + 39 = 226)
D	*Canones diversi super Thema Regium* (67 + 82 + 75 + 45 + 70 = 339)
D	Canon 1 a 2 (44 + 4 = 48)
D	a 2 Violin in Unisono (3 + 76 + 22 + 101 = 202)
D	a 2 *per Motum contrarium* (123 + 125 = 248)
D	a 2 *per Augmentationem contrario Motu* (3 + 37 + 150 + 107 + 65 = 362)
D	*Fuga canonica in Epidiapente* (34 + 57 + 22 + 100 = 213)
D	Regis Iussu Cantio Et Reliqua Canonica Arte Resoluta (56 + 85 + 59 + 24 + 79 + 57 + 42 + 105 = 507)

Here are some compelling findings from Tatlow's investigations, simplified in Table 6.2.[38] In sections E and C the values of the titles 'canon' and 'sonata' (44 and 66) add up to 110.

The word values of the headers in movements B and E – *Thema Regium* and *Quaerendo invenietis* – together equal 330, while the titles in section B, Ricercar and *Canon perpetuus super Thema Regium* (72 + 368), equal 440. Thus: 110: 330: 440. These proportions parallel the number of bars of the canons in sections C and D (220), and the number of bars of the sonata in section C (440). Lastly, there are 660 bars in sections B, D and E, and 1320 bars (2 × 660) in the three parts of the sonata.

Tatlow views these parallel proportions as evidence of a 'close numerical relationship', suggesting that the two key phrases, *Thema Regium* and *Quaerendo invenietis*, may have been the 'source of invention' ('Erfindungsquelle') for the collection as a whole.[39] Thus, she concludes that the *Musical Offering* is a 'perfectly proportioned work, fulfilling clearly two of the three characteristics found in every collection that Bach published: the bar totals of the whole and the parts are multiples of 10, and there are several levels of proportion across the structure'.[40] Also noteworthy is the parallelism between the word value of

---

[38] After Tatlow (2016), 232.
[39] Ibid., 233.
[40] Ibid., 237.

key words and the number of bars. Christoph Wolff's view, that the work is an *opus perfectum* due to its 'well-balanced' characteristics and 'inner connection',[41] is arguably confirmed owing to Tatlow's painstaking research. In the final analysis, the *Musical Offering* has '1980 bars forming a 2:1 proportion: 1320 bars of trio sonata and 660 bars of canon and ricercar. As ... Bach would have designed the manuscript layout for the non-musician engravers, deciding the number of bars per page, per plate and per movement, this numerical design with its proportioning within the sections is without doubt Bach's – it is not a coincidence of random numbers'.[42]

If Bach 'manipulated the number of bars to create perfect proportions in his scores that cannot be heard',[43] the question arises: did he share his method with his children? In this regard, Tatlow recalls J. N. Forkel's observation that Bach's era 'was a period ... when one took all of music to be the main science, when the whole of music theory consisted solely of calculations, and when one believed that all expression and all beauty in art depended solely on the mathematical proportions of tones... But these times are now over, and what happened in excess then, maybe happens too little nowadays'.[44] That said, members of the family certainly continued to spread the Bachian legacy at least by employing the BACH cipher, which, depending on its placement, could be prominently audible. We may conclude by considering some examples, of which a dozen, perhaps more, survive from five members of the family, including four of J. S. Bach's sons – Carl Philipp Emanuel, Johann Christian (the 'London' Bach), Johann Christoph Friedrich Bach and Wilhelm Friedemann – and one nephew – Johann Michael (the 'Wuppertal' Bach).[45]

Not surprisingly, many of these examples pay homage to the family monogram in contrapuntal contexts not unlike J. S. Bach's own style, ranging from a brief sketch by W. F. for a fugal exposition[46] and a twelve-bar canonic draft by C. P. E.[47] to a 'Fughette' by J. C. F.[48] and fully fledged fugues by C. P. E.,[49] J. C.[50] and J. M. Bach.[51] Of these, two stand out for their supplemental prefixes to the cipher.

---

[41] Wolff (1991), 255.

[42] Tatlow (2016), 229.

[43] Ibid., 368.

[44] Ibid., citing Forkel (1788), 30.

[45] See also Schulenberg (2010 and 2014), *passim* for additional examples by W. F. and C. P. E.

[46] See Schering (1924).

[47] See Godt (1979), 157–8.

[48] Fedtke (1984), 18.

[49] Ibid., 14–17.

[50] Ibid., 19–28.

[51] Available online through IMSLP.

Ex. 6.9: C. P. E. Bach, Canonic Cipher Draft

Ex. 6.10: J. C. F. Bach, 'Fughette'

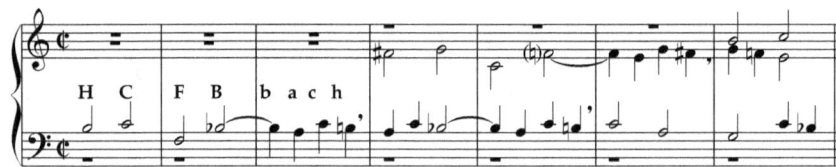

Thus, C. P. E. converted his own initials into pitches by using the Italian version of 'Philipp' ('Filippo'), to produce his signature: C, F, E, B, A, C, H (ex. 6.9).[52]

In a similar way, his brother J. C. F. insinuated those initials into the 'Fughette' by shortening 'Johann' to 'Hans', yielding in turn H C F B A C H (ex. 6.10).

In other examples BACH appears in contexts usually *not* associated with high counterpoint. Thus, J. M.'s fugue serves as the finale of a keyboard concerto in B-flat major, in which he balances the conflicting demands of contrapuntal excursions and virtuosic display. In the case of J. C.'s fugue, fully three fourths of the composition unfold in a conventional manner, but ultimately evolve into a *quasi*-improvisation, with arpeggiated figurations suggestive more of Mozart than J. S. Bach. Finally, C. P. E. seems to have demonstrated the greatest versatility in treating the cipher by working it into the bass line of the first movement of his Sonata in C major H 41 (1744), the opening of the bass line of his setting

---

[52] A convenience he also used in the collection *Psalmen mit Melodien* (1774), No. 41. See Schulenberg (2014), 174.

Ex. 6.11: C. P. E. Bach, Symphony in C major, Adagio (1773), bars 1–4

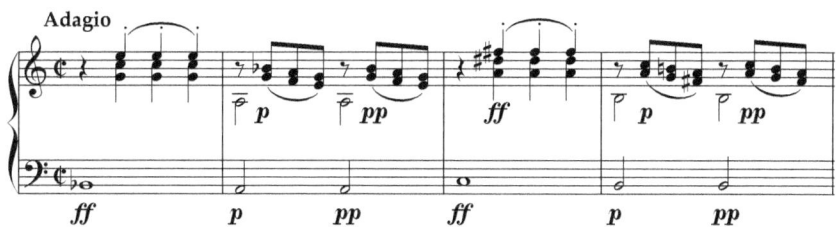

Ex. 6.12: C. P. E. Bach, Rondo in C major (1780), bars 137–9

of C. F. Gellert's Ode for New Year's Day H 686 (1757), again the bass line of the Adagio of the Symphony in C major H 659 (1773) and, finally, the toccata-like flourishes of the Rondo in C major H 260 (1780).[53] Shown here are passages from the symphony (ex. 6.11) and rondo (ex. 6.12).

In the symphony, the Adagio literally interrupts the coursing energy of the first movement by dramatically introducing the cipher in the bass, a highly expressive passage that tests the extremes of the composer's dynamic range, from *fortissimo* to *pianissimo*. And in the rondo, C. P. E. sustains the stark intensity associated with the cipher through a rapidly rising chromatic sequence that

---

[53] In addition, several brief studies on BACH survive in C. P. E.'s hand. See C. P. E Bach (2019), 125–6.

ascends through several iterations of the four-note pattern. There can be little doubt, then, that like other members of his family, C. P. E. was intimately aware of the magnetic power of the cipher. Well before Beethoven, Mendelssohn, Robert Schumann and Brahms would rediscover it, not to mention devoted disciples in the twentieth century, this son of Bach was absorbing the allure of the family name, aware that he was neither the first, nor to be sure, the last.

CHAPTER 7

Enlightened Ciphers, *Ars combinatoria* and Masonic Secrets

> I cannot write in verse, for I am no poet. I cannot arrange the parts of speech with such art as to produce effects of light and shade, for I am no painter. Even by signs and gestures I cannot express my thoughts and feelings, for I am no dancer. But I can do so by means of sounds, for I am a musician.
>
> – Mozart to his father, 8 November 1777[1]

RECOGNISED today as the consummate synthesist of the late Baroque, 'der alte Bach' lived long enough to experience the cultural movement known as the Enlightenment. When he travelled to Potsdam in 1747, he arrived at a Prussian court where Frederick the Great regularly conversed in French with the deist Voltaire and counted among a few other 'enlightened' monarchs (though absolutist, to be sure) who sympathized with *philosophes* such as Rousseau, Diderot, Hume and Kant, and placed their faith squarely in reason and optimism about mankind. The celebrated motto Kant revived from Horace, *sapere aude* ('dare to know'), might well stand for the entire movement. But the desired knowledge now reached beyond the rational, quantifiable world to the murky subjectivities of emotions, domains of human experience that inconveniently resisted 'the control of reason'.[2] The new inquisitiveness also engaged aesthetics, a nascent field recognized by the philosopher A. G. Baumgarten to address how we perceive the beautiful, in turn challenging the centuries-old theory of mimesis, according to which art was like a mirror, imitating the world around it. Precisely how music participated with its sibling arts in this process – what exactly did music imitate? – had never been fully unravelled. If, after Horace, poetry was indeed 'like a painting' (*ut pictura poesis*), only with serious difficulty could music fit into what 'rational' arbiters of taste such as Gotthold Ephraim Lessing viewed as a Procrustean metaphor.

Rational arbiters of taste indeed came to view music less as an imitative and more an expressive agent autonomous from the traditional taxonomy of the arts. And so, at the apex of the Enlightenment Haydn and Mozart were creating

---

[1] Anderson (1985), 363.
[2] Gay (1969), 282.

lustrous scores that, while reflecting on their surface elegantly rational designs, nevertheless could betray deeper currents of meaning. Thus, the First Day of Haydn's oratorio *The Creation* (1798) announced the lifting of darkness through a radiant chorus. But what preceded this chorus was an orchestral overture depicting chaos. Here Haydn reengineered his craft to produce sonic metaphors for an aimless void that disrupted conventional musical parameters – pitch, metre, rhythm, harmony, dissonance treatment, form and timbre – releasing irrational sound masses as destabilizing and frightening as anything created up to that point. Mozart, who, like Haydn, preferred major to minor keys, nevertheless habitually exploited the major–minor exchange in telling psychological ways, as in the emotionally depth-defying Siciliano of the Piano Concerto, K 488 (1786), where, as if to explore the interior psyche of the soloist, he summoned the rare key of F-sharp minor, in contrast to the glistening key of A major for the outer movements. These two examples broached a different aesthetic category altogether – the sublime – which explained 'why [one] could admire that which was not beautiful – storms at sea, ruined castles, terrifying earthquakes. It found room for the irregular, literally unruly, productions of genius'.[3]

Within this paradox of the rational plumbing the 'unruly', Viennese classicism operated. With the eruption of the French Revolution in 1789 and aftershocks of the Terror unleashed in 1793, the high Classical style came to comprise a multi-layered system of musical signs, some readily apparent, but others functioning in cryptic ways, as if to suggest an interior musical realm inscrutably veiled, a type of music, in David Schroeder's memorable phrase, 'rattling at the cage of the Enlightenment'.[4] No surprise, then, that during this period, musical cryptography, word games and codes, and *double entendres* flourished, even if under the guise of the 'rational' pursuit of knowledge.

i

Today we remember the Italian violinist Giuseppe Tartini (1692–1770) as a composer of over one hundred concerti and a smaller number of solo sonatas, among them the celebrated 'Devil's Trill', which depicts a dream about the violinist consummating a compact with the devil. According to the Venetian Count Francesco Algarotti, before composing Tartini customarily read Petrarch to choose poetic subjects that he then painted in tones.[5] What gives Tartini's music its mystique is that he inscribed into his scores motto-like texts, usually concealed through cryptographic means, and thus withheld from public

---

[3] Ibid., 304.
[4] Schroeder (1999), 11.
[5] Dounias (1966), 89.

view. Not until 1935 were they deciphered, a muddle of 'short strokes, crosses, angles, full and half circles and other geometric figures'.[6] By using frequency analysis Minos Dounias transliterated these symbols, which, he discovered, corresponded to the twenty characters of the Italian alphabet. Petrarch did not figure among the authors of these texts; instead, Tartini preferred Pietro Metastasio, the leading eighteenth-century librettist of *opera seria*. Sometimes Tartini jotted down epigram-like quotations in the margins of his manuscripts, but sometimes he underlaid them beneath a theme, so that his music became effectively 'a scarcely disguised setting of the words themselves'.[7] Apart from Tartini's circle, few probably would have grasped the full import of his method, so that for not quite two centuries Tartini's compositions were performed as autonomous instrumental music divorced from their literary prompts.

Not all were as scrupulous in suppressing these deeper levels of meaning from public view. In 1774 the English physician William Hooper published *Rational Recreations*, intended 'to render useful learning, not dull, tedious, and disgustful, not rugged and perplexing, not austere and imperious, but facile, bland, delightful, alluring, captivating'.[8] Among the book's diversions was a card game that preserved the inviolability of the rows, columns and diagonals of a five-by-five magic square, whose sums remained constant.[9] Further on in the volume Hooper considered 'different methods of writing in cipher', including rotating a 'mystical dial' to transmit clandestine messages. By replacing the moveable letters of the inner perimeter of the wheel with pre-selected snippets of one or two musical notes, the encrypted message could become a streaming line of music (Illustration 7.1).

Occasionally the cryptographer might change the time signature or clef of the music, or randomly distribute null-like flats and sharps among the segments to throw cryptologists off the scent. With these 'safeguards' in place, Hooper imagined that the plaintext, 'let me know you are safe and ease my tortured mind', could be 'enclosed in a letter about common affairs, and pass unsuspected' – unless, that is, 'it should fall into the hands of any one who understands composition, for he would very likely surmise, from the odd disposition of the notes, "that more is meant than meets the ear"'.[10] Indeed, what met the ear in Illustration 7.1 were jumbled gestures riven by large leaps lacking melodic cohesion.

---

[6] Ibid., 91.
[7] Brainard (1961), 392.
[8] Hooper (1774), iv.
[9] Ibid., 49.
[10] Ibid., 153.

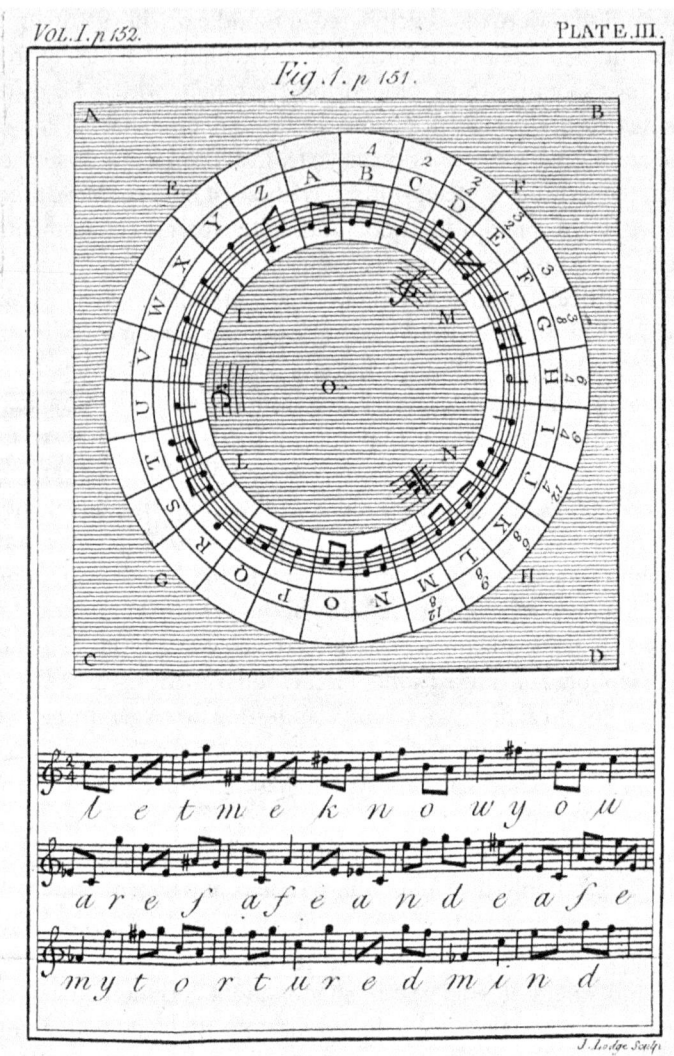

Illustration 7.1: William Hooper, *Rational Recreations* (1774), vol. 1, pl. III (p. 152)

One musical sport by Hooper reaffirmed the 'rationalistic temperament of the time' as well as the 'general public enthusiasm for mathematics'.[11] In No. XXII he posed a challenge that moved the discourse into the realm of combinatorial art: 'To find how many different sounds may be produced by striking on a harpsichord two or more of the seven natural notes at the same time'.[12]

---

[11] Hedges (1978), 180.

[12] Hooper (1774), 64.

One could confirm the answer, 120, by methodically compiling all the possible two-note combinations of, say, the pitches C, D, E, F, G, A and B (21), then the three-note (35), four-note (35), five-note (21), six-note (7) and seven-note (1) simultaneities, and summing them.

The art of combinations (*ars combinatoria*) became a popular eighteenth-century pastime that betrayed the new enthusiasm for 'explaining all events through scientific observation'.[13] As early as 1636 the French Minorite music theorist and mathematician Marin Mersenne (1588–1648) viewed musical composition as a 'sequence and arrangement of consonances',[14] leading him to generate in his *Harmonie universelle* a table of 720 anagram-like permutations of the six hexachordal syllables.[15] There is clear evidence that in the eighth book of the *Musurgia universalis*, in a section titled 'Combinatorial musurgia', Athanasius Kircher borrowed heavily from Mersenne.[16] Then, in 1666, Gottfried Wilhelm Leibniz released *De arte combinatoria* (*Concerning the Art of Combinations*). As noted in Chapter 5, here we read about one particular musical problem that perhaps inspired Hooper's derivation of simultaneities from the notes of a scale, namely, to determine how many possible melodies one could extract from a given number of notes.[17] The philosopher was concerned about whether all knowledge could be reduced to combinations of simple ideas, so that one might propose a universal language (*characteristica universalis*) based upon commonly accepted scientific calculations. Toward this end, Leibniz envisioned an international language of signs, a type of pasigraphy that might admit, for example, not just mathematical symbols but also musical notes.[18]

By the mid-eighteenth century, *ars combinatoria* had descended from Leibniz's lofty philosophical perch to engage considerably more practical applications and began to support a popular culture of musical dilettantism. Because one could 'codify the mechanical [rational] elements of musical composition more clearly than at any other time',[19] the untutored could now avail themselves of musical parlour-room games supported by pre-determined tables of options. By simply rolling dice and consulting tables, they could choose one bar at a time and produce their 'own' musical concoctions. In one game devised by Johann

---

[13] Hedges (1978), 184.
[14] Knobloch (1979), 262.
[15] Mersenne (1636), 117–28; see also Klotz (2006), 66ff.
[16] Knobloch (1979), 266–7.
[17] Klotz (1999), 236.
[18] Klotz (2006) 99–112.
[19] Ratner (1970), 345.

Philipp Kirnberger, *Der allezeit fertige Menuetten – und Polonoisenkomponist* (*The Ever-Ready Minuet and Polonaise Composer*, 1757), fashioning fourteen bars of a polonaise or thirty-two bars of a minuet unlocked for an amateur access to fully 11^{14} or 11^{32} options. As Leonard Ratner noted, 'the entire population of eighteenth-century Europe, working a lifetime on these games could not exhaust the combinations [lying] within Kirnberger's minuets and polonaises'.[20]

Kirnberger may have been the first to systematize musical combinations. Today he is remembered, though, as a pupil of J. S. Bach, with whom Kirnberger studied between 1739 and 1741, and as the author of *Die Kunst des reinen Satzes* (*The Art of Pure Composition*, 1774–9), a two-volume treatise of figured bass, chorale harmonization and counterpoint after Bach's pedagogical method. Though wont to probing the interstitial mysteries of the Thomaskantor's fugues, the theorist revealed another side of his personality in his musical game. One theory is that Kirnberger composed 'conventional' polonaises, then dissected them into individual bars, and entered them into tabular form.[21] Having fixed the harmonic progressions of the dance, Kirnberger provided 'eleven possible melodic variants, corresponding respectively to the eleven numbers that can turn up on a throw of two six-sided dice'.[22] In this way, Kirnberger's colleague Friedrich Wilhelm Marpurg observed, one could generate a dozen dances without 'breaking one's head'[23] (*ohne Kopfzerbrechen*). But this facility did not shield Kirnberger from Charles Burney's rebuke: the theorist was 'more ... an algebraist, than a musician of genius'.[24]

Over the next few decades musical dice games proliferated in Europe,[25] enticing the musically unsophisticated, now able to 'compose' 'without the least knowledge of Musick'. These chance compositions entailed small-scale pieces including marches and dances such as minuets, waltzes, contredanses and ecossaises. But one notable exception was a considerably more esoteric offering from Carl Philipp Emanuel Bach in 1754, *Einfall einen doppelten Contrapunct in der Octave von sechs Tacten zu machen ohne die Regeln davon zu wissen* (*Method for Making Six Bars of Double Counterpoint at the Octave without Knowing the Rules*).[26]

---

[20] Ibid., 344.
[21] Klotz (1999), 238.
[22] Ratner (1970), 343.
[23] Marpurg to Kirnberger, 1 July 1765, in Klotz (1999), 244.
[24] Burney (1775), ii, 123.
[25] For details, see Hedges (1978), 185–7; and Zaslaw (2005).
[26] See further, Helm (1966).

In this case the player entered the domain of cerebral counterpoint, the preserve of the musically learned. Double (invertible) counterpoint required one first to fashion two musical lines that could be performed simultaneously against each other without violating voice-leading rules. Using octave transposition, by flipping the parts so that the top voice became the lower voice (and vice versa), one generated the 'equivalent' in double counterpoint. What Emanuel Bach's game accomplished was to remove the anxiety of committing wayward intervallic combinations, the bane of contrapuntists. To accomplish that, he composed a six-bar exemplar of invertible counterpoint, and supplemented it with eight options, for a total of nine possibilities for the treble and nine for the bass. The layman simply had to spin a top and consult Bach's tables to determine the choices. Composing fifty-four bars of invertible counterpoint cost Bach relatively little effort, but the results spoke for themselves: all told, a player addicted to this game, even if not exactly the musical Wordle of the eighteenth century, could conceivably create 282,429,536,481 error-proof miniatures. Kirnberger's colleague Marpurg calculated this staggering sum when he published Bach's *Einfall* in 1760.[27] Not surprisingly, Marpurg too was a devoted Bachian and seasoned music theorist inclined toward the mathematical side of the art. Indeed, for several decades he served as the director of the Royal Prussian Lottery.

Among other musical chance games of the eighteenth century were three attributed to Joseph Haydn and Mozart, though their celebrity may have incentivized unscrupulous publishers intent upon turning a quick profit to ghostwrite these items. The *Gioco filharmonico* (*Harmonic Game*) ascribed to Haydn appeared in Naples in 1793 and was reprinted in 1812. Its subtitle advertised 'an easy method for composing an infinite number of minuet-trios without any knowledge of counterpoint'. Though there is no evidence of trios in the Naples print, a contemporary, anonymously released *Neues Musikalisches Würfelspiel* (*New Musical Dice Game*) from Vienna not only transmits the same minuet fragments as the *Gioco filharmonico* but supplements them with multiple choices for sixteen-bar trios, emboldening Thomas H. O'Beirne to muse whether, after counting all the permutations, we might justifiably add 940,369,969,152 trios to Haydn's already expansive oeuvre?[28]

There is no hard evidence to corroborate Haydn's direct role in the *Gioco filharmonico*. Still, Leonard Ratner was likely correct when he observed that 'the spirit of the *ars combinatoria* can be felt throughout eighteenth-century music'. Thus, 'the short, well-defined melodic stereotypes available to all composers …

---

[27] Marpurg (1970), iii, 167–81.
[28] O'Beirne (1968).

invited the manipulations, the jugglings and substitutions that make up combinatorial play'.[29] Ratner believed that Haydn's String Quartet in C major, Op. 20 No. 2 and Symphonies Nos. 92 (*Oxford*) and 103 (*Drum Roll*) displayed combinatorial 'permutations of melodic figures', but perhaps a more convincing example is the *Alternativo*, or Trio, of the *Menuetto* from the String Quartet in E-flat major, Op. 76 No. 6. Here, in lieu of a standard binary form with each section repeated, Haydn crafted – most unusually – ninety-six bars apportioned into six cycles of sixteen bars each. Each cycle, in turn, comprises four four-bar sections, and each section announces an unadorned E-flat major scale that rotates from instrument to instrument against ever-changing countersubjects, almost as if chosen from some prefabricated table by rolls of dice.

Thus, the first cycle begins with a descending scale in the cello, imitated in turn by the viola, second violin and first violin. Against these scales the non-scale-bearing instruments introduce variant-like accompaniments. Then, when the second cycle commences, we start the process anew, with the scales in *ascending* (that is, retrograde or inverted) order, and with their own, newly contrived supporting variants. Ex. 7.1 illustrates the sixteen bars of the third cycle, which reinstates the descending scales of the first cycle, though now in the sequence of first and second violins, viola and cello.

In this case, the non-scale variants appear in violin 1, violin 1 and 2, and violin 1, 2 and viola.

Haydn's delight in 'alternative' combinations of voices seduced Mozart as well. Two years after his death, Haydn's younger colleague received credit for two dice games that appeared posthumously in 1793 from J. J. Hummel in Berlin and Amsterdam. Bearing the title *Anleitung* (*Instruction*), they allowed the player to 'compose' as many waltzes or contredanses 'as one desires with two dice, without understanding anything about music or composition'.[30] Despite lack of evidence to validate Mozart's authorship, these games eventually entered the sixth edition of the Köchel *Verzeichnis* as K. Anhang C 30.01, even though their 'persistent dissemination seems the product of combinations and permutations of credulousness, wishful thinking, sloppy scholarship, deliberate obfuscation, and commercial greed'.[31]

Quite another matter, though, is a single autograph leaf preserved in the Bibliothèque Nationale in Paris, and bearing the Köchel number 561f.[32] On the *recto* side Mozart sketched thirty-nine two-bar gestures, a kind of proving

---

[29] Ratner (1970), 359.

[30] Mozart (1793).

[31] Zaslaw (2005), 227.

[32] Collection Charles Malherbe, Mus. Ms. 253. See Noguchi (1990) and Zaslaw (2005).

Ex. 7.1: Joseph Haydn, String Quartet in E-flat major, Op. 76 No. 6, 'Alternativo' (1799)

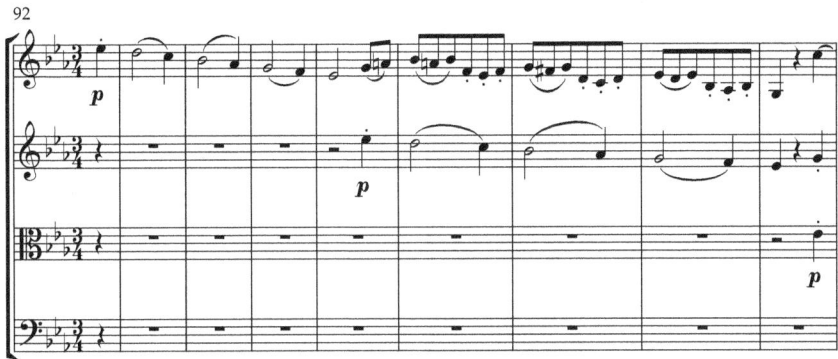

ground for an envisioned minuet. He labelled all but the first with the letters of the alphabet, in the process expending twenty-four lower-case letters (save *j* and *x*), and fourteen upper-case (all but *A, C, E, H, I, J, O, R, U, V, X* and *Y*). Whether some cryptographic design determined Mozart's choice of letters remains unknown, but he may have left a clue about their purpose. On the eighth stave, he selected six two-bar segments and notated them in consecutive order. If we add the identifying letters associated with these motives, the incipient minuet spells '*a f a n c i S*'.

In 1990 the Japanese musicologist Hideo Noguchi investigated whether the letters referred to someone in Mozart's circle. Indeed, the composer appears to have enciphered the answer on the *verso* of the page, where he redoubled efforts to fabricate a patchwork minuet through combinatorial means. Here we find a collection of two-bar modules, this time augmented to forty-nine units somewhat more polished than their counterparts on the *recto* side. Mozart now added rests, fermatas, chromatic pitches and a few slurs, and designed some segments as harmonic progressions. Most conspicuously, he dispensed altogether with the letters and replaced them with an alternating binary series of the numbers 1 and 2. The quantity of these segments, which fill out five and a half staves of the *verso* side, was more than sufficient to consume all the letters of the lower-case alphabet (again, save j and x). Noguchi surmised that Mozart's plan had shifted to create two variants for each letter of the alphabet, which could be labelled $[a]1$, $[a]2$, $[b]1$, $[b]2$, and so forth, continuing all the way through z. By pairing these suppressed letters with the alternating numbers, Noguchi was able to crack the code. Mozart's final notation on the page, a twenty-two-bar continuity draft that used eleven of the forty-nine segments, disclosed the answer (ex. 7.2).

Matching these eleven segments with the restored letters, Noguchi deciphered the name 'Francisca', likely Francisca von Jacquin (1769–1853), daughter of the botanist Nicolaus Josef Baron von Jacquin, and a student of Mozart, who probably wrote the piano part of the Piano Trio in E-flat major ('Kegelstadt'), K 498 for her in 1786.

Mozart never finished his exercise in *ars combinatoria*, and to be sure, K 561f raises more questions than it answers. Are other names lurking in Mozart's manuscripts? Was the whole affair just a 'rational recreation' for his circle, or did it leave a deeper imprint on his scores? As to the second question, we may consider one of Mozart's most familiar minuets, the third movement of the *Jupiter* Symphony, K 551, finished in August 1788, and conveniently in C major, the key of Mozart's sketches for K 561f. Coincidentally or not, a few segments on the *verso* of K 561f closely resemble if not duplicate gestures in the *Jupiter*. Ex. 7.3a–j offers some comparisons.

Example 7.3a: Mozart, K 561f	Example 7.3b: Mozart, K 551
Example 7.3c: Mozart, K 561f	Example 7.3d: Mozart, K 551
Example 7.3e: Mozart, K 561f	Example 7.3f: Mozart, K 551
Example 7.3g: Mozart, K 561f	Example 7.3h: Mozart, K 551
Example 7.3i: Mozart, K 561f	Example 7.3j: Mozart, K 551

Did Mozart repurpose ideas from the *Jupiter* in his minuet game? Or did he compose the minuet of the symphony with the intent to apply combinatorial principles?

Without further evidence, we will likely never know. Nevertheless, the finale of the *Jupiter*, resplendent acme of Mozart's contrapuntal achievements, might corroborate his engagement with combinatorial composition. During the exposition of this dizzying Sonata Form movement Mozart introduces no fewer than four subjects (ex. 7.4), to which a fifth ultimately figures in the breathtaking

ENLIGHTENED CIPHERS 157

Ex. 7.2: Mozart, Musical Game, K 561f

Ex. 7.3: Mozart, Comparisons between K 551 and 561f

Ex. 7.4: Mozart, *Jupiter* Symphony, K 551, Finale, Stretto (1788)

Mozart, 'Jupiter' Symphony, finale, stretto, order to subjects								
fl., vn 1	b. 372	376	380	384	388	392	396	399
fl., vn 1	—	—	4	1	3	(4 dim., 3)	2	1
ob. 1, vn 2	—	4	1	3	(4 dim., 3)	2	4	3
ob. 2, vla	4	1	3	(4 dim., 3)	2	4	1	4
bn 1, cello	1	3	(4 dim., 3)	2	4	1	3	(4 dim., 3)
bn 2, bass	—	—	—	4	1	3	(4 dim., 3)	2

display of quintuple counterpoint that constitutes the peroration of the coda. Once all five subjects are in play, Mozart sustains the contrapuntal intensity for a few additional iterations, as he rotates the subjects in a kaleidoscope of harmonic combinations, the vertical analogue of the horizontal, melodic juxtapositions in K 516f.

It is as though Mozart reaches here for the Kantian mathematical sublime and grasps a precious vision of it, before the celebratory trumpets and drums ring down the curtain in the triumphant closing bars. Not even Haydn, who had experimented with triple and quadruple counterpoint in his String Quartets Op. 20, achieved anything rivalling Mozart's finale.

Non-musical aspects of Mozart's life also betrayed his fascination with combinatorial methodologies. His correspondence reveals a genius who delighted in mathematical sums; deliberate reorderings of syntax; riddle-like word games that included acrostics and anagrams; prose that might veer into nonsensical sequences of rhyming words[33]; polylingual phraseology and macaronic contrivances, etc. – in short, tampering with the conventions of language, whether of words or music. Like his compositions, Mozart's not-quite three hundred letters operate on different levels – there is at first glance the adherence to the mainstream use of his native language (for his music, substitute: 'normal' patterns of the Classical style), but then there is the escape into an alternative linguistic world (for his music, substitute: unpredictable exchanges between the major and minor modes, unexpected harmonic digressions, chromatic saturations of underlying diatonic structures, etc.). Standing quite apart in the correspondence

---

[33] On 31 January 1778 he conceived a letter to his mother in rhyming couplets.

are the nine extant letters to his cousin Maria Anna Thekla (the Bäsle letters, 1777–81), in which Mozart indulges in 'unbridled verbal buffoonery' and 'unrestrained language' allowing a 'faecal-erotic babble of voices to emerge'.[34]

One conspicuous way in which the correspondence documents the exterior and interior realms of the composer's daily world is through his periodic activation of cryptography, which Mozart and his father, Leopold, employed to redact sensitive topics that might attract the prying eyes of censors. Presumably Leopold developed the system, in which 'the Mozarts simply exchanged ten letters of the alphabet with each other',[35] while preserving the rest unaltered:

a=m **b**=b **c**=c **d**=d **e**=l **f**=i/j **g**=g **h**=u **i/j**=f **k**=k **l**=e **m**=a/ä **n**=n **o**=s **p**=p **q**=q **r**=r **s**=o/ö **t**=t **u**=h **v**=v **w**=w **x**=x **y**=y **z**=z

As an example, here is a passage regarding preparations for the Munich premiere of Idomeneo from Mozart's letter to his father of 24 November 1780, alternating between normal and encrypted text:

> Concerning <u>alfnlr splrm</u> <meiner opera/my opera> rest unworried, my dearest father – I hope all of this will go quite well. – <u>lfnl kelfnl Cmbmel</u> <eine kleine Cabale/a little cabal> will no doubt have it taken off – […] – for – I have among the <u>Nsbelool</u> <Noblesse/nobility> the <u>mnolunefcuotln</u> <ansehnlichsten/ most respected and <u>vlrasgefcuotln umholr</u> <vermöglichsten häuser/ wealthiest houses> – and the <u>lrotln Bly dlr ahofck</u> <ersten Bey der musick/first in music> are all for me.[36]

A few months later, Mozart was again resorting to ciphers to conceal his tumultuous dismissal by the Archbishop of Salzburg:

> As long as <the Archbishop> remains here, I shall not <give a concert>. You are altogether mistaken if you think that I shall <get a bad name with the Emperor and the nobility,> for <the Archbishop> is detested here and <most of all by the Emperor.> … Write to me <in cypher> that you are pleased – and indeed you may well be so – <but in public rail at me as much as you like, so that none of the blame may fall on you.>[37]

Even when not relying on encryption, Mozart could summon other types of verbal manipulations to convey private feelings. Thus, the archbishop was

---

[34] Konrad (2015), 2–3.
[35] Ibid., 11.
[36] Ibid.
[37] Anderson (1985), 729.

ridiculed in an acrostic communicated to Leopold on 24 November 1780: 'If only the <u>a</u>ss who smashes a <u>r</u>ing, and by so doing <u>c</u>uts himself a <u>h</u>iatus in his <u>b</u>ehind so that <u>I</u> hear him <u>s</u>— like a castrato with <u>h</u>orns, and with his long ear <u>o</u>ffers to caress the fox's <u>p</u>osterior, were not so ...'[38]

Yet another stratagem was the anagram, as in the answer to this 'Zoroastrian' riddle the composer distributed with others at a Viennese masked ball on 19 February 1786.[39] At the event, held in the Redoutensaal of the Hofburg, Mozart appeared as an oriental philosopher: '*You can have me without seeing me. You may wear me without having me. You can give me without having me.* [Answer:] *D.e.e.h.i.n.ö.r.r.* [horns: *Die Hörner*]'[40] Here Mozart concealed a common metaphor, the cuckold's horns, referenced musically the same year in the first act of *The Marriage of Figaro*, where the servant Figaro, betrothed to Susanna and plotting to thwart Count Almaviva's lascivious designs, sings a cavatina ('Se vuol ballare') in which the French horns allude to his imagined humiliation. In the opera as in the riddle, the listener is left to decipher the meaning.

Related to Mozart's anagrammatizing[41] was his penchant for introducing himself (or signing his name) as Gnagflow Trazom, as he did upon meeting the fortepiano builder Johann Andreas Stein.[42] Sometimes Mozart's verbal reversals extended to dates, for instance in a letter to his sister, Nannerl, of 21 August 1773 ('Oidda. Gnagflow Trazom. Anneiv, Tsugua, ts21, 3771'[43]). Once again, this pseudonymous habit could have real musical consequences, as when in Augsburg in 1777 the composer improvised a fugue on a subject given to him by a monk and presented it in *cancrizans*, which Mozart described as 'arseways'.[44]

All these game-like manipulations disguised Mozart's identity, which the composer could conceal or reveal in manifold ways. The randomizing rearrangement of letters and words in his letters did betray a method, for the 'reshuffling [was] usually symmetrical or ... governed by other rules, for instance, exchanging the first and last word, or two inner ones'.[45] And so, after compiling an extensive, alphabetical list of his 'friends' (some fictitious), Mozart closed his letter of 26 November 1777 to his father with this disjointed bit of prose, deftly translated by Emily Anderson to mimic its syntactic dislocations: 'I can't write

---

[38] Ibid., 672.

[39] See Solomon (1985); Winternitz (1958), 208; and Karhausen (2011), 149–50.

[40] Karhausen (2011), 149.

[41] See also his letter of 13 November 1780, Anderson (1985), 662; and the concert aria K 369, with its acrostic on 'favorita', Rushton (2006), 83.

[42] Letter of 14 October 1777, Anderson (1985), 316.

[43] Ibid., 240. See also Leopold's letter of 1 November 1777 to his son, and Wolfgang's letter to his mother of 31 January 1778, Anderson (1985), 354 and 457.

[44] Letter of 23 October 1777, ibid., 339.

[45] Winternitz (1958), 208.

anything sensible today, as I am rails off the quite. Papa be annoyed not must. I that just like today feel. I help it cannot. Warefell. I gish you nood-wight. Sound sleeply. Next time I'll sensible more writely'.[46] Sometimes these reorderings simulated (or parodied?) musical forms, as in refrain-like recurrences of an individual word, which Winternitz labels the 'rondo device, the interruption of his prose at almost equal intervals by the same word or short phrase repeated over and over again'.[47] Or, for the alphabetical series of Mozart's friends mentioned above, we might add the variation principle – the long list impresses as a burst of verbal riffs on a common theme. In Mozart's music and life, the ever-changing combinations of the one mirrored the disjunctions of the other, even if the composer's epistolary style suggested the 'hasty exhalation[s] of a person hardly able to catch his breath, not the marble respiration of an idealized, fictitious figure'[48] capable of creating profound masterpieces of Western music.

∽ ii

Another significant aspect of Mozart's life – his embrace of Freemasonry – has encouraged scholars to investigate whether the composer was a 'refined numerologist'.[49] On 14 December 1784 he was initiated as an apprentice into the Viennese lodge *Zur Wohltätigkeit* (*Charity*). He quickly rose to become a mason at the lodge *Zur wahren Eintracht* (*True Concord*, on 7 January 1785), then a Master Mason (by 22 April, when his father, Leopold, achieved the same rank). Also relevant, on 11 February 1785 Joseph Haydn was admitted to *Zur wahren Eintracht*. Mozart was unable to attend this ceremony,[50] but the following day a remarkable gathering took place at his residence, where Haydn joined Mozart and two other Masons to read through the new set of six string quartets Mozart dedicated to Haydn. They included the storied 'Dissonance' Quartet in C major, K 465, which triggered debates among theorists well into the nineteenth century. It begins with a lament-like Adagio introduction of twenty-two chromatically magnified bars, among the most dissonant Mozart conceived. Their abrasive cross relations impelled Giuseppe Sarti to admonish that listeners required 'ears lined with iron'.[51] How to make sense of the slow introduction, which, when the Allegro movement proper commences,

---

[46] Anderson (1985), 392.
[47] Winternitz (1958), 212. See Mozart's letter of 19 May 1770, Anderson (1985), 138.
[48] Konrad (2015), 1.
[49] Grattan-Guinness (1992a), 201.
[50] See Irmen (1996), 87ff., 98ff.
[51] See Vertrees (1974).

paradoxically resolves into a luminous, translucent exposition in C major, conspicuous for its elevation of consonance?

Hans-Josef Irmen has read this quartet as a direct response to Mozart's initiation into Freemasonry, that 'system of morals, wrapped in allegories and illuminated by symbols'.[52] For Irmen the deepest levels of the quartet become apparent through numerological analysis of groups of pitches in the Adagio that, when summed, spell out pertinent words related to Masonic rituals. Thus, in the first nine bars the first violin part dispenses eighteen notes, the numerical sum of the word 'acacia'. Mentioned in the ceremony for Mozart's promotion to Master Mason, it refers to a branch that in biblical times marked the grave of Adoniram, to whom Solomon had assigned the building of the temple[53]:

$$A \quad c \quad a \quad c \quad i \quad a$$
$$1 \; +3 \; +1 \; +3 \; +9 \; +1 \; = 18$$

Other numerological acrobatics yield more encoded words, such as 'coffin' (for part of his initiation Mozart was placed in an open coffin), 'death', and by counting the notes of the entire Adagio, the name of the composer's lodge, 'Zur Wohlthätigkeit'.[54] But might these sundry calculations amount to mere happenstance? Irmen is perhaps on firmer ground in examining the title page of the six 'Haydn' quartets, issued late in 1785 by the Viennese firm of Carlo Artaria, Mozart's principal publisher and fellow Mason. Framing the page with its dedication are 'two continuously intertwined ribbons, a symbol known from the ancient mystery cults of Egypt and transmitted in Apuleius' *Metamorphoses* [*The Golden Ass*]',[55] all of which influenced Mozart's most overtly Masonic work from the end of his life, the Singspiel *Die Zauberflöte* (*The Magic Flute*, 1791). For Irmen, the meaning of the framing border is clear enough: 'whatever the quartets enclose is intended only for the initiated'.

If shorn of the most conjectural numerological claims, a Masonic interpretation of the 'Dissonance' Quartet might explain its extraordinary juxtaposition of competing types of music. The laboured slow introduction could represent the trials of the blindfolded postulant, who experiences a symbolic death; the subsequent, affirming turn to C major could mark the triumph of Masonic ideals of benevolence, enlightened knowledge and blissful happiness as he is raised from the coffin and his blindfold removed.[56] Surely the novice initiate

---

[52] Irmen (1996), 7.
[53] Ibid., 99, 114.
[54] Ibid., 99.
[55] Ibid., 100.
[56] See further, Chailley (1970), 84–5.

Haydn would not have missed the symbolism, though he seems not to have pursued Masonic elements in his own music. But Mozart, of course, did, first by composing several works specifically for his lodge, and second, by collaborating on *Die Zauberflöte* with the impresario Emanuel Schikaneder, who had belonged to a lodge in Regensburg.

Not surprisingly, Mozart's late masterpiece has received its full measure of Masonic readings.[57] There is no need to detail its uncontroversial imagery – in the overture, the use of the Masonic key of three flats, E-flat major; the knocking of the petitioner on the temple door, represented by the three chords heard at the opening, then in the middle by the winds, which introduce the characteristic anapaestic rhythm; and the invocation of fugal counterpoint for the trials of the candidate, reenacted in the second act by Tamino and Pamina. But what tests our credulity further is the attempt to discern numerological agents at work in the score.

For Irmen, the 'text of the *Magic Flute* is an astounding linguistic construction that does not only convey the meaning comprehensible on the surface, but also serves to give the musical notation a meta-language which remains veiled from the eyes of the public'.[58] Did Mozart activate that language in his score? For Ivor Grattan-Guinness, the answer is a resounding yes. Drawing upon ancient Egyptian mythology, he begins by identifying primary and secondary groups of significant numbers (3, 6, 5, 8, 2 and 18; and 4, 7 and 30). Of the first group, 'the most dominant was 3, and carried a masculine significance also held by 6; 5 and 8 were feminine; 2 took symbolic forms, especially opposites (male/female, sun/moon, etc.); and 18 held "higher", quasi-religious connotations'.[59] Of the secondary group, '4 is represented especially by the Four Elements which serve as base for the trials undergone by Tamino, Pamina, and Papageno', while '7 takes its place here from … the 7-fold shield of the sun to represent true knowledge, which the [Queen of the Night] instructs Monostatos to steal from Sarastro'.[60] Finally, supplementing these two groups are triangular or pyramidal numbers that periodically come into play, that is, 'sums of integers from 1 onwards'; one in particular, 10, is the pyramidal number to 4 (1 + 2 + 3 + 4 = 10). Furthermore, the trio of 6: 8: 10 represents the Masonic square, a right-angled triangle used by craftsmen who built the medieval cathedrals, and a well-known symbol of Masonic guilds.

Grattan-Guinness adduces considerable 'evidence' to support privileging these numbers. Thus, the Queen of the Night's first aria (No. 4, 'Zum Leiden bin

---

[57] For instance, Nettl (1957), Chailley (1992) and Buch (2004).
[58] Irmen (1996), 249.
[59] Grattan-Guiness (1992a), 205.
[60] Ibid., 206.

Ex. 7.5: Mozart, *Die Zauberflöte*, Overture (1791)

ich auserkoren') projects the feminine side in a melody that divides its opening phrase into 5 + 5 pitches, while her rage aria in Act II (No. 14, 'Der Hölle Rache kocht in meinem Herzen') has a text of eight lines that Mozart sometimes sets in groups of five or eight notes, again emphasizing the feminine. Similarly, 6 and 18 seem relevant for Sarastro – 'the number 18 and its factors feature all over Sarastro's part'.[61] And even the fugal subject of the overture, which draws upon 4, 6 and 8 (ex. 7.5), is not exempt from the accumulating sums.

Grattan-Guinness finds meaning too in the total number of pitches of the subject, 36, the pyramidal number for 8. But once again, are these highlighted relationships evidence of a deliberate numerological design? Do they substantively add to Masonic interpretations of Mozart's Singspiel?

In a recent reevaluation of *Die Zauberflöte*, David Buch has offered a rebuff, arguing that while the libretto and score might obliquely refer to elements of Freemasonry, there is no hard evidence that Schikaneder or Mozart intended to create a 'pervasive masonic allegory'.[62] Instead, Buch proposed fairy-tale operas as sources for many of the numerological and mythological trappings. However one assesses the meanings of *Die Zauberflöte*, its enduring influence is beyond dispute, for it soon inspired reactions, dramatic and musical. The Mason Goethe, for one, began work on an allegorical sequel, to be set as a Singspiel by Paul Wranitzky, but ultimately released as a closet drama in 1807.[63] Before Goethe progressed far, the librettist of Mozart's opera, Schikaneder, conceived his own sequel. *Das Labyrinth oder Der Kampf mit den Elementen: Der Zauberflöte zweyter Theil* (*The Labyrinth or The Struggle with the Elements: The Magic Flute, Part II*) premiered in Vienna in 1798, with Schikaneder reprising his role as Papageno.[64] The composer was Peter von Winter, whose overture began with the ceremonial threefold series of chords; the prominent Mozartean imagery associated with Papageno, including the 'pan-pipe

---

[61] Ibid., 219.

[62] Buch (2004), 219. Possibly among the adherents was Jules Verne, whose novel *Les indes noires* (*The Black Indies*, 1877), has been interpreted as a Masonic allegory modelled on Mozart's Singspiel. Lamy (2007), 51–62.

[63] Wolfgang Amadeus Mozart, *Die Zauberflöte. Oper in zwei Aufzügen. Dichtung von Emanuel Schikaneder. Im Anhang Szenen aus Der Zauberflöte zweiter Teil. Ein Fragment von Johann Wolfgang Goethe* (Stuttgart: 1979), 71–80.

[64] See Henderson (1983).

flourishes and glockenspiel trimmings',[65] was not far behind. Whether the labyrinth further allegorized the idea of Masonic trials remained open to debate,[66] but Goethe revealed his own view in 1827, when he commented to Johann Peter Eckermann, 'Let the crowd of spectators take pleasure in the spectacle; the higher import will not escape the initiated, as has been the case with the "Magic Flute", and other things beside'.[67]

∽ iii

If Masonic readings readily accrued to Mozart's music,[68] the same was not the case with 'Papa' Haydn. Unlike the Mozarts, Haydn did not resort to cryptography in his correspondence, but his brother, whose career transpired largely in Salzburg, did invent a musical alphabet of his own[69] (ex. 7.6).

Ex. 7.6: Michael Haydn, Cipher Key

---

[65] Ibid.
[66] For Henderson, 'no evidence exists to suggest that either Schikaneder or Winter intended to convey any Masonic message', ibid., 202.
[67] Eckermann (2022), 184 (29 January 1827).
[68] Grattan-Guinness proposed that Mozart's final trilogy of symphonies (1788), composed during his thirty-third year, reflect Masonic symbolism: 'Now 33 was an extremely significant number in the Austrian Masonic tradition – probably as the supposed years in Jesus's life in the orthodox interpretation of the Bible … Thus it was imperative for an ardent Mason to do something fundamental in that year; so for Mozart a 3, and of a major form in music, would be a suitable response'. Grattan-Guinness (1992b), 2–3.
[69] Rettensteiner (2006), 52–3, 61.

Ex. 7.7: Michael Haydn, Cipher

B l e i b e n   S i   e

i   m m e   r   m e i n

F   r   e u n d   !

Exploiting a chromatic scale of twenty-eight pitches (including enharmonic spellings) and specifying crotchets for lower-case and minims for upper-case letters, Michael Haydn was able to encode correspondence to his circle in a distinctive, if rudderless form of musical Babel. He made provisions for umlauts (two-note slurred quavers) and even for punctuation marks, so that a semibreve rest might silently mask an emphatic exclamation mark, as in ex. 7.7.

An unusual, early instance of Joseph Haydn's manipulation of letters occurred in 1767, when he completed the cantata *Applausus*, for the anniversary of a Cistercian abbot who had professed monastic vows in Zwettl, Austria. Haydn's score is an allegory about theology and the virtues of temperance, prudence, justice and fortitude, but what attracts our attention is an inscription at the end of the autograph: 'hVnC appLaVsVM feCIt joseph haIDn' ('Joseph Haidn created this Applausus').[70] Here the composer certified his authorship by designing an anagrammatic chronogram, highlighting the relevant letters in upper-case script so that, when placed in proper order, they spelled out 1767, the year of composition (MDCCLVVVII = 1767). To accomplish this goal, he rendered the letter 'u' three times as a 'v', and altered his name, replacing the 'y' with an 'i', lest the year erroneously appear as 1766.

We have already mentioned Haydn's use of a palindrome in Symphony No. 47 (1772; p. 19). In 1791 Haydn revisited retrogression, albeit in a quite different context – settings of the decalogue. For the First Commandment, he apportioned a puzzle canon on three concentric staves of continuous music that could be realized in clockwise or counterclockwise direction, or, by turning the music upside down, in clockwise or counterclockwise motion as well (see Illustration 7.2).[71]

---

[70] Vienna, Gesellschaft der Musikfreunde Sign 111 2724 /1 (Q855).
[71] See further Beduschi (2013).

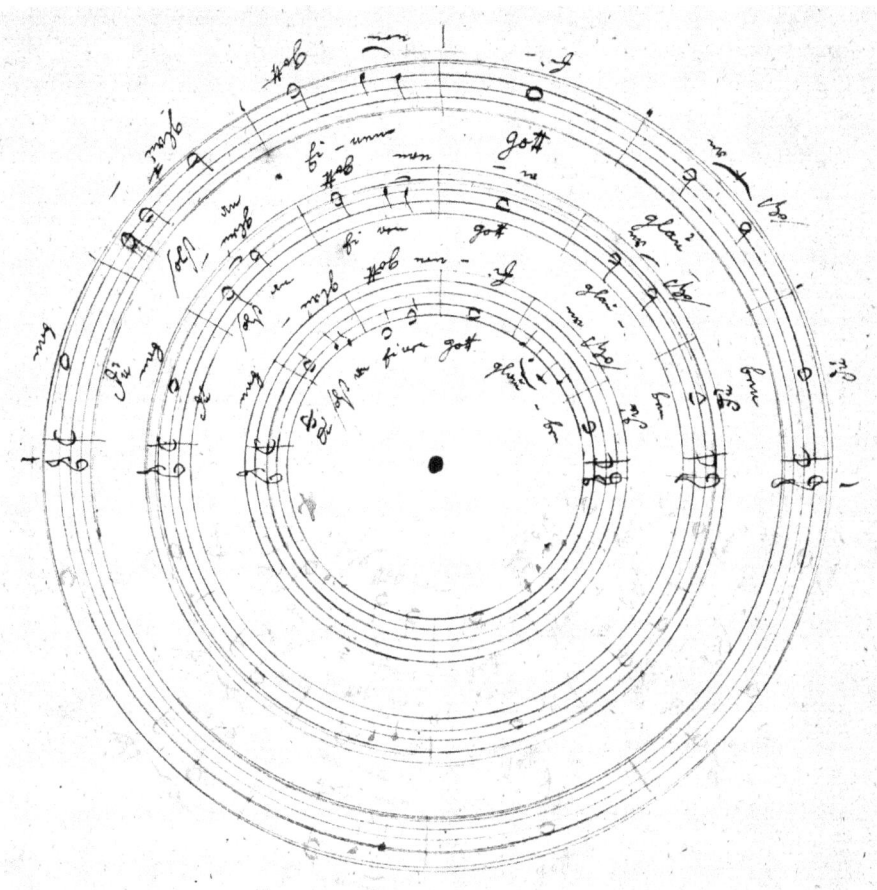

Illustration 7.2: Joseph Haydn, First Commandment (1791), autograph, Mary Flagler Cary Music Collection (The Morgan Library & Museum, New York)

We can situate Haydn's manuscript in the long tradition of puzzle canons that privileged graphic designs.[72] His choice of strict imitation for the Commandments plays on the etymology of the term canon (Greek for 'rule') so that, in the case of the First Commandment, the circular layout accommodates a perpetual canon relating to the idea of divine perfection. The visual riddle recalls too the rich history of verbal canons and their early zenith in the Renaissance polyphony of Franco-Flemish composers (see Chapter 4).

Between 1757 and 1781, Padre G. B. Martini, a celebrated pedagogue who mentored Mozart, sought to document the tradition by publishing *Storia della musica* in three volumes. Though his history treated only the music

---

[72] See Chapter 2, p. 19, and Schiltz (2015), 279–301.

of antiquity, Martini adorned the beginnings and endings of chapters with some seventy illustrative vignettes, all displaying enigmatic canons prefaced by Latin mottoes drawn from classical poets, biblical verses and Renaissance theorists, with some referencing specific works by Ockeghem, Obrecht and Josquin. Then, in the nineteenth century the composer Luigi Cherubini took up Martini's gauntlet, solved all the canons, and notated their solutions in an autograph now in the Bibliothèque Nationale, Paris, recently available in a modern edition.[73]

Be that as it may, there may be other riddles in Haydn's vast oeuvre still awaiting decipherment. For instance, in 1986 László Somfai proposed that the 'Emperor' String Quartet, Op. 76 No. 3, which he read as a quartet *in tempore belli*, was one candidate.[74] At its centre stood the variation movement on the 'Emperor's Hymn', originally composed in 1797 by Haydn for the birthday of Francis II, the last Holy Roman Emperor. Somfai proposed that Haydn encoded the first letters from the hymn's opening line of text, '**G**ott **e**rhalte **F**ranz **d**en **K**aiser', as a cipher in the first violin at the outset of the work, where the composer modified 'K' to 'C' (Caesar), yielding the pitches G-E-F-D-C (ex. 7.8).

To fortify this imperial cipher, he then introduced dotted rhythms in a series of rising scales, a familiar musical topic associated with royalty. Extending the encipherment further, Somfai wondered whether in the development the prominent turn to the mediant, E major, announced by rustic drones in the cello and viola, might refer to the Esterházy princes, the Hungarian nobility closely allied with the Habsburg emperors, and, of course, Haydn's employers. Sure enough, the mediant passage displays too its share of dotted rhythms and markers of the *style hongrois*. In effect, Somfai interprets the first movement as a proto-cipher composition, an homage to Francis II that culminates in the finale, where we encounter dramatic battle music in C minor that inevitably gives way to a victorious conclusion in C major, reviving the telltale rhythms of the original motto from the first movement. But all these readings come with caveats. For one, despite the convenient *pitch alignments* of the original five-note motto with the text of the *Kaiser* hymn, their *rhythms* do not correspond to those of the hymn (ex. 7.9).

If Haydn intended to explore musical encipherments in this quartet, he appears not to have proceeded much further beyond the motto, with its veiled pitch references to the hymn text. The motto itself remains a gesture in search of a theme, which fully materializes only in the second movement.

---

[73] Beduschi (2023).
[74] Somfai (1986).

Ex. 7.8: Joseph Haydn, String Quartet in C major, Op. 76 No. 3, Cipher (1799)

Ex. 7.9: Joseph Haydn, String Quartet in C major, Op. 76 No. 3, 'Emperor's Hymn' (1799)

☙ *iv*

There remains to discuss two events in Haydn's reception history: twice in the twentieth century, his surname spawned clusters of piano pieces constructed from a shared H-A-Y-D-N cipher, first in Paris, during the centenary of his death (1909), then in London, during the semiquincentennial of his birth (1982). By the time of his death 'Papa' Haydn had achieved a durable fame that crossed national borders, impelling Napoleon, then occupying Vienna, to post an honour guard before the composer's residence. Nonetheless, the efflorescence of Romanticism effectively dismantled his reputation through one dismissive cliché after another. 'Roguish', 'childlike' and 'old-worldly' were applied to characterize Haydn's music as thin insofar as emotional content was concerned, and the composer himself as a naïve optimist and wig-adorned servant of the *ancien régime*.[75] Haydn's music was increasingly forgotten until its revival in the twentieth century.

The prime mover behind this effort in France, where a strain of neo-Classicism took hold, was Jules Écorcheville, who studied composition with César Franck in Paris and the nascent field of *Musikwissenschaft* with Hugo Riemann in Leipzig. Ultimately, Écorcheville endured trench warfare before perishing during the First World War in 1915. But six years before, he invited eight composers to contribute cipher pieces for the centenary to the *Revue Musicale de la S.I.M.* Of these, Claude Debussy (*Hommage à Haydn*), Paul Dukas (*Prélude élegaïque*), Reynaldo Hahn (*Thème varié sur le nom d'Haydn*), Vincent d'Indy

---

[75] Proksch (2015), 7.

Ex. 7.10: 'Haydn' Cipher

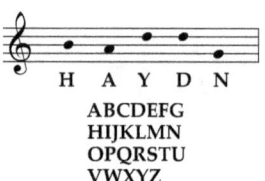

(*Menuet sur le nom d'Haydn*), Maurice Ravel (*Menuet sur le nom d'Haydn*) and Charles-Marie Widor (*Fugue sur le nom d'Haydn*) accepted, while Gabriel Fauré and Camille Saint-Saëns declined.[76] The cipher specified for Haydn's name (B-A-D-D-G) derived from the *clef allemande* shown in ex. 7.10, which retained German conventions for B (B-flat) and H (B-natural), and transformed Y and N to D and G.

H-A-Y-D-N proved musically pliable, for it required only diatonic pitches from the scale of G major; not surprisingly, five of the six composers chose this tonality, while Dukas added another sharp to the key signature of his elegiac *Prélude*, so that it concluded in D major.

On hearing these pieces, listeners encounter diverse styles with few references to Haydn's music. In this regard the variations of Reynaldo Hahn, a Venezuelan composer known for his popular songs, approached Haydn's idiomatic style most closely. Hahn's *thème* falls symmetrically into four-bar phrases, of which the last reaffirms the initial cadential gesture, closing a circular process that Haydn sometimes used to construct his own themes. Moreover, Hahn's pastiche-like variations submit to conventional triadic analysis without challenging the norms of Classical tonality. Similarly, Widor's scurrying three-part fugue on Haydn's name effectively transports us to the eighteenth century, reviving memories perhaps of the fugue in Haydn's String Quartet in C major, Op. 20 No. 2 (1772), though soon enough Widor submerges his diatonic subject in a fluid chromaticism reflective more of his own age.

The remaining four offerings show ample signs of their own decade. Paul Dukas's *Prélude*, for instance, begins with languorously drifting, impressionist sonorities that are tonally ill defined, even as they attempt to undergird the cipher slowly emerging in the upper voice. Of the six contributors, Dukas quotes H-A-Y-D-N most sparingly: it appears but a handful of times, and, indeed, ultimately without its final pitch, G, so that the subdued, D major ending seems somehow contrived. D'Indy's *Menuet*, on the other hand, offers clearer tonal definition: he juxtaposes a minuet in G major with a contrasting

---

[76] Ibid., 81ff.

trio in E-flat major, though in both sections the structural triads appear with supplemental pan-diatonic pitches; thus, the final 'tonic' contains an added A, allowing d'Indy to integrate the complete cipher vertically into the harmony.

Maurice Ravel's *Menuet sur le nom d'Haydn* betrays neo-Classical leanings in its fastidiously balanced phrases. Thus, the opening sixteen-bar period divides evenly into identical eight-bar halves, each of which breaks into two four-bar portions. On the other hand, offsetting this revival of Haydnesque symmetries is Ravel's harmonic language, which again draws liberally on pan-diatonic sonorities refined from the motto itself. What is more, Ravel pursues the potential of the cipher considerably further than his colleagues by insinuating into the middle of the dance retrograde and retrograde-inverted variants, revealing Ravel to be the most cryptographically minded of the six composers.

The outlier of the centenary offerings is Debussy's *Hommage à Haydn*, which, from the perspective of form, is the freest of the collection. While Debussy's colleagues unequivocally invoke eighteenth-century genres (theme and variations, minuet, fugue), Debussy offers what he describes as a 'slow waltz' (*valse lente*). Here we find two leisurely statements of the cipher, before the tempo abruptly shifts to *Vif*, when the cipher abruptly morphs into an obsessive *idée fixe*, methodically spinning dozens of iterations through nimble passagework. Near the end Debussy restores the slow waltz, but only for two bars, before the work evaporates in a fleeting whiff. Aside from the densely enciphered nomenclature, there is little in this music to suggest a link to Haydn or some neo-Classical strategy. Indeed, one wonders whether Debussy's personal views of Haydn align with remarks the French composer made in the 'Open Letter to the Chevalier W. Gluck', where Monsieur Croche pointedly asks: 'Is it more elegant to please King Louis XIV than to please society under the Third Republic? … Your art was essentially in the grand ceremonious style. Common people only participated at a distance … You represented to them, as it were, a wall behind which something was happening'.[77]

By 1982, modern Haydn scholarship had advanced immeasurably with the appearance of Anthony van Hoboken's catalogue, just shy of two thousand pages, finished in 1978.[78] Following this monument came another, the first complete Haydn edition, issued in 113 volumes between 1958 and 2018. When the BBC commissioned musical tributes to Haydn, six English composers answered the call,[79] at least one of them with expertise in Haydn's music, the

---

[77] *Monsieur Croche the Dilettante Hater*, in *Three Classics in the Aesthetic of Music*, trans. B. A. Langdon Davies (New York: 1962), 68–9.

[78] *Joseph Haydn, Thematisch-bibliographisches Werkverzeichnis* (Munich: 1957–78).

[79] George Benjamin, Richard Rodney Bennett, Lennox Berkeley, R. S. Johnson, John McCabe and Edmund Rubbra.

composer/pianist John McCabe, who had recorded the fifty-two keyboard sonatas. McCabe's singular contribution for the 1982 festivities was a *Lamentation Rag*, in his words, 'a lugubrious piece that is softly ragtime, but never really becomes pastiche'. The title referred to Haydn's Symphony No. 26 in D minor (*Lamentatione*), a *Sturm und Drang* work written for Easter probably in 1768. The syncopations of its first movement now reemerged in McCabe's right-hand melody, displaced by a semiquaver against a regular stride rag accompaniment in the left hand. McCabe informs us that 'the melodic line of this short piece [was] entirely derived from the musical transliteration of the name FRANZ JOSEPH HAYDN'. To accomplish that conjuring, McCabe dispensed with the German convention of 'h' as B-natural, and derived his cipher as shown in ex. 7.11, with two slight adjustments for 'a' and 'e'.

Thus, 'Franz' became F-D-A-flat-G-E-*flat*, with the 'a' and 'e' bent to A-flat and E-flat; 'Joseph', C-A-*flat*-E-*flat*-E-B-*flat*-A, with the 'a' 'e', and 'b' lowered; and 'Haydn', A-A-D-D-G, where 'H' was enciphered as A, rather than B-natural, according to the German system. The senior representative of Viennese high Classicism experienced a new incarnation, and made the considerable leap from a courtly symphony composed for the Esterházy prince to the swaying rhythms of twentieth-century ragtime (ex. 7.12).

Of the remaining BBC contributions, three revived the H-A-Y-D-N cipher created by Écorcheville in 1909 – Edmund Rubbra in *Invention on the Name of*

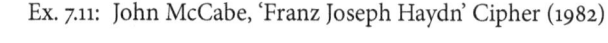

Ex. 7.11: John McCabe, 'Franz Joseph Haydn' Cipher (1982)

Ex. 7.12: John McCabe, *Lamentation Rag* (1982)

Haydn, Op. 160; Richard Rodney Bennett in *Impromptu on the Name of Haydn*; and George Benjamin in *Meditation on Haydn's Name*. Bennett and Benjamin underscored the cipher rhythmically by segregating it into quintuplets, Bennett through gently undulating patterns from which the cipher emerges in the soprano, and Benjamin through an arpeggiated, fixed sonority of five pitches that remains a constant harmonic ostinato.

One other English composer paid homage to Haydn in 1982, the eccentric Robert Simpson, who revisited Haydn's palindromic Minuet from Symphony No. 47 to new extremes in the imposing String Quartet No. 9. Simpson retained intact Haydn's G major theme, including its retrograde, before launching into thirty-two variations, all observing the original binary form, and culminating in a fugue. After the opening theme, Simpson abandoned Classical tonality to pursue a language largely atonal and yet tethered to a pitch-centric plan that largely descended and ascended by whole tones,[80] enabling him to visit all twelve key centres. Motivic scraps of Haydn's minuet melody circulated freely, setting in motion the paradox of winding and rewinding, of revealing and masking that, like the contrived HAYDN ciphers, engaged with the height of modernism in the early 1980s.

---

[80] G, F, E-flat, D-flat, B, A, G, A-flat, B-flat, C, D, E, F-sharp and G.

CHAPTER 8

Censors, *Unsinn*, Nominal Ciphers and *Solrésol*

'If only [the censor] knew about what they were thinking in their music!'

– Grillparzer

EXEMPLIFYING the temper of the times, in 1804 a physician from Lower Saxony, Johann Jacob Heinrich Buecking, released *Anweisung zur geheimen Correspondenz systematisch entworfen* (*Instructions for Secret Correspondence, Systematically Designed*). His manual appeared just before an exhausted Europe lost its grip on a lull in the Napoleonic conflagrations. Buecking's intent was to offer readers ways to encipher messages by exploiting the alphabet: 'With 20–30 letters one could label every idea capable of being grasped and developed and describe it for millions ... For 24 letters could be varied in 2,585,201,673,884,976,640,000 ways, so that they did not follow each other in the exact same order, and so that one letter in each series only appeared once'.[1]

Observing the potential of musical notation as an encrypting device, Buecking included one example on a supplementary plate. In the master key each letter of the alphabet appeared with a short musical motive of three to six notes, with rhythmic values chosen to fill one bar of triple time each (ex. 8.1).

To render the encoded message – the word 'Freund' ('friend') – less susceptible to discovery, he framed it with a few 'null' bars. Those who 'knew' their J. S. Bach would be bemused to find in the penultimate bar of ex. 8.2 a quotation from the Minuet in G major in the Anna Magdalena Bach Notebook, BWV Anh 116 (authorship now uncertain). In this way, one could render 'Freund' as music, 'constructing' the concealed word one letter at a time, a technique somewhat reminiscent of the *ars combinatoria* examined in Chapter 7. So long as the combined prefabricated motives did not generate irremediable ruptures in the musical syntax, Buecking's ruse would likely pass unchallenged, allowing 'now

---

[1] Buecking (1804), 16.

Ex. 8.1: J. J. H. Buecking, *Anweisung zur geheimen Correspondenz* (1804)

Ex. 8.2: J. J. H. Buecking, *Anweisung zur geheimen Correspondenz* (1804)

arias, now rondos and minuets' to materialize that communicated stealthily through their literally 'unspeakable alterations'[2]:

The same year, a spectacular ceremony attended by Pius VII transpired in the Cathedral of Notre Dame in Paris, where on 2 December Napoleon crowned himself Emperor of the French. Though a *cabinet noir* ('black chamber') dedicated to decrypting intercepted intelligence was at his disposal, Napoleon remained sceptical: 'To draw the truth from this mass of chaotic reports is something vouchsafed only to a superior understanding; mediocre ones are lost therein, they tend to believe that the enemy is here rather than there and proceed to evaluate available reports in accordance with their wishes. In this way they commit grave errors that are quite capable of wrecking entire armies and even countries'.[3] Instead, Napoleon preferred to glean information about his enemies' troop movements from the relatively unrestricted English press.[4] Eight years later, at the high watermark of his empire, he invaded Russia, a disastrous campaign hampered by the severe winter of 1812, and superior intelligence assets of the tsar. When the decimated *grande armée* eventually staggered back to France, the largest military force yet assembled in history had lost at least two thirds of its strength.

That same year there appeared in Paris a modest pamphlet titled *Stigmatographie, ou l'art d'écrire avec des points, suivie de la Mélographie, nouvelle manière de noter la musique* (*Stigmatography, or the Art of Writing with Points,*

---

[2] Ibid., 45–6.

[3] Van Creveld (1985), 68.

[4] Andrew (2018), 340.

Followed by Melography, a New Manner of Notating Music).[5] Its author was the pianist/composer Auguste Bertini (1780–1830), who sometime between 1799 and 1804 had dedicated a piano sonata to Napoleon, then acting as 'First Consul'.[6] Accompanying it was a servile preface proclaiming him 'the greatest man of this century'. Musically uninspired, the clichéd march-like rhythms of the sonata impress as a transparent attempt to curry favour with the regime, and yet may help us contextualize the pamphlet of 1812. Like Buecking's *Anweisung*, Bertini's *Stigmatographie/Mélographie* reflected the persistent tremors of a revolutionary age, in particular its constant need to design through cryptography new ways to camouflage secrets.

To 'write with points' Bertini proposed using paper printed with dozens of rows of dots, on which the vowels and consonants of relevant words could be encrypted from two keys. In lieu of dots, one could also resort to music paper, in which case a needle could accurately puncture holes on the lines and spaces of the staves. Yet another option communicated the steganographic message through the ten fingers, in a modern adaptation of the Guidonian hand,[7] in which the five digits of the left hand formed the vowels, and the five of the right, the consonants. Bertini's other invention, *Mélographie*, began with a set of twelve symbols for the pitches of the chromatic scale, supplemented by additional symbols for rhythms, metrical relationships and dynamics. To demonstrate, he concluded by transcribing the popular children's song 'Ah! vous dirai-je, Maman' into his new system (see Illustration 8.1).

Meanwhile, on the other side of the warring nations, Napoleon's elevation from First Consul to hereditary emperor sent shock waves throughout the allies, including the imperial Viennese court, where the Habsburg emperor, Francis II, implemented new procedures to safeguard his reign. Terrified of political instability, Francis directed agents to spy on his own family, and was purportedly suspicious enough of Beethoven's compositions to comment, 'there is something revolutionary about the music'.[8] Attempting to forestall the inevitable – twice French troops occupied Vienna, in 1805 and 1809 – and in 1806 Francis II, pressured by Napoleon, renounced his title as Holy Roman Emperor to become Francis I, Emperor of Austria – the increasingly paranoid ruler initiated a 're-censorship' campaign to quash eruptions of revolutionary fever wherever they might occur.

---

[5] Bibliothèque Nationale Inventaire Vm8 1158.

[6] Piano Sonata in C major, Op. 2.

[7] See p. 120.

[8] Attributed to Johann Doležálek in Kopitz and Cadenbach (2009), vol. 1, 258.

Illustration 8.1: Auguste Bertini, *Mélographie, nouvelle Manière de noter la musique* (1812), p. 11 (Paris, Bibliothèque Nationale)

The campaign's charge was broad, for censorship 'now extended to virtually everything written, including inscriptions on fans, toys, and snuffboxes'.[9] Retroactively the censors proscribed 2,500 books that had already earned the stamp 'admittitur' ('it is admitted'). In relatively short order, the administrative apparatus tightly restricted intellectual liberties until 1848, when the wave of mid-century revolutions succeeded for a while in dissolving Austrian censorship altogether.

Not surprisingly, the censors' authority produced capricious results. Joseph Carl Bernard, an editor at the *Wiener Zeitung* and friend of Beethoven, opined in one of the conversation books, 'The censors here don't have any rules; they make deletions merely according to their own opinion, so as not to be responsible for anything'.[10] Literary celebrities became entangled in the censors' nets, including C. M. Wieland, Franz Grillparzer, Madame de Staël, Friedrich Schlegel and Lord Byron. In 1820 Byron vented from Austrian-controlled Italy to his publisher John Murray: 'Of the state of things here it would be difficult and not very prudent to speak at large, the Huns opening all letters: I wonder if they can read them when they have opened them? If so, they may see … that I think them damned scoundrels and barbarians, their emperor a fool, and themselves more fools than he.'[11]

In 1823 Grillparzer shared with Beethoven the sanguine sentiment that the 'censor cannot harm musicians. If only [the censor] knew about what they were thinking in their music!'[12] But censors *did* directly affect musicians – the premiere of Beethoven's opera *Leonore* was delayed in 1805, and officials balked at the titles of Schubert's Singspiel *Die Verschworenen* (*The Conspirators*, 1823) and final stage effort, the unfinished *Der Graf von Gleichen* (*Count von Gleichen*, 1827; *gleich* can mean 'equal'). In Beethoven's case we may gain further insights by browsing through the *Konversationshefte*, 139 slender volumes which he kept from 1818 for his visitors to record their conversations with him, to which he responded orally. Readers of these documents encounter an aimless 'stream of consciousness without any immediately perceptible relationship to specific place or time'[13]; still, though Beethoven's segments of the dialogues are irretrievably lost, occasionally we obtain some revealing glimpses of his private world, and the realities of Viennese life during the post-Napoleonic

---

[9] Ingrao (2000), 231.
[10] 18 April 1820; Albrecht (2018–2019), ii, 152.
[11] Dowden (1955), 68.
[12] Köhler and Beck (1983), 288.
[13] Albrecht (2020), vol. 3, xix.

Restoration. Thus, in March 1820 Bernard recorded a conversation he had with Beethoven's student Carl Czerny: '[he] told me that the Abbé Gelinek has fulminated at length about them at the Camel [Restaurant]; he said you were a second Sand, [and] that they complained about the Emperor, about the Archduke, about the ministers, and that they would end up on the gallows'.[14] Here the pianist/composer Joseph Gelinek compared his arch-foe to Karl Sand, the German political activist who in 1819 assassinated the reactionary playwright August von Kotzebue, triggering the Carlsbad Decrees that abolished student associations (*Burschenschaften*), further regulated the press and bolstered the surveillance of citizens.

Regrettably, Beethoven's response to Bernard has not survived, but other entries in the conversation books betray the composer's republican sympathies. And so, in 1820 the educator Joseph Blöchinger von Bannholz noted three assertions, separated by lines to cue Beethoven's oral replies:

Now it is again miserable.

———————

It was earlier much better, NB. Before 1813.

———————

The *aristocrats* found support once more in Austria, and the *republican spirit* only just glows in the ashes.[15]

In the case of Beethoven's letter written to the poet G. F. Treitschke *ca.* February 1814, we do not have to read between the lines to tease out Beethoven's political opinions, for here we find this telling comment: 'better to deal with artists than with the Great ones (the small and minuscule)'.[16]

Still, if Beethoven's plain coiffure *à la Titus* and sartorial appearance projected republican sympathies,[17] he was not averse to celebrating the Austrian regime when it suited him. Thus, in November 1814 he organized a 'musikalische Akademie' in which he conducted the patriotic potboiler *Wellington's Victory* Symphony and *Der glorreiche Augenblick* (*The Glorious Moment*), a cantata 'written in fawning tribute to the Congress of Vienna'.[18] The text, by Aloys Weißenbach, is rife with platitudes, including in the fourth movement a reverential reference to Emperor Francis. In privileging celebratory choruses,

---

[14] Köhler and Beck (1972), vol. 1, 339.
[15] Ibid., 345–6; as trans. in Kinderman (2016), 39.
[16] Brandenburg (1996), Bd. 3, 11–12 (No. 699).
[17] See Kinderman (2016), 28–9.
[18] Ibid., 38.

Beethoven's music perhaps meant to allegorize the recent 'Battle of the Nations' in Leipzig, fought in 1813 by some 500,000 troops in unparalleled pitched combat that dealt Napoleon a profound defeat. But Beethoven's embrace of a public, ceremonial idiom in this work did not prevent Francis's agents from filing a confidential report about the composer: 'Factions *pro* and *contra* Beethoven are forming. Against von Rasumovsky, Apponyi [and] Kraft, who worship Beethoven, stands a wide majority surplus of connoisseurs who decline to hear music at all in Herr Beethoven's composition.'[19]

As Beethoven withdrew after the Congress of Vienna into his tomb of total deafness, so did the music of his last decade become increasingly experimental and cryptic. To his contemporaries Beethoven's late style was a vexing riddle in sound that discouraged even the most inquisitive from fathoming his new visions of musical expression and structure. Few, for instance, could make sense of the last cello sonata, Op. 102 No. 2 (1815), with its military fanfares in the first movement, lament-like chorale in the middle movement, and unconventional fugal finale, conceptualized, like the finale of the *Hammerklavier* Sonata Op. 106 (1818), 'with some licences' (*con alcune licenze*), and a level of dissonance surpassed only by the cacophonous remonstrations of the *Grosse Fuge*, Op. 133 (1826). Or, indeed, the late string quartets, displaying an anagrammatic use of motives; the ineffable, wordless *Heiliger Dankgesang* at the centre of Op. 132 (1825); and the puzzling motto that poses the fatalistic question 'Muß es sein?' ('Must it be?') in Op. 135 (1826).

The return to formal counterpoint in Beethoven's late period was one manifestation of his retreat into musical abstractions, as if purely cerebral processing somehow compensated for what his ears could no longer physically apprehend. In this rarefied world Beethoven considered composing an orchestral overture on BACH, yielding preliminary sketches in 1822, and a few more in 1824 and 1825. Gustav Nottebohm was the first to consider this project, now catalogued in the Beethoven *Verzeichnis* as *Unv* (Unfinished) 4.[20] But Nottebohm evidently missed that Beethoven had also woven the cipher into an earlier sketch for the *Agnus Dei* of the *Missa Solemnis*, that sprawling monument composed for his student Archduke Rudolf, installed in 1819 as the Archbishop of Olomouc. In a thematic notation of 1821 probably envisioned for the *Dona nobis pacem*,[21] Beethoven had embedded the telltale chromatic tetrachord, and identified it (ex. 8.3).

---

[19] Fournier (1913), 289.

[20] Nottebohm (1887), 577–80.

[21] Artaria 197, 62; see Beethoven (2010), vol. 2, 82.

Ex. 8.3: Beethoven, Sketch for *Missa solemnis*, 'Dona nobis pacem'

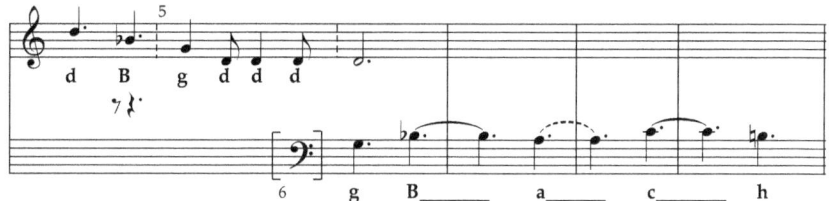

Ex. 8.4: Beethoven, *Grosse Fuge*, Op. 133 (1827)

We next encounter the cipher in the sketches Nottebohm briefly discussed. A few one and two-stave jottings display it prominently, and intimate possible options for a countersubject, but the project did not advance further.

Nevertheless, Peter McCallum has pointed out that in the *Grosse Fuge* of 1827, the BACH cipher literally appears in bars 28 and 29, where Beethoven disguises it in retrograde as HCAB (ex. 8.4).

There is other evidence that Beethoven 'was clearly engaged with the possibilities of permutational and retrograde variations of motives'.[22] We have already commented on one example in the String Quartet Op. 131 (see p. 25), but there are additional reorderings, as in the String Quartet in A minor, Op. 132. Here Beethoven announces the topic of counterpoint in the cello in the first two bars, with an imitative texture drawn from four pitches, G-sharp-A-F-E, that easily betray themselves as an anagram of the same Baroque subject in Op. 131, this time in the order 4, 2, 3, 1. Perhaps not coincidentally, the unison figure near the opening of Op. 133, B-flat-B-natural-A-flat-G, impresses as a slight expansion of the opening of Op. 132 (see ex. 8.4). Finally, Beethoven also posed anagrammatic riddles in the finale of the String Quartet Op. 127. The opening bars project HCAB once again (ex. 8.5), so that even if concealed, Bach's name hovers over Beethoven's late style.

Among the other puzzles of Beethoven's late style is the meaning of the extraordinary 'Heiliger Dankgesang eines genesenen an die Gottheit in der lydischen Tonart' ('Sacred Song of Thanks of a Convalescent to the Godhead

---

[22] McCallum (2009), 131.

Ex. 8.5: Beethoven, String Quartet in E-flat major, Op. 127, Finale (1827)

Ex. 8.6: 'Salvum me fac, Deus'

in the Lydian Mode') that forms the centre of Op. 132. Here, Beethoven introduces a textless, modal chant-like melody that recurs throughout the movement in alternation with more energetic sections in D major marked 'Neue Kraft fühlend' ('Feeling new strength'). The question is whether in 1825 the convalescent Beethoven freely composed this Lydian melody or perhaps modelled it on a liturgical chant. The late Warren Kirkendale searched for plainchant melodies to which Beethoven may have alluded and proposed one candidate for the initial phrase in the Alleluia verse 'Salvum me fac, Deus' ('Make me safe, Lord'; ex. 8.6).[23]

Kirkendale wondered whether Beethoven's choice of the Lydian mode reflected its traditional association as a 'remedy for fatigue of the mind and likewise for that of the body'.[24] But other arguments counter the borrowing hypothesis. For instance, there is no conclusive evidence that Beethoven had access to the plainchant melody; furthermore, the gestation of at least some of the *Dankgesang* melody is traceable to sketches by the composer that document its evolution, perhaps suggesting it was the product of Beethoven's own compositional process, not a cobbling together of preexisting segments from old plainchant. Be that as it may, Beethoven's re-creation of a 'Gregorian style' may have 'succeeded better than he realized',[25] leaving us to wonder about the verbal message Beethoven intended the Lydian melody to deliver. But that code, if indeed there was one, remains undeciphered.

---

[23] Kirkendale (2007).

[24] Ibid., 541, quoting Zarlino, *Institutioni harmoniche* (Venice, 1558), 303.

[25] Ibid., 543.

Ex. 8.7: Schubert, Fugal Sketch (1828)

∞ i

A fervent admirer of Beethoven's late string quartets was his younger contemporary Franz Schubert, who, after requesting a reading of Op. 131 on 14 November 1828, mused whether there was anything left to compose. We might imagine Schubert's keen interest in the motivic combinations and recombinations of its opening fugue, for just days before, he had commenced fugal sketches that he brought on 4 November to Simon Sechter, an erudite music theorist who, it was said, did not let a day pass without composing a fugue.[26] Schubert had always felt insecure about his proficiency in counterpoint. Now, near the end of his tragically abridged life of thirty-one years, having composed nearly a thousand compositions in nearly every musical genre of the time, he resolved to remedy his deficiency by drafting eighteen fugal subjects and answers for Sechter's review.[27]

What concerns us is the final fugal entry (ex. 8.7) for which Sechter crafted the subject from Schubert's name by converting five of its eight characters – S, c, h, b and e – into pitches:

Schubert's assignment was to complete the fugue, but when he died just days later, on 19 November, the task devolved to Sechter, who completed a memorial tribute released on 28 November as his *Fuge in C Moll*, Op. 43 with the Viennese firm of Anton Diabelli, one of Schubert's principal publishers. Sechter

---

[26] Parry (1908), 405.
[27] See Mann (1982); Mann (1986); and Steblin and Stocken (2007).

Ex. 8.8: Abbé Stadler, Fugue in C minor (1828)

was not alone in producing a cryptographic memorial. Diabelli also issued a Fugue in C minor on Schubert's name by Abbé Maximilian Stadler, whose circle included Haydn, Mozart, Beethoven, Schubert and Sechter. Indeed, Stadler's fugue betrays certain similarities to Sechter's. Nevertheless, Stadler derived his own cipher subject, one that employed only four characters – c, h, b and e – to yield a differently profiled subject. Thus, instead of commencing with Sechter's ascending sixth, Stadler chose to highlight the descending chromatic motion, C-B-natural, and B-flat (ex. 8.8).

Both Sechter and Stadler realized that by extending this chromatic descent through the interval of the fourth (C, B-natural, B-flat, A-natural, A-flat, G) they could allude to the *passus duriusculus*, the descending chromatic fourth associated since the Baroque with the lament (see exs. 8.9a–b). Were they aware that in the Fantasy in F minor (D 940), completed just months before in March 1828, Schubert himself had incorporated a fugue that ultimately exhausted itself with a similar reference (ex. 8.9c)?

That might have been the end of Schubertian cryptography. But in 1986, the American composer John Harbison created another *tombeau* in an uncanny, otherworldly chamber work, *November 19, 1828*, for piano and string trio, a late twentieth-century memorial. In four movements, Harbison's music depicts Schubert's transition into the hereafter. The score includes, in the second movement, a suite-like series of musical gestures subjected to mirror inversion to represent the world turned upside down; and, in the third, a recall of a rondo from 1816 that Schubert had left unfinished. With the fourth movement,

Ex. 8.9a: Abbé Stadler, Fugue in C minor (1828)

Ex. 8.9b: Simon Sechter, Fugue in C minor, Op. 43 (1828)

Ex. 8.9c: Schubert, Fantasy in F minor, 1828 (D940)

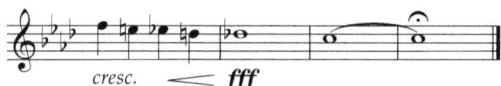

Harbison revives Sechter's subject on Schubert's name, and now allows the string trio to consummate its own realization of the fugue before the piano explores alone further contrapuntal labyrinths Schubert might have encountered in the next life.

The unusual scoring of *November 19, 1828* – instead of a piano quartet Harbison conceived the ensemble as a string trio separate from the piano – carries symbolic meanings. The piano part surely personifies Schubert; the three strings, his circle of Viennese friends, the social network through which he disseminated his music. In effect, Harbison seems intent upon conjuring up a spectral vision of the *Schubertiaden*, the informal gatherings of the composer's circle in which games such as charades were played, music performed, and ideas 'freely' exchanged, at least to the extent possible in Biedermeier Vienna. We now know that Schubert associated with two 'secret' societies, the *Unsinnsgesellschaft* (*Nonsense Society*), to which he belonged in 1817 and 1818, and

Ludlamshöhle (*Ludlam's Cave*),[28] founded in 1819, for which he stood for membership in 1826, until the police summarily closed the organization on suspicion of threatening the state.[29]

The rolls of the *Unsinnsgesellschaft* list between twenty and thirty men, most of them painters, theatrical or literary figures; Schubert may have been the only musician. All the members assumed code names.[30] For example, the anagram Schnautze concealed the actor Eduard Anschütz, while the painter August von Kloeber was known by the moniker Goliath Pinselstiel ('brush handle'). Schubert evidently masqueraded behind several nicknames, including Ritter Cimbal ('knight cymbal'), a play on *Klavizimbel* and cembalo (keyboard), and therefore on Schubert's association with the piano. Possibly related was Chevalier Touchetout ('knight who touches all [the keys]').

The *Unsinnsgesellschaft* produced an illustrated weekly newspaper titled *Archiv des menschlichen Unsinns: Ein langweiliges Unterhaltungsblatt für Wahnwitzige* (*Archive of Human Nonsense: A Boring Entertainment Sheet for Lunatics*). Its tone was decidedly satirical, and, when not featuring scatological reportage, it specialized in parodying government-published accounts in the *Oesterreichischer Beobachter* (*Austrian Observer*), perhaps a factor in the club's sudden demise in 1818, the year of August von Kotzebue's assassination. Schubert arguably composed several works for the society, including 'Das Dörfchen' (D 598) for *a cappella* male quartet, a word play on Ferdinand Dörflinger, a member who adopted as his pseudonym the feminine Elise Gagernadl geborene von Antifi, and appeared in drag in a surviving watercolour of the organization's activities. Steblin has conjectured that Schubert also composed music for *Der Feuergeist* (*The Fire Spirit*), a nonsensical drama 'in four acts with choruses, machinery and flying objects' performed at the club in 1818. In a cryptic entry of 13 August 1818 in the *Archiv* we read: 'According to reports from Spain the Inquisition tribunal there has had Juan *de la Cimbala* arrested since owing to his own confessions for quite some time he has practised the black arts along with his profession'.[31]

To decipher this passage Steblin proposed these interpretations: for Juan de la Cimbala [Cembalo] read Schubert; for Spain, read Hungary, where Schubert had served in 1818 as the music instructor of the Countess Caroline Esterházy; and for the black arts, read a reference to the extraordinary palindromic passage in Schubert's *Die Zauberharfe* (1820, see p. 21), which, Steblin argues, could

---

[28] Named after a play by the Dane Adam Oehlenschläger.
[29] See in particular Castelli (1861), 174–232.
[30] Steblin (1998, 1999 and 2014).
[31] Steblin (1998), 347.

well transmit music originally used in *Der Feuergeist*.³² Both dramas feature roles for the fire-demon Sutur and a magic harp, suggesting that the origins of Schubert's melodrama publicly performed in Vienna in 1820 indeed lay in the private frivolities of the *Unsinnsgesellschaft* two years before.

Much remains unknown about Schubert's club activities and private life in Vienna, including his sexuality and encounters with the police. At least one member of his circle, the political activist and poet Johann Senn, was arrested and incarcerated for a year, before being exiled to the Tyrol. Steblin has scoured the newsletters of the *Unsinnsgesellschaft* and uncovered several words she believes could have been code names or references to Schubert, including *Schuh* (shoe), *Schub* (push) and *Kaleidoskop* (kaleidoscope). In a watercolour by Leopold Kupelwieser a bespectacled figure resembling Schubert peers through a kaleidoscope, the significance of which Gustav Anschütz raised in the society's *Archiv*:

> The undersigned has the honour of faithfully informing the venerated public that he has for sale a kind of kaleidoscope (also known as looking-through-tube) with the unique property that one can use it to see through all kinds of clothing. The great benefit of this optical device should be apparent to everybody since it discloses some items that are at present carefully kept hidden. Especially for young men who like to go walking on the Graben.³³

Anschütz's reference to the Graben, a region of Vienna where the 'Graben nymphs' practised a brisk trade of prostitution, hints at a Viennese demimonde that may well have ensnarled the composer.

∽ ii

While Schubert applied ciphers near the end of his life, other contemporaries were producing chamber music based on their own names. One was the violinist Friedrich Ernst Fesca (1789–1826), who had worked in Kassel after Napoleon absorbed it in 1807 into the newly created Kingdom of Westphalia. After its dissolution in 1813 during the Congress of Vienna, Fesca and a host of other musicians descended upon the imperial capital to partake of the celebrations there. Louis Spohr described what happened on one occasion:

> [Fesca's] quartets and quintets ... took greatly in Vienna and found a ready sale among the publishers there. One of them began in one of its themes with the notes, which form the composer's name:

---

³² Steblin (2014), 11ff.
³³ Steblin (2010), 199.

Ex. 8.10: F. E. Fesca, Theme

This the auditors thought very pretty, and joked [about] the other composers present, *Hummel*, *Pixis* and me, on account of our unusual names. This suggested the idea to me of making something musical out of my name, with the assistance of the abbreviation formerly used of the *piano* into *po*, and of a quarter rest, which when written looks like an r. It was in this form:

Ex. 8.11: Louis Spohr, String Quartet, Op. 29 No. 1

And I immediately took it as a theme for a new violin-quartet, which is the first of the three quartets published in Vienna by Mechetti as Op. 29 and dedicated to Andreas Romberg. When I first played it at my friend's Zizius, it met with great applause, and the originality of the theme, with its descending, diminished *Quarte*, was especially praised. I now called together those who had previously quizzed me for my unmusical name and shewed them (for naturally they had not heard it) the famous thema formed out of my name. They laughed heartily at my artistic trick, and now quizzed the more both Hummel and Pixis, who with all their skill could make nothing musical out of their names.[34]

Fesca's quartet/quintet has not survived and is catalogued as lost.[35] Nevertheless, the slow movement of his String Quartet in B-flat major, Op. 1 No. 3, clearly displays as the first five notes of its second theme the composer's name, lending some credence to Spohr's account (ex. 8.12).

As for his own, cleverly concealed self-reference in Op. 29 No. 1, Spohr developed the cryptogram on other levels throughout the quartet, so that the two pitches of his name influenced the choice of tonalities. In particular, the Scherzo begins in E-flat major, but then pivots in its trio to B major, through an enharmonic transformation of the pitch E-flat into D-sharp; elsewhere, Spohr plays on another enharmonic exchange, whereby B-natural becomes

---

[34] Spohr (1865), 129–30.
[35] Frei-Hauenschild (1998), 566.

Ex. 8.12: F. E. Fesca, String Quartet in B-flat major, Op. 1 No. 3 (1815)

C-flat, again broadening the palette of key relationships. So, what begins as a cryptic musical signature affects the tonal planning of the whole, demonstrating that sometimes a musical cipher casts its influence well beyond the literally encoded pitches.

Among Spohr's circle was the family of the Berlin banker Abraham Mendelssohn Bartholdy, son of the prominent philosopher of the *Haskalah* Moses Mendelssohn and father of two extraordinary musical prodigies, Fanny and Felix Mendelssohn. They had private tutors and benefitted from a rigorous, if conservative, musical instruction that exposed them to many leading musicians of the time, including Spohr. Counterpoint featured prominently in their musical diet, not at all surprising since the Mendelssohns were devotees of the music of J. S. Bach. Indeed, when the piano virtuoso Ignaz Moscheles visited Berlin in 1824, he notated in Fanny's album a *Duett* comprising one line of sixteen bars, in which the second voice was realized by turning the page upside down, reading the accompanying part in retrograde, and placing it beneath the first part.[36]

Some three years before, in June 1821, the Mendelssohns had received at their fashionable residence on the Leipzigerstrasse the painter Carl Joseph Begas (1794–1854), protégé of the French Empire artist Antoine-Jean Gros. After Napoleon's defeat, the Prussian monarch Frederick William III had brought Begas to Berlin, where he executed an oil sketch of Felix[37] and possibly painted Fanny's portrait as well.[38] Their mother, Lea, noted that because Begas was especially passionate about music, he 'felt very much drawn to my children, and they had to compose something for him as a souvenir, for which Fanny quite fortuitously used the letters contained in his name as notes'.[39] Fanny's cipher piece (H-U 41) has survived in an autograph miscellany,[40] where she recorded it on 27 June 1821.

---

[36] See Klein (1993), 153 and illustration 3a.

[37] Bodleian Library, Oxford, M. Deneke Mendelssohn Collection, e. 5.

[38] The *Mädchenbildnis* (*ca.* 1821), in *Begas Haus Heinsberg: Die Sammlung Begas*, ed. Rita Müllejans-Dickmann and Wolfgang Cortjaens (Cologne: 2013), 78–9.

[39] Mendelssohn Bartholdy (2010), vol. 1, 48.

[40] Staatsbibliothek zu Berlin – Preussischer Kulturbesitz, Mendelssohn Archiv Depos. Lohs 1, 45–48.

Ex. 8.13: Fanny Mendelssohn, *Klavierstück* on the Name of Begas, H-U 41 (1821)

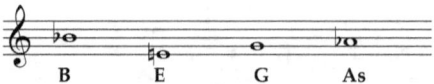

By 1821 Begas had begun to spell his name Begaße (Begasse), allowing Fanny to seize on its unusual feature: all of its letters could convert into six pitches, with two (the *a* and first *s*) serving as A-flat (As), and one (the second *s*) sounding as E-flat, [E]s (ex. 8.13).

As Fanny realized, the first two pitches, B-flat and E, unfolded a dissonant tritone that, when resolved, oriented the music around F minor. But in the third and fourth bars, Fanny was able to redirect the harmony toward A-flat major, establishing a tonal ambiguity between the two keys that anticipated the cryptograms of Robert Schumann, in particular the enigmatic sphinxes of *Carnaval*.[41]

We know that Fanny's brother Felix also composed a piece for Begas (MWV U34),[42] though it has not been identified, nor is there any evidence that he indulged in a play of ciphers on the painter's name. But Felix was already aware of musical cryptography, first through his preoccupation with Bach's music, and second having composed a fugue for string quartet in C minor on 11 April 1821 (MWV R5), barely two months before Fanny's memento. For the beginning of the fugal subject Felix chose the pitches C-E-flat-G-F-sharp, which by themselves might not arouse a cryptologist's suspicion (ex. 8.14).

When transposed to F minor, however, the subject reads in German nomenclature F-As-C-H, spelling out the surname of Carl Friedrich Christian Fasch (1736–1800), founder of the Berlin Singakademie, whose pupils included Carl Friedrich Zelter, composition instructor of Felix and Fanny (ex. 8.15). Sure enough, toward the middle of the fugue Felix devised an entrance of the subject on the subdominant F minor, above which the name Fasch appears, likely in Zelter's hand).[43]

---

[41] See Chapter 9, p. 220, and Todd (2010), 47.

[42] See Wehner (2009), 301–2.

[43] For a facsimile, see John Michael Cooper (2009), 42.

Ex. 8.14: Mendelssohn, Fugue for String Quartet in C minor (1821)

Ex. 8.15: Mendelssohn, Fugue for String Quartet in C minor (1821)

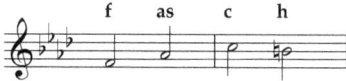

Earlier we mentioned another intellectual pastime of Mendelssohn, contriving brainteasing rebuses for his friends (see p. 31). His attraction to word play also found an outlet in a poetic game known as *Endreim-Spiele* (French, *bouts-rimés*). This literary diversion had originated in France during the seventeenth century; it involved selecting random pairs of rhyming words for which one contrived verses ending with the same rhymes. In German realms the preferred poetry for these games was *Knittelverse*, a type of doggerel that typically contained eight or nine syllables per line with four stresses. Some examples survive from the twelve-year-old Mendelssohn's visit in 1821 to Goethe in Weimar,[44] including one signed *Der schreibsüchtige Reisende F. M.* ('the travelling writing addict F. M.'). The pre-chosen rhyming words appear below in bold script:

Schon höre ich den Frühlings **Sänger**	I already hear the singer of spring
Wie ist sein Ton so süß und **mild**,	How is its tone so sweet and mild,
Wie findet dich ein Vogel**fänger**	How a bird catcher finds you,
Der etwas Böses führt im **Schild**,	Who bears something evil in his shield,
Bei Dir vergißt man allen **Kummer**,	One forgets all sorrows with you,
Doch sieh, da winkt der **Abendstern**	But see, the evening star beckons
Zum sanften, träumereichen **Schlummer**,	To a gentle slumber rich in dreams,
Die holde Nacht ist nicht mehr **fern**.	The lovely night is no longer distant.
Nun Nachtigall, ich will denn **scheiden**,	Now, nightingale, I will then part from you,
Gewiß, ich suche stets dich **auf**,	For sure, I will always visit you,
Und immer hör ich Dich mit **Freuden**,	And always will I hear you with joy,
In meinem ganzen **Lebenslauf**.[45]	Throughout my entire life.

And here is the beginning of another solution for the same rhymes prepared by Ulrike Pogwisch, sister of Goethe's daughter-in-law:

---

[44] See Elvers (1970).
[45] Ibid., 5–6.

Ich kenne einen holden **Sänger**	I know a lovely singer
Und ist er gleich ein bischen **Wild**	and if he is at once a little wild
So bleibt er doch mein Herzens-**Fänger**	so he remains still the conqueror of my heart
Mein Trost und Schutz und Schirm und **Schild**[46]	my comfort, protector, guardian and shield.

The challenge, of course, was to tease out convincing poetic links between paired words ordinarily not associated together.

These intellectual pursuits were harmless enough, but on quite another level was Mendelssohn's life-long effort to revive the music of J. S. Bach. This project played out in several different ways, among them rescuing forgotten works that had lain dormant (most notably, the *St. Matthew Passion*, premiered in Leipzig in 1727 and revived by Mendelssohn in Berlin in 1829); editing Bach's music (for example, the collected organ works for the English publisher Coventry & Hollier, 1845–6); unveiling a sandstone Bach monument near the Leipzig Thomasschule in 1843; and, of course, absorbing Bachian stylistic elements into Mendelssohn's style, whether the extensive reliance on chromaticism, frequent recourse to canonic and fugal counterpoint, or appearances of Lutheran chorales. As a *Neuchrist* baptized when he was seven (auspiciously enough, on Bach's birthday, 21 March 1816), Mendelssohn identified with the Thomaskantor not just musically but spiritually as the epitome of German musical Lutheranism, a perspective that led Hector Berlioz to chide Mendelssohn for being 'a little too fond of the dead'.[47] Mendelssohn's *Bachschwärmerei* also encouraged him to reexplore musical cryptography, and to join the burgeoning list of composers drawn to the BACH cipher. Which brings us to a remarkable organ concert Mendelssohn presented at the Thomaskirche on 6 August 1840.[48]

In 1834 Mendelssohn had read through a piano-duet arrangement of *Art of Fugue*,[49] and the occasion may have made him aware of Bach's plan to conclude that encyclopaedic work with a fugue that introduced his cipher as one of its subjects. Six years later, when Mendelssohn gave his Leipzig organ concert, he ended the programme with a 'freie Phantasie'. Here, according to Robert Schumann, the preeminent organist of his time 'revealed himself in full artistic glory; [the fantasy] … was based on the chorale "O Haupt voll Blut und Wunden," into which he later wove the name Bach and a fugal movement, and rounded out the whole in such a clear and masterful way that it could have been printed as a consummate work of art'.[50]

---

[46] Ibid., 7.
[47] Berlioz (1975), 294.
[48] See Pape (1988).
[49] Letter of Mendelssohn of 17 July 1834; Mendelssohn Bartholdy (2010), 478–9.
[50] *Neue Zeitschrift für Musik* 13 (1840), 56.

Ex. 8.16: Mendelssohn, Chorale Harmonization of 'O Haupt voll Blut und Wunden'

Mendelssohn never published his improvisation, though he may have considered reusing some of its ideas: an autograph folio in Oxford transmits part of a relevant, though unfinished organ composition. It begins with a harmonization of 'O Haupt voll Blut und Wunden', the Passion chorale Bach had interpolated several times into the *St. Matthew Passion*.[51] The fragment then continues with what appears to be the first of several projected variations, suggesting that Mendelssohn had in mind a chorale partita. Could this autograph draft document be part of the 'freie Phantasie'? Of particular interest is his placement of the melody in D minor, a key in which the descending half-step B-flat-A, coincidentally or not the first two pitches of Bach's name, figures several times (ex. 8.16).

Is it far-fetched to imagine that had Mendelssohn completed the torso he may have concluded with a fugal passage on BACH, thus realizing the full potential of the half-step from the chorale? And is it possible that Mendelssohn may have begun drafting this movement as an option for one of his six organ sonatas, Op. 65 (1845), a collection replete with chorales, fugues and fugati, and may even have considered deploying the BACH cipher in what became his principal work for the organ? The same year saw the completion of the *Sechs Fugen über den Namen BACH*, Op. 60 by Robert Schumann, certainly no stranger to musical cryptography (pp. xix, xxi). In the end Mendelssohn did not assign a prominent role to BACH in his Op. 65 (more on that presently), though he later revisited the cipher. On 5 May 1847, during his last London sojourn, he appeared at a Concert of Antient Music in the Hanover Square Rooms under the patronage of Prince Albert to perform a 'Prelude and Fugue on the Name of BACH'.[52] Mendelssohn requested that the work be identified only by 'Bach', not 'Seb. Bach', because, the composer explained, he

---

[51] See Todd (1995).
[52] *The Musical World* 22 (1847), 334–5.

was 'not quite sure whether it is his or one of his sons'.[53] Most likely the work in question was the Prelude and Fugue in B-flat major, formerly attributed to J. S. Bach as BWV 898, though now reclassified with its authorship as uncertain (see also p. 130).

None of Mendelssohn's organ sonatas culminates in a fugue on BACH, but there is one tantalizing passage in Op. 65 No. 1 possibly relevant to our discussion. The transition leading to the finale offers this chromatic sequence (ex. 8.17).

It subsumes two *fortissimi*, transposed, and overlapping statements of the cipher, A-natural-G-sharp-C-flat-B-flat and C-flat-B-flat-D-flat-C. Did Mendelssohn intend them as BACH references a half-step below and half-step above the literally missing, if implied B-flat-A-C-B-natural?

The cases of Mendelssohn and his sister Fanny Hensel are especially compelling, owing to their family's deep involvement in the Bach Revival (it bears emphasis that Felix labelled Fanny the 'Thomaskantor', and that Fanny named her son Sebastian). Scholars such as Christopher Reynolds have proposed examples of BACH ciphers in the Mendelssohns' music, most of which appear at transposed pitch levels.[54] Thus, the first movement of Felix's late String Quartet in F minor, Op. 80 (1847), usually interpreted as a *Nachruf* to his sister, presents one version, B-double flat-A-flat-C-flat-B-flat, that arguably recalls ex. 8.17 and a similar motive in the finale of Fanny's Piano Sonata in C minor (1824), written 'for Felix in his absence'. In another example, from Fanny's Eichendorff setting 'Im Herbst' (H-U 407, 1844), the text refers to a *Bächlein* ('brook'), perhaps for Fanny a word play on *Bach*; indeed, her vocal line obligingly presents the cipher, this time as C-B-D-C-sharp. And finally, when Fanny does introduce the figure at its original pitch level, as in the second movement of her Bachian cantata *Hiob* (1831), she conceals it through a registral displacement, a process that Reynolds describes as a 'tactic of separation', so that the allusion is easily missed (ex. 8.18).[55]

If the siblings were well versed in musical ciphers, they were not prepared for one unexpected cryptological contretemps. Writing on 28 December 1830 from Rome, Felix related that Venetian officials had confiscated his manuscripts in October shortly before his departure for Florence and Rome, and he had retrieved them only 'after much annoyance and writing here and there'.[56]

---

[53] Letter of 30 April 1847 to Henry Rowley Bishop; Mendelssohn Bartholdy (2017), 128.

[54] See Reynolds (2003), 120–1, 131–5.

[55] Ibid., 134.

[56] Mendelssohn Bartholdy (2009), 181.

Ex. 8.17: Mendelssohn, Organ Sonata in F minor, Op. 65 No. 1 (1845)

Ex. 8.18: Fanny Hensel, *Hiob* (1831)

The reason for the seizure, he explained, was that customs agents suspected his music concealed a secret correspondence in ciphers (*Chiffercorrespondenz*), an idea the composer dismissed as a 'wretched stupidity' (*jämmerliche Dummheit*).

∾ iii

Historically speaking, detecting the BACH tetrachord ranks among the most favourite pastimes of musicians with a penchant for cryptanalysis. But what if musical cryptographers pursued a much more ambitious aim, one that went well beyond the occasional nominal cipher to aspire to a systematic, universal language? In this case 'the world would become saturated with hidden meanings',[57] and music might facilitate communication in unforeseen ways. In Chapter 5 we described attempts by Athanasius Kircher, John Wilkins and Francis Godwin in the seventeenth, and Philip Thicknesse in the eighteenth centuries to realize musically transformed forms of speech, not to mention Leibniz's pursuit

---

[57] Collins (2001), 90.

198 THE ART OF MUSICAL CIPHERS, RIDDLES AND SUNDRY CURIOSITIES

of a universal language, one aspect of which might have entailed utilizing all possible melodies. The quest for a universal language now found renewed interest in the nineteenth century, with at least two noteworthy attempts.

The first appeared in Germany in 1830 as *Die Instrumentalton-Sprechkunst* (*The Instrumental Tone Art of Speaking*), a short treatise by B. E. A. Weyrich about how to send 'all news afar through instrumental pitches, in peacetime as well as war, for civil and military purposes, on land and on sea'. Weyrich proposed designing an artificial language with as many musical/verbal correlations as needed to 'provide the public with a means to promote its rapid correspondence'.[58] Sensing that his invention might have applications on the battlefield, he devoted much of the treatise to exploring how instruments could convey military commands over considerable distances, simply by applying a code as in ex. 8.19, in which each letter of the alphabet was encrypted with its own musical marker, requiring only four different pitches that Weyrich repurposed through rhythmic variants.

Meanwhile, in Paris the French violinist François Sudre (1787–1862) was developing *la langue musicale* ('musical language'), eventually known as *Solrésol*. It required only seven consecutive pitches (with additional accidentals for some and rhythmic modifications for others) to generate the requisite number of musical counterparts for the twenty-four letters of the French alphabet[59] (ex. 8.20). Following this key, the cryptographer could 'translate' the word 'j'aime', for instance, into ex. 8.21.

Soon enough Sudre was playing on his violin words, phrases and complete sentences, which a student trained in the language then correctly identified verbally. Word spread of the invention, and a panel of experts convened to judge its utility. The members – five well-known composers, including the director of the Conservatoire, Luigi Cherubini – after conferring, 'recognized that the author has perfectly attained most of what he has proposed, that which we believe is a veritable musical language'.[60]

Demonstrating the innovation's advantages in military applications proved somewhat more challenging, as French generals customarily relayed orders by means of the clarion, a military trumpet that, if capable of emitting piercing sounds, was limited in that it could only produce four different pitches. Undeterred, in 1844 Sudre published *Téléphonie ou Télégraphie acoustique pratiqué au moyen de quatre sons exécutés sur le clairon* (*Telephony or Practical Acoustical Telegraph by Means of Four Pitches Executed on the Clarion*), among the

---

[58] Weyrich (1830), iv.
[59] Quoted in Whitwell (2012), 4.
[60] *Moniteur Universel*, 16 November 1828, trans. in Whitwell (2012), 6.

Ex. 8.19: B. E. A. Weyrich, *Die Instrumentalton-Sprechkunst* (1830)

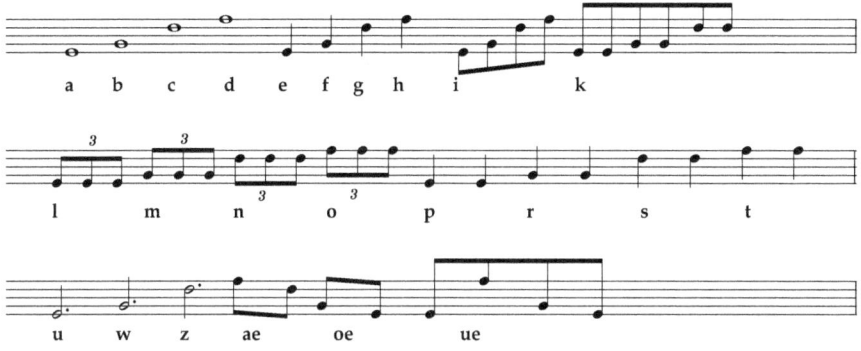

Ex. 8.20: François Sudre, *La langue musicale* (1823)

Ex. 8.21: François Sudre, *La langue musicale* (1823)

earliest uses of the term telephony, decades before Alexander Graham Bell's telephone in 1876. Further demonstrations confirmed the new system's advantages: for example, for vessels fog-bound on the seas. Sudre continued to make improvements, finding ways to adapt his invention for the blind, deaf and mute. In 1830 the *Revue Musicale* published this favourable assessment: '[T]he Musical Language, with respect to that of the telegraph, has the advantage to be able to be put in usage overall, in the rugged places, in the seas, in positions between earth and water and the ability to be easily carried always by the generals or the captains of boats.'[61]

Sudre's *Téléphonie* failed to secure funding, though it did receive the endorsement of one more composer, Hector Berlioz, in the *Journal des Dèbats politiques et littéraires* of 1849. Here we learn that Sudre had reduced the musical pitches to just three (*sol-do-sol*, or g'-d"-g"), which could accommodate 3,159 military orders. To reinforce naval applications of his system, he mustered into service eight tuned cannons that could project a barrage of messages over large distances at sea. But, Berlioz conceded, Sudre was probably destined to follow the lot of many inventors, 'the fatal law to which the unfortunate, bent under the weight of a new idea, have, in all times and in all places, been subjected'.[62]

Berlioz seems to have identified with Sudre as an unrecognized visionary well ahead of his time. Like Sudre, Berlioz imagined futuristic forays. Thus, in the novella *Euphonia*, about a community of 12,000 musical souls inhabiting the slopes of the Harz Mountains five hundred years into the future (2344), he created a 'satirical critique of his own musical environment and an opportunity to express fantasies or fears about how the activities and art of musicians might eventually be transformed by new technologies'.[63] In Euphonia,

> the signal for working-hours, meals, and meetings … as well as for rehearsals in small or large groups, is given by a huge organ situated at the top of a tower rising above all the buildings of the town… The language of the tower organ, this aural telegraphy, is hardly understood by any but Euphonians; they alone are familiar with telephony, an invention whose importance was foreseen by one Sudre in the nineteenth century.[64]

By the mid-nineteenth century, telegraph wires were connecting familiar with unfamiliar landscapes. Some Romantics associated the telegraph with the Aeolian harp, symbol of a spontaneously generated musical force; the telegraph and the harp 'channelled invisible substances (electricity or wind)'.[65] Sometimes the new technology inspired musical responses. Thus, in 1857 Johann Strauss II released his *Telegrafische Depeschen* (Telegraphic Dispatches), Op. 195. It begins in 4/4 time with staccato figures in the strings accompanied by snare drum, meant to imitate the skittering dots and dashes of telegraphic code.[66] Eventually

---

[61] *Revue Musicale*, 4 September 1830, trans. in Whitwell (2012), 14.

[62] *Journal des Dèbats politiques et littéraires*, 17 November 1849, trans. in Whitwell (2012), 33.

[63] Rij (2015), 193.

[64] Berlioz (1973), 285.

[65] Rij (2015), 151.

[66] See further, ibid., 146ff.

Strauss identifies the dispatch as the waltz theme that emerges over the transom, as it were, in 3/4, the music 'hidden' within the code.

In the 1849 testimonial to Sudre Berlioz pursued further his notion of the neglected visionary, who proposed transformative innovations not fully appreciated during his time. Indeed, despite additional endorsements from Victor Hugo and Alexander von Humboldt, and a supportive audience with Napoleon III, the inventor was unable to publish his treatise, *Langue musicale au moyen de la quelle on peut converser sur tous les Instruments* (*Musical Language by Means of Which One Can Converse on All the Instruments*).

That task devolved to his wife, Joséphine, who accomplished it in 1866; a *Grammaire du Solrésol ou Langue universelle de Fr. Sudre* prepared by Boleslas Gajewski followed in 1902. Sudre's system involved using the seven solmization syllables to represent words, beginning with one- and two-syllable combinations (*si* = 'oui'; *do* = 'non'; *dore* = 'je'), and then building up longer conglomerates (*Solrésol* = 'language'). One could play the transformed syllables on any instrument to communicate the meaning to anyone conversant in the language. Sudre classified the seven solmization syllables into different categories into which he could fit entries from his vocabularies, but his system had its constraints. For some words he reversed their meaning by simply articulating them in retrograde (*domisol* = 'Dieu'; *solmido* = 'Satan'), but by and large there was no easy way to organize, let alone acquire fluency in the roughly 12,000 words of the language. By the early twentieth century the limits of *Solrésol* were apparent to the French linguist Louis Couturat: 'There is no need for long reflection to realize how vain it is to express all of humanity's ideas by means of just seven syllables that are always the same'.[67] Nevertheless, it had been Joséphine Sudre's fervent wish 'that music, which is one for all,' would 'be able to become, through its linguistic application, the bond tying together all nations!'[68]

---

[67] Couturat (1903), 37. Couturat later constructed his own artificial language, a forerunner of Esperanto.

[68] Whitwell (2012), 71.

CHAPTER 9

Riddles of the Sphinx

'The soul is a cipher, in the sense of a cryptograph, and the shorter a cryptograph is, the more difficulty there is in its comprehension – at a certain point of brevity it would bid defiance to an army of Champollions.'

– Edgar Allan Poe, 'Sarah Margaret Fuller'[1]

PROVIDING a liberating escape for a generation of Romantics, musical ciphers became a familiar pursuit within the circle of Robert Schumann. Sometimes the 'recipient' tasked with deciphering the 'plaintext' was identified, as in the *FAE* Sonata for violin and piano, which Robert, Albert Dietrich and Johannes Brahms created for Joseph Joachim, who performed it with Clara Schumann on 28 October 1853 and not only decrypted the plaintexts – 'frei aber einsam' ('free but alone') and 'Gisela' – but also identified the authors of the four movements.

To authenticate a cipher generally requires documentation from the composer, though this chapter also considers speculative ciphers for their revealing insights into music as *Beziehungskunst*, an art form intimately tied to relationships.[2] Indeed, within the Schumann circle most ciphers did operate within this context, whether reflecting collegiality, romantic love, multi-amory, opportunities for playful games, or posthumous remembrance.[3]

Clara and Robert Schumann formed the centre of a group of musicians and composers intrigued with ciphers, including Albert Dietrich (1829–1908), a student of Robert in Düsseldorf; Joseph Joachim (1831–1907), the violinist-composer whose acquaintance with the Schumanns began in the 1840s in Leipzig; and Johannes Brahms, whose early piano works Robert famously described in 1853 as *verschleierte Sinfonien* ('veiled symphonies'). In addition, there was the Danish composer Niels Gade and lastly, Franz Liszt, who found his way to the BACH tetrachord, and may have experimented with other ciphers as well.

Robert Schumann's approach to ciphers was intertextual, tilting decidedly toward the literary, and often coyly humorous. For Holly Watkins, 'Schumann's

---

[1] 'The Literati of New York City. – No. IV' (August 1846).
[2] See Borchard (2014).
[3] See Borchard (2018).

music wears concealment on its sleeve'.[4] Among his best-known ciphers are: A-B-flat-E-G-G in the *Abegg* Variations, Op. 1 (1830), which encrypts the last name of Meta Abegg, a fictional character (Meta could be an anagram for Tema); ASCH (spelled variously as A-flat-C-B-natural, A-E-flat-C-B-natural, or, reordered, as E-flat-C-B-natural-A) in *Carnaval*, Op. 9, the plaintexts being 'Aš' (Asch, now in the Czech Republic, the home town of Ernestine von Fricken, to whom Schumann was for a time engaged); and E-flat-C-B-natural-A, the 'musical' letters of his own name.[5] Whereas Abegg is easily decipherable, the last two ciphers, ASCH and SCHA, are somewhat more oblique, given that 'As' stands for A-flat, while 'S' represents E-flat.

The *Abegg* Variations received a witty review by Ludwig Rellstab in the journal *Iris im Gebiete der Tonkunst*. Rellstab confessed that had he not seen the title he would have found the theme 'meandering and monotonous', owing to several similar progressions in its first half, which Schumann then varied slightly in the second half. Pointing to the motive A-B-flat-E-G-G, Rellstab criticized the theme's limited presentation, and lamented its lack of contrapuntal elaboration. The theme seemed rather like a 'musical gag' (*musikalischer Scherz*), indeed probably just as Schumann had intended (ex. 9.1).[6]

Rellstab concluded by proposing other cipher-friendly subjects: the usual suspect Bach, but also 'Fasch,[7] ice [*Eis*], coffee [*Caffé*],[8] fish [*Fische*], rabbit [*Hase*], and sheep [*Schaf*]', waggish suggestions probably not lost on Schumann's circle.

Rellstab's critique aside, Schumann's Op. 1 is rich in sparkling virtuosity – *and* humour. Grasping that the musical potential of a name alone can generate a playful game for the contestant, Schumann took up the challenge by using the second half of the theme to present his cipher in retrograde (G-G-E-B-flat-A). In the following variations *ABEGG* is largely swept away by mounting and cascading *bravura* displays, excepting one brief passage of two sustained chords in which the lowest notes are released one by one, faintly tracing the original motive.

Another frequently discussed cipher-like motive is the bell-like tolling of the pitches E, B-natural and E, which spell 'Ehe' ('marriage') in *Mondnacht (Moonlit Night)* from the Eichendorff *Liederkreis*, Op. 39 No. 5.[9] This song's intertextuality hints at 'Ehe' on more than one level. Eichendorff's hypnotic poem

---

[4] Watkins (2011), 86.

[5] ASCH and SCHA also appear in Schumann's *Faschingsschwank aus Wien*, Op. 26 (1839).

[6] Schumann (1971), 107–8.

[7] See p. 192.

[8] See p. 4.

[9] Uhde and Todd (2018), 25; also see Daverio (2002), 76.

Ex. 9.1: Robert Schumann, *Abegg* Variations, Op. 1 (1830)

speaks of the union of earth and sky ('It was as if heaven had quietly kissed the earth'); also, during the year of composition, 1840, Robert and Clara wed after a protracted legal battle with her father, Friedrich Wieck. Whether Schumann's attraction to the three pitches betrays a legitimate cipher is almost beyond the point, though the frequent repetitions of the somnolent bass motive suggest that the composer was fully aware of its verbal meaning; indeed, in a letter to Clara of 15 April 1838 he averred that 'Ehe' is a 'very musical word', one, furthermore, containing the consonance of a perfect fifth.[10]

A key element of Robert Schumann's approach to ciphers was the paradox of masking and unmasking musical content. In this regard Schumann's cipher manipulations resembled another technique he and Clara frequently used in their music – playing on allusions versus quotations.[11] Here we might imagine a continuum on which clear quotations populate one extreme – one thinks, for example, of Robert's deployments of the *Marseillaise* in *Faschingsschwank aus Wien*, Op. 26, *Die beiden Grenadiere*, Op. 49 No. 1 and *Hermann und Dorothea* Overture, Op. 136, and his self-quotation of the opening of *Frauenliebe- und leben* in the Andante and Variations, Op. 46, fifth variation. Moving along the continuum we encounter less precise references that gradually slide to the other extreme: all too general 'references' in which Robert masks his intentions, leaving the listener to wonder if there is indeed any relevant allusion. The entire process can thus mirror the art of musical encryption: just as Schumann can generate an explicit cipher, as in the six BACH fugues for organ, Op. 60, or mask the cipher so that at best it impresses as implicit, so can he weave into his musical textures quotations that easily blend into less specific references that appear to lose their identity altogether.

Perhaps the *locus classicus* of this process in Schumann's music is the Fantasy for piano, Op. 17 (1837), a work written for an initiative to raise funds for the Beethoven monument in Bonn, unveiled in 1845. At the time of composition, Robert and Clara were separated, and Schumann contrived a way to ally Beethovenian reminiscences in the first movement of his fantasy with his pressing

---

[10] Schumann (2012), 294.
[11] See Todd (1994 and 2026).

Ex. 9.2: Robert Schumann, Fantasy, Op. 17, First Movement (1837)

need 'to write just one thought everywhere, with large letters and chords: Clara'.[12] In bars 156–60 he introduced 'a veiled allusion … eventually clarified as a Beethovenian quotation.'[13] The phrase in question gradually moves from an allusion to a more or less clear borrowing from Beethoven's *An die ferne Geliebte* (*To the Distant Beloved*), Op. 98, presented three times in succession in the closing bars of the movement, and yielding, in the end, to block chords (see ex. 9.2).

This allusion/quotation pairing has provoked some controversy. The late Anthony Newcomb remarked that not until the twentieth century did scholars notice the similarities, so that the entire nineteenth century somehow remained oblivious to them.[14] Still, discounting the comparison altogether seems unjustified, for Schumann reused the phrase (with modifications) in several other works, including the song cycle *Frauenliebe- und leben*, Op. 42 No. 6, and the finales of the String Quartet in F major, Op. 41 No. 2 and Second Symphony, Op. 61.[15] What is more, the young Brahms adapted the phrase in the original version of his Piano Trio No. 1 in B major, Op. 8 (1854), though whether he was alluding to *An die ferne Geliebte*, to the first movement of Schumann's Fantasy, or to both, is unclear.[16] Possibly, Schumann did not intend to revive Beethoven's song cycle; but surely the phrase bore some special significance. Whether an

---

[12] Letter of 9 October 1837, Weissweiler (1994), vol. 1, 32.
[13] Todd (1994), 93.
[14] Newcomb (2004), 295.
[15] Bars 31ff., 36ff. and 294ff. respectively.
[16] Bars 104ff. and 424ff. of Brahms's finale, first version.

Ex. 9.3: Robert Schumann, *Carnaval*, Op. 9, Sphinxes (1837)

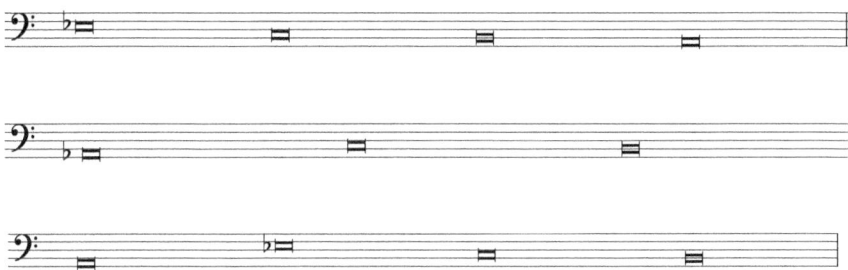

allusion or quotation, as Nicholas Marston has asserted, 'both are forms of reference, means of bringing into a work material which exists independently of the work itself'.[17] And the Fantasy is no stranger to the process, beginning as it does, before the downbeat is struck, with the quotation from Friedrich Schlegel's poem *Die Gebüsche*, and its reference to a 'gentle tone drawn for him who eavesdrops secretly'. Like this literary unmasking, the playful use of musical references, whether literal quotations or elusive allusions, resembles the riddles of musical ciphers, impelling us to consider once again 'the popular belief that [Schumann] often approached his art as a kind of cryptography in tones'.[18]

Among Schumann's most perplexing ciphers are the three 'sphinxes' in *Carnaval*, Op. 9, a chain-like composition comprising twenty miniatures whose titles, from 'Pierrot' to 'Arlequin', 'Eusebius' to 'Florestan', explore diverging musico-literary worlds, real and imagined. Many of the movements derive their material in some way from the sphinxes. The revelation comes after the eighth piece, *Réplique*, where the pianist first encounters the phlegmatic symbols (ex. 9.3).

Carnaval then resumes, as if nothing has happened. The three musical 'sphinxes' – *Es-C-H-A*, *As-C-H* and *A-Es-C-H* – and their plaintexts (Sch[um]a[nn], Asch and Asch) are not the most puzzling aspect. Rather, it is their appearance – how they are made explicit in the middle of the composition, though having been present in the music all along; and whether they should be performed or left as soundless *Augenmusik*. The 'sphinxes' seem to breathe the air of 'a vague musical past'[19] with their obsolescent rhythmic values as square breves.

Holly Watkins has argued that sphinxes can 'point toward meaning without connecting all the dots, solving some mysteries (the source of certain harmonic

---

[17] Marston (1992), 34.
[18] Daverio (2007), 73.
[19] Watkins (2011), 86.

and motivic features of *Carnaval*) while creating others (what do the ciphers mean?)'.[20] How do performers respond to the sphinxes? Some pause, merely acknowledging these hieroglyphs in silence but not playing them, while others perform them as written. Then there was Rachmaninoff, who in his famous 1929 recording provided a rumbling tremolo accompaniment, as if trying to activate some supernatural agency hidden within the dormant creatures. Regarding Schumann's inspiration for these and other ciphers, different theories have been advanced, the most widespread view asserting that what elicited these ciphers was his love and knowledge of literature (and word games),[21] his fascination with cryptography and his Romantic view of music as autobiography.

How did Schumann develop his enciphering techniques? One proposal by the inveterate cryptologist Eric Sams is that Schumann was familiar with Johann Ludwig Klüber's *Kryptographik: Lehrbuch der Geheimschreibekunst (Chiffrir- und Dechiffrirkunst) in Staats- und Privatgeschäften* (*Cryptography: Manual of the Art of Secret Writing (Enciphering and Deciphering) in Official and Private Affairs*), which appeared in 1809. The composer's father, August, was a bookdealer and publisher in Zwickau, and conceivably possessed a copy of the *Lehrbuch*. According to Sams, Robert 'had a copy by him all his life'.[22] If he did, he would have read Klüber's claim to have summarized 'if not all, still by far the most interesting of the presently used methods to write secretly'.[23]

For us, the relevant portion of Klüber's manual is the fifth chapter of the third part, titled 'Musical Notation or Music Ciphers, and Writing with Circular Disks'.[24] Here the author describes musical ciphers as *musique parlante* ('speaking music') and explains how to use a cipher wheel. It contains two circles, a fixed outer and moveable inner circle. The inner circumference displays twenty-six one- and two-note musical motives; the outer circle, the letters of the alphabet. Each letter of the outer circle thus aligns with a musical motive which may be changed by adjusting the smaller disc. Klüber's example pairs motives with letters that spell the phrase 'c'est avec beaucoup de satisfaction'. To render the encipherment secure, he recommends that the cryptographer arrange in advance with the decipherer to rotate the inner wheel one step to the right or left *after each word*, so that different letters correspond to each musical motive, for 'a letter written entirely according to this method can only be read by someone who has before him a disk set up exactly that way'.[25]

---

[20] Ibid.
[21] Schumann (1971), 107–8.
[22] Sams (1969–70), 114.
[23] Klüber (1809), ii.
[24] Ibid., 264.
[25] Ibid., 267.

Klüber's example produces nonsensical music, though he seems unconcerned by its appearance, and blithely recommends adding sharps, flats and time signatures, without realizing that the musically literate might cringe at the result. Thus, Klüber randomly employs accidental signs before the pitches E and A, in an excerpt ostensibly in C major/A minor that ordinarily would not require sharps or flats.

Let us now return to Schumann's ciphers. One late example is *FAE*, for 'frei aber einsam' ('free but alone'), particularly rich in intertextuality, owing to the members of the circle who exploited it. Schumann worked this cipher into the second and fourth movements of the *FAE* Sonata; his colleagues Dietrich and Brahms supplied the first and third movements, with the former using the cipher more transparently than the latter. Furthermore, Joachim relied heavily upon it in his own music. In fact, he was first to use *FAE*; he derived the cipher in 1853, when he was a reluctant bachelor, and routinely returned to it as his proxy signature in many works. Tekla Babyak has argued that Joachim's 'autobiographical cipher' alludes to the 'absence of reciprocal love',[26] not to the letters of his own name. In short, *FAE* is separate from other ciphers in Schumann's circle that do encode names: in addition to *SCHA* (E-flat-C-B-A) for Robert Schumann, there are *BAHS* (B-flat-A-B-E-flat) for Brahms; *Gis-E-La* (G-sharp-E-A, the mirror inversion of *FAE*), for Gisela von Arnim, object of Joachim's infatuation; *GADE* for Niels Gade; and, possibly for Ferdinand David in Schumann's late Violin Sonata in D minor, Op. 121, *DAFD* and *DADEF* (the latter, *FErDinAnD* in reverse). Schumann was inspired by the musical potential of FAE and set it against G-sharp-E-A (plaintext Gis-E-La) in the last movement of the *FAE* Sonata. But Joachim was the first to explore the pairing in July 1853 in his *Drei Stücke* for violin and piano, Op. 5, dedicated to Gisela von Arnim. Whether Schumann knew those pieces by October 1853, he was aware of Joachim's passion for Gisela, which the violinist did not conceal.

The Intermezzo, Schumann's second movement of the *FAE* Sonata, expends no fewer than ten statements of the cipher within forty-six bars, or about one every four or five bars, split between the violin and piano. But one mystery remains: did he also have in mind a second cipher for Joachim's name, the pitches A, C and B-natural (ex. 9.4)? The third *FAE* statement, intoned in the bass of bars 12–13, coincides with those notes (plaintext, ACH) accented in the treble. There is evidence that Schumann reflected on the individual syllables of Joachim's name, reading 'Jo' as Jove, or the god Jupiter, and 'achim' as Achim, that is, the poet Ludwig Achim von Arnim. Writing to Joachim on 13 October 1853 Schumann revealed: 'Recently I proposed a toast with a glass of wine in the form of charades. Three syllables: the first a god loves, the two others many

---

[26] Babyak (2024), 81.

Ex. 9.4: Robert Schumann, *FAE* Sonata, Intermezzo (1853)

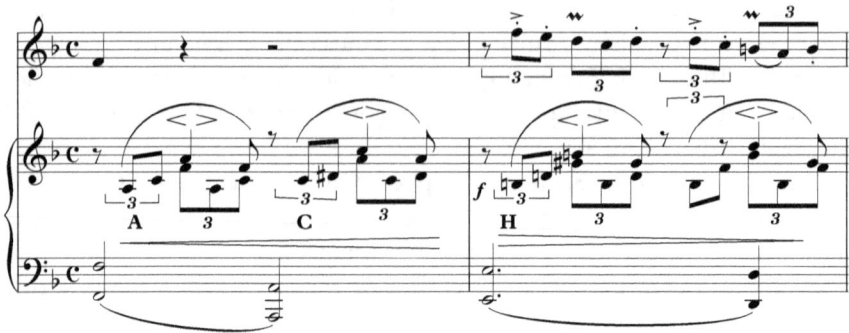

readers love, the whole [word] all of us love; the entirety should live' (solution: Jo-Achim).[27]

One of Schumann's collaborators was Albert Dietrich, who dispatched the first movement. Dietrich incorporated only four appearances of the cipher into the violin part of the sonata, at the beginning of the exposition, the end of the development, after the beginning of the reprise, and in the final bars. In each case the cipher appeared explicitly; nevertheless, in comparison to Schumann's dense packing of the Intermezzo with *FAE*, Dietrich's four ciphers impress as sparse and restrained.

The member of the Schumanns' circle who pursued musical cryptography with determined doggedness was Joseph Joachim. *FAE* protrudes in many of his compositions, in letters to Gisela von Arnim and Brahms, and also in a signature to several of Joachim's entries in Brahms's *Schatzkästlein* ('treasure chest') of literary aphorisms (Nos. 225, 228 and 230),[28] which date from 1850 to 1854 and include 'seventeen quotations ascribed to Joseph Joachim, most identified by the initials "f.a.e." or their pitch equivalents'.[29] Here we can contrast his approach to ciphers with that of his friends, for Joachim divulges his 'secrets' with such force as if his goal were to lay bare his innermost feelings.[30]

---

[27] Moser (1910), vol. 1, 85–6.

[28] Uhde (2018), 145.

[29] Daverio (2002), 104.

[30] Thus, in a letter of 23 April 1856 to Gisela Joachim writes: '[in everything] I have thus far composed, I have surrendered to a certain fatalism of emotion to such a degree that I considered it unjust to give my mind any other task than to detect and recognize; its task was to gather what had been bred in the warmth of our emotions and save it from the abyss.' Joachim (1911b), 97.

When in 1853 he finished the overture to *Hamlet*, Joachim had just moved from Weimar, where he had worked as Liszt's concertmaster, to Hanover, where he felt lonely and isolated. But this period also coincided with Joachim's desire for intimacy with Gisela von Arnim (daughter of Bettine) whom he had met in Weimar in the autumn of 1852. Joachim used the cipher *FAE* to sign the autograph of *Hamlet* in March 1853, revealing his identification with the overture – it was worthy of his signature – and that he finished the work 'free but alone'. Other than one passage that features the pitches F-A-flat-E in a seemingly endless loop of tremolos, the most exposed presentation of *FAE* occurs in the accompaniment to the exposition's secondary theme, where we hear unbroken iterations of *E-F-A-E-F*.

In *Drei Stücke* for violin and piano, Op. 5, composed in July 1853, Joachim explored the cipher further. In particular, he saturated the second piece, 'Abendglocken' ('Evening Bells'), with ciphers, and applied blue ink to accentuate statements of *FAE* in the score.[31] Op. 5 also featured as a second cipher the three pitches G-sharp, E and A, which had debuted the year before, in 1852, in a letter to Gisela after he first set eyes on her in Weimar. While his letter notates the pitches as a rising sixth and falling fifth, 'Abendglocken' presents them as a descending third and rising fourth, in constant alternation with *FAE*.

The opening of 'Abendglocken' at once establishes a sombre mood by isolating the ciphers from each other through the notational device of a framing 'double bar'. Then, in the central B section, Joachim contrasts the reality of his situation with the desired alternative: '… his original intention was to call the Op. 5 pieces *Wirkliches und Geträumtes* (*The Real and Imagined*), but finally decided against this option. The B section also portrays the ciphers in an exaggerated, repetitive manner, bordering on obsession. With five to seven repetitions each, they alternate between the left and right hands, with *FAE* in the left, and *Gis-E-La* in the right, and yet, remain separated as if by "an inevitable fate"'.[32]

The intensity with which Joachim's ciphers in Op. 5 evoke his personal discontent is probably incomparable. In 1859, a good six years after Joachim had met Gisela von Arnim, the drama took its decisive turn. Herman Grimm, a close friend of Gisela since their childhood days, and Joachim's close friend during the early-to-mid 1850s, married her, thus ending their triangular relationship.

Joachim returned to the cipher pair G-sharp-E-A and FAE in his *Variations on an Original Theme* for viola and piano, Op. 10 (1855), weaving Gisela's signature conspicuously into the opening of the theme, and ultimately signing the finale with his own cipher. Further applications of the pair obtained in the *Kleist*

---

[31] Hamburg, Staats- und Universitätsbibliothek MS BRA: Ac 25.
[32] Uhde (2018), 153.

Overture (1856), *Notturno* (1858) and Violin Concerto in G major (1889). These six notes – first used by Joachim in July 1853 and then by Robert Schumann in the finale of the *FAE* Sonata in October 1853 – engendered a variety of pieces by Joachim and another composer in the Schumanns' circle – Brahms. To understand Brahms's ciphers and interest in *FAE* and its variants, we turn now to his friendship with Joachim.

The Brahms–Joachim relationship extended from their first encounter in Hanover (April 1853) through meetings in Göttingen and Düsseldorf to the well-documented counterpoint exchange (1856–61), the famous collaboration on Brahms's Violin Concerto Op. 77 (1878), for which Joachim provided critical feedback and a cadenza, and beyond.[33] Their time together in Göttingen and Düsseldorf was especially connected to ciphers – in Düsseldorf, of course, Joachim received the *FAE* Sonata, including Brahms's scherzo.

From the Göttingen period in 1853 dates an amusing composition by Brahms for his friend, the *Hymne zur Verherrlichung des großen Joachim* ('Hymn in Adulation of the Great Joachim').[34] Brahms composed it for Joachim's birthday, then believed to fall on 24 July,[35] and took the opportunity to quote generously from his compositions, including Op. 2 No. 1 and Op. 5. The former, a romance without ciphers, was already published, while the latter, teeming with *Gis-e-la* and *FAE* ciphers, was just being composed in Göttingen. Thus, Brahms's quotation from Op. 5 No. 3 provides a convenient date stamp for Joachim's Op. 5, of which No. 2, 'Abendglocken', is especially laden with ciphers. Brahms conceived those in his birthday offering in a 'spirit of jest'[36]; the hymn's importance, though, lies less in the piece itself, and more in the arresting presence of ciphers from almost the first day of Brahms's and Joachim's friendship, prompting us to view the spoof as further evidence of *Beziehungskunst*. Just as the *Hymne* was a collaborative effort in which Joachim's ciphers encircled Brahms's music, so the *FAE* Sonata was a shared project of five friends, Robert Schumann, Dietrich, Brahms, Clara Schumann and Joachim. It was created, according to the autograph, 'In Erwartung der Ankunft des … Freundes' ('While awaiting the arrival of the friend') – that is, as a 'rearrangement' of *FAE*.[37]

Among Joachim's and Brahms's other collaborations was their counterpoint exchange. David Brodbeck has investigated this productive period in the life of the historically curious Brahms, for whom studying Renaissance and Baroque

---

[33] See Uhde (2021).

[34] See Sholes (2020), 63.

[35] Michelmann (1930), 99.

[36] Sholes (2020), 62.

[37] Stadtbibliothek zu Berlin, Signatur Mus.ms. autogr. Schumann, R. 26.

Ex. 9.5: Brahms, Double Concerto in A minor, Op. 102, First Movement (1887)

music came more easily than for the not so contrapuntally inclined Joachim.[38] Indeed, Joachim, who balanced his career as a virtuoso, composer, conductor and concertmaster in Hanover, laboured mightily over these exercises, signing in frustration one letter 'Dein unkontrapunktischer J. J.'[39] Brahms supplied feedback and corrected quite a number of Joachim's exercises, many of which contained *FAE*, *Gis-e-la* and *BACH* ciphers.

Though Brahms's own contributions to the exchange do not employ *FAE* or *Gis-e-la*, he may have experimented with Joachim's reordered *EAF* cipher of 22 April 1856. Brahms's possible reorderings of the *FAE* ciphers and their modifications have caused considerable speculation, such as the distinctive, possibly anagrammatic *FEA* motive in the first movement of the Double Concerto in A minor for violin and cello, Op. 102 (ex. 9.5).

In general, supporting the legitimacy of Brahms's ciphers is a relatively small amount of evidence. Not in dispute are ciphers, some in plaintext and some in their pitch equivalents, found in Brahms's collection of aphorisms, *Des jungen Kreislers Schatzkästlein*. Equally uncontroversial are *FAE* ciphers in the finale of the Piano Sonata No. 3 in F minor, Op. 5 (bar 39), and *Agathe* ciphers in 'Und gehst du über den Kirchhof', Op. 44 No. 10 and String Sextet No. 1 in G major, Op. 36. The muse behind the last two was the soprano Agathe von Siebold, whom Brahms met in Göttingen during the summer of 1858.

Her cipher comprises the pitches A, G, A, B and E ('Aga[t]he'), which Daverio likens to a 'soggetto cavato'. In the choral part-song 'Und gehst du über den Kirchhof', for Sams a 'threnody for lost love',[40] Daverio describes the cipher's treatment in bars 1–6 as an ostinato; an 'almost identical' motivic *Gestalt* appears in the first movement of Brahms's Op. 36 'at the climax of the second group', where we hear three consecutive statements (ex. 9.6).

Among scholars who value strong supporting documentation for a cipher, Daverio nevertheless concedes that the 'documentary evidence for the link between Agathe and the musical cipher … comes three decades after the fact, in

---

[38] Brodbeck (1994).
[39] Joachim to Brahms, 21 March 1856, Moser (1908), V:125.
[40] Sams (2000), 14.

Ex. 9.6: Brahms, Sextet No. 1 in G major, Op. 36, First Movement (1865)

Ex. 9.7: Agathe Cipher in Joachim's Letter to Brahms of 27 September 1894

a letter of 27 September 1894 from Joachim, who has recently visited Brahms's old flame while on holiday in Göttingen' (ex. 9.7).[41]

Thus, what triggered the cipher seems to have been a romance that occurred in 1858 and 1859. Would Agathe von Siebold have been the 'recipient'? To judge by her memoirs, it would seem so: 'I loved Johannes Brahms very much, and for a short while, he loved me'.[42]

Among the compositions Brahms completed in Göttingen were five songs, the *Fünf Gedichte*, Op. 19, of which four date from 1858, the year of his courtship of Agathe. Not surprisingly, scholars have read the composer's selection of the poems, by Hölty, Uhland and Mörike, as concerning Brahms's unfulfilled relationship with her.[43] To that end, William Horne found a significant clue in the original versions of two of the Uhland settings, Nos. 2 ('Scheiden und meiden') and 3 ('In der Ferne'), which Brahms initially placed in the keys of E minor and E major, before transposing them down a whole-step for the published version. Noting that the vocal lines of the original versions begin with a perfect fifth and fourth (E-B-E), Horne conjectured, reasonably enough, that Brahms had borrowed Robert Schumann's encryption of *Ehe* ('marriage'), but disguised the allusion first by presenting the pitches in *ascending* order rather than Schumann's descending lunar rays, and second by transposing the songs, so that *Ehe* appeared as D-A-D (see ex. 9.8).[44]

Apparently unnoticed, though, is that all five *Gedichte* privilege the motive of a perfect fifth and fourth melodically or harmonically, so that the desired union with Agathe plausibly runs threadlike through the entire opus.

What about whether Brahms constructed the subject of his Fugue in A-flat minor for organ, WoO 8 (1856), from his own surname? Daverio finds it

---

[41] Daverio (2002), 105.
[42] Küntzel (1985), 94.
[43] Horne (2012), 241–7.
[44] Ibid., 242–3.

Ex. 9.8: Brahms, *Fünf Gedichte*, Op. 19 No. 3, 'In der Ferne' (1858)

Ex. 9.9: Brahms, Fugue in A-flat minor, WoO 8 (1856)

'probable' on the strength of the evidence, whereas Brahms's scherzo from the *FAE* Sonata reveals only an 'oblique relationship to [the] plaintext'.[45] Regarding the fugue, in July 1856 Brahms wrote to the music critic Adolf Schubring, 'The [enclosed] music is at once a reply [to an earlier letter from Schubring] and my signature, because I'm really not inclined to inscribe the latter at the bottom of the page. You will certainly be able to perceive the name.'[46] Daverio views 'Brahms' as the most likely signature; he finds in the fugal subject (ex. 9.9) four musical letters from the composer's last name: B-flat (B), B-double flat or A (A), Cb/B (H) and E-flat (S).[47] But once again, Brahms was apparently intent upon covering his tracks: he scrambled the pitches' order, forming an anagram of his surname, H, B, S and A.

A possibly intentional, if well-hidden cryptic nod from Brahms to Joachim may lurk in the String Quartet in C minor, Op. 51 No. 1 (1873), which, unlike its sibling in A minor, Op. 51 No. 2 that announces unmistakably A*FAE* at the opening, is not usually mentioned in discussions about ciphers (ex. 9.10). As part of the primary thematic group in the first movement we hear in the first violin the three-note combination F-D-flat-C (bar 11), picked up by the second violin (bar 15), now in the tonic (C-A-flat-G) and supported by the cello with

---

[45] Daverio (2002), 104.
[46] Ibid., 106.
[47] Ibid.; see also Sams (2000), 20.

Ex. 9.10: Brahms, String Quartet in C minor, Op. 51 No. 1, First Movement (1873)

an ascending gesture, G-B-C. We can recognize a mirroring process here: C-A-flat-G is a transposed mirror inversion of G-B-C.

This device, in turn, recalls *FAE* and *Gisela*, which, if slightly reordered (*AFE* and *E-G-sharp-A*), produce the same intervallic shapes as Brahms's motivic manipulations.

In searching for cipher pairings, we are probably on firmer ground in Brahms's Intermezzo in A minor, Op. 116 No. 2 (published in 1892). Its mysterious middle section, *Non troppo presto*, 'introduces in the left hand a persistent figure of thirds that are repeated with a quiet insistence that borders on an obsession reminiscent of 'Abendglocken'. What is more, the thirds link together the *Gis-e-la* and *FAE* ciphers, with *FAE* embedded in the pattern in its retrograde version' (ex. 9.11).[48]

William Horne's tantalizing suggestion that Op. 116 No. 2 may be based 'on a now lost sarabande'[49] from the 1850s strengthens the hypothesis of the fifty-nine-year-old Brahms recalling nostalgically his youthful friendship with Joachim, though this intriguing allusion, of course, could also be a coincidence.

What about purely speculative Brahmsian ciphers that lack supporting documentation concerning the composer's intentions? One famous case, the so-called 'frei aber froh' cipher ('free but happy', *FAF*), appears to have been the construction of Max Kalbeck.[50] Equally disputed are the ciphers in which Brahms, like Robert, may have uttered 'Clara' in tones. Let us begin with 'frei aber froh'. Brahms allegedly composed it into his Third Symphony in F major, Op. 90, and into his String Quartet in A minor, Op. 51 No. 2; the *Balladen* for piano, Op. 10; First Piano Concerto in D minor, Op. 15; First Symphony in C minor, Op. 68; and *Tragic* Overture, Op. 81. Michael Musgrave and John Daverio have both challenged the legitimacy of the cipher, and lack of rigor in its

---

[48] Uhde and Todd (2018), 36. The slow movement of Brahms's String Quintet in G major Op. 111, offers a comparable case: in the opening viola motive, F-A-G-sharp-E, the composer combines F-A-E and G-sharp-E-A.

[49] Horne (1989), 270.

[50] Musgrave (1980), 252.

Ex. 9.11: Brahms, Intermezzo in A minor, Op. 116 No. 2 (1892)

application.[51] Daverio argues that because *FAF* appears nowhere in its basic form but rather in 'derivative' forms, 'fundamental rules' of cipher compositions that Brahms and Joachim followed are disregarded. Daverio also refutes Brahms's supposed use of FEA (a reordering of *FAE*) in the Double Concerto – once again, the *Ur*-motive is nowhere to be found. Only if we accept that Brahms 'completely altered' his approach by tolerating well-hidden 'derivations' of ciphers, 'nestled in the middle of longer phrases', could we perhaps reappraise those ciphers as 'intended' by the composer.

No less problematic is the notorious *Clara* cipher. As Daverio reminds us, 'the documentary evidence for Brahms's encipherment of *Clara* is nil'. But this lack of evidence has not stopped scholars from extending Sams's investigations, and reading the cipher (C-B-A-G-sharp-A) into a variety of Brahms's works[52] – for example, the scherzo of the Piano Trio No. 1, Op. 8; Variations for Piano, Op. 9; finale of Brahms's First Piano Concerto, Op. 15; third movement of the Second Serenade, Op. 16; and others,[53] not to mention Eric Sam's hypothesis that Robert Schumann used the turn figure in a variety of works for his wife, including the Piano Concerto in A minor, Op. 54. Though Musgrave has compellingly shown how C-B-A-G-sharp-A relates to one of the 'basic shapes' of Brahms's First Symphony,[54] more recent scholarship about musical cryptograms has tightened the definition of what constitutes a cipher. Motives that are hidden, transposed or operate without the composer's confirming 'stamp of approval' now garner more scepticism than several decades ago.

One final questionable Brahms cipher pertains to arguably his most substantial composition, the *German Requiem*, Op. 45 (1869). According to Benjamin Locke, the pitches C, B, A and E (*CHAE*) encipher the plaintext Christiane, a

---

[51] Musgrave (1983); Musgrave (1980), 251–2.
[52] Daverio (2002), 112.
[53] For a full list, and arguments refuting each cipher, see ibid.
[54] Musgrave (1983), 121.

reference to the composer's mother, whose passing in 1865 inspired the work. Locke traces this germinal motive in the first (soprano and alto, bars 21–3), fifth (first violin, bars 1–4), sixth (alto, bars 208–10) and seventh movements (bars 40–8). Known for Brahms's 'idiosyncratic text selection' – one that expresses more 'personal resonances' of an 'agnostic view of Christian doctrine' rather than a traditional Christian approach to the requiem genre – Op. 45 may feature a novel cipher technique, for example of splitting up *CHAE* between the soprano and alto lines.[55] But once again, in the absence of further documentation, this cipher too remains conjectural.

Among the few composers whose surname accommodated a 'complete encipherment' was Niels Gade, the most prominent nineteenth-century Danish composer and Mendelssohn's deputy in Leipzig. Devotees of Schumann also acknowledged Gade for his brief appearance in the *Album für die Jugend*, Op. 68 (1848), where No. 41, titled 'Nordisches Lied' and subtitled '(Gruss an G.)', sang the pitches G, A, D and E in the soprano line (ex. 9.12).

But by the time Schumann penned his Nordic testimonial, Gade had already translated his own name into music.

Thus, his Violin Sonata No. 1 in A major, Op. 6 (1843) contains *GADE* in the second movement, where it appears in retrograde, transposed down a wholestep to D-C-G-F (ex. 9.13).

The outer movements too betray glimpses of GADE as melodic source material: the first movement's theme showcases the descending fourth A-E (second and fourth letters of 'Gade'). The third movement, a rondo in A minor, plays most explicitly with the four letters by showing a train of partly unordered, partly ordered GADE formations, yielding in the violin part the consecutive line G-A-D-E-G-D-A-D-E-G-D, before returning to the opening refrain. This last example is reminiscent of Gade's Symphony No. 5 in D minor, Op. 25 (1852), 'a wedding present for his fiancée, which appears to incorporate an anagrammatic rewriting of GADE as ADEG.'[56]

When the musician arrived in Leipzig in 1843, Schumann 'revelled in the musicality (G-A-D-E) of his new friend's name.'[57] Gade encountered too Mendelssohn and Joachim; the latter, like Gade, studied composition with Moritz Hauptmann, Kantor of the Thomaskirche. Gade combined his own cipher with BACH in a contrapuntal setting, *Drei kleine Clavierstücke*, Op. 2a, dedicated to his friend Oluf BACHlin, who may have been 'no more than a contrived literary character, perhaps in the tradition of E. T. A. Hoffmann's Kreisler, embraced so

---

[55] Locke (1998), 10.
[56] Todd (2023), 52.
[57] Jensen (2012), 15.

Ex. 9.12: Robert Schumann, 'Nordisches Lied', Op. 68 No. 41 (1848)

Ex. 9.13: Niels Gade, Violin Sonata No. 1 in A major, Op. 6, Second Movement (1843)

warmly by Robert Schumann and Brahms. If so, that might explain why each of the three pieces juxtaposes the two ciphers, so that GADE appears alongside BACH, with the latter understood as a double entendre, so that it might refer to J. S. Bach or Oluf Bachlin.'[58]

Gade was much more explicit with his signature in *Gaade i 4 bundne Toner* (*Puzzle in 4 Obligatory Notes*) than in his early violin sonata. Here the four pitches emerge in the melodic soprano line. The third piece, *Silent Thoughts*, transposes his surname up a whole-step to A-B-E-F-sharp. Another piece, *Rebus* (1875), 'introduced a new phase in Gade's cipher treatments – in addition to appearances of *GADE*, melodically and harmonically, the composer also employed the familiar *BACH* motive, initially in minims, then crotchets, and finally quavers.'[59]

In 1893 Gade's former pupil Edvard Grieg memorialized his teacher in one of six *Lyric Pieces*, Op. 57. Unlike Schumann's *Nordisches Lied*, with its literal *GADE* cipher but non-specific subtitle 'Gruß an G', Grieg's Op. 57 No. 2 bore the explicit title 'Gade' but concealed its cipher first by setting the composition in A major, and rearranging the order of the Dane's name as A-B-F-sharp-E (that is, transposition of G-A-E-D), in a process reminiscent of Gade's

---

[58] Todd (2023), 56.
[59] Ibid.

Ex. 9.14: Grieg, *Lyric Pieces*, Op. 57 No. 2 (1893)

transformations of his own name, and Schumann's conjuring of the sphinxes in *Carnaval* (ex. 9.14).

Thus did one generation pay musical homage to another.

We turn now to a less intimate member of Schumann's circle, Franz Liszt, who at various times was on friendly terms with the Schumanns, and with Joachim between 1850 and 1852, during the violinist's tenure in Weimar. But after Mendelssohn's death in 1847, the Schumanns became alienated from Liszt, and Joachim declared his antipathy toward Liszt's aesthetic views in 1857. Clara and Joachim took issue with what they viewed as the tawdriness of Liszt's virtuosity. In 1840, Liszt had dedicated his *Études d'exécution transcendante d'après Paganini* to Clara, and in 1854, the Piano Sonata in B minor to Robert. By then, though, Robert had entered the asylum in Endenich, and Clara could not muster any enthusiasm for the work; 'nothing but noise – there is not a wholesome thought...', she was reported to have reacted.[60]

It is this masterpiece of Liszt, however, that David Brown and Alan Walker have subjected to programmatic readings, including ciphers. Despite its 'bald title',[61] the sonata has been interpreted as a 'portrait of the Faust legend', in which the diabolical and divine are in conflict, suggested by the mordant tritones in the primary theme doubled in octaves, and the pan-diatonic second theme associated with the chant *Crux fidelis* ('Faithful Cross'). There are other 'hidden meanings', if speculative, that Walker has read into the work.[62] Brown argues that the sonata contains at least one detail pointing toward a cipher, 'that the second of the two descending scales ... had not only been based on one of the ciphers ... used in the following year in the *Faust* Symphony, but had also exemplified the same process of linkage and overlapping to generate melodic growth.' Brown's theory of ciphers in the sonata prompts an intriguing hypothesis. On 28 March 1854, Joachim received feedback from Liszt about the *Drei Stücke*, Op. 5. The elder musician humorously labelled the pieces 'Gisellen' (pun on 'Gisela'), and thus acknowledged that her cipher had not escaped him.

---

[60] Litzmann (1913), vol. 2, 74.

[61] David Brown (2003), 6.

[62] Walker (1989), 149ff.

Ex. 9.15: Proposed Ferenc Liszt Cipher (after David Brown)

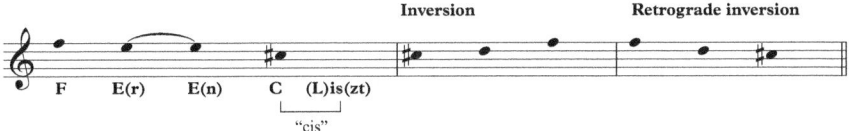

Ex. 9.16: Proposed Ferenc Liszt Cipher (after David Brown)

Ex. 9.17: Liszt, Piano Sonata in B minor, First Movement (1854)

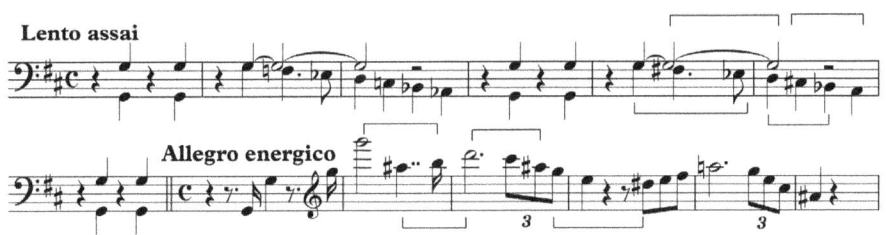

Though the ciphers in Liszt's Sonata, and, for that matter, the *Faust* Symphony, remain conjectural, let us pursue Brown's theory further. He believes that Liszt used the Hungarian version of his Christian name, Ferenc, and his last name to construct a combined 'Ferenc Liszt' cipher: 'Ferenc … [is] followed by Liszt … where the "is" in the surname, now appended to the final "c" of Ferenc, raised that pitch to C-sharp' (see ex. 9.15).

Further, the 'Ferenc Liszt cipher has a second viable form [ex. 9.16] … and it seems clear that both forms were recruited to provide the nuclei that propagated the first six pitches of the Sonata's *Allegro energico* first subject' (ex. 9.17).[63]

In addition, Brown suggests that the sonata also refers to the 'composer's relationship with Carolyne [*née* Karolina] zu Sayn-Wittgenstein' (see ex. 9.18).[64] She had taken up residence with him in Weimar, where he dedicated the twelve symphonic poems composed there (1848–57) to her. Though they desired to marry – she tried to have her union with the Russian Prince Nicolaus von

---

[63] David Brown (2003), 6–7.
[64] Ibid., 7.

Ex. 9.18: Cipher for Carolyne zu Sayn-Wittgenstein (after David Brown)

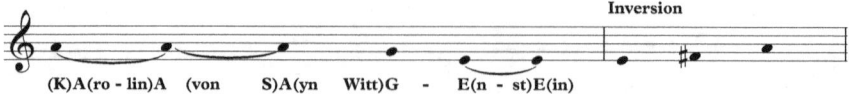

Sayn-Wittgenstein annulled by the pope – that plan failed in 1861. Nevertheless, they remained close until Liszt's death. According to Brown's reading, the sonata relates their love story through four themes: the first appears in bars 9–13; the second (*grandioso*) outlines the first part of the second subject; the third (*Allegro energico*) is 'Liszt's love theme'; and the fourth (*cantando espressivo*), 'Karolina's love theme'.[65]

There is another work by Liszt that relies on a cipher and relates directly to the Schumanns' circle, the *Präludium und Fuge über das Thema B-A-C-H* for organ (1856; revised, 1870). Liszt was probably unaware of Brahms's brief citation of BACH in the cadenza he composed for Beethoven's Fourth Piano Concerto, let alone Gade's innocent play on the name 'Oluf Bachlin' discussed earlier, but almost surely Liszt would have known Robert Schumann's six Organ Fugues on BACH (1845), a collection with as many variants of the tetrachord. Liszt fabricated his own distinctive version of the cipher (ex. 9.19). In unorthodox fashion, his fugue 'begins' a major third below B-flat, with the cipher on G-flat followed by its 'correct' appearance on B-flat. Together, these two entrances traverse two thirds of the chromatic scale, the eight pitches spanning F to C in ascending order. The four missing pitches then appear in descending order (E-natural, E-flat, D and D-flat), allowing Liszt to traverse the total chromatic scale.

Like the fugue, Liszt's prelude is impregnated with the cipher's chromaticism. Already from its opening the motive rumbles in the pedals, forming an obsessively repeating chromatic cluster. One passage displays the ciphers prominently via a composed-out ritardando; their incessant circling now gradually decelerates from semiquavers to quavers, crotchets and minims, then to dotted minims and semibreves (ex. 9.20).

These two techniques – exhausting *BACH* as a trapped motive, and systematically unwinding it through a written-out ritardando – bring Liszt's music close to Joachim's idiosyncratic cipher style. As for trapped motives, there is no more compelling example than his 'Abendglocken', Op. 5 No. 2 (see ex. 9.21), and both Joachim's *Hamlet* and *Demetrius* Overtures feature composed-out ritardandi.[66]

---

[65] Ibid., 9.
[66] Uhde (2015) and (2018), 122ff.

Ex. 9.19: Liszt, *Präludium und Fuge über das Thema B-A-C-H* (1856)

Ex. 9.20: Liszt, *Präludium* (1856)

Ex. 9.21: Joachim, 'Abendglocken', Op. 5 No. 2 (1853)

Though by 1856 Joachim was diverging significantly from Liszt's visions of the musical future, nothing would have stopped Liszt from tacitly acknowledging his younger virtuoso friend, especially since the older musician received copies of Joachim's Op. 5 pieces and *Hamlet* Overture from the composer himself.[67]

Other aspects of Liszt's sensational life involved variable, cipher-like concealments. For Joanne Cormac, he was a 'multinational chameleon' who practised the art of code-switching – abruptly changing languages amidst his conversations and correspondence 'to create a sense of intimacy with the recipient'.[68]

---

[67] Liszt to Joachim of 28 March 1854; Joachim (1911b), I:178.

[68] Cormac (2013), 243.

Liszt was born in the small, German-speaking town of Raiding, Hungary (near the Austrian border), and never learned Magyar, though his countrymen hailed him as a national hero, a role he assumed by appearing in a Hungarian officer's uniform. But early on French became his *lingua franca*, even if he was known to slip from French or German into English, Italian or Latin. He was constantly '[adjusting] his use of languages … to manipulate the way he was perceived by others'.[69] This cosmopolitan manner informed his music as well, so that the symphonic poem *Héroïde funèbre* (1857) began in a Hungarian style that metamorphosed into an Italianate *cantilena* style, before crossing borders again to allude to the *Marseillaise*.[70]

In his correspondence with women, Liszt occasionally resorted to cipher-like initials and codes. Writing from Russia to his mistress Marie d'Agoult he cautioned, 'When certain things have to be said, resort to our usual hieroglyphics',[71] and he signed several letters to Princess Carolyne with 'BB' (*bons bessons*, 'or good twin lambs, i.e. soul-mates').[72] But Liszt's infatuation with Agnes Street-Klindworth, daughter of Metternich's master spy Georg Klindworth, activated the clandestine side of the composer to a new level. Shortly after arriving in 1853 in Weimar, she joined her father's agents tracking insurgents hiding there after the failed revolution of 1848, and between piano lessons with Liszt began a torrid affair with him, 'one of the best kept secrets of the Weimar years'.[73] Then, in 1855, she abruptly departed the duchy, but continued to correspond with him; their letters reveal cryptic glimpses of secret lives preoccupied with ciphers and cabbalistic numerology. Thus, on 6 December 1863 Liszt wrote, 'All the same, you would be wronging me in presuming that I have forgotten our childish little cabala of the *Karls-Platz* staircase'; and, in the same letter, 'the double *cypher* still retains all its luminous magic'.[74]

A few years before, in May 1849, a furtive man '37–38 years old, of medium height, [who] has brown hair and wears glasses' arrived in Weimar at Liszt's villa, the Altenburg. His future son-in-law, Richard Wagner, had fled Dresden after the Prussian military suppressed the short-lived uprising there against the Saxon monarchy. Fearing extradition, the fugitive now assumed the identity of 'Professor Werder from Berlin' before arranging, with Liszt's backing, to reach safety in Switzerland and begin an eleven-year exile.

---

[69] Ibid., 231.

[70] Ibid., 245.

[71] Pocknell (2000), xliv.

[72] Ibid., xliii.

[73] Walker (1986), 47.

[74] Pocknell (2000), 222.

One might imagine that Wagner, who had 'demanded the obliteration of the aristocracy, the imposition of universal suffrage, the elimination of usury',[75] and associated in Dresden with the Russian anarchist Mikhail Bakunin (*aka* Dr. Schwartz), was versed in cryptography, and that his own need for secrecy spilled over into his music. As far as we know, though, he never experimented with musical cryptograms, ciphers, anagrams and the like. But when he designed the plot of *Das Rheingold*, prologue to the *Ring of the Nibelungen*, he devised a theatrical palindrome for its two inner scenes, in which Wotan and Mime descend from the heavens above the Rhein to Nibelheim in the bowels of the earth, capture the dwarf Alberich and his purloined gold, and return to their lofty abode. The clangourous toiling of the anvils, heard during the descent and again during the ascent, audibly impresses as a symmetrical reversal. Even if the music, unlike the experiments of Schubert in *Die Zauberharfe* and Berg in *Lulu* (see pp. 188 and 345), does not unfold an exact palindrome, Wagner's stage direction, 'The scene changes itself, only in retrograde manner, as before', clarifies his intentions to advance the dramatic argument only to uncoil it.

Beyond this example, there are also Wagner's *Leitmotive* ('leading motives'), intricate networks of arguably cipher-like musical tags that inhabit the sprawling dimensions of the *Ring*. Wagner himself mostly avoided the term; it came into currency after the premiere of the *Ring* at Bayreuth in 1876, with the publication of Hans von Wolzogen's *Thematischer Leitfaden* (*Thematic Guide*) to the *Ring*. An ardent Wagnerian, Wolzogen 'uncovered' no fewer than ninety motives, from the 'Motive of the primeval element' in the opening of *Das Rheingold* to the 'Salvation of love' in the closing of *Götterdämmerung*. They comprised 'the fundamental forms of the musical action'.[76] To reduce Wagner's staggering twenty hours of music to seven or so dozen recurring motives was, of course, problematic; as Wagner understood, and as Arnold Whittall and Christian Thorau have argued,[77] the motives' power lay in their ability to transform themselves, as if susceptible to alternate musical encryptions. Indeed, what Wolzogen viewed as the 'Salvation of love' motif at the end of the *Ring* Wagner evidently conceived as the 'glorification of Brünnhilde'.

There is, finally, one aspect of Wagner's *Ring* that did conceal a private meaning *not* divulged to the public. When in 1854 from the asylum of exile the composer commenced the autograph draft for the first act of *Die Walküre*, he 'inserted here and there comments on which clear light fell onto so many of his personal relationships as well as the particular circumstances of his creation'.[78]

---

[75] Ross (2020), 21.
[76] Wolzogen (1876), 9.
[77] Whittall (2001), 527; Thorau (2009), 162.
[78] Strobel (1932), 151.

And so we find six sets of elliptical initials that Otto Strobel decoded in 1932, demonstrating that they concerned the composer's involvement with Mathilde Wesendonck, poet and wife of another confirmed Wagnerian, the affluent silk merchant Otto Wesendonck. Thus, in the opening scene, just after Siegmund sings 'The sun smiles now on me again', we encounter 'I[ch]. l[iebe]. d[ich]. gr[enzenlos]!!' ('I love you endlessly'); and, just before the conclusion of the scene, as Siegmund and Sieglinde, unaware that they are siblings, look at each other, 'L[iebst]. d[u]. m[ich]. M[athilde].?' ('Do you love me, Mathilde?').[79] In short, Wagner too, it seems, like Schumann's circle, practised his own variety of *Beziehungskunst*.

By century's end, the major schism in German music – between the *Zukunftsmusiker* ('musicians of the future') supporting Wagner and Liszt, and the '*Brahmins*' ['*Brahmaner*'], a closely drawn, for some cultish circle around Brahms – was well defined. Most musicians aligned with one of these camps, though Arnold Schoenberg comfortably traced his roots to both sides, so that Brahms emerged as a 'progressive' composer.[80] Another musician who explored each faction was Max Reger (1873–1916), for Antonius Bittmann a determined practitioner of 'historicist modernism'. In 1900 Reger produced his *Phantasie und Fuge über BACH*, Op. 46, an imposing organ work that drew upon 'conservative' *and* 'progressive' directions in German music, here represented by Robert Schumann and Franz Liszt. Earlier we considered how in the *Präludium und Fuge über das Thema B-A-C-H* Liszt in 1856 was already exploiting the full chromatic gamut. If anything, Reger's fantasy from the turn to the new century intensified his predecessor's chromatic forays; what is more, Reger's fugal subject betrayed clear similarities to Liszt's (ex. 9.22).

But Reger's homage to Bach was unimaginable too without its taut relationship to Robert Schumann's organ fugues on BACH (1845), especially to the endpoints of that cycle, Nos. 1 and 6 (ex. 9.23).

Not only are the subjects similar, but, like Schumann's two fugues, Reger's is an accelerando fugue; furthermore, like Schumann, Reger introduces his subject in retrograde.[81]

Reger dedicated Op. 46 to another confirmed Bachian, Josef Rheinberger, who in 1884 had contributed a short *Fughetta* in C major on BACH 'in the strict style'. But Reger could write music that heralded the modernism of the new century as assertively as it reaffirmed links to historical models. Thus, in the Violin Sonata No. 4 in C major, Op. 72 (1903), he produced 'a manifesto

---

[79] Ibid., 152.

[80] Schoenberg (1984), 398.

[81] Reger, bars 55–7, 60–2.

Ex. 9.22: Reger, *Phantasie und Fuge über BACH*, Op. 46 (1900)

Ex. 9.23: Robert Schumann, Organ Fugues on *BACH*, Op. 60 Nos. 1 and 6 (1845)

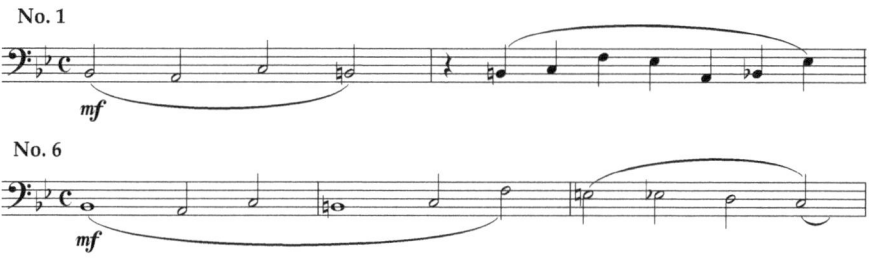

Ex. 9.24: Reger, Violin Sonata No. 4 in C major, Op. 72 (1903)

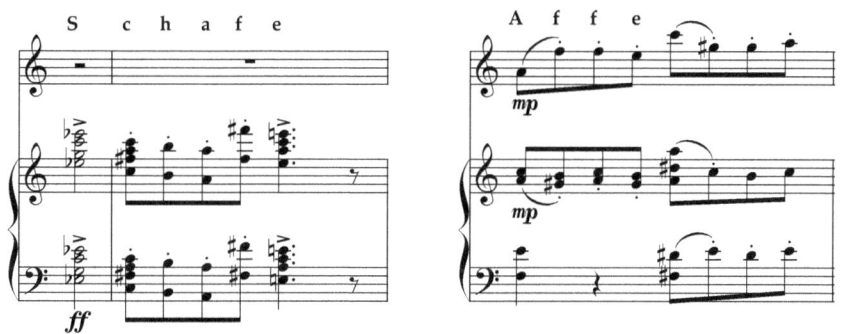

of perverse modernism'[82] that in all but the title, a few harmonically translucent passages, and sometimes 'artificial' final cadences, aggressively strained against tonal moorings. Here Reger drew in equal measure upon Brahms's Violin Sonata No. 1 in G major, Op. 78 (*Regen*) and, from the New Germans, Richard Strauss's tone poem *Ein Heldenleben* (*A Hero's Life*) to lampoon critics on both sides of the aisle. Reger's weapons of choice were musical cryptograms for 'sheep' and 'ape' (*Schafe*, E-flat-C-B-A-F-E; *Affe*, A-F-F-E), deployed throughout the sonata (ex. 9.24).

---

[82] Bittmann (2004), 708.

These ciphers provided a backstory for music that brazenly if paradoxically declared its autonomy from, and yet preservation of, the Brahmsian ideal of 'absolute' music. Perhaps the clairvoyant Robert Schumann would have been amused; Brahms, we might imagine, bemused?

CHAPTER 10

Stenographic Mysteries, Dark Sayings, Magic Squares and Foul Balls

'The Enigma I will not explain – its "dark saying" must be left unguessed.'

– Edward Elgar

O F course, Wagner's cryptic initials were meant for his eyes alone, like furtive diary entries projecting onto Sieglinde's and Siegmund's illicit union the composer's inner turmoil over his liaison with Mathilde Wesendonck. In the nineteenth century initialism also appeared in literature, including the novels of Charles Dickens, who early on became a 'professional language player'.[1] From a letter of 1833 signed 'Charles I.B.L.K.Y.N. Dickens'[2] to a wall inscription at Staple Inn

P
J T
1747

contemplated by Hiram Grewgious in *The Mystery of Edwin Drood* (1870),[3] Dickens indulged in word games. Both examples remain unsolved, though Dickens did offer some options for the second – 'Perhaps John Thomas', 'Pretty Jolly Too' and 'Possibly Jabbered Thus'.[4] Elsewhere, he was more forthcoming. For example, early in *Pickwick Papers* (1837) we encounter 'P.V.P.M.P.C.' and 'G.C.M.P.C', identified in the author's footnotes as 'Perpetual Vice-President – Member Pickwick Club' and 'General Chairman – Member Pickwick Club'. Later in the novel, Pickwick encounters Peter Magnus, who proffers his business card: '"Curious circumstance about those initials, sir"' … "you will observe – P.M. – post meridian … I sometimes sign myself 'Afternoon'. It amuses my friends very much, Mr. Pickwick"'.[5]

---

[1] Bowles (2019), 66.
[2] Storey (1982), I, 31.
[3] Chapter 11.
[4] Douglas-Fairhurst (2011), 62.
[5] *Pickwick Papers*, Chapter 22.

Admittedly, Dickens himself was 'biscriptal – able to read and write in two graphic codes',[6] conventional Roman script and shorthand, which he mastered by 1829, intending to find employment as a freelance court reporter in London. Shorthand had been established in England since at least the late sixteenth century. Among its practitioners were Sir Isaac Newton and Samuel Pepys, who relied upon the stenography of Thomas Shelton known as tachygraphy (Greek for 'fast writing'). Dickens's textbook was the *Brachygraphy* ('short writing') of Thomas Gurney (1705–70); the character David Copperfield described it as a 'savage, stenographic mystery'.[7] Two features that rendered Gurney's shorthand difficult were: first, it dispensed with punctuation; and second, it relied on consonants, compelling the reader to insert missing vowels into prickly lists of consonants. Thus, in a speech to Parliament 'mst al dply afd w so s los' emerged as 'but you must all have been deeply affected with so severe a loss'.[8]

Hugo Bowles has recently plumbed the relationship between Dickens's shorthand and his manipulation of language and concluded that 'Dickens's spelling [often] reflects the principles of Gurney shorthand'.[9] As any Dickensian knows, the author frequently used non-standard spellings to capture his characters' idiolects, recalling the reductive qualities of the shorthand method that he practised. Indeed, Bowles assembles 173 'deviant' spellings in *Pickwick Papers* alone, including, for instance, *buzzim* for 'bosom' and *fernomenon* for 'phenomenon'.[10]

Like the Victorian Dickens, the Edwardian Sir Edward Elgar often played verbal games, and fairly 'wallow[ed] in words'.[11] He solved cryptographic puzzles[12] and wrote playful letters to his daughter, Carice, whose name derived from his wife's forenames, **Car**oline **A**l**ice**. The Elgars' residence, Craeg Lea, concealed the composer's surname in reverse (**Craeg Le**a) and an anagram of his wife's initials, 'C. A. E.' (**Cra**e **L**ea). His correspondence teems with deliberate misspellings, puns and other verbal manipulations, for instance, 'zu' for 'you' and 'faser' for 'father'. Craig Bauer has culled many more mind-twisting word pairings from Elgar's letters to Carice, including 'Histish englory', 'dimple sinner' and 'oracular jerkations',[13] all of which test the boundaries of verbal meaning and cryptographic nonsense.

---

[6] Bowles (2019), 2.
[7] *David Copperfield*, Chapter 43.
[8] Cited in Douglas-Fairhurst (2011), 62.
[9] Ibid., 122.
[10] Ibid., 167–71.
[11] *David Copperfield*, Chapter 43.
[12] Buckley (1905), 41.
[13] Bauer (2017), 153–4.

One puzzle that engaged Elgar and his daughter in 1902 was a triple 'Botanical Acrostic'; its solution was a slightly irregular five-by-five square, with words formed as uprights by the first (acrostic), third (mesostic) and fifth (telestich) columns.[14] Here are the clues:

1. Of iron peculiarly may be; with noise and fury equally.
2. To say that food is this is scanty praise.
3. Its gorgeousness may well attract our gaze.
4. A Grecian land will here assistance lend.
5. A narrow strip, in fine, pronounced the end.

The solution reveals the intersections of words that can be read vertically and horizontally:

1. S c R a P
2. E d I bl E
3. P a G ean T
4. A c H ae A
5. L i T tora L

Among Elgar's favourite diversions was the cryptic crossword. Enigmatologists generally credit Edward Powys Mathers (1892–1939) for inventing it, in which the clues themselves require decipherment – for example, they might employ anagrams puns, or homonyms.[15] Mathers, whose penname was Torquemada, after the fifteenth-century Spanish Grand Inquisitor, began issuing cryptic crosswords in *The Observer* in 1926, prompting the composer to write just a few months later: 'Although Sir Edward Elgar would rather adorn a stake than venture to disturb unduly the august meditations of TORQUEMADA, he dares to suggest and hope that, on the completion of the first year of the weekly [w]rackings … the puzzles may be collected and published with the answers in one volume'.[16]

Elgar expended effort not only in solving puzzles, but also in creating them, perhaps most famously the 'Dorabella' Cipher, preserved in a note from 1897 written for Dora Penny, daughter of the Reverend Alfred Penny of Wolverhampton. The composer recorded three lines of squirming squiggles for 'Dorabella' (after Dorabella in Mozart's *Così fan tutte*) and dated them below.[17] The eighty-

---

[14] Ibid., 44–5.

[15] In 1968 and 1969 the lyricist/composer Stephen Sondheim introduced cryptic puzzles to American audiences in the *New York Magazine*, gathered together in a volume released in 1980.

[16] Elgar (2014), 320.

[17] Powell (1937), 98.

seven scrawls comprise single, double and triple semicircular shapes susceptible to rotation or inversion, so that, for example, a 'u'-like shape may appear as an 'n', or an 'm'-like shape as a 'w'. Because several appear to resemble the letter 'E' or its repositioning, we might deduce that Elgar drew them from his own initials, E. W. E. (Edward William Elgar); another conjecture is that he employed a mono- or polyalphabetic substitution system, not unlike the stick figures in Sir Arthur Conan Doyle's *The Adventure of the Dancing Men* (1903), one of four Sherlock Holmes mysteries to employ cryptography.[18] Like Doyle, Elgar made his cipher more difficult to crack because the squiggles flow in a continuous sequence, without spaces separating individual words (Illustration 10.1)

There have been several attempts to decode this message, beginning in 1970 with Eric Sams,[19] who proposed, in part, 'Larks! It's chaotic, but a cloak obscures my new letters, A, B'. More recently, in 2007, Tony Gaffney (*alias* Jean Palmer) began his 'solution' with the equally unconvincing 'B (Bella) hellcat i.e. war using??'[20] Then, in 2009, Tim S. Roberts of Central Queensland University of Australia claimed to have discovered a key Elgar used to produce the ciphers, 'LADPENNY WRITIGIC OSWYKPBU', or, with adjustments, 'Lady Penny, writing in code is a way to keep busy'.[21] A second stage of decrypting generated by this key then yielded 'P.S. Now droop beige weeds set in it', a reference, Roberts suggested, to Elgar's garden. But even Roberts's results caused the sceptical Bauer to observe, 'real solutions rarely require explanations'.[22] There the matter rested until Wayne Packwood introduced another perspective in 2020, arguing that Elgar embedded two dots in the three rows of ciphers, as if to suggest the movements of a conductor's baton, so that the rows should be read vertically rather than horizontally. Packwood's ultimate solution read: 'A woman is like chess one has to make sacrifices for its queen it is victory that she commands not do better'.[23]

Compounding the mystery is that elsewhere Elgar applied similar squiggles.[24] In April 1886 he attended a concert at the Crystal Palace honouring Franz Liszt, then visiting England just months before his death, when Elgar heard a

---

[18] Along with *The Adventure of the Gloria Scott* (1893), *The Adventure of the Red Circle* (1911) and *The Valley of Fear: The Tragedy of Birlstone* (1914).

[19] Sams (1970a) 151–4.

[20] Macnamara.

[21] Roberts, 'Solving the Dorabella Cipher' (https://unsolvedproblems.org/S36b.pdf). [Accessed 3 February 2025]

[22] Bauer (2017), 133.

[23] Packwood (2020).

[24] For instance, an autograph note in Elgar's hand sold by Sotheby's in May 2016 (Lot 92) bears the notation 'Wrote to Hill offering to purchase Gagliano' followed by the English pound sign and a few squiggles. Presumably this document dates from 1891, the year Elgar bought the violin from the luthier W. E. Hill.

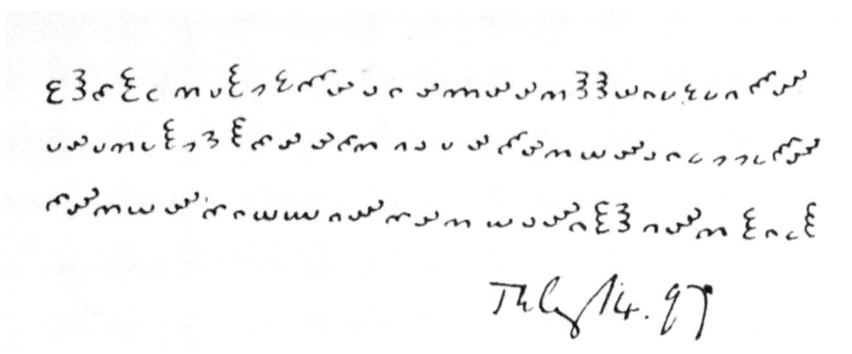

Illustration 10.1: Elgar, Dorabella Cipher (1897), Powell (1937), 98

performance of the symphonic poem *Les Préludes*. In the margin of the concert programme he noted eighteen ciphers, purportedly solved in 1977 by Anthony Thorley to read: 'Gets you to joy, and hysterious'.[25] 'Hysterious' suggests a portmanteau from 'hysteria' and 'mysterious', a conceit in keeping with Elgar's word plays, not to mention that the sentiment accords with the programmatic content of Liszt's first symphonic poem, and what he described as a series of transitional 'preludes to that "unknown hymn"'. But no one has yet shed much light on how Thorley hit upon his reading,[26] or whether it might use the same key as the Dorabella cipher.

There is another crucial piece of evidence concerning Elgar's glyphs. In a notebook from the 1920s the composer recorded several cryptographic annotations, where we again encounter the wriggling squiggles in their upright, horizontal and sloping positions and inclinations.[27] Elgar provided a key for these jottings, with twenty-four different figures arranged above the letters of the alphabet.[28] The key reveals a plan: the squiggles fall into recurring groups of three, with ascending number of curvilinear shapes from one to three in each group. Thus, for the letter 'a' Elgar began with a semicircular shape resembling 'c'; for the letter 'b' he added a second semicircle to produce a sign resembling 'E'; and for the letter 'c' appended yet another semicircle to produce 'X'. For the next three letters, 'd', 'e' and 'f', he simply rotated the symbols for 'a', 'b' and 'c' to the right by forty-five degrees. The remaining groups of letters then continued to revolve through six more adjustments of forty-five degrees each, so that 'x', 'y' and 'z' completed the circle of the pattern (ex. 10.1).

---

[25] See Moore (1984), 114.
[26] See further Bauer (2017), 135.
[27] Elgar Will Trust and Elgar Birthplace Museum, Lower Broadheath, Worcestershire.
[28] The letters 'i' and 'j' share the same figure, as do 'u' and 'v'.

Ex. 10.1: Elgar's Cryptograms and Key

```
c E Ec E Enmmɔ³³ ɔ³³ɔɔ³u www cE E
A B C D E F G H I J   K L M N O P Q R S T U V W X Y Z
```

Beneath the key Elgar recorded three short, easily transcribable encrypted messages. The first, 'Marco Elgar', refers to the composer's dog; the second reads 'A very old cypher'; the third, 'Do you go to London?'

Nevertheless, as intriguing as Elgar's key is, it provides no solution for the 'Dorabella' cipher, only gibberish. Did Elgar devise different keys for his ciphers? Here, the cryptographic plot thickens, for at the bottom of the same notebook page, Elgar drew four clock-like circles, each divided into quadrants, with each containing hash marks, pointing outside or inside the circle, to the right or left of the vertical line and above or below the horizontal line that divide the circle into semicircles. Were these circles designed to orient the squiggles according to their matching rotations, to provide varying options for aligning them with the letters of the alphabet? Alas, Elgar did not reveal how he placed the twenty-four letters next to these squiggles, so that they might change into credible characters and form meaningful words.

Once again, we are left to our own devices. Using trial and error, we may now consider the key presented in ex. 10.2.

According to this scheme, the letter 'A' appears midway and proceeds in reverse through Elgar's ternary squiggles, from 'A' to 'M', leaving the second half of the alphabet, 'N' to 'Z', to unfold in retrograde from the end. Applying this key, we may now begin to transcribe the 'Liszt' Cipher. Happily, the first three squiggles produce the word 'GET', the fourth, 'S', the fifth, 'U', and the sixth, 'T', or "GETS U T". With a little imagination, we may read this beginning as "Gets [you] t[o]", that is, the very opening of the solution proposed by Thorley in 1977. Proceeding a bit further, the seventh symbol could be a 'J', though its orientation is somewhat ambiguous. But the next two squiggles seem to produce 'H' and 'E', throwing us off the track. Still, if we persevere with the remaining squiggles, we find "DHSTEARWP". Here the 'D' could stand for '[an]d', leaving 'HSTEARWP' to be read possibly as 'H[i]stearwp'. Setting aside 'WP', which remains enigmatic, 'H[i]stear' brings us close to Thorley's solution: 'GETS YOU TO JOY, AND HYSTERIOUS', which arguably 'married "hysteria" with "mysterious" through a "tear"'.[29]

Elgar may well have used shorthand-like abbreviations, word plays, etc. to conceal his plaintext, adding layered masks that for over a century have

---

[29] Moore (1984), 114.

Ex. 10.2: Possible Key to Elgar's Liszt Cipher

successfully guarded his plaintext. Until another, more convincing solution to the Liszt Cipher presents itself, 'GETS YOU TO JOY, AND HYSTERIOUS' remains the most plausible. We concur with David Copperfield, who admitted in the midst of his shorthand travails, '... the wonderful vagaries that were played by circles; the unaccountable consequences that resulted from marks like flies' legs; the tremendous effect of a curve in the wrong place; not only troubled my waking hours, but reappeared before me in my sleep'.[30] Meanwhile, the 'Dorabella' Cipher remains as secretive as in 1937, when Mrs. Richard Powell (*née* Dora Penny) published a facsimile, with this admission: 'I have never had the slightest idea what message it conveys; [Elgar] never explained it and all attempts to solve it have failed. Should any reader of this book succeed in arriving at a solution it would interest me very much to hear of it'.[31]

ʚ *i*

In matters cryptological, turnaround is only fair play, so we may consider Elgar's solution of a nettlesome cryptogram that appeared in 1896, one year before he penned the 'Dorabella' Cipher. The occasion was the release of four articles by John Holt Schooling, a statistician and writer whose interests included graphology (he analysed Dickens's handwriting) and calculating the size of the wide-ranging British Empire. For the *Pall Mall Magazine* Schooling authored a serialized history of cryptography, 'Secrets in Cipher', from antiquity to late-Elizabethan times, through the mid-Stuart period, from Charles II to George II, and finally up to the closing decade of the nineteenth century. Here Elgar would have read about the Spartan scytale and the decryption methods of Elizabeth's chief spymaster, Francis Walsingham. There was also an example of a string cypher, in which a ball of twine was periodically knotted so that when one attached the unwound twine to a special frame bearing the alphabet at the top, a secret message materialized.[32] Elgar may have recognized this method from Rudyard Kipling's story 'The Man Who Would Be King' (1888), which

---

[30] *David Copperfield*, Chapter 38.
[31] Powell (1937), 98.
[32] Schooling (1896), 246–7.

Ex. 10.3: J. H. Schooling, Musical Cipher from the Time of George II (1796)

refers to its use by the poor in the Punjab. And, finally, Schooling presented one musical cipher from the time of George II (1727-60), shown in ex. 10.3, and not unlike the cryptogram by Philip Thicknesse (see p. 126).[33]

Each of Schooling's first three articles ended with a cryptogram for the reader to crack before the author revealed its solution in the next instalment. But the entire series culminated in a still more challenging puzzle, deliberately left undeciphered, emboldening Schooling to assert that 'the meaning ... will never be solved by anyone'.[34] Here is the ultimate gauntlet Schooling cast down and Elgar accepted – two rows of numbers, concluding with two tantalizing question marks:

36	49	97	65	45	43	30	24	76	88	66
54	45	26	44	55	59	57	22	36	?	?

It was an example of a so-called nihilist cipher, used by Russian anarchists plotting against the tsar near the close of the century. Earlier in the fourth instalment, Schooling had presented a similar puzzle and provided its solution, which involved a five-by-five lettered square and a key word. But he failed to disclose the key word for his final puzzle and presumed that no one would be able to defeat the cipher. Elgar proved otherwise.

How did he accomplish the task? Nine annotated cards preserved at the Elgar Birthplace Museum in Worcestershire disclose his incremental progress.[35] First, Elgar wrote out a grid that allowed him to convert numbers to letters:

---

[33] Ibid., 459.
[34] Ibid., 618.
[35] Fully explained in Bauer (2017), 136–47.

	1	2	3	4	5
1	A	B	C	D	E
2	F	G	H	I	K
3	L	M	N	O	P
4	Q	R	S	T	U
5	V	W	X	Y	Z

Then, focusing on the number 22 in Schooling's cryptogram, Elgar noticed that the plaintext and key word for that number could be produced only by adding 11 + 11,[36] that according to the grid 11 corresponded to the letter A, and that, therefore, he could insert A as part of the plaintext *and* repeating key word for the number 22. In a similar way, the number 30 in the first row could only result from adding 15 + 15: in other words, the letter E. Other numbers in the puzzle admitted multiple options, so Elgar had to test different possibilities. Eventually he determined that the key word had seven letters, in the order - - - - A - E.

The breakthrough came when he identified it as COURAGE. Writing out Schooling's original numbers in a row and beneath it on the second row the repeating key word COURAGE then allowed Elgar to produce for the third row the corresponding numbers for COURAGE. Thus, the first letter, C, corresponded to 13, the second letter, O, to 34, the third letter, U, to 45, and so on. These he then subtracted from Schooling's original numbers to produce yet another series for the fourth row (for example, 36 − 13 = 23; 49 − 34 = 15, etc.), which he could then easily transcribe (by replacing 23 with H, 15 with E, etc.) to divulge the plaintext: 'He who fears is half dead'. That left the final two question marks in Schooling's puzzle as superfluous nulls. Here is a summary of all these numerical gyrations, with Schooling's numbers marked in bold:

36	**49**	**97**	**65**	**45**	**43**	**30**	**24**	**76**	**88**	**66**	**54**	**45**	**26**	**44**	**55**	**59**	**57**	**22**	**36**
C	O	U	R	A	G	E	C	O	U	R	A	G	E	C	O	U	R	A	G
13	34	45	42	11	22	1	13	34	45	42	11	22	15	13	34	45	42	11	22
23	15	52	23	34	21	15	11	42	43	24	43	23	11	31	21	14	15	11	14
H	e	w	h	o	f	e	a	r	s	I	s	h	a	l	f	d	e	a	d

Elgar thus played both sides of the cryptanalytical coin: he could construct *and* solve seemingly impenetrable riddles. Now the numbers in Schooling's cipher might encourage us to consider whether numbers may have also played a role

---

[36] Of course, 22 is also the sum of, for example, 14 + 8, but there is no 8 in the five-by-five grid.

in the squiggles Elgar devised in 1897 for Dorabella – that is, could they have represented numbers that, in turn, converted by means of some grid into letters? Perhaps, though a cursory inspection would seem to produce more dead ends. The 'Dorabella' Cipher employs no fewer than twenty-one different symbols, so exactly how Elgar might have aligned them with a grid that accounted for all ten digits from 0 to 9 poses further challenges. For now, we shall allow 'Dorabella' to rest in peace and proceed to yet another beguiling aspect of Elgar's music – whether he employed *musical* cryptograms.

The short answer is yes. As early as 1885 he composed an *Allegretto* for violin and piano for two daughters of the Reverend William Gedge, violin pupils of the composer. As Elgar realized, the Gedge surname lent itself readily to encipherment, and so he designed a five-note cipher displayed beneath the title in so many breves, as if to recall the antiquarian sphinxes in the *Carnaval* of Robert Schumann, to whom the young composer referred as 'my ideal'.[37] Elgar worked some thirty odd references to the 'Misses Gedge' into his offering of just under one hundred bars, or about one every three bars, a level of saturation reminiscent of Schumann's technique of cipher manipulations. Ex. 10.4 illustrates one passage in which the ciphers appear at their most dense, occurring every bar.

According to Anthony Thorley, Elgar employed a cipher in *The Dream of Gerontius* (1900), in which the composer pilloried his rival Charles Villiers Stanford as 'Satanford' in the Demons' Chorus of Part II.[38] 'Satanford' would be another credible example of Elgar's word games, but exactly how he may have translated this parody into musical terms is unclear. Yet another encipherment, this one readily apparent, was the octave e'-e" on a treble stave (ex. 10.5), which Elgar occasionally enlisted as a substitute for his initials.[39] So the composer certainly practised musical cryptography, which brings us to the final Elgarian riddle, the most refractory of all – the *Enigma* Variations of 1899.

Elgar's daughter Carice observed that when 'her father had finished a Sunday cryptic crossword it was as if he had completed one of his big scores'.[40] One wonders if the obverse were true – that for Elgar dispatching a major composition was comparable to solving an arduous puzzle. For more than a century the Variations have defied attempts to explicate their enigma(s), the 'dark saying[s]' Elgar refused to reveal. Having successfully solved Schooling's puzzle of 1896, Elgar now constructed his own musical riddle, filling the score with

---

[37] Letter of 1 July 1883 to Dr. Buck, cited in Moore (1984), 97. On Elgar's awareness of Schumann's sphinxes, see also Trowell (1993), 306–7 (147n).

[38] Moore (1984), 299.

[39] Moore (1987), vol. 1, 148, 182.

[40] Sams (1998), 414.

Ex. 10.4: Elgar, *Allegretto* for Violin and Piano (1885)

Ex. 10.5: Elgar's Musical Signature

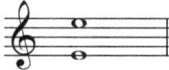

layers of extra-musical significance – vignette-like portraits of friends identified only by their initials or by cryptic headings such as Nimrod, Ysobel and Romanza, not to mention the overarching mystery behind the theme of the composition, and the possibility that it served as a foil to a much more widely known theme never literally stated in the music, even though it somehow cast a shadow over the work.

There is irony that the original title for the composition was far less forthcoming – Variations; there was no mention of 'Enigma' until Elgar's editor and close friend at Novello's, August Jaeger, immortalized as Nimrod[41] in the ninth variation, added the word above the opening bars of the autograph score. What Elgar had playfully described as 'a set of Variations (orkestry) on an

---

[41] After the biblical hunter in Genesis 10: 8–12; 'Jaeger' is the German for 'hunter'.

original theme'⁴² now took on a far more serious purpose, made more oracular by Elgar's revealing, yet vexing comments printed with the programme for the premiere conducted by Hans Richter in London on 19 June 1899:

> It is true that I have sketched for their amusement and mine, the idiosyncrasies of fourteen of my friends, not necessarily musicians; but this is a personal matter, and need not have been mentioned publicly. The Variations should stand simply as a 'piece' of music. The Enigma I will not explain – its 'dark saying' must be left unguessed, and I warn you that the connexion between the Variations and the Theme is often of the slightest texture; further, through and over the whole set another and larger theme 'goes', but is not played ... So the principal Theme never appears, even as in some late dramas – e.g., Maeterlinck's 'L'Intruse' and 'Les sept Princesses' – the chief character is never on the stage.⁴³

In time, the identities of the fourteen characters became public,⁴⁴ so that the framing variations were understood to represent Elgar's wife, Caroline Alice Elgar (C. A. E.) and the composer himself (E. D. U. for Edward, or 'Edoo', Caroline's nickname for him), with the intervening variations depicting twelve friends. Details such as Dorabella's stutter (tenth variation) and the bark of the bulldog Dan who belonged to the Hereford organist George Robertson Sinclair (eleventh variation) did not escape notice. Even the three inscrutable asterisks of the thirteenth variation were unmasked to reveal Lady Mary Trefusis (*née* Lygon), who in 1899, Elgar believed, had voyaged to New South Wales in Australia, prompting him to incorporate into her music a quotation from Mendelssohn's *Calm Sea and Prosperous Voyage* Overture.⁴⁵

But for every secretive detail of the composition, the principal enigma has remained largely a closed book, notwithstanding determined efforts to advance this or that theme to fit with the opening bars of Elgar's composition. Proposals over the years have included 'Auld Lang Syne', 'Loch Lomond', 'God Save the Queen', 'For He's a Jolly Good Fellow', 'A Mighty Fortress is Our God' and the slow movements of Mozart's *Prague* Symphony K 504 and Beethoven's *Pathétique* Sonata Op. 13.⁴⁶ Among the most novel is that Elgar's 'theme' (see ex. 10.7), which begins on the third scale degree followed by the first, fourth and

---

⁴² Elgar to Jaeger, 24 October 1898, in Moore (1987), vol. 1, 95.

⁴³ From the programme notes of Charles Ainslie Barry for the London premiere, cited in Rushton (1999), 65.

⁴⁴ See Elgar (1947).

⁴⁵ Regarding the identity of the asterisks, see Rushton (1999), 75–6.

⁴⁶ For attempts to solve the 'Enigma' through 1991, see Lee (1994), 254–5, and Rushton (1999), 89–93.

second, encodes the irrational constant Pi (3.14159).[47] But perhaps we should take seriously Elgar's admonishment that the variations may stand 'simply as a "piece" of music', that the link between them and the theme is 'often of the slightest texture'. Perhaps the search for an external theme that fits, hand in glove, in counterpoint with Elgar's theme is a fool's errand, even though the composer expressed surprise that Dora(bella) Powell 'of all people' had not guessed it.[48]

There is another possibility. What if the enigma concerns not Elgar's 'theme' – the first violin part of bars 1–6, with its drooping melodic thirds – but rather the bass line, with its stepwise, scale-like ascent (ex. 10.6a)?

That a bass line could radiate an aura of mystery had been demonstrated by the appearance of a curious *scala-rebus* in a Milanese music journal in 1888 (ex. 10.6b),[49] the inspiration for Giuseppe Verdi's *a cappella Ave Maria* that applied the scale as a foundational *cantus firmus* in all four voices, and fashioned against it counterpoints drawn from its pitches (ex. 10.6c).

The *Ave Maria* appeared as the first of the *Quattro pezzi sacri* (*Four Sacred Pieces*) in 1898, just a year before the *Enigma* Variations' premiere. Fittingly, the

Ex. 10.6a: Elgar, *Enigma Variations*, Op. 36 (1899), Bass Line

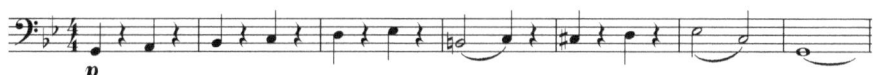

Ex. 10.6b–c: *Scala enigmatica*; Verdi, *Ave Maria* (1898)

---

[47] Santa and Santa (2010).
[48] Powell (1937), 23.
[49] *Gazzetta musicale di Milano* (5 August 1888).

Ex. 10.7: Elgar, *Enigma* Variations, Op. 36 (1899)

scala-rebus became known as the *scala enigmatica*; in 1905, Verdi's treatment of it was described as producing 'queer counterpoint … far-fetched and difficult of intonation'.[50] Though unlikely that this 'enigma' could have had some connection with Elgar, it continued to intrigue composers, among them Luigi Nono, well into the twentieth century and beyond.[51]

That said, in 1993 Brian Trowell pointed out similarities between Elgar's bass line and a fugato-like passage from his cantata *Caractacus*, Op. 35, also released in 1898[52] (ex. 10.6a, 10.8).

Salient here is that both bass lines traverse the interval of the sixth through ascending stepwise motion before they descend. So, may Elgar have been exploring an allusion to his cantata, set in the Malvern Hills, in the composer's native Worcestershire, where, according to legend, the chieftain Caractacus had made his last stand in the first century CE against Roman invaders? Setting aside the cantata, we might note that the *Enigma* bass line has similarities too to the finale of a major orchestral work that Elgar would have known – Brahms's Fourth Symphony Op. 98 (1885), celebrated for its revival of the passacaglia through fully thirty variations plus coda, in which a rising ostinato figure recurs not only in the bass but occasionally in the treble as well (ex. 10.9).

Admittedly, Brahms's template ascends through a perfect fifth, *not* the sixth in *Caractacus* and the *Enigma* Variations. What's more, Brahms fills in the whole-step from the fourth to fifth scale degree, A to B, with the chromatic passing tone A-sharp, a detail missing in Elgar's bass line, where the comparable adjustment would have been a C-sharp between the C and D (bars 2–3). Brahms's ostinato pattern (transposed to G minor) does not work against Elgar's theme, likely the reason why Op. 98 has not received much press in the

---

[50] Hadow (1905), vol. 6, 223.
[51] See Nielinger-Vakil (2015), *passim*.
[52] Trowell (1993), 312.

Ex. 10.8: Elgar, *Caractacus*, Op. 35 (1898)

Ex. 10.9: Brahms, Fourth Symphony, Op. 98 (1885)

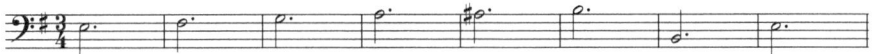

search for the enigma, though Julian Rushton has discussed the similarities and suggested the first and fourth movements of the symphony as tentative models for Elgar.[53] There is, though, another piece of evidence to consider. Elgar's bass line reveals that in fact he *did* make use of the raised fourth like Brahms, though not in bars 2–3, where its similarity to Op. 98 would have been perhaps too readily apparent. Rather, the C-sharp appears in bar 5, as if to strengthen through hindsight the general allusion in the earlier bars to Brahms. Perhaps this was Elgar's way of having another, 'larger theme' present, even though it is not literally heard; as in two of Maeterlinck's dramas of the 1890s, 'the chief character is never seen on the stage'.

Another question remains: did Elgar, given his penchant for riddles, apply musical cryptograms in the variations? Might we wonder, for instance, if the spinning three-note string figures in the Dorabella variation (ex. 10.10) form sounding complements to the swirling ternary squiggles in the Dorabella cipher? Also conjectural, might the stream of initials afforded by the subtitles of Elgar's variations harbour some hidden message relating to the 'dark saying' of the whole? No one, it seems, has investigated these possibilities, though the significance of encrypting initials into a musical composition was not lost on Elgar's younger colleague, Granville Bantock, who conducted the second performance of the *Enigma* Variations in 1899. The next year he composed his own series of twelve orchestral *Helena* Variations, dedicated to his wife, Helena Francesca Bantock, and offered as 'my thoughts and reflections on some of your moods'.[54]

---

[53] Rushton (1999), 25–6.
[54] Bantock (1972), 44.

Ex. 10.10: Elgar, *Enigma* Variations, Op. 36 (1899)

Ex. 10.11: Granville Bantock, *Helena* Variations (1900)

In a letter of 22 October 1899 the composer specified them as 1) Valkyrie, 2) woman, 3) a light mood, 4) ascetic and church, 5) imp, 6) inward wrestlings, 7) meditation, 8) love, 9) rage, 10) Eastern mood, 11) melancholy mood and 12) climax.[55] Binding the whole together were his wife's initials, H. F. B., enciphered as B-natural, F and B-flat, appearing at the opening of the theme (ex. 10.11), and undergoing transformations throughout the composition.

As Bantock realized, the three-note motive presented its own conundrum: a dissonant tritone, B-F, is juxtaposed with a perfect fifth, F-B-flat, before the tritone fully resolves by contrary motion to the sixth B-flat to G-flat. From Helena's initials Bantock built a composition culminating in a radiant final variation in the major recalling the finale of Elgar's set from the previous year. Perhaps Granville intended his conclusion as a self-portrait, as if to follow Elgar's precedent by framing the *Helena* Variations with the spouses. But unlike Elgar, who chose to interpret his theme through an extended circle of friends introduced in the internal variations, Bantock dwelled throughout his work on Helena's personality and her various moods, all drawn from the three-pitch cipher; the social character of Elgar's music thus yielded to more private, personal reflections about a marital relationship.

ii

Musically encrypted letters also figured in Gustav Holst's orchestral suite *The Planets*, premiered in 1920. The composer contrived a four-note cipher (G,

---

[55] Worcestershire Archive, Worcester; we are grateful to Jennifer Oates of Carroll College for this information.

Ex. 10.12: Holst, *The Planets*, 'Uranus' (1920)

E-flat and A from **Gusta**ve and B-natural from **H**olst), announced in the brass straightaway in the penultimate movement, 'Uranus the Magician' (ex. 10.12).

A mystic whose interests embraced theosophy, phrenology and Sanskrit, Holst became a serious student of astrology, then experiencing a revival in England, owing in part to the publication of Alan Leo's *The Art of Synthesis* (1912). Quite likely, this book influenced Holst's masterpiece.[56] Not only did Leo treat each heavenly body separately,[57] but he provided as well descriptive headings, one of which Holst absorbed into his suite, 'Neptune the Mystic'. Why Holst associated Uranus with magic is not clear, but he underscored the association by working into his conjuring music a memorable solo for three bassoons that recalled a similar passage in Paul Dukas's *The Sorcerer's Apprentice* (1897).

Why did Holst begin 'Uranus' with his own cipher? The answer may lie in the composer's astrological natal chart.[58] Here we find that the dominant planets for his birthdate, 21 September 1874 (at 4:24 p.m., under the sign of Virgo), were Saturn, the Moon and, notably, Uranus. Holst did not compose a lunar movement, leaving us with Saturn and Uranus. The question now becomes whether he manipulated his cipher into the music for Saturn as well as Uranus. Indeed he did, though in a slightly less obvious way. The senescent music for Saturn begins with no fewer than twenty-six iterations of slowly pendulating chords that, clocklike, mark the passage of time (ex. 10.13).

These chords contain five pitches from a whole-tone scale, E-flat-F-G-A-B, that in turn engulf Holst's tetrachord in 'Uranus': G-E-flat-A-B. The effect is to link the movements, so that the harmonically disguised cipher in 'Saturn' becomes fully clarified thematically in 'Uranus'. Were these 'mood pictures', as Holst described the movements of his suite, thus somehow autobiographical in nature? And did astrology play a role in Holst's selection of 'Saturn' as his favourite movement?[59] Raymond Head has argued that it did, and that the Golden Section, commonly used in horoscopes to calculate various degrees of

---

[56] See further, Head (1993).

[57] Ten in total, including the Sun and Moon, but not Pluto, discovered in 1930, then reassessed in 2006 as a dwarf planet.

[58] See https://www.astrotheme.com/astrology/Gustav_Holst [Accessed on 19 February 2023].

[59] Greene (1995), 57.

Ex. 10.13: Holst, *The Planets*, 'Saturn' (1920)

inter-planetary relationships, played a significant role, for '*Saturn* proves to be the Golden Section point and the core of the entire suite'.[60]

Other twentieth-century British composers cultivated musical ciphers, including Gordon Jacob, who memorialized the English hornist Aubrey Brain in the Sextet for piano and winds (1956), through a motive drawn from his name, ABEBA. British musicians succumbed to the allure, too, of the BACH cipher, now filtered through modernist lenses. Thus, in 1935 Ralph Vaughan Williams identified as a quintessential motive of his Fourth Symphony a 'crushed' version of the four notes, B-A-H-B (B-flat-A-B-natural-B-flat), or, transposed to the principal tonality of the symphony, F-E-G-flat-F.[61] From this figure Vaughan Williams extracted the ninth F-G-flat, transposed it to C-D-flat and featured it in the harsh sonority of the very opening, a reference, it turns out, to the tumultuous beginning of the finale to Beethoven's Ninth Symphony.[62] To be sure, BACH appears sporadically in its original guise in the Fourth Symphony, but is overshadowed by persistent reiterations of its compressed version, especially in the fugal finale, so that the whole impresses as 'a peculiarly modernist struggle between organic unity and fragmentation',[63] yielding 'a twisted version of "The Great German Masterpiece"'.[64]

The altered BACH is one means by which Vaughan Williams 'subverts Beethovenian symphonism',[65] a technique not dissimilar, perhaps, to William Walton's unexpected invocation of the cipher, this time unaltered, in his *Variations on a Theme by Hindemith* (1963). There, in the fifth variation, Walton subjects a portion of Hindemith's theme (from the slow movement of his Cello Concerto of 1940) to mirror inversion, in the process accidently producing the BACH

---

[60] Head (1993), 22. As a postscript to *The Planets*, in 2015 Libby Larsen composed *Earth (Holst Trope)*, an orchestral 'essay from space' that added the 'missing … essential planet'. Creating 'a sense of moving towards and away from Earth, while rotating', the music communicates through Morse Code embedded references to 'earth', 'water' and 'air'.

[61] Saylor (2022), 146.

[62] Vaughan Williams to Olin Downes, 25 September 1943; Ryan Ross (2019), 127.

[63] Barone (2008), 61.

[64] Saylor (2022), 147.

[65] Ryan Ross (2019), 128.

Ex. 10.14: Walton, *Variations on a Theme by Hindemith* (1963)

Ex. 10.15: Humphrey Searle, Symphony No. 1, Op. 23 (1953)

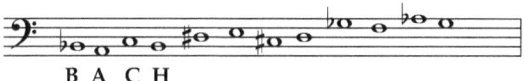

cipher; it appears twice in the winds, their timbres distorted by doubling string tremolos marked *sul ponticello* (at rehearsal 26; ex. 10.14).

To his editor Walton downplayed the reference: '[Variation] V goes backwards & arse over tippet as well & of course the inversion of bar 24 produces that fetish B.A.C.H. Why it has this mystic significance beats me. For my part it is purely a fluke & has about as much interest to me as Boo-Cie and Hawkes!'[66]

Yet another revival of BACH appears in the opening of Humphrey Searle's Symphony No. 1, Op. 23 (1953), where the four pitches form the first tetrachord of the undergirding twelve-tone row (ex. 10.15).

This row was the same deployed by Anton Webern in his String Quartet, Op. 28 (1938). Searle had studied with Webern in Vienna and was among the first to become familiar with Webern's new composition, which paid homage to Bach by encrypting his name into the serial substructures of the music. It was a fraught time for the Austrian composer, whose music the Nazis banned as degenerate (*entartet*) in 1938, the year of Hitler's *Anschluss* of Austria. Five years later, at the height of the Second World War, Searle dedicated his Op. 2, *Night Music*, to Webern on his sixtieth birthday. Quite plausibly, Searle conceived his first symphony as a memorial to Webern, by reviving one of the composer's most distinctive rows, and in the process revitalizing Webern's own homage to Bach. The symphony was not Searle's only foray into cipher composition. For Schoenberg's seventy-fifth birthday in 1949, the British composer offered a short piece for string quartet titled *Passacaglietta*, Op. 16, and subtitled 'In Nomine Arnold Schoenberg', with a musical cipher printed above his name (ex. 10.16).

---

[66] Walton to Alan Frank, 12 December 1962; *William Walton Edition*, vol. 15, Orchestral Works 1, ed. James Brooks Kuykendall (Oxford: 2007), viii. 'Boo-Cie and Hawkes' refers to the music publisher Boosey & Hawkes.

Ex. 10.16: Humphrey Searle, *Passacaglietta*, Op. 16 (1949)

Ex. 10.17: Humphrey Searle, *Passacaglietta*, Op. 16 (1949)

By adding four pitches to the eight already prescribed by the cipher, Searle generated a tone row which served as the basis for the tribute (ex. 10.17), recalling Alban Berg's encipherment of his teacher's name in the *Kammerkonzert* (1925) for Schoenberg's fiftieth birthday (see p. 341).

There was yet another opportunity for Searle to explore cryptography. In 1977 the BBC commissioned him to provide music for a radio broadcast about Thomas Mann's novel *Doctor Faustus: The Life of the German Composer Adrian Leverkühn as Told by a Friend* (1947). The protagonist (understood as modelled after Schoenberg), invents a new system of composition based upon rows derived 'from the twelve steps of the tempered semitone alphabet', and manipulated through inversion, retrograde and retrograde-inversion to yield 'forty-eight different forms'.[67] One of Leverkühn's compositions, a set of songs on texts by Clemens Brentano, employs a motive of five pitches, B-E-A-E-E-flat, or in German H-E-A-E-Es, a musical cipher derived from the butterfly **Het-ae**r**a** **E**smeralda, Leverkühn's sobriquet for a prostitute from whom he contracts syphilis.[68] This motive produces 'an oddly melancholy sound that pervades [Leverkühn's] music in a variety of harmonic and rhythmic disguises, assigned now to one voice, now to another, often in its inverted form, as if turned on its axis, with the intervals still the same, but with the notes in reverse sequence'.[69] Leverkühn is able to expand the cipher into a complete tone row (the procedure Searle employed in his *Passacaglietta* for Schoenberg). Nearly three decades later, Searle endeavoured to bring Leverkühn's fictional music to life by assigning the butterfly cipher a prominent role in his score for the BBC.[70] To para-

---

[67] Thomas Mann (1999), 205, 206.

[68] Ibid., 166.

[69] Ibid.

[70] Ziolkowski (2012), 842.

Ex. 10.18: Thea Musgrave, *Homage to B.A.C.H.* (2013)

phrase Mann, '[Searle] was not the first composer, nor … the last … to insert secret messages as formulas or logograms in his work, revealing music's innate predilection for superstitious rites and observances charged with mystic numbers and alphabetical symbols'.[71]

Like Vaughan Williams, Walton and Searle, the nonagenarian Scottish composer Thea Musgrave ruminated about the BACH cipher as an act of commemoration, in her *Largo in Homage to B.A.C.H.* for string orchestra (2013). Playing on the pitches of the cipher, she organized her work into four sections, controlled harmonically by B-flat, A and C major, and B minor. Leading each portion is a different soloist, rising in register from the double bass to cello, viola and violin. In addition, the music is suffused with what Musgrave terms a 'misty overlay', created by a series of foundational octatonic scales[72] that slowly evolve; as detailed in ex. 10.18, each scale contains a few pitches from the cipher, but also the pitches of the relevant tonal triad.

---

[71] Thomas Mann (1999), 166.

[72] Scales that alternate between half-steps and whole-steps.

In the third section, the solo violist introduces chromatic scales, in preparation for the surprise of the final section: here the mist lifts as the music turns to B minor, and a quotation of the first phrase from the chorale 'O Haupt voll Blut und Wunden' before reaching a final cadence in B major. In a note to the score Musgrave elaborates: 'although the overall feeling of the four sections alters to travel spontaneously and "organically" through the arc of the piece, each section (B.A.C.H.) is rigorously organized and controlled with similar internal ingredients as well as within a "master plan". This, for me, is the essence of Bach'.

At least two other compositions by Musgrave display musical ciphers. Most recently, the short solo cello piece *D.E.S.* (2016) commemorates Dame Ethel Smyth, the British composer, suffragette and author, first by concluding its three sections with the pitches **D, E** and **E-flat**, and second by labelling those sections **D**esolate, **E**nergized and **S**tormy. But a far more extensive play with cryptograms obtains in her Chamber Concerto No. 3, written for the eightieth birthday of Nadia Boulanger in 1967. Cast in five movements framed by a short *Dedicatio* and *Envoi*, this concerto offers a modernist review of the composers of the First and Second Viennese schools through ciphers derived from their names. They appear in two groups – first Haydn, Mozart, Beethoven and Schubert; then Schoenberg, Webern and Berg (ex. 10.19).

Musgrave's ciphers for the last three are borrowed from the opening bars of Berg's *Kammerkonzert*, with a few rhythmic adjustments. One peculiarity is that **Schub**ert and **Sch**o**e**n**b**erg share several pitches, so that Schubert becomes, as it were, an accidental link between the two schools. In the five following movements, arranged in a symmetrical, arch-like pattern, different instruments execute virtuosic cadenzas drawn from the ciphers. Thus, Haydn and Mozart are assigned to the first violin, Beethoven to the clarinet, Schubert and Schoenberg to the horn and viola, Webern to the bassoon, contrabass and cello, and Berg to the second violin. When all is said and done, Musgrave then signs her work in the *Envoi* by having the cello present her own cipher (see ex. 10.20).

All eight instruments thus impress as so many historical characters identified by their cryptographic transformations.

Among other major British composers who turned to musical ciphers was Benjamin Britten. Some examples: an early set of variations from 1929 on the initials of his sister, Charlotte Elizabeth (C. E. B.); a self-portrait for viola and strings (E. B. B.), written in 1930 but unpublished until 1997 as the second of the *Two Portraits*[73]; *Variations on a Theme by Frank Bridge* (1937), in which the initials of his teacher (F. B.) are announced in the opening bars; the

---

[73] The pitches E, B and B appear in the solo viola and first violin in bars 10 and 22.

Ex. 10.19: Thea Musgrave, Chamber Concerto No. 3 (1967)

Ex. 10.20: Thea Musgrave, Chamber Concerto No. 3 (1967)

(possible) appearance of the Shostakovich cipher (transposed) in *Rejoice in the Lamb* (1943) and *Rape of Lucretia* (1946)[74]; the short fanfare for David Webster, Administrator of the Royal Opera House, using a cycle of fifths that incorporates his name, C-E-G-**D-A-E-B** (1970); the twelve-bar *Scherzettino-A.B.* for the eightieth birthday of Sir Arthur Bliss (1971); and the *Tema 'Sacher'* for solo cello on the name of the conductor Paul Sacher, portrayed by the pitches E-flat, A, C, B, E and D (1976; see p. 354).

Mervyn Cooke has argued that Britten was preoccupied 'with tonal symbolism and conceptual musical puns',[75] and, further, that several of his operas reflect through code-like musical means one defining aspect of his personality: 'his (at times rather uneasy) mixture of conformism and nonconformism, public and private personae, observance of official responsibilities and desire for personal freedom'.[76] As a homosexual and conscientious objector, Britten came of age with the outbreak of the Second World War, and, playing on the initials of his name, 'made symbolic use of the pitch classes B-flat and B-natural in certain works – relating the former to oppression and discipline, and the latter to free will'.[77] Thus, in *Billy Budd* (1951) – coincidentally or not the protagonist of Herman Melville's novella shares initials with the composer – Britten associated B-flat ('be flat') major with military discipline and B ('be natural') minor with freedom and the threat of mutiny. And in *Peter Grimes* (1945), Britten again privileged B-flat major, for instance in the coroner's inquest about

---

[74] Though aware of Shostakovich's music since at least the 1930s, Britten met him in 1960; regarding the Shostakovich cipher, see also p. 280.

[75] Mervyn Cooke (2013), 104.

[76] Ibid., 124.

[77] Ibid., 121.

the title character with which the opera begins. Cooke adduces other examples of tonal encoding from *Albert Herring* (1947), *Gloriana* (1953), *Noye's Fludde* (1957) and *The Prodigal Son* (1968), so that overall Britten's operas captured in their tonal organization the public/private dichotomy of his life across a significant span of his career.

The singular case of Peter Maxwell Davies (1934–2016) offers one final example of a British musician steeped in musical enigmas. Having explored a hard-edged serialism, Davies withdrew into a monkish existence in the Orkney Islands, where he kept a diary written in his own runic-like script based on an invented alphabet, especially difficult to decipher as it 'included German words with Greek grammar'.[78] Starting in 1975 with the chamber work *Ave maris stella*, he developed a new system based upon transformed magic squares, which now largely controlled his selection of pitches and rhythmic durations. As Davies himself disclosed, he drew inspiration from alchemy and its association with magic squares linked to the Ptolemaic planets. Thus, the chamber work *Mirror of Whitening Light* (1978) referred to 'the purification or "whitening" process by which a base metal may be transformed into gold and, by extension, to the purification of the human soul'. Here Davies employed an 8×8 square associated with Mercury, while *Ave maris stella* ('Hail, star of the sea') explored the 9×9 square of the Moon, (often coupled with Diana, and, in the Catholic tradition, the Virgin Mary). Other squares included Saturn (3×3), Jupiter (4×4), Mars (5×5), the Sun (6×6) and Venus (7×7), each with its own numerical constant obtained by adding any of the individual rows, columns or diagonals. Extending the series, Davies appears to have resorted to a square for Uranus (10×10) in the *Strathclyde* Concerto No. 4 (1990), as well as a 12×12 square for *Spinning Jenny* (1999).[79]

In several compositions, Davies extracted pitch material from Gregorian chants in the *Liber usualis*, the compendium of liturgical melodies for the Catholic Mass and Office. Rather than cite a complete chant, however, he preferred to filter it through a sieve-like process, selecting just a few pitches that might either meet the requirements of the square or that he might supplement as needed (for example, five pitches from the chant plus three additional, freely chosen pitches for, say, an 8×8 square). As a result, the original chant rarely appeared intact; instead, paraphrased portions protruded from the swirling textures.

---

[78] McGregor (2000), 6. For a reconstruction of Davies's alphabet, see ibid., 29.
[79] For a list of Davies's magic squares, see McGregor (2009), 242–54.

Ex. 10.21a–b: *Ave maris stella*; Peter Maxwell Davies, *Ave maris stella* (1975)

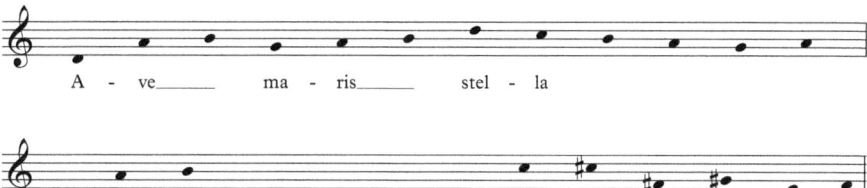

In the case of *Ave maris stella*, the composer initially selected nine pitches, the first three of which recalled the opening of the chant, while the others were unrelated (ex. 10.21a–b).[80]

Next, Davies used the nine pitches to generate a 9×9 square, by writing down the series in the top row and first column and completing the remaining eight rows as transpositions of the same. The third step was to notate another 9×9 square, this time rotating the series so that it began on the sixth pitch (F-sharp), and continued with the seventh through ninth, and first through fifth. The remaining eight rows of the grid materialized through a process of diagonal manipulations within the square, so that the second row began with the (transposed) seventh pitch, the third with the eighth, and so on. After numbering these eighty-one pitches in order row by row (for example, row 1: 1–9; row 2: 10–18), Davies was ready to bring into play the 9×9 magic square of the Moon (ex. 10.22).

Ex. 10.22: 9×9 Magic Square

37	78	29	70	21	62	13	54	5
6	38	79	30	71	22	63	14	46
47	7	39	80	31	72	23	55	15
16	48	8	40	81	32	64	24	56
57	17	49	9	41	73	33	65	25
26	58	18	50	1	42	74	34	66
67	27	59	10	51	2	43	75	35
36	68	19	60	11	52	3	44	76
77	28	69	20	61	12	53	4	45

---

[80] See further Jones and McGregor (2020), 76–82, and Griffiths (1982), 72ff.

Ex. 10.23: Peter Maxwell Davies, Magic Square for *Ave maris stella* (1975)

C♯	F	C	E	B	G♯	A	F♯	D
A	G♯	C	G	B	F♯	D♯	E	C♯
D♯	B	A♯	D	A	C♯	G♯	F	F♯
G	E	C	B	E♭	B♭	D	A	F♯
G	A♭	F	D♭	C	E	B	E♭	B♭
D♯	B♯	C♯	B♭	F♯	F	A	E	G♯
B♭	F	D	E♭	C	A♭	G	B	G♭
D♯	F♯	C♯	A♯	B	G♯	E	D♯	G
G♯	D♯	G	D	B	C	A	F	E

By applying the numbers from the magic square of the Moon to the rotated pitch square, the composer achieved his goal – converting the lunar numbers into pitches (ex. 10.23).

Thus, since the first row of ex. 10.22 began with the numbers 37, 78 and 29, Davies located their corresponding pitches in the rotated square as C-sharp, F and C. Ultimately the process yielded the grid of pitches that in turn generated materials for his chamber work. 'Composing' *Ave maris stella* essentially entailed choosing alternate paths through the grid, perhaps starting in the upper left-hand corner, moving around the successively shrinking perimeter to reach the centre; pursuing the reverse process (spiralling outward from the centre to the corners); or tracing diagonal courses through the square. No less pre-determined were Davies's rhythmic values, for which he also produced a 9 × 9 grid, with shifting rows of numbers (*modulo* 9) ranging from 1 to 9 quavers in duration.[81]

For the most part, the original Marian chant remains well concealed – only well into the score does the alto flute play the opening of the chant in sustained notes, where it begins to emerge almost as a *cantus firmus*.[82] There is a trace here of the cryptic experiments of the fifteenth-century Franco-Flemish composers, who, as we saw (Chapter 4), often subjected their source material to cerebral refinements, generating a series of puzzles to be solved. As Davies himself conceded, 'I've got a crossword-puzzle musical mentality anyway and … I enjoy working with it, and doing that does present little challenges, which I like'.[83]

---

[81] See Griffiths (1982), 73.
[82] At rehearsal mark C2.
[83] Griffiths (1982), 121.

❧ *iii*

When musical cryptography arrived in the American colonies is unclear, though the need for cryptography abruptly increased with the outbreak of the War of Independence in 1775. The commander of the Continental Army, George Washington, firmly valued military intelligence, and Thomas Jefferson developed his own polyalphabetic cipher wheel to safeguard personal correspondence. In literature, the fascination with espionage helped launch the career of the novelist James Fenimore Cooper, whose novel *The Spy* (1821), set during the war, was a bestseller, even if it did not introduce specific cryptograms into the plotline.

Cooper's younger compatriot Edgar Allan Poe, though, did incorporate them into some of his short stories, and what is more, expended considerable effort in cryptanalysis, first in *Alexander's Weekly Messenger* and then *Graham's Magazine*, both published in Philadelphia. Poe invited his readership to submit encrypted puzzles for him to 'unravel', including a daunting specimen submitted from, yes, Limerick (Ohio), in which the correspondent had employed 'seven distinct alphabets in the concoction of his cypher'. Nevertheless, Poe met the challenge: it was, he revealed, an enciphered version of 'The Siege of Belgrade' (1828), an alliterative, abecedarian poem by Alaric Alexander Watts about the Austrian victory over the Turks in 1789.[84] Here are the opening lines, in rhyming couplets:

> An Austrian army, awfully arrayed,
> Boldly, by battery, besieged Belgrade;
> Cossack commanders cannonading come,
> Dealing destruction's desolating doom.

In 1843 Poe published *The Gold Bug*, one of his 'tales of ratiocination' – the prototypes, as Sir Arthur Conan Doyle later acknowledged, of detective mysteries. Set on Sullivan's Island near Charleston, South Carolina, the story centres around a secret message encrypted on a sheet of vellum that maps the hidden treasure of Captain Kidd. The first clue is an image of a young goat that materializes when heat is applied to the vellum, a pun on the pirate's name. The message itself comprises a relatively simple substitution cipher that the protagonist, William Legrande, easily cracks through frequency analysis, for 'circumstances, and a certain bias of mind, have led me to take an interest in such riddles, and it may well be doubted whether human ingenuity can construct an enigma of the kind which human ingenuity may not, by proper application, resolve'.[85]

---

[84] *Alexander's Weekly Messenger*, 19 February 1840.
[85] Levine and Levine (1976), 170.

Among significant American composers partial to musical enigmas was the rugged individualist from Danbury, Connecticut, Charles Ives. Even before matriculating at Yale College in 1894, his non-conformist habits were in full earshot – bracing applications of polytonality in several keys clashing simultaneously; mashups of quotations from hymn tunes and popular songs careening within modernist compositional frames; and all in all, a persistent, relentless chafing against European art music. Ives's music exudes sphinx-like mysteries – for example, *The Unanswered Question* (1909; revised 1930s), with its neutral tonal wash of background strings evoking the 'silence of the Druids, who know, see and hear nothing'; the sevenfold 'Perennial Question of Existence' posed by the solo trumpet; and the ructious woodwinds, the 'fighting answerers' who vainly attempt to respond.[86]

In the case of the *Three-Page Sonata* (1905–7), Ives's motivation was 'to knock the mollycoddles out of their boxes and to kick out the softy ears'.[87] A special target was the American music critic William James Henderson, whose *What is Good Music?* offered advice 'for Persons Desiring to Cultivate a Taste in Musical Art'. Here Ives would have read of 'two ... contrasted themes [in] modern sonata writing' as a '*sine qua non*'.[88] In reaction, the composer challenged the conventions of the well-made sonata, and produced if not an 'anti-sonata',[89] at least music confronting 'the idea of the sonata'.[90] His curt response to Henderson begins with a 'first theme' that is anything but: we hear the B-A-C-H cipher that occasionally reappears in different voices at different transposition levels or in mirror inversion, but generally disappears into the grating, chromatic sound. Instead of a contrasting second theme, Ives offers an abridged second movement, where we do encounter a 'contrasting' lyrical theme against an arpeggiated accompaniment. The third 'movement' then erupts in a boisterous, strident march that features trios in syncopated jazz idioms before the whole affair concludes with an anomalous C major chord. What had begun as a modernist reflection on the BACH cipher ends with an emasculated tonal gesture at once hollow and anti-climactic.

The disorienting surface of his music often covered hidden meanings. If the inspiration for the *Three-Page Sonata* was BACH, to which Ives alluded in other works,[91] in the case of the middle movement of the Piano Trio (1909–10) the composer contrived the title *TSIAJ*, baffling until one understands its deflating

---

[86] Ives (1953), foreword.

[87] Ives (1991), 155.

[88] W. J. Henderson (1935), 47; see also Baron (1987), 14–18.

[89] Hitchcock (1977), 44.

[90] Baron (1987), 13.

[91] As in *Thanksgiving* from the *Holidays Symphony* and the *Concord Sonata*. See Antony Cooke (2015): 207, 307.

acronym: 'This Scherzo *Is A Joke*'. Offering a rancorous medley of melodies, the movement nevertheless 'encodes a nostalgia that is undeniable'.[92] Among the quotations and allusions are fraternity and Civil War songs, Stephen Foster's *My Old Kentucky Home*, the hymn *In the Sweet Bye and Bye* and Fountain, *Dixieland*, and, near the end, the (secret) fraternity song *The Gods of Egypt Bid Us Hail*.[93] Often Ives 're-forms old tunes by obscuring, fragmenting, layering, distorting, and even reinventing', so that in the scherzo they are 'not merely disguised but fairly obliterated',[94] even if hiding in plain view.

Also in 'plain' view was Ives's use of palindromic techniques,[95] realized most strikingly in the miniature chamber composition *All the Way Around and Back* (1905–7). In one minute, he captures musically an event in a baseball game from his youth: when the batter hits a pitch deep down the foul line, the runner on first base advances to second and third, only to retrace his steps back to first when the umpire rules that the ball fell in foul territory. The familiar sequence inspired a rhythmic palindrome in which the forward and retrograde motions of the runner were captured by subdividing a semibreve into minims, a triplet, crotchets, quintuplet, septuplet and undecatuplet, before the process reversed itself. The result: a sonic snapshot perhaps not unrelated to early reverse film sequences (see p. 256) already being screened in the United States in 1897.[96]

For some two decades Ives enjoyed his most creative phase before retiring from composition in 1924. The world had changed irreversibly in June 1914 with the outbreak of the First World War. For a while the United States avoided the conflagration, but in January 1917 British intelligence intercepted an encrypted dispatch from the German Foreign Office to its ambassador in Mexico. Known as the Zimmermann Telegram, it proposed a German-Mexican alliance should the United States enter the First World War against the Central Powers. Within a few months the document's release precipitated the American declaration of war. Ives volunteered to drive an ambulance but was turned down for medical reasons. But another American musician, the composer/pianist Amy Beach, had already been near the hostilities; in 1911, she had embarked on an extended concert tour of Germany, then delayed her homecoming until September 1914, a month or so after the general military mobilizations. Upon her return Beach made 'strongly pro-German statements to the American press, although ... her allegiance was to the musical, not the militaristic Germany'.[97]

---

[92] Feder (1999), 209–10.
[93] At Yale Ives had belonged to Wolf's Head, a secret society founded in 1884.
[94] Feder (1999), 210.
[95] See Lambert (1997), 65ff.
[96] Tohline (2015), 44.
[97] Block (1998), 196.

Ex. 10.24: Amy Beach, Prelude and Fugue, Op. 81 (1918)

Among the compositions drafted during her German sojourn was the Prelude and Fugue for piano solo, Op. 81 (1918), a cipher composition based on her name, which in German nomenclature generated the six-note subject A-B-flat-E-A-C-B-natural, boldly announced at the opening of the prelude in bass octaves and then recycled as the first subject of the double fugue. The pairing of a thematically related prelude and fugue alluded to J. S. Bach's frequent practice in the *Well-Tempered Clavier*, and underscored Beach's 'allegiance' to German music; furthermore, as she doubtlessly realized, her name encased within its pitch sequence the eponymous BACH cryptogram (ex. 10.24).

But the virtuosic writing in the prelude, marked *quasi improvvisazione* and bristling with challenging octaves and double thirds, triggered memories of Liszt's *Präludium und Fuge über das Thema B-A-C-H* for organ (see p. 222). Finally, Beach's double fugue, constructed from two subjects introduced separately and then combined, traversed rhythmic shifts to quaver triplets and semiquavers, orienting her music in the tradition of the accelerando fugue extending back to the finale of Beethoven's Piano Sonata Op. 110. One cipher thus generated another, enabling the American to explore her own connections to the revered traditions of Bachian counterpoint from the perspective of 1918, the end of what H. G. Wells termed the 'war to end war'.

Beach was not the only American to celebrate the Thomaskantor through ciphers. From 1940 dates Walter Piston's *Chromatic Study on the Name of Bach* for organ, in which, following Webern's precedent, Piston absorbed Bach's name into a twelve-tone row, partitioned into four trichords instead of three tetrachords. The BACH cipher also figured fifteen years later in the slow movement of Lukas Foss's *Symphony of Chorales* (1958), where the composer contraposed it against the penitential chorale 'Herr, ich habe mißgehandelt'. And Bach had been on the mind of Charles Loeffler, whose *Partita* for violin and piano (1930), a four-movement work originally envisioned for viola d'amore and harpsichord, captured in its first two movements 'the great beauty of moods expressed by titles as well as by charm and delight in the great Cantor of Leipzig[']s 6 Partitas'.[98] To be sure, Loeffler did not apply the BACH cipher in this singular

---

[98] Knight (1993), 240.

work, which begins with an *Intrada* and neo-Baroque 'merry fugue' followed by variations on a sarabande by Johann Mattheson, and then leaps from the eighteenth century to a *divertissement* of 'minstrel, ragtime, tango, and other jazzy elements'[99] before concluding with a *finale des tendres adieux* set in a fuzzy impressionist style. But Loeffler did employ another cipher to unify his score, this one drawn from the initials of **E**lizabeth **S**prague **C**oolidge, the American patroness to whom he dedicated the work. Thus, the three-note motto **E**-e(**S**)-flat-**C** appears early in the *Intrada* and midway in its prime and inverted forms, and ultimately returns in the closing bars of the finale.[100]

In 1964 Donald Martino created a cryptographic, three-movement sonatina for the Brazilian cellist Aldo Parisot. Titled *Parisonatina al'Dodecafonia*, this work included a motto and cadenza on solmization syllables drawn from Parisot's names, with 'Al-' represented by 'la' (A), 'do-' by C, 'ri-' by 're' or D (altered to D-sharp), 'so-' by 'sol' or G, and 't' by 'ti' or B, all blended into a twelve-tone work. Two years later, for the fiftieth birthday of Milton Babbitt, Martino produced *B,A,B,B,I,T,T* for solo clarinet with paper tubes of various lengths to extend the instrument's range; Babbitt's name is spelled out letter by letter over wide registral displacements and sliding glissandi. Other examples of American musical cryptography include Robert Moran's *32 Cryptograms for Derek Jarman* (1995); Samuel Adler's *Four Composer Portraits* (2002), with cipher-inspired treatments of Milton Babbitt, Ned Rorem, Gunther Schuller and David Diamond[101]; Mark Applebaum's *40 Cryptograms* (2008), for the fortieth birthday of the jazz percussionist Terry Longshore; and Derek Jenkins's *We Seven* (2016), in which ciphers encrypt the names of the Mercury astronauts.

In a separate category was the extraordinary centenarian Elliott Carter (1908–2012), whose late style of the 1990s and 2000s exhibited a notable turn toward simplification of means. Until recently, this music was 'generally treated as "Carter light": shorter pieces, thinner textures, less complicated rhythms and forms'.[102] But its surfaces could be deceptive. In several works spanning 1996 and 2007 he relied upon ciphers to add levels of meaning, even if positioning only a solitary, memorial B ('H') to conclude his *Boston Concerto* (2002), *Instances* (2012) and *Epigrams* (2012), symbolizing his wife of more than sixty years, Helen Frost-Jones Carter.[103] The eightieth birthday of Robert Mann, founder

---

[99] Ibid.

[100] The same cipher figures prominently in another commission from Coolidge, *Three Variations on a Theme* for string quartet by Roy Harris (1933), though usually in the reordered sequence E-flat-C-E-natural.

[101] See further, Gowen (2022).

[102] Link (2022), 19.

[103] Ibid., 18.

of the Juilliard Quartet, inspired *Rhapsodic Musings* for solo violin (2000), in which the prominent pitches D and E (*Re* and *Mi*) substituted for his initials,[104] while in *HBHH* for solo oboe (2007) Carter employed B, B-flat, B and B as a framing device to spell 'Happy Birthday, Heinz Holliger'. For the duet *Au quai* for viola and bassoon (2002) a verbal pun commemorated the fiftieth birthday of the composer/conductor Oliver Knussen, while in *A 6 Letter Letter* for English horn (1996) Carter revived the celebratory Sacher-hexachord cipher for the ninetieth birthday of Paul Sacher (see also p. 354).

There remains *Réflexions* for chamber orchestra (2004), for the eightieth birthday of Pierre Boulez. On earlier occasions, for his sixtieth, seventieth and seventy-fifth birthdays, Carter had deployed a tetrachord fashioned from Boulez's surname: **B-flat** (B) O **C** (Ut) **A** (La) **E** (E) Z,[105] one of only two tetrachords that contained all six basic interval classes.[106] In *Réflexions* Carter assigned the pitches G-sharp and D-sharp for the letters O and Z, yielding the sequence B-flat, G-sharp, C, A, E and D-sharp. Here the expanded cipher allowed him to work with hexachords, in particular the unique all-trichord hexachord that subsumed all twelve possible three-note segments in their basic forms.[107] Musical cryptography and set theory thus combined in a satisfying, meaningful alliance.

Finally, recently John Corigliano has employed in *The Lord of Cries* (2021) as a melodic and harmonic cipher the pitches E-A-B-C-C-A-B-flat to spell EAHCCAB (BACCHAE in reverse). Along with Bram Stoker's *Dracula* (1897), Euripides's ancient tragedy provides the storyline, set in Victorian England, the latest incarnation of the vaunted genre of vampire literature.[108] But well before his opera, Corigliano approached more indirectly the ghost-like sound world of musical ciphers in Symphony No. 1 (1990), written to commemorate friends lost during the AIDS epidemic. Here Corigliano created a musical hauntology, incorporating into the third movement several eulogies, with the 'words' removed, so that audiences might revisit their own experiences of loss, and of imaginary futures never realized.

---

[104] Ibid., 71 and 417.

[105] In *Esprit rude/Esprit doux* (1984), *Esprit rude/Esprit doux II* (1994) and *Retrouvailles* (2000). See further, Link (2022), 243.

[106] That is, the minor second (A-B-flat), major second (B-flat-C), minor third (A-C), major third (C-E), perfect fourth (E-A) and tritone (B-flat-E).

[107] See Link (2022), 36ff.

[108] See Alex Ross's review in *The New Yorker*, 16 August 2021.

CHAPTER 11

Queer Liaisons, Mystic Chords, *DSCH* and Tombstone Monograms

'Too many riddles weigh men down on earth. We must solve as we can, and try to keep a dry skin in the water.'

Fyodor Dostoyevsky, *The Brothers Karamazov*, III, Ch. 3

THE Russian composer Peter Ilyich Tchaikovsky (1840–93) encountered at least one weighty Dostoyevskian riddle – his sexuality. It affected his posthumous reception, when the question arose whether he died of cholera or by suicide mandated by a hastily convened court of honour or one of his ardent admirers, Tsar Alexander III, to forestall a scandal about the composer's pederastic trysts. As recently as 2018 this debate triggered renewed attention after the sensational release of a trove of family correspondence. For much of the twentieth century, the Soviet government had methodically groomed the composer's official commemoration: '… it would have been unthinkable to accept the idea that Pyotr Ilyich Tchaikovsky, Russia's national treasure, was a homosexual. Therefore, he wasn't.'[1] Nevertheless, the composer's diaries, released in 1945 as the Second World War came to its tumultuous close, contained one compelling passage from 23 April 1884: 'There was much Z. Oh, what a monster of a person I am!'[2] In a footnote the editor of the diaries, Wladimir Lakond, surmised: 'This was the secret symbol that, it appears, Tchaikovsky employed to refer to his homosexuality.'[3] An entry from the previous day regarding the composer's thirteen-year-old nephew Vladimir Luovich Davidov prompted this annotation: 'Tchaikovsky was very attached to him from his childhood and there is reason to believe that in his late years the attachment was more than platonic.'[4]

---

[1] Kostalevsky (2018), x.
[2] Tchaikovsky (1945), 27.
[3] For a different reading see Taruskin (2009), 97.
[4] Tchaikovsky (1945), 26.

Some seventy years later, with the appearance of the unexpurgated *Tchaikovsky Papers*, the musical world finally gained access to documents that disclosed in unprecedented detail the composer's intimate life and homoerotic desires. Consider, for example, this episode in a letter of 1 March 1879 to the composer's brother Modest, written from Paris. Here Tchaikovsky acknowledged that he had

> caught sight of a nice young girl ['Louise'], of very pleasant appearance, dressed cheaply but cleanly … After talking for a while I saw that she was a perfectly decent girl and not out to rob me, and at her suggestion, took her to a little hotel in *Rue St. Denis*, and rented a room. I spent a pleasant evening but couldn't help worrying about whether someone might come in.[5]

Modest, who was also gay,[6] would have understood that 'Louise' was likely a cover for a male partner, an example of Tchaikovsky's habit of devising feminized names for his correspondence, sometimes to mask erotic dalliances.[7] Thus, in a letter of [24] September 1871 one object of his attention, the architect Ivan Klimenko, became Klimena: 'But can you, the most beloved of the concubines of my harem, you, the beautiful and at the same time young Klimena, doubt for even a single moment my love for you?'[8]

The question of Tchaikovsky's sexual identity precipitated another: did the composer allude to it in his music? For several scholars the answer is yes. Turning to the composer's songs, Philip Ross Bullock offers nuanced readings to show how the music might 'encode in aesthetic form aspects of same-sex desire'.[9] As it happens, several texts Tchaikovsky set treat the trope of self-imposed silence; in that negation of sound, whether poetic or musical, Bullock finds 'the presence of something hidden and unspoken, even unspeakable … In the case of Tchaikovsky's songs, homosexuality constitutes one particular formative absence, a homosexuality that is simultaneously suspected yet undisclosed.'[10]

Timothy L. Jackson pursues a note-centred approach by orienting the composer's 'homosexual problem' in 'unbridgeable disjunctions, between the unorthodox (read "homosexual") and orthodox (read "heterosexual") worlds',[11]

---

[5] Kostalevsky (2018), 161.

[6] See Poznansky (1991), 76–7.

[7] See also Wiley (2009), 79–80.

[8] Cited in Poznansky (1991), 139.

[9] Bullock (2008), 105.

[10] Ibid., 102.

[11] Timothy L. Jackson (1995), 4.

so 'that the overtly heterosexual plots in the [symphonic poems], operas and ballets may convey coded messages relevant to the "homosexual problem"'.[12] Examples of the *double entendre* may occur in the Fourth, Fifth and Sixth Symphonies as 'significant departures from the norm' that are 'programmatically connected with the composer's musical representation of tragic Destiny, a destiny sealed by triumphant homosexuality'.[13] And so, Jackson isolates in the late symphonies unusual features, including a 'partial reversal of the recapitulation' – reintroducing elements of the second theme *before* the first – that might suggest a '"deformation" of standard sonata form'. Jackson then finds in the Fourth Symphony what he labels a '"homosexual" tritonal deformation of "normative" diatonic harmony'.[14] Here Tchaikovsky privileges the raised subdominant (♯IV) and lowered dominant (♭V), creating large-scale tritones between F minor and B major, and F minor and C-flat major, that militate against the conventional choices of the subdominant B-flat minor and dominant C major.

There are few signs that anytime soon scholars will divorce Tchaikovsky's music from his extraordinary life and relationships. The composer himself left the matter open in a short sketch he drafted for the program of the Fifth Symphony: 'Total submission before fate, or, what is the same thing, the inscrutable designs of Providence. Allegro. 1) Murmurs, doubts, laments, reproaches against … XXX. 2) Shall I cast myself into the embrace of *faith*??? A wonderful programme, if only it can be fulfilled.'[15] Here again, we encounter a coded cipher, raising the question of whether Tchaikovsky's music betrays any further examples of the device. David Brown proposed that Tchaikovsky explored networks of ciphers in several compositions, including the symphonic poem *Fatum* (1868), Piano Concerto No. 1 (1875), Symphony No. 3 (1875), String Quartet No. 3 in E-flat minor (1876) and Suites Nos. 1 in D minor (1879) and 2 in C major (1883).

Of these, *Fatum* and the iconic Piano Concerto betray strong connections to the Belgian singer Désirée Artôt, whom Tchaikovsky met in 1868[16]; the two considered marriage until Artôt wed another singer in 1869. As Brown noted in 1978, Artôt's name readily lent itself to musical encipherment (ex. 11.1).

Tchaikovsky could have impressed the second of these ciphers, outlining the diminished fourth D-flat-A, into the first movement of the concerto, where the second theme, in D-flat major, highlights the interval (ex. 11.2).

---

[12] Ibid., 5.
[13] Ibid., 6.
[14] Ibid., 13. See also Timothy L. Jackson (1999) regarding the Sixth (*Pathétique*) Symphony.
[15] Quoted in David Brown (1991), IV, 148.
[16] David Brown (1982), II, 23.

Ex. 11.1: Désirée Artôt Cipher

D É(S) SI RÉ E A(RTÔT)

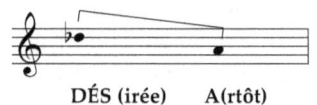

DÉS (irée)   A(rtôt)

Ex. 11.2: Tchaikovsky, Piano Concerto No. 1, Op. 23, First Movement (1875)

For that matter, the unorthodox prominence of D-flat major in that work – the concerto begins in B-flat minor only to pivot within a few bars to its mediant, an unusual deviation that, along with other anomalies, likely caused Nikolai Rubinstein to reject the work – could have been another reference to *Dés*-irée, as might the choice of D-flat major for the key of the second movement. Similarly, the love theme in the overture-fantasy *Romeo and Juliet* (1870–80) is also in D-flat major, made more unconventional by its appearance in an exposition centred largely on B minor. More problematic, though, is Brown's first Désirée cipher, in which her forename is spelled out musically letter by letter, to which the pitch A is added for the surname. If we segregate the final four pitches, B-D-E-A, and transpose them down by a step, we obtain the sequence A-C-D-G: as it happens, the opening motive of *Fatum* (*Fate*, ex. 11.3).

But do these pitches convey a cryptographic meaning? If so, at the least, this 'cipher' is far more veiled than its sibling, the diminished fourth D-flat-A-natural, so that with the six-note sequence we may be chasing a phantom. Be that as it may, Tchaikovsky's symphonic poem certainly remains among his most enigmatic, least-known compositions. Premiered in 1869, it provoked a rebuke from Mily Balakirev, the intended dedicatee, on account of its peculiar final cadence, in which an ambiguous augmented triad (B-flat-D-F-sharp) moves through unmediated parallel motion to a C-major triad (ex. 11.4).[17]

---

[17] Separating the two is the passing tone B-natural, which compounds the voice-leading by implying bald parallel fifths.

Ex. 11.3: Tchaikovsky, *Fatum*, Op. 77 (1869)

Ex. 11.4: Tchaikovsky, *Fatum*, Op. 77 (1869)

The exact significance of this gesture, and whether it concerned Tchaikovsky's relationship to Désirée Artôt – we could view the augmented fifth as the transposed inversion of Désirée's diminished fourth – remains unclear, although the cadence surely impresses as a fatalistic justification of the title, as if the unnamed protagonist of the work (Tchaikovsky?) bends to some omnipotent force. Ultimately, the composer rejected the work and, indeed, destroyed his autograph score. But somehow the performing parts survived, allowing the work's posthumous release in 1896 as Op. 77.

Among other possibilities for Tchaikovsky's deployment of ciphers is a descending four-note sequence drawn from his own name, E-C-B-A (P**e**ter T**cha**ikovsky). Quite likely, the composer was aware of Robert Schumann's sphinxes in *Carnaval*, one of which, E-flat-C-B-A (**Sch**um**a**nn), shares several pitches. Now if we transpose the presumed Tchaikovsky moniker up by a semitone to F-D-flat-C-B-flat, we obtain the opening pitches of the Piano Concerto No. 1 (ex. 11.5).

That this motive facilitates a turn to D-flat major, Désirée's key, might suggest a planned pairing of the two former lovers; there is some evidence presented by Helen Elizabeth Rudeforth, too, that the composer's cipher operates in at least one of his last works, the Six Romances, Op. 73 of 1893.[18]

Ex. 11.5: Tchaikovsky, Piano Concerto No. 1, First Movement, Op. 23 (1875)

---

[18] Rudeforth (1998), 183.

Ex. 11.6: Tchaikovsky, Suite No. 1 in D minor, Op. 43 (1878)

Still other cryptograms may populate Tchaikovsky's scores, including the Third Symphony, where the diminished fourth associated with Artôt is present[19]; the end of the funeral march in the Third String Quartet, *in memoriam* to the Czech violinist Ferdinand Laub (**Ferd**i**n**a**nd**, transposed up a step to G-flat-F-E-flat-B-flat)[20]; and the Suites Nos. 1 and 2, where the composer may have enciphered the names of several relatives, and, perhaps most significantly, of his patroness, Madame von Meck,[21] with whom he maintained a platonic, epistolary relationship for some thirteen years. The two exchanged over one thousand letters but met only once (accidentally), before she abruptly ended their friendship in 1890. In the first orchestral suite the opening movement plausibly encrypts the phrase 'Nadejda Filaretoffna, mily drug' ('Nadezhda Filaretovna, dear friend'), so that it serves as the subject of a formal fugue (ex. 11.6).

Could Tchaikovsky have thus emblazoned his patroness within a display of counterpoint? While working on the Fourth Symphony in September 1878 he wrote to her: 'Because I was constantly thinking of you while I was composing this piece, at every stage was asking myself whether this or that bit would please you … I cannot dedicate it to anyone other than *my best friend*'.[22] To gauge the depth of her feelings for the composer we may turn to one of her letters from 1877, described by David Brown as a 'confession of love (for such, in its bizarre way, it was)': 'for several days I was as one delirious, and I could do nothing to free myself from this state. I must tell you that I cannot separate the musician from the man, and in him, the servant of such a high art, even more than in other people, I wish and expect to find those human qualities which I worship'.[23]

↬ *ii*

As a graduate of the first class of the St. Petersburg Conservatory in 1866, Tchaikovsky was aware that his music would be measured against European art music. Even more significant, then, his willingness to explore non-normative

---

[19] David Brown (1982), II, 43.

[20] Ibid., II, 65–6.

[21] David Brown. (1991), III, 62–3, 241–2.

[22] Cited in David Brown, III, 19–20.

[23] Ibid., II, 134–5.

procedures in his orchestral works. Other Russian musicians pursued a different path: separating themselves from European models to boost their nationalist identities. One group, centred around Mily Balakirev in St. Petersburg and known as the 'mighty little bunch' (*moguchaya kuchka*), were non-professionals, 'the last generation of aristocratic autodidacts'.[24] They included Alexander Borodin, an internationally recognized organic chemist; César Cui, a military engineer; Modest Mussorgsky, a civil servant; and Nikolai Rimsky-Korsakov, a naval officer. A second group later coalesced around the timber merchant Mitrofan Belyayef, who established a chamber-music series in St. Petersburg and a music publishing firm to advance Russian music. Among the composers he supported were Cui, Rimsky-Korsakov, Borodin, Anatoly Lyadov, Alexander Glazunov, Alexander Kopylov and Nikolai Sokoloff (the last two, students of Rimsky-Korsakov).

All these musicians resorted to ciphers, whether individually or, in one instance, collaboratively. Cui, a music critic and feuilletonist who published articles anonymously with the asterism ⁂, ventured into print as a composer in 1857 with the appearance of his Scherzo for piano duet, Op. 1. Its playful primary motive derived from the name of a Lithuanian aristocrat, the singer Malvina Bamberg, whom he married the following year. Undergirding her cipher, B-flat-A-B-flat-E-G (**Bamberg**), were persistent drumming repetitions of the pitch C in the bass, representing Cui's own initials, **CC** (ex. 11.7).

On the other hand, Rimsky-Korsakov, despite his association with the *kuchka*, experienced an academic conversion in 1871 when he joined the faculty

Ex. 11.7: Cui, Scherzo, Op. 1 (1857)

---

[24] Taruskin (2005), vol. 3, 786.

of the St. Petersburg Conservatory.[25] Undertaking remedial self-study in harmony and counterpoint, he approached the BACH cipher, first in a double fugue from 1875, and on two other occasions in 1878. The *Six Variations sur le thème BACH* Op. 10 comprises a Schumannesque suite of character pieces, including a waltz, intermezzo, scherzo, nocturne and highly chromatic prelude and fugue, each constructed from the Thomaskantor's name, printed in stark octaves at the head of the composition. There he stood watch like a silent sphinx. Thus, in the waltz we count sixteen statements of BACH in the bass; in the intermezzo, twenty-four in the soprano; in the scherzo, again twenty-four, though now in the tenor; and in the duet-like, Chopinesque nocturne, twelve in the alto – all told, a frequency that rivals the cipher experiments of Robert Schumann and Joseph Joachim.

If the *Six Variations* transport us from nineteenth-century genres back to Bach's fugues, in one miniature Rimsky-Korsakov revived the Thomaskantor's name in a most unlikely context – a series of *Paraphrases* for piano solo on the popular children's tune 'Chopsticks'. Alongside other offerings by Borodin, Cui and Lyadov, Rimsky-Korsakov fashioned a nondescript *fughetta* on BACH that contraposes a few fugal gestures against the elementary expanding patterns of the musical hobbyhorse (ex. 11.8).

Meanwhile, Rimsky-Korsakov's pupil and colleague Alexander Glazunov applied ciphers in two virtuoso piano compositions. The *Walzer*, Op. 23 (1890), dedicated to the soprano Nadeschda Sabela, drew upon a five-note theme that spelled her surname by employing German nomenclature for the first four letters and the solmization syllable *la* for the last two: E(**s**)-flat-**A**-**B**-flat-**E**-(**l**)**A**. The earlier Suite, Op. 2 (1883), took for its theme 'Sascha' (E(**s**)-flat-**A**-E(**s**)-flat-**C**-**H**-**A**), a diminutive form of Alexander, which shared several pitches with Robert Schumann's cipher in *Carnaval* for Asch (A-E-flat-C-B; see p. 204). Perhaps for that reason Glazunov followed Rimsky-Korsakov's lead in the *Six Variations* in producing a chain-like series of pieces reminiscent of Schumann's piano cycles. Like the *Variations*, Glazunov's suite included a scherzo, nocturne and waltz, all prefaced by an introduction and prelude, though dispensing with fugal entanglements.

Yet another group of cipher compositions offered a homage to the Russian music publisher Belyayev (Belaieff), whose name generated the compact motive B-flat-A-F (**B**-flat-**la**i-**eff**). Among them were the *Sérénade* Op. 3 for string quintet by Nikolay Sokoloff (1887) along with the *Andantino* Op. 7 (1888) and Prelude and Fugue Op. 11 (1889) for string quartet by Alexander Kopylov. Once again, a salient feature of these cipher pieces was their concentration on

---

[25] See further Maes (2002), 169ff.

Ex. 11.8: Rimsky-Korsakov, *Paraphrases*, 'Chopsticks' (1879)

the cryptogram; thus, Sokoloff's *Sérénade* began with six consecutive statements of B-flat-A-F in the second violin followed by no fewer than seventeen more an octave above in the first violin.

By far the most ambitious work generated from Belyayev's name, though, was the collaborative four-movement string quartet written to celebrate his fiftieth birthday (1886) by Rimsky-Korsakov, Lyadov, Borodin and Glazunov. In this case the Sonata Form endpoints encouraged Rimsky-Korsakov and Glazunov to treat the cipher at various transposed and inverted levels, as the formal process allowed. Lyadov's second-movement scherzo, propelled by nimble staccato iterations of the cipher (B-flat-A-F), anticipated the animated scherzo of Debussy's String Quartet in G minor (1893), with its persistent highlighting of the pitches G, F-sharp and D. For three summers (1880–2) Debussy had visited Russia in the employ of Madame von Meck. Whether a decade later he was simply revisiting memories of Russian music or responding to Lyadov's scherzo – Debussy's motive transposes Lyadov's down a third (exs. 11.9a and b) – is unclear. Perhaps relevant, though, is that inaugurating Debussy's scherzo are several plucked G major chords, seemingly recalling Borodin's pizzicato chords in the third movement of the collaborative quartet that simulate a Spanish

Ex. 11.9a–b: Lyadov, String Quartet, Scherzo (1886); Debussy, String Quartet in G minor, Scherzo (1893)

guitar (*Serenata alla Spagnola*), against which Belyayev's cipher emerges in a *cantabile* melody assigned to the viola.

As a risible cryptographic postscript to Lyadov's scherzo we might mention his student Nikolai Myaskovsky, who in his String Quartet in D minor, Op. 33 No. 3 enciphered a 'joke at the expense of Lyadov'.[26] After the professor repeatedly disparaged Grieg's music, Myaskovsky concealed the Norwegian's name in the opening bars ('Edfard Gr[ie]g') and then the monitory Russian phrase 'beregis Lyadova' ('beware of Lyadov') in the contrasting second theme of the first movement (ex. 11.10). The target remained oblivious to the deception.[27]

Among the most eccentric musicians to enjoy Belyayev's patronage was the sensualist, symbolist and messianist Alexander Scriabin (1872–1915), whose mature music exploited the 'chord of the pleroma', a term borrowed from Gnosticism to invoke the fullness of divine power. Comprising a series of fourths, some chromatically altered (C-F-sharp-B-flat-E-A), this 'mystic chord' (ex. 11.11) lived 'near the octatonic and whole-tone collections in a "homogeneous land"'.[28] Just as five of the six pitches derived from a whole-tone scale on C, so also did five emanate from an octatonic scale on C. One other feature of the scales, and of the chord, was the plurality of tritonal relationships,[29] explored perhaps most fully by Scriabin in his orchestral work *Prometheus, the Poem of Fire* (1908–10), for which a special keyboard instrument projected a spectrum of colours coordinated with particular tonalities (see Chapter 2, p. 36). Scriabin now jettisoned from his scores the conventional diatonic

---

[26] Ikonnikov (1946), 69.

[27] Ibid., 70; representing the letter 'r' is *re*.

[28] Morrison (2022), 12.

[29] For example, within the whole-tone scale C-F-sharp, D-G-sharp and E-B-flat; within the octatonic scale, C-F-sharp, D-G-sharp and E-flat-A.

Ex. 11.10: Myaskovsky, String Quartet in D minor, Op. 33 No. 3 (1930)

Ex. 11.11: Scriabin, Mystic Chord

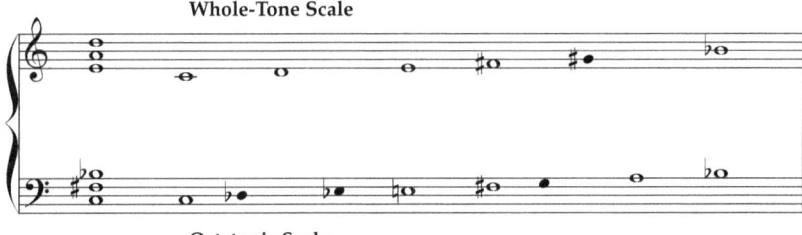

scale and its familiar consonant triads, in deference to a new music that aimed toward the 'transcendence of the ego', the 'revelation of the supernatural' and a 'new hierarchy of the divine world completely shorn of earthly reality'.[30]

In 1905 Scriabin had discovered the writings of Helena Blavatsky (1831–91), including *The Secret Doctrine* (1888), a central text of the occult movement known as theosophy ('divine wisdom') that enjoyed a remarkable vogue during the Russian Silver Age, the period of the last two tsars, Alexander III and Nicholas II, spanning the 1880s to the outbreak of the First World War. Madame Blavatsky was 'an expatriate Russian woman with an enthusiasm for Buddhist thought and a genius for self-promotion'.[31] Her new movement, which quickly became international, with headquarters in Adyar, India, interpreted theosophy broadly, by relating all existence to a God-centred reality. The human soul 'transmigrates through an enormous number of lifetimes, first downward into matter, then upward into spirit, each incarnation shaped by the karma

---

[30] Maes (2002), 215.
[31] Carlson (1993), 3.

generated by good or evil acts'.³² Ever cyclic in nature, the universe has proceeded through billions of years alternating between *manvantaras*, or periods of activity and manifestation, and *pralayas*, periods of rest and dormancy. As part of the all-encompassing divine unity, man is a god who, having temporarily succumbed to the negative attraction of matter, aspires to return to a positive spiritual existence.

This idea resonated with Scriabin, who as early as 1904 or 1905 recorded in one of his notebooks: 'I am, and there is nothing outside me. I am nothing, I am everything, I am unity and the uniform multiplicity within it'.³³ Theosophy encouraged Scriabin to realize in his music an overarching metaphor for the *manvantara*, 'the return of mankind and nature to God, followed by the absorption of time and space in the Deity'. Many of his later scores exhibit what his brother-in-law and early biographer, Boris de Schloezer, described as a 'uniform succession of states – languor, longing, impetuous striving, dance, ecstasy, and transfiguration', a 'series of upswings, with each successive wave rising higher and higher toward a final effort, liberation, and ecstasy'.³⁴ If music remained the centre of Scriabin's theurgic project, his ultimate vision, *Mysterium*, would have dwarfed all that he – or anyone else – had previously envisioned: an eschatological 'vision of an apocalyptic ecstasy'.³⁵ All five senses were to partake of an orgiastic demonstration of thousands, as Scriabin's 'Omni-art' would unfold over seven days in a newly designed temple situated near the Himalayas. For years the composer contemplated this final, all-consuming effort, and in 1914, the year before he died, began sketching ideas for the *Acte préalable*, the prologue to the event. But ultimately, while the horrors of the First World War raged, *Mysterium* remained an unsolved mystery, Scriabin's unfulfilled 'image of cosmic death in a state of ecstasy'.³⁶

∾ *iii*

After Scriabin, the next two generations produced 'the last great *Russian* composer', Sergei Prokofiev (1891–1953), a prodigy and virtuoso pianist who pursued a cosmopolitan career in Europe and the United States before repatriating

---

³² Ibid., 115.
³³ Nicholls and Pushkin (2018), 66, 68.
³⁴ De Schloezer (1987), 97.
³⁵ Ibid., 177.
³⁶ Ibid., 292.

Ex. 11.12: Prokofiev, Third Piano Sonata, Op. 28 (1917)

in 1936 to the new Soviet Union; and 'the first great *Soviet* composer',[37] Dmitri Shostakovich (1906–75), whose career transpired under the new regime. Prokofiev employed a musical cipher in his Third Piano Sonata, Op. 28, premiered at the St. Petersburg Conservatory in 1918, months after the eruption of the Bolshevik Revolution. But the subtitle of the sonata, 'From the Old Notebooks', betrays its origins in an unpublished piece from 1907, in which Prokofiev ruminated on the name of Sofia Esche, a classmate at the Conservatory, deriving first the pitches E-E-flat-C-B-E from her surname,[38] and ten years later simplifying it to E-C-B-E (Eche), the beginning of the contrasting theme in the one-movement sonata (ex. 11.12).

In contrast, Dmitri Shostakovich was a confirmed cryptographer who habitually massaged ciphers into his music, especially the four-note series D-E-flat-C-B-natural (**DSCH**), extracted from a Germanized version of his name (**D**imitrij **Sch**ostakowitsch). Prominent in the composer's later music, this cipher readily prompts comparison to **BACH**, also comprising four pitches: the third and fourth pitches of each cipher are identical, and each coheres around a central minor third, framed on either side by a semitone. While **BACH** fills out the chromatic span between A and C, **DSCH** expands the compass by one semitone, in the process omitting the pitch D-flat in the chromatic scale between B and E-flat (ex. 11.13).

Along with **BACH**, other candidates have been advanced to explain the origins of Shostakovich's cipher. **DSCH** shares three pitches with Robert Schumann's **ASCH** sphinx; furthermore, the fugal subject of the second

Ex. 11.13: **BACH** and **DSCH** Ciphers

---

[37] Medić (2020), 88.
[38] See O'Shea (2013), 142; and the diary entry of 20 September 1907 in Prokofiev (2006), 8–9.

Ex. 11.14: Stravinsky, *Symphony of Psalms*, Second Movement (1930)

movement of Stravinsky's *Symphony of Psalms* (1930) has been viewed as a 'compelling potential influence'.[39] Not only do the first four pitches reuse **DSCH**, even if in altered order (C-E-flat-B-natural-D, ex. 11.14), but, as we know, Shostakovich prized Stravinsky's score, and prepared a four-hand arrangement for personal use.

Stephen C. Brown argues that as early as the 1920s Shostakovich was exploiting several compositional elements that may have led him independently to the cipher.[40] They included the octatonic scale; Jewish musical modes and idioms; modal lowering of individual degrees of a scale; modal clash, or juxtaposing a scale degree in its conventional *and* lowered forms; and scalar tightening, or contracting a portion of a scale into a more compressed space, all of which can generate **DSCH**. Some examples: Violin Concerto No. 1 in A minor, Op. 77 (1948), where the cipher appears, slightly rearranged, in the first two movements; Fugue No. 15 in D-flat major, Op. 87 (1952), based on a wedge-like subject that expands from a semitone to a fifth, in the process germinating **DSCH**; Fifth String Quartet in B-flat major, Op. 92 (1952), where a viola motive embeds the cipher; and Sixth String Quartet in G major, Op. 101 (1956), where the cipher appears harmonically in the closing sonorities of each movement.

Whatever its origins, this distinctive cipher, exploited by Shostakovich *and* many of his students and colleagues, produces 'an unmistakable "Shostakovich sound"',[41] but also a metaphor for an artist working within the Soviet totalitarian state. And therein lies the rub, for 'we know a great deal about him, and he remains largely invisible to us'.[42] Was Shostakovich, who periodically glorified the Soviet state according to the dictates of socialist realism in programmatic symphonies – thus, Nos. 2 (*To October*, 1927), 3 (*First of May*, 1930), 5 ('Soviet artist's reply to just criticism', 1937), 7 (*Leningrad*, 1942), 11 (*The Year 1905*, 1957) and 12 (*The Year 1917*, 1961) – an acquiescent comrade of the workers' paradise? Or was Shostakovich, whose opera *Lady Macbeth of the Mtsensk*

---

[39] Stephen C. Brown (2006), 96, also 97–8.
[40] Ibid., 82.
[41] Ibid., 69.
[42] Lesser (2011), 2.

District Stalin reviled in 1936; who was publicly criticized again in 1948 along with Prokofiev and others for lapsing into Western formalism; who routinely slept with a packed suitcase at his side, assuming he would be exiled to Siberia; and who was pressured to join the Communist Party in 1960, rather a dissident who layered his music with content critical of the government – thus, Symphony No. 13 (*Babi Yar*, 1962), from all appearances about the Nazi massacre of tens of thousands of Jews near Kyiv in 1941, yet also broaching through Yevgeny Yevtushenko's protest poetry topics controversial enough to trigger a backlash against the composer and poet during the Khrushchev Thaw (*Ottepel*)?

Because of the prominence of **DSCH** in Shostakovich's music and the long shadow it cast on his reception – the motto is etched on his tombstone in Moscow, and since 1994 has heralded the masthead of the *DSCH Journal* devoted to his life and works – many have read below the surface the uncompromising critique of 'an embittered dissident who, in the line of the old Russian tradition of the *yuródiviy* – the "holy fool" who had the privilege of telling the tsar the truth with impunity' – now 'proclaimed his real and devastating opinion of the pernicious regime through hidden codes in his music'.[43] In 1979 this revisionist agendum gained compelling force with the appearance of *Testimony*, released by the *émigré* Soviet musicologist Solomon Volkov, who claimed to have transcribed memoirs the composer had dictated between 1971 and 1974. Unabashedly, Volkov now 'revealed' hidden undercurrents in his subject's music. Thus, the Fifth Symphony, which had triumphantly restored Shostakovich's reputation in 1937 and brought him back into the official Soviet fold, was a duplicitous example of doublespeak: 'The rejoicing [in the symphony] is forced, created under threat, as in *Boris Godunov*. It's as if someone were beating you with a stick and saying, "Your business is rejoicing, your business is rejoicing," and you rise, shakily, and go marching off, muttering, "Our business is rejoicing, our business is rejoicing"'.[44] Similarly, the Eleventh Symphony (1957), ostensibly about the Revolution of 1905, actually concealed a protest against the Soviet intervention in Hungary one year before in 1956. What was heard 'in this music was not the police firing on the crowd in front of the Winter Palace in 1905, but the Soviet tanks roaring in the streets of Budapest'.[45]

Soon after the publication of *Testimony* doubts arose about its authenticity. Volkov provided no hard proof that Shostakovich had substantiated

---

[43] Maes (2002), 344.
[44] Volkov (1979), 183.
[45] Volkov (1995), 169.

the bombshell claims, and sceptics did not remain silent. In the estimation of Laurel Fay, *Testimony* was 'a poor source for the serious biographer. The embittered, "deathbed" disclosures of someone ravaged by illness, with festering psychological wounds and scores to settle, [were] not to be relied upon for accuracy'.[46] On the other hand, in *Shostakovich Reconsidered*, Allan B. Ho, Dmitri Feofanov and seventeen other contributors ardently supported the case for Shostakovich as a 'closet dissident rather than political toady'.[47] In Francis Maes's assertive phrasing, he was a 'lifelong dissident, who behind the official façade of his music had been making ironic comments about the Soviet regime the whole time'.[48] There the matter has rested, with the experts continuing their debate, leaving us to consider here the **DSCH** cipher and its spread beyond the music of Shostakovich.

According to conventional wisdom, Shostakovich first unveiled the cipher in the Tenth Symphony in E minor Op. 93, which premiered in December 1953, nine months after the death of Stalin on 5 March (the very day that Prokofiev passed). Shostakovich revealed the cipher gradually over the course of the symphony. Thus, in its opening bars we hear in the contrabass the figure E-F-sharp-G-D-sharp, a transposed, anagram-like reordering of F-sharp-G-E-D-sharp (ex. 11.15).

Two movements later, in the *Allegretto*, Shostakovich transposes the anagram to C-D-E-flat-B-natural before finally unmasking the cipher in the flute and piccolo at its 'correct' pitch level, D-E-flat-C-B-natural (ex. 11.16), as if to announce the composer's arrival in the score.

Further on, the French horn introduces a beguiling second cipher, E-A-E-D-A, for Elmira (**E-L**[a]-**Mi-R**[e]-**A**) Nazirova (ex. 11.17), an Azerbaijani pianist who studied composition with Shostakovich at the Moscow Conservatory in 1947.[49]

These two ciphers then gradually approach each other, separated by shorter intervening intervals until the two appear briefly together in a *fortissimo* climax. The 'hidden' narrative seems clear enough: the third movement alludes to Shostakovich's relationship with the 'unattainable' Elmira, who also remained totally 'unknown' for decades after the premiere of the symphony until 1994, when the Israeli musicologist Nelly Kravetz identified her encrypted cipher.[50]

---

[46] Fay (2000), 4; also, Fay (1980).

[47] Ho and Feofanov (1998), 47–8.

[48] Maes (2002), 347.

[49] Huseinova (2003).

[50] Huseinova (2002); see also Kravetz (2000).

Ex. 11.15: Shostakovich, Tenth Symphony, First Movement (1953)

Ex. 11.16: Shostakovich, Tenth Symphony, Third Movement (1953)

Ex. 11.17: Shostakovich, Elmira Cipher (1953)

If we believe the account in *Testimony*, the Tenth Symphony conveys other submerged references beyond the composer's personal life to his conflicted identity as a Soviet musician:

> I couldn't write an apotheosis to Stalin, I simply couldn't. I knew what I was in for when I wrote the Ninth [Symphony, 1945]. But I did depict Stalin in music in my next symphony, the Tenth. I wrote it right after Stalin's death, and no one has yet guessed what the symphony is about.[51]

The frantic second movement scherzo, marked by militant percussive effects, shrill, siren-like wailing, and massed blocks of raw sound, erupts with brutish energy – Shostakovich's portrait of Stalin? In B-flat minor, the scherzo unleashes a muscular motive that consumes the pitches B-flat, C, D-flat and E-flat, just two degrees of separation from the composer's personal cipher, which we may expose by rearranging the pitches as D-flat, E-flat, C and B-flat, and then

---

[51] Volkov (1979), 141.

chromatically raising the endpoints, thus: D-natural-E-flat-C-B-natural. Quite likely, Shostakovich's decision to place this movement in B-flat minor was significant. That key lies a tritone, tonally speaking the furthest removed, from E major, the ultimate tonic of the symphony, which in the end releases unbridled iterations of **DSCH** in the four timpani, asserting once again the individual against the totalitarian state, and offering 'the ultimate act of personal defiance'.[52]

Arguably Shostakovich's most gnomic creation from a cryptographic point of view was the Eighth String Quartet, composed in just days in 1960 after the composer, willingly or not, joined the Communist Party. In no other work did he saturate his music with so many monograms, privileged in all five connected movements, so much so that the composition impresses patently as musical autobiography. For Volkov **DSCH** played 'the function of Virgil, leading the listener through the circles of the composer's hell – through music that is sometimes unbearably gloomy, sometimes supernaturally tranquil and translucent, sometimes nervous, even paranoid'.[53] Supporting this interpretation is an extensive series of self-quotations that circulate throughout the composition; among them, from the composer's First Symphony (1926), *Lady Macbeth* (1932), Fifth Symphony (1937), Second Piano Trio (1944), film score *The Young Guard* (1948) and First Cello Concerto (1959).[54] There are also allusions to other composers whom Shostakovich revered.[55] The opening of the quartet, for example, presents four successive entries of the cipher in imitative counterpoint, plausibly a nod to the opening fugue of Beethoven's String Quartet in C-sharp minor, Op. 131. If slightly reordered, Beethoven's subject, G-sharp-B-sharp-C-sharp-A, can be heard as B-sharp-C-sharp-A-G-sharp, just one semitone off from the transposed equivalent of **DSCH**, B-sharp-C-sharp-A-sharp-A-natural.

Somewhat more challenging to interpret is the quotation in the fourth movement of the revolutionary Russian funeral song 'Tortured by Great Misery', a melody, according to Shostakovich/Volkov, 'known to all Russians'.[56] In 1998 the Soviet musicologist Lev Lebedinsky commented that here Shostakovich was describing himself: 'His life was full of torture … And precisely what was it that tortured him? More than anything else, captivity. A freedom-loving democrat, he was forced to live and work under a totalitarian regime which crushed him in its oppressive machinery'.[57] No stranger to controversy in the

---

[52] Mishra (2008), 205.
[53] Volkov (2004), 270.
[54] See ibid., 235–6.
[55] For a detailed list, see Fanning (2004a), 54–5.
[56] Volkov (1979), 156. See also Fanning (2004a), 114.
[57] Lebedinsky (1998), 476.

Shostakovich wars – the composer's son, Maxim, for one, rejected these claims – Lebedinsky went further, and 'revealed' that 'a few of the composer's closest friends knew that after finishing the [quartet], Shostakovich had intended to kill himself; luckily, they managed to persuade him not to do it'.[58] So, in Lebedinsky's reading, the quartet, officially dedicated 'to the victims of fascism and war', was not just a 'wrenching human document'[59] but considerably more: a hyper-emotional suicide letter, complete with a memorial review of significant works in the composer's career and provided with his envisioned funeral march, all threaded together with the ubiquitous monogram.

Two other enigmatic facets of the composer's music deserve mention. First, his decades-long engagement with Soviet cinema, from *The New Babylon* (1928, about the Paris Commune of 1871) to *King Lear* (1971), has recently received scholarly attention from Joan Titus, for whom Shostakovich's scores were 'interstitial, continuing code traditions from opera and melodrama into cinema, and crossing regions, just as his music does today'.[60] Before establishing his career, Shostakovich had worked as a pianist in silent-film theatres, where he improvised from his 'own internal musical dictionaries', a few vestiges of which survive in early Soviet silent film music manuals that typically offered 'charts with suggestions on how to accompany a film'.[61] The shifting images on the screen thus found audible counterparts in the quicksilver play of apposite *intonatsii*, or 'musical intonations' – code-like gestures that were 'undoubtedly communicative, regardless of the concept of socialist realism'.[62]

Finally, an especially cryptic turn in Shostakovich's late style was his recognition in 1967 of twelve-tone techniques, a remarkable development, given his prior towing 'the official Soviet line' by criticizing Western serialism.[63] Shostakovich was perhaps responding to the 'unofficial' work of a younger generation of composers, who adopted twelve-tone composition as 'a form of resistance for … small Soviet audiences' assembling in 'small, out-of-the-way locations'.[64] Shostakovich's first row appeared in the sixth song of the cycle *Seven Verses of Aleksander Blok*, Op. 127, titled, provocatively enough, 'Mysterious Signs'. Here

---

[58] Ibid., 477. See also the composer's letter of 19 July 1960 to Isaak Glikman: 'I wrote this ideologically flawed quartet which is of no use to anybody. I started thinking that if some day I die, nobody is likely to write a work in memory of me, so I had better write one myself.' Glikman (2001), 90–1.

[59] Taruskin (2000), 27.

[60] Titus (2016), 6.

[61] Ibid., 6–7.

[62] Ibid.

[63] Schmelz (2004), 303.

[64] Ibid., 304, 330.

the ambiguous atonal trajectory of the row evoked the secrets of the Russian symbolist's apocalyptic imagery of 'oppressive dreams' portending 'war and flames'.[65] Nevertheless, Shostakovich did not embrace orthodox serialism. He availed himself of no retrograde or inverted forms of the row, but only one prime form to reuse a few times without altering its pitch sequence.

For a few years until his death in 1975 Shostakovich experimented with serial manipulations in several late works, including the final three string quartets and two symphonies.[66] Had he lived longer would he have accepted the rigorous strictures of serialism, following Stravinsky's new path in the 1950s and 60s? Perhaps. But it is a relatively safe wager that Shostakovich would have continued to exploit ciphers, as he did in the Fifteenth Symphony (1971), where at the outset the flute intones the name of his grandson, Sascha (e**S**-**A**s-**C**-**H**-**A**; E-flat-A-flat-C-B-A-natural), and in the third movement of the Fourteenth String Quartet (1973), dedicated to the cellist of the Beethoven Quartet, Sergei Shirinsky, whose name required a more elaborate code. In the third movement, we hear the motive D-sharp-E-D-natural-E-G-A, a veiling of the familiar version of Sergei, 'Seryozha': E**s** (the German E-flat, enharmonically redefined here as D-sharp) for 'S'; **E** for 'e'; the solfège syllable **Re** or D-natural for 'r'; the Cyrillic **Ë** (pronounced '**Yo**') for the pitch E; ; the Cyrillic **Ж** (pronounced like a soft G) for '**zh**'; and **A** for 'a'. To supplement this well-masked reference, Shostakovich later quotes an aria from his opera *Lady Macbeth* in which the character Sergei is addressed as 'Seryozha'. A cryptogram and self-reference thus underscore a double pun, just one demonstration of the rich art of Shostakovich, who remained to the end not so much an *apparatchik* as a skilled practitioner of his own Aesopian musical riddles.[67]

What added gravitas to **DSCH** was its widespread adoption by composers outside and within the Soviet Union, too many to consider here.[68] Examples from non-Russian composers include some that might seem coincidental, such as Benjamin Britten's *Rejoice in the Lamb* ('And the watchman strikes me with his staff', 1943; F-sharp-G-E-D-sharp) and *Rape of Lucretia* ('Give him this orchid', 1946; F-sharp-G-E-D-sharp), dating well before the composers' first meeting in 1960. More convincing examples occur in the third movement (toccata) of Witold Lutosławski's Concerto for Orchestra (1954) and slow movement of Malcolm Arnold's Symphony No. 3 (1957), where the transposed

---

[65] See Gillies (2022), 65–72.

[66] In addition to Schmelz (2004) see Henderson (2008b), 426–34.

[67] See further, Zak (1998).

[68] For a discussion through 1988 see Hulme (2002), 567–75.

cipher appears as A (for 'Arnold'?)-A-sharp-G-F-sharp. Both examples postdate Shostakovich's Tenth Symphony (1953), in which **DSCH** first emerged into public view; what is more, Arnold was part of the British delegation in 1957 to the Prague Spring Festival, where he met Shostakovich.

Probably the most ambitious application to date of the cipher has been the *Passacaglia on DSCH* by Ronald Stevenson (1963), a monumental piano work exceeding one hour in duration. Constructed upon a thirteen-note ostinato patterned from the cipher, the composition traverses a spectrum of variations, including a Sonata Form, set of dances and culminating triple fugue on **DSCH**, **BACH** and the *Dies irae* (to the victims of the Holocaust), all of which conveniently contain the defining intervallic nexus of a semitone and minor third (ex. 11.18).

DSCH and **BACH** also figure in Stevenson's Piano Concerto No. 2 (*The Continents*, 1972), where they generate a fugue and assume their place in a Baedeker-like review of world music. Finally, four years later, Stevenson penned the introspective memorial tribute *Recitative and Air for Shostakovich*.

More recently, the Italian composer Lorenzo Ferrero has revived the cipher in *DEsCH* for oboe, bassoon, piano and orchestra (2006, the Shostakovich centenary), and in the singular *Op. 111 – Bagatella su Beethoven* (2009). Here the pianist begins *in medias res* by paraphrasing a turbulent passage from the first movement of Beethoven's final piano sonata (1822) before isolating the motive of a minor third and diminished fourth (C-E-flat-B-natural) and adding the pitch D to yield our cipher. The motive has even penetrated mass-media markets and found its place in Danny Elfman's film score for *Dolores Claiborne* (1995) and the single 'Hammer, Stirrup, and Anvil' from the final album of the English rock band Chumbawamba, *ABCDEFG* (2010), where the revealing line 'My name is Dmitri' announces the composer's symbolic presence. Most recently, the Armenian jazz pianist Tigran Hamasyan has woven the cipher into the driving, angular rhythms of 'Ara Resurrected' from his album *The Call Within* (2020).

Ex. 11.18: Ronald Stevenson, *Passacaglia on DSCH* (1963)

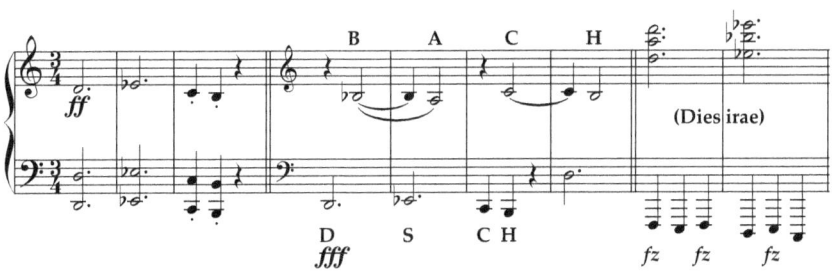

Inside the Soviet and post-Soviet states generations of composers after Shostakovich paid homage through the cipher. Whether or not his pupil German Galynin deliberately incorporated the motive into the third movement of his First Piano Concerto (1946) is debatable,[69] but there is little doubt about the extra-musical narrative of Boris Tishchenko's Symphony No. 5 (1967) – it arguably chronicles a musical dialogue between him and his mentor/friend, with significant quotations from several works by both composers, and extensive use of **DSCH**. Other Soviet tributes to Shostakovich include Mieczysłav Weinberg's Symphony No. 12 (1976), again filled with quotations from Shostakovich but (surprisingly) no instances of **DSCH**,[70] and the Ninth String Quartet (1978) by the Georgian Sulkan Tsintsadze, based heavily on **DSCH** and displaying allusions to his friend's Eighth String Quartet of 1957. Another chamber work, the *Postlude DSCH* (1981) by Valentyn Silvestrov, is set for soprano *vocalise* and piano trio.[71]

In another category are two works by Edison Denisov (1929–96), who during the late 1940s and 50s found a strong supporter in Shostakovich, and was one of the first to assimilate the tetrachord fully into the asperities of twelve-tone composition. Denisov became a central figure in underground Soviet music during the 1960s and 70s that pursued 'spiritual emancipation from the ideological pressures of the ruling system'.[72] Thus, in his Saxophone Sonata (1970) **DSCH** spawned the first four pitches of the row (D-E-flat-C-B-C-sharp-A-flat-A-B-flat-G-F-sharp-E-F), while in a slightly earlier work, *1969 DSCH*, for clarinet, trombone, cello and piano, the cipher and its transposition by tritone accounted for eight pitches of the row (D-E-flat-C-B-G-sharp-A-F-sharp-F-natural-E-G-C-sharp-B-flat; ex. 11.19).

Denisov seized too upon cryptographic symmetries camouflaged in his own name, so that the motive E-D-E-flat (**Edis**on) and its inversion D-E-E-flat (**Denis**of) became his 'signature-tune'.[73] He folded these cyphers into many works,[74] including the *Requiem* (1980), where at the very end the three pitches serve as an autobiographical marker in a pandiatonic sonority based on the fifth G-D. Here the pitch G stood for 'Gott', the D for *Deus, Domine* and Denisov, all part of a 'universalizing gesture' connecting the 'personal and the impersonal'.

---

[69] See Fanning (2004), 291–2.

[70] Elphick (2019), 208.

[71] Silvestrov later encoded his wife's name, Larissa, into the closing bars of Symphony No. 6 (2000). In 2022 the composer numbered among the millions of refugees fleeing Ukraine during the sudden escalation of the Russo–Ukrainian conflict.

[72] Kholopov and Tsenova (1995), xiv. See also, Schmelz (2009), 131ff., 275ff.

[73] Kholopov and Tsenova (1995), 80n. 9.

[74] Ibid., 80n. 9, 112 and 147n. 6.

Ex. 11.19: Edison Denisov, *1969 DSCH* (1969)

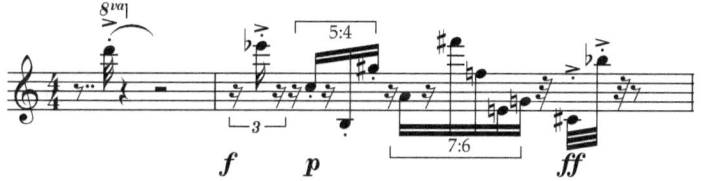

As the composer confessed, 'I sign at the end', to prepare the work 'for an imaginary museum, thereby insuring its future'.[75]

The case of Denisov illustrates that **DSCH** not only paid tribute to Shostakovich but also encouraged the proliferation of ciphers. Almost inevitably **DSCH** prompted new germinations of **BACH**, causing the Estonian Arvo Pärt, for instance, to invoke the Thomaskantor in at least three works in which serialism 'cohabit[ed] with [tonality], in a free association of styles'[76]: 1) *Collage on the Theme BACH* (1964) for oboe, strings, harpsichord and piano, which quotes intact in its middle movement the sarabande from Bach's sixth English Suite; 2) *Wenn Bach Bienen gezüchtet hätte* (*If Bach Had Been a Beekeeper*, 1976), in which chromatic clusters swarming around the cipher at different pitch levels create apian sound effects; and 3) *Concerto piccolo über BACH* (1994) for trumpet, strings, harpsichord and piano, a recasting of *Collage*. Similarly, Sofia Gubaidulina (p. 35) could not resist the allure of **BACH** in a variety of works, including *Reflections on the Theme BACH* for string quartet, based on *Contrapunctus* 14 from *Die Kunst der Fuge* (2002), in which **BACH** emerges in the closing chorale,[77] and *So sei es* (2013), for violin, contrabass, percussion and piano, written to commemorate her colleague Viktor Suslin, and alluding to **BACH** and the subject of the Fugue in C-sharp minor (*Well-Tempered Clavier*, Book 1) as symbols of the cross.

The potency of these familiar musical ciphers inevitably encouraged the derivation of new musical cryptograms. Among the novelties were examples from Rodin Shchedrin (**SHCHED**), Sofia Gubaidulina (**EsG**) and Alfred Schnittke (**ADSCH**).[78] Of these, the last elevated ciphers, which Schnittke termed monograms, to a wholly new level of compositional strategy. No longer 'an occasional curiosity', they became a fully integrated 'source of pitch material … deeply

---

[75] Adamenko (2007), 132, 133, 134.
[76] Henderson (2008a).
[77] See Straus (2020).
[78] Cherniak (2019), 303.

connected to the circumstances of his works' creation'.⁷⁹ Schnittke now cast his cipher net out just about as far as possible, to encrypt not just dozens of composers from the fifteenth through twentieth centuries, but also performers who premiered his compositions, and words such as 'Deutschland', 'Leipzig', 'Thomaskirche', 'Hamburg', 'die Erde' ('earth') and 'das Böse' ('evil'). The last materialized in the third movement of his Third Symphony (1981) as a series of eight notes: D(**D**)-A(**A**)-E-flat (e**S**)-A-flat (**AS**)-B-flat (**B**)-E (ö [**oe**])-D-sharp (e**S**)-E(**E**), with a pitch redundancy for the 's' of 'Das' (E-flat *and* A-flat).

Having chosen his minacious theme, Schnittke subjected it to a whirlwind of transformations 'to create allusions to various historical styles, as well as to some landmark composers' personal styles, or even to their particular works'.⁸⁰ Examining the composer's sketches for the symphony (Juilliard Manuscript Collection, New York), Ivana Medić determined that Schnittke intended to accumulate into his score at least fifteen different 'stylistic layers', generating a historical review of not quite a millennium of music. Thus, 'evil' surfaces in the symphony through several allusions marshalled in chronological order, beginning with twelfth-century medieval organum, hocket and fifteenth-century fauxbourdon, then the style of chorales followed by more specific reminiscences – for example, Mozart (Piano Concerto in D minor, K 466), Beethoven (*Egmont* Overture) and Wagner – before venturing forward through Mahler and twentieth-century serialism to the avant-garde.⁸¹ After this polystylistic panorama, Schnittke reverses the allusions, in effect tracing their origins before combining them *ad libitum*, as the movement clangorously concludes on the pitch B-flat, the link to the finale's first and principal monogram, **BACH**.

How to interpret this narrative of musical time-travelling, propelled forward and back by the jarring din of competing monograms? Medić proposes that 'Schnittke's moral here is that evil ... has always existed and always will'.⁸² But why the concentration on monograms for German composers⁸³ and cities, not to mention the obsessive composing-out of 'das Böse' in so many distinctive variants of a common monogram? Relevant here is that Schnittke, whose

---

⁷⁹ Segall (2013), 254.

⁸⁰ Medić (2013), 191.

⁸¹ Ibid., 191–6.

⁸² Ibid., 197.

⁸³ Schnittke's sketches display monograms for Walter von den Vogelweide, Hans Sachs, Heinrich Isaac, Buxtehude, Pachelbel, Froberger, Mattheson, Telemann, J. A. Hasse, W. F. Bach, C. P. E. Bach and J. C. Bach, among others; furthermore, in the first movement there are three 'waves' of twenty-seven monograms formed around composers from Bach to Mozart, Beethoven to Johann Strauss, and Mahler to Mauricio Kagel. Medić (2013), 177, 183.

ancestry was Volga German, was half-Jewish, half-German, so that he was 'a foreigner everywhere'.[84] Also relevant is that his favourite novel was *Doctor Faustus* of Thomas Mann, that expatriate's searing 'critique of Germany, the country that had "sold its soul to the Devil"'.[85] In this reading, the culminating appearances of **BACH** in the symphony represented for Schnittke 'one of those magical formulas [that] could be used to overcome the confusion of the world and to "structure" both the world and individual consciousness'.[86] The composer was recalling his own line of descent from German music history – as it happened, the Third Symphony was premiered by Kurt Masur at the Leipzig Gewandhaus on 5 November 1981 – and, furthermore, likely offering his own 'clandestine critique of German culture', viewed as '[having] reached its pinnacle and been in the state of decline since the onset of modernism and avant-garde'.[87]

What Alexander Ivashkin labelled the Schnittke Code[88] comprised several constituent parts: monograms that could divulge directly their plaintext (thus B-C-A-G-E for John **Cage**) or remain vexingly laconic (for example, the pitch G for Lui**g**i Nono); monograms that could hide as subsets of others, or as portions of complete twelve-tone rows; familiar and yet seemingly out of place triads appearing in non-tonal contexts; and unpredictable, jumbled juxtapositions of disparate historical styles.

Surveying the whole of Schnittke's career, Gavin Dixon apportioned it into four phases, with some overlap between the third and fourth:

1. an early serial period (1963–1971), in which the composer absorbed the methods of the Second Viennese School, at first cautiously but then extending his proficiency to serializing pitch *and* non-pitch parameters,
2. a turn to commemorative spiritual music (1972–1980), which relied heavily upon monograms, employed Catholic plainchant and Znamenny chant of the Orthodox Church, and embedded representations of the cross,
3. a liberal exploration of *polystylism* (1968–1991), Schnittke's term to designate the use of quotations and allusions in a commingling of styles from the Western traditions of art and popular music, all chosen to

---

[84] Ivashkin (1996), 10.
[85] Ibid., 198.
[86] Ivashkin (2017), 202.
[87] Medić (2013), 209.
[88] Ivashkin (2017).

explore through pastiche good and evil, order and chaos, and to reaffirm the centrality of Bach, and

4. a late style (1985–1994), precipitated by strokes the composer suffered beginning in July 1985; during this period Schnittke opted for an intuitive approach to composition, and inserted into his music moments of silence as symbols of absence, eerily anticipating the musical paradox chiselled into his gravestone after his death: a semibreve rest notated with a fermata and the dynamic marking *ff*.[89]

Numerous compositions of Schnittke illustrate these four phases; here, we review a few examples, beginning with the Violin Concerto No. 2 (1966), from the early serial period.

What stands out in this score is Schnittke's decision not to pursue orthodox twelve-tone serialism. While he viewed dodecaphony as a necessary alternative to tonality, he did not uniformly subscribe to the prohibition of pitch repetition before exhausting all twelve pitches of the row. To be sure, the principal material on which he based his concerto *is* a tone row that, emerging from the introductory violin solo, is taken up by the string section. But the pitches of that row – G-F-sharp-G-sharp-A-F-B-flat-B-E-C-D-flat-E-flat and D – accumulate only gradually, for they are interrupted by persistent repetitions of the open G-string, an anchoring pedal-point that returns at the end of the concerto to impose a circular unity onto the music.

Few members of the audience at the premiere in 1966 suspected that Schnittke assigned a symbolic significance to his tone row. Though initially reluctant to share this subtext, the composer later revealed that the twelve pitches represented the apostles of Christ, physically reinforced by the twelve string instruments of the chamber orchestra. The soloist, who ordains the row and spreads the Gospel through the apostles, is Christ; the double bass, the last of the strings to enter, is the 'anti-soloist', Judas, who betrays the Saviour through distortions, caricatures and relegation to the murky low registers. The programmatic outlines of a Gospel narrative thus come into focus: the concerto depicts the gathering of the disciples, Last Supper and betrayal by Judas, arrest and judgment of Christ, procession to Calvary and crucifixion, last words (in the high register of the solo violin) and death and, following, a timpani roll to render the earthquake, burial and resurrection.[90] The concerto thus advances a Christological morality tale of good versus evil.

---

[89] For a fuller treatment of these phases see Dixon (2022), 449.

[90] Dixon (2022), 140–3.

The deaths of Igor Stravinsky in 1971, Schnittke's parents in 1972 and 1975, and Shostakovich in 1975, followed by the composer's baptism into the Catholic faith in 1982, led to several commemorative works during his second stylistic phase. If he generated the short *Canon in memoriam Igor Stravinsky* for string quartet from the monogram G, F, E, D, E-flat, C, B, E-flat, A, E-flat (I**G**or **FED**orovi**SCH** St**r**A**v**in**S**k**y**), supplemented by the four missing pitches (F-sharp, G-sharp, A-sharp and C-sharp) to complete the chromatic aggregate,[91] in the *Prelude in memoriam Dmitri Shostakovich* for two violins (the second concealed *behind* a curtain) Schnittke derived his material largely from **DSCH** and **BACH**, to which he added a plucked open D-string – 'Dmitri' – as an ostinato. Relying heavily upon monograms, including one for '**ges**torben' ('dead'; G, E, E-flat), Schnittke no longer felt bound to strict serial procedures. In the end, **DSCH** and **BACH** simply merged through their two common pitches, C and B-natural, again reaffirming the 'idea of Bach as a source point for musical history'.[92]

Other works from this second period brought Schnittke's music into the domain of the sacred. Thus, he envisioned the Piano Quintet, begun after his mother's passing but not completed until 1976, after his father's death, as an instrumental Requiem, with five movements paralleling the principal parts of the Mass for the dead. In a similar way, Symphony No. 2 (*St. Florian*, 1979), inspired by Schnittke's visit in 1977 to Anton Bruckner's tomb, was designed as an 'invisible mass'; most of the six symphonic movements, corresponding to the *Kyrie, Gloria, Credo, Crucifixus, Sanctus/Benedictus* and *Agnus Dei*, begin with a chorus singing chants from the *Graduale Romanum*, to which the orchestra responds. As the composer acknowledged, 'representations of the cross do permeate the entire Symphony',[93] with intersecting horizontal and vertical displays in the score, and the circular figure (*circulatio*) of C-sharp-D-sharp-B-sharp-C-sharp (reworked from the *Crucifixus* of J. S. Bach's Mass in B minor), not to mention the ubiquitous, cross-like **BACH** monogram.

As early as 1971 Schnittke started recording ideas about 'polystylistic tendencies in modern music'[94] that over the next two decades would become the defining trademark of his mature third phase. He differentiated between quotation techniques, which could range from reproducing 'stereotypical micro-elements of an alien style, belonging to another age or another national tradition ', to 'exact or reworked quotations or pseudo-quotations', and allusions, 'subtle hints

---

[91] Ibid., 198–9.
[92] Ibid., 31; see also 210–11.
[93] Medić (2017), 29.
[94] Schnittke (2002), 87–90.

and unfulfilled promises that hover on the brink of quotation but do not actually cross it'.[95] In Schnittke's view, polystylism had 'always existed in concealed form in music', but by the 1970s was emerging as 'a conscious device', though not without complications. One issue was just 'how many levels of stylistic polyphony listeners [could] perceive simultaneously'. Still, polystylism '[widened] the range of expressive possibilities, [and facilitated] the integration of "low" and "high" styles, of the "banal" and "recherché" to create a ... general democratization of style'.[96] During the waning years of the Soviet Union, this last view resounded forcefully among Schnittke's generation, motivated as it was by the renewed push for artistic freedom from outworn, threadbare Soviet ideology.

Thus, in the Third String Quartet (1983) Schnittke posed three quotations 'separated by centuries', yet placed adjacently in the opening bars, that over the course of the composition met and ultimately merged, as if to 'bring all times together'.[97] These quotations revived a cadential passage from Orlando di Lasso's *Stabat mater* (1585), then leaped ahead to the subject of Beethoven's *Grosse Fuge*, Op. 133 (1827), and finished by invoking the Shostakovich cipher. Schnittke labelled each quotation in the score.

Despite their historical separation, the quotations share intervallic similarities, so that 'Beethoven' and 'Shostakovich' engulf 'Lasso'; and 'Beethoven', 'Shostakovich'. Schnittke buttresses his quotations with monograms, including the familiar **DSCH** and **BACH**, and new ciphers for Lasso (OrlAnDo Di LASSo, or A, D, D, A, E-flat, A-flat) and Beethoven (LuDwiG vAn BEetHoven, or D, G, A, B-flat, E, B). Of these two, the Beethoven monogram, prominent in the second movement, is richly allusive, and thus explores the other side of the quotation-allusion continuum of polystylism. Scholars have compared the first four notes to a Mannheim rocket (a rising arpeggiated figure associated with the centre of early Classicism), and to the rondo theme from Beethoven's *Pathétique* Sonata, Op. 13.[98] But the monogram might also allude to the finale of Beethoven's *Tempest* Sonata, Op. 31 No. 2, or the finale of his String Quartet, Op. 132 (ex. 11.20).

If Schnittke indeed had in mind here Op. 132, that might explain why in the middle movement of his quartet he shifts to a chorale-style texture reminiscent of the *Heiliger Dankgesang*.

---

[95] Ibid., 87, 88.
[96] Ibid., 89, 90.
[97] Quoted in Dixon (2022), 194.
[98] See ibid., 195.

Ex. 11.20: Schnittke, Third String Quartet (1983)

LuDwiG vAn B   E ethH   oven

Hartmut Schick has proposed that we can interpret Schnittke's Third Quartet as a 'musicological reflection' about the history of the string quartet.[99] In contrast, in the Concerto grosso No. 3 he turned his attention to five composers from the seventeenth, eighteenth and twentieth centuries with centennial anniversaries in 1985: Heinrich Schütz (1585–1672), J. S. Bach (1685–1750), G. F. Handel (1685–1759), Domenico Scarlatti (1685–1757) and Alban Berg (1885–1935). Admittedly, the music betrays little that might allude to Schütz's music, though Schnittke afforded that composer, along with the other four, a personalized monogram subsequently fleshed out into a complete twelve-tone row. The composition begins as a tonal neo-Baroque concerto grosso in G minor in the style of Bach's *Brandenburg* Concerti, but within a few minutes, 'the museum explodes, and we are standing with the scraps of the past (quotations) before a dangerous and uncertain present'.[100] Now traversing atonal realms, the music swerves to modernist styles reminiscent of Alban Berg's Violin Concerto, opposed occasionally by tubular bells pitched to intone **BACH**; one nod to Berg is a rising sequence of four whole tones, likely a reference to the chorale Berg quotes, 'Es ist genug', that Bach had harmonized in the finale of his cantata *O Ewigkeit, Du Donnerwort* (BWV 60). And yet, ultimately these stylistic contradictions yield to a distant echo of the opening movement in 'iridescent strings, undergirded by comforting, clockwork pizzicato, surrounded by a halo of celesta and chimes'.[101]

Finally, what of Schnittke's fourth, late phase, summarized by Evgenia Chigareva as 'more introspective, more confessional, and, generally speaking … simpler, clearer, and more transparent'?[102] Impressed too upon this visionary music of the late 1980s and 1990s is a fundamentally new concept of time:

> Previously when I composed I started with the form … and gradually filled it up with details, but now I compose more with the feeling that every moment is

---

[99] See Schick (2002).
[100] Köchel (1994), 102.
[101] Schmelz (2019), 124.
[102] Chigareva (2017), 178.

living and changeable. The endlessness of each second ... was revealed to me... I know that the work is formally finished, but in reality it is never finished. There is no final full stop.[103]

Perhaps no other late work epitomizes Schnittke's re-conception of time more powerfully than the finale of the Cello Concerto No. 2, written for Mstislav Rostropovich in 1990. Here, in a 'suppressed polystylism'[104] that basks in a lush, neo-Romantic C minor, Schnittke unfolds a passacaglia with twenty-six repetitions of an eight-bar subject, against which the solo cello offers an 'unending recitative', with each statement celebrating the infinity of each second, taking its place in the eternal chain, and moving the clock-like apparatus to an 'inaudible, eternal tintinnabulation'.[105]

---

[103] Quoted in ibid., 179.
[104] Dixon (2022), 169.
[105] Köchel (1994), 97.

CHAPTER 12

Hommages, Tombeaux, Triskaidekaphilia and *Langage communicable*

> The diverse languages that we know are, above all, agents of communication ... One could very well imagine a language based on movements, images, colours, scents.[1]
>
> – Olivier Messiaen

EXAMPLES of French cipher-plying musicians continued to accumulate after the offerings for the Haydn centenary in 1909, when the *Revue musicale* inaugurated six new piano compositions based on his name (see Chapter 7). In contrast to this neo-Classical revival, French composers did not wait a centenary to adopt **BACH**, the universal musical symbol of the Thomaskantor. Among examples is one by Vincent d'Indy in the *Tableaux de voyage*, Op. 33 (1888), a suite of thirteen piano pieces depicting his travels in Germany. The eleventh, 'Beuron', illustrates a Benedictine abbey in the Black Forest, which drew from d'Indy a chromatic fugue in a severe, 'high' style. Here he committed the final bars to four statements of **BACH**.

More fugal treatments followed from French composers in the twentieth century, in particular in 1932, when Arthur Honegger's *Prélude, Arioso et fughetta sur le nom de Bach* and Albert Roussel's *Prélude et fugue sur le nom de Bach*, Op. 46 appeared in a supplement to a special Bach issue of the *Revue musicale*.[2] The Swiss Honegger, pupil of Widor and d'Indy, alluded in the title to two late nineteenth-century piano works by César Franck, the *Prélude, Choral et Fugue* (1885) and *Prélude, Aria et Final* (1886). But while Franck's pieces were cipher-free, Honegger allowed **BACH** to permeate all three movements of his composition. First, in the toccata-like prelude, he dispersed the four, chromatically adjacent pitches over a span of two octaves, transforming the half-steps into expansive sevenths (ex. 12.1).

---

[1] Messiaen (1973), Foreword.

[2] With other contributions by Alfredo Casella and Francesco Malipiero (see p. 357), and Francis Poulenc (see below).

Ex. 12.1: Honegger, *Prélude, Arioso et Fughetta sur le nom de Bach* (1932)

Next, he led the motive through ascending and descending sequences, while the bass line traversed a climbing, chromatic slide (B-flat, B-natural, C ... B-flat and B-natural) before reversing direction, collapsing the cipher to its normal range of a minor third. Four statements of **BACH** then introduced the internal *Arioso*, where the cipher now functioned as an ostinato figure stated fifteen times in the tenor, soprano and bass against expressive melodic arabesques. In the *fughetta* Honegger reinvigorated his experiments in register by opening the tetrachord so that instead of sevenths it now spanned ninths and tenths. He concluded with one further surprise: though the numerous iterations of **BACH** privileged B-flat as a quasi-tonic, in the last four bars (*Largamente*) the final cadence unexpectedly 'tonicized' the final pitch of the cipher, B-natural, as the root of an unalloyed B-major sonority. The tonal 'progress' of the composition from B-flat to B major thus anchored the shifting chromatic textures by supporting the endpoints of the cipher.

Another pupil of d'Indy, the seafaring Frenchman Albert Roussel, whose exotic voyages took him to Vietnam before he committed to composition, also participated in the *Revue musicale* supplement in 1932. But whereas Honegger fully embraced the **BACH** motive at the outset of his prelude, in the *Prélude et Fugue sur le nom de Bach*, Op. 46 Roussel deferred the cipher until the fugue, which displayed in its subject a paradoxical mixture of conjunct and disjunct motion – here the half-step B-flat-A proceeded, after a small leap of the minor third A-C, by an ascending seventh, C-B-natural. Meanwhile a third contributor, Poulenc, avoided fugal complications altogether in his *Valse-Improvisation sur le nom de BACH*, dedicated to Vladimir Horowitz. It was as if Bach's polyphonic sublime collided with the banal, represented by a whirling, somewhat pedestrian waltz from the 1930s, though still invested with considerable artistry (ex. 12.2).

As if mismatched for the waltz, the phlegmatic pitches of the cipher generated just its beginning, whereupon the dance pursued its own unpredictable course. At the climactic midpoint, Poulenc then quoted the cipher in retrograde (**HCAB**), as if to undo its Bachian associations. In the end, **BACH** evaporated in a high, chromatic cluster before the final chord on E, a tritone away and thus at furthest remove from B-flat, bringing the madcap proceedings to their close.

Ex. 12.2: Poulenc, *Valse-Improvisation sur le nom de Bach* (1932)

Quite a different treatment of **BACH** emerged from the cinephile Charles Koechlin, who, as we saw in Chapter 1, had converted three silver-screen actors' names into cryptograms in the seductive score of the *Seven Stars' Symphony* (1933). A pupil of Gabriel Fauré, Koechlin was a devoted contrapuntist who nevertheless insisted that 'counterpoint for the eye alone signifies nothing … the coming together of all the parts must remain musical'.[3] The art of the discipline, he maintained, resided in deftly manoeuvring within constricted spaces to discover untapped, expressive edges of the music. For Koechlin, the supreme contrapuntist of all time, J. S. Bach, had achieved just that, and so in 1942, the year the Nazis consolidated their control of France, the French composer emulated his predecessor in an extraordinary, monumental act of wartime homage, the *Offrande musicale sur le nom de Bach*, Op. 187. This was a full-scale rehearing of *The Musical Offering* (1747), in which Koechlin replaced the 'royal theme' of Frederick the Great (see p. 140) with **BACH**. The cipher appears in sixteen newly composed movements brimming with contrapuntal displays that emulated the imposing architecture of Bach's *summa*.

Like Bach, Koechlin designed his composition around ricercar-like movements supported by canons (among them, perpetual, retrograde, augmentation and mirror varieties) and other erudite movements, affirming Koechlin's conviction that **BACH** 'gave rise to all sorts of harmonies that one would not think of writing unless led towards them by the theme itself'.[4] One novelty was the eleventh movement, a *fugue symétrique*. Invented in the 1930s by the French general Emile Duchêne, this genre featured subjects that rotated around symmetrical tritonal axes. As ex. 12.3 illustrates, Koechlin's subject began with **BACH**, extended sequentially through transposition so that it touched all twelve chromatic pitches before yielding to the answer,[5] which, commencing

---

[3] Koechlin (1926), 1.

[4] Koechlin to Jules Guieysse, 17 November 1942, cited in Orledge (1989), 197.

[5] See further Nies (2010), 53–4, who profitably compares Koechlin's subject to that of Bach's Fugue in B minor, *Well-Tempered Clavier*, Book I.

Ex. 12.3: Koechlin, *Offrande musicale sur le nom de Bach*, Op. 187 (1942)

on the pitch E, replicated the process exactly and returned through the reverse tritonal shift to the point of origin, B-flat.

In 1942 Koechlin drafted his conception in a *particella*, or short score. He had no illusion about an official premiere in occupied France, which 'would have been terribly misunderstood' and 'contrary to the attitude of the musician during the war'.[6] But in a mere two weeks in 1946 he orchestrated the music for a large ensemble of 106 musicians. From this extended palette he extracted an affluence of instrumental combinations, drawing on techniques reminiscent of Webern's exploration of *Klangfarbenmelodie* (sound-colour-melody) a few years earlier in 1935, when the Austrian had made his orchestral arrangement of the six-part ricercar from *Das musikalische Opfer*, preserving intact the 'royal theme', but relying on constantly shifting instrumental tints to produce a variegated timbral counterpoint. Sadly, Koechlin did not live to hear his contribution to the twentieth-century Bach revival; the premiere was delayed until 1973, and the work not recorded until 2008.[7]

---

[6] Cathé (2010), 437.

[7] See the Foreword in Koechlin (2011), xi–xv.

Not the seminal composer of the high Baroque but the city of Barcelona provided the subject of the *Rhapsodie sur des airs Catalans* of the French organist Eugène Gigout (1844–1925), from 1897. Alluding to snatches of popular tunes, all loosely bound by a recurring fanfare-like motive contrived from letters of the dedication, '**A** l**a** vi**lle** de **Barce**lone',[8] Gigout acknowledged the Catalonian nationalist movement awakening at century's end. Among his circle were Gabriel Fauré, Albert Roussel and Paul Dukas, all of whom would receive their own nominal encryptions, including a collaborative *tombeau* for Dukas in 1936. The most senior was Fauré, who, ironically, seems not to have used ciphers himself.[9] Nevertheless, his name inspired several cipher creations, first a collaborative string quartet by Maurice Ravel, Raoul Bardac, Paul Ladmirault and J. J. A. Roger-Ducasse (1902); then tributes by Ravel, Ladmirault, Roger-Ducasse, Koechlin, Louis Aubert, George Enescu and Florent Schmitt, for a celebratory issue of the *Revue musicale* (1922); and finally the *Suite on the Name of Gabriel Fauré* by Sir Arnold Bax (1945). Most of this music is still relatively unfamiliar; its abundance persuades us to pause to consider the 'Fauré' cryptogram from the perspective of his 2024 centenary.

i

Relatively little is known about the collaborative string quartet of 1902 undertaken by four students in Fauré's composition class at the Conservatoire.[10] The internal second and third movements by Bardac and Ladmirault are no longer traceable, though the outer movements by Ravel and Roger-Ducasse did reemerge as the first movement of Ravel's String Quartet (1904) and finale of Roger-Ducasse's String Quartet No. 1 (1909). According to Jean-Michel Nectoux, the keys of the four movements – F, A, G and D[11] – symbolized Fauré's cipher, usually transliterated as **FAGD**, and generated two other variants, **FAGDE** (again representing 'Fauré') and **GABDBEE FAGDE** ('Gabriel Fauré'), from the table below, in which 'u' evolved into G; 'i' into B; and 'l' into E:

A	B	C	D	E	F	G
H	I	J	K	L	M	N
O	P	Q	R	S	T	U
V	W	X	Y	Z		

---

[8] Moulded with some liberties into the sequence A-A-E-B-A-C-sharp-E-E.
[9] See also p. 14 and p. 170 above.
[10] See Nectoux (1980), 20–1; Nectoux (1991), 427; and Nichols (1977), 245.
[11] Nectoux (1980), 21.

296   THE ART OF MUSICAL CIPHERS, RIDDLES AND SUNDRY CURIOSITIES

Ex. 12.4: Roger-Ducasse, String Quartet No. 1, Finale (1902)

If the quartet's key sequence projected Fauré's name over the entire composition, his cipher figured even more conspicuously in the finale of Roger-Ducasse's String Quartet, where it appears at the head of his movement as **FAGD**, with the annotation, 'sur les lettres du nom "Fauré"'. What is more, Roger-Ducasse meticulously documented throughout his score specific instances of the cipher, of which ex. 12.4 summarizes a handful. Thus, the four pitches appear as the bass line of the opening slow introduction (a), the soprano of stopped chords in the violins (b), with a chromatic adjustment (c) and in augmentation (d).

There remains the first movement of Ravel's String Quartet in F, dedicated 'a mon cher maître Gabriel Fauré'. Could this music betray traces of the collaborative tribute to Fauré in 1902? Unlike Roger-Ducasse, Ravel did not tag themes literally based on the pitch sequence F, A, G and D; and yet, a closer look reveals some tantalizing evidence that the cipher's pitch content, if not its order, did influence Ravel's music melodically *and* harmonically. To begin with, he may have noticed that the Fauré cipher contained all three pitches of the D minor triad (D, F and A) as well as two pitches of the F major triad (F and A),

Ex. 12.5: Ravel, String Quartet, First Movement (1903)

a)
p

b)
pp *espr.*

c)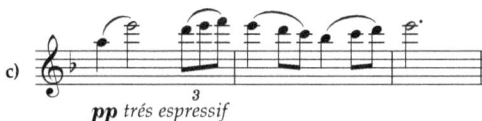
pp *trés espressif*

d)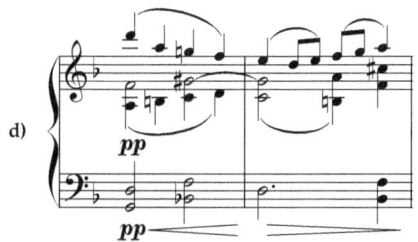
pp
pp

so that it could easily support pandiatonic mixtures of the two. This feature may explain why in the exposition Ravel chose to place his second theme in D minor and then, without transposing its pitch level in the recapitulation, in F major, where he simply reharmonized the same theme.

If we analyze the thematic contents of the first movement, we find that they do tend to favour pitches from the Fauré ciphers (**F, A, G, D** and **F, A, G, D, E**), albeit in mixed orders. For example, the first theme – A, G, A, E, D, A, F, C, E and D – draws exclusively, save for the C, on the five pitches. Example 12.5 illustrates this theme and others from the bridge and second theme. There is also a passage (bars 9ff.) that features a repeating ninth chord; its pitches – G, D, F and A – effectively reorient the four-note version of the cipher into a harmonic sonority.

It may be that in 1902 Ravel, Bardac, Ladmirault and Roger-Ducasse formulated a plan by which Ravel began their quartet with general allusions to Fauré's cipher while Roger-Ducasse absorbed specific citations in the finale. But such a trajectory remains conjectural. Still, Ravel was quite capable of trading in ciphers, including **FAGDE**. That occasion was another special issue of the *Revue musicale* brainstormed by the journal's founder, Henry Prunières, to honour Fauré in 1922, two years before his death. Prunières invited seven composers to write variations on a theme by Fauré; ultimately, they chose instead as their common theme Fauré's enciphered name.[12] Turning to the genre of the berceuse, Ravel crafted an exquisite miniature for muted violin and piano in G major, allowing the primary theme to represent 'Gabriel' (**GABDBEE**) as well as 'Fauré' (**FAGDE**, ex. 12.6), and thus to encrypt his complete name.

Ravel assigned the cryptogram to both instruments and imbued it with chromatically inflected harmonies. Instead of cadencing in G major, the final bar lingered on an unresolved dissonance, as if to suggest a child drifting off to sleep. Fauré was deeply affected by the tribute, 'a source of joy and pride', he wrote Ravel, 'for your old professor'.[13]

Among the other pieces for Fauré was Koechlin's 'Choral sur le nom de Fauré', in which **FAGDE** functions as a moveable *cantus firmus*, appearing now in this voice, now that. This expressive, if studious, essay impresses as an imaginary page from Koechlin's *Précis des Règles du contrepoint*, an illustration of how to adapt florid species counterpoint in modernist, twentieth-century contexts. All told, Koechlin's contribution comprised eleven different ways to treat the static cipher as a *cantus firmus*, several of which concluded by cadencing in E major, for the final letter of his teacher's name. On the other hand, Paul Ladmirault's treble-dominated *Hommage à Gabriel Fauré* played on modal ambiguity between D minor and F major, with a contrasting, internal trio in B-flat major, the third below D minor. In the trio, Ladmirault reharmonized the original cipher, **FAGDE**, without transposing it, recalling Ravel's similar device in the first movement of his string quartet.

Either by accident or design, in the *Esquisse sur le nom de Fauré*, Louis Aubert retained Ladmirault's revamping of the cipher in his trio, and the key of B-flat major. Beginning straightaway with the cipher in the treble, Aubert immediately subjected it to an anagrammatic reordering, so that 'Fauré' momentarily became 'Fu(f)aré' (ex. 12.7).

After one more unaltered statement in the treble, Fauré's name disappeared within a fog of softly dappled sonorities that blurred the B-flat major triad with the pandiatonic pitches C and G. As Aubert's title suggested, this 'sketch' remained incomplete, depending for its effect more on intimations than explicit confessions.

Two more piano compositions from the special issue, *Pièce pour piano sur le nom de Fauré* by the Romanian George Enescu and *Hommage sur le nom de Fauré* by Florent Schmitt, explored Fauré's abstract late style, in which he had pursued a 'radical self-renewal involving a lightening of instrumental textures,

---

[12] For details, see Nectoux (1980), 18–20.

[13] Fauré to Ravel, 15 October 1922, cited in ibid., 86.

Ex. 12.6: Ravel, Berceuse (1922)

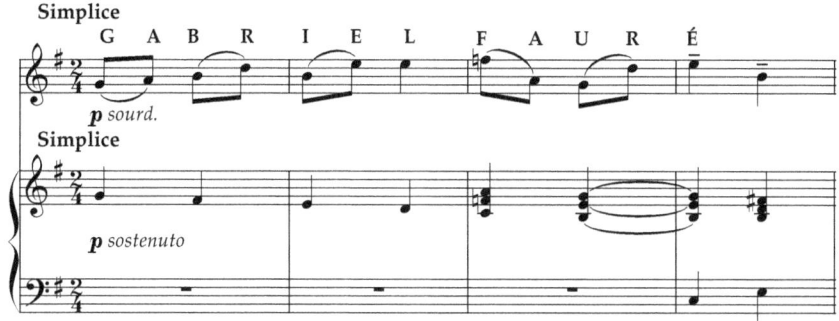

Ex. 12.7: Aubert, *Esquisse sur le nom de Fauré* (1922)

a stiffening of melodic lines and a still greater harmonic audacity resulting from a more consistent emphasis on counterpoint'.[14] And so Enescu subjected the five-note cipher **FAGDE** to a dozen or so tonally ambiguous harmonizations supported by susurrant accompaniments, marked 'harmonious and veiled' (*harmonieux et voilé*), of arpeggiated quintuplets that punned rhythmically on the letters of Fauré's name. In the end, Enescu superimposed the five pitches into delicate vertical sonorities that resolved into a moment of tonal stability – a pure, widely spaced C major sonority.

Such clarity was not the primary concern of Florent Schmitt, whose *Hommage* collided with a brashly dissonant realm of elliptical harmonies lacking 'secure' root-position triads and careening metrically from conflicting time signatures. Lending some coherence to the welter of sound was the periodic appearance of two contrasting ciphers, one for 'Fauré' (**FAGDE**), asserted in bass octaves, and one for 'Gabriel' (**GABDBEE**), singing in a more intimate style in the treble. The ciphers appeared in immediate succession near the end,

---

[14] Nectoux (1991), 294–5.

spelling out for the only time his complete name. In 1935 Schmitt found occasion to repurpose the *Hommage* as the scherzo-like second movement of *In memoriam* Op. 72, a commemoration of Fauré for full orchestra.[15] If the first movement drew upon distant thematic memories from Fauré's opera *Pénélope* (1913), the second enlisted cipher techniques to connect 'new creativity to the past, specifically to a deceased composer'.[16]

The most substantial of these musical panegyrics for Fauré was Roger-Ducasse's *Poème symphonique*, which appeared in piano reduction in the 1922 supplement to *La Revue musicale*. Here the reference to the Lisztian orchestral genre confirmed that the poem offered unabashedly programmatic music; furthermore, its subject, the cipher **FAGDE**, was notated at the head of the music. But piquing our critical understanding of the music too was Roger-Ducasse's short quotation in the full score from a poem by the symbolist Paul Verlaine: 'La note d'or que fait entendre, / Le cor, dans le lointain des bois' ('The golden note that is heard, / The horn in the distance of the woods'). In 1894 Fauré had set this poem and eight others from Verlaine's *La bonne chanson* as a song cycle, Op. 61, then arranged the music for voice, piano and string quintet (1898), and finally reworked its material into an enchanting version for solo harp, *Une châtelaine en sa tour* (*A Lady of the Castle in Her Tower*), Op. 110 (1918). Roger-Ducasse followed suit and produced his own nacreous, symbolist score that played not just on Fauré's cipher but also subtly alluded to the perfumed world of his songs and revelled, like the delicate tissues of Verlaine's verses, 'in the associations aroused by the beloved's name'.[17]

As for the cipher, it is found nowhere in the opening of Roger-Ducasse's music. Rather, he sets in motion a search for it that gradually identifies the cipher's pitches. First, we hear in the bass clarinet the pitches F, C, A-flat, E-flat and D-flat (ex. 12.8). We might perceive a distant approximation of **FAGDE**, though we might also imagine that A-flat, E-flat and D-flat allude (through transposition) to Fauré's Op. 110.

The entrance of the high strings in bar 6 subtly modifies the figure to F, C, A-natural, G, D and E-flat, and thus approaches the cipher more closely. Nearly thirty bars later it emerges in full as F, A, G, D and E-natural, first in a *fortissimo* outburst from the flutes and piccolo, then in a sustained statement in the strings (ex. 12.9).

From this point, the cipher intermittently draws into focus; though, unlike Koechlin or Enescu, Roger-Ducasse never saturates his textures with the monogram, preferring instead to cite it sparingly.

---

[15] Lorent (2012), 105.

[16] Minors (2019), 98.

[17] Rumph (2020), 109.

Ex. 12.8: Roger-Ducasse, *Poème symphonique* (1922)

Ex. 12.9: Roger-Ducasse, *Poème symphonique* (1922)

Two decades after Fauré's death, the British composer Sir Arnold Bax honoured the Frenchman with yet another cryptographic concoction, *Suite on the Name of Gabriel Fauré* for piano, composed for the 1945 centenary of Fauré's birth, and rescored for harp and strings in 1949, the twenty-fifth anniversary of his passing. Self-described as a 'brazen romantic', Bax apportioned his suite into five lushly tonal movements with modal flavourings ('Prélude', 'Barcarolle', 'Polka', 'Storm' and 'Quodlibet'), all deriving thematic material from the familiar 'Fauré' ciphers explored in 1922.

Meanwhile, in 1929, the sixtieth birthday of Albert Roussel had prompted another celebration in the *Revue musicale* with a collection of musical tributes for piano solo. In this case, Poulenc, Honegger and Jacques Ibert availed themselves of cryptograms, though by applying different methods. Poulenc's *Pièce brève sur le nom d'Albert Roussel* betrayed its process readily enough – it derived the pitch sequences A-D-B-flat-E-B-flat-D for 'Albert' and B-flat-G-E-C-E-D for 'Roussel' from this common French key:

A	B	C	D	E	F	G	H
I	J	K	L	M	N	O	P
Q	R	S	T	U	V	W	X
Y	Z						

Poulenc labelled the references in the score, including a few appearances of 'treblA'. Quite another matter, though, was Honegger's *Hommage à Albert Roussel*, for which the Swiss composer designed his own cryptographic method (ex. 12.10).

Ex. 12.10: Honegger, *Hommage à Albert Roussel* (1929), Key

He began by aligning the letters of the alphabet with twenty-five ascending pitches above, divided into four segments: 1) eight natural pitches (excepting B, or B-flat) for A–H; 2) six sharps for I–N; and 3) seven flats for O–U; leaving 4) four recycled natural pitches for V–Z (omitting W). Honegger then carved out the thirteen pitches for 'Albert Roussel', yielding this angular melody (Ex. 12.10).

Next, he coupled the cipher with two quotations from Roussel's music, the *valse* from the pantomime-ballet *Le Festin de l'araignée* (*The Spider's Banquet*, 1913) and, in the coda, a phrase from the slow movement of the Piano Concerto, recently completed by Roussel in 1928.[18] That Honegger revealed his own, idiosyncratic cipher methodology leads us to wonder whether the *Hommage* was a unique cryptographic experiment, or among other examples of a hidden system in his music.

Be that as it may, yet another mystery resides in Ibert's *Toccata sur le nom d'Albert Roussel*. Its busy opening highlights in the soprano voice the seven pitches D, A, G, F-sharp, F-sharp, E and D, a recurring figure in the piece that presumably translates the seven letters of 'Roussel'. Now if we attempt to solve 'Roussel' according to the key introduced earlier in this chapter (p. 291), we find that 'R', 'o' and 'u' indeed become D, A and G. But according to the key, 's' should convert to E, not Ibert's F-sharp. While the penultimate letter of 'Roussel' would remain E, the final 'l' should correspond to E, though Ibert notates D. So, Ibert either erred, took liberties while constructing his cipher, or employed some yet unrevealed cryptographic key.

With the passing in 1935 of Paul Dukas, the 'Degas of music,'[19] the *Revue musicale* devoted one issue to the composer as a *tombeau*, to which nine of Dukas's students contributed. Descended from literary laments dating back several centuries, the *tombeau* emerged as a musical genre in seventeenth-century

---

[18] Halbreich (1999), 243.
[19] *La Revue Musicale* 157 (1936), 3.

Ex. 12.11: Honegger, *Hommage à Albert Roussel* (1929)

France before falling out of favour in the eighteenth. Maurice Ravel revived it in his *Tombeau de Couperin* (1917), a suite-like set of dances dedicated to six friends killed during the First World War. In 1920 and 1924 the *Revue musicale* produced two *tombeaux*, one for Debussy, who had died in 1918 during the waning months of the war, and one for Pierre de Ronsard, whose quadricentenary fell in 1924. Dukas contributed to both.[20] Though neither piece employed ciphers, in 1909 the composer had released one that did, the *Prélude élégiaque sur le nom de Haydn*,[21] among Dukas's few works to appear in print. Now, in 1936, his pupils Gabriel Pierné and Guy Ropartz honoured him by fabricating cipher pieces (ex. 12.12).

If Pierné's *Prélude sur le nom de Paul Dukas* presented the cryptogram on two different rhythmic levels – a melody above in minims supported by winding quavers in the accompaniment – Ropartz's *À la Mémoire de Paul Dukas*

Ex. 12.12: Pierné, *Prélude sur le nom de Paul Dukas* (1936)

---

[20] See Watson (2019), 230–7.

[21] See p. 169; and Watson (2019), 136–9.

Ex. 12.13a–d: Ropartz, *À la Mémoire de Paul Dukas* (1936); Dukas, *L'Apprenti sorcier* (1897); Dukas, *La Péri* (1912); Dukas, Symphony in C (1896)

divided the cryptogram into two portions ('Paul' and 'Dukas'), the first assigned to the treble, and the second, to the bass accompaniment (ex. 12.13a). Later in the composition, he introduced three discreet references to his teacher's music, all marked with quotation marks. The first is easy to unmask – it is a reharmonized echo of the bassoon solo from *L'Apprenti sorcier* (*The Sorcerer's Apprentice*, 1897; ex. 12.13b). The second recalls the Peri's theme from the ballet *La Péri* (1912; ex. 12.13c), while the more ambiguous third possibly paraphrases the climax of the slow movement of Dukas's Symphony in C (1896; ex. 12.13d).

Ropartz's blended techniques of citation and allusion seem to have simulated Dukas's own compositional strategy. Thus, in *La Plainte, au loin, du faune* (*The Lament from Afar of the Faun*), written for the *Tombeau de Debussy*, Dukas had revived the celebrated opening flute solo of his predecessor's *Prélude à l'après-midi d'un faune* (*Prelude to the Afternoon of a Faun*, 1894), but in a way so that the reference also highlighted similarities to the Peri theme from Dukas's own *La Péri*.[22] In this way the musical allusions of one generation encouraged the next to unlock the past. If Debussy's flute arabesques signified 'memories of erotic gratification' in Mallarmé's poem, by the time of Dukas's brief remembrance in 1920 – virtually the last music he created – the arabesques stood for 'the desire of desire', 'a kind of posthumous work itself'[23] reactivated by Ropartz's memorial of Dukas in 1936.

~ ii

Among the musical circle of Gabriel Fauré was the precocious but tragically short-lived composer Lili Boulanger (1893–1918), who, the Frenchman attested, exhibited perfect pitch at age two. In 1913, at age nineteen, she became the first woman to win the coveted Prix de Rome that had sent generations of male

---

[22] See Watson (2019), 199, 230–4.
[23] Castro (2019), 80, 81.

French composers (though neither Ravel nor Dukas) to the French Academy at the Villa Medici atop the Spanish Steps. But the outbreak of the First World War and Lili's chronically frail health impelled her to return to Paris, where she succumbed at age twenty-four to Crohn's disease. Though she had begun to garner publishing contracts, much of Boulanger's sensual, aromatic music fell into neglect until its revival during the closing decades of the twentieth century.

Some accounts of her personal affairs (corroborated by her sister, Nadia) indicate that Lili indulged in numerology, ciphers and word games.[24] According to Miki Piré, she identified with the number thirteen, which affected her life in various ways. Her name contained thirteen letters, so she chose as a monogram for the covers of her printed scores an ambigram designed as an encircled glyph-like figure that read either as 'LB' or the number '13' (Illustration 12.1).

When she won the Prix de Rome – in 1913 – she competed along with twelve other entrants, and she secured the prize by a margin of thirty-one votes (13 backwards). Then, as if acknowledging numerological destiny, she destroyed thirteen of her compositions. Among her projects were settings of Psalms 130, 131, 137, and 1 Corinthians 13.

If Schoenberg, who died on Friday, 13 July 1951, was a confirmed triskaidekaphobe, Lili Boulanger was an aspiring triskaidekaphile. In this regard, the work that has elicited numerological readings is her exquisite song cycle *Clairières dans le ciel* (*Clearings in the Sky*), finished in 1914 and released posthumously in 1919.[25] For its texts she chose thirteen poems from a cycle of twenty-four titled *Tristesses* (*Sadnesses*, 1905) by the symbolist Francis Jammes, and arranged them into a narrative about lost love. Here the poet remembers his lover, who has suddenly disappeared, through various images: she was 'a Madonna at the foot of his bed, two columbines on a hillside, the sight of a country landscape, a keepsake medal given him by his love, a memory of last year's lilacs, and a sudden rainstorm'.[26] Lili seems to have identified with this anonymous lover, to whom the poet refers solely through the pronoun 'elle', which the composer may have reread as a pun on her first initial. In addition, the opulent floral imagery throughout the cycle could well symbolize Lili, as in the opening song, a distant memory of the lover having descended to a meadow 'with plants of which the roots like to grow in water' (*des plantes dont la tige aime à pousser dans l'eau*) – that is, water *lilies*. Almost certainly, Boulanger noticed that Jammes's verses privileged the Alexandrine, traditionally a line of twelve syllables, though here he allowed its *thirteen*-syllable cousin a significant role.

---

[24] See especially Dopp (1994), on which the following discussion draws.

[25] There also survives an unfinished orchestral version from probably 1915. See Fauser (1990), 10.

[26] Rosenstiel (1978), 172.

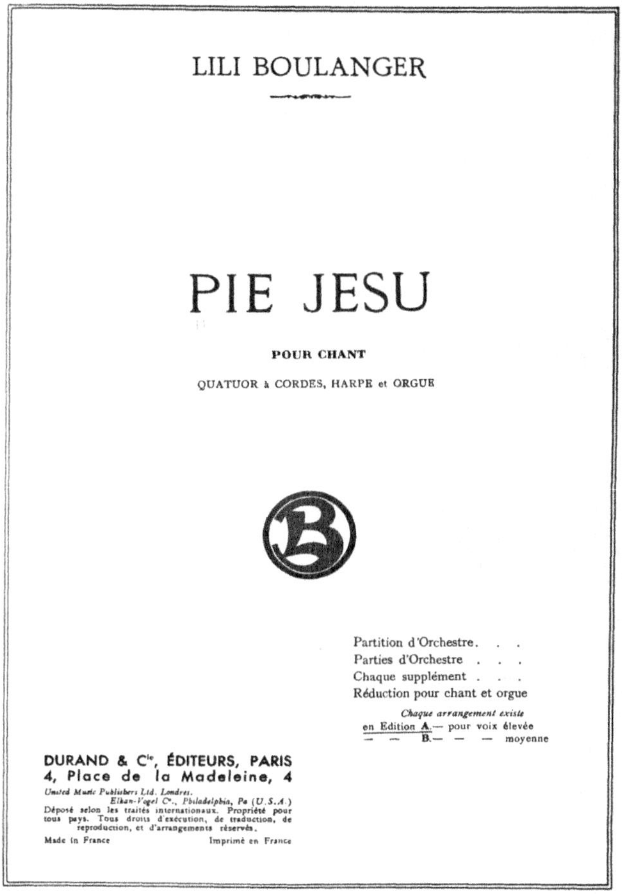
LILI BOULANGER

PIE JESU

POUR CHANT

QUATUOR à CORDES, HARPE et ORGUE

Partition d'Orchestre. . .
Parties d'Orchestre . . .
Chaque supplément . . .
Réduction pour chant et orgue

Chaque arrangement existe
en Edition A.— pour voix élevée
— — B.— — — moyenne

DURAND & Cie, ÉDITEURS, PARIS
4, Place de la Madeleine, 4

United Music Publishers Ltd. Londres.
Elkan-Vogel C^o., Philadelphia, Pa (U.S.A.)
Déposé selon les traités internationaux. Propriété pour tous pays. Tous droits d'exécution, de traduction, de reproduction, et d'arrangements réservés.
Made in France Imprimé en France

Illustration 12.1: Lili Boulanger, Monogram, title page, *Pie Jesu* (first edition, 1922)

The number thirteen also left harmonic traces in Boulanger's songs. If commentators have noticed her predilection for ninth and eleventh chords, the question remains whether she extended her harmonic vocabulary to experiment with *thirteenth* chords (*accords de treizièmes*), which Charles Koechlin found 'very usable'.[27] As Bonnie Jo Dopp observes, the thirteenth is the 'final addition in the accumulation of thirds that utilizes all seven pitch classes of a diatonic scale'.[28] That is, if we regard the opening piano sonority of the song cycle as a gapped ninth chord, E-G-sharp-B-[D-natural]-F-sharp, we can

[27] Koechlin (1925), 617.

[28] Dopp (1994), 563.

Ex. 12.14: Lili Boulanger, *Clairières dans le ciel*, 'Elle était descendue' (1919)

extrapolate a fully cyclic thirteenth chord that expends all seven basic pitch names by adding thirds above, A and C-natural (ex. 12.14).

Now Boulanger does not place such a chord in her first bar. But if we consider bar 2 – a transposition of bar 1 down a whole-step – and combine the two parallel ninth chords (E-G-sharp-B-[D-natural]-F-sharp and D-F-sharp-A-[C-natural]-E), together they do unfurl the thirteenth chord horizontally.

In bar 6, at the reference to the water lilies, Boulanger shifts her harmonic preference from ninth chords to enriched eleventh chords (B-flat-D-[F]-A-flat-C-E). Then, at the midpoint of the song (bar 12, *très expressif et soutenu*), which references the meadow in full blossom ('toute fleurie'), she achieves a sounding thirteenth chord (E-flat-G-B-flat-D-flat-F-[A-flat]-C), realizing an unrestrained, floral extravagance that embraces the complete sequence of thirds (ex. 12.15).

More sonorities of the thirteenth accrue in the second half of the song before the fan-like process reverses itself, returning us through an eleventh chord to the ninth chords of the opening.

And what about Boulanger's possible interests in musical ciphers? Again, the first song offers intriguing, if not conclusive, evidence. Cryptographically speaking, Lili's name transforms itself into the pitch sequence E-B-E-B (see pp. xxi and 306); perhaps not coincidentally, the bass of the piano part obligingly presents four statements of the open fifth E-B, or 'Lili'. Granted, one might grumble that the French usually accepted the German reading of B as B-flat and H as B-natural, so that one might expect 'Lili' to convert instead to the tritone E-B-flat-E-B-flat. There is a prominent tritonal relationship in the first six bars: if we extract the bass line, we see that it descends (a play on 'Elle était descendue') by whole tones from E to D-natural, C-natural and finally

Ex. 12.15: Lili Boulanger, *Clairières dans le ciel*, 'Elle était descendue' (1919)

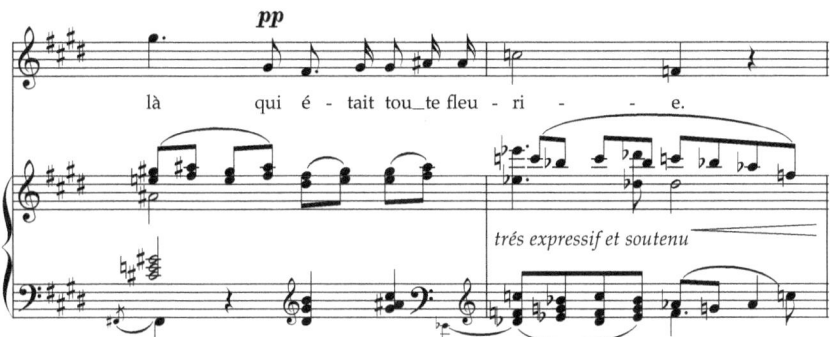

B-flat at the exact point where Boulanger enriches her harmonies as eleventh chords. So perhaps the prominent fifths, whether perfect (E-B) or diminished (E-B-flat), offer a veiled allusion to the composer's name, intimated in the text by references to 'Elle' and the water lilies. Of course, the B-flat could also refer to the 'B' of 'Boulanger'.

There is one other conspicuous detail about 'Elle était descendue': she dedicated it '*Au Maître GABRIEL FAURÉ*'. Could she have impressed his name into the music by using ciphers? Transposed to E major, the key of 'Elle était descendue', we might expect, then, pitch complexes containing E-F-sharp-G-sharp-B-G-sharp-C-sharp-C-sharp or E-G-sharp-F-sharp-C-sharp-D-sharp. Admittedly, fully realized ciphers for Fauré do not leap off the page, but is it mere coincidence that the piano part begins by spelling in its chord the first four letters (transposed) of 'Gabriel' and first three of 'Fauré'?

A few other songs of the cycle also have dedications to Boulanger's friends. The antepenultimate eleventh, 'Par ce que j'ai souffert' ('Because I have suffered'), bears the heading '*A DAVID DEVRIES*', the tenor who sang the role of Faust in *Faust et Hélène*, Boulanger's prize-winning cantata for the Prix de Rome. According to Léonie Rosenstiel, 'the entire cycle was inspired by the voice of David Devriès'[29]; Dopp has gone even further, to propose that the singer was 'Lili's secret lost love'.[30] In this reading, the poet/protagonist of Jammes's verses would be Devriès; the absent lover, Lili herself. Dopp points out that for the title page of the cycle, published in 1919 by Ricordi after the composer's death, the logo acquired a new design (presumably created by Lili during the last months of her life) so that it now admitted three plausible readings:

---

[29] Rosenstiel (1978), 189.
[30] Dopp (1994), 574.

Ex. 12.16: Lili Boulanger, *Clairières dans le ciel*, 'Par ce que j'ai souffert' (1919)

'LB', for 'Lili Boulanger'; '13', for her preferred number; and, contained within the uppercase letter 'B', two D's, the tenor's initials. Perhaps we should not be surprised, then, to find in the music a persistent emphasis on the pitch D, not just in the vocal line, but also the piano part, where Boulanger establishes an obsessively static pedal point doubled at the octave (d'-d"), seemingly for *David Devriès* (ex. 12.16).

If Lili Boulanger's ciphers remained to some extent conjectural, others produced well-documented examples of the art. One was the organist Maurice Duruflé, whose *Prélude et Fuge sur le nom d'A.L.A.I.N* (**ADAAF**; 1943) honoured the organist Jehan Alain, pupil of Dukas and Roger-Ducasse, who had fallen at the Battle of Saumur in 1940. Another was the pianist/composer Robert Casadesus, who wrote cipher pieces for the quadricentenary of the birth of Pierre de Ronsard (1924), the violinist Claude Pasquier (1939),[31] and centenary of the birth of Ernest Chausson (1955). Casadesus's Prelude Op. 5 No. 5, *sur le nom de Ronsard*, invoked the sixteenth-century Pléiade poet with the cipher **DAGEADD**, which appeared in transposition and retrograde, measured out in the archaic metre of 4/1. For the *Hommage à Chausson* Op. 51 (1954) Casadesus derived the cipher **CBAECCGF**, split between the violin and piano. Here are the two keys employed for the three ciphers:

A	B	C	D	E	F	G	H		A	B	C	D	E	F	G
I	J	K	L	M	N	O	P		H	I	J	K	L	M	N
Q	R	S	T	U	V	W	X		O	P	Q	R	S	T	U
Y	Z								V	W	X	Y	Z		

Alain = **ADAAF**   Ronsard = **DAGEADD**   Chausson = **CBAECCGF**

---

[31] See Yudha (2012), 28–30.

Ex. 12.17: Langlais, Symphonie n°2, ©1977 Editions Combre, Paris. All right reserved. Used by permission

```
A B C D E F G H
I J K L M N O P
Q R S T U V W X
```

A more unusual case was the music of the blind organist Jean Langlais (1907–91), a pupil of Dukas who used the braille system while composing, and then dictated the final version to his wife.[32] Langlais embedded ciphers for his friends and intimate relationships into his works, and, for the bicentenary of Jean-Philippe Rameau, incorporated an acrostic on the Baroque composer's name into the six movements of a *Hommage* (1964).[33] Five years later, in the third organ voluntary (subtitled *Sainte Trinité*) Langlais devised a cryptogram of his close friend Olivier Messiaen, and in the *Deuxième Symphonie* (1976), written *à la Webern*, began by enciphering the words 'Dieu' ('God') and 'Marie' ('Mary') into the score (ex. 12.17), before contributing a few years later *B.A.C.H.*, six organ pieces on the cipher, for the Bach tricentenary.

↜ iii

'The wellspring for his vast creative output is, of course, his undoubting religious faith, a frame of mind more common in the Middle Ages than in our century.'[34] So observed David Palmer on Olivier Messiaen's eightieth birthday. A devout Catholic who served for sixty years in Paris as organist at the Church of the Holy Trinity (*Sainte-Trinité*), Messiaen committed much of his music to exploring articles of faith, to pondering the ineffability of God, which, the composer imagined, might be partially perceptible through occasional bursts of blazing insights. Unlike the angels, who, according to the Thomist view, could communicate 'without language, without convention, and still more astonishing, without regard for time or place',[35] humans were dependent on

---

[32] Labounsky (2000), 71.

[33] Ibid., 156, 190–2. The titles of the movements are 'Remembrance, Allegretto, Meditation, Evocation, As a Fugue and United Themes'.

[34] Palmer (1988), 10.

[35] Messiaen, foreword to *Méditations* (1973), 'Le langage communicable'.

the imprecision of language; even music, formidable though it might be, did 'not express anything directly. It [could] suggest, arouse a sentiment, a state of the soul, touch the subconscious, stimulate the faculties of dreaming, and these [were admittedly] immense powers; but it absolutely [could not] "speak," inform with precision'.[36]

Attempting to approach the ultimately unknowable in his music, the 'charm of impossibilities',[37] Messiaen developed a multi-layered, syncretic style with verbal and non-verbal layers of meaning, sometimes revealed by the composer, sometimes not. For Messiaen, 'God was present everywhere and in all sound'.[38] This musical synaesthete viewed his art as a 'theological rainbow', in which 'all colours have their place. What may to human eyes appear as utter heterogeneity is a "single reality, seen from different angles" in the light of God's infinite plenitude'.[39]

For instance, one might find in the same composition swaths of plainchant from the Catholic liturgy and complex rhythmic patterns (*decî-tâlas*) from classical Indian music, as in the *Méditations sur le mystère de la Sainte Trinité* (1969). Or, in the monumental *Des canyons aux étoiles...* (*From the Canyons to the Stars...*, 1974), nestled among the colourful crags of atonal chords Messiaen might place A major harmonies that ultimately coalesced into 'a supernova of A major, billowing into the lowest and highest reaches of the orchestra and whiting out in *fortissimo* strings'.[40] In the landscapes of Messiaen's protean harmonies, A major triads impressed as anomalous, for the composer did not prop them up with further references to common-practice tonality or its major/minor scales. Instead, he turned to 'modes of limited transpositions' – symmetrical, scale-like divisions of the octave that produced only a few transpositions before the original mode reemerged. Messiaen was intrigued too with 'non-retrogradable' rhythms – motives or themes that were rhythmically palindromic, the same forwards and backwards – and, finally, with 'interversions', 'free shuffling[s] of the order within a series of objects'.[41] When not regulating pitch and rhythm, Messiaen might momentarily succumb to jazz-inflected harmonies,

---

[36] Ibid.

[37] Messiaen (1956), 13; see also the illuminating study by Wu (1998).

[38] Ross (2007), 488.

[39] Bannister (2012), 174; Messiaen (1956), 21, 63; and Goléa (1960), 41.

[40] Ross (2007), 496. According to the composer, A major was the key that appeared most frequently in his music; he associated it with the colour blue. Rößler (1986), 118.

[41] Fabbi (1998), 60. For example, a series of four notes, labelled 1, 2, 3 and 4, can be interverted from the centre outward to produce 3, 2, 4, 1 and 4, 2, 1, 3 before the next interversion reverts to 1, 2, 3, 4.

as in the early piano cycle *Vingt regards sur l'enfant Jesus* (*Twenty Aspects of the Infant Jesus*, 1944), or amass grating chords of twelve pitches that absorbed the total chromatic, as in *Catalogue d'oiseaux* (*Catalogue of the Birds*, 1958).

This last-named work celebrated the multifarious language of birdsong, a mainstay, from the 1950s onwards, of the composer's creative process. Nearly three hours in length, the *Catalogue d'oiseaux* transferred to the piano a chattering, nattering aviary. In other works, he expanded his purview to survey additional species, meticulously transcribing into notation their songs over the course of his travels through Europe, Israel and the United States, where he marvelled at the preternatural, otherworldly canyons of Utah. Messiaen viewed birdsong as the 'archetype of clarity, weightlessness and agility',[42] and birds as 'the greatest musicians on our planet',[43] though he had no illusions about the limits of Western notation in capturing their nuanced musical language. Because birds sing in shrill tessituras, bend their melodies through microtonal inflections, and often perform in rapid tempi, Messiaen was obliged to transpose their music one or more octaves lower, approximate their diminutive intervals with half-steps, and ease their breakneck communications into more leisurely flows – all to produce a 'transposition of what I heard, but on a more human scale'.[44]

One bird that particularly entranced Messiaen was the yellowhammer (*bruant jaune*), whose bursts of short notes followed by a sustained note frequent the pages of several scores. In music history, this bird first came to fame in a celebrated anecdote of Carl Czerny, that Beethoven had found the dramatic opening of the Fifth Symphony (1808) in the creature's dynamic/static call.[45] For Messiaen, though, the music of the yellowhammer assumed an extra-worldly significance as 'the last earthly sound before heaven, a kind of intermediary between the two places'[46]; thus, four of the nine movements of the *Méditations* conclude with its signature – seven clipped pitches eclipsed by a solitary long, perhaps an inkling of the hereafter.

Many of Messiaen's compositional strategies came to fruition in the imposing organ work *Méditations sur le mystère de la Sainte Trinité*, a cycle laden with Trinitarian symbolism. This composition was his ninth for organ solo; its nine movements, the square of *three*. For Janette Fishell, the composer evoked

---

[42] van Maas (2002), 322.
[43] Samuel (1994), 85.
[44] Ibid., 95.
[45] See further, Bowden (2008).
[46] Shenton (2008), 63.

'through music and text a sense of the mystery of the Trinity'[47]; for Paul Thissen, the numerological layers of the score projected nothing less than 'sounding theology' (*klingende Theologie*).[48] To realize it, Messiaen now developed the *langage communicable*, which he applied to only three compositions – *Méditations*, *Des canyons aux étoiles…* and *Livre du Saint Sacrement* (1984), a culminating cycle of eighteen (3 × 6) pieces for organ on the subject of the Eucharist. The principal elements were: 1) a musical alphabet in which Messiaen assigned each letter from *a* to *z* to a fixed pitch, rhythm and register; 2) an elementary grammar that devised short musical *formulae* for the auxiliary verbs 'to have' and 'to be', and reactivated the case endings of classical Latin; and 3) a code-like series of leitmotifs with extra-musical meanings. Through these means, Messiaen was able to encrypt texts from the thirteenth-century *Summa Theologiae* of Thomas Aquinas, and encode relevant concepts; all, he explained, 'without desiring to imitate the cabalist in search of a meaning hidden beneath the letters of the words or the numerical values of those letters'.

Ex. 12.18 illustrates the composer's key for the musical alphabet.

Here we see that the letters from *a* to *h* correspond to conventional pitch names in ascending, scale-like order, with *b* rendered as B-flat, and *h* as B-natural. In contrast, the remaining eighteen letters range over several octaves, dispersing, as it were, the orderly half-steps into a spray of chaotic leaps for *i*–*z*. Because Messiaen's alphabet consumes all twelve pitches of the chromatic scale, a few letters duplicate the same pitches, albeit in different registers. For example, the pitch F serves three different letters, including *f*, as one would expect, but also *s* and *z*. Rhythmically, Messiaen employs ten different values, built up incrementally from one to eleven semiquavers in duration.

Having expended twelve different pitches, ten rhythms and five registers, Messiaen next outlined grammatical rudiments of his new language, all elucidated in the preface to *Méditations*. To limit the number of words in texts chosen for encryption, he omitted articles, pronouns, adverbs and prepositions, retaining only nouns, adjectives and verbs. To save more words, he revived Latin case endings, using simple musical *formulae* to specify the genitive, dative, accusative or ablative case designated by the text. Two short three-note motives[49] – one descending for *être* ('to be'), the other ascending in exact mirror inversion for *avoir* ('to have') – symbolized the divine, for 'all that *is* comes [down] from God', and 'we can always *have* more by elevating ourselves to God' (ex. 12.19).

---

[47] Fishell (1988), 12.

[48] Thissen (1996), 129.

[49] Perhaps not coincidentally, each motive spanned the interval of a ninth (3 × 3).

Ex. 12.18: Messiaen, *Méditations*, Musical Alphabet

Ex. 12.19: Messiaen, *Méditations*, 'Être' and 'Avoir' Motives

Finally, recalling how Champollion had discovered in cartouches of Egyptian hieroglyphs the names of pharaonic royalty, Messiaen created his own musical oblong, a theme for the 'Divine Name ... a real theme (Wagner would have called it a Leitmotiv) ... to express that God is equally immense and eternal, without beginning or end, in space as in time'. This *Dieu* theme appeared in two forms, 'one in forward motion, the other in retrograde, like two extremes that regard each other, from which one might recoil indefinitely'.

Of course, without Messiaen's brief guide to his *langage communicable* and without a score, listeners would not be able to discern these layers of meaning. But with the annotated score in hand, musicians could acquire some expertise in the composer's system, parse the syntax of the encrypted text, and ponder other referents that Messiaen marked, be they encoded words, birdsongs, Hindu talas or leitmotifs. We may demonstrate by summarizing the third *Méditation*, one of *three* movements that 'converse' in the new language. Here the constituent textual/musical elements include a short passage from Aquinas transliterated in the treble by the right hand (*Summa Theologiae*, Part I, *Question* 28), and repetitions of various talas executed by the left hand and the pedal part.

Rather than render Aquinas's complete text into music, Messiaen first prepared a condensed French paraphrase:

Aquinas's Latin: 'et sic manifestum est quod relatio realiter existens in Deo est idem essentiae secundum rem' ('And thus, it is manifest that a real relation in God is in reality identical with nature.')[50]

Messiaen's French paraphrase: 'Relation [réelle] en Dieu est [réellement] identique à essence de Dieu' ('The relation with God is identical to the essence of God'.)

To transform this paraphrase into music he then set 'relation' according to his alphabet (see ex. 12.18), 'en' by using a four-note formula for the locative case, and 'Dieu' by resorting to his pre-determined leitmotif (ex. 12.20).

Subsequently, the verb 'est' activated the three-note descending pattern of ex. 12.19, the adjective 'identique' and noun 'essence' found their musical counterparts in Messiaen's alphabet, and the prepositions 'à' and 'de' mobilized the dative and genitive cases, each according to its respective four-note cell. Finally, the last word, 'Dieu', reprised the leitmotif heard earlier, but now in its retrograde version, reminding us that God is 'without beginning or end'.

Thus, Messiaen meditated on different aspects of the Trinity, labelling Aquinas's texts with superscripts in the score, and revealing their meanings, like flares of illuminating dazzlement (*éblouissement*). Constructed from the alphabet, case endings and leitmotifs, the *langage musicale* was a highly selective system that tested music's ability to transmit complex verbal meanings.[51] Perhaps that explains why Messiaen seldomly explored it; after the *Méditations*, he resorted to it in just two of the twelve movements of *Des canyons aux étoiles…*, and three of the eighteen movements of *Livre du Saint Sacrement*. For example, in the third movement of *Des canyons*, Messiaen introduced the Aramaic words 'men', 'tekel' and 'parsin', which only the Old Testament prophet could read at the court of Belshazzar (Daniel 5: 25–8). As Messiaen explained, 'these three fateful words ... astonishingly ... produced an extraordinary and blood-curdling melody for the brass instruments, which I can do nothing about, it's merely the result yielded by the letters'.[52]

Exactly what led him to explore music as a proto-language remains unclear. Andrew Shenton has suggested that there was some precedent for Messiaen's experiments in the relatively little-known music of his student François-Bernard Mâche, a musician with interests in linguistics and semiotics, and founder of zoomusicology, a subdiscipline that studied musical communication among animals.[53] As early as 1959 Mâche had composed *Safous Mélè*, a cantata-like

---

[50] Aquinas (1965), 30–1.
[51] Shenton (1998), 236.
[52] Rößler (1986), 69–70.
[53] See Grabócz (1993); and Grabócz and Mathon (2018).

Ex. 12.20: Messiaen, *Méditations*, 'Relation en Dieu est identique à essence de Dieu' (1969)

setting of Greek texts by Sappho that applied a linguistic model to transcribe phonemes of words into Roman letters, which he then assigned to specific pitches to produce a 'type of sonorous cryptogram'.[54] Years later he divulged details of the method,[55] noting that while the Greek metre 'in effect furnished a melodic/rhythmic scheme of two pitches and two rhythms' for the vocal line, the instrumental accompaniment '[rested] on … phonetic correspondences, largely a matter of convention, and often even arbitrary'.[56] Mâche provided a phonological table of front and back vowels, palatal and occlusive consonants, paired with Greek letters and aligned beneath four partitions of sounds for the piccolo, oboe, harp and tambourine, leaving the sibilant clashes of the cymbal to capture the alveolar/fricative consonant 's'.

If Mâche refocused cryptographic efforts at the level of phonemes, others observed older practices. Thus, in 1956, when the French pianist Marguerite Long celebrated her jubilee, eight countrymen – Jean Françaix, Henri Sauguet, Darius Milhaud, Jean Rivier, Henri Dutilleux, Jean-Yves Daniel-Lesur, Francis Poulenc and Georges Auric – contributed an orchestral suite of 'variations' based on her surname, which spelled the cryptogram EAGG[57]:

A	B	C	D	E	F	G
H	I	J	K	L	M	N
O	P	Q	R	S	T	U
V	W	X	Y	Z		

At least two, Rivier and Dutilleux, folded into their pieces the pianist's complete name; ex. 12.21 gives the cipher devised by Rivier.

---

[54] Mâche (1992), 65–6.
[55] Ibid.
[56] Mâche (1992), 65; see also Shenton (2008), 77–8.
[57] Dunoyer (1993), 186–7.

Ex. 12.21: Jean Rivier, *Nocturne* (1956)

The suite has now lapsed into obscurity, though Poulenc's penultimate offering achieved some status. Meanwhile, between 1969 and 1972 the prolific Georges Migot produced a rash of cipher pieces for various scorings (piano, organ, cello, flute, flute and harp, string quartet) that he described as 'nominé', that is, based on the names of their dedications; Migot's cryptograms remain largely unpublished.[58]

There remains the case of Pierre Boulez (1925–2016), *enfant terrible* of the post-war French avant-garde. A student of Messiaen committed to 'total serialism', Boulez pursued the *ultra*-modern, in the process rejecting many twentieth-century pioneers in composition, whether Schoenberg, Stravinsky, Messiaen himself, or even John Cage, whose unlocking of aleatoric methodologies captured Boulez's attention. As if reviving Voltaire's imperative *écrasez l'infâme* ('crush the loathsome'), Boulez thrived on polemics, leading Messiaen to observe that his former pupil was 'in revolt against everything'.[59] And yet, when Stravinsky died in November 1971, the Frenchman joined an eclectic group of composers, among them Elisabeth Lutyens, Aaron Copland, Elliott Carter, Alexander Goehr, Roger Sessions and Darius Milhaud, to pay tribute to the cosmopolitan Russian in the contemporary music journal *Tempo*.[60] Boulez's contribution was ... *explosante-fixe* ... (after a text by the surrealist André Breton), a work of unspecified scoring divided into sections labelled 'originel' ('original') and 'transitoire' ('transient'). The order of these sections varied from performance to performance; a series of arrows offered optional pathways through the score, leading the ensemble now from this 'originel' to that 'transitoire'.

Offering a degree of structural coherence was Boulez's use of a seven-note row – E-flat, G, D, A-flat, B-flat, A and E – of which the first, E-flat (eS), invoked Stravinsky's initial, though the remaining pitches did not derive from a special key. Indeed, Boulez viewed the symbolic eS as mere coincidence:

> the entire central part of the flute ... is organized around the pitch E-flat which, at least in German, is said as *es*. For *es* (S) is the initial of Stravinsky. But then

---

[58] Chailley (1981), 74; Honegger (1977), xxvii, 9–10, 16, 23, 26, 39.

[59] Samuel (1976), 111.

[60] 'In Memoriam: Igor Stravinsky. Canons & Epitaphs, set 2', *Tempo* (1972), No. 98.

again, no one can detect it; it is not, in the final judgment, so important. It is a phenomenon of coincidence, of cryptography or of a musical cryptogram of which one finds so much; it possesses no musical significance, but simply a personal significance.[61]

Boulez redeployed the materials of ... *explosante-fixe* ... in 1975, when he composed another *tombeau*, *Rituel*, this time for his colleague Bruno Maderna. Here Boulez scored for eight groups of instruments, mingling Western woodwind, brass and strings with percussive non-Western bells, woodblocks, cymbals and gongs. Beginning modestly with one and then two groups, Boulez gradually built up the ensemble before initiating a 'retrograde and symmetrical process of ... paring down', tracing 'an arch whose descending slope resounds like a slow death struggle'.[62] The same seven-note row, freely applied in pitch order, presumably stood for the letters of Maderna's name, though once more, a cryptographic key did not occasion those pitches. Of course, one would not expect Boulez, who devoted himself to severing links to the past, to preserve older French approaches to musical cryptography. All the greater irony, then, that in 1976, to celebrate the career of the Swiss conductor Paul Sacher, Boulez produced a composition based on a six-note cipher on Sacher's name, one that Boulez reemployed in several more works through the end of the century.

---

[61] Boulez (1976), 139–40.
[62] Jameux (1990), 355.

CHAPTER 13 (12A)

Mystics, Numerologists and Modernists

'There must be secret laws that direct our destiny, that should remain secret.'

– Strindberg, *A Blue Book*

'The world revolves within; what bursts out is merely the echo – the world of art.'

– Arnold Schoenberg

No one, perhaps, captured the paradoxes of late nineteenth-century music more cogently than Eduard Hanslick, who opined in the Viennese *Neue Freie Presse* on 26 February 1885 about Anton Bruckner, heir to the symphonic legacies of Beethoven and Schubert, and the chromatically sodden edifices of Wagner: 'It remains a psychological enigma, how this gentlest and most peaceable of men ... at the moment of composing turns into an anarchist, who mercilessly sacrifices everything one would call logic and clarity of development, unity of form and tonality'.[1] As century's end approached, Bruckner's music exuded the autumnal Romanticism of the recent past *and* whirling 'progress' of the present. Many found an irreparable disconnect between his rustic *Weltanschauung* and ability to produce colossal symphonies Hanslick likened to strangulating boa constrictors.[2] A provincial organist from Upper Austria, Bruckner seemed out of place in cosmopolitan Vienna. Even his successor Gustav Mahler described him as 'a simpleton – half genius, half imbecile' (*halb Genie, halb Trottel*).[3]

Dominating Bruckner's personal life were odd, obsessive behaviours, in particular the need to count – bricks in a building, leaves on a tree, stars in the heavens. These enumerating disorders affected his devotional life as well. A pious Catholic, Bruckner summarized his daily prayers in diaries, using a code-like series of abbreviations, with 'V' for 'Vater unser' (Lord's Prayer), 'A'

---

[1] Orel (1953), 132; trans. in Floros (2011), 42.

[2] Eduard Hanslick, *Neue freie Presse*, 30 March 1886.

[3] Pfohl (1973), 15. On Mahler's relationship to Bruckner, see Korstvedt (2017).

for 'Ave Maria', underscored by horizontal lines to indicate the quantity.[4] For the composer, music was no less than the 'occult revelation of the highest insights'.[5]

There was also the issue of Bruckner's interest in cadavers. As early as 1867 this morbid fascination seized him when Maximilian I, younger brother of the Austrian emperor Francis Joseph and emperor of Mexico for three short years, was executed by a Republican firing squad, memorialized in Franz Liszt's *Marche funèbre* (1867) and Édouard Manet's *Execution of Emperor Maximilian* (1869). When the body arrived in Vienna for interment in the imperial Capuchin crypt, Bruckner inquired whether the Habsburg royal would lie in state for public viewing.[6] Then, two decades later, when Schubert's and Beethoven's remains were exhumed, Bruckner attended the ceremonies and attempted to cradle their skulls in his hands.

These behaviours suggest that Bruckner suffered from obsessive-compulsive personality disorder, in which recurring, controlling thoughts caused him to act out compensatory behaviours to restore stability in his world, only to experience loop-like re-triggering of the obsession. His arithmomania is of special interest here because it 'expose[d] a psychological and political substrate',[7] and, furthermore, left clear traces in his scores that directly affect how we might interpret his music.

Indeed, the autographs of Bruckner's symphonies reveal that the counting fixation was essential to his compositional process. One only must peruse the bottom of each page to see how he religiously jotted down numerical series, partitioning the music into phrases that, in the aggregate, cohered into more substantial periods and paragraphs. Timothy L. Jackson has likened Bruckner's numbers to a 'metrical grid' that 'pinpoint[ed] the "downbeat," i.e., first accented measure of the individual phrase'.[8] Bruckner relied primarily on multiples of four-bar units, 'the equation of counting mania with quadratic phrasing'.[9] If eight-bar phrases breaking into four plus four bars were the norm, inevitably the creative process produced 'anomalies' that obliged him to make adjustments.

One example is the scherzo of the Ninth Symphony (1894).[10] Its principal subject, which fully materializes only at the upbeat to bar 43, comprises an

---

[4] See Elisabeth Maier (1997).
[5] Eckstein (1936), 157.
[6] Floros (2011), 45; Auer (1967), 199.
[7] Horton (2004), 93.
[8] Timothy L. Jackson (1990), 102.
[9] Williamson (2004), 6.
[10] Österreichische Nationalbibliothek Mus. Hs. 19.481 b A/Bruckner 152.

eight-bar phrase that is immediately repeated, forming a sixteen-bar period. However, the forty-two bars comprising the introduction betray a greater variety of metrical organization in Bruckner's counting. First, the composer releases this 'boa constrictor' of 760 bars with nearly two bars of rest, so that the movement literally begins *ex nihilo*. That brief silence led Bruckner to count two two-bar units before enumerating a full eight-bar phrase with *pizzicato* strings: 1 2/ 1 2/ 1 2 3 4 5 6 7 8. Then, as if starting anew in bar 13, he inserted another two-bar morsel before proceeding with two 'normative' eight-bar phrases followed by an extended span of twelve bars. At this point (bar 42), the macabre theme erupts in full, brutish force, in lockstep with the grim procession of two eight-bar portions, marked *fortissimo* and *arco*, and unleashed with adamantine repetitions of the tonic pitch D.

Only owing to the holographs Bruckner bequeathed to the Austrian national library are we afforded admission into his creative workshop. When the first edition of the Ninth Symphony appeared in 1903, none of these numerical annotations were mentioned by the editor, Ferdinand Löwe. Nor was one other unusual feature of the score – Bruckner's placement of rehearsal letters in the third movement. Two hundred and forty-three bars in length, this slow movement required every letter of the alphabet, from A to Z, ostensibly providing practical cues for use during rehearsals. But closer inspection reveals an oddity that may relate yet again to the composer's counting fixation. By bar 219 Bruckner had annotated his score with rehearsal letters from A to T. With only twenty-five bars remaining, he then shortened the distance between the final seven letters, allowing him to reach Z with just bars to spare before the end. Apparently, completing the alphabet afforded him a sense of closure.

One could adduce other evidence of Bruckner's 'monomaniacal' musical habits; the determined motivic repetitions that dominate the scherzo of the Eighth Symphony (1890) come to mind, for instance. But a larger question remains: does Bruckner's number obsession betray just his psychoneurotic profile, or does it also concern deeper levels of musical meaning? Harry Halbreich and Wolfgang Grandjean believed so.[11] Halbreich argued that the overarching structure of the Sixth Symphony (1881) rested upon the greater and lesser Golden Section (the ratios .618 and .382).[12] Grandjean went further: 'The Golden Section and Fibonacci numbers in the movements of the Sixth Symphony can be no coincidence, for the values are too exact. One must assume therefore that Bruckner consciously (not intuitively) employed them'.[13]

---

[11] Halbreich (1983), and Grandjean (2001).
[12] Halbreich (1983), 87–8.
[13] Grandjean (2001), 267.

324   THE ART OF MUSICAL CIPHERS, RIDDLES AND SUNDRY CURIOSITIES

In 1936, Bruckner's former pupil Friedrich Eckstein recalled that the number eleven had played a 'significant role' in the composer's 'numerical fantasies'. A row of objects separated by the same spacing could trigger the composer's *Zählmanie*, and the rhythm of his counting affected him like some magical pronouncement of destiny.[14] For Gunnar Cohrs, who viewed Bruckner as a supreme 'musical architect',[15] the composer had predicated at least two symphonies, the Fifth (1877) and Ninth, upon *Grundzahlen* (fundamental numbers) that shaped their formal proportions, just as centuries before, nameless artisans of Gothic cathedrals had selected basic numbers to govern the dimensions and architectonic details of their soaring creations.[16] So the possibility of numerological exegeses of Bruckner's music arose, and he joined other composers – for example, Ockeghem, Josquin, J. S. Bach, Mozart, Bartók and Gubaidulina – not immune to the power of sounding numbers.

In the case of the Fifth Symphony, Cohrs amassed evidence that seven represented the *Grundzahl*. To begin with, the lengths of the four movements either approximated or matched exact multiples of seven: in the first movement, 511 bars (73×7); second movement, 211 bars ($30 \times 7 + 1$, off by one bar); third movement, scherzo, 338 bars ($48 \times 7 + 2$, off by two bars), and trio, 148 bars ($3 \times 7 \times 7 + 1$, off by one bar); and finale, 635 bars ($90 \times 7 + 5$, off by five bars, though Bruckner reached the final chord in bar 629, which he stated *seven* times). Also relevant, the principal theme of the second movement privileged the melodic interval of the seventh, with ten concentrated sevenths in the treble and bass of bars 15–17, eclipsed by thirteen consecutive sevenths in bars 23–6 (ex. 13.1).

But why the highlighting of seven? Cohrs reminds us that in Catholicism the number symbolized the veneration of Mary, and that the Baroque monastery of St. Florian, where Bruckner worked for several years, was a centre of Marianism. The composer's diaries document that he habitually recited among his prayers *Ave Maria* and *Salve Regina*. He would have been familiar with the Seven Sorrows and Joys of Mary; probably not happenstance, then, that when he set *Ave Maria* as a motet (1861), he scored the composition for *seven* parts – sopranos, first and second altos, first and second tenors, and first and second basses.

Admittedly, one might dismiss these observations as 'idle speculation', were it not for substantial evidence that Bruckner constructed another symphony, the unfinished Ninth, by applying multiple *Grundzahlen*, in this case

---

[14] Eckstein (1936), 168.

[15] Cohrs (1990).

[16] Ibid., 21; and, in detail, Cohrs (1992). See also Nowak (1985), 45, who argued that in the finale of the Fifth Symphony Bruckner had 'intuitively' based the formal proportions on the number thirty.

Ex. 13.1: Bruckner, Fifth Symphony, Adagio (1877)

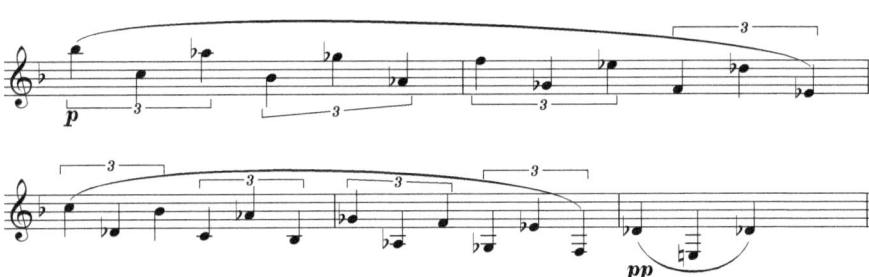

the numbers 7; 9, a possible reference to the Trinity (3 × 3); and 37, drawn from the dimensions of St. Stephen's Cathedral in Vienna. Cohrs's approach entailed compiling a list of the multiples of these three numbers between 1 and 567, and then seeking relevant relationships within the music. But that evidence was not confined to dry counting of numbers. Cohrs found a symbolic use of 9, for instance, in the prominent ninths and ninth chords of the first movement. Thus, in bar 19, where Bruckner inflected the first theme by unexpectedly introducing the chromatic pitch E-flat, the interval of the minor ninth is exposed in the horn call; similarly, Cohrs interprets a motive stated nine times in the horns (bar 493) as a symbolic 'cross figure' (*Kreuzsymbol*) that again spans a minor ninth, which also figures prominently in the poignant theme of the third movement (ex. 13.2a–b).

As for the prime number 37, the width of the nave is 111 feet (1 × 3 × 37); the total width, 222 feet (2 × 3 × 37); the total length, 333 feet (3 × 3 × 37); and the height of the tower, 444 feet (4 × 3 × 37). For Cohrs, the symphony reflects this *Grundzahl* in a variety of ways. For instance, each of the three surviving movements concludes with a 'final building block' (*Schlußbaustein*) of exactly 37 bars. In addition, each movement divides into 37 subsections, all detailed by Cohrs in a table,[17] most of which align with Bruckner's rehearsal letters. And finally, there is a mathematical 'coincidence'. If we impose upon the bars of all three movements a 'basic unit of time' (*Grundzeiteinheit*), whereby one bar of the first movement (*Feierlich*) = two bars of the scherzo (*Lebhaft*) = four bars of the still faster trio (*Schnell*) = half a bar of the slow third movement (*Langsam*), the calculations yield: 567 (first movement) + 125 (250/2, scherzo proper) + 66 (264/4, trio) + 125 (250/2, scherzo *Da capo*) + 486 (2 × 243, third movement) = 1,369. That grand sum is exactly the square of 37.[18]

---

[17] Cohrs (1992), 69–75.
[18] Ibid., 45.

Ex. 13.2a–b: Bruckner, Ninth Symphony, First and Third Movements (1894)

There is yet more supporting evidence. Its trail begins with a report in the Stuttgart *Neue Musikzeitung* regarding the composer's planning for the Ninth Symphony in 1892: 'Our Anton Bruckner, the symphonist, intends to add to his nine symphonies a tenth, namely the "Gothic." To find the right mood, for days he has been spending hours in and around St. Stephen's Church in Vienna studying its noble designs'.[19] To this piece of evidence Cohrs adds another: a single autograph sheet formerly possessed by Bruckner's pupil August Stradal, on which the composer recorded several enigmatic numbers and ratios, which Stradal attested was 'a calculation of the relationships of measures in the last movement of the new symphony by Bruckner.'[20]:

30	<u>10</u>	×	12
	33		
	<u>12</u>	10 = 30	
	66		
<u>33</u>	5 = 15		
496	4		

Here we encounter another riddle that, like Elgar's *Enigma* Variations, has remained unsolved for a century and more. Stradal received the sheet from the composer in 1895, so perhaps the reference to the 'last movement' was to the sketches Bruckner left for the envisioned *fourth* movement?[21]

---

[19] *Neue Musikzeitung* 13 (1892), No. 16, 187.

[20] Cohrs (1990), 25–6. Österreichische Nationalbibliothek, Vienna, Bogen S. M. 38.846.

[21] The autograph of the third movement bears the dates 31 October and 30 November 1894.

i

Though little remembered today, the versatile Friedrich Eckstein (1861–1939) was a significant figure in Bruckner's life and link to Viennese modernism. Eckstein met Bruckner in 1881, became his private pupil in harmony and counterpoint, then his personal secretary and early advocate. In 1923, Eckstein published his memoirs of Bruckner, with a detailed account of the composer's pedagogical and analytical methods. After noting his reliance on metrical grids in his symphonies, Eckstein revealed that Bruckner employed the *Grundbass* ('fundamental bass'), an inaudible, imaginary bass line moving by fourths and fifths, that, 'acting behind the scenes like a *spiritus rector*',[22] traced the roots of the underlying harmonic progressions. In the 1720s the French composer Jean-Philippe Rameau had introduced this analytical tool, adopted by two theorists in the orbit of J. S. Bach, Johann Philipp Kirnberger and Friedrich Wilhelm Marpurg, and later exploited in the nineteenth century by the Austrian theorist Simon Sechter, with whom Bruckner studied counterpoint. According to Eckstein, Bruckner often notated the fundamental bass by jotting down stemless, filled-in noteheads or letters to indicate the underlying harmonic relationships in his music.

When not championing Bruckner's works, Eckstein pursued other interests, such as a vegetarian lifestyle that attracted both Hugo Wolf and Gustav Mahler, who responded to Richard Wagner's flirtation with the movement. Neither Wolf nor Mahler was smitten by numerology, but, like Bruckner, they were confirmed Wagnerians. According to Constantin Floros, Mahler based his symphonies on 'inner programs, which he shared publicly up to the Fourth Symphony', in an attempt to 'thematize existential questions'.[23] But after 1900, Mahler began withdrawing his verbal programmes, partly because they were 'vulnerable to gross misunderstandings', partly because 'they were too personal to publicize'.[24] Encouraged by clues the composer embedded in his scores, curious admirers did not hesitate to advance programmatic interpretations of his instrumental works. These clues included Mahler's repurposing textless quotations from his own songs, allowing popular musical styles to intrude into his symphonies, and exploring the symbolic use of unusual timbres – thus, Mahler revealed, the cowbells in the Sixth and Seventh Symphonies (1904 and 1905) approximated the distant, earthly din beneath one (Mahler? The artist?) who stood 'at the highest summit in the face of eternity'.[25] Mahler appears to have captured the idea of transcendence, of leaving the earth for a transformed,

---

[22] Eckstein (1923), 12.
[23] Floros (2021), 114.
[24] Ibid., 114, 115.
[25] Floros (2013), 249–50.

Ex. 13.3: Mahler, *Ewigkeit* Motive

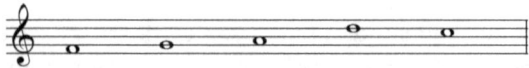

spiritual existence, through the use of a rising figure, the *Ewigkeitmotiv* ('eternity motive'), that appears either in prime or inverted form throughout his musical corpus (ex. 13.3).

Philip Barford counted no fewer than ninety-two examples of this 'thematic archetype' throughout Mahler's oeuvre, and suggested that it 'crystallize[d] a kind of religious longing, boundless aspiration frequently associated with texts of a mystical character'.[26] Associated with the love duet 'Ewig, ewig' in the third act of Wagner's *Siegfried*, the motive surely held a special significance for the composer, though he never publicly revealed its purpose.

Like Mahler, Eckstein was a confirmed Wagnerian. In 1882, to attend the premiere of Wagner's *Parsifal*, Eckstein performed a salvific 'penitential pilgrimage'[27] – walking nearly three hundred miles from Vienna to Bayreuth, since travelling less arduously by train seemed 'undignified' (*unwürdig*).[28] But Eckstein's chief role in our narrative played out a few years later in another aspect of Viennese culture. In 1887, he founded the Vienna Theosophical Society, which gained a small but secure foothold among liberal intelligentsia in *fin-de-siècle* Vienna, a seething cauldron of modernism.

Eckstein was deeply drawn to the occult – not just to theosophy but its more radical, racially tinged offshoot of anthroposophy,[29] spiritualism, clairvoyance and paranormal phenomena – which now enjoyed a surge in interest. He had met Madame Blavatsky, whose writings, we have seen, captured the attention of Scriabin and Holst (cf. pp. 271 and 245); furthermore, Eckstein's circle included the English physicist Lord Rayleigh, the Nobel Prize laureate *and* spiritualist who discovered argon and believed in the diurnal interventions of spirits, because they were visible to him.[30] Even the founder of psychoanalysis, Sigmund Freud, whose *Interpretation of Dreams* (1899) opened the secretive subconscious realm to 'scientific' inquiry, maintained a 'reserved, groping interest' in telepathy, not to mention his susceptibility to numerological superstitions[31] that plagued him, as they did Arnold Schoenberg and Alban Berg. The diverse circle around Eckstein was indeed at least tolerant of, if not actively committed to, pseudo-scientific

---

[26] Barford (1960), 298; see also de la Grange (1997), 143–4, 167–8.
[27] Ross (2020), 255.
[28] Eckstein (1936), 213.
[29] See Luhrssen (2012), 13–18.
[30] Eckstein. (1936), 69.
[31] Gay (1988), 58, 354–5, 443.

approaches and beliefs. In 1910 Freud advised Mahler about marital crises with his wife, Alma; furthermore, one of Freud's early patients was Eckstein's sister Emma,[32] and Eckstein himself was mentioned anonymously in Freud's *Civilization and Its Discontents* (1930).[33] While the extent of Mahler's occult interests remains murky, that was not the case with one seminal pioneer of musical modernism, Arnold Schoenberg (1874–1951), whose life and work were inseparable from mysticism and numerology, not to mention musical cryptograms.

∾ *ii*

In 1909, Schoenberg recorded an aphorism that might stand as a manifesto for pantonality (soon mislabelled by critics as atonality), the radically new type of music he began to explore in transformative works such as the Second String Quartet Op. 10 (1908) and *Drei Klavierstücke* Op. 11 (1909): 'The world revolves within; what bursts out is merely the echo – the world of art.'[34] One might presume that his music's powerfully churning cross-currents reflected Schoenberg's innermost emotional states, a working out, as it were, of deeply seated Freudian drives. Indeed, creations such as the monodrama *Erwartung* Op. 17 (1909), in which the composer represented 'in *slow motion* everything that occurs during a single second of maximum spiritual excitement, stretching it out to half an hour',[35] frequently encouraged psychoanalytic interpretations.[36] But often underestimated is the degree to which Schoenberg's new aesthetic, with its emancipation of dissonance and removal of triadic references, may well have drawn sustenance from mysticism and the occult.

From all appearances, Schoenberg believed 'that music [could] somehow penetrate into another and higher spiritual realm'.[37] John Covach traced this attitude to Schoenberg's readings of the philosopher Arthur Schopenhauer, theosophist Rudolf Steiner (1861–1925) and Swedish theologian/scientist/mystic Emanuel Swedenborg (1688–1772), to whom we might add the Swedish playwright August Strindberg, with whom, as Schoenberg was likely aware, the composer shared initials. Of these figures, Swedenborg seems to have influenced Schoenberg in a pivotal way, through Honoré de Balzac's novella *Séraphita* (1834), an exploration of the Swede's mysticism and doctrine of correspondences, according to which the natural world mirrors a higher, spiritual existence.

---

[32] Ibid., 84–5.
[33] Freud (1961), 19.
[34] Reich (1971), 56–7.
[35] Schoenberg (1984), 105.
[36] See for example Wickes (1989) and Carpenter (2004).
[37] Covach (1995), 13.

Set along a Norwegian fjord, *Séraphita* concerns a mysterious, androgynous figure about to ascend through death into a purely spiritual realm. Séraphita/Séraphitus is beloved by Wilfred and Minna, who in the final chapter witness the angel's assumption, and experience a transient vision of Swedenborg's heaven, an alternate cosmos in which time, space and death do not exist. Schoenberg gave serious thought to setting Balzac's vision, either as an oratorio (1912) or a symphony (1914) that would have exceeded the personnel requirements for Mahler's colossal Eighth ('Symphony of a Thousand'). In a third gestation, *Séraphita* was to form part of Schoenberg's ultimately unrealized oratorio *Die Jacobsleiter* (*Jacob's Ladder*, 1915), where it would 'chronicle the transition of a group of characters, under the guidance of the Archangel Gabriel, from life to death and spiritual rebirth'.[38] Schoenberg himself crafted the text for this project, which began with these lines, heavily influenced by Balzac's Swedenborg and theosophical/anthroposophical attitudes of the time: 'Whether right or left, forward or backward, up or down – one has to go further, without questioning what lies before or behind. That should remain hidden: you ought to, must forget it to fulfil your task.'

Schoenberg's engagement with Swedenborg extended well beyond these musical torsos. In 1913, when the composer drafted the first of the *Four Orchestral Songs* Op. 22, he chose the poem *Seraphita* by the English Decadent poet Ernest Dowson (1896), translated into German by Stefan George. Over its liquescent verses 'hovers ... the protagonist of Balzac's novel of the same name, angel-like and hermaphroditic, who embodies the perfect union of intellect and love, and expounds Emanuel Swedenborg's spiritual cosmology of a paradise freed from earthly constraints.'[39] This rarely performed song belonged to Schoenberg's last opus before his decisive turn to twelve-tone composition. One can almost sense in the opening clarinet melody of Op. 22 No. 1 the inevitability of Schoenberg's progression toward full dodecaphony. The first and second melodic phrases fall prophetically into two segments of twelve pitches each, with minimal pitch duplication, so that they impress as proto-twelve-tone rows that would yield to the genuine article a few years later in 1921, when Schoenberg produced his first rigorously serial pieces, the Prelude and Intermezzo of the Suite for Piano, Op. 25.

Schoenberg occasionally referenced in his writings and correspondence Balzac's novella,[40] nowhere more cogently than in a lecture the composer delivered on twelve-tone music in Los Angeles at UCLA in 1941. Pausing to consider the fatalistic motive 'Muß es sein?' ('Must it be?') from Beethoven's final String

---

[38] McKee (2005), 137. See also, Bailey (1984), 81–2.
[39] MacDonald (2008), 251.
[40] Covach (1998), 13–14.

Quartet, Op. 135, and its manipulation through mirror inversion and retrograde motion, two of the cardinal processes in serial music, Schoenberg commented, 'It should be mentioned that the last century considered such a procedure cerebral, and thus inconsistent with the dignity of genius'. 'But', he continued, 'the validity of this form of [serial] thinking is also demonstrated by the previously stated law of the unity of musical space, best formulated as follows: *the unity of musical space demands an absolute and unitary perception.* In this space, as in Swedenborg's heaven (described in Balzac's *Séraphita*), there is no absolute down, no right or left, forward or backward'.[41]

In short, the new order of Schoenberg's twelve-tone music, predicated upon an 'absolute' unity of musical space, may well have arisen to offer a 'spiritual glimpse of the world that "lies behind" tonality'.[42] The way had been prepared by the plunge into atonality, announced in 1908 by the Second Quartet, a work that deceptively commenced with a traditional F-sharp minor triad, destabilized by the removal of residual tonal ephemera, so that the last movement grasped free atonality, ushered in with the poem *Entrückung* (*Rapture*) by Stefan George, sung by a soprano, with its astral opening line: 'Ich fühle Luft von anderem Planeten' ('I feel fragrance from another planet').

The invention of dodecaphony in the 1920s afforded Schoenberg the opportunity to achieve a new musical order that, he believed, would insure the supremacy of German music for a century. Others were less sanguine, including Thomas Mann, another *émigré* who had resettled in Los Angeles. In *Doktor Faustus* (1947), Mann's sweeping critique of German culture and the Third Reich, he modelled the fictitious composer Adrian Leverkühn, who invents a radically new type of music clearly like the twelve-tone method, on Schoenberg himself. But while Leverkühn conceded that audiences will not grasp 'the precise, detailed awareness of the *methods* by which the highest and strictest order, like that of the stars, a cosmic order and regularity, is achieved', he still insisted that they 'would hear the order itself, and the perception of it would provide an unknown aesthetic satisfaction'.[43] Nonetheless, through the novel's narrator, Serenus Zeitblom, Mann rejected Leverkühn's mystical vision as something 'that really belongs more to astrology. The rationalism you call for has a great deal of superstition about it – of a belief in something impalpable and vaguely demonic that's more at home in games of chance ... Contrary to what you say, your system looks to me as if it's more apt to resolve human reason into magic'.[44]

---

[41] Schoenberg (1984), 223.
[42] Covach (1995), 8.
[43] Thomas Mann (1999), 206.
[44] Ibid., 207–8.

Superstition or mystical clairvoyance? In August 1946 Schoenberg suffered a nearly fatal heart attack, lost consciousness, and was resuscitated only after being administered digitalis. Weeks before, he had begun sketching what would become the String Trio, Op. 45, a twelve-tone composition in five sections alternating between three main parts and two episodes, the whole contraposing conventional *arco* passages (with the bow) against a battery of special, otherworldly effects – eerie *sul ponticello* (on the bridge), rasping *col legno* (bowing with the wood of the bow), and ethereal, disembodied harmonics. As he later documented in his memoir 'My Fatality' ('Mein Todesfall'),[45] the Trio abstracted his experiences throughout the ordeal, including frantic attempts to revive him. Mann was among the first to whom Schoenberg confided 'experiences ... secretly woven into the composition – experiences of which the work was a kind of fruit'.[46] Did the 'magic' of Schoenberg's score somehow convey his out-of-body existence during the illness, his vision of the afterlife?

Schoenberg would live nearly five more years before uttering the word 'Harmonie' and expiring in 1951. His 'second' *Todesfall* was laden with unpropitious numerology. Born on 13 September 1874, he had lived most of his adult life a triskaidekaphobe, only to succumb on Friday, 13 July 1951, just minutes – possibly thirteen – before midnight and the 'safe haven' of 14 July, at an age that added up to thirteen ($7 + 6 = 13$). Schoenberg was increasingly prone to anxiety in years associated with thirteen or its multiples, and so warily divided his life span into thirteen-year segments: 1874–86, 1887–99, 1900–12, *1913–25*, 1926–38 and *1939-1951*. As early as 1913 his pupil Webern was documenting the gravitas of the fateful number in Schoenberg's scores: thus, the primary theme of the String Quartet in D minor, Op. 7 was thirteen bars long, the vocal part of *Gurrelieder* began on the thirteenth page, and so on.[47] The years 1926 (13×2; age 52, or 13×4) and 1939 (13×3; age 65, or 13×5) brought the composer renewed apprehension. Sometime around 1909 he attempted to confront his phobia by numbering the thirteenth bars of his scores '12a'. The composer scrupulously declined the spelling 'Aaron' in his unfinished opera *Moses und Aron*, lest the title contain thirteen letters.[48] Schoenberg seems to have regarded the spelling with twelve letters as satisfying the needs of a strict twelve-tone composition; indeed, none of Schoenberg's compositions bear titles with thirteen letters.[49]

---

[45] Bailey (1984), 152–4.
[46] Thomas Mann (1961), 172.
[47] Webern to Schoenberg, 16 September 1913, cited in Gratzer (1993), 211.
[48] Haimo (2007), 385, 393n. 4.
[49] Ibid.

In 1993 Schoenberg's numerological compulsions inspired a monograph by the composer Colin Sterne, who believed that numbers permeated 'every aspect of [Schoenberg's] life and his art', and hardly could have been 'a casual, part-time pursuit'.[50] Drawn initially to Schoenberg's iconic expressionist melodrama *Pierrot lunaire* Op. 21 (1912), conceived as three groups of seven poems each, Sterne began by investigating whether 3, 7 and their product, 21, were 'structural determinants' of the composition. Finding nothing in the music that indicated such a basis, he then turned to a popular book about numerology by Florence Evylinn Campbell, an American astrologer and cartomancer, *Your Days Are Numbered*, that had appeared in New York in 1931, two years before Schoenberg arrived in the United States. In her system, 'the number most closely associated with 3 and 7 is their sum, 10, not their product, 21, and ... in numerological reduction, 10 becomes 1 by adding its digits'.[51] Drawing on a new series of numbers – 3, 7, 1, 11 and 22 – Sterne now began to make 'breakthroughs' that revealed Schoenberg's covert method, so that 'there was no aspect of the time element in [*Pierrot*] which did not relate to [the five numbers]'.[52] Sterne's conclusions impressed one of Schoenberg's former students, John Cage, who wrote that by giving 'all numbers their own place in his work, Schoenberg made his work breathe as it does in what often seems to be an excess of expressivity, or an expressivity at least that exceeds that of any other music'.[53] But there was no hard evidence that Schoenberg ever read Campbell, or drew upon her additive numerology.

However one assesses Schoenberg's numerology, there is ample evidence that it played a significant role in his aesthetic outlook, as it did in the music of his devoted student Alban Berg. These two shared as well an interest in musical cryptograms as a further means of disguising meaning in their compositions. It appears that Schoenberg himself devised what has become known in the literature as the 'Eschbeg' set, a motive of six pitches derived from the letters of his surname (E-flat [e**S**], **C**, B-natural [**H**], B-flat [**B**], **E** and **G**), sometimes supplemented with A (for **A**rnold).[54]

Perhaps the most sensational, though for decades concealed, cryptographic example obtained in the scherzo of Schoenberg's Second String Quartet, Op. 10 (1908). At the time the composer had developed a friendship with the young Austrian expressionist painter Richard Gerstl (1883–1908), who offered Schoenberg instruction in painting. When the composer's first wife, Mathilde, began to

---

[50] Sterne (1993), vi, vii.
[51] Ibid., v.
[52] Ibid.
[53] Ibid., i.
[54] See Forte (1978) and Taruskin (2005), 314–16.

model for Gerstl, their relationship developed into a perfervid affair, and precipitated a crisis when she eloped with the painter before, after the intervention of Anton Webern, returning to her marriage and children. In despair, Gerstl burned his paintings and stabbed and hanged himself in his studio. Schoenberg responded by weaving into the trio of his scherzo the opening phrase of the popular Viennese tune 'O, du lieber Augustin'; its recurring text, 'alles hin' ('all is gone'), served as a poignant allusion to the drama in his life. As he likely realized, the three principals of the triangle shared the letters A and D in their forenames (**A**rnol**d** = A-D; **R**ic**h**ar**d** = C-B[H]-A-D; and **M**at**hild**e = A-B[H]-D-E), encouraging him to introduce personalized ciphers into the quartet, though in Mathilde's case one disguised through an anagrammatic adjustment (ex. 13.4).

But surely none of these relationships was perceived at the riotous premiere in Vienna on 21 December 1908 by the audience, incited much more by the disorienting entrance of 'O, du lieber Augustin', the intrusion of George's texts in the third and fourth movements and, of course, the composer's embrace in the finale of peculiar harmonies from a 'different planet'.

There was, though, one member of Schoenberg's inner musical circle aware of the emotional subcurrents flowing through the Second Quartet – Alexander von Zemlinsky (1871–1942), who had advised his largely autodidactic colleague in composition before becoming his brother-in-law when Mathilde Zemlinsky married Schoenberg in 1901. Despite the strained circumstances of 1908, Zemlinsky endeavoured to help mend the rift musically in 1917 by completing his own Second String Quartet Op. 15, not only dedicated to Schoenberg but featuring cello-centric textures (Schoenberg was a cellist), as well as a motive drawn from the tritone A-E-flat (A-eS, for his initials), and the same Mathilde cipher Schoenberg had used in his Op. 10.[55]

Less than a year after Mathilde's death in 1923, Schoenberg married Gertrud Kolisch, sister of the violinist Rudolf Kolisch, and conceived the Suite for Seven Instruments, Op. 29 (1925), as a wedding present. Here Schoenberg crafted a twelve-tone row that began with the pitches E-flat and G, that is, her initials, e(S) and G. Among the forty-eight forms of the row, two prime forms and their retrogrades along with two inverted forms and their retrogrades positioned E-flat and G either as their first and second, or eleventh and twelfth pitches (ex. 13.5).

By favouring these eight rows, Schoenberg was able to imprint Gertrud's initials into the first and last bars of the four movements. In most cases he concealed the two pitches within chords, but in the third and fourth movements, he brought E-flat and G into sharper focus. Thus, the brisk subject of

---

[55] See Beaumont (2000), 229–30, 234.

Ex. 13.4: Schoenberg, String Quartet No. 2, Scherzo (1908)

Ex. 13.5: Schoenberg, Suite, Op. 29 (1925)

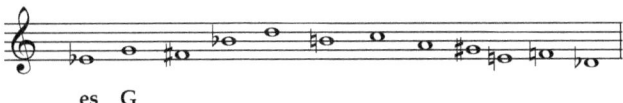

the concluding Gigue announces straightaway the two pitches melodically, and in the extraordinary third movement, a set of variations on Friedrich Silcher's nineteenth-century song *Aennchen von Tharau*, the piano presents them as the downbeat of the first bar, where they are impossible to miss.

The first lines of Silcher's love song read 'Ännchen von Tharau ist, die mir gefällt, / sie ist mein Leben, mein Gut und mein Geld', or, in Henry Wadsworth Longfellow's translation, 'Annie of Tharaw, my true love of old, / she is my life, and my goods, and my gold'. Schoenberg's challenge was to present this familiar melody, set in E major, within the context of a twelve-tone composition. The solution was to highlight the theme in the bass clarinet as a series of dotted-crotchet syncopations that gently rubbed against the piano as it unfolded in the first few bars the original prime form followed by its retrograde, inversion and retrograde-inversion (ex. 13.6).

The first few pitches of the tune, B, C-sharp and B, served double duty as the sixth and twelfth pitches of the prime row, and seventh of its retrograde. In this way, Schoenberg achieved a strict row composition that nonetheless projected,

Ex. 13.6: Schoenberg, Suite, Op. 29 (1925)

Ex. 13.7: Schoenberg, Variations, Op. 31 (1928)

B   A   C   H   B   C   A   H   E   F#   D#   F♮

as if in bas relief, an otherwise hidden tonal artefact. The theme emerged briefly from the 'welter' of atonal sonorities before deferring in the variations to Schoenberg's serial manipulations.

The composer explored a somewhat similar technique in his orchestral Variations, Op. 31 (1928). Here the theme of the nine variations and finale was rigorously twelve-tone, but embedded in the row was an anagrammatic reworking, this one of the familiar BACH cipher, in the order of BCAH, or B-flat, C, A, B-natural,[56] disguised further through transposition to E, F-sharp, E-flat, F (ex. 13.7).

Schoenberg had already used the cipher in retrograde, HCAB, in the neo-Baroque Suite for piano, Op. 25 (1923), where the four pitches form the conclusion of the basic row; later, he would tuck another reference to BACH into his Fourth String Quartet, Op. 37 (1936).[57] Striking about the Variations is the degree to which he first masked the Bachian cipher, only to raise its profile gradually over the course of the work, until it ultimately appeared in its familiar historical guise; for instance, in this stentorian passage from the finale (ex. 13.8, bars 334–9).

There is further evidence, too, that, in the words of the late Richard Taruskin, Schoenberg's row was 'covertly tailored to a Bachian purpose'.[58] Ethan Haimo has pointed out that in addition to the embedded BACH cipher, the fifth through ninth pitches of the row may echo uncannily the subject of Bach's *Art of Fugue*,[59] to which we might observe that the ninth through twelfth pitches might hint at the subject of *The Musical Offering* (ex. 13.9).

---

[56] For readers sceptical of musical anagrams: the composer named his son Ronald R. Schoenberg, born in 1936, after an anagram of Arnold, as he did on the birth of his son Roland in 1941, before changing his name on the advice of the astrologer Oskar Adler to Lawrence Adam. Ronald Schoenberg's son, E. Randol Schoenberg, born in 1966, carried on the family tradition.

[57] Boss (2014), 309.

[58] Taruskin (2005), 703.

[59] Haimo (1990), 162.

Ex. 13.8: Schoenberg, Variations, Op. 31, BACH (1928)

Ex. 13.9: J. S. Bach, *Art of Fugue*, *The Musical Offering*; Schoenberg, Variations, Op. 31, Tone Row (1928)

Operating behind the surface permutations of the rows in the Variations was a more deeply lying narrative thread that traced Schoenberg's relationship with the music of Bach; arguably, the twentieth-century Bach revival was the subject of the work, first concealed, then revealed.

∞ iii

Like Schoenberg, Alban Berg (1885–1950) was steeped in the fatalism of numerology and the occult. The parallels between the two composers are telling, indeed. As Wolfgang Gratzer has detailed,[60] the composer absorbed the theories of Swedenborg, first through Balzac's *Séraphita* – Berg contemplated a symphonic work on the novella – and then through the writings of his favourite contemporary author, August Strindberg, whose dramas exuded a 'celestial greatness' ('*überirdische Größe*').[61] Berg faithfully collected the Swede's works, and underlined in a copy of Strindberg's *A Blue Book* (1907–12), a late collection of aphoristic reflections on Swedenborgian mysticism, 'There must be secret laws that direct our destiny, that should remain secret', a reference to the theosophical notion that 'all suffering is just punishment for offences committed in previous incarnations'.[62]

---

[60] Gratzer (1993).
[61] Berg to Webern (29 July 1929), cited in Gratzer (1993), 29.
[62] Ibid., 48.

Other authors whom Schoenberg's circle avidly read included the philosopher Otto Weininger, whose metaphysical musings in *Über die letzten Dinge* (*On Last Things*, 1904) Berg interpreted as confirming Swedenborg's theory of correspondences.[63] Though relatively unknown today, Weininger's essays caused a sensation when they appeared the year after he rented a room in Vienna at Schwarzspanierstrasse Nr. 15 (Beethoven's final residence) and committed suicide. In the case of the architect Adolf Loos, whose lecture *Ornament und Verbrechen* (*Ornament and Crime*, 1908) offered an earnest critique of the florid designs of Art Nouveau and its German counterpart, *Jugendstil*, Berg and his colleagues embraced an unapologetic supporter of their music. Berg would likely have taken to heart Loos's assertion that 'Beethoven's symphonies would never have been written by a man who was obliged to go about in silk, velvet and lace ... Lack of ornament is a sign of spiritual strength'.[64]

A special mark of Berg's affection for Loos was a double acrostic the composer crafted for the architect's sixtieth birthday in 1930. Here Berg implanted 'ADOLF LOOS' vertically in the initial letters of the lines from top to bottom, and 'alban berg' at the ends of the lines:

    Adolf Loos: diese neun
                          Buchstaben, sind sie etw**a**
    Deut- und vergleichbar der Musen A-
                          polls, des Lichtgottes, Neunzah**l**;
    Oder sind sie – zerlegt –,
                          zieht man die ersten fünf a**b**,
    Lebenspendend die vier Ele-
                          mente: ohn' Ornament!, d**a**
    Feuer, Wasser und Luft –
                          So wie die Erde – erst dan**n**-
    Liegt's an des Vornamens Fünf? – den fünf
                          Sinnen geben den Maßsta**b**;
    Oder wirken die drei
                          Silben – gleich Grazien – Magi**e**?
    Oft – auch im Scherz – wär' der endlichen
                          Zahlen Spiel wiederholba**r**. –
    Scherz dabei! Denn un-
                          endlich geht weiter Dein We**g**.[65]

---

[63] See ibid., 100–1.

[64] Münz and Künstler (1966), 231.

[65] *Adolf Loos zum 60. Geburtstag am 10. Dezember 1930* (Vienna, 1930), 67; in Gratzer (1993), 233. A free translation: 'Adolf Loos, these nine letters, are they perhaps interpretable and comparable to the muses of Apollo, God of light, nine in number;

As Berg realized, the two names contained nine letters each, dividing into five and four, with three syllables (two for the forenames and one for the surnames). Using 3, 4 and 5 as factors, Berg could have produced 60 as the relevant number for Loos's anniversary ($3 \times 4 \times 5$), though in his poem the composer chose to liken 3 to the number of Graces; 4 to the elements; 5 to the senses; and 9 to the Muses.[66]

Yet another member of Berg's circle was the physician, violinist and astrologer Oskar Adler (1874–1955), a close friend of Schoenberg, whose lectures coalesced in 1935 into the *Einführung in die Astrologie als Geheimwissenschaft* (*Introduction to the Secret Knowledge of Astrology*). Adler's ideas were influencing Berg by 1914. There is evidence that Adler may have prepared a natal horoscope for the composer; according to Louis Krasner, who premiered Berg's Violin Concerto in 1936, Viennese artists and intellectuals of the 1930s were 'all conscious ... of the vibrations that emanated from [Adler] ... and his astrological charts were sought by all of the twelve-tone circle'.[67] Geoffrey Poole has theorized that if Berg indeed received a horoscope from Adler, the composer may have discovered that on his birth date, 9 February 1885, at a time of birth around 6:07 a.m., number 23 was 'blazoned from all four corners of the natal chart, on its East-West and North-South axes'.[68]

That realization might have been enough for Berg to regard 23 as his fateful number, which surfaced frequently in his correspondence beginning in 1914.[69] But other factors could have activated his numerical sensitivities: for instance, his first attack on 23 July 1908 of bronchial asthma, a debilitating condition with which he would contend for much of his life.[70] Yet another justification for privileging 23 may have been his encounter in 1915 with the (pseudo-scientific) research of Wilhelm Fliess, an otolaryngologist and close colleague of Freud, who had propounded 'a scheme of biorhythmic cycles of 23 and 28 days, to which males and females were subject and which, he believed, would permit

---

or are they broken down if one takes away the first five, the four life-giving elements: without ornament!, then fire, water and air, as well as earth – only then – is it because of the first-named five – the five senses provide the standard measure; or do the three syllables – like the graces – work magic? Often – even in jest – the game of finite numbers could be repeated. – Just kidding! Because your path continues indefinitely'.

[66] Ibid., 234–6.
[67] Jarman (1989), 182.
[68] Poole (1991), 5.
[69] Gratzer (1993), 215–17.
[70] Reich (1965), 26.

the physician to diagnose all sorts of conditions and ailments'.[71] And finally, according to Berg's pupil Willi Reich, who co-founded in 1932 the music journal *23. Eine Wiener Musikzeitschrift*, the number, though ostensibly referring to the twenty-third paragraph of an Austrian press law, was chosen to recognize Berg's *Schicksalszahl*.[72]

Just as Schoenberg was obsessed with the number 13, so was Berg preoccupied with 23. He became an inveterate numerologist, finding his number in relatively insignificant street addresses, telegrams and hotel rooms, but also in significant dates, as when Schoenberg and Berg began using the familiar *Du* in their correspondence (23 June 1918),[73] and when Berg completed important compositions (*Chamber Concerto*, on 23 July 1925; the concert aria *Der Wein*, 23 July 1929; and the Violin Concerto, 23 July 1935).[74] Little wonder, then, that Berg's numerological leanings tumbled over into his music. In 1967 the Hungarian scholar András Pernye culled evidence that in the *Lyric Suite* (1926), for instance, 23 played the decisive role in determining the lengths of the movements and choices of tempi. Thus, five of the six movements were exactly divisible by 23 (69, 138, 69, 460, 46), as were the composer's metronome markings.[75]

Unable to detect a conspicuous application of 23 in Berg's first opera, *Wozzeck*, Pernye pursued a different approach. Recalling that the drama from which Berg derived his libretto, Georg Büchner's *Woyzeck* (1836), had been based on a historical event, the eponymous soldier's murder of his lover in 1821, Pernye added together the number of bars of Berg's three acts, which summed to 1,927. Subtracting six silent bars marked in the score (four at the end of Act II, two at the beginning of Act III) then yielded a total of 1,921 *sounding* bars, corresponding to the centenary of the murder, and the year during which Berg completed *Wozzeck*. Pernye then considered the number 21 (common to 1821 and 1921) and its factors, 7 and 3, and extracted further discoveries that tended to reinforce a large-scale numerological reading of the opera: *Wozzeck* was released as Berg's Op. 7; the fourth scene of Act I (Doctor's study) comprised a passacaglia on a subject of seven bars with twenty-one variations; the first scene of Act III (Marie's room) offered seven variations and a fugue on a seven-bar theme; the second scene of Act III (path by the lake), in which Wozzeck stabs Marie, consisted of 49 (7×7) bars; and the final scene (street by Marie's room), in which her orphaned child remains on stage, expended 21 (7×3) bars.

---

[71] Gay (1988), 56; Gratzer (1993), 182.
[72] Reich (1965), 81.
[73] Gratzer (1993), 215.
[74] Pernye (1967), 141.
[75] Ibid., 148–9.

Ex. 13.10: Berg, 'Über den Bergen' (1905)

No less compelling was Berg's pursuit of musical cryptography. Early on, he was likely aware of Robert Schumann's cipher for the *Abegg* Variations (A-B-flat-E-G-G), which, shorn of the repeated G, prophetically replicated Berg's own name. Not coincidental, then, was the ubiquitous spelling of 'A. Berg' in the early song 'Über den Bergen' ('Beyond the Mountains', 1905), in which the A and B-flat form a neighbour-note figure in the bass, while the pitches B-flat, E, D (*Ré*) and G appear within a half-diminished sonority above.[76] The piano accompaniment thus punned repeatedly on 'Alban Berg' (**Alban Berg**) and 'Bergen' (**Berg**en), beyond which, Karl Busse's poem reads, 'lives happiness' (ex. 13.10).

Ciphers populated several of Berg's major works, usually in tandem with numerology. For the *Kammerkonzert* (*Chamber Concerto*, 1925), he prepared an 'Open Letter' to Schoenberg, explaining that the music celebrated his fiftieth birthday, Berg's fortieth birthday, and the twentieth year of the colleagueship of Schoenberg, Berg and Webern.[77] These three events played out in the very opening of the work, a short introduction that presented three characteristic ciphers on the composers' names.[78] The work comprised three movements, which Berg envisioned as 'Friendship' (*Freundschaft*), 'Love' (*Liebe*) and 'World' (*Welt*), in the order of theme and variations, ternary *ABA* slow movement and rondo. Berg's summary diagram of the concerto divulged how the lengths of the principal sections and subsections fell into multiples of three; thus, the first

---

[76] See further, Adams (2008), 330.

[77] The letter appeared in the Viennese music periodical *Pult und Taktstock* in February 1925, and is reproduced in Reich (1963), 135–40.

[78] For **Arnold Sch**ö**n**berg, A, D, E-flat, C, B, B-flat, E and G; for **Anton Webern**, A, E, B-flat and E; and for **Alban Berg**, A, B-flat, A, B-flat, E and G.

and second movements were each 240 bars in length; the finale, their sum, or 480 bars, yielding *in toto* 480 + 480, or 960 bars. Indeed, the number three 'determined virtually every aspect of the concerto's construction, including … the duration, the instrumentation, the organization of rhythm and metre, the types of thematic and harmonic material, the formal structures, and the methods used to amalgamate the first two movements in the finale'.[79]

Other details, though, Berg did not disclose, especially a private programme for the slow movement, which memorialized the decline of Mathilde Schoenberg after the Gerstl affair, her illness and death. Berg deployed ciphers on her name (A-B-D-E) similar to those her husband and Zemlinsky had explored in their second string quartets and worked into the movement quotations from Schoenberg's tone poem after Maeterlinck's *Pelléas et Mélisande* (1903), which concerned a love triangle. In Berg's rehearing, Gerstl, Mathilde and Schoenberg stood for Pelléas, Mélisande and Golaud. Berg also expanded the movement so that its second half formed a palindrome of the first, stopping and reversing its forward course, as if to depict 'Mathilde's moment of death and ascent into heaven'.[80]

In the *Lyric Suite* for string quartet (1926) he concealed a decidedly autobiographical content. Though scholars had assumed the work offered purely 'absolute music', that reading abruptly changed half a century later in 1977, when George Perle made a sensational discovery – an annotated copy of the printed score Berg had prepared for Hanna Fuchs-Robettin, wife of the Prague industrialist Herbert Fuchs-Robettin.[81] As this source made clear, Berg had begun a romantic relationship with her in 1925, and sublimated his desire for the one he likened to Beethoven's 'Immortal Beloved'[82] by composing the *Lyric Suite*, a narrative of their relationship 'from its innocent beginnings (first movement), to their declaration of love (third movement) and in the sixth movement, to the recognition of the impossibility of its ever developing into anything more permanent'.[83]

In 2008, the full extent of the Berg/Fuchs-Robettin liaison was exposed by the release of their correspondence, including fourteen letters from Berg to Fuchs, with this acknowledgment: 'Will the music be powerful enough, despite its modernity, to speak to you and speak as forcibly and unambiguously as it is intended? Intended as a confession (one that concerns no one but you!) of

---

[79] Dalen (1989), 141.
[80] Covach (1998), 18.
[81] See Perle (1977 and 1981).
[82] Letter of July 1925 from Berg to Hanna Fuchs, in Floros (2008), 19.
[83] Jarman (1997), 167.

Ex. 13.11: Wagner, *Tristan und Isolde*, Vorspiel (1859)

our encountering love!'[84] Here and elsewhere we learn that the *Lyric Suite* was 'full of secret references to our numbers 10 and 23 and our initials H F A B'[85]; that the second movement (*Andante amoroso*) enciphered Hanna's daughter Dorothea, known affectionately as 'Do-do', with the pitches C, C; that the third movement (*Allegro misterioso*) cited themes from Zemlinsky's *Lyric Symphony*, including one set to the words 'Du bist mein eigen' ('You are my own!')[86]; and that the finale (*Largo desolato*) was a *Lied ohne Worte*, inspired by the poem 'De Profundis' from Baudelaire's *Les fleurs du mal* (translated by George), written into Berg's copy of the score for Hanna, but suppressed in the published score. The opening verses read: 'To you, O sole beloved, go my cries/ Out of the dark abyss, down which my heart has fallen.'[87] In the same movement Berg interwove quotations from *Tristan und Isolde*,[88] and he made sure to write out separately the celebrated first three bars of Wagner's *Vorspiel*, sharing with Hanna that their initials were entwined in another drama about illicit love[89] (ex. 13.11).

This revelation gave new meaning to Adorno's assertion that whenever Berg encountered a piano, he would play the opening of Wagner's iconic score.[90]

Of course, the composer withheld these hidden meanings. Apart from Hanna, most likely his pupil Theodor Adorno was among the few aware of the affair. Adorno had served as a *postillion d'amour*, delivering letters to her, and as early as 1937, without revealing the *dramatis personae*, he coyly described the *Lyric Suite* as a 'latent opera'.[91] In an analysis prepared for the Kolisch Quartet,

---

[84] Letter of 23 October [1926], in Floros (2008), 36.

[85] It remains unclear why 10 was Hanna's special number; one theory is that her name had ten characters.

[86] See Floros (1981), 25, 27, 28.

[87] As translated in ibid., 21.

[88] Ibid., 35, 37.

[89] Floros (2008), 37.

[90] See Baragwanath (1999), 62n.

[91] Adorno (1991), 104.

who gave the Viennese premiere in 1927, Berg himself left this ambiguous comment about the character of the music, summed up as 'suffering fate' (*Schicksal erleiden*).[92] But the secret programme remained hidden for decades, leaving musicians to ponder instead the mysteries of the score, of which roughly half was based on a twelve-tone row that underwent metamorphosis, while the other half was freely composed.

Ex. 13.12 illustrates the original row of the *Lyric Suite*.

Framing it are F and C-flat, for **Fuchs, Hanna**; in addition, the first hexachord can be heard as reinforcing the scale of F major while the second hexachord tilts (enharmonically) toward B major, further alluding to her symbolic presence. The second hexachord is a retrograde of the first transposed by a tritone. And finally, the entire row is an example of an all-interval set, meaning that it contains every interval (or inversional equivalent) within the octave – a minor second/major seventh (F-E), major second/minor seventh (A-G), minor third/major sixth (C-A), major third/minor sixth (E-C), perfect fourth/perfect fifth (G-D) and tritone (D-A-flat) that divides the octave symmetrically in half.

By manipulating the row's order, Berg was able to bring the lovers' initials into focus. For the second movement, he exchanged the tenth and fourth pitches, before transposing the row a minor third higher, so that it began on A-flat, with the result that **A**, **B**, **F** and **H** now appeared consecutively as the fourth through seventh pitches. In the third movement, by shifting the altered row a major second higher, Berg transferred the four initials, so they appeared prominently at the beginning of the series (ex. 13.13a–b).

Though Gottfried Scholz has rightly commented that 'numbers and letters form the main vocabulary'[93] on which Berg relied, there is another technique (already encountered in the *Kammerkonzert* and *Lyric Suite*) that came to represent a hallmark of his art – retrograde patterns and palindromes. Like Schoenberg and Webern, Berg was attracted to the idea that recursive motion could serve to reinforce symmetry and unity, but in Berg's case palindromic designs assumed a disproportionate weight. As Douglas Jarman has noted, excepting 'the Violin Concerto, there is not a single major work [by Berg] written after the Op. 5 Clarinet Pieces [1913] that does not include' a 'large-scale retrograde'.[94] And even in the concerto (1935), Berg exploited the final few bars to reverse the violin arpeggiations of the introduction, as if to suggest that a palindrome framed the music.

---

[92] Rauchhaupt (1971), 105.

[93] Scholz (1998), 59.

[94] Jarman (1997), 167.

Ex. 13.12: Berg, *Lyric Suite*, Tone Row (1926)

Ex. 13.13a–b: Berg, *Lyric Suite*, Tone Rows, Second and Third Movements (1926)

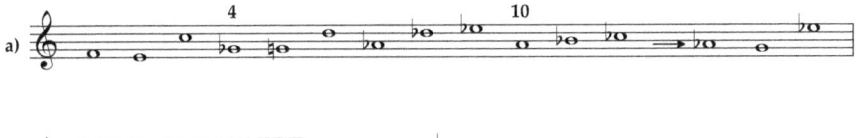

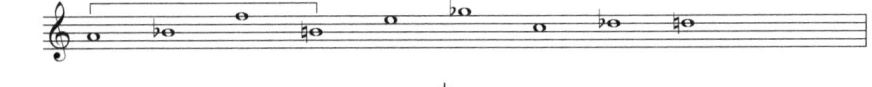

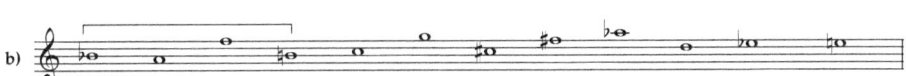

Whatever meaning the composer attached to the device, in the *Kammerkonzert*, *Lulu* and *Der Wein*, he ensured that the pivot points of his symmetrical structures were visually conspicuous in the scores' layouts, by instructing the compositor to place the midpoints exactly in the centre of the printed page. Through the lens of *Augenmusik*, then, one could visually compare the spooling and unspooling of the palindrome, even if all its details could not be audibly apprehended during a performance. In *Lulu*, the purpose of the reversible musical interlude separating the two scenes of Act 2 was clear enough (see p. 21). In the *Kammerkonzert*, Berg did not publicly reveal the symbolism of the expanded, palindromic slow movement, but we now know that it concerned the death of Mathilde Schoenberg (see p. 342).

Finally, in the through-composed concert aria *Der Wein* (1929), settings of three Anacreontic poems by Baudelaire translated by Stefan George ('The Spirit of Wine', 'The Wine of Lovers' and 'The Wine of the Desolate'), Berg retraced in retrograde some thirty bars from the end of the second song as a transition to the third song. The text for this section reads:

> Softly we lie on the wings,
> Of wind racing onward with free rein,
> Both with the same passion.
> Away, sister, arm in arm.
> We take flight with no rest or pause,
> Into my land of dreams![95]

---

[95] As translated in Simms and Erwin (2021), 311.

Here the palindromic hinge interrupts the lovers' escape into the 'land of dreams', as Berg ruefully admitted in a letter to Hanna of 4 December 1929, when he disclosed the special musical symbolism at the midpoint, her initials, H and F: 'So also when I sang of wine – as I did this past summer – whom else does it concern but you, Hanna … and these words die away in the softest accord of H [B] and F major! [bars 140 and 141] – What follows after that can only be the song of the "Wine of the Desolate."' He then signed his letter, 'Aye, that I am and that I remain, but also remain wholly and eternally thine'.

CHAPTER 14

Round Trips, Gothic Skyscrapers, Thunderwords and Fallen Angels

'Cypherjugglers going the highroads. Seekers on the great quest.'

– Joyce, *Ulysses* (195.21)

'messages are essentially private, deciphered by each according to the influence of the moment.'

– Pierre Boulez, *Messagesquisse*

Excepting Schoenberg and Berg, active German cypherjugglers included Hanns Eisler (1898–1962), who experienced firsthand the advent of twelve-tone serialism as Schoenberg's student during the early 1920s. When Eisler's music was banned in 1933, he fled Germany and settled in Los Angeles, where he composed dozens of film scores. Because of his communist sympathies Eisler was blacklisted in Hollywood, interrogated by the House Committee on Un-American Activities, and deported in 1948. He spent his final years in East Berlin, where he resumed a lifelong friendship with Bertolt Brecht, and composed the national anthem of the German Democratic Republic.

Like many composers tied to East Germany,[1] Eisler drew inspiration from the BACH cipher, as in the *Präludium und Fuge über BACH* for string trio, Op. 46 (1934), in which the tetrachord generates through two transpositions an entire tone row.[2] But, as Eisler explained, 'the choice of the "B-A-C-H" motto is not meant to honour Johann Sebastian Bach ... The choice ... should connect much more to the bourgeois mysticism of the common musicians, who often only understand no more of Bach than the letters B-A-C-H.'[3] Another work, *Fourteen Ways to Describe the Rain* Op. 70 (*Vierzehn Arten den Regen zu beschreiben*) originated in a score for Joris Ivens's silent film *Rain* (*Regen*, 1929), but was repurposed for Schoenberg's seventieth birthday in 1944. Here Eisler not

---

[1] See Häcker (1989) and Calico (2011), who discusses ciphers by Paul Dessau.
[2] See also Hart (2018), 81–2, 129–30.
[3] Ibid., 82.

only employed a chamber-music ensemble reminiscent of *Pierrot lunaire* (1912) but introduced in an opening *Anagramm* Schoenberg's name. Thus, the violin asserted A and E-flat for the initials A and eS, while the cello's low D stood for the last letter of 'Arnold'. In the following variations, the anagrams congealed into a twelve-tone row. There was also evidence of numerological planning: while *Pierrot lunaire*, Schoenberg's Op. 21, comprised twenty-one movements in three groups of seven (3 × 7), Eisler released his composition as Op. 70 (10 × 7), with an *Anagramm* of seven bars followed by fourteen (2 × 7) variations.

Eisler's contemporary Paul Hindemith (1895–1963) did not adopt twelve-tone serialism, but did explore retrograde motion. Hindemith was a modernist who never fully jettisoned triadic tonality from his scores but explored key relationships based upon the overtone series, starting with the fifth and fourth, then proceeding through thirds and sixths, seconds and sevenths, and ending with the most distant, the tritone. In *Ludus tonalis* (*Tonal Game*, 1942), a piano cycle of twelve fugues, he graphed these relationships into a spiralling design, with increasing space between the tonic, C, and eleven other tonalities, like a solar system: 'As the distance increases, the warmth, light and power of the sun diminish, and the tones lose their closeness of relationship'.[4]

Hindemith's musical order revived centuries-old Pythagorean ideas that 'harmony is based on numbers, usually in the form of ratios that stand for intervals ... and that mathematics should therefore be understood as an ontological mediator between ideas and phenomena'.[5] These principles profoundly influenced Plato, Ptolemy and Boethius, before finding an advocate in the astronomer Johannes Kepler (1571–1630), whose *Harmonices mundi* (*Harmonies of the World*, 1618) inspired Hindemith to compose a symphony (1951) and opera (*Die Harmonie der Welt*, 1957) about the life of the astronomer.

Notwithstanding tonal centricities in his music, Hindemith did analyze according to his system Schoenberg's serial *Klavierstück* Op. 33a.[6] In addition, Hindemith composed several works in which reversible motion was a significant component. Thus, in the Clarinet Quintet Op. 30 (1923/revised 1954), the fifth movement formed the retrograde of the first, while in the Horn Concerto (1950) the slow third movement was broadly palindromic around a poem written by the composer, 'declaimed' wordlessly in recitative style by the soloist. Similarly, in *Ludus tonalis* the third fugue, in F, was palindromic. Framing the entire cycle were a *Praeludium* and *Postludium*, the latter generated by reproducing the prelude in retrograde-inversion.

---

[4] Hindemith (1941), vol. 1, 57.

[5] Bruhn (2005), 16.

[6] Hindemith (1941), vol. 1, 217–19.

No less remarkable was Hindemith's operatic scene *Hin und zurück* (*Round Trip*, 1927), written during the waning years of silent film. Here the drama rewound itself from the midpoint. After a husband murders his adulterous wife, her body is removed, and he leaps out a window. Then, a mysterious sage-like figure uncoils the action. Previous portions of text return with the order of their phrases exchanged, and the wife revives, restoring the *status quo ante*. Throughout the whole, an aunt knits a garment that increases in size, despite the negation of the plot. So, Hindemith juxtaposes two colliding temporal processes, one teleological, the other a nullifying turning around, and in the process draws upon filmic techniques. The rewinding of the plot imitates retrograde procedures in films of the 1920s, while the appearance of leitmotif-like figures coded with extra-musical meanings recalls anthologies of musical cues from the 1920s for improvising live music in theatres during screenings.[7]

Hindemith's extensive catalogue of chamber works – between 1935 and 1955 he wrote seventeen sonatas for instruments – includes one curiosity, the Sonata for Althorn and Piano (1943). A member of the saxhorn family, the althorn was eventually replaced by the alto saxophone. Playing on the double meaning of 'alt' ('alto' and 'old'), Hindemith explored in this sonata a narrative of old versus new, supplemented by eighteen lines of his own verses, this time read aloud by the performers before the finale. Titled 'Das Posthorn', the dialogue likens the althorn to the old post horn that announced the arrival of mail coaches, when speed was 'counted by straining horses' gallop', not by 'lightning prisoned up in [telegraph] cables'. The poem explains one enigmatic passage in the second movement, where Hindemith introduces persistent rhythms in Morse Code for the letters *N, k, a* and *w*, an acronym for 'Niemand kann alles wissen' ('No one can know all'; ex. 14.1).[8]

In Chapter 2 (see p. 45) we introduced Hindemith's older contemporary Béla Bartók as a Hungarian modernist who arguably applied the Golden Section and Fibonacci Series in several compositions. He was preoccupied too with symmetry on multiple levels, including mirror-like combinations of motives, themes and harmonies displaying tritonal axes, and scales (some drawn from his ethnomusicological research in Hungary and Central Europe).[9] Though not rivalling the ailihphilia of Berg, Bartók employed broadly palindromic arch forms for some major works, including the opera *Bluebeard's Castle* (1911) and ballet *The Wooden Prince* (1917), and anticipated their symmetries as early as 1909 in the Bagatelle, Op. 7 No. 12.[10] With the Fourth and Fifth String Quartets (1928

---

[7] Monchick (2012), 530, 536n.

[8] Concerning the acronym, traced to drawings of Niklaus Manuel Deutsch (*ca.* 1484–1530), see Hemken (2015), 11–21; Ehrstine (2002), 210; and Koerner (1993), 419.

[9] See Hentschel (1997) and Jyrkiäinen (2012).

[10] Fischer (2000), 282–3.

Ex. 14.1: Hindemith, Sonata for Althorn and Piano (1943)

and 1934), the composer developed five-movement plans arranged around a core third movement, mapping correspondences between the first and fifth, and second and fourth movements in tempos, themes and other elements.

To suggest an all-embracing symmetry in a composition, Bartók might design individual movements so that their internal structures reflected the macro-palindromic design of the whole. One example was the opening Allegro of the Fifth String Quartet, a Sonata Form movement with three thematic areas in the exposition (*a*, *b* and *c*) that reappeared in the recapitulation in mirror inversion *and* reverse order (*c*, *b* and *a*). The result was a seven-part arch form,[11] with a tonal scheme that traversed an ascending whole-tone scale:

	Exposition			Development	Recapitulation mirror inversion		
themes	*a*	*b*	*c*		*c*	*b*	*a*
pitch centres (whole-tone scale)	B♭	C	D	E	F♯	A♭	B♭
bar numbers	1	25	44	59	133	146	159

The movement began and ended with strident repetitions of the pitch B-flat in octave doublings, launching a graduated ascent of key areas by whole-steps; the development marked the midpoint of the process – E – the tritone that divides the octave into two equal portions. Might there be any significance to Bartók's decision to choose B-flat as the endpoints of this structure? Here we enter the realm of conjecture, though one piece of largely overlooked evidence may lead us to cryptography.

Among Bartók's unpublished *juvenilia* is a Scherzo in B-flat minor for piano solo from 1900, known as the Scherzo 'F. F. B. B.', written when the young composer was infatuated with Felicie Fábián, a classmate at the Liszt Academy in Budapest. The opening of this scherzo introduces their initials with octave leaps[12] (ex. 14.2).

---

[11] See Bartók's analysis of the quartet (1935), in Suchoff (1976), 414–15.

[12] For a facsimile of the first page, see Dille (1976), 290. Regarding Fábián, see David Cooper (2015), 18.

Ex. 14.2: Bartók, Scherzo in B-flat minor (1900)

Indeed, we know that in his schoolbooks from the 1890s Bartók occasionally contrived musical references to names, including the violinist Fränzl Ágost (August Fränzl), whose cipher and initials figure in the finale of the Piano Sonata BB 12 (1898).[13] Furthermore, around 1897, Bartók sketched ten bars of a fugue, the subject of which spelled the pitches D, A, C and B-natural, or 'Dach' (German for 'roof').[14] Third, Bartók would have been aware of ciphers in the music of his older contemporary Ernst von Dohnányi. A self-described 'Schumann Robber', the young Dohnányi derived sphinx-like ciphers on the pitch sequence B-natural, E, D and A from the forename of Heda Pongrácz in six piano pieces of 1891.[15] Bartók was perhaps unaware of them, though he probably knew well Dohnányi's piano cycle *Winterreigen* (*Winter Dances*, 1905). Its third piece, 'An Ada', prominently displays a dozen or so iterations of A-D-A; and in the tenth, a postlude titled *Ade*, Dohnányi dwells on the pitches A-D-E (Latin for 'Farewell').

The Hungarian scholar László Somfai has documented how in the second movement of the First String Quartet (1909) Bartók planned to insinuate BACH in transposition, but then, perhaps at the urging of Zoltán Kodály, removed it.[16] Two years later, though, in *Bluebeard's Castle*, Bartók did introduce the cipher into the transition to the postlude that follows the culminating scene of the Seventh Door, albeit in transposed guise as G-flat, F, A-flat and G-natural, against an organ pedal point on B-flat, leading László Vikárius to propose that the static pitch possibly symbolized Bártok *and* Bach.[17] These references to the Thomaskantor, along with allusions to the *St. Matthew Passion* in the *Cantata profana*,[18] beg the question whether Bartók later intentionally incorporated BACH into the opening fugal subject of the *Music for Strings, Percussion and*

---

[13] Somfai (1996), 38.
[14] Dille (1976), 192.
[15] Wong (2010), 107ff.
[16] Somfai (2019).
[17] Communication from Dr. Vikárius of 15 October 2023.
[18] Vikárius (2022).

Celesta (see p. 26). That work from 1936, two years after the Fifth String Quartet, returns us to its first movement, and the stubborn B-flat octaves that frame it. Could they refer to the composer's initials? Could the prominent reference to E in the development, midpoint of the movement, form part of a large-scale cipher highlighting the letters 'B' and 'é' in Béla?

∞ i

Another seminal modernist, Igor Stravinsky, resisted neither the magnetism of musical symmetry nor BACH, especially in works from 1951 and beyond, when he committed to dodecaphony. His privileging of symmetry is evident, for instance, in several occurrences of what Joseph Straus labelled 'retrograde symmetry' and 'inversional pairings of rows'.[19] Thus, in the Cantata (1952) we find palindromic melodic lines, scrupulously bracketed in the score, and mirror canons. In the *Canticum sacrum* (1955) and *Threni* (1958), Stravinsky elaborated symmetrical five-part plans inspired by the bejewelled architecture of St. Mark's in Venice, with its pentagram of domes; in the former, premiered in the cathedral, the fifth movement unfolds as the retrograde of the first, while in the latter, the second and fourth movements display retrograde canons. Among other examples is the television drama *The Flood* (1962), in which Stravinsky released the deluge through a strict palindrome. Here the 'retrograde symmetry ... seems to imply continuation in both directions, toward both a time before and a time after the flood ... with the beginning and end only implied'.[20]

The music of Webern, likened to 'a perpetual Pentecost for all who believe in music',[21] proved decisive for Stravinsky's adoption of serialism. Webern's String Quartet Op. 28 (1938), based on a tone row emanating from the BACH tetrachord, may well have renewed Stravinsky's interest in the cipher and its potential for treatment within serial contexts[22] (ex. 14.3).

As early as 1930, Stravinsky had instilled in the fugal subject for the second movement of the *Symphony of Psalms* three chromatic tetrachords that impress as anagram-like reorderings of BACH. And if we extract the uppermost pitches of the third and fourth bars, we discover that Stravinsky traced the retrograde of the cipher, HCAB (ex. 14.4).

Stravinsky became preoccupied with these four pitches, which appear in various combinations in several tone rows. Thus, in *Canticum sacrum*, which

---

[19] Straus (2001).

[20] Ibid., 134.

[21] Stravinsky and Craft (1960), 98.

[22] Similarly, the Polish composer Krzysztof Penderecki incorporated BACH in two twelve-tone rows of the *Passion according to Luke* (1966), where it appears as the final tetrachord of the series. Schwinger (1989), 203.

Ex. 14.3: Webern, String Quartet, Op. 28, Tone Row (1938)

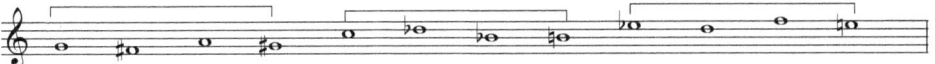

Ex. 14.4: Stravinsky, *Symphony of Psalms*, Second Movement (1930)

exhibits his first twelve-tone row, the first four pitches are A, B, C and B-flat. In later works he reordered the same content in rows for *Agon* and *The Flood* (B, A, B-flat, C), *A Sermon, a Narrative, and a Prayer* and *Requiem Canticles* (C, B, A, B-flat), and *The Dove Descending Breaks the Air* (A, B-flat, C, B). What unites these respellings are their symmetries, consisting of a whole-step, half-step and whole-step, or a half-step, whole-step and half-step, recalling Webern's fascination with miniature, crystalline formations.[23]

Stravinsky composed one other serial work in which the row subsumed the BACH cipher, though in a more unusual way. For *In memoriam Dylan Thomas* (1954) he limited the prime form to just five pitches filling out the chromatic space within the *major* third C and E – E, E-flat, C, C-sharp and D. The original prime row thus concealed the cipher as C-sharp, C, E-flat and D, rendering the remaining E, cryptographically speaking, a null pitch (ex. 14.5).

The question remains, why did Stravinsky limit his row to five pitches? The answer lies in Dylan Thomas's poem 'Do not go gentle into that good night', which, set for tenor and string quartet, formed the centre of the memorial, framed by solemn dirge canons for four trombones and string quartet. In short, 'the number *five* [served] as an underlying structural determinant of the text'.[24] Thus, Thomas's poem was a villanelle, with *five* tercets and one quatrain. His chosen metre was iambic pentameter, in verses of ten syllables comprising *five* iambs

Ex. 14.5: Stravinsky, *In memoriam Dylan Thomas* (1954)

---

[23] See Smyth (1999).

[24] Gauldin and Benson (1985), 168.

each. And he developed rhyming patterns involving *five* words – 'right ... bright ... flight ... sight ... height', and 'they ... bay ... way ... gay ... pray'. Restricting the row to five pitches was one way to reflect musically the poet's numerology. Other strategies included placing the dirge canons in the metre of 5/4, designing the song so that it contained fifty-five bars (5 × 11), and organizing the framing canons (with intervals of *five* beats between the trombones' entries) so that they alternated between *five* trombone canons and *five* ritornelli for string quartet. Furthermore, Robert Gauldin and Warren Benson suggested that Stravinsky selected E as the first pitch of his prime row because it was the *fifth* letter of the alphabet.[25]

Did Stravinsky secrete other hidden meanings through letter-number equivalents? Noticing that he specified timings of 1'27", 4'30" and 1'23" for the three movements, Gauldin and Benson proposed that 27" could be read as the sum of 9" + 18", or in letters, 'I.S.'; and 23", of 4" + 19", or 'D.T.'. Also, 4'30" prescribed for the middle movement was exactly 270", or, again, 'I.S.'.[26] From these initialisms there was but a short leap to the numbers 14 and 41, with their numerological connections to J. S Bach. So perhaps Stravinsky in his last years turned not only to palindromic symmetries, ciphers and numerology, but also to the esoteric pursuit of musical gematria. In retrospect, the composer's decision in 1958 to produce as his first completely twelve-tone composition *Threni*, based on the Lamentations of Jeremiah, was significant: the textual acrostic formed from the letters of the Hebrew alphabet from *aleph* to *tav* likely resonated with a composer who found meaning and solace in puzzles, large and small.

ii

Among Stravinsky's patrons was the Swiss conductor and philanthropist Paul Sacher, at the time among the wealthiest individuals in the world, who commissioned the Concerto in D (1947) and *A Sermon, a Narrative, and a Prayer* (1962). Stravinsky did not live long enough to participate in the celebration organized for the benefactor's seventieth birthday (1976) by the Russian cellist Mstislav Rostropovich.[27] For that occasion, eleven composers furnished works for solo cello, joined by a twelfth, Pierre Boulez, who wrote a piece for solo cello supported by an ensemble of six. Shared by the dozen contributions was a six-note cipher drawn from Sacher's name – E-flat (e**S**), **A**, **C**, B-natural (**H**), E and D (**Re**); ex. 14.6.

In duration, these offerings range from Benjamin Britten's *Tema Sacher* (*ca.* one minute) to Klaus Huber's *Transpositio ad Infinitum* (*ca.* twelve minutes).

---

[25] Ibid., 178.

[26] Ibid., 179.

[27] See further, Rostropovich (1976) and Dunnagan (2011).

Ex. 14.6: Sacher Cipher

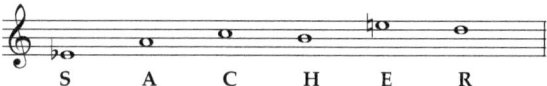

S   A   C   H   E   R

Almost all cite the motto literally, identified by letters next to the relevant pitches in the scores. Only Henze does not employ the complete cipher in his *Capriccio*, asserting that the enciphered letters are 'more or less recognizable as such … manifesting themselves in the most varied forms and continually changing into different constellations'.[28] There is considerable range, too, in the cipher's frequency, with just a few allusions by Henze compared to generous applications in Witold Lutosławski's *Sacher-Variation*.

Though the original plan was to assemble variations on the shared cipher, the pieces reference other historical forms and genres, and explore high modernist, extended cello techniques. Thus, Heinz Holliger exploits the Sacher hexachord in recurring *basso ostinato* figures that recall distant Baroque antecedents, while Wolfgang Fortner's *Zum Spielen* includes three internal variations, of which one is a strict canon.[29] And Luciano Berio's *Les mots sont allés* (*The Words Have Gone*) impresses as a 'speaking', if textless, accompanied recitative.

In a separate category is the Argentine 'neo-expressionist' Alberto Ginastera's *Puneña No. 2*, Op. 45; here the hexachord conjures up the Puna, the highlands of the Andes, and 'the sonorous world of this mysterious heart of South America that was the Inca empire'.[30] In two movements, the first (*Harawi*) offers a pensive love song that alternates between the cipher and a transformed folk theme from Cuzco (the ancient Incan capital) filling out the total chromatic by privileging the six pitches *not* in the cipher. The second movement (*Wayno Karnavalito*) celebrates a 'tumultuous Carnival dance on the principal theme "eSA-CHERe", full of rhythms of charangos [small Andean lutes] and Indian drums, coloured costumes, ponchos and masks, as well as of Indian corn alcohol'.[31] Enhancing the exoticism of the score is a battery of special effects, including nuanced quarter tones and indeterminate pitches, all reinforcing the symbolic encounter between European and pre-Columbian cultures.

At least four compositions, by Klaus Huber, Holliger, Henri Dutilleux and Boulez, extend encrypted meanings beyond the Sacher hexachord. In *Transpositio ad Infinitum* Huber incorporates four intermezzo-like passages marked

---

[28] Prefatory note to *Capriccio*.

[29] In 1950 Fortner had treated BACH contrapuntally in the *Phantasie über die Tonfolge b-a-c-h für zwei Klaviere, neun Solo-Instrumente und Orchester*.

[30] From Ginastera's prefatory note to the score.

[31] Ibid.

Piano dolce con espressione*, *Aliquote*, *Undertones* and *Lento*,** forming an acrostic on Sacher's first name. Holliger's *Chaconne* concludes with a ***Post Scriptum that appends the conductor's initials. And in *Trois strophes sur le nom de Sacher* Dutilleux adds a brief quotation from Bartók's *Music for Strings, Percussion and Celesta*, which Sacher had premiered in Basel in 1937. Here Dutilleux revives the symmetrical fugal subject from Bartók's first movement, presented in its prime form atop its inversion (ex. 14.7), yielding a wedge-like gesture that, Dutilleux noted, embraced the Sacher cipher in *Trois strophes*.[32]

Dutilleux was sufficiently intrigued by the cipher to pursue it in a later work commissioned by Sacher, *Mystère de l'instant* (1989), the ninth movement of which was titled *Métamorphoses (sur le nom de Sacher)*. In the case of *Messagesquisse*, Boulez contrived a portmanteau word play ('message(s)-sketch') that he interpreted in a dedicatory note to Sacher:

Les messages sont souvent secrets	Messages are often secrets
La musique a cet avantage: point de mots,	Music claims this advantage: no words,
les messages sont essentiellement personnels,	messages are essentially private,
déchiffrés par chacun selon l'emprise du moment.	deciphered by each according to the influence of the moment.

By scoring for seven celli, Boulez was able to accumulate six-part vertical alignments of the Sacher hexachord in the supporting celli, freeing the principal cello to embellish the cipher. The seven musicians symbolized an aliquot of seventy ($7 \times 10 = 70$) that alluded to the anniversary of the septuagenarian.[33] There may be other, undisclosed 'messages' in this score; to be sure, the cipher was meaningful enough to Boulez that he reused it in *Répons* (1981), *Dérive 1* (1984), *Incises* (1994) and *sur Incises* (1996, for Sacher's *ninetieth* birthday).[34]

The Sacher project replenished the tradition of cryptographic homage. In a similar way, several modern Italian composers perpetuated Bach's name, furthering the nineteenth-century precedent of Arrigo Boito, whose cryptogram for the Thomaskantor – *Fede a Bach* ('Trust in Bach') – was set in 1888 as an organ fugue by Marco Enrico Bossi (ex. 14.8).

In 1910 Feruccio Busoni unleashed his *Fantasia contrappuntistica*, a virtuoso juggernaut for piano in the Lisztian tradition that placed a chorale at either end framing fully four fugues (two of them constructed on the BACH cipher and subject and countersubjects from *Die Kunst der Fuge*), supplemented by several

---

[32] Potter (1997), 76.

[33] Hirsbrunner (1985), 160.

[34] Whittall (2016), 366–7.

Ex. 14.7: Dutilleux, *Trois strophes sur le nom de Sacher* (1976)

Ex. 14.8: M. E. Bossi, Fugue (1888)

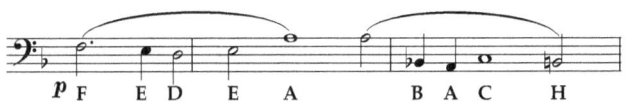

internal variations and a cadenza. Busoni made no fewer than four versions, the last (1922), for two pianos. Bach's imposing edifices of sound triggered for many of Busoni's generation powerful associations with the Gothic, leading him to imagine not only soaring arches of medieval cathedrals, but also their modern counterparts in the rising skyscrapers of Chicago encountered during his American concert tour of 1910.[35] At some point Busoni, who aspired to become an architect, made a sketch of the fourteenth-century Palace of Popes in Avignon, with the sections of its façade labelled so that they corresponded to the divisions of the *Fantasia*.

In the culmination of the score the chorale returns in the high treble over percussive repetitions of the tetrachord in the bass that arguably left their mark two decades later on the second *Ricercar sul nome 'Bach' (Ostinato)* of Alfredo Casella, released in 1932 along with the *Prélude à une fugue imaginaire sur le nom de Bach* by Bossi's pupil Gian Francesco Malipiero in a Bach issue of *La Revue musicale* (ex. 14.9).

Ex. 14.9: G. F. Malipiero, *Prélude à une fugue imaginaire sur le nom de Bach* (1932)

---

[35] Roberge (1996).

Then, in 1949, Malipiero's student Bruno Maderna based his *Fantasia per due pianoforte* on the cipher,[36] while in 1952, the serialist Luigi Dallapiccola completed for his daughter the collection *Quaderno musicale di Annalibera*, eleven short piano pieces that recalled the aphoristic gestures of Webern's piano Variations, Op. 27 and Schoenberg's citations of BACH in his orchestral Variations, Op. 31. Dallapiccola manipulated his row to construct webs of Bachian ciphers, and in 1954 made an orchestral arrangement of the piano work, *Variazioni*, that further confirmed his debt to Schoenberg. In the *Canti di liberazione* (*Songs of Liberation*, 1955), Dallapiccola continued to mine the BACH tetrachord,[37] and yet found his own voice in a 'soundscape' that was 'distinct, with gentle rhythms and mercurial gestures, softer dynamics, and, above all, a "tonal" surface'.[38]

More recently, in 2015, Carlotta Ferrari memorialized Bach's name in a chaconne for solo violin that, through the magic of scordatura retuned the four open strings from G-D-A-E to B-natural-C-A-B-flat. The composition contains uncanny repetitions of minimalist scraps – a single pitch, unassuming half-step or whole-step – distributed across the four strings, and then in overlapping patterns. Ferrari purposefully limited these snippets to four *notated* pitches – B-flat, A, C and B – so that the soloist reading the score was constantly reminded of the Thomaskantor's 'presence' through *Augenmusik*. But because of the scordatura, the b-flat" played on the E-string sounds a tritone below, as e"; the pitch c" on the D-string, a second below, or b-flat'; and the pitch b on the G-string, a major third above as d-sharp' (since the A-string is not retuned, there is no change for pitches played on that string). In short, the audience hears not literal repetitions of the BACH cryptogram at their original pitch level, but distortions caused by the adjusted tunings. That Ferrari chose to write a chaconne for solo violin is surely no coincidence – the title alludes to the Chaconne in D minor from Bach's second Partita (BWV 1004), now recalled in ghost-like communications from the past.

Ferrari cast her cipher net further into the past to capture the seventeenth-century madrigalist Carlo Gesualdo, Prince of Venosa, whose name inspired a *Ciaconna e fuga* for organ (2016).[39] But no post-modern (or modern) Italian composer rivalled the avid cryptography of Mario Castelnuovo-Tedesco (1895–1968). Between 1953 and 1967 he crafted fifty-two 'Greeting Cards' for different scorings, from solo piano or guitar to duets and string quartet, all based

---

[36] See Fearn (1987).

[37] Dallapiccola (2000), 13ff.

[38] Alegant (2010), 33.

[39] In this case she derived a *soggetto cavato*: Car (fa = F) – lo (sol = G) Ge (re = D) – su (ut = C) – al (la = A) – do (sol = G) Da (fa = F) V (ut = C) – e (re = D) – no (sol = G) – sa (fa = F).

Ex. 14.10: Castelnuovo-Tedesco, Greeting Card No. 4 (Walter Gieseking)

on the names of friends, colleagues and students that he gathered into his Op. 170. The recipients included André Previn, Jascha Heifetz, Gregor Piatigorsky, Walter Gieseking, Andrés Segovia, Luigi Dallapiccola and many others. The composer relied upon a simple method to generate these 'alphabet pieces': first, he wrote out ascending and descending chromatic scales from a to a", and then added the alphabet letters from 'a' to 'z' below.

Because the descending scale formed the retrograde (or inversion) of the ascending form, each name yielded two different musical options. Also, because the placement of the letters arbitrarily determined the pitch sequence of the cryptograms, encipherments could produce angular melodic contours that strained against tonal readings. In Greeting No. 4 (Walter Gieseking), the cipher emerged as a nine-note pandiatonic arabesque reminiscent of the music of Debussy and Ravel, staples of the German pianist's repertoire (ex. 14.10).

Castelnuovo-Tedesco chose to title this gift *Mirage*, a verbal double entendre, as it conflated Debussy's *Image* and Ravel's *Miroirs*.

❧ iii

While composers in the twentieth century and beyond continued to manipulate verbal cryptograms in their music, during the 1920s and 30s the Irish novelist and poet James Joyce pursued the obverse art: hiding musical allusions within *literary* contexts. After developing stream of consciousness techniques, he abandoned linear narratives and submerged his prose into free sequences of characters' thoughts, usually in first-person present or third-person past tense. 'Je suis au bout de l'anglais' ('I am at the end of English'), he quipped to the Swiss sculptor August Suter: 'I really could not … use words in their ordinary connections … [T]hey do not express how things are in the night, in the different stages – conscious, then semi-conscious, then unconscious … When morning comes of course everything will be clear again … I'll give them back their English language'.[40] And so, Joyce created a radically new, multi-layered prose style into which he buried puns, acrostics, anagrams, acronyms, semagrams, number symbolism[41] and steganographic sleights of hand,[42] not to mention cryptograms and code-like sigla recorded in notebooks for the principal characters.[43] To his brother, Stanislaus, Joyce wryly observed, 'After all, the Holy Roman Catholic Church was built on a pun' – presumably a reference to Matthew 16:18: 'Thou are Peter [*Petrus*] and upon this rock [*petram*] I will build my church'. When asked to reveal the schema for the *Penelope* episode from *Ulysses*, Joyce demurred, though he admitted that he had 'put in so many enigmas and puzzles that it will keep the professors busy for centuries arguing over what I meant, and that's the only way of insuring one's immortality'.[44]

Musical techniques informed Joyce's now mellifluous, now rasping prose. There are no better examples than the ten onomatopoetic 'thunderwords' introduced periodically throughout *Finnegans Wake*. These breathless, sesquipedalian concatenations comprise 100 and, in one case, 101 run-on letters, sometimes combined into composite polylingual blends that may be parsed as individual linguistic units or apprehended as sweeping pseudo-musical gestures possessing their own rhythmically rhyming energy. Thus, the first thunder word, announcing the fall of the hod carrier Finnegan, breaks like a resounding thunderclap, with an initial reference to the Tower of Babel that then descends into jumbled variants of the word 'thunder' in Hindi, Arabic, Japanese, Greek, French, Italian, English, Portuguese, Swedish, Irish and Danish: ('bababadalgharaghtakamminarronnkonnbronntonnerronntuonnthunntrovarrhounawnsakawntoohoohoordenenthurnuk!)'.[45] It is the all-encompassing 'voice of God made audible through the noise of Finnegan's fall'.[46]

Joyce possessed, like his father, a distinctive tenor voice, and seriously considered music as a career. He grew up steeped in choral music, Irish folksong and the world of 'old Italian operas that seemed to have been written especially

---

[40] Ellmann (1982), 546.

[41] For Joyce's use of numbers in *Ulysses*, see Bulson (2020).

[42] See Wawrzycka (2018).

[43] Sixty-six notebooks containing preliminary ideas and working drafts for the novel, with well over 10,000 pages of material, are preserved at SUNY-Buffalo. Regarding the sigla, see McHugh (1976).

[44] Ibid., 521.

[45] Kark, gargarahat (Hindi), ra'd (Arabic), kaminari (Japanese), brontê (Greek), tonnerre (French), tuono (Italian), thunn (English), trovão (Portuguese), åska (Swedish), scan (Irish), torden (Danish), tórnach (Irish).

[46] Campbell and Robinson (2005), 16.

for Irish tenors'.⁴⁷ Almost inevitably, he was drawn to the cult of Wagnerism.⁴⁸ Not surprisingly, Joyce adopted Wagner's leitmotif techniques, and filled *Ulysses* and *Finnegans Wake* with specific references to Wagner's music and his circle.⁴⁹ Some were readily evident, but others sufficiently veiled to remain ambiguous. Thus, in *Finnegans Wake* (149.13): 'And I suppose you heard I had a wag on my ears?', interpreted by Paul Martin to refer to 'Wagner', but by Roland McHugh, to 'earwig'.⁵⁰

The range of the author's musical references in his novels was broad indeed. In *Joyce's Grand Operoar* Matthew Hodgart and Ruth Bauerle teased out operatic allusions in *Finnegans Wake*, the lion's share concerning (in descending order) Wagner and Verdi, Mozart, Meyerbeer and Puccini, with representation of Donizetti, Gilbert and Sullivan, Gounod, Handel, Mascagni and Rossini.⁵¹ Of modernists the authors garnered entries for Berg, Busoni (whom Joyce met in Zurich), Debussy, Fauré, Holst, Janáček, Schoenberg, Richard Strauss, Stravinsky and Kurt Weill. On another level of analyzing what Joseph Campbell labelled 'a gigantic wheeling rebus',⁵² there is evidence that in the novel Joyce concealed several references to solmization syllables. Consider, for instance, this befuddling passage early in Part I:

> 566 A.D. On Baalfire's night of this year after deluge a crone that hadde a wickered Kish for to hale dead turves from the bog lookit under the blay of her Kish as she ran for to sothisfeige her cowrieosity and be me sawl but she found hersell sackvulle of swart goody quickenshoon and small iligant brogues, so rich in sweat. (13.36–14.4)

'Be me sawl' can be *heard* (*not* read) as a transformation of 'B, mi, sol', the pitches B (or B-flat), E (mi) and G (sol).⁵³ Was Joyce slipping into his prose pitches from actual musical motives circling in his ear? For Joyce, B, E and G, or, say, a descending fifth and ascending third, would have offered a gesture replete with possible musical sources. Here Hodgart and Bauerle proposed the dramatic passage from Act I, Scene 3 of Wagner's *Die Walküre*, in which Siegmund discloses his identity to Sieglinde: 'Siegmund heiss ich, und Siegmund bin ich' ('My name is Siegmund, and Siegmund I am'). Obligingly, his

---

⁴⁷ Imbs (1936), 109.
⁴⁸ See further, Ross (2020), 469ff.
⁴⁹ See the appendix to Martin (1991), 185–221.
⁵⁰ Martin (1991),187; McHugh (2016),149.
⁵¹ Hodgart and Bauerle (1997).
⁵² Campbell and Robinson (1944), 3.
⁵³ Hodgart and Bauerle (1997), 118.

part indeed began with a descending fifth and ascending third, but traversing the pitches F-sharp, B, D and G, and thus at a different transposition level than 'B, mi, sol'.

Before we clamber off the slippery slope of solmization, there is yet another piece of evidence in the second part of Book II, the children's study hour, annotated in the margin of p. 260 as 'IMAGINABLE ITINERARY THROUGH THE PARTICULAR UNIVERSAL'. Here Joyce's impenetrable prose refers to the medieval trivium (Grammar, Logic and Rhetoric) and quadrivium (Arithmetic, Music, Geometry and Astronomy),[54] but there is also a listing of great men ('menly about peebles', that is, 'mainly about people'), where we find 'under Guido d'Arezzo's Gadeway' (260.12–13), a reference to the eleventh-century inventor of the musical alphabet (see p. 63). Then, just pages later (272.12–14) we read: 'Please stop if you're a B.C. minding missy, please do. But should you prefer A.D. stepplease'. Linking the two is an entry in the left margin of p. 272, where we discover a bit of musical notation – aptly enough, the four pitches B, C, A, D (ex. 14.11) – confirmation that Joyce was familiar with musical cryptography, and its roots in Guidonian solmization. At the least, this cryptogram arouses our suspicion that other musical ciphers, even if not explicitly notated, but transmitted through homonymic plays of assonance and consonance, are active in the novel.[55] They could well represent the author's broader strategy of engaging cryptography to conceal 'secret knowledge from all but the few', to 'delight in [the] deliberate obfuscation [that] can be seen on nearly every page of the book'.[56]

One other (musical) example of 'deliberate obfuscation' dominates the celebrated Sirens episode of *Ulysses*, set largely in the Ormond Hotel in Dublin, from which the barmaids Douce and Kennedy observe a cavalcade along the River Liffey. They are the Sirens who flirt with customers. Resisting their seductive charms is Leopold Bloom, who arrives at the hotel after visiting several Dublin shops. Much of the episode alternates between the Ormond and Bloom's meanderings, seemingly forming a linear narrative, although the events occur simultaneously, and thus create a type of verbal counterpoint. For as Joyce explained in 1919, he conceived the entire episode as a *fuga per canonem*, as he 'did not know in what other way to describe the seductions of music beyond which Ulysses travels'.[57]

---

[54] Campbell and Robinson (1944), 163ff.

[55] For further possibilities, see Hodgart and Bauerle (1997), 122, 130, 138, 141, 146, 164, 181, 193, 199, 224, 227, 229 and 234.

[56] Staples (1965), 167, 168.

[57] Letter of 6 August 1919; Gilbert (1966), 129.

Ex. 14.11: James Joyce, *Finnegans Wake* (1939)

Fuga per canonem ('fugue through canon'), a recondite term found in counterpoint treatises, has prompted questions largely unanswered until 2013,[58] when Susan Sutliff Brown revealed Joyce's source to be the entry for 'Fugue' in the second edition of *Grove's Dictionary of Music and Musicians* (1906).[59] Its author was Ralph Vaughan Williams (see p. 246), who invoked the term and others Joyce recorded in a copybook, now in the National Library of Ireland, that preserves a partial draft of the Sirens episode.[60] Here we find in Joyce's Italianized summary 'tela contrappuntistica' ('contrapuntal web'), 'raccorciamento' ('diminution') and 'stretto maestrale' ('masterly stretto'), all from Vaughan Williams's article.[61]

How Joyce's episode unfolds a rigorous fugue is not clear, though he may have provided a clue by inserting the lines 'Done. Begin!' a page and a half into the episode and, at its very end, '*Done.*' Perhaps the imperative marks the beginning of the fugue; the ending of the episode, its conclusion. What about the prefatory material before 'Begin!'? If he intended his fugue to simulate one of J. S. Bach, then Joyce might have been thinking of a prelude and fugue, after the forty-eight of the *Well-Tempered Clavier*, Books I and II. And, he may have been aware that Bach often linked preludes to fugues by recycling motivic elements that appear in the preludes and then reemerge in more refined versions in the fugues. Perhaps significantly, the opening words of *Sirens*, 'bronze by gold', return to mark the putative entrance of the fugue. Furthermore, as Heath Lees pointed out, 'the first four sentences of "Sirens" begin with initial letters (**B**ronze, **C**hips, **H**orrid and **A**nd) that form an anagram of Bach's name'.[62]

Whether the *Sirens* was in some sense a homage to Bach will likely remain unanswered, as will whether Joyce's fugal machinations were in response to Vaughan Williams's sketch of a prototypical fugue by the Thomaskantor. But, to return to the chase, how might we perceive the subject and answer in Joyce's breathless 'flight' (*fuga*) of voices?

Of the parade of characters in *Sirens* the principals are the two barmaids, identified as 'bronze' (Lydia Douce) and 'gold' (Mina Kennedy), and the roving

---

[58] Susan Sutliff Brown (2013).
[59] Reprinted in Vaughan Williams (1987), 286–302.
[60] See Ferrer (2013), 328ff.
[61] Ibid., 296, 298.
[62] Lees (1984).

Bloom. Like a fugal subject the barmaids appear throughout the 'composition' in a range of nominal variations (that is, 'musical' transpositions – 'bronze by gold', 'gildedlettered', 'goldbronze', 'bronze gigglegold', 'goldenly', 'bronze whiteness', 'goldwhisky', 'Girlgold', 'gilded arch', 'bronze and rose' and 'weary gold'). If the barmaids represent the fugal subject,[63] then plausibly Bloom is the fugal answer. Here, too, Joyce leads his protagonist through a variety of 'statements', including 'Bloowho', 'Bloowhose', 'greaseaseabloom', 'Old Bloom', 'Blue Bloom', 'Wise Bloom', 'Bloohimwhom', 'Bloo smi', 'soft Bloom', 'lonely Bloom', 'bootsboy Bloom' and 'Bloom alone'. Venturing further, we might detect a few specialized fugal techniques, including diminution of the subject, in which 'gold' and 'bronze' are run together or closely juxtaposed: 'In a giggling peal young goldbronze voices blended, Douce with Kennedy your other eye. They threw young heads back, bronze gigglegold, to let freefly their laughter' (260.6–9). On the other hand, Joyce might have had augmentation in mind when he designed these examples of more leisurely, spacious prose: 'Yes, gold from anear by bronze from afar' (264), and 'Gold in your pocket, brass in your face' (285). Next, stretto, from the Italian for 'strait' or 'narrow', may have determined the tightly packed 'Bloom. Old Bloom. Blue Bloom is on the rye' (262). And finally, Joyce perhaps marked the arrival and intensification of a pedal point with the tapping cane of the blind piano tuner. It evolves from 'Tap' on p. 281 to 'Tap. Tap. Tap. Tap. Tap. Tap. Tap. Tap' and 'A stripling, blind, with a tapping cane, came taptaptapping' on p. 289. Here the tuner has returned to the hotel to retrieve his tuning fork; for Anthony Burgess, 'his stick [symbolizes] the fixed and unchanging note of the fork itself, holding all the divergent strands of counterpoint together'.[64] These examples illustrate some ways that Joyce brought his freighted prose into the abstract realm of music, 'toward a playfulness with the sound of language without much regard for a coherent narrative'.[65]

By the time Joyce died in 1941, two years after releasing *Finnegans Wake*, composers had begun distilling the fragrant musicality of his work.[66] The results ranged from a relatively conventional song setting by Frank Bridge of 'Goldenhair' (1925) from Joyce's poetry collection *Chamber Music*, to Luciano Berio's *Tema (Omaggio a Joyce)* (1958), an electronic tape piece featuring the voice of Cathy Berberian, who read material from the prelude of the 'Sirens' episode in *Ulysses*. Here the 'text' 'consists entirely of dislocated phrases from the text. They tell no story, so there is nothing to distract the reader from

---

[63] Another possibility is that they symbolize two different subjects, so that *Sirens* unfolds as a double fugue.

[64] Burgess (1973), 85.

[65] Hastings (2022), 124.

[66] For a list, see http://www.waywordsandmeansigns.com/about/james-joyce-music/

texture and rhythm – save that the mind, confronted with isolated images, begins to build hypothetical bridges between them, generating new meanings'.[67] Arguably the epitome of Berio's Joycean pursuits, though, was *Sinfonia* (1968), specifically its scherzo, in which the third movement from Mahler's Second Symphony formed the backdrop, like a 'river running through a constantly-changing landscape, disappearing from time to time underground, only to emerge later totally transformed'.[68] Into this current Berio infused a collage of quotations from Bach, Beethoven, Berlioz, Brahms, Debussy, Mahler, Schoenberg, Berg, Webern, Richard Strauss, Ravel, Stravinsky, Hindemith and Boulez[69] that offered a compressed 'history of music'.[70] Against this display eight amplified soloists presented various texts, largely spoken and drawn from Samuel Beckett, though including oblique references to Joyce.

Among other responses was the *Joyce Book* (1932), an early collaborative song anthology that tapped his *Pomes penyeach* (1927), with contributions by thirteen composers, among them Arnold Bax, Albert Roussel, John Ireland, Roger Sessions, Arthur Bliss, Herbert Howells and George Antheil. The last, the self-proclaimed 'Bad Boy of Music', enjoyed a special relationship with Joyce. In 1923 the author attended a piano recital by Antheil that sparked a riot, and a private hearing of the composer's 'ultra-modern' work, *Ballet mécanique*, a futurist vision of mechanical noise originally meant to accompany a post-cubist film by Fernand Léger. When the *Ballet* premiered at the Théatre des Champs Elysées in 1926 as a concert piece with an 'orchestra' of player pianos, xylophones, electric bells, propellers, bass drums, tam-tam and siren, it too provoked a disturbance, impelling Ezra Pound to exclaim to the audience, 'Vous *êtes* tous des imbéciles' ('You are all imbeciles').[71] Joyce was quite impressed by the novel cacophony, and somehow even found one passage 'like Mozart'.[72] Antheil later recalled that Joyce 'had an encyclopaedic knowledge of music'.[73] The two contemplated a collaboration, and settled on a new opera about the Cyclops episode in *Ulysses*. Antheil envisioned an ambitious work four hours in duration, but the project soon floundered – only three pages in score survived, treating just the first line of Joyce's text. Once again Antheil intended the orchestra to

---

[67] Osmond-Smith (1991), 61–2.

[68] Losada (2004), 31.

[69] For details, see Osmond-Smith (1985), 7–71.

[70] Ibid., 107.

[71] Imbs (1936), 101.

[72] Ibid., 57.

[73] Antheil (1945), 153.

generate mechanical effects, reinforced this time by an amplified gramophone recording and an invisible chorus hidden beneath the stage.[74]

How he would have responded in *Mr. Bloom and the Cyclops* to Joyce's concealed allusions we will never know, but during the Second World War Antheil found another way to apply cryptography by collaborating with the actress Hedy Lamarr. The two invented a device for improving Allied radio-directed submarine torpedoes. To counter the enemy's attempts to jam communications, in 1942 they secured a patent for encrypting a signal over a range of eighty-eight frequencies (like the keys of a piano), randomly altered in a process resembling what Antheil had implemented in the piano rolls for *Ballet mécanique*.

Of other composers drawn to Joyce, the young neo-Romantic Samuel Barber (1910–81) turned to *Chamber Music*, *Ulysses*, and *Finnegans Wake*.[75] With the exception of *Fadograph of a Yestern Scene* Op. 44 (1971), a late orchestral commentary on a 'punning' text from *Finnegans Wake* (7.15),[76] Barber set eight other texts as songs. Quite another matter was the music of Tōru Takemitsu (1930–96), the prolific Japanese autodidact whose fascination with Western culture was quickened by his reading of Joyce and dedication to musical ciphers. The trichord E-flat-E-A (see ex. 14.12), a half-step and perfect fourth spelling **S**(eS)-**E**-**A**, figured prominently in an extended series of water-themed works; the pitches also appeared in retrograde in his surname (Ta**k**e**m**itsu).[77]

For some twenty years he developed this compact cipher in 'Waterscape', a cycle of works that, 'like their subject, pass[ed] through various metamorphoses, culminating in a sea of tonality'.[78] They included *Garden Rain* (1974), *Waves* (1976), *Waterways* (1978), *Towards the Sea* (1981), *Rain Tree* (1981), *Rain Coming* (1982), *Rain Spell* (1982), *Rain Tree Sketch* (1982), *Wavelength* (1984), *The Sea Is Still* (1986), *Rain Dreaming* (1986), *riverrun* (1987), *I Hear the Water Dreaming* (1987), *Rain Tree Sketch II* (1992) and *Between Tides* (1993). Takemitsu subjected the ubiquitous *SEA* motive to transpositions and, furthermore, expanded the three pitches into a larger family of six or more, as if intent upon constructing an entire tone row.

---

[74] See Martin (1999).

[75] Similarly, Barber's younger American colleagues, Donald Martino (1931–2005) and David Del Tredici (1937–2023), were unable to resist Joyce's allure. Among their contributions was Del Tredici's *Syzygy* (1966), for soprano, horn and orchestra, a setting of *Ecce Puer* (1932), written on the birth of Joyce's grandson, not long after the death of his father.

[76] The neologism 'fadograph' may be read as 'faded photograph'. 'Fado' is Irish for 'old'; 'yestern', a modification of 'gestern' (German for 'yesterday').

[77] Burt (2006), 177.

[78] Preface to *Rain Coming* (1982).

Ex. 14.12: Tōru Takemitsu, SEA Cipher

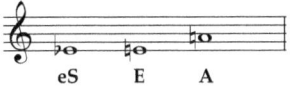

In one composition from 'Waterscape', *riverrun* for piano and orchestra, he associated the aquatic images of his cycle with Joyce by recalling the very first word of *Finnegans Wake*, a reference to the River Liffey.[79] In *Far Calls. Coming, Far!* for violin and orchestra (1980) and *A Way a Lone* for string quartet (1981), Takemitsu further pursued his Joycean project by reviving words from the closing lines of the novel. Just as the author had observed in 1926 that *Finnegans Wake* 'ends in the beginning of a sentence and begins in the middle of the same sentence',[80] so did Takemitsu's scores seem boundless, unconstrained, so that one might imagine the conclusion of *A Way a Lone* flowing naturally into the beginning of *riverrun*. By extending the *SEA* cipher with pitches a major or minor third above – for example, in its prime form, E-flat-E-A-C-sharp-F-A-flat – Takemitsu admitted some tonal markers, in this case, the triads A-C-sharp-E and C-sharp (D-flat)-F-A-flat – subcurrents of a musical 'river flowing into the sea.'[81] Curiously, while the cipher emerged and disappeared in numerous transpositions and inversions, generally Takemitsu avoided presenting it on E-flat, and thus explicitly re-spelling 'sea'. Perhaps this playing with pitch was his answer to Joyce's word games, acrostics, puns, etc.[82] In the end, pulsating through the ever equivocal music and polysemous prose were Takemitsu's own 'recirculations' of Joyce's phonocentric imagery.

Only fourteen when the war abruptly terminated in the infernos of Hiroshima and Nagasaki, the young Takemitsu sought escape in Western music. During the 1960s and beyond he came under the sway of the American musical iconoclast John Cage (1912–92), then deconstructing the meaning of music through Zen Buddhism and the *I Ching*, the Chinese book of divination, which led him to introduce elements of chance into his works. Like Takemitsu, Cage was profoundly affected by *Finnegans Wake*, and among the first to set its lines to music, in 'The Wonderful Widow of Eighteen Springs' (1942), composed three years after the novel's publication.[83] Unprecedented in conception, this

---

[79] The work in turn inspired John Luther Adams's *Eros Piano* (1989), which begins where Takemitsu's music ends.

[80] Gilbert (1966), 246.

[81] Takemitsu (1995), 112.

[82] See Miller (1998), 23ff.

[83] Cage fashioned the text from p. 556. Two Joycean pendants to the song, 'In the Name of the Holocaust' (p. 419; 1942) and 'Nowth upon Nacht' (also p. 556; 1985) would follow.

song required only three pitches for the vocal line, and specified that the piano be closed, so that the 'performer' could generate percussive rhythmic effects on its lid or underside.

Cage's most extensive engagements with Joyce came much later in his career, first in 1979, with *Roaratorio, An Irish Circus on Finnegans Wake*, for radio broadcast, deemed 'the most thoroughly Joycean work of music yet written'.[84] There followed the fantasy *James Joyce, Marcel Duchamp, Erik Satie: An Alphabet* (1982).[85] To realize it Cage created a four-step protocol: 1) choosing a book (*Finnegans Wake*); 2) selecting a key text (primarily 'James Joyce', supplemented in *An Alphabet* by 'Marcel Duchamp' and 'Erik Satie'); 3) excerpting words in the book that contained individual letters in the key text; and 4) assembling a severely abridged text so that the key letters could appear as mesostics – acrostics positioned in the middle of the lines:

> mummurrlubeJubes
> mOtherpeributts up
> lethargY's love at the end of it all
> Community
> sEnior

Cage culled these words from pages 396 and 397 of *Finnegans Wake*, where they are dispersed over fourteen lines. Here is the beginning of Joyce's text, with Cage's curtailments in italics and the first two letters of 'Joyce' in bold: 'Ah now, it was tootwoly terrific, the *mummurr-lubeJubes*! And then after that they used to be so forgetful, counting *mOtherpeributts up*.' Anyone reading Cage's redacted prose could visually apprehend the implanted vertical mesostic, while anyone listening to the performance could not. If Joyce's prose preserved some semblance of syntax, Cage's version, which 'condensed' the six hundred plus pages of the novel to a few dozen, devolved into seemingly random associations of words stripped bare of logocentric significance. Not yet satisfied, Cage added new layers to this neo-Joycean confusion by recording lists of places and sounds mentioned in *Finnegans Wake* as well as traditional Irish music, all set against his own reading of the newly crafted mesostic texts and interacting simultaneously in random counterpoint throughout the hour-long performance.

Among Cage's admirers were Pauline Oliveros, who feted him in 1986 with *Dear John: A Canon on the Name of Cage*, and Simon Jeffes, who memorialized

---

[84] Scott W. Klein (1999), 152. Cage found his title in this phrase on p. 41 of *Finnegans Wake*: 'of this longawaited Messiah of roaratorios'.

[85] See further Fetterman (1996), 216ff.; and Knowles (1999), 151–70.

the emancipator of aleatoric music in 1992 with the haunting *CAGE DEAD*, written for the avant-pop band Penguin Café Orchestra. Both compositions used ciphers, so that, implausibly enough, Cage, the zealous expunger of determinism in music, joined the select list of the Bachs, Fasch, Gade, Beach, Berg and Paul Sacher – all linked by the cryptographic affinities of their names.

∾ *iv*

To conclude this farrago of musical ciphers, riddles and other curiosities, let us consider four works from the last half century that have engaged enigmas through different means. We begin with the Greek composer Iannis Xenakis (1922–2001), whose music broached issues of continuity and discontinuity by drawing on probability theory to generate a radically new art form – stochastic music. Trained in mathematics and civil engineering, Xenakis initially showed aptitude for science rather than music. His early attempts in composition reveal experimentation with the Fibonacci Series and Golden Section,[86] but also a desire to preserve native folk music by becoming a 'Greek Bartók'[87] (during the Second World War Xenakis joined the Greek resistance and assumed a false identity[88]). After the war he found employment in the Paris studio of the architect Le Corbusier, whom Xenakis helped design the futuristic Philips Pavilion for the World's Fair of 1958 in Brussels. Mirroring the building's nine swooping, concrete hyperbolic paraboloids were his musical designs of careening string glissandi that animated the orchestral work *Metastasis* (*Beyond Immobility*, 1954).

For Xenakis the binary pair of determinism/indeterminism epitomized the paradox of modern music. There was first the striving for continuous control, as in the rigorous determinism of the serialists, in which 'the same cause [the tone row] always ha[d] the same effect', with 'no deviation, no exception'.[89] In opposition was discontinuity – 'continuous change', ultimately leading to 'absolute chance'.[90] To connect the pair Xenakis turned to kinetic gas theory and the laws of probability governing the random movements of molecules, so that 'the riddle was suddenly solved and everything fell into place'.[91]

---

[86] Harley (2004), 5, 6, 30.
[87] Ibid., 7.
[88] Varga (1996), 19.
[89] Ibid., 76.
[90] Ibid., 76, 77.
[91] Ibid., 76.

The results opened new sonic vistas. While architecture and music 'found an intimate connection'[92] between space and time in *Metastasis*, elsewhere Xenakis assembled clusters of pitches that morphed into 'arborescences', tree-like shapes that, when rotated on a pitch/time graph, produced evolving variants. He might recycle a cluster from one composition to another, thus ensuring a degree of continuity through self-quotation. Concurrently, he developed the idea of music clouds – undifferentiated, nebulous noise that could dissolve into individual pitches. Xenakis explored continuous change in another way in *Palimpsest* (1979), a chamber work for eleven musicians, named after the practice in classical antiquity and the Middle Ages of reusing tablets or parchments by scraping off old texts and inscribing new material over them. The result was a music of four tiers (wind, piano, percussion and strings), each of which could emerge now and then as a foregrounded 'text' only to recede into the background din and disappear entirely, allowing vestiges of other texts to reemerge. Or, the entire ensemble could align in a moment of clarity, playing a simple melody in rhythmic unison, as if the ensemble were 'reading' from the same page. Xenakis chose the title for this multivalent work only after completing it, but, as James Harley has affirmed, the title's relevance for understanding the music was evident on at least three levels: first, 'the idea of deriving a proliferating welter of lines from an initial contour relates to the notion of writing over an existing text. Second, there is the layering of rhythms and instrumental lines, along with the juxtaposition of instrumental groups. Third, the temporal unfolding, in which blocks of related material succeed one another ... reflects the historical succession of texts on a parchment'.[93]

If Xenakis enciphered abstract metaphors for the paradox of continuity and discontinuity, other composers confronted historical events of contemporary significance. In 1970 George Crumb (1929–2022) released *Black Angels*, for electrified string quartet with supporting percussion and special sound effects, described as a 'parable on our troubled contemporary world'. Symbolism of many kinds informs this extraordinary work, as in the prominent quotations from Schubert's *Death and the Maiden* Quartet in the centre, and Tartini's *Devil's Trill* and the *Dies irae* in the surrounding movements. Conceived 'in time of war' (*in tempore belli*), the quartet appeared at the height of the Vietnam conflict, and unfolded a numerological scheme based on the values of seven and thirteen. Crumb dated his score on Friday, 13 March 1970, associating thirteen with the devil-music of angels cast out of heaven; on the other hand, the number seven represented the antipode, God-music.

---

[92] Xenakis (1992), 10.

[93] Harley (2004), 125.

These numbers play out throughout the composition. Most literally, Crumb periodically instructs the four musicians to count from one to seven in different languages, including German, French, Russian, Hungarian, Japanese and Swahili. If we consider the two intervals that consume seven and thirteen half-steps, we may isolate the perfect fifth and minor ninth, for example C-G and C-C-sharp (octave above). Their difference, six (13–7), yields the tritone (*diabolus in musica*, or 'devil in music'), in this case G-C-sharp. These are the intervals that form the numerological substrate of the music.

Crumb revealed considerably more numerical symbolism in a synoptic diagram of *Black Angels* published with the score. The work comprises 'thirteen images from the dark land' grouped into three sections – *Departure*, *Absence* and *Return* – signifying the 'fall from grace', 'spiritual annihilation' and 'redemption'.[94] They project a programmatic narrative that betrays antecedents in J. S. Bach's *Capriccio on the Departure of a Beloved Brother* (BWV 992) and Haydn's *Farewell* Symphony, but also in Beethoven's Piano Sonata Op. 81a (*Das Lebewohl*, 1810), the three movements of which bear subtitles similar to Crumb's – *Farewell*, *Absence* and *Reunion* – on the departure from and return to Vienna of Archduke Rudolf during the Napoleonic Wars. Crumb's three sections subdivide asymmetrically into five, four and four movements, with the centrepiece, the seventh movement, forming the hinge of a palindrome in which the endpoints, the second and twelfth, third and eleventh, fourth and tenth, fifth and ninth, and sixth and eighth movements align programmatically. To underscore this symmetry, Nos. 1, 7 and 13 are titled Threnody I, II and III, with Nos. 1 and 13 specified as *Night of the Electric Insects*, Crumb's searing image of American attack helicopters in Vietnam transformed into grotesque distortions in the high strings, and No. 7, as *Black Angels!* The composer incorporates yet another reference to the reversible design by varying and organizing the scoring of the movements, marked tutti, trio, duo or solo:

scoring:	4	3	2	1	2	3	4	3	2	1	2	3	4
movement:	1	2	3	4	5	6	7	8	9	10	11	12	13

Finally, each movement betrays different manipulations of the numbers seven and thirteen, all reversed, as one might expect, during the second half of the quartet.[95] Thus, in No. 1 (7×13), Crumb brackets pitch groups meant to be repeated for seven seconds, while in No. 13 (13×7), events lasting for thirteen

---

[94] Bruns and Ben-Amots (2005), 302.
[95] See Adamenko (2007), 42.

seconds tend to dominate. Elsewhere, in No. 3, thirteen notes appear over seven, while in its counterpart, No. 11, he superimposes seven over thirteen.

While Crumb privileged numerology and recursive motion in *Black Angels*, the Polish composer Henryk Górecki (1933–2010) resorted to numerology and ciphers in several works from the 1970s on. A boy when the Nazis invaded Poland in 1939, Górecki came of age during the post-war Warsaw Pact. At that time a generation of young Polish composers, including Górecki, Lutosławski and Penderecki, were emboldened after Stalin's death in 1953 by the thaw in the Eastern bloc, and found a relative degree of artistic freedom in the Western avant-garde, whether the cerebral byways of total serialism or unmediated spontaneity of aleatoric music.

By the 1970s, this liberating trend had largely run its course, so that Górecki now developed an accessible style based upon simple, often minimalist means that might draw upon modal or triadic formations. He began to 'harness his discoveries to overtly expressive and sometimes highly personal compositions'.[96] Thus, in *Ad matrem* Op. 29 (1972), for soprano solo, chorus and orchestra, on a short phrase from the *Stabat mater* ('Mater mea, lacrimosa dolorosa'), Górecki encoded several dates pertinent to his mother's life and death in the beat patterns of the bass drum.[97] And in *Beatus vir*, Op. 38 (1979), for baritone solo, chorus and orchestra, he submerged more dates in a repeating ostinato figure and pendulating series of pealing chords. This work was a commission by Cardinal Wojtyła of Cracow for the nine-hundredth anniversary of the martyrdom of St. Stanislaus on 11 April 1079. As it happened, the cardinal became pope on 16 October 1978, so Górecki commemorated numerologically in his score that month and day as well as that of Stanislaus's death.[98] The premiere occurred on 9 June 1979, during John Paul II's pilgrimage to his country – but at a cost to the composer. The officially atheist communist regime withheld official recognition, and effectively denied that his music had succeeded in linking the patron saint of Poland to the country's first pope.

Górecki's interest in ciphers, which, 'being usually a private matter, normally [remained] undetected',[99] peaked during the 1980s and 90s. The examples include *Good Night*, Op. 63, for soprano, alto flute, three tam-tams and piano (1990), a memorial to Michael Vyner, director of the London Sinfonietta,[100] and *Recitativa i Ariosa 'Lerchenmusik'*, Op. 53, for clarinet, piano

---

[96] Ibid., 70.

[97] Ibid.

[98] Ibid., 99n. Communication from Mikołaj Górecki of 4 February 2024.

[99] Ibid., 125n.

[100] See ibid., 132–4.

Ex. 14.13: Górecki, Fourth Symphony, *Tansman Episodes* (2014)

and cello, premiered in 1986. Commissioned by Louise Lerche-Lerchenborg, '*Lerchenmusik*' prompted a pun on the German word for lark ('Lerche'), hence 'lark music', leading Górecki to imitate bird calls by embellishing his melodic lines with avicular imagery. But he also indulged in a play of ciphers, generating the motives E-C-B and B-flat-G, excerpted from her name: L**erch**e-Lerchen**b**org. Surrounding this letter symbolism were allusions to the opening of Beethoven's Piano Concerto No. 4, Op. 58, which gradually came more and more into focus as a clear quotation.

Górecki's most substantial cipher composition was Symphony No. 4, Op. 85 (*Tansman Epiodes*), completed in short score in 2006; the full score, realized by his son, Mikołaj, received its premiere in London in 2014. The idea for the symphony originated from a festival in Łódź, where Alexandre Tansman, the 'musical plenipotentiary of Poland in the Western world',[101] was born in 1897. On the first page of the autograph Górecki revealed how he generated a cryptogram from 'Aleksander Tansman' by using the readily available letter names and four solfège syllables for 'l' (*la*), 'r' (*re*), 't' (*ut*) and 'm' (*mi*), leaving only two letters, 'k' and 'n', as null values. The resulting melody (ex. 14.13) exhibited two salient features.

First, the prominence of the pitch A, heard five times, established a tonal centre for the work, which began in A minor and ended in A major, reactivating the traditional minor-to-major trope. And second, the cryptogram unfolded a nearly exact palindrome around the second 'e' of 'Aleksander'.

The Tansman cipher totally dominates the first movement, where it emerges in small, cell-like units, each repeated several times, lending the music an inexorable quality ruptured only by *fff* drum strokes at the end of each unit. These obsessive repetitions enable Górecki to dispense with developing thematic material in favour of a 'static' music that gathers its potency from the accretive force of sheer massed sound. Then, when the cipher fully reemerges in the finale, Górecki unexpectedly introduces near the end the 'Siegfried' motive from Wagner's *Ring*. Its purpose is no less clear than the Beethoven reference in *Lerchenmusik*, and thus remains another unsolved riddle. But when the final, A major chord (*sffff*) reverberates after eighteen crunching, dissonant chords, one suspects that Górecki relies not just upon cryptography and

---

[101] Slonimsky (2004), 2.

extrinsic quotations, but also on numerology, as signalled by the composer's perseverating repetitions, a counting phenomenon that reinforces the symphony's unusual breadth and architectonic durability.

Our final musical conundrum is the orchestral work *Become Ocean* by the American composer John Luther Adams, awarded a Pulitzer Prize in 2014. Its title derives from a mesostic poem by John Cage in tribute to the experimentalist composer (and mentor of Adams) Lou Harrison, whose music Cage compared to a river flowing into a delta. A musical environmentalist who spent decades in the Alaskan interior, Adams experienced firsthand global warming and anthropogenic damage to the planet. His art centres on transforming concert halls into vessels of imaginary music inspired by natural soundscapes, of which three, *Become Ocean* (2013), *Become River* (2013) and *Become Desert* (2017) form a trilogy. Adams views himself as a sensualist *and* formalist,[102] so that the beguiling, ostensibly formless surface of his music conceals more deeply lying geometrical structures. Distributed among three ensembles (strings, woodwind and brass), the various layers cohere into a natural, seamless organism that now advances, now withdraws. Looking at the score of *Become Ocean*, one notices first the rising/falling septuplet figures that swell and ebb in the piano part throughout the composition. These are sonorous *and* (through *Augenmusik*) visual waves, elemental motions mirrored by slower quintuplet and triplet patterns in the woodwind and brass, so that, numerologically speaking, Adams bases his score on the prime numbers three, five and seven. Moving like crosscurrents through much of the score, these temporal planes merge into three 'tsunamis of sound'[103] before receding into near silence. There is yet another dimension of Adams's formal logic: the entire score, it turns out, is a palindrome around its midpoint that ends by returning to its origins. Our journey, in short, is fully circular; we are immersed in a force much larger than ourselves, as we become one with ocean.

∾ v

For almost two millennia in the West, musical riddles have challenged and tapped the deepest layers of our common humanity, ensnaring us in layers of sound instead of tissues of words. Like words, music can be frivolous in character and offer no more than harmless diversions, and yet it can also address considerably weightier matters, be they acts of espionage, authorship, courtship or homage (perhaps most recently, in 2023, in the coronation music for

---

[102] Interview with the composer: https://www.youtube.com/watch?v=SNyMNdnYZ5s [Accessed 3 February 2025].

[103] Ibid.

Charles III[104]), let alone occasional attempts to treat music as a 'universal language'. Whatever the motivation, 'cypherjugglers' and practitioners of the musical curiosities discussed in these pages have remained engaged over the centuries, cajoling, rebuffing and yet informing us, whether immediately aware or not, of the indispensable role of music in our lives, of its eternal mysteries and clairvoyant truths – of what Schoenberg unapologetically viewed as necessity, not superstition.

---

[104] On 6 May 2023, when a cipher on his name appeared in an arrangement of the Irish hymn 'Be Thou My Vision'.

Bibliography

Abele, Ute, 'Der Schleier – Zu Bildern und Verfahren in der Musik des 15. und 16. Jahrhunderts', *Studien zur Musikwissenschaft* 14 (Hamburg: 2008)

Adamenko, Victoria, *Neo-Mythologism in Music: From Scriabin and Schoenberg to Schnittke and Crumb* (Hillsdale, NY: 2007)

Adams, Sara Ballduf, 'The Development of Alban Berg's Compositional Style: A Study of His *Jugendlieder* (1901–1908)' (Ph.D. diss., Florida State University: 2008)

Adorno, Theodor W., *Alban Berg: Master of the Smallest Link*, trans. Juliane Brand and Christopher Hailey (Cambridge: 1991)

Agee, Richard J., 'Costanzo Festa's *Gradus ad Parnassum*', *Early Music History* 15 (1996), 1–58

Albert, Giacomo, 'Weakening Structures or Structuring Mistakes? Brian Ferneyhough's Manipulation of the Fibonacci Sequence in his Second String Quartet', *Mitteilungen der Paul Sacher Stiftung* 28 (April 2015), 55–60

Albrecht, Theodore, ed. and trans., *Beethoven's Conversation Books*, vol. 2 (Suffolk: 2018–2019)

_____, ed. and trans., *Beethoven's Conversation Books*, vol. 3 (Suffolk: 2020)

Alegant, Brian, *The Twelve-Tone Music of Luigi Dallapiccola* (Rochester, NY: 2010)

Al-Kadi, Ibrahim A., 'Origins of Cryptography: The Arab Contributions', *Cryptologia* 16 (1992), 97–126

Allen, Steward Lee, *The Devil's Cup: A History of the World According to Coffee* (New York: 1999)

Ambros, August Wilhelm, *Geschichte der Musik* (Leipzig: 1909; Hildesheim: 1968), 5 vols.

Anderson, Emily, ed., *The Letters of Mozart and His Family* (New York: 1985), 3rd ed.

Andrew, Christopher, *The Secret World: A History of Intelligence* (New Haven, CT: 2018)

Anheim, Étienne, 'Les calligrammes musicaux de Baude Cordier', in Martine Clouzot and Christine Laloue, eds., *Les représentations de la musique au Moyen Âge* (Paris: 2005), 46–55

Antheil, George, *Bad Boy of Music* (Garden City, NY: 1945)

Aquinas, Thomas, *Summa Theologiae*, ed. and trans. Ceslaus Velecky (London: 1965), vol. 6: *The Trinity*

Atlas, Allan, 'Gematria marriage numbers and golden sections in Dufay's "Resveillés vous"', *Acta Musicologica* 59 (1987), 111–26

Auer, Max, *Anton Bruckner: Sein Leben und Werk* (Vienna: 1967)

Babyak, Tekla, 'Between the Cipher and the *Idée Fixe*: Joachim, Berlioz, and the Lovestruck Psyche,' in Katharina and Michael Uhde, eds., *Joseph Joachim: Identities | Identitäten* (Hildesheim: 2024), 77–94

Bach, C. P. E., *The Complete Works*, ed. Peter Wollny, VIII:1 (Los Altos: 2019)

Bachmann, Tibor and Peter J. Bachmann, 'An Analysis of Béla Bartók's Music through Fibonaccian Numbers and the Golden Mean', *The Musical Quarterly* 65 (1979), 72–82

Bacon, Francis, *Of the Advancement and Proficience of Learning*, trans. Gilbert Wats (Oxford: 1640)

Bailey, Walter B., *Programmatic Elements in the Works of Schoenberg* (Ann Arbor, MI: 1984)

Bain, Jennifer, '"… Et mon commencement ma fin": Genre and Machaut's Musical Language in His Secular Songs', in Deborah McGrady and Jennifer Bain, eds., *A Companion to Guillaume de Machaut* (Leiden: 2012), 79–101

⸻, *Hildegard of Bingen and Musical Reception: The Modern Revival of a Medieval Composer* (Cambridge: 2015)

Bannister, Peter, 'Olivier Messiaen (1908–1992)', in Christopher S. Anderson, ed., *Twentieth-Century Organ Music* (New York: 2012), 171–93

Bantock, Myrrha, *Granville Bantock: A Personal Portrait* (London: 1972)

Baragwanath, Nicholas, 'Alban Berg, Richard Wagner, and Leitmotivs of Symmetry', *19th-Century Music* 23 (1999), 62–83

Barford, Philip T., 'Mahler: A Thematic Archetype', *Music Review* 21 (1960), 297–316

Barney, Stephen A., W. J. Lewis, J. A. Beach and Oliver Berghof, trans., *The Etymologies of Isidore of Seville* (Cambridge: 2006)

Baron, Carol Kitzes, 'Ives on His Own Terms: An Explication, a Theory of Pitch Organization, and a New Critical Edition for the "3-Page Sonata"' (Ph.D. diss., City University of New York, 1987)

Barone, Anthony, 'Modernist Rifts in a Pastoral Landscape: Observations on the Manuscripts of Vaughan Williams's Fourth Symphony', *The Musical Quarterly* 91 (2008), 60–88

Bauer, Craig P., *Unsolved! The History and Mystery of the World's Greatest Ciphers from Ancient Egypt to Online Secret Societies* (Princeton, NJ: 2017)

Beaumont, Antony, *Zemlinsky* (Ithaca, NY: 2000)

Bede, *The Reckoning of Time*, trans. Faith Wallis (Liverpool: 1999)

Beduschi, Luciane, 'Joseph Haydn's *Die heiligen zehn Gebote* als Canons and Sigismund Neukomm's *Das Gesetz des alten Bundes, oder die Gesetzgebung auf Sinai*: Exemplification of Changes in Musical Settings of the Ten Commandments during the Eighteenth and Nineteenth Centuries', in Dominik Markl, ed., *The Decalogue and Its Cultural Influence* (Sheffield: 2013), 296–317

Beethoven, Ludwig van, *A Sketchbook from the Year 1821 (Artaria 197)*, ed. William Drabkin (Bonn: 2010), 2 vols.

Bellamy, William, *Shakespeare's Verbal Art* (Newcastle upon Tyne: 2015)

Bent, Margaret, 'Deception, Exegesis and Sounding Number in Machaut's Motet 15', *Early Music History* 10 (1991), 15–27

Benthem, Jaap van, 'Text, Tone, and Symbol: Regarding Busnoys's Conception of *In hydraulis* and Its Presumed Relationship to Ockeghem's *Ut heremita solus*', in Paula Higgins, ed., *Antoine Busnoys: Method, Meaning, and Context in Late Medieval Music* (Oxford: 1999), 215–53

Berlioz, Hector, *Evenings with the Orchestra*, trans. and ed. Jacques Barzun (Chicago: 1973)

_____, *The Memoirs of Hector Berlioz*, trans. and ed. David Cairns (New York: 1975)

Bernac, Pierre, *Francis Poulenc: The Man and His Songs*, trans. Winifred Radford (New York: 1977)

Bernstein, Lawrence F., 'Ockeghem as the Bach of His Day', in G. Filocamo and M. J. Bloxam, eds., *Uno gentile et subtile ingenio: Studies in Renaissance Music in Honor of Bonnie J. Blackburn* (Turnhout: 2009), 577–91

Bertini, Auguste, *Stigmatographie, ou L'art d'écrire avec des points, suivie de la Mélographie, Nouvelle manière de noter la musique* (Paris: [1812])

Bilak, Donna, 'Chasing Atalanta: Maier, Steganography, and the Secrets of Nature', in Maier (2020)

Bittmann, Antonius, 'Brahms, Strauss, Sheep, and Apes: Reger's "Heroic" Struggle with Tradition', *The Musical Quarterly* 87 (2004), 708–31

Blackburn, Bonnie J., 'The Corruption of One is the Generation of the Other: Interpreting Canonic Riddles', *Journal of the Alamire Foundation* 4 (2012), 182–203

Blackburn, Bonnie J. and Leofranc Holford-Strevens, 'Juno's Four Grievances: The Taste for the Antique in Canonic Inscriptions', in Ulrich Konrad, Jürgen Heidrich and Hans Joachim Marx, eds., *Musikalische Quellen – Quellen zur Musikgeschichte: Festschrift für Martin Staehelin zum 65. Geburtstag* (Göttingen: 2002), 159–74

Block, Adrienne Fried, *Amy Beach, Passionate Victorian: The Life and Work of an American Composer, 1867–1944* (New York: 1998)

Blumenberg, Heike, 'Ein musikalisches Bildrätsel', *Die Musikforschung* 45 (1992), 163–5

Boogaart, Jacques, '*Speculum mortis*: Form and Signification in Machaut's Motet *Hé! Mors/ Fine Amour/ Quare non sum mortuus* (M3)', in Leach (2003), 13–30

──────────, 'Sound and Cipher: Number Symbolism in Machaut's Motets', in Lawrence Earp and Jared C. Hartt, eds., *Poetry, Art, and Music in Guillaume de Machaut's Earliest Manuscript (BnF fr. 1586)* (Turnhout: 2021), 377–95

Borchard, Beatrix, 'Musik als Beziehungskunst – ein Blick zurück, zwei nach vorne', in Martin Tröndle, ed., *Das Konzert: Neue Aufführungskonzepte für eine klassische Form* (Bielefeld: 2014), 219–38

──────────, 'Ernst und Joachim – Virtuose Selbstdarstellung versus sachbezogene Interpretationshaltung?', in Christine Hoppe et al., *Exploring Virtuosities: Heinrich Wilhelm Ernst, Nineteenth-Century Musical Practices and Beyond* (Hildesheim: 2018), 53–74

Boss, Jack, *Schoenberg's Twelve-Tone Music: Symmetry and the Musical Idea* (Cambridge: 2014)

Boulez, Pierre, *Conversations with Célestin Deliège* (London: 1976)

Bowden, Sylvia, 'The Theming Magpie: The Influence of Birdsong on Beethoven Motifs', *The Musical Times* 149 (2008), 17–35

Bower, Calvin M., ed., *The Liber Ymnorum of Notker Balbulus* (London: 2016), 2 vols.

Bowles, Hugo, *Dickens and the Stenographic Mind* (Oxford: 2019)

Boyd, Malcolm, ed., *Oxford Composer Companions: J. S. Bach* (Oxford and New York: 1999)

Brainard, Paul, 'Tartini and the Sonata for Unaccompanied Violin', *Journal of the American Musicological Society* 14 (1961), 383–93

Brandenburg, Sieghard, ed., *Ludwig van Beethoven Briefwechsel* (Munich: 1996), vol. 3

Braun, Werner, 'Visuelle Elemente in der Musik der frühen Neuzeit: Rastralkreuze', in Gerhard F. Strasser and Mara R. Wade, eds., *Die Domänen des Emblems: Außerliterarische Anwendungen der Emblematik* (Wiesbaden: 2004), 135–55

Brodbeck, David, 'The Brahms-Joachim Counterpoint Exchange; or, Robert, Clara, and "the Best Harmony between Jos. and Joh."', *Brahms Studies* 1 (1994), 30–80

Brothers, Lester D., 'The Hexachord Mass: 1600–1720' (Ph.D. diss., University of Los Angeles, 1973)

Brown, David, *Tchaikovsky: A Biographical and Critical Study*, vol. 2: *The Crisis Years (1874–1878)* (London: 1982); vol. 4: *The Final Years (1885–1893)* (London: 1991)

──────────, 'Deciphering Liszt', *The Musical Times* 144 (2003), 6–15

Brown, Stephen C., 'Tracing the Origins of Shostakovich's Musical Motto', *Intégral* 20 (2006), 69–103

Brown, Susan Sutliff, 'The Mystery of the "Fuga per Canonem" Solved', *European Joyce Studies* 22 (2013), 173–93

Bruhn, Siglind, *The Musical Order of the World: Kepler, Hesse, Hindemith* (Hillsdale, MI: 2005)

_____, ed., *Encrypted Messages in Alban Berg's Music* (London: 1998)

Bruns, Steven and Ofer Ben-Amots, eds., *George Crumb & the Alchemy of Sound: Essays on His Music* (Colorado Springs: 2005)

Buch, David, '*Die Zauberflöte*, Masonic Opera, and Other Fairy Tales', *Acta Musicologica* 76 (2004), 193–219

Buckley, Robert J., *Sir Edward Elgar* (London: 1905)

Buecking, Johann J., *Anweisung zur geheimen Correspondenz systematisch entworfen* (Wolfenbüttel: 1804)

Bukofzer, Manfred, 'The Fountains Fragment', in *Studies in Medieval and Renaissance Music* (New York: 1950), 86–112

Bullock, Philip Ross, 'Ambiguous Speech and Eloquent Silence: The Queerness of Tchaikovsky's Songs', *19th-Century Music* 32 (2008), 94–128

Bulson, Eric, *Ulysses by Numbers* (New York: 2020)

Burckhardt, Jacob, *The Civilisation of the Renaissance in Italy*, trans. S. G. C. Middlemire (London: 1892)

Burgess, Anthony, *Joysprick: An Introduction to the Language of James Joyce* (London: 1973)

Burney, Charles, *The Present State of Music in Germany, the Netherlands, and United Provinces* (London: 1775), 2nd ed.

_____, *A General History of Music from the Earliest Ages to the Present Period (1789)*, ed. Frank Mercer (New York: 1957)

Burt, Peter, *The Music of Tōru Takemitsu* (Cambridge: 2006)

Butchart, David S., 'A Musical Journey of 1567: Alessandro Striggio in Vienna, Munich, Paris and London', *Music & Letters* 63 (1982), 1–16

Butler, Christopher, *Number Symbolism* (London: 1970)

Calico, Joy H., 'Musical Threnodies for Brecht', in *Edinburgh German Yearbook* 5 (2011), 163–81

Campbell, J. and H. M. Robinson, *A Skeleton Key to* Finnegans Wake (New York: 1944)

Campbell, Joseph and Henry Morton Robinson, *A Skeleton Key to* Finnegans Wake: *Unlocking James Joyce's Masterwork* (Novato, CA: 2005)

Carlson, Maria, *'No Religion Higher Than Truth': A History of the Theosophical Movement in Russia, 1875–1922* (Princeton, NJ: 1993)

Carpenter, Alexander, '*Erwartung* and the Scene of Psychoanalysis: Interpreting Schoenberg's Monodrama as a Freudian Case Study' (Ph.D. diss., University of Toronto, 2004)

Castelli, J. F., *Memoiren meines Lebens: Gefundenes und Empfundenes, Erlebtes und Erstrebtes* (Vienna and Prague: 1861), vol. 2

Castro, Paulo F. de, 'A Network of Meaning(s): Paul Dukas's *La Plainte, au loin, du faune* ... as an Intertextual Case Study', in Helen Julia Minors and Laura Watson, eds., *Paul Dukas: Legacies of a French Musician* (London: 2019), 71–85

Cathé, Philippe, 'Contrepoint et fugue: Charles Koechlin, *L'Offrande musicale sur le nom de Bach*, douze mouvements pour orchestre, orgue et piano, Op. 187, le "retour à Bach"', in Marie-Hélène Benoit-Otis, ed., *Charles Koechlin: Compositeur et Humaniste* (Paris: 2010), 435–45

Céard, Jean and Jean-Claude Margolin, *Rébus de la Renaissance: Des images qui parlent* (Paris: 1986), 2 vols.

Chailley, Jacques, 'Joseph Haydn and the Freemasons', in H. C. Robbins Landon, ed., *Studies in Eighteenth-Century Music: A Tribute to Karl Geiringer on His Seventieth Birthday* (New York: 1970), 117–24

―――――, 'Anagrammes musicales et "langages communicables"', *Revue de musicologie* 67 (1981), 69–79

―――――, *The Magic Flute Unveiled: Esoteric Symbolism in Mozart's Masonic Opera* (Rochester, VT: 1992)

Cherniak, Yevhennia, Irena Barantsova, Maryna Biletska, Viktoriia Mitlytska and Tetyana Pidvarko, 'Transformation of Sound Cipher Complexes in the History of Musical Art and Their Specific Manifestations in the Work of Composers of the 17th–21st Centuries', *Journal of History, Culture and Art Research* 8 (2019), 301–9

Cheshire, Gerard, 'The Language and Writing System of MS408 (Voynich) Explained', *Romance Studies* 37 (2019), 30–67

Chigareva, Evgenia, 'On the Late Style of Alfred Schnittke (the Instrumental Works)', in Dixon (2017), 178–96

Cintas, Pedro, 'Francis Bacon: An Alchemical Odyssey through the *Novum Organum*', *Bulletin for the History of Chemistry* 28 (2003), 65–75

Clarke, Barry R., *Francis Bacon's Contribution to Shakespeare: A New Attribution Method* (New York: 2019)

Clegg, Brian, *The First Scientist: A Life of Roger Bacon* (London: 2003)

Clemens, Raymond, ed., *The Voynich Manuscript* (New Haven, CT: 2016)

Cohen, Judith, *The Six Anonymous* L'homme armé *Masses* (Rome: 1968)

Cohrs, Gunnar, 'Der musikalische Architekt: Zur Bedeutung der Zahlen in Bruckners 5. und 9. Sinfonie', in *Neue Zeitschrift für Musik* 151 (1990), 19–26

―――――, 'Zahlenphänomene in Bruckners Symphonik: Neues zu den Strukturen der Fünften und Neunten Symphonie', *Bruckner Jahrbuch 1989/90* (Linz: 1992), 35–75

Colker, M. L., 'A Discussion of Cryptography in a Late Medieval Codex', *Manuscripta* 15 (1971), 85–8

Collins, Paul, *Banvard's Folly: Thirteen Tales of People Who Didn't Change the World* (London: 2001)

Columbro, Sister Mary Electa, S. N. D., 'Ostinato Technique in the Franco-Flemish Motet: 1480–ca. 1562' (Ph.D. diss., Case Western Reserve University, 1974), 2 vols.

Cooke, Antony, *Charles Ives's Musical Universe: Unlocking the Code … Reassessing his Provenance* (West Conshohocken, PA: 2015)

Cooke, Mervyn, 'Be Flat or Be Natural? Pitch Symbolism in Britten's Operas', in Philip Rupprecht, ed., *Rethinking Britten* (New York: 2013), 102–27

Cooper, David, *Béla Bartók* (New Haven, CT: 2015)

Cooper, John Michael, 'Mendelssohn's Fugues for String Quartet', *Ad Parnassum* 7 (2009), 37–69

Cormac, Joanne, 'Liszt, Language, and Identity: A Multinational Chameleon', *19th-Century Music* 36 (2013), 231–47

Cornelius, Paul, *Languages in Seventeenth- and Early Eighteenth-Century Imaginary Voyages* (Geneva: 1965)

Coron, Antoine, *Avant Apollinaire: Vingt Siècles de Poèmes Figurés* (Marseilles: 2005)

Couturat, Louis, *La Logique de Leibniz d'après des documents inédits* (Paris: 1901; repr. Hildesheim: 1961)

_____ and Léopold Leau, *Histoire de la langue universelle* (Paris: 1903; repr. Hildesheim: 2001)

Covach, John, 'Schoenberg's Turn to an "Other World"', *Music Theory Online* 1 (1995), 1–11

_____, 'Balzacian Mysticism, Palindromic Design, and Heavenly Time in Berg's Music', in Siglind Bruhn, ed., *Encrypted Messages in Alban Berg's Music* (New York: 1998), 5–29

Dalen, Brenda, '"Freundschaft, Liebe, und Welt": The Secret Programme of the Chamber Concerto', in Douglas Jarman, ed., *The Berg Companion* (London: 1989), 141–80

Dallapiccola, Luigi, 'Notes for an Analysis of the Canti di Liberazione', trans. F. Chloë Stodt, *Perspectives of New Music* 38 (2000), 5–24

D'Anghiera, Pietro Martire, *De Orbe Novo: The Eight Decades of Peter Martyr d'Anghera*, trans. Francis Augustus MacNutt (New York: 1912), 2 vols.

Daverio, John, 'Brahms's Musical Ciphers: Acts of Homage and Gestures of Effacement', in John Daverio, *Crossing Paths: Schubert, Schumann, and Brahms* (New York: 2002), 103–24

_____, 'Piano Works I: A World of Images' in Beate Perrey, ed., *The Cambridge Companion to Schumann* (Cambridge: 2007), 65–85

David, Hans T. and Arthur Mendel, eds., *The New Bach Reader: A Life of Johann Sebastian Bach in Letters and Documents*, rev. Christoph Wolff (New York: 1998)

David, Tenney L., trans., *Roger Bacon's Letter Concerning the Marvelous Power of Art and of Nature and Concerning the Nullity of Magic* (Easton: 1923)

Davies, H. Neville, 'The History of a Cipher, 1602–1772', *Music & Letters* 48 (1967), 325–9

_____, 'Bishop Godwin's "Lunatique Language"', *Journal of the Warburg and Courtauld Institutes* 30 (1967), 296–316

Dawkins, Peter, *The Shakespeare Enigma* (London: 2004)

Debussy, Claude, *Lettres de Claude Debussy à son éditeur* (Paris: 1927)

_____, *Correspondance 1872–1918*, ed. François Lesure, Denis Herlin and Georges Liébert (Paris: 2005)

De Luca, Elsa, 'Musical Cryptography and the Early History of the "Léon Antiphoner"', *Early Music History* 36 (2017), 1–54

De Luca, Elsa and John Haines, 'Medieval Musical Notes as Cryptography', in Ellison and Kim (2018), 30–47

Dentler, Hans-Eberhard, *Johann Sebastian Bachs 'Kunst der Fuge': Ein pythagoreisches Werk und seine Verwirklichung* (Mainz: 2004)

Devlin, Keith J., *Finding Fibonacci: The Quest to Rediscover the Forgotten Genius Who Changed the World* (Princeton, NJ: 2017)

Devos, Jérôme P., *Les chiffres de Philippe II (1555–1598) et du despacho universal durant le XVIIe siècle* (Brussels: 1950)

Devrient, Eduard, *My Recollections of Felix Mendelssohn-Bartholdy, and His Letters to Me*, trans. Natalia Macfarren (London: 1869, repr. Cambridge: 2013)

Dille, Denis, *Thematisches Verzeichnis der Jugendwerke Béla Bartóks 1890–1904* (Kassel: 1976)

Dittmer, Luther, ed., *Firenze Biblioteca Mediceo-Laurenziana, Pluteo 29, 1* (Brooklyn, NY: 1960)

Dixon, Gavin, *The Routledge Handbook to the Music of Alfred Schnittke* (London: 2022)

_____, ed., *Schnittke Studies* (London, 2017)

Doe, Paul, 'Tallis's "Spem in Alium" and the Elizabethan Respond-Motet', *Music & Letters* 51 (1970), 1–14

Dopp, Bonnie Jo, 'Numerology and Cryptography in the Music of Lili Boulanger: The Hidden Program in *Clairières dans le ciel*', *The Musical Quarterly* 78 (1994), 556–83

Douglas-Fairhurst, Robert, *Becoming Dickens: The Invention of a Novelist* (Cambridge, MA: 2011)

Dounias, Minos, *Die Violinkonzerte Giuseppe Tartinis als Ausdruck einer Künstlerpersönlichkeit und einer Kulturepoche* (Wolfenbüttel: 1935; repr. Wolfenbüttel, Zürich: 1966)

Dowden, Wilfred S., 'Byron and the Austrian Censorship', *Keats-Shelley Journal* 4 (1955), 67–75

Drosnin, Michael, *The Bible Code* (New York: 1997)

Dufourcet-Hakim, Marie-Bernadette, 'Figures et symbols dans les motets de Guillaume de Machaut', in Jacqueline Cerquiglini-Toulet and Nigel Wilkins, eds., *Guillaume de Machaut* (Paris: 2002), 71–89

Dunnagan, Ryane, 'An Examination of Compositional Style and Cello Techniques in *12 Hommages à Paul Sacher*' (D.M.A. diss., University of Georgia, 2011)

Dunoyer, Cecilia, *Marguerite Long: A Life in French Music, 1874–1966* (Bloomington, IN: 1993)

Durante, Sergio, 'On *Artificioso* Compositions at the Time of Frescobaldi', in Alexander Silbiger, ed., *Frescobaldi Studies* (Durham, NC: 1987), 195–217

Durling, Robert M., ed. and trans., *Petrarch's Lyric Poems* (Cambridge: 1976)

Eckermann, Johann Peter, *Conversations with Goethe*, trans. Allan Blunden (London: 2022)

Eckstein, Friedrich, *Erinnerungen an Anton Bruckner* (Vienna: 1923)

_____, *'Alte unnennbare Tage!' Erinnerungen aus siebzig Lehr- und Wanderjahren* (Vienna: 1936)

Ehrstine, Glenn, *Theater, Culture, and Community in Reformation Bern, 1523–1555* (Leiden: 2002)

Einstein, Albert, 'Augenmusik im Madrigal', *Zeitschrift der Internationalen Musikgesellschaft* 14 (1912–13), 8–21

El-Daly, Okasha, *Egyptology: The Missing Millennium; Ancient Egypt in Medieval Arabic Writings* (London: 2005)

Elders, Willem, *Symbolic Scores: Studies in the Music of the Renaissance* (Leiden: 1994)

_____, 'Did Josquin Use a Musical "Signature?"' *Tijdschrift van de Koninklijke Vereniging voor Nederlandse Muziekgeschiedenis* 62 (2012), 29–63

_____, *Josquin des Prez and His Musical Legacy: An Introductory Guide* (Leuven: 2013)

Elgar, Edward, *My Friends Pictured within: The Subjects of the Enigma Variations as Portrayed in Contemporary Photographs and Elgar's Manuscript* (London: 1947)

_____, *Darling Chuck: The Carice Letters*, in Martin Bird, ed., *Edward Elgar: Collected Correspondence* (Rickmansworth: 2014), Series 2, vol. 1

El-Hibri, Tayeb, *The Abbasid Caliphate: A History* (Cambridge: 2021)

Ellison, Katherine and Susan Kim, eds., *A Material History of Medieval and Early Modern Ciphers: Cryptography and the History of Literacy* (London: 2018)
Ellmann, Richard, *James Joyce* (New York: 1982)
Elphick, Daniel, *Music Behind the Iron Curtain: Weinberg and his Polish Contemporaries* (Cambridge: 2019)
Elvers, Rudolf, *Endreim-Spiele mit Felix Mendelssohn* (Berlin: 1970)
Ernst, Thomas, 'The Numerical-Astrological Ciphers in the Third Book of Trithemius's Steganographia', *Cryptologia* 22 (1998), 318–41
Fabbi, Roberto, 'Theological Implications of Restrictions in Messiaen's Compositional Processes', in Siglind Bruhn, ed., *Messiaen's Language of Mystical Love* (New York: 1998), 55–84
Fallows, David, *Josquin*, 2nd ed. (Turnhout: 2020)
Fanlo, Jean-Raymond, 'Le traicté des chiffres et sécrètes manières d'escrire de Blaise de Vigenère', in Daniel Martin, Pierre Servet and André Tournon, eds., *L'énigmatique à la Renaissance: Formes, significations, esthétiques: Actes du colloque organisé par l'association Renaissance, Humanisme, Réforme (Lyon, 7–10 septembre 2005)* (Paris: 2008), 27–39
Fanning, David, 'Shostakovich and His Pupils', in Laurel E. Fay, ed., *Shostakovich and His World* (Princeton, NJ: 2004a), 275–302
_____, *Shostakovich: String Quartet No. 8* (Aldershot: 2004b)
Fauser, Annegret, 'Die Musik hinter der Legende: Lili Boulangers Liederzyklus *Clairières dans le Ciel*', *Neue Zeitschrift für Musik* 151/11 (1990), 9–14
Fay, Laurel, 'Shostakovich versus Volkov: Whose Testimony?' *Russian Review* 39 (1980), 484–93
_____, *Shostakovich: A Life* (New York: 2000)
Fearn, Raymond, 'At the Doors of Kranichstein: Maderna's "Fantasia" for 2 Pianos', *Tempo* 163 (1987), 14–20
Feder, Stuart, 'This Scherzo Is [Not] a Joke', in James W. Barron, ed., *Humor and Psyche: Psychoanalytic Perspectives* (Hillsdale, NJ: 1999), 203–17
Fedtke, Traugott, ed., *B-A-C-H, Fugen der Familie Bach für Orgel und andere Tasteninstrumente* (Leipzig: 1984)
Ferrer, Daniel, 'What Song the Sirens Sang … Is No Longer beyond All Conjecture: A Preliminary Description of the New "Proteus" and "Sirens" Manuscripts', *James Joyce Quarterly* 50 (2013), 319–33
Fetterman, William, *John Cage's Theatre Pieces: Notations and Performances* (Amsterdam: 1996)
Fischer, Victoria, 'Bartók's Fourteen Bagatelles Op. 6, for Piano: Toward Performance Authenticity', in Elliott Antokoletz, Victoria Fischer and Benjamin Suchoff, eds., *Bartók Perspectives: Man, Composer, and Ethnomusicologist* (New York: 2000), 273–86

Fishell, Janette, 'Old Symbols – New Language: An Examination of Olivier Messiaen's *Méditations sur le Mystère de la Sainte Trinité*', *Diapason* 79 (December 1988), 12–15
Floros, Constantin, 'Das esoterische Programm der Lyrischen Suite von Alban Berg: Eine semantische Analyse', in Rainer Riehn and Heinz-Klaus Metzger, eds., *Musik-Konzepte 4 – Alban Berg Kammermusik 1* (Munich: 1981), vol. 1, 5–48
_____, *Alban Berg and Hanna Fuchs: The Story of a Love in Letters*, trans. Ernest Bernhardt-Kabisch (Bloomington, IN: 2008)
_____, *Anton Bruckner: The Man and the Work*, trans. Ernest Bernhardt-Kabisch (Frankfurt am Main: 2011)
_____, *Gustav Mahler and the Symphony of the 19th Century*, trans. Neil K. Moran (Frankfurt am Main: 2013)
_____, 'Mahler and Program Music', in Charles Youmans, ed., *Mahler in Context*, (Cambridge: 2021), 110–17
Forkel, Johann Nikolaus, *Allgemeine Geschichte der Musik* (Leipzig: 1788), vol. 1, in Othmar Wessely, ed., *Die grossen Darstellungen der Musikgeschichte in Barock und Aufklärung* (Graz: 1967), vol. 8
Forshaw, Peter J., 'Michael Maier and Mythoalchemy', in *Furnace and Fugue: A Digital Edition of Michael Maier's 'Atalanta fugiens' (1618) with Scholarly Commentary* (Charlottesville, VA: 2020) [https://doi.org/10.26300/bdp.ff.forshaw]
Forte, Allen, 'Schoenberg's Creative Evolution: The Path to Atonality', *The Musical Quarterly* 64 (1978), 133–76
Fournier, August, *Die Geheimpolizei auf dem Wiener Kongress: Eine Auswahl aus ihren Papieren* (Vienna: 1913)
Frei-Hauenschild, Markus, *Friedrich Ernst Fesca (1789–1826): Studien zu Biographie und Streichquartettschaffen* (Göttingen: 1998)
Freud, Sigmund, *Civilization and Its Discontents*, trans. James Strachley (New York: 1961)
Frisius, Rudolf, *Karlheinz Stockhausen II: Die Werke 1950–1977; Gespräch mit Karlheinz Stockhausen: 'Es geht aufwärts'* (Mainz: 2008)
Fuhrmann, Wolfgang, 'A Humble Beginning? Three Ways to Understand Brumel's *Missa Ut re mi fa sol la*', *Journal of the Alamire Foundation* 7 (2015), 22–49
Gajewski, Boleslas, *Grammaire du solrésol ou langue universelle de François Sudre* (Paris: 1902)
Galilei, Vincenzo, *Dialogo della musica antica, et della moderna* (Florence: 1581; facs. Rome: 1934)
Gauldin, Robert, 'The Magic Squares of the Third Movement of Webern's Concerto Op. 24', *In Theory Only* 2 (1977), 32–42

Gauldin, Robert and Warren Benson, 'Structure and Numerology in Stravinsky's *In Memoriam Dylan Thomas*', *Perspectives of New Music* 23 (1985), 166–85

Gay, Peter, *The Enlightenment: An Interpretation, Volume II: The Science of Freedom* (New York: 1969)

_____, *Freud: A Life for Our Time* (New York: 1988)

Gerbino, Giuseppe, *Canoni et enigmi: Pier Francesco Valentini e l'artificio canonico nella prima metà del Seicento* (Rome: 1995)

Gilbert, Stuart, *Letters of James Joyce* (New York: 1966), vol. 1

Giles, Roseen, 'Physicality and Devotion in Heinrich Ignaz Biber's *Rosary Sonatas*', *Yale Journal of Music & Religion* 4 (2018), 68–104

Gillies, Richard Louis, *Singing Soviet Stagnation: Vocal Cycles from the USSR, 1964–1985* (London: 2022)

Glarean, Heinrich, *Dodecachordon*, trans. and ed., Clement A. Miller (Dallas: 1965), 2 vols.

Glidden, Hope H., 'Babil/Babel: Language Games in the *Bigarrures* of Estienne Tabourot', *Studies in Philology* 79 (1982), 242–55

Glikman, Isaak, *Story of a Friendship: The Letters of Dmitry Shostakovich to Isaak Glikman 1941–1975*, trans. Anthony Phillips (Ithaca, NY: 2001)

Gloag, Kenneth and Nicholas Jones, *Peter Maxwell Davies Studies* (Cambridge: 2009)

Godt, Irving, 'C. P. E. Bach His Mark', *College Music Symposium* 19 (1979), 154–61

Godwin, Bishop Francis, *The Man in the Moon*, ed. John Anthony Butler (Ottawa: 1995)

Godwin, Joscelyn, ed., *Michael Maier's* Atalanta Fugiens *(1617): An Edition of the Fugues, Emblems and Epigrams* (Tysoe: 1987)

_____, *Athanasius Kircher's Theatre of the World: His Life, Work, and the Search for Universal Knowledge* (Rochester, VT: 2015)

Goléa, Antoine, *Rencontres avec Olivier Messiaen* (Paris: 1960)

Gouk, Penelope, 'Music and the Sciences', in Tim Carter and John Butt, eds., *The Cambridge History of Seventeenth Century Music* (Cambridge: 2005), 132–57

Gowen, Bradford, *A Performer's Guide to the Piano Music of Samuel Adler* (Rochester, NY: 2022)

Grabócz, Marta, 'The Demiurge of Sounds and the poeta doctus: François-Bernard Mâche's Poetics and Music', *Contemporary Music Review* 8 (1993), 131–82

_____ and Geneviève Mathon, eds., *François-Bernard Mâche: le compositeur et le savant face à l'univers sonore* (Paris: 2018)

Grandjean, Wolfgang, *Metrik und Form bei Bruckner* (Tutzing: 2001)

Grange, Henry-Louis de la, 'Music about Music in Mahler: Reminiscences, Allusions, or Quotations?' in Stephen E. Hefling, ed., *Mahler Studies* (Cambridge: 1997)

Grattan-Guinness, Ivor, 'Counting the Notes: Numerology in the Works of Mozart, Especially *Die Zauberflöte*', *Annals of Science* 49 (1992a), 201–32

_____, 'Why Did Mozart Write Three Symphonies in the Summer of 1788?', *Music Review* 53 (1992b), 1–6

Gratzer, Wolfgang, *Zur 'wunderlichen Mystik' Alban Bergs: Eine Studie* (Vienna: 1993)

Gray, Cecil, *The History of Music* (New York: 1931)

Greene, Richard, *Holst: The Planets* (Cambridge: 1995)

Griffiths, Paul, *Peter Maxwell Davies* (London: 1982)

Grimm, Julius Otto, *Zukunfts-Brahmanen-Polka: dem lieben Johanni Kreislero juniori (Pseudonymo Brahms) dediziret*, ed. Otto Biba (Tutzing: 1983)

Grosser, Felix, 'Ein neuer Vorschlag zur Deutung der Sator-Formel', *Archiv für Religionswissenschaft* 24 (1926), 165–9

Guyot, Edmé-Gilles, *Nouvelles récréations physiques et mathématiques* (Paris: 1769–70), 4 vols.

Häcker, Werner, 'Erberezeption im Sozialismus: Das Tonsymbol B-A-C-H im Musikschaffen der DDR', *Beiträge zur Musikwissenschaft* 31 (1989), 266–78

Hadow, William Henry, *The Oxford History of Music*, 2nd ed. (Oxford: 1905), vol. 6, 223

Hahn, David C., '"Numerical composition": A Study of Pythagorean-Platonic Ideas in the Making of the Rondeaux of Guillaume de Machaut' (Ph.D. diss., Stanford University, 1993)

Haimo, Ethan, *Schoenberg's Serial Odyssey: The Evolution of His Twelve-Tone Method, 1914–1928* (Oxford: 1990)

_____, 'Schoenberg, Numerology, and *Moses and Aron*', *Opera Quarterly* 23 (2007), 385–94

Haines, John, 'On *Ligaturae* and Their Properties: Medieval Music Notation as Esoteric Writing', in John Haines, ed., *The Calligraphy of Medieval Music* (Turnhout: 2011), 203–22

Halbreich, Harry, 'Bruckners Sechste kein Stiefkind mehr', in Othmar Wessely, ed., *Bruckner-Symposion: 'Bruckner-Interpretation' Bericht Linz 1982* (Linz: 1983), 85–92

_____, *Arthur Honegger*, trans. Roger Nichols (Portland, OR: 1999)

Hankins, Thomas L., 'The Ocular Harpsichord of Louis-Bertrand Castel: Or the Instrument That Wasn't', *Osiris* 9 (1994), 141–56

Hanses, Mathias, 'Love's Letters: An Amor-Roma Telestich at Ovid, *Ars armatoria* 3.507–10', in Phillip Mitsis and Ioannis Ziogas, eds., *Wordplay and Powerplay in Latin Poetry* (Berlin, Boston: 2016), 199–212

Haresnape, Geoffrey, 'An ABC by Geoffrey Chaucer', *English Academy Review: Southern African Journal of English Studies* 32 (2015), 152–9

Harley, James, *Xenakis: His Life in Music* (New York: 2004)

Harris, Stephen J., 'Anglo-Saxon Ciphers', in Ellison and Kim (2018), 65–79
Hart, Heidi, *Hanns Eisler's Art Songs: Arguing with Beauty* (Rochester, NY: 2018)
Hastings, Patrick, *The Guide to James Joyce's Ulysses* (Baltimore: 2022)
Hatter, Jane D., *Composing Community in Late Medieval Music: Self-Reference, Pedagogy, and Practice* (Cambridge: 2019)
Haupenthal, Gerhard, *Geschichte der Würfelmusik in Beispielen* (Diss., Universität des Saarlandes, 1994), 2 vols.
Head, Raymund, 'Holst – Astrology and Modernism in "The Planets,"' *Tempo* 187 (1993), 15–22
Hedges, Stephen A., 'Dice Music in the Eighteenth Century', *Music & Letters* 59 (1978), 180–7
Helm, Eugene, 'Six Random Measures of C. P. E. Bach', *Journal of Music Theory* 10 (1966), 139–51
Hemken, Jennifer Ann, 'The Mystery of the Althorn (Alto Horn) Sonata (1943) by Paul Hindemith' (D.M.A. diss., North Texas State University, 2015)
Henderson, Donald G., 'The "Magic Flute" of Peter Winter', *Music & Letters* 64 (1983), 193–205
Henderson, Lyn, 'A Solitary Genius: The Establishment of Pärt's Technique (1958–68)', *The Musical Times* 149 (2008a), 81–8
_____, 'Shostakovich, the Passacaglia, and Serialism', in Mishra (2008b), 409–34
Henderson, W. J., *What is Good Music?* (New York: 1935)
Hentschel, Frank, *Funktion und Bedeutung der Symmetrie in den Werken Béla Bartóks* (Lucca: 1997)
Henze, Marianne, *Studien zu den Messenkompositionen Johannes Ockeghems* (Berlin: 1968)
Herodotus, *The Histories*, trans. Aubrey de Sélincourt (Baltimore: 1965)
Hewitt, Helen, 'The Two Puzzle Canons in Busnois's Maintes femmes', *Journal of the American Musicological Society* 10 (1957), 104–10
Higgins, Paula, '*In hydraulis* Revisited: New Light on the Career of Antoine Busnois', *Journal of the American Musicological Society* 39 (1986), 36–86
_____, 'Parisian Nobles, a Scottish Princess, and the Woman's Voice in Late Medieval Song', *Early Music History* 10 (1991), 145–200
Higley, Sarah L., *Hildegard of Bingen's Unknown Language: An Edition, Translation, and Discussion* (New York: 2007)
Hildegard von Bingen, *Lieder nach den Handschriften*, ed. Pudentiana Barth OMB, M. Immaculata Ritscher OSB and Joseph Schmidt-Görg (Salzburg: 1969)
Hillebrand, Jörg, *Igor Markevitch: Leben, Wirken und kompositorisches Schaffen* (Kassel: 2000)

Hilton, James, *Chronograms: 5000 and More in Number Excerpted Out of Various Authors and Collected at Many Places* (London: 1882)
Hindemith, Paul, *The Craft of Musical Composition*, trans. Arthur Mendel (New York: 1941)
Hintermaier, Ernst, 'The Missa Salisburgensis', *The Musical Times* 116 (1975), 965–6
Hirsbrunner, Theo, *Pierre Boulez und sein Werk* (Laaber: 1985)
Hitchcock, H. Wiley, *Ives* (Oxford: 1977)
Ho, Allan B. and Dmitry Feofanov, eds., *Shostakovich Reconsidered* (London: 1998)
Hodgart, Matthew J. C. and Ruth Bauerle, *Joyce's Grand Operoar: Opera in Finnegans Wake* (Urbana, IL: 1997)
Hoepffner, Ernest, 'Anagramme und Rätselgedichte bei Guillaume de Machaut', *Zeitschrift für romanische Philologie* 30 (1906), 401–13
Hofstadter, Douglas R., *Gödel, Escher, Bach: An Eternal Golden Braid* 20th Anniversary Edition (London: 2000)
Hoke, Hans Gunter, *Zu Johann Sebastian Bachs* Die Kunst der Fuge (Leipzig: 1979)
Honegger, Marc, *Catalogue des oeuvres musicales de Georges Migot* (Strasbourg: 1977)
Hooper, William, *Rational Recreations: In Which the Principles of Numbers and Natural Philosophy Are Clearly and Copiously Elucidated by a Series of Easy, Entertaining, Interesting Experiments, Among Which Are All Those Commonly Performed with the Cards* (London: 1774), vol. 1
Hopkinson, Cecil, *A Bibliographical Thematic Catalogue of the Works of John Field, 1782–1837* (London, 1961)
Hoppin, Richard H., *Medieval Music* (New York: 1978)
Horace, *Satires, Epistles and Ars Poetica*, trans. H. Rushton Fairclough (Cambridge, MA: 1942)
Horne, William, 'Brahms's Düsseldorf Suite Study and His Intermezzo, Opus 116, No. 2', *The Musical Quarterly* 73 (1989), 249–83
_____, 'Recycling Uhland: Brahms and the "Wanderlieder"', *Notes of the Music Library Association* 69 (2012), 217–59
Horton, Julian, 'Recent Developments in Bruckner Scholarship', *Music & Letters* 85 (2004), 83–94
Howat, Roy, *Debussy in Proportion: A Musical Analysis* (Cambridge: 1983a)
_____, 'Review-Article: Bartók, Lendvai and the Principles of Proportional Analysis', *Music Analysis* 2 (1983b), 69–95
Hughes, Indra M. N., 'The Mathematical Architecture of Bach's "The Art of Fugue"' (D.M.A. diss., University of Auckland: 2006)

Hulme, Derek C., *Dmitri Shostakovich: A Catalogue, Bibliography, and Discography*, 3rd ed. (Lanham, MD: 2002)

Huot, Sylvia, *From Song to Book: The Poetics of Writing in Old French Lyric and Lyrical Narrative Poetry* (Ithaca, NY: 1987)

Huseinova, Aida, 'The Heart of the Tenth Symphony', *DSCH Journal* 17 (2002), 38–40

―――――, 'Shostakovich's Tenth Symphony: The Azerbaijani Link – Elmira Nazirova', *Azerbaijan International* 11 (Spring 2003), 54–9

Ikonnikov, Alexei A., *Myaskovsky: His Life and Work* (New York: 1946)

Imbs, Bravig, *Confessions of Another Young Man* (New York: 1936)

Ingrao, Charles W., *The Habsburg Monarchy 1618–1815*, 2nd ed. (Cambridge: 2000)

Irmen, Hans-Josef, *Mozart's Masonry and the Magic Flute* (Essen: 1996)

Ivashkin, Alexander, *Alexander Schnittke* (London: 1996)

―――――, 'The Schnittke Code', in Gavin Dixon, ed., *Schnittke Studies* (London: 2017), 197–207

Ives, Charles, *The Unanswered Question* (New York: 1953)

―――――, *Memos*, ed. John Kirkpatrick (New York: 1991)

Jackson, Paul R. W., *The Life and Music of Sir Malcolm Arnold: The Brilliant and the Dark* (Aldershot: 2003)

Jackson, Philip T., 'Two Descendants of Josquin's "Hercules" Mass', *Music & Letters* 59 (1978), 188–205

Jackson, Timothy L., 'Bruckner's Metrical Numbers', *19th-Century Music* 14 (1990), 101–31

―――――, 'Aspects of Sexuality and Structure in the Later Symphonies of Tchaikovsky', *Music Analysis* 14 (1995), 3–25

―――――, *Tchaikovsky: Symphony No. 6 ('Pathétique')* (Cambridge: 1999)

Jaffe, Jane Vial, 'Eduard Marxsen and Brahms' (Ph.D. diss., University of Chicago, 2009), 2 vols.

Jameux, Dominique, *Pierre Boulez* (Cambridge, MA: 1990)

Jarman, Douglas, 'Alban Berg, Wilhelm Fliess, and the Secret Programme of the Violin Concerto', in Douglas Jarman, ed., *The Berg Companion* (London: 1989), 181–94

―――――, 'Secret Programmes', in Anthony Pople, ed., *The Cambridge Companion to Berg* (Cambridge: 1997), 167–79

―――――, '"Remembrance of Things That Are to Come": Some Reflections on Berg's Palindromes', in Christopher Hasty, ed., *Alban Berg and His World* (Princeton, NJ: 2010), 195–221

Jensen, Eric Frederick, *Schumann* (New York: 2012)

Jerphanion, Guillaume de, *La voix des monuments: Études d'archéologie, nouvelle série* (Paris: 1938), 38–94

Joachim, Johannes, ed., *Joseph Joachims Briefe an Gisela von Arnim* (Göttingen: 1911a)

_____, and Andreas Moser, eds., *Briefe von und an Joseph Joachim* (Berlin: 1911b)

Johnson, Graham, *Poulenc: The Life in the Songs* (New York: 2020)

Jones, Nicholas and Richard McGregor, *The Music of Peter Maxwell Davies* (Woodbridge: 2020)

Jong, H. M. E. de, *Michael Maier's* Atalanta Fugiens: *Sources of an Alchemical Book of Emblems* (Leiden: 1969)

Jyrkiäinen, Reijo, *Form, Monothematicism, Variation and Symmetry in Béla Bartók's String Quartets* (Helsinki: 2012)

Kaczynski, Bernice M., *Greek in the Carolingian Age: The St. Gall Manuscripts* (Cambridge: 1988)

Kahn, David, *The Codebreakers: The Story of Secret Writing* (New York: 1996)

Karhausen, Lucien, *The Bleeding of Mozart: A Medical Glance on His Life, Illnesses and Personality* (Bloomington, IN: 2011)

Kass, Robert E., 'Introduction to "Solving the Bible Code Puzzle"', *Statistical Science* 14 (1999), 149.

Kellman, Herbert, ed., *The Treasury of Petrus Alamire: Music and Art in Flemish Court Manuscripts 1500–1535* (Ghent: 1999)

Kellner, Herbert Anton, 'Welches Zahlenalphabet benützte der Thomaskantor Kuhnau?' *Die Musikforschung* 33 (1980), 124–5

_____, 'Zum Zahlenalphabet bei Guillaume de Machaut', *Musik und Kirche* 51 (1981), 29

Kholopov, Yuri and Valeria Tsenova, *Edison Denisov*, trans. Romela Kohanovskaya (Chur: 1995)

Keyte, Hugh, 'Hugh Keyte Replies', *Early Music* 9 (1981), 345

Kinderman, William, 'Beethoven and Napoleon: A Reassessment', in Bernhard R. Appel, Joanna Cobb Biermann, William Kinderman and Julia Ronge, eds., *Beethoven und der Wiener Kongress (1814/15): Bericht über die vierte New Beethoven Research Conference Bonn, 10. bis 12. September 2014* (Bonn: 2016), 23–46

King, David A., *The Ciphers of the Monks: A Forgotten Number-Notation of the Middle Ages* (Stuttgart: 2001)

Kircher, Athanasius, *Musurgia universalis* (Rome: 1650; repr. Hildesheim: 1970), 2 vols.

_____, *China Illustrata: With Sacred and Secular Monuments, Various Spectacles of Nature and Art and Other Memorabilia*, trans. Charles D. Van Tuyl (Indianapolis: 1987)

Kirkendale, Warren, 'Gregorian Style in Beethoven's String Quartet Op. 132', in Warren and Ursula Kirkendale, *Music and Meaning: Studies in Music History and the Neighbouring Disciplines* (Florence: 2007)

Klein, Hans-Günter, '"... dieses allerliebste Buch": Fanny Hensels Noten-Album', *Mendelssohn Studien* 8 (1993), 151–67

Klein, Scott W., 'The Euphonium Cagehaused in Either Notation: John Cage and *Finnegans Wake*', in Knowles (1999), 151–67.

Klotz, Sebastian, '*Ars combinatoria* oder "Musik ohne Kopfzerbrechen": Kalküle des Musikalischen von Kircher bis Kirnberger', *Musiktheorie* 14 (1999), 231–45

_____, *Kombinatorik und die Verbindungskünste der Zeichen in der Musik zwischen 1630 und 1780* (Berlin: 2006)

Klüber, Johann Ludwig, *Kryptographik: Lehrbuch der Geheimschreibekunst (Chiffrir- und Dechiffrirkunst) in Staats- und Privatgeschäften* (Tübingen: 1809)

Knight, Ellen, *Charles Martin Loeffler: A Life Apart in American Music* (Urbana, IL: 1993)

Knobloch, Eberhard, '*Musurgia universalis*: Unknown Combinatorial Studies in the Age of Baroque Absolutism', *History of Science* 17 (1979), 258–75

Knowles, Sebastian G. D., ed., *Bronze by Gold: The Music of Joyce* (New York: 1999)

Knox, Ronald, *A Book of Acrostics* (London: 1924)

Köchel, Jürgen, *Alfred Schnittke zum 60. Geburtstag – eine Festschrift* (Hamburg: 1994)

Koechlin, Charles, 'Evolution de l'harmonie', in Albert Laignac and Lionel de la Laurencie, eds., *Encyclopédie de la musique* (Paris: 1925), Part II, 617–23

_____, *Précis des Règles du Contrepoint* (Paris: 1926)

_____, *Offrande musicale sur le nom de Bach Opus 187* (Paris: 2011)

Koerner, Joseph Leo, *The Moment of Self-Portraiture in German Renaissance Art* (Chicago: 1993)

Köhler, Karl-Heinz and Dagmar Beck, eds., *Ludwig van Beethovens Konversationshefte* (Leipzig: 1972 and 1983), vols. 1 and 3

Köhler, Reinhold, 'Sator-Arepo-Formel', *Zeitschrift für Ethnologie* 13 (1881), 301–6

Konrad, Ulrich, 'Mozart the Letter Writer and His Language', in Simon P. Keefe, ed., *Mozart Studies* 2 (Cambridge: 2015), 1–22

Kopitz, Klaus Martin and Rainer Cadenbach, eds., *Beethoven aus der Sicht seiner Zeitgenossen in Tagebüchern, Briefen, Gedichten und Erinnerungen* (Munich: 2009), vol. 1

Korstvedt, Benjamin M., 'Mahler's Bruckner, between Devotion and Misprision', *Journal of the American Musicological Society* (2017), 357–432

Kostalevsky, Marina, ed., *The Tchaikovsky Papers: Unlocking the Family Archive* (New Haven, CT: 2018)

Kravetz, Nelly, 'A New Insight into the Tenth Symphony of Dmitry Shostakovich', in Rosamund Bartlett, ed., *Shostakovich in Context* (Oxford: 2000), 159–74

Krenek, Ernst, 'Anton Weberns magisches Quadrat', *Wiener Zeitschrift Forum* 12/141–2 (August / September 1965), 395–6

Krenek, Ernst, *Johannes Ockeghem* (New York: 1953)

Küntzel, Hans, *Brahms in Göttingen: Mit Erinnerungen von Agathe Schütte, geb. von Siebold* (Göttingen: 1985)

Labounsky, Ann, *Jean Langlais: The Man and His Music* (Portland, OR: 2000)

Ladewig, James, 'Bach and the *Prima prattica*: The Influence of Frescobaldi on a Fugue from the *Well-Tempered Clavier*', *Journal of Musicology* 9 (1991), 358–75

Lambert, Philip, *The Music of Charles Ives* (New Haven, CT: 1997)

Lamy, Michel, *The Secret Message of Jules Verne: Decoding His Masonic, Rosicrucian, and Occult Writings*, trans. Jon E. Graham (Rochester, NY: 2007)

Large, Brian, *Smetana* (London: 1970)

Leach, Elizabeth Eva, ed., *Machaut's Music: New Interpretations* (Woodbridge: 2003)

Lebedinsky, Lev, 'Code, Quotation and Collage: Some Musical Allusions in the Works of Dmitry Shostakovich', in Ho and Feovanov, 472–82

Lee, Gordon, 'Another Piece in the Jigsaw: A Retrospective Survey of Past Attempts at Solving the "Enigma" and Some Further Thoughts on Elgar's XIIIth Variation', *Elgar Society Journal* 8 (1994), 252–65

Lee, Jung-Min, 'National Identity Formation and Musical Modernism in Post-World War II Korea' (Ph.D. diss., Duke University, 2017)

Lees, Heath, 'The Introduction to "Sirens" and the Fuga per Canonem', *James Joyce Quarterly* 22 (1984), 39–54

Leibniz, Gottfried Wilhelm, *Dissertatio de arte combinatoria* (Leipzig: 1666)

———, *Opera omnia*, ed. Ludovic Dutens (Geneva: 1768)

Lendvai, Ernő, *Béla Bartók: An Analysis of His Music* (London: 1971)

Leo, Domenic, 'Authorial Presence in the Illuminated Machaut Manuscripts' (Ph.D. diss., New York University, 2005)

Lesser, Wendy, *Music for Silenced Voices: Shostakovich and His Fifteen Quartets* (New Haven, CT: 2011)

Lesure, François and Richard Langham Smith, eds., *Debussy on Music* (New York: 1977)

Levine, Stuart and Susan Levine, eds., *The Short Fiction of Edgar Allan Poe* (Urbana, IL, 1976)

Levison, Wilhelm, *England and the Continent in the Eighth Century* (Oxford: 1973)

Lindmayr, Andrea, 'Ein Rätseltenor Ockeghems: Des Rätsels Lösung', *Acta musicologica* 60 (1988), 31–42

Lindmayr-Brandl, Andrea, 'Ockeghem's Motets: Style as an Indicator of Authorship: The Case of *Ut heremitas solus* Reconsidered', in Philippe Vendrix, ed., *Johannes Ockeghem: Actes du XLe Colloque international d'études humanistes, Tours, 3–8 février 1997* (Paris: 1998), 499–520

Link, John, *Elliott Carter's Late Music* (Cambridge: 2022)

Litzmann, Berthold, *Clara Schumann: An Artist's Life, Based on Material Found in Diaries and Letters*, trans. Grace E. Hadow (London: 1913), vol. 2

Locke, Benjamin, 'Christiane: Cryptography in Brahms's *Ein deutsches Requiem*', *Choral Journal* 39/2 (1998), 9–14

Lombard, Maurice, *The Golden Age of Islam*, trans. Joan Spencer (Princeton, NJ, 2004)

Long, Michael, 'Symbol and Ritual in Josquin's *Missa Di Dadi*', *Journal of the American Musicological Society* 42 (1989), 1–22

Looze, Laurence de, '"Mon nom trouveras": A New Look at the Anagrams of Guillaume de Machaut: The Enigmas, Responses, and Solutions', *Romanic Review* 79 (1988), 537–57

_____, *Pseudo-Autobiography in the Fourteenth Century: Juan Ruiz, Guillaume de Machaut, Jean Froissart, and Geoffrey Chaucer* (Gainesville, FL: 1997)

Lorent, Catherine, *Florent Schmitt* (Paris: 2012)

Losada, Cristina Catherine, 'A Theoretical Model for the Analysis of Collage in Music Derived from Selected Works by Berio, Zimmermann, and Rochberg' (Ph.D. diss., City University of New York, 2004)

Ludwig, Loren, 'John Farmer's Sundry Waies: The English Origin of Michael Maier's "Alchemical Fugues"', in *Furnace and Fugue: A Digital Edition of Michael Maier's 'Atalanta fugiens'* (1618) with Scholarly Commentary (Charlottesville, VA: 2020) [https://doi.org/10.26300/bdp.ff.ludwig]

Luhrssen, David, *Hammer of the Gods: The Thule Society and the Birth of Nazism* (Lincoln, NE: 2012)

Lukomsky, Vera and Sofia Gubaidulina, '"My Desire Is Always to Rebel, to Swim against the Stream!"' *Perspectives of New Music* 36 (1998), 5–41

Lyons, Stuart, *Horace's Odes and the Mystery of Do-Re-Mi* (Oxford: 2007)

_____, *Music in the Odes of Horace* (Oxford: 2010)

Maas, Sander van, 'The Reception of Aquinas in the Music of Olivier Messiaen', in Paul van Geest, Harm Goris and Carlo Leget, eds., *Aquinas as Authority* (Leuven: 2002), 317–31

Macdonald, Hugh, *Skryabin* (Oxford: 1978)

MacDonald, Malcolm, *Schoenberg* (New York: 2008)
Macey, Patrick, 'Frescobaldi's Musical Tributes to Ferrara', in Kerala J. Snyder, ed., *The Organist as Scholar: Essays in Memory of Russell Saunders* (Stuyvesant, NY: 1994), 197–231
Machaut, Guillaume de, *The Judgment of the King of Navarre*, ed. and trans. R. Barton Palmer (New York: 1988)
_____, *The Tale of the Alerion*, ed. and trans. Minnette Gaudet and Constance B. Hieatt (Toronto: 1994)
_____, *Le Livre dou Voir Dit (The Book of the True Poem)*, ed. Daniel Leech-Wilkinson, trans. R. Barton Palmer (New York: 1998)
_____, *La Prise d'Alexandre (The Taking of Alexandria)*, ed. and trans R. Barton Palmer (New York: 2002)
Mâche, François-Bernard, *Music, Myth and Nature, or the Dolphins of Arion*, trans. Susan Delaney (Chur: 1992)
Machiavelli, Niccolò, *The Art of War*, trans. Henry Neville (Mineola, NY: 2006)
Macnamara, Mark, 'The Artist of the Unbreakable Code', *Nautilus* (https://nautil.us/the-artist-of-the-unbreakable-code-234588/). [Accessed 3 February 2025]
Maes, Francis, *A History of Russian Music from Kamarinskaya to Babi Yar*, trans. Arnold J. Pomerans and Erica Pomerans (Berkeley, CA: 2002)
Maier, Elisabeth, 'A Hidden Personality: Access to an "Inner Biography" of Anton Bruckner', in Timothy L. Jackson and Paul Hawkshaw, eds., *Bruckner Studies* (Cambridge: 1997), 32–53
Maier, Michael, *Atalanta Fugiens. An Edition of the Emblems, Fugues and Epigrams*, trans. and ed. Joselyn Godwin (Grand Rapids, MI: 1989)
_____, *Furnace and Fugue: A Digital Edition of Michael Maier's 'Atalanta fugiens' (1618) with Scholarly Commentary*, ed. Tara Nummedal and Donna Bilak (Charlottesville, VA: 2020)
Mann, Alfred, 'Schubert's Lesson with Sechter', *19th-Century Music* 6 (1982), 159–65
_____, *Schuberts Studien*, in Franz Schubert, *Neue Ausgabe sämtlicher Werke* (Kassel: 1986), Serie VIII: Supplement Band 2
Mann, Thomas, *The Story of a Novel: The Genesis of DOCTOR FAUSTUS*, trans. Richard and Clara Winston (New York: 1961)
_____, *Doktor Faustus: The Life of the German Composer Adrian Leverkühn as Told by a Friend*, trans. John E. Woods (New York: 1999)
Marinoni, Augusto, *I Rebus di Leonardo da Vinci, raccolti e interpretati* (Florence: 1954)
Marpurg, Friedrich Wilhelm, *Historisch-kritische Beyträge zur Aufnahme der Musik* (Berlin: 1754–60; repr. Hildesheim: 1970)

Marschall, Veronika, *Das Chronogramm: Eine Studie zu Formen und Funktionen einer literarischen Kunstform, dargestellt am Beispiel von Gelegenheitsgedichten des 16. bis 18. Jahrhunderts aus den Beständen der Staatsbibliothek Bamberg* (Frankfurt am Main: 1997)

Marston, Nicholas, *Schumann Fantasie, Op. 17* (Cambridge: 1992)

Martial, *Epigrams*, ed. and trans. D. R. Shackleton Bailey (Cambridge: 1993), vol. 1

Martin, Paul, *Joyce and Wagner: A Study of Influence* (Cambridge: 1991)

_____, '"Mr. Bloom and the Cyclops": Joyce and Antheil's Unfinished "Opéra Mécanique"', in Sebastian D. G. Knowles, *Bronze by Gold: The Music of Joyce* (New York: 1999), 91–105

Mason, Wilton, 'Father Castel and His Color Clavecin', *The Journal of Aesthetics and Art Criticism* 17 (1958), 103–16

McCallum, Peter, 'The Process within the Product: Exploratory Transitional Passages in Beethoven's Late Quartet Sketches', in William Kinderman and Joseph E. Jones, eds., *Genetic Criticism and the Creative Process: Essays from Music, Literature, and Theater* (Rochester, NY: 2009), 123–50

McCarthy, Kerry, *Tallis* (New York: 2020)

McGregor, Richard, 'Reading the Runes: Deciphering Maxwell Davies's Secret Language', *Perspectives of New Music* 38 (2000), 5–29

_____, 'Source Material Used in the Works of Peter Maxwell Davies, 1957–2006', in Gloag and Jones (2009), 242–54

McHugh, Roland, *The Sigla of Finnegans Wake* (Austin: 1976)

_____, *Annotations to Finnegans Wake*, 4th ed. (Baltimore: 2016)

McKay, Brendan, Dror Bar-Natan, Maya Bar-Hillel and Gil Kalai, 'Solving the Bible Code Puzzle', *Statistical Science* 14 (1999), 150–73

McKee, Eric, 'On the Death of Mahler: Schoenberg's Op. 19, No. 6', *Theory and Practice* 30 (2005), 121–51

Meconi, Honey, *Pierre de la Rue and Musical Life at the Habsburg-Burgundian Court* (Oxford: 2003)

Medić, Ivana, 'The Sketches for Alfred Schnittke's Symphony No. 3, and What They (Don't) Tell Us', *Musicology* 15 (2013), 169–213

_____, '"Crucifixus etiam pro nobis": Representations of the Cross in Alfred Schnittke's Symphony No. 2, "St. Florian"', in Gavin Dixon, ed., *Schnittke Studies* (London: 2017), 3–29

_____, 'Prokofiev and Shostakovich: A Two-Way Influence', in Rita McAllister and Kristina Guillaumier, eds., *Rethinking Prokofiev* (New York: 2020), 87–106

Meinel, Christoph, 'Alchemie und Musik', in Christoph Meinel, ed., *Die Alchemie in der europäischen Kultur- und Wissenschaftsgeschichte* (Wiesbaden: 1986), 201–25

Meister, Aloys, 'Musiknoten als Geheimschrift im 16. Jahrhundert', *Musica sacra* 25 (1892), 100

_____, *Die Anfänge der modernen diplomatischen Geheimschrift: Beiträge zur Geschichte der italienischen Kryptographie des XV. Jahrhunderts* (Paderborn: 1902)

_____, *Die Geheimschrift im Dienste der päpstlichen Kurie von ihren Anfängen bis zum Ende des XVI. Jahrhunderts* (Paderborn: 1906)

Melamed, Daniel R., 'A Thirty-Six Voice Canon in the Hand of C. P. E. Bach', in Daniel R. Melamed, ed., *Bach Studies 2* (Cambridge: 1995), 107–18

_____, 'Rethinking Bach Codes', in Bettina Varwig, ed., *Rethinking Bach* (New York: 2021), 227–50

Mendelssohn Bartholdy, Felix, *Sämtliche Briefe* Band 2, ed. Uta Wald; Band 3, ed. Uta Wald; Band 4, ed. Lucian Schiewitz and Sebastian Schmideler; Band 12, ed. Stefan Münnich, Lucian Schiewietz and Uta Wald (Kassel: 2009, 2010, 2011 and 2017)

Mendelssohn Bartholdy, Lea, *'Ewig die deine': Briefe an Henriette von Pereira-Arnstein*, ed. Wolfgang Dinglinger and Rudolf Elvers (Hanover: 2010), 2 vols.

Mersenne, Marin, *Harmonie universelle* (Paris, 1636)

Messiaen, Olivier, *The Technique of My Musical Language*, trans. John Satterfield (Paris: 1956)

_____, *Méditations sur le mystère de la Sainte Trinité pour Orgue* (Paris: 1973)

Meyer, Heinz and Rudolf Suntrup, *Lexicon der mitteralterlichen Zahlenbedeutungen* (Munich: 1987)

Michelmann, Emil, *Agathe von Siebold: Johannes Brahms' Jugendliebe* (Göttingen: 1930)

Milka, Anatoly P., 'Warum endet die Fuga a 3 Soggetti BWV 1080/19 in Takt 239?', *Bach Jahrbuch* 100 (2014), 11–26

_____, *Rethinking J. S. Bach's The Art of Fugue*, trans. Marina Ritzarev, ed. Esti Sheinberg (Abingdon: 2016)

Miller, Lynette, 'The Sound of Dreams: Tōru Takemitsu's *Far Calls. Coming. Far!* and James Joyce's *Finnegans Wake*' (M.A. thesis, McGill University, 1998)

Milsom, John, 'English Polyphonic Style in Transition: A Study of the Sacred Music of Thomas Tallis', 2 vols. (Ph.D. diss., Oxford University, 1983)

_____, 'The Nonsuch Music Library', in Chris Banks, Arthur Searle and Malcom Turner, eds., *Sundry Sorts of Music Books: Essays on the British Library Collections Presented to O. W. Neighbour on his 70th Birthday* (London: 1993), 146–82

Minors, Helen Julia, '*Le Tombeau de Paul Dukas* in *La Revue musicale*', in Helen Julia Minors and Laura Watson, eds., *Paul Dukas: Legacies of a French Musician*, (London: 2019), 86–109
Mishra, Michael, ed., *A Shostakovich Companion* (Westport, CT: 2008)
Monchick, Alexandra, 'Paul Hindemith and the Cinematic Imagination', *The Musical Quarterly* 95/4 (2012), 510–48
Moore, Jerrold Northrup, *Edward Elgar: A Creative Life* (Oxford: 1984)
_____, ed., *Elgar and his Publishers: Letters of a Creative Life* (Oxford: 1987), 2 vols.
Moroney, Davitt, 'Alessandro Striggio's Mass in Forty and Sixty Parts', *Journal of the American Musicological Society* 60 (2007), 1–69
Morrison, Simon, 'About That Chord, and about Scriabin as a Mystic', in Kenneth Smith and Vasilis Kallis, eds., *Demystifying Scriabin* (Woodbridge: 2022), 11–25
Moser, Hans Joachim, *Joseph Joachim: Ein Lebensbild* (Berlin: 1910), 2 vols.
_____, ed., *Johannes Brahms im Briefwechsel mit Joseph Joachim*, 3rd ed. (Berlin: 1908; reprint, Tutzing: 1974)
Mozart, Wolfgang Amadeus, *Anleitung so viel Englische Contre Tänze mit zwei Würfeln zu componiren als man will, ohne etwas von der Musik oder der Composition zu verstehen* (Berlin: 1793)
_____, *Anleitung Walzer oder Schleifer mit zwei Würfeln zu componiren als man will, ohne etwas von der Musik oder der Composition zu verstehen* (Berlin: 1793)
Münz, Ludwig and Gustav Künstler, *Adolf Loos: Pioneer of Modern Architecture*, trans. Harold Meek (London: 1966)
Musgrave, Michael, '*Frei aber Froh*: A Reconsideration', *19th-Century Music* 3 (1980), 251–8
_____, 'Brahms's First Symphony: Thematic Coherence and Its Secret Origin', *Music Analysis* 2 (1983), 11–33
Nectoux, Jean-Michel, 'Fauré, Henry Prunières et *La Revue musicale*', *Études fauréennes* 17 (1980), 17–24
_____, *Gabriel Fauré: A Musical Life*, trans. Roger Nichols (Cambridge: 1991)
_____, ed., *The Correspondence of Camille Saint-Saëns and Gabriel Fauré: Sixty Years of Friendship*, trans. J. Barrie Jones (Burlington, VT: 2004)
Nettl, Paul, *Mozart and Masonry* (New York: 1957)
Newbould, Brian, 'A Schubert Palindrome', *19th-Century Music* 15 (1992), 207–14
Newcomb, Anthony, 'Schumann and the Marketplace: From Butterflies to *Hausmusik*', in R. Larry Todd, ed., *Nineteenth-Century Piano Music* (New York: 2004), 2nd ed., 258–315

Newes, Virginia, 'Writing, Reading and Memorizing: The Transmission and Resolution of Retrograde Canons from the 14th and Early 15th Centuries', *Early Music* 18 (1990), 218–34

Newman, Barbara, review of Higley, in *Pneuma* 35 (2013), 459

Nicholls, Simon and Michael Pushkin, trans., *The Notebooks of Alexander Skryabin* (New York: 2018)

Nichols, Roger, *Ravel* (London: 1977; New Haven, CT: 2012)

Nielinger-Vakil, Carola, *Luigi Nono: A Composer in Context* (Cambridge: 2015)

Niemöller, Klaus Wolfgang, 'Zum Paradigmenwechsel in der Musik der Renaissance: Vom *numerus sonorus* zur *musica poetica*', in Philippe Vendrix, ed., *Music and the Renaissance: Renaissance, Reformation, and Counter-Reformation* (London: 2011), 93–121

Nies, Otfrid, 'Le rêve des horizons lointains: un parcours de l'oeuvre de Charles Koechlin', in Marie-Hélène Benoit-Otis, ed., *Charles Koechlin: Compositeur et Humaniste*, ed (Paris: 2010), 17–62

Noguchi, Hideo, 'Mozart – Musical Game in C K. 516f', *Mitteilungen der Internationalen Stiftung Mozarteum* 38 (1990), 89–101

Nosow, Robert, 'Le proporzioni temporali in due messe di Dufay: *Se la face ay pale* e *Ecce Ancilla domini*', *Rivista italiana di musicologia* 28 (1993), 53–77

Nottebohm, Gustav, *Zweite Beethoveniana: Nachgelassene Aufsätze* (Leipzig: 1887), 577–80

Nowak, Leopold, 'Anton Bruckners Formwille, dargestellt am Finale seiner V. Symphonie', in *Über Anton Bruckner: Gesammelte Aufsätze 1936–1984* (Vienna: 1985), 43–6

O'Beirne, Thomas H., '940, 369, 969,152 Dice-Music Trios', *The Musical Times* 109 (1968), 911–13

Oesch, Hans, 'Webern und das SATOR-Palindrom', *Veröffentlichungen der Paul Sacher Stiftung* 2 (1991), 101–56

Orledge, Robert, 'Charles Koechlin and the Early Sound Film 1933–38', *Proceedings of the Royal Musical Association* 98 (1971–2), 1–16

_____, *Charles Koechlin (1867–1950): His Life and Works* (London: 1989)

O'Shea, Gary, 'Prokofiev's Early Solo Piano Music: Contexts, Influences, Forms, Performance' (Ph.D. diss., University of Sheffield, 2013)

Osmond-Smith, David, *Playing on Words: A Guide to Luciano Berio's Sinfonia* (London: 1985)

_____, *Berio* (Oxford: 1991)

Ovid, *Metamorphoses*, trans. Mary M. Innes (Baltimore: 1955)

_____, *The Art of Love and Other Poems*, trans. J. H. Mozley (Cambridge: 1962)

Packwood, Wayne, 'Elgar as Cryptographer – Tuning and Turing', *Musical Opinion* 143 (2020), 34–7

Palisca, Claude V., ed., Warren Babb, trans., *Hucbald, Guido, and John on Music: Three Medieval Treatises* (New Haven, CT: 1978)

Palmer, David, 'Olivier Messiaen: A Tribute on His 80th Birthday', *Diapason* 79 (December 1988), 10–11

Pape, Matthias, *Mendelssohns Leipziger Orgelkonzert 1840* (Wiesbaden: 1988)

Pares, Martin, 'The Northumberland MS., the Promus, and the Long Word', *Baconiana* 43 (1960), 66–86

Parry, C. H. H., 'Sechter', in J. A. Fuller Maitland, ed., *Grove's Dictionary of Music and Musicians* (London: 1908), 405

Pater, Walter, *Selected Essays*, ed. Alex Wong (Manchester: 2018)

Paule, Maxwell Teitel, *Canidia, Rome's First Witch* (London, 2017)

Perkins, Leeman L., 'Ockeghem's "Prenez sur moi": Reflections on Canons, Catholica, and Solmization', *Musica Disciplina* 44 (1990), 119–83

Perle, George, 'The Chansons of Antoine Busnois', *Music Review* 11 (1950), 89–97

_____, 'The Secret Program of the *Lyric Suite*', *The International Alban Berg Society Newsletter* 5 (1977), 4–12

_____, 'Das geheime Programm der Lyrischen Suite', in Heinz-Klaus Metzger and Rainer Riehn, eds., *Alban Berg: Kammermusik I. Musik-Konzepte 4. 1978* (Munich: 1981), 49–74

Pernye, A[ndrás], 'Alban Berg und die Zahlen', *Studia Musicologica Academiae Scientiarum Hungaricae* 9 (1967), 141–61

Pesce, Dolores, *Guido d'Arezzo's* Regule Rithmice, Prologus in Antiphonarium, *and* Epistola ad Michahelem: *A Critical Text and Translation* (Ottawa: 1999)

Pesic, Peter, 'The Clue to the Labyrinth: Francis Bacon and the Decryption of Nature', *Cryptographia* 24 (2000), 193–221

Pfohl, Ferdinand, *Gustav Mahler: Eindrücke und Erinnerungen aus den Hamburger Jahren*, ed. Knud Martner (Hamburg: 1973)

Pike, Lionel, 'Towards a Study of Musical Motion: Robert Simpson's Variations and Finale on a Theme of Haydn (1948)', *The Music Review* 54 (1993), 137–48

_____, *Hexachords in Late-Renaissance Music* (Aldershot: 1998)

Planchart, Alejandro Enrique, 'The Origins and Early History of "L'homme armé"', *Journal of Musicology* 20 (2003), 305–57

_____, *Guillaume Du Fay: The Life and Works* (Cambridge: 2018), 2 vols.

Platen, Emil, 'Über Bach, Kuhlau und die thematisch-motivische Einheit der letzten Quartette Beethovens', in Sieghard Brandenburg and Helmut Loos, eds., *Beiträge zu Beethovens Kammermusik: Symposion Bonn 1984* (Munich: 1987), 152–64

Platt, Isaac Hull, *Are the Shakespeare Plays Signed by Francis Bacon?* (Philadelphia: 1897)

Plutarch, *The Rise and Fall of Athens: Nine Greek Lives*, trans. Ian Scott-Kilvert (Baltimore: 1964)

Pocknell, Pauline, ed. and trans., *Franz Liszt and Agnes Street-Klindworth: A Correspondence, 1854-1886* (Hillsdale, NY: 2000)
Poe, Edgar A., 'A Few Words on Secret Writing', *Graham's Magazine* 19 (1841), 33-8, 96, 192, 306-8
Poole, Geoffrey, 'Alban Berg and the Fateful Number', *Tempo* 179 (December 1991), 2-7
Pople, Anthony, 'Secret Programmes: Themes and Techniques in Recent Berg Scholarship', *Music Analysis* 12 (1993), 381-99
Porta, Giambattista della, *De furtivis literarum notis vulga, De ziferis libri IIII* (Naples: 1563 and 1602)
Potter, Caroline, *Henri Dutilleux: His Life and Works* (Aldershot: 1997)
Powell, Mrs. Richard [Penny, Dora], *Edward Elgar: Memories of a Variation* (London: 1937)
Powell, Newman W., 'Fibonacci and the Golden Mean: Rabbits, Rumbas and Rondeaux', *Journal of Music Theory* 23 (1979), 227-73
Poznansky, Alexander, *Tchaikovsky: The Quest for the Inner Man* (New York: 1991)
Price, Derek J., ed., *The Equatorie of the Planetis Edited from Peterhouse Ms. 75.I* (Cambridge: 1955)
Prinz, Ulrich, Joachim Dorfmüller and Konrad Küster, 'Die Tonfolge B-A-C-H in Kompositionen des 17. bis 20. Jahrhunderts: ein Verzeichnis', in *300 Jahre Sebastian Bach* (Tutzing: 1985), 389-419
Prokofiev, Sergey, *Diaries 1907-1914: Prodigious Youth*, trans. Anthony Phillips (Ithaca, NY: 2006)
Proksch, Bryan, *Reviving Haydn: New Appreciations in the Twentieth Century* (Rochester, NY: 2015)
Rand Schmidt, Kari Anne, *The Authorship of the* Equatorie of the Planetis (Cambridge, 1993)
Ratner, Leonard G., '*Ars Combinatoria* Chance and Choice in Eighteenth-Century Music', in H. C. Robbins Landon, ed., *Studies in Eighteenth-Century Music: A Tribute to Karl Geiringer on His Seventieth Birthday* (New York: 1970), 343-63
Rauchhaupt, Ursula von, ed., *Schoenberg, Berg, Webern: Die Streichquartette der Wiener Schule: Eine Dokumentation* (Munich: 1971)
Reed, Jay, '*Mora* in the *Aeneid*', in Mitsis, 87-106
Reeds, Jim, 'Solved: The Ciphers in Book III of Trithemius's *Steganographia*', *Cryptologia* 22 (1998), 291-317
Rees, Owen, 'Machaut's Mass and Sounding Number', in Leach (2003), 95-110
Reich, Willi, *Alban Berg*, trans. Cornelius Cardew (New York: 1965)
_____, *Arnold Schoenberg: A Critical Biography*, trans. Leo Black (New York: 1971)

Rescher, Nicolaus, *On Leibniz: Expanded Edition* (Pittsburgh: 2013)
Rettensteiner, Werigand, Joseph Otter and Georg Schinn, *Biographische Skizze von Michael Haydn* (Salzburg: 1808; repr. Stuttgart: 2006)
Revue musicale 4/11 (1922); Louis Aubert, Georges Enesco, Charles Koechlin, Paul Ladmirault, Maurice Ravel, Jean Jules Aimable Roger-Ducasse and Florent Schmitt, *Homage musical à Gabriel Fauré, Sept pièces de piano sur le nom de Fauré F*fa *A*la *U*sol *R*ré *É*mi, supplement to *La Revue musicale*
Revue musicale 10/7 (1929); R. Chalupt, 'Le reflet du monde extérieur dans l'oeuvre d'Albert Roussel', 20–8
Revue musicale 17/1 (1936); Joaquin Rodrigo, 'Le Tombeau de Paul Dukas', 8–17
Reynolds, Christopher Alan, *Motives for Allusion: Context and Content in Nineteenth-Century Music* (Cambridge: 2003)
Rij, Inge van, *The Other Worlds of Hector Berlioz: Travels with the Orchestra* (Cambridge: 2015)
_____, '"A Living, Fleshy Bond": The Electric Telegraph, Musical Thought, and Embodiment', *19th-Century Music* 39 (2015), 142–66
Roberge, Marc-André, 'Ferruccio Busoni, His Chicago Friends, and Frederick Stock's Transcription for Large Orchestra and Organ of the "Fantasia contrappuntistica"', *The Musical Quarterly* 80 (1996), 302–31
Roberts, Tim S., 'Solving the Dorabella Cipher' [https://unsolvedproblems.org/S36b.pdf]
Robertson, Anne Walters, 'The Mass of Guillaume de Machaut in the Cathedral of Reims', in Thomas Forrest Kelly, ed., *Plainsong in the Age of Polyphony* (Cambridge: 1992), 100–37
_____, *Guillaume de Machaut and Reims: Context and Meaning in His Musical Works* (Cambridge: 2002)
Rößler, Almut, *Contributions to the Spiritual World of Olivier Messiaen, with Original Texts by the Composer*, trans. Barbara Dagg, Nancy Poland and Timothy Tikker (Duisburg: 1986)
Rosenstiel, Léonie, *The Life and Works of Lili Boulanger* (Madison, WI: 1978)
Ross, Alex, *The Rest Is Noise: Listening to the Twentieth Century* (New York: 2007)
_____, *Wagnerism: Art and Politics in the Shadow of Music* (New York: 2020)
Ross, Ryan, '"Blaspheming Beethoven?": The Altered BACH Motive in Vaughan Williams's Fourth Symphony', *Acta Musicologica* 91 (2019), 126–45, 191
Rostropovich, Mstislav, ed., *Dank an Paul Sacher: zum 28. April 1976* (Zurich: 1976
Rudeforth, Helen Elizabeth, 'Words, Ideas and Music: A Study of Tchaikovsky's Last Completed Work, the *Six Songs*, Opus 73' (Ph.D. diss., University of Birmingham, 1998)

Rumph, Stephen, *The Fauré Song Cycles: Poetry and Music, 1861–1921* (Berkeley, CA: 2020)
Rushton, Julius, *Elgar: 'Enigma' Variations* (Cambridge: 1999)
_____, *Mozart* (Oxford: 2006)
Ruthven, K. K., *Faking Literature* (Cambridge: 2001)
Sams, Eric, 'The Tonal Analogue in Schumann's Music', *Proceedings of the Royal Musical Association* 96 (1969–70), 103–17
_____, 'Elgar's Cipher Letter to Dorabella', *The Musical Times* 111 (1970a), 151–4
_____, 'Variations on an Original Theme (Enigma)', *The Musical Times* 111 (1970b), 258–62
_____, 'Elgar's Enigmas', *The Musical Times* 111 (1970c), 692–4
_____, 'A Schumann Primer?' *The Musical Times* 111 (1970d), 1096–7
_____, 'Brahms and His Musical Love-Letters', *The Musical Times* 112 (1971), 329–30
_____, 'Brahms and His Clara Themes', *The Musical Times* 112 (1971), 432–4
_____, 'Musical Cryptography', *Cryptologia* 3 (1979), 193–201
_____, *The Songs of Robert Schumann*, 3rd ed. (Bloomington, In: 1993), 22–6
_____, 'Elgar's Enigmas', *Music & Letters* 78 (1998), 410–15
_____, *The Songs of Johannes Brahms* (New Haven, CT: 2000)
_____, 'Cryptography, Musical', in Stanley Sadie, ed., *The New Grove Dictionary of Music and Musicians* (London: 2001), vol. 6, 753–8
Samuel, Claude, *Conversations with Olivier Messiaen*, trans. Felix Aprahamian (London: 1976)
_____, *Olivier Messiaen: Music and Color, Conversations with Claude Samuel and Olivier Messiaen* (Portland, OR: 1994)
Sandresky, Margaret Vardell, 'The Golden Section in Three Byzantine Motets of Dufay', *Journal of Music Theory* 25/2 (1981), 291–306
Santa, Charles Richard and Matthew Santa, 'Solving Elgar's Enigma', *Current Musicology* 89 (2010), 75–89
Sayers, Dorothy L., *Whose Body?* (New York: 1923)
Saylor, Eric, *Vaughan Williams* (New York: 2022)
Schenk, Eva-Maria, *Das Bilderrätsel* (Diss., University of Cologne, 1968)
Schenkman, Walter, 'Tatlow's Bach and Bach's Signatures in the Goldberg Variations', *Bach: The Journal of the Riemenschneider Bach Institute* 34 (2003), 63–106
[Schering, Arnold], 'Zwei Stammbuchblätter von W. Friedemann und C. Phil. Em. Bach', *Bach Jahrbuch* 21 (1924), 139

Schick, Hartmut, 'Musikalische Konstruktion als musikhistorische Reflexion in der Postmoderne: Zum 3. Streichquartett von Alfred Schnittke', *Archiv für Musikwissenschaft* 59 (2002), 245–66

Schiltz, Katelijne, 'A Space Odyssey: The Mensuration Signs and the Lunar Cycle', in Sabine Rommeveaux, Philippe Vendrix and Vasco Zara, eds., *Proportions: Science – Musique – Peinture & Architecture* (Turnhout: 2011), 217–29

_____, 'Visual Pictorialism in Renaissance Musical Riddles', *Journal of the Alamire Foundation* 4 (2012), 204–21

_____, *Music and Riddle Culture in the Renaissance* (Cambridge: 2015)

Schloezer, Boris de, *Scriabin: Artist and Mystic*, trans. Nicholas Slonimsky (Berkeley, CA: 1987)

Schlötterer-Traimer, Roswitha, *Johann Sebastian Bach: Die Kunst der Fuge* (Munich: 1966)

Schmelz, Peter J., 'Shostakovich's Twelve-Tone Compositions and the Politics and Practice of Soviet Serialism', in Laurel E. Fay, ed., *Shostakovich and His World* (Princeton, NJ: 2004), 303–54

_____, *Such Freedom, If Only Musical: Unofficial Soviet Music during the Thaw* (New York: 2009)

_____, *Alfred Schnittke's Concerto Grosso No. 1* (New York: 2019)

Schnapp, Jeffrey T., 'Virgin Words: Hildegard of Bingen's Lingua Ignota and the Development of Imaginary Languages Ancient to Modern', *Exemplaria* 3 (1991), 267–98

Schnittke, Alfred, *A Schnittke Reader*, ed. Alexander Ivashkin, trans. John Goodliffe (Bloomington, IN: 2002)

Schoenberg, Arnold, *Style and Idea: Selected Writings of Arnold Schoenberg*, ed. Leonard Stein, trans. Leo Black (Berkeley, CA: 1984)

Scholz, Gottfried, 'More on Secret Programs in Berg's Instrumental Music', in Bruhn (1998), 45–65

Schooling, John Holt, 'Secrets in Cipher', *Pall Mall Magazine* 8 (1896): 'I. From Ancient Times to Late Elizabethan Days', 119–29; 'II. From Late-Elizabethan Days to Mid-Stuart Times', 245–56; 'III. From the Times of Charles II to the Second George', 453–62; 'IV. From the Time of George II to the Present Day', 609–18

Schott, Gaspar, *Schola steganographica in classes octo distributa* (Nuremberg: 1665)

Schroeder, David, *Mozart in Revolt: Strategies of Resistance, Mischief and Deception* (New Haven, CT: 1999)

Schulenberg, David, *The Music of Wilhelm Friedemann Bach* (Rochester, NY: 2010)

_____, *The Music of Carl Philipp Emanuel Bach* (Rochester, NY: 2014)

Schulze, Hans-Joachim, 'Rätselhafte Auftragswerke Johann Sebastian Bachs: Anmerkungen zu einigen Kantatentexte', *Bach Jahrbuch 2010*, 69–93

Schumann, Robert, *Tagebücher, Band I: 1827–1838*, ed. Georg Eismann (Leipzig: 1971)

_____, *Schumann Briefedition: Serie I Familienbriefwechsel*, Band 4, ed. Anja Mühlenweg (Cologne, 2012)

Schwartz, W., 'Der Zauber des "rückwärts" Singens und Spielens', *Zeitschrift für Ethnologie* 15 (1883), 113–22

Schwenter, Daniel, *Steganologia & steganographia nova: Geheime, magische, natürliche Red und Schreibkunst* (Nuremberg: 1620)

_____, *Deliciae physico- mathematicae oder Mathemat. und philosophische Erquickstunden* (Nuremberg: 1636)

Schwinger, Wolfram, *Krzysztof Penderecki: His Life and Work*, trans. William Mann (London: 1989)

Seay, Albert, 'The *Conditor Alme Siderum* by Busnois', *Quadrivium* 12 (1971), 225–34

Segall, Christopher, '*Klingende Buchstaben*: Principles of Alfred Schnittke's Monogram Technique', *Journal of Musicology* 30 (2013), 252–86

Selenus, Gustavus, *Cryptomenytices et Cryptographiae Libri IX in quibus & planißima Steganographiae a Johanne Trithemio ... conscriptae, Enodatio traditur ...* (Lüneburg: 1624)

Shaffer, Melanie, 'Finding Fortune in Motet 13: Insights on Ordering and Borrowing in Machaut's Motets', *Plainsong & Medieval Music* 26 (2017), 115–39

Shapiro, Barbara, *John Wilkins 1614–1672: An Intellectual Biography* (Berkeley, CA: 1969)

Shattuck, Roger, *The Banquet Years: The Arts in France – Alfred Jarry, Henri Rousseau, Erik Satie, Guillaume Apollinaire* (New York: 1958)

Shawn, Allen, *Leonard Bernstein: An American Musician* (New Haven, CT: 2014)

Sheldon, Rose Mary, 'The Sator Rebus: An Unsolved Cryptogram?' *Cryptologia* 27 (2003), 233–87

Shenton, Andrew, 'Speaking with the Tongues of Men and of Angels: Messiaen's "langage communicable"', in Siglind Bruhn, ed., *Messiaen's Language of Mystical Love* (New York: 1998), 225–45

_____, *Olivier Messiaen's System of Signs: Notes Toward Understanding His Music* (London: 2008)

Sheppard, H. Fleetwood, 'Tallis and His Song of Forty Parts', *The Musical Times* 19 (1878), 97–8

Sherr, Richard, '*Illibata Dei Virgo Nutrix* and Josquin's Roman Style', *Journal of the American Musicological Society* 41 (1988), 434–64

Sholes, Jacquelyn, 'Music for Birthdays: Commemorative Birthday Pieces in Johannes Brahms's Circle (1853–1854) and Elsewhere', in Katherine Haldane Grenier and Amanda R. Mushal, eds., *Cultures of Memory in the Nineteenth Century: Consuming Commemoration* (Cham: 2020), 61–80

Shumaker, Wayne, *Renaissance Curiosa: John Dee's Conversations with Angels, Girolamo Cardano's Horoscope of Christ, Johannes Trithemius and Cryptography, George Dalgarno's Universal Language* (Binghamton, NY: 1982)

Simms, Bryan and Charlotte Erwin, *Alban Berg* (New York: 2021)

Sleeper, Helen Joy, 'The Alchemical Fugues in Count Michael Maier's *Atalanta Fugiens*', *Journal of Chemical Education* 15 (1938), 410–15

Slim, H. Colin, 'Dosso Dossi's Allegory at Florence about Music', *Journal of the American Musicological Society* 43 (1990), 43–99

Slocum, Kay Brainerd, '*Speculum musicae*: Jacques de Liège and the Art of Musical Number', in Robert L. Surles, ed., *Medieval Numerology: A Book of Essays* (New York: 1993), 10–37

Slonimsky, Nicholas, *Writings on Music*, ed. Electra Slonimsky Yourke (New York: 2004), vol. 1, Friedrich, *Joh. Seb. Bach: Kirchen-Kantaten* (Berlin-Dahlem: 1947–9), vol. 3 (*vom 8. Sonntag nach Trinitatis bis zum Michaelis-Fest*), 5–21

Smyth, David H., 'Stravinsky's Second Crisis: Reading the Early Serial Sketches', *Perspectives of New Music* 37 (1999), 117–46

Solomon, Maynard, 'Mozart's Zoroastrian Riddles', *American Imago* 42 (1985), 345–69

Somfai, László, '"Learned Style" in Two Late String Quartet Movements of Haydn', *Studia Musicologica* 28 (1986), 325–49

_____, *Béla Bartók: Composition, Concepts, and Autograph Sources* (Berkeley, CA: 1996)

_____, 'With or without the B-A-C-H Motive? Bartók's Hesitation in Writing his First String Quartet', *Studia Musicologica* 60 (2019), 15–22

Spitta, Philipp, *Johann Sebastian Bach* (Leipzig: 1880)

Spohr, Louis, *Selbstbiographie* (Kassel: 1860–1), trans. as *Louis Spohr's Autobiography* (London: 1865)

Staples, Hugh B., 'Joyce and Cryptology: Some Speculations', *James Joyce Quarterly* 2 (1965), 167–73

Steblin, Rita, *Die Unsinnsgesellschaft: Franz Schubert, Leopold Kupelwieser und ihr Freundeskreis* (Vienna: 1998)

_____, 'Schubert's Role in the Unsinnsgesellschaft as Revealed by Clues from Schiller and Aschenschlägel', in Eva Badura-Skoda, Gerold W. Gruber, Walburga Litschauer and Carmen Ottner, eds., *Franz Schubert und seine Freunde* (Vienna: 1999), 238–45

_____, 'New Thoughts on Schubert's Role in the Unsinnsgesellschaft', *Schubert: Perspektiven* 10 (2010), 199–223

_____, 'Schubert: The Nonsense Society Revisited', in Christopher H. Gibbs and Morten Slovik, eds., *Franz Schubert and His World* (Princeton, NJ: 2014), 1–37

_____ and Frederick Stocken, 'Studying with Sechter: Newly Recovered Reminiscences about Schubert by His Forgotten Friend, the Composer Joseph Lanz', *Music & Letters* 88 (2007), 226–65

Sterne, Colin C., *Arnold Schoenberg, The Composer as Numerologist* (Lewiston, ME: 1993)

Stewart, Alan, 'The Case for Bacon', in Paul Edmondson and Stanley Wells, eds., *Shakespeare beyond Doubt* (Cambridge: 2013), 16–28

Stewart, John L., *Ernst Krenek: The Man and His Music* (Berkeley, CA: 1991)

Stinson, Russell, *Bach's Legacy: The Music as Heard by Later Masters* (New York: 2020)

Storey, Graham et al., eds., *The Pilgrim Edition of the Letters of Charles Dickens* (Oxford: 1982), vol. I

Strasser, Gerhard F., 'The Noblest Cryptologist: Duke August the Younger of Brunswick-Lüneburg (Gustavus Selenus) and His Cryptological Activities', *Cryptologia* 7 (1983), 193–217

_____, *Lingua Universalis: Kryptologie und Theorie der Universalsprachen im 16. und 17. Jahrhundert* (Wiesbaden: 1988)

_____, 'Musik und Kryptographie', in *Die Musik in Geschichte und Gegenwart* Sachteil 6 (Kassel: 1997), 783–90

_____, 'Musik(noten)chiffren oder die "widernatürliche" Kunst, Musik zu geheimer Kommunikation zu verwenden', in Hartmut Laufhütte, ed., *Künste und Natur in Diskursen der Frühen Neuzeit* (Wiesbaden: 2000) 1107–21, vol. 2

_____, 'The Rise of Cryptography in the European Renaissance', in Karl de Leeuw and Jan Bergstra, eds., *The History of Information Security: A Comprehensive Handbook* (Amsterdam: 2007), 277–325

_____, 'Ninth-Century Figural Poetry and Medieval Easter Tables – Possible Inspirations for the Square Tables of Trimethius and Vigenère?' *Cryptologia* 34 (2010), 22–6

_____, 'Wolfenbüttel, a Minor German Duchy but a Major Centre of Cryptology in the Early Modern Period', *Tatra Mountains Mathematical Publications* 70 (2017), 1–40

Straus, Joseph N., *Stravinsky's Late Music* (Cambridge: 2001)

_____, 'Historical and Stylistic Reconciliation in Sofia Gubaidulina's *Reflections on the Theme BACH*', in Inessa Bazayev and Christopher Segall, eds., *Analytical Approaches to 20th-Century Russian Music: Tonality, Modernism, Serialism* (New York: 2020), 229–42

Stravinsky, Igor and Robert Craft, *Memories and Commentaries* (Garden City, NY: 1960)
Streich, Hildemarie, 'Music, Alchemy and Psychology in "Atalanta fugiens" of Michael Maier', in Godwin (1987), 9–64
Strobel, Otto, 'Wagners Leben im Lichte der Randbemerkungen seiner Originalhandschriften', *Allgemeine Musikzeitung* 59 (1932), 151–3
_____, 'Die Kompositionsskizze zur "Walküre". Zu unserer Notenbeilage', *Zeitschrift für Musik* 100/7 (1933), 710–11
Strohm, Reinhard, '"La harpe de Melodie", oder das Kunstwerk als Akt der Zueignung', in H. Danuser *et al.*, eds., *Geschichte, Ästhetik, Theorie: Festschrift Carl Dahlhaus zum 60. Geburtstag* (Laaber: 1988), 305–16
_____, '*De plus en plus*: Numbers, Binchois, and Ockeghem', in Suzannah Clark and Elizabeth Eva Leach, eds., *Citation and Authority in Medieval and Renaissance Musical Culture: Learning from the Learned* (Woodbridge: 2005), 160–73
Strunk, Oliver, ed., *Source Readings in Music History*, Leo Treitler, rev. ed. (New York: 1998)
Suchier, Hermann, 'Das Anagramm in Machaut's *Voir Dit*', *Zeitschrift für romanische Philologie* 21 (1897), 541–5
Suchoff, Benjamin, ed., *Béla Bartók Essays* (London: 1976)
Sudre, F[rançois], *Téléphonie ou Télégraphe acoustique pratiqué au moyen de quatre sons exécutés sur le clairon* (Paris: 1844)
_____, *Langue musicale universelle* (Paris: 1866)
_____, *Langue musicale au moyen de laquelle on peut converser sur tous les instruments* (Paris: n.d.)
Sudre, Joséphine, *Théorie et pratique de la langue musicale* (Tours: 1883)
Suetonius, *The Twelve Caesars*, trans. Robert Graves (Harmondsworth: 1965)
Sylvestre, Loïc and Marco Costa, 'The Mathematical Architecture of Bach's "The Art of Fugue"', *Il saggiatore musicale* 17 (2010), 175–6
Tabourot, Étienne, *Les bigarrures et Touches du Seigneur des Accords* (Rouen: 1584)
_____, *Les bigarrures du seigneur des accords avec les apophthegmes du sieur Gaulard et les escraignes dijonnoises, revus sur les éditions originales de 1583, 1584, 1585, 1586 et 1588 augmentés de notes de divers commentateurs et précédés de la vie de l'auteur, Estienne Tabourot, par Guillaume Colletet, publiée pour la première fois* (Brussels: 1866)
Takemitsu, Tōru, *Confronting Silence: Selected Writings*, trans. and ed. Yoshiko Kakudo and Glenn Glasow (Berkeley, CA: 1995)
Taruskin, Richard, 'Shostakovich and Us', in Rosamund Bartlett, ed., *Shostakovich in Context* (New York: 2000).

_____, *The Oxford History of Western Music*, vol. 1: *Music from the Earliest Notations to the Sixteenth Century*; vol. 3: *Music in the Nineteenth Century*; vol. 4: *Music in the Early Twentieth Century* (New York: 2005)

_____, *On Russian Music* (Berkeley, CA: 2009).

Tatlow, Ruth, 'J. S. Bach and the Baroque Paragram: A Reappraisal of Friedrich Smend's Number Alphabet Theory', *Music & Letters* 70 (1989), 191–205

_____, *Bach and the Riddle of the Number Alphabet* (Cambridge: 1991)

_____, 'Text, the Number Alphabet and Numerical Ordering in Bach's Church Cantatas', in *Bachs 1. Leipziger Kantatenjahrgang* (Dortmund: 2002), 121–33

_____, 'The Use and Abuse of Fibonacci Numbers and the Golden Section in Musicology Today', *Understanding Bach* 1 (2006), 69–85

_____, 'Collections, Bars and Numbers: Analytical Coincidence or Bach's Design?' *Understanding Bach* 2 (2007), 37–58

_____, *Bach's Numbers: Compositional Proportion and Significance* (Cambridge: 2016)

_____, 'Parallel Proportions, Numerical Structures and *Harmonie* in Bach's Autograph Score', in Yo Tomita, Robin A. Leaver and Jan Smaczny, eds., *Exploring Bach's B-minor Mass* (Cambridge: 2020), 142–62

Tchaikovsky, Peter Ilyich, *The Diaries of Tchaikovsky*, trans. Wladimir Lakond (New York: 1945)

Thicknesse, Philip, *A Treatise on the Art of Decyphering, and of Writing in Cypher with an Harmonic Alphabet* (London: 1772)

Thissen, Paul, 'Zahlensymbolik im Orgelwerk von Olivier Messiaen', *Kirchenmusikalisches Jahrbuch* 80 (1996), 115–31

Thorau, Christian, 'Guides for Wagnerites: Leitmotifs and Wagnerian Listening,' in Thomas S. Grey, ed., *Richard Wagner and his World* (Princeton, NJ and New York: 2009), 161–77

Thucydides, *The Peloponnesian War*, trans. Rex Warner (Baltimore: 1966)

Tilton, Hereward, *The Quest for the Phoenix: Spiritual Alchemy and Rosicrucianism in the Work of Count Michael Maier (1569–1622)* (Berlin: 2003)

Titcomb, Caldwell, 'The Josquin Acrostic Re-Examined', *Journal of the American Musicological Society* 16 (1963), 47–60

Titus, Joan, *The Early Film Music of Dmitry Shostakovich* (New York: 2016)

Todd, R. Larry, 'Retrograde, Inversion, Retrograde-Inversion and Related Techniques in the Masses of Jacobus Obrecht', *The Musical Quarterly* 64 (1978), 50–78

_____, 'Joseph Haydn and the *Sturm und Drang*: A Revaluation', *Music Review* 41 (1980a), 172–96

_____, 'The Genesis of Webern's Opus 32', *The Musical Quarterly* 66 (1980b), 581–91

———, 'On Quotation in Schumann's Music', in R. Larry Todd, ed., *Schumann and His World* (Princeton, NJ: 1994), 80–112

———, 'New Light on Mendelssohn's *Freie Phantasie* (1840)', in Geoffrey C. Orth, ed., *Literary and Musical Notes: A Festschrift for Wm. A. Little* (Bern: 1995), 205–18

———, *Fanny Hensel: The Other Mendelssohn* (New York: 2010)

———, 'The Musical Cryptography of Niels Gade, or, What's in a Name?' in Ulrich J. Blomann, David B. Levy, Ralph P. Locke and Frieder Reininghaus, eds., *Music, a Connected Art: Die Illusion der absoluten Musik: A Festschrift for Jürgen Thym on his Eightieth Birthday* (Baden-Baden: 2023), 49–58

———, 'The Elusive Clara Schumann: Quotations and References, Allusive and Illusive', in Joe Davies and Roe-Min Kok, eds., *The Schumanns in Context* (Cambridge: 2026)

Tohline, Andrew M., 'Towards a History and Aesthetics of Reverse Motion' (Ph.D. diss., Ohio University, 2015)

Trithemius, Johannes [Johann Heidenberg], *Polygraphiae libri sex* (Oppenheim: 1518)

———, *Steganographia: ars per occultam scripturam* (Frankfurt: 1606)

Trowell, Brian, 'Proportion in the Music of Dunstable', *Proceedings of the Royal Musical Association* 105 (1978), 100–41

———, 'Elgar's Use of Literature', in Raymond Monk, ed., *Edward Elgar: Music and Literature* (Aldershot: 1993)

Tsenova, Valeria, 'Number and Proportion in the Music of Sofia Gubaidulina', *Mitteilungen der Paul Sacher Stiftung* 14 (2001), 23–8

———, *Zahlenmystik in der Musik von Sofia Gubaidulina* (Berlin: 2001)

———, 'Magic Numbers in the Music of Sofia Gubaidulina', *Muzikologija* 2 (2002), 253–61

Turrentine, Herbert C., 'The Tombstone of Guillaume Dufay: A Reflection of Early Renaissance Hagiolatry', *Explorations in Renaissance Culture* 12 (1986), 19–35

Uhde, Katharina, 'Of "Psychological Music", Ciphers, and Daguerreotypes: Joseph Joachim's *Abendglocken* Op. 5 No. 2 (1853)', *Nineteenth-Century Music Review* 12 (2015), 227–52

———, *The Music of Joseph Joachim* (Woodbridge: 2018)

———, 'Joachim and Brahms: Formative Influences and Performative Identities Reconsidered, April to July 1853', in Nicole Grimes and Reuben Phillips, eds., *Rethinking Brahms* (New York: 2021), 156–76

——— and R. Larry Todd, 'Joachim and Musical Solitude, or the Beginnings of the Ciphers F-A-E and Gis-e-la', in Jonathan Kregor, ed., *Nineteenth-Century Programme Music: Creation, Negotiations, Reception* (Turnhout: 2018), 25–38

Van Creveld, Martin, *Command in War* (Cambridge, MA: 1985)
Varga, Bálint András, *Conversations with Iannis Xenakis* (London: 1996)
Vaughan Williams, Ralph, *National Music and Other Essays*, 2nd ed. (Oxford: 1987)
Vellekoop, Kees, 'Zusammenhänge zwischen Text und Zahl in der Kompositionsart Jacob Obrechts: Analyse der Motette *Parce domine*', *Tijdschrift van de Vereniging voor Nederlandse Muziekgeschiedenis* 20 (1966), 97–119
Vertrees, Julie Anne, 'Mozart's String Quartet K. 465: The History of a Controversy', *Current Musicology* 17 (1974), 96–114
Vigenère, Blaise de, *Traicté des chiffres, ou Secrètes manières d'escrire* (Paris: 1586)
Vikárius, László, 'Béla Bartók's "Cantata Profana" (1930): A Reading of the Sources', *Studia Musicologica* 35 (1993–4), 249–301
_____, 'Bartók's Bach Borrowings', *Revue Belge de Musicologie* 76 (2022), 251–68
Volkov, Solomon, *Testimony: The Memoirs of Dmitri Shostakovich*, trans. Antonina W. Bouis (New York: 1979)
_____, *St. Petersburg: A Cultural History*, trans. Antonina W. Bouis (New York: 1995)
_____, *Shostakovich and Stalin: The Extraordinary Relationship between the Great Composer and the Brutal Dictator* (New York: 2004)
Wälli, Silvia, *Melodien aus mittelalterlichen Horaz-Handschriften* (Kassel: 2002)
Walker, Alan, 'Liszt and Agnes Street-Klindworth: A Spy in the Court of Weimar?', *Studia Musicologica* 28 (1986), 47–63
_____, *Franz Liszt Volume 2: The Weimar Years: 1848–1861* (New York: 1989)
Walther, Johann Gottfried, *Musikalisches Lexicon oder musikalische Bibliothek*, ed. Richard Schaal (Leipzig: 1732; repr. Kassel: 1953)
Warren, Charles W., 'Brunelleschi's Dome and Dufay's Motet', *The Musical Quarterly* 59 (1973), 92–105
Watkins, Holly, *Metaphors of Depth in German Musical Thought* (Cambridge: 2011)
Watson, Laura, *Paul Dukas: Composer and Critic* (Woodbridge: 2019)
Wawrzycka, Jolanta, 'Newspapers, Print, Language: Steganography', in William S. Brockman, Tekla Mecsnóba and Sabrina Alano, eds., *Publishing in Joyce's Ulysses: Newspapers, Advertising and Printing* (Leiden: 2018), 57–76
Webern, Anton von, *Letters to Hildegard Jone and Josef Humplik*, ed. Josef Polnauer (Bryn Mawr: 1959)
_____, *Sketches (1926–1945): Facsimile Reproductions from the Composer's Autograph Sketchbooks in the Moldenhauer Archive*, ed. Hans Moldenhauer and Ernst Krenek (New York: 1968)

Wegman, Rob C., 'Busnoys' "Anthoni usque limina" and the Order of Saint-Antoine-en-Barbefosse in Hainaut', *Studi musicali* 17 (1988), 15–31

⸻, 'Jacobus de Ispania and Liège', *Journal of the Alamire Foundation* 8 (2016), 253–74

Wehner, Ralf, *Felix Mendelssohn Bartholdy: Thematisch-systematisches Verzeichnis der musikalischen Werke (MWV)* (Wiesbaden: 2009)

⸻, '"Mit Deinen Rebusen machst Du uns doch alle zu Eseln." Zu einigen Bilderrätseln von Felix Mendelssohn Bartholdy', *Mendelssohn Studien* 20 (2017), 111–25

Weiss, Stefan, 'Musikalische Kryptographie: Eine Ergänzung', *Die Musikforschung* 46 (1993), 287–8

Weissweiler, Eva, ed., *The Complete Correspondence of Clara and Robert Schumann*, trans. Hildegard Fritsch and Ronald L. Crawford (New York: 1994), vol. 1

Weyrich, B. E. A., *Die Instrumentalton-Sprechkunst oder Anleitung, durch Instrumentaltöne alle Nachrichten in die Ferne zu geben, sowohl im Frieden als im Kriege, beim Civile und Militair, auf dem Lande und Meere* (Leipzig: 1830)

Whittall, 'Leitmotif', in Stanley Sadie, ed., *The New Grove Dictionary of Music and Musicians* (London: 2001), vol. 14, 527.

Whittall, Arnold, 'Pierre Boulez and the Suspension of Narrative', in Edward Campbell and Peter O'Hagan, eds., *Pierre Boulez Studies* (Cambridge: 2016), 354–72

Whitwell, David, *La Téléphonie and the Universal Musical Language*, 2nd ed. (Austin: 2012)

Wickes, Lewis, 'Schoenberg, *Erwartung*, and the Reception of Psychoanalysis in Musical Circles in Vienna until 1910/11', *Studies in Music* 23 (1989), 88–106

Wiley, Roland John, *Tchaikovsky* (New York: 2009)

Wilkins, Ernest H., 'Maria ... Prete', *Italica* 28/2 (June 1951), 101–3.

Wilkins, John, *Mercury: or the Secret and Swift Messenger. Shewing How a Man May with Privacy and Speed Communicate his Thoughts to a Friend at any Distance* (London: 1641; repr. Philadelphia: 1984)

Williams, Peter, *The Organ Music of J. S. Bach* (Cambridge: 1985), 3 vols.

Williamson, John, 'Introduction: A Catholic Composer in the Age of Bismarck', in John Williamson, ed., *The Cambridge Companion to Bruckner* (Cambridge: 2004), 3–14

Winternitz, Emanuel, 'Gnagflow Trazom: An Essay on Mozart's Script, Pastimes, and Nonsense Letters', *Journal of the American Musicological Society* 11 (1958), 200–16

⸻, 'Leonardo and Music', in Ladislao Reti, *The Unknown Leonardo* (New York: 1974), 110–35

Wolff, Christoph, *Bach: Essays on His Life and Music* (Cambridge, MA: 1991)

_____, *Johann Sebastian Bach: The Learned Musician* (New York: 2000)
Wolff, Helmut Christian, *Telemanns Beschreibung einer Augen-Orgel (1739)* (Blankenburg: 1982)
Wolzogen, Hans von, *Guide through the Music of R. Wagner's "The Ring of the Nibelung" (Der Ring des Nibelungen)*, trans. Ernst von Wolzogen (Leipzig: n.d. [after 1876])
Wong, Wendy H. W., 'The "Imperial and Royal-Court Schumann Robber": The Unpublished Piano Cycles of Ernst von Dohnányi', *Fontes Artis Musicae* 57 (2010), 86–114
Wright, Craig, 'An Example of Musical Inversion from the Circle of Dufay', in Alan W. Atlas, ed., *Papers Read at the Dufay Quincentenary Conference* (Brooklyn, NY: 1976), 144–8
_____, 'Dufay's *Nuper rosarum flores*, King Solomon's Temple, and the Veneration of the Virgin', *Journal of the American Musicological Society* 47 (1994), 395–439
_____, *The Maze and the Warrior: Symbols in Architecture, Theology and Music* (Cambridge: 2001)
Wu, Jean Marie, 'Mystical Symbols of Faith: Olivier Messiaen's Charm of Impossibilities', in Siglind Bruhn, ed., *Messiaen's Language of Mystical Love* (New York: 1998), 85–120
Wuidar, Laurence, 'Les *Geroglifici Musicali* du Padre Lodovico Zacconi', *Revue belge de musicologie* 61 (2007), 61–87
Xenakis, Iannis, *Formalized Music: Thought and Mathematics in Composition* (Stuyvesant, NY: 1992)
Yates, Frances, *The Rosicrucian Enlightenment* (London: 1972)
Yearsley, David, *Bach and the Meanings of Counterpoint* (Cambridge: 2002)
Yudha, Cicilia, 'Pianist and Composer Robert Casadesus: *Huit Études*, Opus 28 and Toccata, Opus 40' (D.M.A. diss., University of North Carolina at Greensboro, 2012)
Zak, Vladimir, 'Shostakovich's Idioms', in Ho and Feofanov (1998), 495–520
Zarlino, Gioseffo, *Le istitutioni harmoniche: A Facsimile of the 1558 Venice Edition* (New York: 1965)
Zaslaw, Neal, 'Mozart's Modular Minuet Machine', in László Vikárius and Vera Lampert, eds., *Essays in Honor of László Somfai on His Seventieth Birthday: Studies in the Interpretation and the Sources of Music* (Lanham, MD: 2005), 219–35
Zimmerman, Nadya, 'Musical Form as Narrator: The Fugue of the Sirens in James Joyce's "Ulysses,"' *Journal of Modern Literature* 26 (2002), 108–18
Ziolkowski, Theodore, 'Leverkühn's Compositions and Their Musical Realizations', *The Modern Language Review* 107 (2012), 837–56

Index

Bold numbers refer to pages with musical examples.
Italicized numbers refer to pages with illustrations.
Bold and italicized numbers refer to pages with tables.

A
acronym, 73
acrostic(s), 21–23, 100, 231
   mesostich, 231, 368
   musical, 22–23, 73, 90, 93, 231
   telestich, 17, 231
Adler, Oskar, 339
   Einführung in die Astrologie als Geheimwissenschaft (*Introduction to the Secret Knowledge of Astrology*, 1935), 339
Adler, Samuel, 259
   Four Composer Portraits (2002), 259
Adorno, Theodor W., 343
aesthetics, 147
   Baumgarten, Alexander Gottlieb, 147
Agricola, Johann Friedrich, 137
Agricola, Martin, 27
   Suavissimae et iucundissimae harmoniae (*Sweetest and Most Delightful Harmonies*, 1567), 27
Alain, Jehan, 310. *See also* Duruflé, Maurice.
Alberti, Leon Battista, 79
   De componendis cifris (*On Composing Ciphers*, 1466), 79
   substitution system, polyalphabetic, 79
   volvelle, 79
alchemy, 108, 110
Algarotti, Count Francesco, 148
Al-Khalīl, 54
Al-Kindī, 54
   Manuscript on Deciphering Cryptographic Messages, A, (ninth century), 54
alphanumeric code(s), 2, 37
Altnikol, Johann Christoph, 138

American colonies, 255
anagram(s), 7, 17–18, 21, 23–28, 70–73, 84, 100, 115–117, 160, 166, 188, 230–231, 336n, 363
   musical anagram(s), 23–**26**, 166, 182–**183**, 204, **213**, **215**, 218, 276, 298, **336**, 348, 352
Andrews, Julie, 67
Anglican Church, 103
   Anglican Reformation, 101
   Book of Common Prayer, 103–104
Antheil, George, 365–366
   Ballet mécanique (1924), 365–366
   Joyce, James, 365
   Lamarr, Hedy, 366
   signal encryption, 366
Antiphoner, Léon, 57–58
   musical neumes, 57
Apollinaire, Guillaume, 32–33
   Calligrammes: Poèmes de la paix et de la guerre, 1913–1916 (1918), 32
   'Mon Coeur pareil à une flame renversée' ('My heart resembles an inverted flame'), 33
Applebaum, Mark, 259
   40 Cryptograms (2008), 259
Apuleius, 162
   Metamorphoses, 162
Aquinas, Thomas, 315–316
   Summa Theologiae, 315–316
Aristotle, 98
   Nichomachaen Ethics, 98
Arne, Thomas, 126
   'Rule Britannia', 126
Arnim, Gisela von, 209–211. *See also* Joachim, Joseph.

Arnold, Malcolm, 3–4, 280–281
  Fantasy on a Theme by John Field, Op. 116, 3–**4**
  Symphony No. 3, 280–281
Ars antiqua (*Ancient Art*), 69
Ars combinatoria (art of combinations), 151–158, 175
  culture of musical dilettantism, 151
  in music, 151–158
Ars nova (*New Art*), 69
  de Liège, Jacques, 69
Ars subtilior, 34
Artaria, Carlo, 162
Aubert, Louis, 295, 298–**299**
  Esquisse sur le nom de Fauré, 298–**299**
Augenmusik (eye music), 32–37, **207**, 374
  See calligram(s), colour music and picture song(s).
August the Younger, Duke of Brunswick-Lüneburg (pseud. Selenus, Gustavus), 84–**86**, 115
  Bibliotheca Augusta (Wolfenbüttel), 84
  Cryptomenytices et Cryptographiae Libri IX (*Secret Intimations and Secret Writings in Nine Books*, 1624), 84–**86**
Auric, Georges, 317
  Long, Marguerite, 317
Avignon, 34, 357

B
Bach, Carl Philipp Emanuel (C. P. E.), 21, 130, 137–138, 143–146, 152–153
  cipher on his initials (C. P. E.), **144**
  Einfall einen doppelten Contrapunct in der Octave von sechs Tacten zu machen ohne die Regeln davon zu wissen (*Method for Making Six Bars of Double Counterpoint at the Octave without Knowing the Rules*, 1754), 152–153
  Rondo in C major (H 260, 1780), **145**
  Sonata in C major (H 41, 1744), 144
  Symphony in C major (H 659, 1773), **145**
BACH cipher, **1**–2, 24, 26–**27**, 31, 46–47, 129–**135**, **137**, 143–146, 182–**183**, 194–**197**, 203, 205, 213, 218–219, 222, 226–**227**, 246–**247**, **249**, 256, **258**, 268, 273, **281**, 283–285, 287–289, 291–**294**, **336**–**337**, 347, 351–**353**, 356–358, 363. *See* BACH tetrachord and *Kreuzsymbol*.
  music of Bach, Johann Sebastian, 130–**135**
  music of Bach's family, 2, 130, 143–146
  music of other composers (non-Bach family), 2, 24, 26–**27**, 31, 46–47, 127–130, 182–**183**, 205, 213, 218–219, 222, 226–**227**, 246–**247**, **249**, 256, 258, 268, 273, 281, 283–285, 287–289, **291**–**294**, **336**–**337**, 347, 351–**353**, 356–358
Bach, Johann Christian ('London Bach'), 130, 143–144
Bach, Johann Christoph Friedrich ('Bückeburg Bach'), 138, 143–**144**
  cipher on his initials (H. C. F.), **144**
Bach, Johann Michael ('Wuppertal Bach'), 143–144
Bach, Johann Sebastian, 1–4, 18–19, 22, 24–**26**, 35, 38–39, 46, 91, 121, 127, 129–144, 147, 152, 175, 219, **247**, 250, 258, 283, 286–287, 289, **293**, 311, 324, 327, **337**, 347, **357**, 363
Bach revival, 2, 194, 294, 337
Berg, Alban, 289
Canonic Variations on 'Vom Himmel hoch da komm' ich her' (BWV 769, 1748), 132–134
Cantatas:
  Coffee Cantata (BWV 211 ca. 1734), 4
  Nach Dir, Herr, verlanget mich (BWV 150, 1707), 22
  O Ewigkeit, Du Donnerwort (BWV 60, 1723), 289
Capriccio on the Departure of a Beloved Brother (BWV 992, 1704), 371
chorale prelude for organ, BWV 668, 46
Concertos:
  Brandenburg Concertos, 289
  Brandenburg No. 2 in F major (BWV 1047, 1719–1720), 130–**131**
crab canon, 19
Das wohltemperierte Clavier (*The Well-Tempered Clavier*), Books I and II (BWV 846–893; I., 1720, rev. 1722; II. c. 1740, rev. 1739–42), 25–**26**, 134, 258, 363
Die Kunst der Fuge (*The Art of Fugue*, BWV 1080), 130, 134–139, 194, **336**–**337**
English Suite No. 6 in D minor (BWV 811), 131–**132**
'Es ist genug', *O Ewigkeit, Du Donnerwort* (BWV 60, 1723), 289
Forkel, Johann Nikolaus, 91
  gematria, 38–39
Goldberg Variations (1741), 91, 134, 136

INDEX 419

Henrici, C. F. (Picander), 39
'Herr, ich habe mißgehandelt' (chorale, BWV 330), 258
La Revue musicale, 291–292
Marpurg, Friedrich Wilhelm, 91
Mass in B minor, 3, 38, 287
Mendelssohn Bartholdy, Felix, 194
Minuet in G major, Anna Magdalena Bach Notebook, BWV Anh 116 (1725), 175
Musikalisches Opfer (*Musical Offering*, BWV 1079, 1747), 19, 139–143, 293–294, 336–**337**
numerology, 132, 136
'O Haupt voll Blut und Wunden' (chorale from the *St. Matthew Passion*), 194–**195**, 250
Partita No. 2 for solo violin (BWV 1004), 258
Prelude and Fugue in B-flat major (BWV 898), 196
St. Matthew Passion (BWV 244, 1727), 39, 194–195, 351
significance of the number fourteen, 132
Sinfonia No. 9 in F minor (BWV 795), 131, **133**
sons, 130, 137–138, 143
tricentenary of birth (1985), 311
representations of the cross in the sacred music, visual, 35
'Wenn wir in höchsten Nöten sein' (BWV 668), 138
BACH tetrachord, 197, 203, 352. *See* Bach cipher.
Bach, Wilhelm Friedemann, 130, 143
Bacon, Sir Francis, 114–118
  Bacon, Elizabeth, 121
  cipher, bilateral, 114–115
  Novum Organum (1620), 114
  Of the Advancement and Proficience of Learning (1605), 114
  Shakespeare Authorship Question (SAQ), 115–117
Bacon, Roger, 56
  Voynich Manuscript, 56
Balakirev, Mily, 264, 267
  Belyayev, Mitrofan, 267
  Glazunov, Alexander, 267
  Kopylov, Alexander, 267
  Lyadov, Anatoly, 267
  mighty little bunch (*moguchaya kuchka*), 267
  Sokoloff, Nikolai, 267

Balbalus, Notker, 57
  Liber hymnorum (*Book of Hymns*), 57
  St. Gallen, 57
  sequences, 57
Balzac, Honoré de, 329–331, 337
  Séraphita (1834), 329–331, 337
Bantock, Granville, 243–**244**
  Elgar, Edward, 243
  Helena Variations, 243–**244**
Barber, Samuel, 366
  Fadograph of a Yestern Scene, Op. 44 (1971), 366
Bardac, Raoul, 295, 297
  Quartet, String (collaborative, 1902), 295, 297. *See also* Ladmirault, Paul; Ravel, Maurice and Roger-Ducasse, Jean.
Bartók, Béla, 26–**27**, 43–46, 130, 324, 349
  Bagatelle, Op. 7 No. 12 (1909), 349
  Bluebeard's Castle (1911), 349
  Cantata profana (1930), 351
  Contrasts (1938), 44
  Divertimento (1939), 44
  Fibonacci Series, 349
  Golden Section, 349
  Music for Strings, Percussion and Celesta (1936), 26–**27**, 44–46, 351–352, 356
  palindromic arch form(s), 349–**350**
  Quartet, String:
    No. 1 (1909), 351
    No. 4 (1928), 349
    No. 5 (1934), 359–350, 352
  Scherzo in B-flat minor (1900), 350–**351**
  Sonata BB 12 (1898), 351
  Sonata for Two Pianos and Percussion (1937), 44
  Wooden Prince, The (1917), 349
Baudelaire, Charles, 343, 345
  Les fleurs du mal (1857), 343
Baumgarten, Alexander Gottlieb, 147
Bax, Arnold, Sir, 295, 301
  Suite on the Name Gabriel Fauré (1945), 295, 301
Beach, Amy, 130, 257–**258**
  cipher on her name, 258
  Prelude and Fugue, Op. 81 (1918), **258**
Beckett, Samuel, 365
Bede, Venerable, 55
  De temporum ratione (*The Reckoning of Time*), 55
Beethoven, Ludwig van, 21, 24–**26**, 146, 178, 180–185, 206, 222, 246, 258, 278, 281, 288–**289**, 313, 321–322, 330–331, 338, 342, 373

An die ferne Geliebte, Op. 98 (1816), 206
Bernard, Joseph Carl, 180–181
censors, 178, 180
Concerto, Piano, No. 4 in G major,
  Op. 58 (1806), 222, 373
Czerny, Carl, 181, 313
deafness, 182
Der glorreiche Augenblick, Op. 136 (*The Glorious Moment*, 1814), 181
Grosse Fuge, Op. 133 (1826), 182–183, 288
'Immortal Beloved', 342
Konversationshefte (conversation books), 180
'Kühl, nicht lau' (WoO 191), **24**
late style, 182
Leonore, Op. 72 (1805), 180
Overture on BACH, sketches for, 182
Quartet, String:
  No. 12 in E-flat major, Op. 127 (1825), 183–**184**
  No. 14 in C-sharp minor, Op. 131 (1826), **25**, 185, 278
  No. 15 in A minor, Op. 132 (1825), 182–184, 288
  No. 16 in F major, Op. 135 (1826), 182, 330–331
Sonata, Cello, D major, Op. 102 No. 2 (1815), 182
Sonatas, Piano:
  No. 8 in C minor, Op. 13 (*Pathétique*, 1799), 288
  No. 17 in D minor, Op. 31 No. 2 (Tempest, 1802), 288
  No. 26 in E-flat major, Op. 81a (Das Lebewohl, 1810), 371
  No. 29 in B-flat major, Op. 106, (Hammerklavier, 1818), 21, 182
  No. 31 in A-flat major, Op. 110 (1821), 258
  No. 32 in C minor, Op. 111 (1822), 281
Symphony:
  No. 1 in C major, Op. 21 (1801), 25–**26**
  No. 5 in C minor, Op. 67 (1808), 313
  No. 9 in D minor, Op. 125 (1824), 246
Wellingtons Sieg, Op. 91 (1814), 181
Begas (Begaße), Carl Joseph, 191–**192**
  Frederick William III, King of Prussia, 191
  Mendelssohn Bartholdy, Fanny, **191**
  Mendelssohn Bartholdy, Felix, 192
Belyayev (Belaieff), publisher, 268
  Belyayev cipher, 268–270
Benevoli, Orazio, 105
  Missa Salisburgensis, 105

Benjamin, George, 173
  Meditation on Haydn's Name (1982), 173
Bennett, Richard Rodney, 173
  Impromptu on the Name of Haydn (1982), 173
Berg, Alban, 21, 47, 225, 248, 250, 289, 333, 337–347, 349
  Adler, Oskar, 339
  Concerto, Violin (1935), 289, 339–340, 344
  Fuchs-Robettin, Dorothea, 343. See also *Lyric Suite*.
  Fuchs-Robettin, Hanna, 342, 344, 346. See also *Lyric Suite* and *Der Wein*.
  Kammerkonzert (*Chamber Concerto*, 1925), 248, 250, 340–342, 344–345
  Krasner, Louis, 339
  Loos, Adolf, 338
  Lulu, 21, 225, 345
  Lyric Suite (1929), 340, 342–**345**. See also Fuchs-Robettin, Dorothea and Hanna.
  palindromic designs, 21
  Reich, Willi, 340
  Schicksalszahl, 340. See significance of the number 23.
  Schoenberg, Arnold, 248, 341–342
  Schoenberg (née Zemlinsky), Mathilde, 342
  significance of the number 23, 47, 339–340
  'Über den Bergen' (1905), **341**
  Vier Stücke, Op. 5 (1913), 344
  Webern, Anton, 341
  Der Wein (1929), 340, 345–346
  Wozzeck (1922), 340. See also Büchner, Georg.
  Zemlinsky, Alexander von, 343
Bergerac, Cyrano de, 125
  Voyage dans la Lune, 125
Berio, Luciano, 364
  Les mots sont allés (*The Words Have Gone*, 1976), 355
  Sinfonia (1968), 365
  Tema (*Omaggio a Joyce*), 1958, 364
Berlioz, Hector, 194, 200–201
  Euphonia, 200
Bernac, Pierre, 33. See also Poulenc, Francis.
Bernstein, Leonard, 39
  Dybbuk (1974), 39
  interest in gematria, 39
  interest in the Kabbalah, 39

Bertini, Auguste, 178–179
　Mélographie, 178
　Sonata, Piano, in C major, Op. 2, 178
　Stigmatographie, ou l'art d'écrire avec des points, suivie de la Mélographie, nouvelle manière de noter la musique (Stigmatography, or the Art of Writing with Points, Followed by Melography, a New Manner of Notating Music, 1812), 177–**179**
Beziehungskunst, 203, 212, 226
Biber, Heinrich, 35
　Missa Salisburgensis, 105
　Rosary Sonatas, 35
Bible, Hebrew, 21, 52–53
　hidden biblical codes, 52–3
Biedermeier Vienna, 187
Bilderrätsel, 30–31. See also picture-puzzles and rebus.
Binchois, Gilles, 92
　'De plus en plus', 92
Bingen, Hildegard von, 57–63
　Liber divinorum operum (Book of Divine Works), 61
　lingua ignota, 57–61
　Melismenfreudigkeit ('melismatic joyfulness'), 60
　'O orzchis Ecclesia' (antiphon), 61–63.
Blavatsky, Helena, 271, 328
　Secret Doctrine, The (1888), 271
　theosophy, 271
Bliss, Sir Arthur, 251
Boccaccio, Giovanni, 22
　Amorosa visione (The Amorous Vision, 1343), 22
Boethius, 69
Boito, Arrigo, 356
　Fede a Bach ('Trust in Bach'), 356
Bolshevik Revolution, 273
Bonaparte, Louis Napoleon (Napoleon III), 201
Boniface, Archbishop of Mainz, 55
Borodin, Alexander, 267–269
　Quartet, String on the Theme B-la-f (1886), 269. See also Belyayev; Glazunov, Alexander; Lyadov, Anatoly and Rimsky-Korsakov, Nikolai.
Bossi, Marco Enrico, 356
　Fugue (1888), 356–**357**
Boulanger, Lili, 305–311
　ambigram, 306–**307**

Clairières dans le ciel (Clearings in the Sky, 1914), 306, **308–310**
Devriès, David, 309–310
Fauré, Gabriel, 309
Faust et Hélène, 309
monogram, 306–**307**
Prix de Rome, 305, 309
triskaidekaphilia, 306–307
water lilies, 306, 308
Boulanger, Nadia, 250
Boulez, Pierre, 260, 318–319, 354, 356
　Carter, Elliott, 260
　Dérive 1 (1984), 356
　…explosante-fixe… (1971), 318–319
　Incises (1994), 356
　Maderna, Bruno, 319
　Messagesquisse (1976), 356
　Répons (1981), 356
　Rituel (1975), 319
　Sacher cipher, 256
　Sacher, Paul, 319
　Stravinsky, Igor, 318
　Sur Incises (1996), 356
　ultramodernism, 318
boutsrimés, 193. See Endreim-Spiele and Knittelverse.
Bow, Clara, 12
Brahms, Johannes, 130, 146, 203, 206, 209–210, 212–219, 222, 227–228, 242–243
　Agathe cipher, 213–**214**
　anagram, 215
　BACH cipher, 222
　BAHS cipher, 209, 214–**215**
　Balladen for piano, Op. 10 (1854), 216
　Brahms, Christiane, 217–218
　Clara cipher, 217
　Concerto, Piano, No. 1 in D minor, Op. 15 (1858), 216–217
　Concerto, Violin, D major, Op. 77 (1878), 212
　Des jungen Kreislers Schatzkästlein, 210, 213
　Double Concerto in A minor, Op. 102 (1887), 213, 217
　Ein deutsches Requiem, Op. 45 (1868), 217–218
　FAE cipher, 213, 215
　FAF cipher ('frei aber froh'), 216–217
　Fünf Gedichte, Op. 19 (1858), 214–**215**
　Fugue in A-flat minor for organ, WoO 8 (1856), 214–**215**
　Gis-E-La cipher, 216

Hymne zur Verherrlichung des großen Joachim ('Hymn in Adulation of the Great Joachim', 1853), 212
Intermezzo in A minor, Op. 116 No. 2 (1892), 216–**217**
Joachim, Joseph, 212, 214, 215
Kalbeck, Max, 216
Quartet, String:
   No. 1 in C minor, Op. 51 (1873), 215–**216**
   No. 2 in A minor, Op. 51 (1873), 215–216
Schubring, Adolf, 215
Serenade, No. 2 in A major, Op. 16 (1859), 217
Sextet, String, No. 1 in G major, Op. 36 (1865), 213–**214**
Siebold, Agathe von, 213
Sonata, *FAE* (1853), 203, 209, 215. *See also* Dietrich, Albert; Joachim, Joseph; and Schumann, Robert.
Sonata, Piano, No. 3 in F minor, Op. 5 (1853), 213
Sonata, Violin, No. 1 in G major, Op. 78 (*Regen*, 1879), 227
Symphony:
   No. 1 in C minor, Op. 68 (1876), 216
   No. 3 in F major, Op. 90 (1883), 216
   No. 4 in E minor, Op. 98 (1885), 242–**243**
   Tragic Overture, Op. 81 (1880), 216
Trio, Piano, No. 1 in B major, Op. 8 (1854), 206, 217
'Und gehst du über den Kirchhof', Op. 44 No. 10 (1858), 213
Variations on a Theme by Robert Schumann, Op. 9 (1854), 217
Brecht, Bertold, 347
Breton, André, 318
Bridge, Frank, 32, 250, 364
   'Goldenhair' (1925), 364
   Rebus (1940), 32
British Broadcasting Corporation (BBC), 171–173, 248
Britten, Benjamin, 250–252, 280
   Albert Herring (1947), 252
   Billy Budd (1951), 251
   Britten, Charlotte Elizabeth, 250
   Elizabeth Variations (1929), 250
   Fanfare for D. W. (1970), 251
   Gloriana (1953), 252
   Noye's Fludde (1957), 252
   Peter Grimes (1945), 251
   Prodigal Son, The (1968), 252
   Rape of Lucretia (1946), 251, 280
   Rejoice in the Lamb (1943), 251, 280
   Scherzettino-A.B. (1971), 251
   Tema Sacher (1976), 354
   tonal encoding, 252
   Two Portraits (1930), 250
   Variations on a Theme by Frank Bridge (1937), 250
Brucci, Rudolf, 130
Bruckner, Anton, 35, 287, 321–327
   arithmomania, 322. See *Zählmanie*.
   autograph manuscripts of symphonies, 322
   Ave Maria (1861), 324
   Eckstein, Friedrich, 324, 327
   Fibonacci sequence, 323
   Golden Section (GS), 323
   grid, metrical, 322
   Grundbass (fundamental bass), 327
   Grundzahl (fundamental number), 324–324
   interest in cadavers, 322
   Löwe, Ferdinand, 323
   Mary, veneration of, 324
   obsessive-compulsive personality disorder, 322
   St. Stephen's Cathedral (Vienna), 325–326
   significance of the number eleven, 324
   Symphony:
      No. 5 (1877), 324–**325**
      No. 6 (1881), 323
      No. 8 (1890), 323
      No. 9 (1894), 322–**326**
   Zählmanie, 324
Brumel, Antoine, 120–122
   Missa Ut re mi fa sol la, 120, 122
Büchner, Georg, 340
   Woyzeck (1836), 340
Buecking, Johann Jacob Heinrich, 175–178
   Anweisung zur geheimen Correspondenz systematisch entworfen (*Instructions for Secret Correspondence, Systematically Designed*, 1804), 175–178
   encryption, musical, 175
Bull, John, 121
   Fitzwilliam Virginal Book, 121
   Ut, re, mi, fa, sol, la, 121
Burney, Charles, 91, 106, 108, 152
Bus, Gervais de, 73
   Roman de Fauvel, 73

INDEX   423

Busnois, Antoine, 92–96
　Anthoni usque limina, 92–94
　Beatrice of Aragon, Queen of Hungary, 95
　Charles the Bold, 92
　d'Aqueville, Jacqueline, 93
　In hydraulis, 93–**94**. *See also* Ockeghem, Johannes and Pythagorean theory.
　Maintes femmes, 94
　Missa L'homme armé, 95
　Ockeghem, Johannes, 92–94
　Order of St. Anthony, 93
　St. Anthony the Abbot, 94
Busoni, Feruccio, 130, 356–357
　Fantasia contrappuntistica (1910), 356
Busse, Karl, 341
Bussotti, Sylvano, 130
Byrd, William, 101, 121
　Bacon, Elizabeth, 121
　My Ladye Nevells Booke (1591), 121
Byzantine Empire, 41
　Constantine I ('the Great'), 41
　Constantinople, fall of (1453), 41

C

Cage, John, 318, 333, 367–368, 374
　James Joyce, Marcel Duchamp, Erik Satie: An Alphabet (1982), 368
　I Ching, 367
　Roaratorio, An Irish Circus on Finnegans Wake (1979), 368
　'The Wonderful Widow of Eighteen Springs' (1942), 367
　Zen Buddhism, 367
calligram(s), 32–33. *See* poèmes figures and picture song(s).
　Apollinaire, Guillaume, 32
　Cordier, Baude, 33
　Poulenc, Francis, 32
　Senleches, Jacob, 33
Cambell, Florence Evylinn, 333
　Your Days Are Numbered (1931), 333
canon, puzzle, 24, 31, 34–35, 105, 166–167
　Dossi, Dosso, 34
　Haydn, Franz Joseph, 166–167
　Kuhlau, Friedrich, 24
　Micheli, Romano, 105
　Senfl, Ludwig, 35
Carlsbad Decrees, 181
　Burschenschaften (student associations), 181
　Sand, Karl, 181
　Kotzebue, August von, 181, 188

Carol, Lewis, 22
　Alice's Adventures in Wonderland, 22
　Through the Looking Glass, 22. *See also* Chin, Unsuk, and Del Tredici, David.
Carter, Elliot, 259–260, 318
　A 6 Letter Letter (1996), 260
　Au quai (2002), 260
　Boston Concerto (2002), 259
　Epigrams (2012), 259
　Frost-Jones Carter, Helen, 259
　HBHH (2007), 260
　Instances (2012), 259
　Réflexions (2004), 260
　Rhapsodic Musings (2000), 260
Casadesus, Robert, 310
　Hommage à Chausson Op. 51 (1954), 310
　Prélude sur le nom de Ronsard, Op. 5 No. 5 (1924), 310
Casals, Pablo, 129
Casella, Alfredo, 130, 357
　Ricercari sul nome 'Bach' (*Ostinato*, 1932), 357
Castel, Louis Bertrand, 36
　clavessin pour les yeux, 36. *See* colour-music.
Castelnuovo-Tedesco, Mario, 358–**359**
　'Greeting Cards', Op. 170 (1953–1967), 358–**359**
Cathedral of Notre Dame (Paris), 18, 177
Cerone, Pietro, 34
　El Melopeo (1613), 34
Champollion, Jean-François, 49
　Rosetta Stone, 49
chance games, musical, 153. *See* dice games, musical.
chant, Gregorian, 252
　Liber usualis, 252
Chaplin, Charlie, 12–16
　Circus, The (1928), 14, 16
　Gold Rush, The (1925), 14
　Modern Times (1936)
　pantomime, silent, 12
characteristica universalis (universal language), 106, 118–119, 123–**125** 151, 197–**199**, 210, 375
　Godwin, Francis, 123, 197
　Kircher, Athanasius, 106, 119, 151, 197
　Leibniz, Gottfried Wilhelm, 118, 151, 198
　Sudre, François, 198–210
　Weyrich, B. E. A., 198–**199**
　Wilkins, John, Bishop of Chester, 124–**125**, 197

Charles the Bold, 92
Chaucer, Geoffrey, 22, 56–57
  An ABC (1369?), 22
  Equatorie of the Planetis, 56
  Treatise on the Astrolabe (1391), 56–57
Chausson, Ernest, 310
  centenary of birth (1955), 310
Cherubini, Luigi, 198
Chin, Unsuk, 22–23
  Akrostichon-Wortspiel (*Acrostic Word Play*), 22–23
Christian symbolism in music, 35, 40, 47, 70, 76–77, 89–91, 110–111, 286
  Gubaidulina, Sofia, 47
  Ockeghem, Johannes, 91
chronogram, 24, 26–28, 166
  Hilton, James, 26–27
  music, 27–28, 166
Chumbawamba (band), 281
  'Hammer, Stirrup, and Anvil', *ABCDEFG* (2010), 281
cipher (non-musical), 51, 54, 84, 114–116, 236, 255
  Bacon, Sir Francis, 114
  bilateral, 114–115
  Caesar, 51, 84
  de Vigenère, Blaise, 83–84
  digraphic, 81
  etymology of, 54
  nihilist, 236
  Shakespeare Authorship Question (SAQ), 115–117
  substitution, 50, 52, 55, 78–81, 84, 115, 232, 255
    atbash, 52
    mlecchita-vikalpa, 50
    monoalphabetic system, 79, 232
    non-alphabetic system, 78
    polyalphabetic system, 79, 84, 232, 255
  volvelle, 79
  xenocrypt, 57
Clementi, Aldo, 130
Colonna, Marco Antonio, 84
colour-music, 36–37
  Castel, Louis Bertrand, 36
  Gubaidulina, Sofia, 37
  Scriabin, Alexander, 36–37
  Wallace Rimington, Alexander, 36
Columbus, Christopher, 78
Congress of Vienna, 182, 183
Conradi, Wilhelm, 130
Copland, Aaron, 318
Corbusier, Le, 369

Cordier, Baude, 33
  'Belle, bonne, sage' ('Beautiful, good, wise [lady]'), 33
  'Tout par compass suy composés' ('Entirely from a compass am I made'), 33
Corigliano, John, 260
  Lord of Cries, The (2021), 260
  Symphony No. 1 (1990), 260
Cortés, Hernán, 78
  substitution system, non-alphabetic, 78
Coulthard, Jean, 130
Council of Nicaea (325 AD), 57
cross, visual representations, 35, 55
  literature, 55
  music, 35
Crumb, George, 32, 370–372
  Black Angels (1970), 370–372
  Makrokosmos I and *II* (1972, 1973), 32
cryptanalysis, 53–54, 56, 77, 83, 255. See also cryptology.
  Poe, Edgar Allan, 255
  Venetian, 77
  Viète, François, 78
cryptology, 54–55, 57, 77–78, 83–84. See also cryptanalysis.
  August the Younger, Duke of Brunswick-Lüneburg, 84
  Ferrara, 77
  Florence, 77
  Milan, 77
  Vatican, 78
Cui, César, 267, 268
  Scherzo, Op. 1 (1857), **267**
culture of musical dilettantism, 151
  Ars combinatoria, 151

D
Dallapiccola, Luigi, 130, 358
  Canti di liberazione (*Songs of Liberation*, 1955), 358
  Quaderno musicale di Annalibera (1952), 358
d'Arezzo, Guido, 63–67, 85, 87, 94, 120–122, 178, 362
  antiphoner, 63
  Epistola de ignotu cantu (*Letter Concerning an Unknown Chant*), 64
  Guidonian hand, 120, 178
  Guidonian hexachord, 94, 120–121
  Micrologus (post 1026), 63
  musical staff, 64
  Regule Rithmice, 67

solmization syllables, 64, 85, 87, 94, 120, 122, 362
Ut queant laxis, 64-**66**
David, Ferdinand, 209
  Schumann, Robert, 209
Debussy, Claude, 43-44, 169, 171, 269-**270**, 303, 305, 359
  death (1918), 303
  Hommage à Haydn (1909), 169, 171
  Images I (1905), 43
  'Jardins sous la pluie' (1903), 44
  La mer (1905), 43
  La Revue musicale, 303, 305
  Meck, Nadezhda von, 269
  'Open Letter to the Chevalier W. Gluck', 171
  Prélude à l'après-midi d'un faune (*Prelude to the Afternoon of a Faun*, 1894), 305
  Quartet, String, in G minor (1893), 269-**270**
Del Tredici, David, 22
  Final Alice (1976), 22
Denisov, Edison, 282-**283**
  1969 DSCH, 282-**283**
  cipher on his name, 282
  Requiem (1980), 282
  Sonata, Saxophone (1971), 282
Devrient, Eduard, 129
Diabelli, Anton, 185-186
dice games, musical, 152-154. See musical chance games, 153
  Bach, Carl Philipp Emanuel, 152-153
  Gioco filharmonico (*Harmonic Game*), 153
  Kirnberger, Johann Philipp, 151-152
  Mozart, W. A., 153-154
Dickens, Charles, 229-230
  biscriptal, 230
  Pickwick Papers (1837), 229
  shorthand, 230
  Mystery of Edwin Drood, The (1870), 229
Dies irae, 281, 370
Dietrich, Albert, 203, 209-210, 212
  Sonata, *FAE* (1853), 203, 210. *See also* Brahms, Johannes; Joachim, Joseph; Schumann, Clara; and Schumann, Robert.
Dietrich, Marlene, 12-14
  Der blaue Engel (*The Blue Angel*, 1930), 13
d'Indy, Vincent, 130, 291-292
  Tableaux de voyage, Op. 33 (1888), 291
Dohnányi, Ernst von, 351

Six Piano Pieces (1891), 351
Winterreigen (*Winter Dances*, 1901), 351
Dossi, Dosso, 34
  Allegory of Music, 34
Dounias, Minos, 149
  frequency analysis, 149
  Tartini, Giuseppe, 149
Dowson, Ernest, 330
  Seraphita, 330
Doyle, Arthur Conan, Sir, 232, 255
  Adventure of Dancing Men, The (1903), 232
  cryptography, 232
  Sherlock Holmes mysteries, 232
Drosnin, Michael, 52
  Bible Code, The, 52
Duchamp, Marcel, 368
  An Alphabet, 368
Duchêne, Emile, 293
  Fugue symétrique, 293
Du Fay, Guillaume, 29, 38, 41-42, 90
  gematria, 38
  Inclita stella maris, 90
  Missa L'homme armé, 90
  Nuper rosarum flores (1436), 41, 42
  Resvellies vous et faits chiere lye (1423), 42
Dukas, Paul, 169-170, 245, 295, 302-**305**, 310-311
  L'Apprenti sorcier (1897), 245, 304
  La Péri (1912), **304-305**
  Pierné, Gabriel, 303
  La Plainte, au loin, du faune (*The Lament from Afar of the Faun*, 1920), 305
  Prélude élégiaque sur le nom de Haydn (1909), 169-170, 303
  La Revue musicale, 295
  Ropartz, Guy, 303-305
  Symphony in C (1896), **304-305**
Dunstable, John, 40-41, 95
  isorhythmic motets, 40-41
  Veni sancta spiritus et emitte, 95
Durand, Jacques, 44
Duruflé, Maurice, 310
  Prélude et Fuge sur le nom d'A.L.A.I.N. (1943), 310
Dutilleux, Henri, 316, 355-356
  Long, Marguerite, 317
  Mystère de l'instant (1989), 356
  Trois strophes sur le nom de Sacher (1976), 356-**357**

E

Eckstein, Friedrich, 324, 327-328
  Bruckner, Anton, 324, 327

vegetarianism, 327
Vienna Theosophical Society, 328
Écorcheville, Jules, 169, 172
  La Revue Musicale de la S. I. M., 169
Eisler, Hanns, 130, 347
  communist sympathies, 347
  House Committee on Un-American Activites, 347
  Präludium und Fuge über BACH, Op. 46 (1934), 347
  Vierzehn Arten den Regen zu beschreiben (*Fourteen Ways to Describe the Rain*, Op. 70, 1941), 347
Elders, Willem, 40
Elfman, Danny, 281
  Dolores Claiborne (1995)
Elgar, Carice, 230, 231, 238. See Elgar, Sir Edward.
Elgar, Caroline Alice, 230, 240. See Elgar, Sir Edward.
  C. A. E., 230, 240
  Craeg Lea, 230
Elgar, Sir Edward, 230-**244**, 326
  Allegretto for violin and piano (1885), **238-239**
  Botanic Acrostic, 231
  Caractacus, Op. 35, 242-**243**
  Craeg Lea, 230
  crossword(s), cryptic, 231, 238
  cryptograms, musical, 238
  Dorabella cipher, 231, 233-**235**, 238, 243. See also Powell (née Penny), Dora.
  Dream of Gerontius, The (1900), 238
  Elgar Birthplace Museum, 236
  Enigma Variations, Op. 36 (1899), **238-244**, **326**
  E. W. E. (initials), 231
  GEDGE cipher, 238
  Jaeger, August, 239
  Liszt cipher, 233-**235**
  Malvern Hills, 242
  puzzle(s), cryptographic, 230
  Schooling, Jason Holt, 235-238
  Schumann, Robert, 238
  shorthand, 234
  signature, musical, **239**
Elizabeth I, Queen of England, 78, 103-104, 115, 235
  Act of Uniformity, 104
  Babington Conspiracy of 1586, 78, 104
  Mary, Queen of Scots, 78
  Ridolfi, Roberto, 104
  Spanish Armada, 78

Walsingham, Sir Francis, 78, 104, 235
Ende, Michael, 22
  Die unendliche Geschichte (*The Neverending Story*, 1979), 22
Endreim-Spiele, 193. See *boutrimés* and *Knittelverse*.
Enescu, George, 295, 298-300
  Pièce pour piano sur le nom de Fauré (1922), 298-299
Ercole I d'Este, Duke of Ferrara, 87, 90, 96
equatorium, 56
Equidistant Letter Sequence (ELS), 53
Esterhàzy family, 168
Evangelium Series, 46
  Gubaidulina, Sofia, 46

F
Farmer, John, 113
  Divers & Sundry Waies of Two Parts in One, to the Number of Fortie upon one Playnsong, 113
Fasch, Carl Friedrich Christian, 192
  Berlin Singakademie, 192
Fauré, Gabriel, 13-14, 170, 293, 295-**301**, 305, 309
  centenary of birth (1945), 301
  Fauré cipher, **295-301**
  La bonne chanson, Op. 61 (1894), 300
  La Revue musicale, 297-298
  Pénélope (1913), 300
  Une chatelaine en sa tour (*A Lady of the Castle in Her Tower*), Op. 110 (1918), 300
Fenimore Cooper, James, 255
  Spy, The (1821), 255
Ferneyhough, Brian, 43
  Quartet, String, No. 2 (1980), 43
Ferrara, 120-123
Ferrari, Carlotta, 358
  Ciaconna e fuga (2016), 358
  Ciaconna sul nome di Bach (2015), 358
Ferrero, Lorenzo, 281
  DEsCH (2006), 281
  Op. 111 – Bagatella su Beethoven (2009), 281
Fesca, Friedrich Ernst, 189-**191**
  Quartet, String, in B-flat major, Op. 1 No. 3, 190-**191**
Fibonacci sequence (Fibonacci series), 41-47, 92, **135**, 349, 369. See also Golden Section (GS).
  Bach, J.S., **135**
  Bartók, Béla, 44-**45**, 349

Bruckner, Anton, 323
Debussy, Claude, 43
Ferneyhough, Brian, 43
Gubaidulina, Sofia, 45–47
Krenek, Ernst, 45
Ockeghem, Johannes, 92
origins of, 43
Pisa, Leonardo da (*alias* Fibonacci), 43
Smirnov, Dmitri, 45
Stockhausen, Karlheinz, 45
Xenakis, Iannis, 369
Field, John, 3–4
BEEF CABBAGE cipher, 3
Nocturne No. 7 in C major (1821), 3
film music, 12
films, silent, 12
'talkies', 12
First World War, 257, 271–272, 302, 306
Zimmerman Telegram, 257
FitzAlan, Henry, twelfth Earl of Arundel, 104
Arundel House, 104–105
Nonsuch Palace, 104–105
Florence, 77, 103
Machiavelli, Niccolò, 77
Medici family, 77, 103
Striggio, Alessandro, the elder, 103
Florence Cathedral, 41, 90
Brunelleschi, Filippo, 41
Forkel, Johann Nikolaus, 91, 142
Bach, J.S., biography of, 91
Ockeghem, Johannes, 91
Fortner, Wolfgang, 355
Zum Spielen (1976), 355
Foss, Lukas, 258
Symphony of Chorales (1958), 258
Françaix, Jean, 317
Long, Marguerite, 317
Francis I, Emperor of Austria, 178, 181. *See* Francis II, Holy Roman Emperor.
censorship campaign, 178, 180
Francis II, Holy Roman Emperor. *See* Francis I, Emperor of Austria.
Franck, César, 169, 291
Prélude, Aria et Final (1886), 291
Prélude, Choral et Fugue (1885), 291
Franco-Flemish composers, 18, 87, 90, 100–101, 167, 254. *See also* Binchois, Giles; Brumel, Antoine; Busnois, Antoine, Du Fay, Guillaume; Josquin des Prez; Obrecht, Jacob and Ockeghem, Johannes.
Franz Joseph I, Emperor of Austria, 332

Frederick the Great, King of Prussia, 4, 140, 147, 293
royal theme, 140–141, 293–294. See *The Musical Offering* under Bach, J.S.
Freemasonry, 161–162
French Revolution, 65, 148
Reign of Terror, 148
French cipher system (musical), 13–14, 301
French Wars of Religion (1562–1598), 78
Frescobaldi, Giralomo, 121–123
Capricci (1624), 122
d'Este family, 121
Ferrara, 121–123
Fiori musicali (1635) 122–123
Rome, 121
Freud, Sigmund, 328–329, 339
Civilization and Its Discontents (1930), 329
Interpretation of Dreams, The (1899), 328
Mahler, Gustav, 329

G
Gabrieli, Andrea, 105
Gabrieli, Giovanni, 34, 105
Gade, Niels, 31, 203, 209, 218–219, 222
Drei kleine Clavierstücke, Op. 2a (1841), 218–219
Gaade I 4 bundne Toner (*Puzzle in 4 Obligatory Notes*, 1875), **219**
GADE cipher, 31, 209, 218–**219**
Hauptmann, Moritz, 218
Rebus (1875), 31, 219
Schumann, Robert, 218–**219**
Sonata, Violin, No. 1 in A major, Op. 6 (1843), 218–**219**
Symphony No. 5 in D minor, Op. 25 (1852), 218
Galilei, Vincenzo, 34
Garbo, Greta, 12. See also *The Seven Stars' Symphony*, Op. 132 under Koechlin, Charles.
stage name as an acrostic, 12
gematria, 37–47
Christianity, early, 37–38
Kabbalah, 37
musical (number symbolism), 38–47
Bach, J.S., 38
Bernstein, Leonard, 39
Du Fay, Guillaume, 42
Franco-Flemish composers, 38
Josquin des Prez, 40
Kuhnau, Johann, 39
Machaut, Guillaume de, 38, 40

George, Stefan, 330–331, 343, 345
　Dowson, Ernest, 330
　Schoenberg, Arnold, 331
German Democratic Republic, 347
Gesualdo, Carlo, 358
Gigout, Eugène, 295
　Rhapsodie sur des airs Catalans (1897), 295
Ginastera, Alberto, 130, 355
　Puneña No. 2, Op. 45 (1976), 355
Glareanus, Heinrich, 88–89
Glazunov, Alexander, 267–269
　Quartet, String, on the Theme B-la-f (1886), 269
　Sabela, Nadeschda, 268
　Suite, Op. 2 (1883), 268
　Walzer, Op. 23 (1890), 268
Godowsky, Leopold, 130
Godwin, Francis, 123–125, 197
　de Bergerac, Cyrano, 125
　Man in the Moone, or a Discourse of a Voyage Thither, The (1638), 123–**124**
　universal language, 123
Goehr, Alexander, 130, 318
Goethe, Johann Wolfgang von, 164
　Freemasonry, 164
golden mean, 92. *See* Golden Section (GS).
　Xenakis, Iannis, 369
golden ratio, 135. *See* Golden Section (GS).
Golden Section (GS), 41–44, 46, 74, 135, 245–246, 323, 349, 369. *See* Fibonacci sequence and golden ratio.
　Bartók, Béla, 44, 349
　Bruckner, Anton, 323
　Debussy, Claude, 43
　Du Fay, Guillaume, 42
　Euclid, 42
　Gubaidulina, Sofia, 46
　Holst, Gustav, 245–246
　Machaut, Guillaume de, 74
　nombre d'or, 44
　Ockeghem, Johannes, 92
Goldsmith, Oliver, 126–127
　Deserted Village, The, 126–127
Górecki, Henryk, 372–374
　Ad matrem, Op. 29 (1972), 372
　Beatus vir, Op. 38 (1979), 372
　Good Night, Op. 63 (1990), 372
　Recitativa I Ariosa 'Lerchenmusik', Op. 53, 372–373
　Symphony No. 4, Op. 85 (*Tansman Episodes*, 2014), 373

Graham Bell, Alexander, 199
　telephone, 199
graphology, 235
Graun, Carl Heinrich, 132
Grieg, Edvard, 219, **220**, 270
　Lyric Pieces, Op. 57 (1893), 219–**220**
Grillparzer, Franz, 180
Grove's Dictionary of Music and Musicians (1906), 363
Gubaidulina, Sofia, 35, 37, 43, 45–47, 130, 283, 324
　Alleluia (1990), 37. *See also* colour-music.
　cipher on her name, 283
　Gerade und Ungerade (*Even and Odd*, 1991), 46
　Heute früh, kurz vor dem Erwachen (*Early in the Morning, Right Before Awakening*, 1993), 46
　Im Anfang war der Rhythmus (*In the Beginning Was Rhythm*, 1984), 46
　In croce (1979), 35.
　interest in numerology, 43, 45–46
　Meditation on the Bach Chorale 'Vor Deinen Thron tret ich hiermit' (1993), 46–47. *See also* Chorale prelude for organ, BWV 668, under Bach, Johann Sebastian.
　Reflections on the Theme BACH (2002), 283. *See also Die Kunst der Fuge* under Bach, Johann Sebastian.
　Sieben Worte (*Seven Last Words*, 1982), 35
　So sei es (2013), 283. *See also Well-Tempered Clavier*, Book I, under Bach, Johann Sebastian.
Gurney, Thomas, 230
　Brachygraphy, 230

H
Hahn, Reynaldo, 169–170
　Thème varié sur le nom de Haydn (1909), 169–170
Hamasyan, Tigran 281
　'Ara Resurrected', *The Call Within* (2020), 281
Handel, George Frideric, 132, 289
Hanslick, Eduard, 321
Harbison, John, 186–187
　November 19, 1828 (1986), 186–187
Harlow, Jean, 13. *See also Epitaphe* under Koechlin, Charles.
Harvey, Lilian, 12. *See also* music for film stars under Koechlin, Charles.

Haydn, Franz Joseph, 14, **19**, 21, 25–**26**,
    147–148, 153–**155**, 158, 161–163,
    165–173, 291, 371
  Cantatas:
    Applausus (1767), 166
  centenary of death (1909), 14, 169, 291
  Creation (1798), 148
  Freemasonry, 161–162
  HAYDN cipher, 169–173, 291
  Hoboken, Anthony van, 171
  La Revue Musicale, Haydn centenary
    issue, 169–171
  Quartet, String:
    C major, Op. 20 No. 2 (1772), 154–155,
      158, 170
    E-flat major, Op. 76 No. 3, 'Emperor'
      (1797), 168–**169**
    E-flat major, Op. 76 No. 6 (1797),
      154–**155**
    F minor, Op. 20 No. 5 (1772), 25–**26**
  reception, 169–173
  semiquincentennial of his birth (1982),
    19, 169
  Symphony:
    No. 26 in D minor (*Lamentatione*,
      1770), 172
    No. 45 in F-sharp minor (*Farewell*,
      1772), 371
    No. 47 in G major (*Palindrome*, 1772),
      19, 166, 173
    No. 92 in G major, (*Oxford*, 1789), 154
    No. 103 in E-flat major (*Drum Roll*,
      1795), 154
Haydn, Michael, 165–**166**
  musical alphabet, **165–166**
Henry IV (of Navarre), 78
  Viète, François, 78
Henry VIII, King of England, 104
  Nonsuch Palace, 104
Hensel (*née* Mendelssohn Bartholdy),
    Fanny, 191–**192**, 196–**197**
  Hiob (1831), 196–**197**
  'Im Herbst' (H-U 407, 1844), 196
  Klavierstück on the Name of Begas, H-U
    41 (1821), 192
  Sonata, Piano, in C minor (1824), 196
  Zelter, Carl Friedrich, 192
Henze, Hans Werner, 355
  Capriccio (1976), 355
Herring, Carl Gottlieb, 5
  CAFFEE cipher, 5
hexachord(s), 131
  Brumel, Antoine, 120–122

Bull, John, 121
Byrd, William, 121
Cabanilles, Juan, 121
Fasolo, Giovanni Battista, 121
Frescobaldi, Giralomo, 121
Froberger, Johann Jakob, 121
Strozzi, Gregorio, 121
Sweelinck, Jan Pieterszoon, 121
Trabaci, Giovanni Maria, 121
hieroglyph(s), Egyptian, 49–50, 107
  demotic, 49–50
  Egyptology, 49
  Rosetta Stone, 49
Hilton, James, 26–27
  *Chronograms Collected: More than 4,000
    in Number* (1882), 26–27
Hindemith, Paul, 246, 348–**350**
  Cello Concerto (1940), 246
  Clarinet Quintet, Op. 30
  Die Harmonie der Welt (1951), 348
  Die Harmonie der Welt (1957), 348
  Hin und zurück (*Round Trip*, 1927), 349
  Horn Concerto (1950), 348
  Ludus tonalis (*Tonal Game*, 1942), 348
  Sonata for Althorn and Piano (1943),
    349–350
Hoffmann, Ernst Theodor Amadeus, 218
Hollandt, Friedrich, 85–87. See also
  August the Younger, Duke of
  Brunswick-Lüneburg.
Holliger, Heinz, 260, 355–356
  Chaconne (1976), 355–356
Holst, Gustav, 244–**246**
  astrology, 245
  Planets, The (1920), 244–**246**
Honegger, Arthur, 130, 291–**292**, 301–**303**
  Hommage à Albert Roussel (1929),
    301–**303**
  *Prélude, Arioso et fughetta sur le nom de
    Bach* (1932), 291–**292**
Hooper, William, 149–**150**
  Rational Recreations (1774), 149–150
Horace, 65–67, 147
  carmina (songs), 66–67
  'Ode to Phyllis' from the *Odes*, 65–67.
    See also *Ut queant laxis* under
    d'Arezzo, Guido.
Howard, Thomas, fourth Duke of Norfolk,
    104–105. See also Tudor, Mary
    ('Bloody').
Huber, Klaus, 354–355
  Transpositio ad Infinitum (1976), 354–355
Hugo, Victor, 201

Humboldt, Alexander von, 201

I
Ibert, Jacques, 302
  Toccata sur le nom d'Albert Roussel (1929), 302
d'Indy, Vincent, 169–170
  Menuet sur le nom d'Haydn (1909), 170
Isidore of Seville, Archbishop, 55
  Etymologiae (*Etymologies*), 55
Ivens, Joris, 347. See also Eisler, Hanns.
  Regen (*Rain*, 1929), 347
Ives, Charles, 130, 256–257
  All the Way Around and Back (1905–7), 257
  Henderson, William James, 256
  Piano Trio (1909–10), 256–257
  Three-Page Sonata (1905–7), 256
  Unanswered Question, The (1909), 256

J
Jacob, Gordon, 246
  Sextet for piano and winds (1956), 246
Jammes, Francis, 306
  Tristesses (*Sadnesses*, 1905), 306
Jannings, Emil, 13–14
Jeffes, Simon, 368–369
  CAGE DEAD (1992), 369
Jenkins, David, 259
  We Seven (2016), 259
Joachim, Joseph, 203, 209–215, 218, 220, 222–**223**, 268
  Arnim, Gisela von, 209–211
  BACH cipher, 213
  Brahms, Johannes, 210, 212–214, 226
  Concerto, Violin, in G major (1889), 212
  Demetrius Overture, Op. 6 (1854), 222
  Drei Stücke, Op. 2 No. 1 (1852), 212
  Drei Stücke, Op. 5, No. 2, 'Abendglocken' (1853), 209, 211–12, 220, 222–**223**
  FAE cipher ('frei aber einsam'), 203, 209–211, 213, 216
  Gis-E-La cipher, 203, 209, 213
  Hamlet Overture, Op. 4 (1853), 211
  Kleist Overture, Op. 13 (1856), 212
  Liszt, Franz, 211, 220
  Notturno, Op. 12 (1858), 212
  Sonata, FAE (1853), 203, 209
  Variations on an Original Theme, Op. 10 (1855), 211
Josquin des Prez, 22, 34, 38, 40, 84, **87**–**90**, 106, 122, 168
  canon, puzzle, 34
  gematria, 38
  Illibata dei virgo nutrix (1508), 22, 88
  Masses:
    Missa Faysant Regretz, 88
    Missa Hercules Dux Ferrarie (ca. 1480–1505), **87–88**
    Missa La sol fa re mi (1502), 88–89, 122
    Missa Pange lingua, 40
    Nymphes de bois (1497), 34, 92. See also *Augenmusik* and Ockeghem, Johannes.
    Ut Phoebi radiis, 89
Joyce, James, 359–368
  Antheil, George, 365
  Chamber Music, 364, 366
  Finnegans Wake, 360–**363**, 366–368
  Joyce Book (1932), 365
  Pomes penyeach (1927), 365
  Ulysses, 360–366
  Wagnerism, 361

K
Kabbalah, 8, 37, 39, 83
Kamasutra, 50
  Vātsyāyana, 50
  Mlecchita-vikalpai, 50
Kant, Immanuel, 147
  mathematical sublime, 158
Kepler, Johannes, 348
  Harmonices mundi (*Harmonies of the World*, 1618), 348
Kipling, Rudyard, 13, 235
  Jungle Books, The, 13
  'The Man Who Would Be King' (1888), 235
Kircher, Athanasius, 7, 106–107, 118–**120**, 125, 151, 197
  China Monumentis qua Sacris qua Profanis … Illustrata (*China Illustrated in Sacred and Secular Monuments*, 1667) 125
  cryptography, 118
  'Fama latere nequit' (1650), **120**
  Guidonian syllables, 120
  Musurgia universalis, sive Ars Magna Consoni et Dissoni (*Universal Musicmaking, or the Great Art of Consonance and Dissonance*), 106, 119, 151. See also *Harmonie. universelle* under Mersenne, Marin.
  Obelisci Aegyptiaci (*Egyptain Obelisks*, 1666), 107
  steganography, 119

Kirnberger, Johann Philipp, 141, 151–153, 327
  Bach, J.S., 152
  Der allezeit fertige Menuetten – und Polonoisenkomponist (*The Ever-Ready Minuet and Polonaise Composer*, 1757), 151–152
  Die Kunst des reinen Satzes (*The Art of Pure Composition*, 1774–9), 152
Kittel, Johann Christian, 130
  'Fugue on the Name BACH', BWV 898, 130–**131**
Klüber, Johann Ludwig, 208–209
  Kryptographik: Lehrbuch der Geheimschreibekunst (Chiffrir- und Dechiffrirkunst) in Staats- und Privatgeschäften (*Cryptography: Manual of the Art of Secret Writing (Enciphering and Deciphering) in Official and Private Affairs*, 1809), 208
Knittelverse, 193. See also *boutsrimés* and *Endreim-Spiele*.
Koechlin, Charles, 13–**16**, 293–295, 298, 300
  Chaplin, Charlie, **15–16**
  'Choral sur le nom de Fauré' (1922), 298
  Dietrich, Marlene, **15**
  Epitaphe, 13
  Jannings, Emil, **15**
  music for film stars, 13
  Offrande musicale sur le nom de Bach, Op. 187 (1942), 293–**294**
  Précis des Règles du contrepoint (1926), 298
  Seven Stars' Symphony, The, Op. 132 (1933), **13**–16, 293
Kolisch, Rudolf, 334
Kolisch Quartet, 344
Kopylov, Alexander, 267–268
  Andantino, Op. 7 (1888), 268
  Prelude and Fugue, Op. 11 (1889), 268
  Sokoloff, Nikolai, 268
Krenek, Ernst, 9, 45
  Fibonnaci Mobile (1964), 45
Kreuzsymbol, 129. See BACH cipher.
Kruschev Thaw (*Ottepel*), 275
Kuhlau, Friedrich, 21, 24–**25**. See also 'Kühl, nicht lau' (WoO 191) under Beethoven, Ludwig van.
  Lento al rovescio, 21
  'Musikalisches Anagramm' (1819), 24–**25**. See also anagram(s).

Kuhnau, Johann, 39
  Musicalische Vorstellung einiger Biblischer Historien (*Biblical Sonatas*, 1700), 39

L
Ladmirault, Paul, 295, 297–298
  Hommage à Gabriel Fauré, 298
  Quartet, String (collaborative, 1902), 295, 297. See also Bardac, Raoul; Ravel, Maurice and Roger-Ducasse, Jean.
Lamarr, Hedy, 366
Landowska, Wanda, 129
Langlais, Jean, **311**
  B.A.C.H: Six pièces, pour orgue (1985), 311
  Hommage à Rameau (1964), 311
  Symphony No. 2 (1976), 311
  Trois méditations sur la Sainte-Trinité, pour orgue (1971), **311**
Lasso, Orlando di, 34, 87n, 288
  Stabat mater (1585), 288
Leibniz, Gottfried Wilhelm, 118, 151, 198
  calculus, discovery of, 118
  characteristica universalis, 118, 151, 198
  De arte combinatoria (*Concerning Combinatorial Art*, 1666), 118, 151
  Leopold I, 118
  machina deciphratoria, (cryptological machine), 118
Leo, Alan, 245
  Art of Synthesis, The (1912), 245
Léonin, 18
  Magnus liber, 18
Lerche-Lerchenborg, Louise, 373. See also *Recitativa I Ariosa 'Lerchenmusik'*, Op. 53, under Górecki, Henryk.
Lessing, Gotthold Ephraim, 147
Liège, Jacques de, 69–70
  Ars nova, 69
  'Iaocobus', 70
  Speculum musicae (*The Mirror of Music*, ca. 1330), 69–70
ligature, etymology of, 58
Lippius, Johannes, 113
  Maier, Michael, 113
  Synopsis Musicae Novae (*Synopsis of New Music*, 1612), 113
Liszt, Franz, 130, 203, 211, 220–224, 226, 232–233, 258, 322
  d'Agoult, Marie, 224
  Études d'exécution transcendante d'après Paganini (1840), 220
  Faust Symphony (1854), 220–221

'Ferenc Liszt' cipher, 221
Héroïde funèbre (1857), 224
Marche funèbre (1867), 322
multinational chameleon, 223
Präludium und Fuge über das Thema B-A-C-H (1856), 222–**223**, 226, 258
Les Préludes (1853–58), 233
Sayn-Wittgenstein, Carolyne (*née* Karolina) zu, Princess, 221–**222**, 224
Sonata, Piano, in B minor (1854), 220–**221**
Street-Klindworth, Agnes, 224
virtuosity, 220
Loeffler, Charles, 258
  Partita for violin and piano (1930), 258–259
  Sprague Coolidge, Elizabeth, 259
Lombardi, Luca, 130
Long, Marguerite, 317
  jubilee, 317
  Variations sur le nom de Marguerite Long (1956), 317
Loos, Adolf, 338
  Art nouveau, 338
  Jugendstil, 338
  Ornament und Verbrechen (*Ornament and Crime*, 1908), 338
Louis XIII, King of France, 106
Lucas Series, 43
  Sofia Gubaidulina, 46
Lumière, Louis, 15
  La demolition d'un mur (1896), 15
Luther Adams, John, 374
  Become Desert (2017), 374
  Become Ocean (2013), 374
  Become River (2013), 374
Luther, Martin, 87
Lutosławski, Witold, 280, 355, 372
  Concerto for Orchestra (1954), 280
  Sacher-Variation (1976), 355
Lutyens, Elisabeth, 318
  Stravinsky, Igor, 318
Lyadov, Anatoly, 267–**270**
  Myaskovsky, Nikolai, 270
  Quartet, String, on the Theme B-la-f (1886), 269–**270**

M

McCabe, John, **172**
  Lamentation Rag, **172**
Machaut, Guillaume de, 18, 24, 38, 40, 69–77

anagram(s), 71–72
dit(s), 71–72
  Dit de l'alerion (*The Tale of the Alerion*), 70, 72
  Dit de la Harpe (*Story of the Harp*), 72
  Dit du Lyon (*Story of the Lion*), 72
  La Prize d'Alexandre (*The Taking of Alexandria*), 72
  Le Voir Dit (*The True Poem*), 71
  Remede de Fortune (*The Remedy of Fortune*), 72
  Le jugement du Roy de Behaigne (*The Judgment of the King of Bohemia*), 72
  Le jugement dou Roy de Navarre (*The Judgement of the King of Navarre*), 72, 76
literary anagrams, 24
Mass (ca. 1360s), 40
motets, 70
  significance of the number twenty-three, 70
  'Amours qui ha le povoir/Faus samblant/Vidi dominum', 40
  'Tans doucement/Eins que ma dame/ Ruina', 73
Musica poetica (music as poetry), 77
numerology, 70–71
numerus sonorous (sounding number), 74, 77, 100
Péronne, 71
pseudonyms, 72–73
Reims Cathedral, 76
Roman de Fauvel, 73
rondeau, 18, 24, 71, 74–76
  'Cinq, un, treze, wit, nuef d'amour fine', 74
  'Ma fin est mon commencement' ('My end is my beginning'), 18, 24, 74–76
  'Quant en moy', 74
  'Vos doulz resgars', 74
Mâche, François-Bernard, 316–317
  Safous Mélè (1959), 316–317
  zoomusicology, 316
Machiavelli, Niccolò, 77
  Dell'arte della Guerra (*The Art of War*, 1520), 77
McKay, Brendan, 53. See also Equidistant Letter Sequence (ELS).
Maderna, Bruno, 358
  Fantasia per due pianoforte (1949), 358
madrigal, Italian, 34

Mahler, Gustav, 321, 327–329, 365
  Ewigkeitmotiv, **328**
  Freud, Sigmund, 329
  Symphony:
    No. 2 (1894), 365
    No. 4 (1900), 327
    No. 6 (1904), 327
    No. 7 (1905), 327
    No. 8 ('Symphony of a Thousand', 1907), 330
Maier, Michael, 108–113
  Atalanta fugiens: Emblemata Nova De Secretis Naturae Chymica (The Fleeing Atalanta: New Chemical Emblems Concerning the Secrets of Nature, 1617), 108–113
  Farmer, John, 113
  Lippius, Johannes, 113
Malpiero, Gian Francesco, 357
Manet, Édouard, 322
  Execution of Emperor Maximilian (1869), 322
Mann, Thomas, 32, 248–249, 285, 331–332
  Doktor Faustus: The Life of the German Composer Adrian Leverkühn as Told by a Friend (1947), 32, 248, 285, 331
Marenzio, Luca, 34
  'Occhi, dolci e suave' ('Sweet and suave eyes', 1587), 34
Markevitch, Igor, 31
  Rébus (1931), 31–32
Marpurg, Friedrich Wilhelm, 91, 152–153, 327
Martini, Padre Giovanni Battista, 167–168
  Mozart, W. A., 167
  Storia della musica, 167
Martino, Donald, 32, 259
  B, A, B, B, I, T, T (1966), 259
  Augenmusik: A Mixed Mediocritique (1972), 32
  Parisonatina al'Dodecafonia (1964), 259
Marxsen, Eduard, 5
  Fantasia 'alla moda' über den Kaffee (1831), 5
Mary, Queen of Scots, 78. See also Elizabeth I, Queen of England.
  Babington Conspiracy of 1586, 78
  'En ma fin est mon commencement', 78
Mathers, Edward Powys, 231
  cryptic crossword(s), 231
  Observer, The, 231
  Torquemada (penname), 231

Maurus, Rabanus, 55
  De laudibus sanctae crucis (*Concerning the Praises of the Sacred Cross*), 55
  poems in perfect squares, 55
Maximilian I, Emperor of Mexico, 322
Maxwell Davies, Peter, 252-**254**
  alchemy, 252
  Ave maris stella (1975), 252-**254**
  Gregorian chant, 252
  Mirror of Whitening Light (1978), 252
  Spinning Jenny (1999), 252
  square, magic, 252–254
  Strathclyde Concerto No. 4 (1990), 252
Meck, Nadezhda von, 266, 269
Mendelssohn Bartholdy, Abraham, 191
Mendelssohn Bartholdy, Felix, 30–31,129–130, 146, 191-**197**, 218, 220, 240
  BACH cipher, 194–196
  Bach revival, 194, 196
  Begas, Carl Joseph, 191
  Bilderrätsel, 30–31
  Calm Sea and Prosperous Voyage Overture, Op. 27 (1828), 240
  Endreim-Spiele, 193
  Fasch, Carl Friedrich Christian, 192
  Fugue for String Quartet in C minor (MWV R5, 1821), 192-**193**
  Goethe, Johann Wolfgang von, 193
  London sojourn(s), 195
  MWV U34, 192
  rebus(es), 193
  Six Organ Sonatas, Op. 65 (1845), 195-**197**
  Quartet, String, No. 6 in F minor, Op. 80 (1847), 196
  Zelter, Carl Friedrich, 192
Mendelssohn Bartholdy, Lea, 191
Mendelssohn, Moses, 191
Mengozzi, Fabio, 11
  SATOR (2019), 11–12
mensural notation, 58
Mersenne, Marin, 119, 151
  Harmonie universelle, 119, 151
Messiaen, Olivier, 311–318
  Catalogue d'oiseaux (*Catalogue of the Birds*, 1958), 313
  Church of the Holy Trinity, 311
  Des canyons aux étoiles… (*From the Canyons to the Stars…*, 1974), 312, 314, 316
  langage communicable, 314–316
  Le Livre du Saint Sacrement (1984), 314, 316

Long, Marguerite, 317
Méditations sur le mystère de la Sainte Trinité (1969), 312–**317**
Milhaud, Darius, 317–318
Stravinsky, Igor, 318
Vingt regards sur l'enfant Jesus (*Twenty Aspects of the Infant Jesus*, 1944), 313
Metastasio, Pietro, 149
opera seria, 149
Metternich, Klemens von, 224
Micheli, Romano, 105–107
Canon angelicus, 105–106
'Maria est fons signatus divinae gratiae; Maria est fons misericordiae' (Mary is the sealed spring of divine grace; Mary is the spring of mercy'), 106–**107**
Migot, Georges, 318
Missa L'homme armé, 90, 95–96
Busnois, Antoine, 95
Crusades, 90
Du Fay, Guillaume, 90
Obrecht, Jacob, 96
Order of the Golden Fleece, 90
Philip the Good, Duke of Burgundy, 90
Mizler, Lorenz Christoph, 132, 139
Correspondierende Societät der musikalischen Wissenschaften (*Corresponding Society of Musical Sciences*), 132, 139
Moran, Robert, 259
32 Cryptograms for Derek Jarman (1995), 259
Morse code, 349
Moscheles, Ignaz, 191
Moscow Conservatory, 276
Mount Vesuvius, 8
Mozart, Leopold, 159–161
Freemasonry, 161
letters to Mozart, W. A., 159–161
Mozart, Wolfgang Amadeus, 144, 147–148, 153–165, 167, 231, 324
Anleitung (*Instruction*), K. Anhang C 30.01 (1793), 154
Artaria, Carlo, 162
Colloredo, Hieronymus von, Archbishop of Salzburg, 159
Concerto, Piano, No. 23 in A major, K. 488 (1786), 148
Così fan tutte (1790), 231
Freemasonry, 161–165
Idomeneo (1780), 159
K. 561f, 154–158

Le nozze di Figaro (*The Marriage of Figaro*, K. 492, 1786), 160
letters, 158–161
Mozart, Leopold, 159–161
Mozart, Maria Anna (Nannerl), 160
Quartet, String:
Nos. 14–19, 'Haydn' (1785), 162
No. 19 in C major, K. 465, 'Dissonance' (1785), 161–162
Symphony No. 41 in C major, K. 551 (1788), 156–**158**
Thekla, Maria Anna, 159
Trazom, Gnagflow (*alias*), 160
Trio, Piano, in E-flat major ('Kegelstadt', K 498, 1786), 156
word games, in correspondence, 158–160
Die Zauberflöte (*The Magic Flute*, 1791), 162–**164**
Musgrave, Thea, **249–251**
Chamber Concerto No. 3 (1967), 250–**251**
D. E. S. (2016), 250
Homage to B. A. C. H. (2013), **249**
Myaskovsky, Nikolai, 270–**271**
Quartet, String, in D minor, Op. 33 No. 3 (1930), 270–**271**

N
Napoleon Bonaparte, 49, 65, 169, 177, 178, 182, 189, 371
Egyptian campaign of 1799, 49
Emperor of France, 177
First Consul, 65, 178
Grand armée, 177
invasion of Russia, 177
Napoleonic Wars, 371
Nazi(s), 129, 247, 275, 293, 372
entartete Musik (*degenerate music*), 247
New Germans, 227
Newton, Isaac, 36, 38, 52, 118
calculus, discovery of, 118
comparison to Bach, J.S., 38
'Concerning the Language of the Prophets', 52
Opticks (1704), 36
Nolan, Christopher, 12
Nottebohm, Gustav, 182–183
Novello (publisher), 239
numerology, musical, 37–47, 70, 88, 92–93, 100–105 *See* gematria, musical.
Bach, J.S., 38–39
Busnois, Antoine, 92
Du Fay, Guillaume, 38, 41
Dunstable, John, 40–41

Franco-Flemish composers, 38, 92
Josquin des Prez, 40, 88
Machaut, Guillaume de, 40, 70
Ockeghem, Johannes, 92
Tallis, Thomas, 103–105

O

Obrecht, Jacob, 38, 92n, 96–**99**, 120, 168
   gematria, 38
   Masses:
      Missa De tous biens plaine, **98–99**
      Missa Graecorum (*Mass of the Greeks*),
        96–97
      Missa L'homme armé, 96
      Missa Maria zart, 96
      De tous biens plaine, 96
   verbal canons, 96
Ockeghem, Johannes, 34, 38, 91–94, 168,
    324
   Binchois, Gilles, 92
   Forkel, Johann Nikolaus, 91
   Josquin des Prez, 34, 92
   Marpurg, Friedrich, 91
   Masses:
      Missa cuiusvis toni (*Mass in Any Mode*), 91
      Missa De plus en plus, 92
      Missa Prolationum (*Mass of Prolations*), 91
   gematria, 38
   Prenez sur moy, 91
   Ut heremita solus, 94. See also Busnois, Antoine.
Oliveros, Pauline, 368
   Dear John: A Canon on the Name of Cage, 368
Oratory College of Troyes, 65
   Pithou, Pierre, 65
Ovid, 7, 17–18, 67, 76
   Ars armatoria (*The Art of Love*), 17–18
   Metamorphoses, 7, 76, 108

P

Pachelbel, Johannes, 27
   Hexachordum Apollinis (1699), 27
Pärt, Arvo, 283
   Collage on the Theme BACH (1964), 283
palindrome(s), 6, 12, 17–18, 21, 44, 74, 76, 166, 225, 257, 352
   Bartók, Béla, 44
   Berg, Alban, 21, 225
   emordnilap, 6, 17–18
   Haydn, Franz Joseph, 166

Ives, Charles, 257
labyrinth, association with, 76
Machaut, Guillaume de, 74
origin, possible, 17
Roma-amor, 17–18
Schubert, Franz, 21, 225
Stravinsky, Igor, 352
Wagner, Richard, 225
Pasquier, Claude, 310
passacaglia, 242, 290
passus duriusculus, 186
Pater, Walter, 27
Payer, Hieronymous, 5
   Variationen über das Buchstaben-Thema C, A, F, F, E, E, Op. 139 (1844), 5
Pearl Harbor, 129
Penderecki, Krzysztof, 372
Pesciolini, Biagio, 107
   'Surrexit pastor bonus', 107
Petrarch, 123, 148–149
philosophes, 147
picture-puzzles, 28. See *Bilderrätsel* and rebus.
Pierné, Gabriel, **303**
   Prélude sur le nom de Paul Dukas (1936), **303**
Pisa, Leonard (*alias* Fibonacci) da, 43
   Liber abbaci (*Book of Calculations*, 1202), 43
Piston, Walter, 258
   Chromatic Study on the Name of Bach (1940), 258
Pithou, Pierre, 65
Plautus, 22
Poe, Edgar Allan, 51, 54, 255
   Alexander's Weekly Messenger, 255
   Caesar cipher, 51
   cryptanalysis, 255
   Gold Bug, The (1843), 255
   Graham's Magazine, 51
   scytale, 51
poèmes figures, 32. See calligram(s), 32
polystylism, 13, 130, 284–285, 287–288, 290
   Schnittke, Alfred, 284–285, 287–288, 290
Pompeii, 8
Porta, Giambattista della, 80-1
   De occultis literarum notis (*Concerning the Hidden Signs of Letters*, 1606), 81
   cipher(s), digraphic, 81
Poulenc, Francis, 32–33, 292–**293**, 301, 317–318
   Calligrammes, FP 140 (1948), 32–33. See also Apollinaire, Guillaume.

436　INDEX

Long, Marguerite, 317
Pièce brève sur le nom d'Albert Roussel (1929), 301
Roussel, Albert, 301
Valse-Improvisation sur le nom de BACH (1932), 292–**293**
Powell (*née* Penny), Dora, 231, 235, 240–241
　Elgar, Sir Edward, Sir, 231, 240
　Penny, Alfred, Reverend, 231
　Powell, Richard, 235
Prokofiev, Sergei, 272–**273**, 276
　death of, 276
　Esche, Sofia, 273
　Sonata, Piano, No. 3, Op. 28 (1917), **273**
　Soviet Union, repatriation to, 272–73
Pythagorean theory, 37, 42, 44, 69, 93–**94**, 139, 348
　Bach, J. S., 139
　Boethius, 69
　Busnois, Antoine, 93–**94**
　Du Fay, Guillaume, 42
　Hindemith, Paul, 348
　music of the spheres, 37
　Pythagoras, 37
　Rameau, Jean-Philippe, 44
　ratios, Pythagorean, 37, 42, 94

R
Rameau, Jean Philippe, 44, 311, 327
Ravel, Maurice, 170–171, 295–**299**, 303, 305, 359
　Berceuse, 298–**299**
　Menuet sur le nom d'Haydn (1909), 170–171
　Quartet, String (collaborative, 1902), 295, 297. *See also* Bardac, Raoul; Ladmirault, Paul and Roger-Ducasse, Jean.
　Quartet, String, in F major (1904), 295–297
　Le Tombeau de Couperin (1917), 303
rebus, 28–32, 115. *See* picture puzzles and *Bilderrätsel*.
　Alamire, Petrus (Imhoff, Petrus), 29
　Bridge, Frank, 32
　da Vinci, Leonardo, 28–29
　de la Rue, Pierre, signature of, 29
　Du Fay, Guillaume, tombstone of, 29
　Gade, Niels, 31
　Markevitch, Igor, 31–32
　Mendelssohn Bartholdy, Felix, *30*–31
　origins of, 28
　Pipelare, Mattaeus, signature of, 29
　Schumann, Robert, 31
　Tabourot, Étienne, 28
Rees, Owen, 40
Reger, Max, 130, 226–**227**
　modernism, historicist, 226
　Phantasie und Fuge über BACH, Op. 46 (1900), 226–**227**
　Violin Sonata No. 4 in C major, Op. 72 (1903), 226–**227**
Rellstab, Ludwig, 204
Rescher, Nicholas, 118
Restoration, post-Napoleonic, 180
　censorship, 178, 180
La Revue musicale, 291–292, 297–298, 300–302
　1920 *tombeau* for Debussy, 303
　1922 Fauré supplement, 298, 300
　1924 *tombeau* for de Ronsard, 303
　1929 tribute to Roger-Ducasse, 301
　1929 tribute to Roussel, Albert, 301
　1932 Bach supplement, 291–292
　1936 *tombeau* for Dukas, 302
　Prunières, Henry, 297–298
Rheinberger, Josef, 226
　Fughetta in C major on BACH (1884), 226
Ridolfi, Roberto, 104
Riemann, Hugo, 169
Rimsky-Korsakov, Nikolai, 267–**269**
　Kopylov, Alexander, 267
　Paraphrases (1879), 268–**269**
　Six Variations sur le theme BACH, Op. 10 (1878), 268
　Sokoloff, Nikolai, 267
　Quartet, String, on the Theme B-la-f (1886), 269. *See also* Belyayev; Borodin, Alexander; Glazunov, Alexander and Lyadov, Anatoly.
Rivier, Jean, 317–**318**
　Long, Marguerite, 317–**318**
Rodgers and Hammerstein, 67
Roger-Ducasse, Jean, 295–297, 300–**301**, 310
　Poème symphonique (1922), 300–**301**
　Quartet, String (collaborative, 1902), 295, 297. *See also* Bardac, Raoul; Ladmirault, Paul and Ravel, Maurice.
　Quartet, String, No. 1 (1909), 295–296
Roman de Fauvel, 73
　de Bus, Gervais, 73
　Fauvel as an acronym, 73

Ronsard, Pierre de, 303, 310
  quadricentenary, 303, 310
  1924 *tombeau*, *La Revue musicale*, 303
Ropartz, Guy, 303–305
  À la Mémoire de Paul Dukas (1936), 303–**304**
Rosenkreuz, Christian, 110
  Rosicrucians, 110, 114, 117
Rosetta Stone, 49
  Ptolemy V Epiphanes, Pharoah, 49
Rostropovich, Mstislav, 290, 354
Roussel, Albert, 291–292, 295, 301–302
  Le Festin de l'araignée (*The Spider's Banquet*, 1913), 302
  La Revue musicale, 301
  Prélude et fugue sur le nom de Bach, Op. 46 (1932), 291–292
Rubbra, Edmund, 172–173
  Invention on the Name of Haydn, Op. 160 (1982), 172–173
Rubinstein, Anton, 22
  Akrostichon, Op. 37 (1856) and Op. 114 (1890), 22
Rudolf II, Holy Roman Emperor, 108
  Kunstkammer, 108

S
Sacher, Paul, 25, 260, 251, 260, 354–356
  Berio, Luciano, 355
  Boulez, Pierre, 355–356
  Britten, Benjamin, 251, 354
  Carter, Elliot, 260
  celebration, seventieth birthday, 354
  Dutilleux, Henri, 355–356
  Fortner, Wolfgang, 355
  Ginastera, Alberto, 355
  Henze, Hans Werner, 355
  Holliger, Heinz, 355–356
  Huber, Klaus, 354–355
  Lutosławski, Witold, 355
  Rostropovich, Mstislav, 354
  Sacher cipher, 251, 269, 354–356, 354–356
St. Petersburg Conservatory, 266, 268, 273
Saint-Saëns, Camille, 14, 170
Sams, Eric, 3, 232
Sarum rite, 102, 105, 113
Satie, Erik, 368
Sauguet, Henri, 317
  Long, Marguerite, 317
scala enigmatica, **241**–242. See *scala-rebus*.
scala-rebus, 241–242. See *scala enigmatica*.
Scarlatti, Domenico, 289

Scheibe, Johann Adolf, 129
Schering, Arnold, 136
Schikaneder, Emanuel, 163, 164
  Das Labyrinth oder Der Kampf mit den Elementen: Der Zauberflöte zweyter Theil (*The Labyrinth or The Struggle with the Elements: The Magic Flute, Part II* (1798), 164
  Die Zauberflöte, 164
  Freemasonry, 163–164
Schmitt, Florent, 295, 298–300
  Hommage sur le nom de Fauré (1922), 298–300
  In memoriam, Op. 72 (1935), 300
Schnittke, Alfred, 35, 130, 283–290
  baptism (into Catholicism), 287
  Canon in memoriam Igor Stravinsky (1971), 287
  cipher on his name (ADSCH), 283
  Concerto, Cello, No. 2 (1990), 290
  Concerto Grosso No. 3 (1985), 289
  Concerto, Violin, No. 2 (1966), 286
  Mann, Thomas, 285
  phases of his career, 285, 289
  polystylism, 284, 287–288, 290
  Prelude in memoriam Dmitri Shostakovich, 287
  Quartet, String, No. 3 (1983), 288–**289**
  Quintet, Piano (1976), 287
  quotation(s), 287–288
  Schnittke Code, 285
  Symphony:
    No. 2, 'Invisible Mass' (1979), 35, 287
    No. 3 (1981), 284–285
Schoenberg, Arnold, 9, 21, 47, 226, 247–**248**, 250, 306, 318, 329–342, 344–345, 347–348, 375
  Drei Klavierstücke, Op. 11 (1909), 329
  Erwartung, Op. 17 (1909), 329
  Eschbeg set, 333
  Four Orchestral Songs, Op. 22 (1913), 330
  Gerstl, Richard, 333–334, 342
  Gurrelieder (1911), 332
  Die Jacobsleiter (*Jacob's Ladder*, 1915), 330
  Klavierstück, Op. 33a (1923), 348
  lectures, UCLA, 330
  Moses und Aron (1932), 332
  numerology, 332–333
  palindrome, 21
  pantonality, 9, 329
    atonality, 9, 329
    dodecaphony, 9, 330–331

serial music (serialism), 130, 279–280, 286, 331, 347
    twelve-tone music, 330–331
Pelléas et Mélisande, Op. 5 (1903), 342
Pierrot lunaire, Op. 21 (1912), 333, 348
Quartet, String:
    No. 1 in D minor, Op. 7 (1905), 332
    No. 2 in F-sharp minor, Op. 10 (1908), 329, 331, 333–**335**
    No. 4, Op. 37 (1936), 336
Schoenberg (*née* Kolisch), Gertrude, 334
Schoenberg (*née* Zemlinsky), Mathilde, 333–334, 342, 345
Searle, Humphrey, 247–**248**
Suite for Piano, Op. 25 (1921–23), 330, 336
Suite for Seven Instruments, Op. 29 (1925), 334–**335**
Trio, String Op. 45 (1946), 332
triskaidekaphobia, 47, 306, 332, 340
Variations, Op. 31 (1928), **336–337**
Schooling, Jason Holt, 235–238
    Pall Mall Magazine, 235
    'Secrets in Cipher', 235–**236**
Schopenhauer, Arthur, 329
Schott, Daniel, 81–83
    Schola Steganographica in Classes Octo Distributa (*School of Steganography Distributed into Eight Categories*, 1665), 82
Schott, Gaspar, 120
Schubert, Franz, 2, 21, 180, **185**–189, 225, 250, 321–322, 370
    Biedermeier Vienna, 187
    'Das Dörfchen' (1817), 188
    Diabelli, Anton, 185
    Die Verschworenen (*The Conspirators*, 1823), 180
    Die Zauberharfe (*The Magic Harp*, 1820), 2, 21, 188, 225
    Esterházy, Caroline, 188
    Fantasy in F minor (1828), 186–**187**
    Freundeskreis (circle of friends), 187
    fugal sketch, **185**
    Der Graf von Gleichen (*Count von Gleichen*, 1827), 180
    Harbison, John, 186–187
    Ludlamshöhle (*Ludlam's Cave*), 188
    Quartet, String, No. 14, D minor, *Death and the Maiden* (1824), 370
    Schubertiade(n), 187
    Sechter, Simon, 185
    Senn, Johann, 189
    Unsinnsgesellschaft (*Nonsense Society*), 187–189
Schumann, Clara, 203, 205, 212, 220
    allusion in the music of, 205
    'Ehe', 204–205
    intertextuality, 203
    quotation in the music of, 205
    Sonata, *FAE* (1853), 203. *See also* Brahms, Johannes; Dietrich, Albert; Joachim, Joseph; and Schumann, Robert.
Schumann, Robert, **31**, 130, 146, 192, 194, 203–**210**, 212, 214, 216–220, 222, 226–228, 238, 265, 268, 273, 341
    Abegg Variations, Op. 1 (1830), 204–**205**, **341**
    Album für die Jugend, Op. 68 (1848), 31, 218–**219**
    Andante and Variations, Op. 46 (1843), 205
    Beethoven, Ludwig van, 206
    Carnaval, Op. 9 (1835), 192, 204, **207**–**209**, 220, 238, 265, 268
    Sphinxes, 192, 207, 220, 238, 265
    ciphers, musical, 204
    ABEGG cipher, 204–205
    ASCH cipher, 204, 268, 273. *See also* SCHA cipher.
    BACH cipher, 205
    Clara cipher, 217
    EHE cipher, 204–205
    SCHA cipher, 204, 207, 209
    Concerto, Piano, in A minor, Op. 54 (1845), 217
    Die beiden Grenadiere, Op. 49 No. 1 (1840), 205
    Endenich, 220
    Fantasy, Op. 17 (1836–38), 205–207
    Faschingsschwank aus Wien, Op. 26 (1839–40), 205
    Frauenliebe- und leben, Op. 42 (1840), 205–206
    Fricken, Ernestine von, 204
    Hermann und Dorothea Overture (1851), Op. 136, 205
    Klüber, Johann Ludwig, 208–209
    Liederkreis, Op. 39 No. 5 (1840), 204–205
    Quartet, String, in F major, Op. 41, No. 2 (1842), 206
    Sams, Eric, 208
    Schumann, August, 208
    Six Fugues for Organ on B. A. C. H., Op. 60 (1845), 205, 222, 226–**227**

Sonata, *FAE* (1853), 203, 209–**210**, 212. *See also* Brahms, Johannes; Dietrich, Albert; Joachim, Joseph; and Schumann, Clara.
Sonata, Violin, in D minor, Op. 121 (1851), 209
Symphony No. 2 (1846), Op. 61, 206
Schütz, Heinrich, 289
Schwenter, Daniel, 81, 120
Scriabin, Alexander, 36–37, 270–272
  Mysterium, 272
  mystic chord, 270–**271**
  Prometheus: The Poem of Fire, Op. 60 (1910), 36, 270. *See also* colour-music.
  theosophy, 36, 271
Searle, Humphrey, **247**–249
  Night Music, Op. 2 (1943), 247
  Passacaglietta, Op. 16 (1949), 247–**248**
  Radio broadcast (BBC), 248
  Schoenberg, Arnold. 247–248
  Symphony No. 1, Op. 23 (1953), **247**
  Webern, Anton, 247
Sechter, Simon, 185–**187**, 327
  Fuge in C Moll, Op. 43 (1828), 185, **187**
  Schubert, Franz, 185
Second Viennese School, 9, 21, 250. *See also* Berg, Alban; Schoenberg, Arnold and Webern, Anton.
Selenus, Gustavus, 84, 115. *See* August the Younger, Duke of Brunswick-Lüneburg.
Senfl, Ludwig, 35
  canons, puzzle, 35
Senleches, Jacob, 33
  'La harpe de melodie' ('The harp of song'), 33
Sessions, Roger, 318
  Stravinsky, Igor, 318
Shakespeare Authorship Question (SAQ), 115–117
  bacon, 117
  Bacon, Delia, 116
  Bacon, Sir Francis, 116
  Clarke, Barry R., 117
  collaborative authors, 117
  Durning-Lawrence, Sir Edwin, 116
  Early English Books Online (EEBO), 117
  Emerson, Ralph Waldo, 116
  honorificabilitudinitatibus, 116
  James, Henry, 116
  Marlowe, Christopher, 117
  Platt, Isaac Hull, 116–117
  Rare Collocation Profiling (RCP), 117
  Shakspere William, 115
  Stanley, William, 117
  Twain, Mark, 116
  Vere, Edward de, 117
  Whitman, Walt, 116
Shakespeare, William, 23–24, 78, 116–117
  Gesta Grayorum (1688), 117
  Love's Labor's Lost, 116–117
  Merry Wives of Windsor, The, 117
  Richard II, 116
  Richard III, 78, 116
  Twelfth Night, 23–24
Shostakovich, Dmitri, 273–283, 287–288
  Chumbawamba (band), 281
  Communist Party, 275, 278
  Concerto, Cello, No. 1 in E-flat major, Op. 107 (1959), 278
  Concerto, Violin, No. 1 in A minor, Op. 77 (1948), 274
  DSCH cipher, 273–278, 280–**283**, 287–288
  DSCH Journal, 275
  Fugue No. 15 in D-flat major, Op. 87 (1952), 274
  Galynin, German, 282
  holy fool (*yuródiviy*), 275
  King Lear (1971), 279
  Lady Macbeth of the Mtsensk District (1932), 274–275, 278, 280
  late style, 279
  Nazirova, Elmira, 276–**277**
  New Babylon, The (1928), 279
  Quartet, String:
    No. 5 in B-flat major, Op. 92 (1952), 274
    No. 6 in G major, Op. 101 (1956), 274
    No. 8 in C minor, Op. 110 (1960), 278, 282
    No. 14 in F-sharp major, Op. 142 (1973), 280
  Sascha cipher, 280
  self-quotations, 278
  Seven Verses of Aleksander Blok, Op. 127 (1967), 279
  Shirinsky, Sergei, 280
  Shostakovich, Maxim, 279
  Soviet realism, 274
  Stalin, Joseph, 277
  Stravinsky, Igor, 274
  Symphony:
    No. 1 in F minor, Op. 10 (1926), 278

No. 2 in B major, Op. 14 (*To October*, 1927), 274
No. 3 in E-flat major, Op. 20 (*First of May*, 1930), 274
No. 5 in D minor, Op. 47 (1937), 274–275, 278
No. 7 in C major, Op. 60 (*Leningrad*, 1942), 274
No. 9 in E-flat major, Op. 70 (1945), 277
No. 10 in E minor, Op. 93 (1953), 276–**277**, 281
No. 11 in G minor, Op. 103 (*The Year 1905*, 1957), 274–275
No. 12 in D minor, Op. 112 (*The Year 1917*, 1961), 274
No. 13 in B-flat minor, Op. 113 (*Babi Yar*, 1962), 275
No. 15 in A major, Op. 141 (1971), 280
tombstone, 275
'Tortured by Great Misery', 278
Trio, Piano, No. 2 in E minor, Op. 67 (1944), 278
Volkov, Solomon, 275
Young Guard, The (1948), 278
Siebold, Agathe von, 213–214. *See also* Brahms, Johannes.
Silvestrov, Valentyn, 282
Postlude DSCH (1981), 282
Simpson, Robert, 19, 173
Quartet, String:
No. 1 (1952), 19
No. 9 (1982), 19, 173
Symphony No. 2 (1956), 19
Variations and Finale on a Theme of Haydn (1948), 19
Smend, Friedrich, 2–3, 136
Smetana, Bedřich, 28
album leaf for piano in C major (1862), 28
Smirnov, Dmitri, 45
Symphony No. 3 (*Voyages*, 1995), 45
Smythe, Dame Ethel, 250
soggetto ostinato, 89. *See also soggetto cavato* under Zarlino, Gioseffo.
Sokoloff, Nikolai, 267–269
Belyayev cipher, 268
Sérénade, Op. 3 (1887), 268–269
Sound of Music, The (film, 1965), 67
Andrews, Julie, 67
Rodgers and Hammerstein, 67
von Trapp children, 67

Soviet Union, 288
Soviet states, 282
Spitta, Philipp, 136
Spohr, Louis, 189–191
Quartet, String, Op. 29 No. 1, **190**–191
square, magic, 6–12, 15, 110, 149, 231, **252**–254. *See* square, perfect and square, SATOR.
Hooper, William, 149
Maier, Michael, 110–111
Maxwell Davies, Peter, **252**–254
relationship to alchemy, 111, 252
Square, SATOR, 6–10
Webern, Anton, **9**–**12**, 17, 21
square, perfect. *See* magic square and square, SATOR.
Square, SATOR, 6–12
Arepo, 6, 12
association with magic, 7
Christological interpretations, 7–8
earliest specimens, 8
hidden message (Sator-Arepo-Formel), 6
Pompeii, ruins of, 8–9
origins, roman antiquity, 6
Stadler, Maximilian, Abbé, 186
Fugue in C minor (1828), **186**
Stalin Joseph, 276–277, 372
Stanford, Charles Villiers, 238
Steiner, Rudolf, 329
stenography, 50, 79, 81–**82**, 110, 115, 119–120, 178, 230, 360
Dickens, Charles, 230
Gurney, Thomas, 230
Newton, Isaac, Sir, 230
Pepys, Samuel, 230
shorthand, 230
Stockhausen, Karlheinz, 45
Adieu (1966), 45
Klavierstück IX (1954–55), 45
Mixtur (1964), 45
Stein, Johann Andreas, 160
Stevenson, Ronald, **281**
Concerto, Piano, No. 2 (*The Continents*, 1972), 281
Passacaglia on DSCH (1963), **281**
Recitative and Air on DSCH: In Memoriam Shostakovich (1976), 281
Strauss, Johann, II, 200–201
Telegrafische Despeschen (*Telegraphic Dispatches*), Op. 195 (1857), 200–201
Strauss, Richard, 227
Ein Heldenleben (*A Hero's Life*), 227

INDEX 441

Stravinsky, Igor, 25–**26**, **274**, 280, 287, 318, 352–354
  Agon (1957), 353
  Cantata (1952), 352
  Canticum sacrum (1955), 352
  Concerto in D (1947), 354
  death (1971), 318
  Flood, The (1962), 352, 353
  In memoriam Dylan Thomas (1954), **353**
  Requiem Canticles (1966), 353
  serialism, 352
  A Sermon, a Narrative, and a Prayer (1962), 353–354
  Symphony in C (1940), 25–**26**
  Symphony of Psalms (1930), **274**, 352–**353**
  Threni (1958), 352, 354
Striggio, Alessandrio, the elder, 103–105
  Florence, 103
  Medici family, 103
  Missa sopra Ecco sì beato giorno, 103–105
Strindberg, August, 329, 337
  Blue Book, A (1907–1912), 337
Sudre, François, 198–201
  Grammaire du Solrésol ou Langue universelle de Fr. Sudre, 201
  La langue musicale (Solrésol), 198–**199**, 201
  Langue musicale au moyen de la quelle on peut converser sur tous les Instruments (Musical Language by Means of Which One Can Converse on All the Instruments), 201
  Téléphonie ou Télégraphie acoustique pratiqué au moyen de quatre sons executes sur le clairon (Telephony or Practical Acoustical Telegraph by Means of Four Pitches Executed on the Clarion), 198–200
Sudre, Josephine, 201
Susato, Tilman, 27
  chanson (1543), 27
Swedenborg, Emanuel, 329–331, 337–338
  theory of correspondences, 338
Swift, Jonathan, 35, 123. See also *Gulliver's Travels Suite* under Telemann, Georg Philipp.

T
tachygraphy, 230
  Pepys, Samuel, 230
  Shelton, Thomas, 230
Takemitsu, Tōru, 366–**367**
  Far Calls. Coming, Far! (1980), 367

  Joyce, James, 367
  SEA motive, 366–**367**
  'Waterscape' cycle (1980s), 366–367
Tallis, Thomas, 101–105, 113
  Missa Puer natus est nobis ('Unto us a child is born'), 101–102
  Spem in alium (c. 1570), 102–105
Tansman, Alexandre, 373. See Symphony No. 4 under Górecki, Henryk.
Tartini, Giuseppe, 148–149
  Algarotti, Francesco, Count, 148
  Metastasio, Pietro, 149
  motto-like texts, 148–149
  musical cryptography, 148
  Petrarch, 148–149
  Sonata, Violin, in G minor, GT 2.g05, 'Devil's Trill', 148
Tchaikovsky, Peter Ilyich, 261–**266**
  Alexander III, Tsar of Russia, 261
  Artôt, Désirée, 263–266
  cipher on his name, 265
  Concerto, Piano, No. 1 in B-flat minor, Op. 23 (1875), 263–**265**
  Fatum (1868), 263–**265**
  homosexuality, 261–263
  Laub, Ferdinand, 266
  Meck, Nadezhda von, 266
  Quartet, String, No. 3 in E-flat minor, Op. 30 (1876), 263, 266
  Romeo and Juliet Overture-Fantasy (1870–1880), 264
  St. Petersburg Conservatory, 266
  Six Romances, Op. 73 (1893), 265
  Suite:
    No. 1 in D minor, Op. 43 (1879), 263, **266**
    No. 2 in C major, Op. 53 (1883), 263
  Symphony:
    No. 3 in D major, Op. 29 (1875), 263, 266
    No. 4 in F minor, Op. 36 (1878), 263, 266
    No. 5 in E minor, Op. 64 (1888), 263
    No. 6 in B minor, Op. 74 (1893), 263
Tchaikovsky, Modest, 262
Tchaikovsky Papers, 262
Telemann, Georg Philipp, 35, 132
  Gulliver's Travels (1728), 35. See also Swift, Jonathan.
Temple of Solomon, 41, 90, 162
Tenet (2020 film), 12
theosophy, 36, 245, 271–272, 328
  Blavatsky, Helena, 271
  Eckstein, Friedrich, 328

Holst, Gustav, 245
Scriabin, Alexander, 36, 271–272
Thicknesse, Philip, **126–127**, 197, 236
   Arne, Thomas, 126
   Gainsborough, Thomas, 126
   Goldsmith, Oliver, 126–**127**
   Treatise on the Art of Decyphering, and of Writing in Cypher, A (1772), 126
Tishchenko, Boris, 282
   Symphony No. 5 (1967), 282
Trithemius, Johannes, 55, 79–**81**, 115
   polyalphabetic substitution cipher system, 55
   Polygraphia libri sex (*Polygraphy in Six Books*, 1518), 79
   Steganographia (*Secret Writing*, ca. 1500), 79–81, 115
Trowell, Brian, 40
Tsintsadze, Sulkan, 282
   Quartet, String, No. 9 (1978), 282
Tudor, Mary ('Bloody'), 104
   Howard, Thomas, fourth Duke of Norfolk, 104
Turing, Alan, 56

V
Valentini, Pier Francesco, 108–**109**, 120
   canon(s), 108
      'Amor, quis maior patet', 108–**109**
      Canone nel nodo Salomonis (*Canon on Solomon's Knot*), 108
      Canone sopra le parole del Salve Regina, 108
Vatican, 78
   Great Schism, 78
Vaughan Williams, Ralph, 246, 249, 363
   Symphony No. 4 in F minor (1934), 246
Venice, 77
   Doge of, 77
   San Marco, 105, 352
Verdi, Giuseppe, 241–242
   Quattro pezzi sacri (*Four Sacred Pieces*, 1898), 241
Verlaine, Paul, 300
   La bonne chanson, 300
Vigenère, Blaise de, 83–84
   Traicté des chiffres, ou Secrètes manières d'escrire (*Treatise concerning Ciphers, or Secret Manners of Writing*), 83
Volkov, Solomon, 275
   Testimony, 275–277
Voltaire, 318

Voynich Manuscript, 56
   author(s), possible, 56
   Chesire, Gerard, 56

W
Wagner, Richard, 224–226, 229, 315, 321, 327–328, **343**, 361, 373
   Der Ring des Nibelungen, 225, 373
      Das Rheingold, 225
      Die Walküre, 225, 361
      Götterdämmerung, 225
      Siegfried (1876), 328
   Dresden Uprising (1849), 224–225
   exile, Switzerland, 224
   Leitmotiv(en), 225, 315
   Parsifal (1882), 328
   'Professor Werder', 224
   Siegfried motive, 373
   Tristan und Isolde (1859), **343**
   Wesendonck, Mathilde, 226, 229
   Wesendonck, Otto, 226
   Wolzogen, Hans von, 225
Wallace Rimington, Alexander, 36
   organ, colour, 36. *See also* colour-music.
Walther, Johann Gottfried, 2–3, 129
Walton, William, 246–**247**, 249
   Variations on a Theme by Hindemith (1963), 246–**247**
Webern, Anton, 247
War of Independence (American), 255
   Continental Army, 255
   Jefferson, Thomas, 255
   Washington, George, 255
Warsaw Pact, 372
Webern, Anton, 9–**12**, 17, 21, 247, 258, 294, 311, 332, 334, 341, 344, 352–**353**, 358
   Bach, J.S., 247
   Concerto, Op. 24 (1934), 10
   'Das Sonnenlicht', Op. 32, 11–**12**
   Klangfarbenmelodie, 294
   Quartet, String, Op. 28 (1938), 352–**353**
   Square, SATOR, 9–12, 17, 21
   TENET, 10–**11**
   Variations, Op. 27 (1936), 358
Webster, David, 245
Weinberg, Mieczysław, 282
   Symphony No. 12 (1976), 282
Werner, G. J., 19, 21, 27
   Menuetto cancrizante, in *Neuer und sehr curios- Musicalischer Instrumental-Calender* (*New and Very Curious Musical Instrumental Calendar*, 1748), 19, **27**

Weyrich, B. E. A., 198–**199**
  Die Instrumentalton-Sprechkunst (*The Instrumental Tone Art of Speaking*, 1830), 198–**199**
Widor, Charles-Marie, 170, 291
  Fugue sur le nom d'Haydn (1909), 170
Wilkins, John, Bishop of Chester, 124–**125**, **197**
  Mercury, or the Secret and Swift Messenger, Shewing How a Man May with Privacy and Speed Communicate his Thoughts to a Friend at Any Distance (1641), 124–**125**. *See also* Godwin, Francis, 123–124, 197
Willaert, Adrian, 84
Wolf, Hugo, 327
Wolzogen, Hans von, 225
  Thematischer Leitfaden durch die Musik zu Richard Wagner's Festspiel Der Ring des Nibelungen, 225

X
Xenakis, Iannis, 369–370
  Fibonnaci Series, 369
  Golden Section (GS), 369
  indeterminism, 369
  Metastasis (*Beyond Immobility*, 1954), 369–370
  Palimpsest (1979), 370

Y
yellowhammer bird, 313
  Beethoven, Ludwig van, 313
  Messiaen, Olivier, 313

Z
Zacconi, Lodovico, 107
  Canoni Musicali, 107
  Prattica di Musica (*The Practice of Music*), 107
Zarlino, Gioseffo, 87, 106
  soggetto cavato dale vocali, 87, 100, 106, 122, 192, 213
Zelter, Carl Friedrich, 192
  Hensel (*née* Mendelssohn Bartholdy), Fanny, 192
  Mendelssohn Bartholdy, Felix, 192
Zemlinsky, Alexander von, 334, 342–343
  Lyric Symphony, Op. 18 (1923), 343
  Schoenberg, Arnold, 334
  Quartet, String, No. 2 Op. 15 (1915), 334
Zemlinsky, Mathilde von, 334. *See* Schoenberg (*née* Zemlinksy), Mathilde under Schoenberg, Arnold.

www.ingramcontent.com/pod-product-compliance
Lightning Source LLC
Chambersburg PA
CBHW070804300426
44111CB00014B/2417